PUBLIC LAW
AND
POLITICAL CHANGE
IN KENYA

PUBLIC LAW

AND

POLITICAL CHANGE

IN KENYA

A Study of
the Legal Framework of
Government from
Colonial Times
to the Present

Y.P. GHAI

and

J.P.W.B. McAUSLAN

Nairobi London New York
OXFORD UNIVERSITY PRESS
1970

OXFORD UNIVERSITY PRESS, ELY HOUSE, LONDON W.1

Glasgow New York Toronto Melbourne Wellington
Cape Town Salisbury Ibadan Nairobi Dar es Salaam Lusaka Addis Ababa
Bombay Calcutta Madras Karachi Lahore Dacca
Kuala Lumpur Singapore Hong Kong Tokyo

OXFORD UNIVERSITY PRESS, P.O. BOX 12532, NAIROBI, KENYA

MADE AND PRINTED IN EAST AFRICA

Preface

There are so many reasons for not writing a book on the public law of an African state, not least that much of the subject matter of the book tends to be somewhat ephemeral, as several authors (and publishers) have found to their cost, that a book on such a topic might be thought to require some justification. Further justification may appear to be needed for the choice of the subject: public law, more particularly constitutional law, is seldom seen as a helpful guide to the understanding of political or governmental structures in Africa, and more often than not tends to hide the realities of the situation. In any case it might be argued that even if the subject is worth writing about, lawyers are hardly qualified to do so.

A straightforward reason for this book is that somewhat surprisingly, in view of the great interest a colonial Kenya inspired in political scientists, lawyers and historians, no book on the policies and government of an independent Kenya written by political scientists or historians was, so far as we could discover, in the offing, and this seemed to be a gap which it was worth trying to fill, if only from a lawyer's perspective.

But there were other reasons as well. Both of us felt some considerable dissatisfaction, as teachers of public law in East Africa and elsewhere, with the style and content of books on African constitutional law. With very few exceptions, they have tended to eschew politics, a discussion of how the constitution is working in practice, a consideration of the administration, or comment on any of these matters, and have concentrated instead on a broad survey of the text of the constitution, other relevant laws, and the few cases that have arisen in the courts on the constitution. They have tended to present the constitution as a static phenomenon, frozen at a particular moment in time, in a photograph from which the background has been carefully excluded, other than a faint rosy hue. The result has been that not merely the books themselves but constitutional law and lawyers are thought of now as almost irrelevant in much academic discussion of political and economic development in Africa.

We are convinced that such exclusion of lawyers is a mistake and that legal scholarship and public lawyers have much to contribute to these topics, but that this will never appear to be the case if we lawyers continue to produce formal analyses of legal texts, which, like so much modern packaged food, has been processed and packaged in a vacuum, and is consequently tasteless. With somewhat less conviction, we would also think that it is a mistake of equal proportions for lawyers, in a desperate effort to prove their relevance to other social scientists in this field, to go overboard for the latest methodology and systems analysis of those social sciences, oblivious of the fact that they are derived from years of empirical work on individual countries, and need skills which we do not yet adequately possess, to be utilized effectively.

What is needed in our view is country by country, or where relevant, area by area, studies of aspects of public law set in their historical, political and economic context so that, first, the role the law has played, is playing, and may in the future play in the development of the polity may begin to be perceived, and secondly, the way the polity has developed, is developing and may in the future develop, may to some extent be seen through the perspective of the law. Naturally, in such studies, both empirical and more traditional techniques of legal research will be needed.

History is important because the law was one of the major tools used by the colonial power to establish its presence, and create the colonial society in which today's leaders of African states grew up, and to which they succeeded at independence. The law created an on-going system of government which was not likely to be, nor was it, in fact, overthrown at independence or thereafter; this is true for all Anglophone African states with the possible exception of Zanzibar. The law at independence therefore is the base-line from which all independent African states have started, and to ignore that base-line and its development is to tell less than half the story.

The political context is important because in many African states, particularly those whose systems of public law are derived from England, the operation of many of the institutions of the state, such as government, legislatures, courts and public corporations, can only be understood if it is appreciated that the reality is that key interpretations of the law are given by politicians, or within a political rather than a legal framework, and that the courts play an insignificant role in the development of public law, or at most a negative role, as the law is sometimes altered to overcome an inconvenient decision. In Kenya, for instance, the constitutional interpretations of the Speaker, given on rulings in the National Assembly, are infinitely more important in the evolution of Kenya constitutionalism than decisions of the High Court. Disapproval of this attitude to public law—itself a legacy of colonialism—should not blind one to the need to relate one's work to it.

The economic context is important because we must constantly remind ourselves of the fact of underdevelopment and what that means, and the plans the governments are making for economic development when discussing these societies. The lack of schooling and literacy, and the lack of adequate means of communication, both affect the viability of the constitutional system as likewise does the lack of capital, the viability of the Development Plan, and the utility of a massive administrative system. The economic beliefs of governments are also relevant to the question of the use to which the law is to be or has been put in political and economic development.

We have attempted here to adopt such an approach as we have outlined above. It follows therefore that this book deliberately departs from the more traditional texts on African constitutional law. Because of the need to explore the historical development of public law, breadth of coverage has had to be sacrificed. There is no consideration of local government and its forebear native administration, very little discussion of the reception of English law, and the whole field of economic law—planning, central banking, credit, foreign investment and development corporations have scarcely been touched on. These omissions are deliberate. In part, the reasons are the size of the book—already large—and the fact that, at least in the case of reception, there is a good deal of writing on the subject, which if not specifically on Kenya, deals with legal problems which have arisen or could arise in Kenya. But it must be squarely admitted that our choice of topics to be left out, as well as to be dealt with, represents a value judgement on our part of what should be looked at in Kenya's legal development if the role of public law in the present polity of Kenya is to be understood, and thus a contribution made towards a fuller understanding of the political development of Kenya. The existence of institutions of native administration is less important than the way colonial administrators exercised judicial and administrative powers over Africans, and it is these latter matters that are therefore considered here. So, too, the organization, powers, and performance of the central administration tell us more about political developments in Kenya than a consideration of equivalent matters at the local level. Again, this is a book on the interrelation of law and political, not economic, development (so far as they can be separated) and thus somewhat regretfully, economic law has been displaced by the need to give full consideration to that matter.

Thus, while we might be criticized as being over-ambitious in our attempt to chart a new course for books on the public law of African states, and so re-establish the validity of a distinctive legal approach to some of the problems of developing states, we would claim an essentially modest aim for the substance of the book; it is not a substitute for either a full scale political analysis or a full scale history of Kenya but an attempt at an analysis and critique of Kenya's development since early colonial times as seen through the processes of the law and the eyes of lawyers.

Two further points need to be made. We hope that this book may be of some use to law students, yet, as we have said, it does not purport to give a complete description of all the current public law of Kenya, nor is it devoid of judgements on past and present legal developments. We make no apology for this. We have never understood the function of the law teacher or writer to be the mere reciter of rules whose merit is to be gauged by the quantity of information he can relay. All African countries have great need for lawyers who can take their eyes off the books of rules, who can see more to law than a set of statutes and law reports, and who can understand something of the workings of the legal system in a fast-changing society, and the contribution the law can make to those changes. Basic principles must of course be understood, but understanding comes from a consideration of those principles within the context of the society in which they operate, and not from learning them parrot-fashion from an alien textbook. The law student must constantly be brought up against questions such as: is this a satisfactory rule here; what is this law designed to achieve; what set of beliefs lie at the back of this law; why do law and practice diverge and so on. In short, a text should aim to stimulate, even aggravate, not stupify, and that is what we have tried to do here.

Secondly, the book contains value judgements in places. Where we have made an adverse criticism both of the colonial past, and the independent present, it has usually been on the basis that the practice has not measured up to the principles espoused by the practitioners, be they lawyers, politicians or administrators, that this failure is sometimes reprehensible, and always a danger to the long-term future of Kenya's development. There are, alas, some countries in which sycophancy is regarded as objective and adverse criticism as sedition; we do not believe Kenya to be such a country, and we would stress that if our judgements are regarded as austere the standards employed are for the most part those set by the leaders of Kenya themselves, and if they are regarded as erroneous they should be seen, not as motivated by ill-will, but as a stimulant to debate on public matters in Kenya.

Finally, one or two points of terminology must be mentioned. All legislation, whatever its origin, is now an Act in Kenya (Legal Notice No. 2 of 1964); before 1964, legislation passed prior to independence was an Ordinance. We have used the term Ordinance in the first four historical chapters regardless of whether the legislation is still in force, and the term Act in the rest of the book regardless of whether the legislation has been repealed. This is not strictly correct, but probably more convenient for the reader. Kadhi is spelt thus throughout the book as that is now the official Kenyan spelling as reflected in the Constitution, and the term Muslim law is used throughout the book for the same reason. The word native has been used where it is part of a recognized expression as in native courts, local native council or in direct quotation; otherwise, the more preferable word African has been used even though that word was not used in legislation or official reports.

Over the four or more years in which this book has been taking shape our debt to our colleagues, and our Universities, has been enormous, to say nothing of the debt to the numerous public servants who have talked with us or penned reports on public matters in Kenya on which we have been able to draw in writing this book. Professor Ghai would like to thank the University College of Dar es Salaam for granting him study leave for the academic year of 1965–6, the Rockefeller Foundation for a fellowship for that year and Nuffield College, Oxford for providing him with a stimulating environment to work in England. Mr. McAuslan would like to thank the University College of Dar es Salaam for leave of absence in the first half of 1965 and Wadham College, Oxford for giving him a temporary lectureship in that period which enabled him to work on the early legal history of Kenya; the London School of Economics and Political Science for agreeing so readily to allow him to return to East Africa in the summer of 1967 to continue research on and writing of the book, and the staff of the Library of the Commonwealth and Foreign Office for their unfailing help. We would both like to thank the University of East Africa for its financial support through a generous grant from the Ford Foundation, towards the cost of publishing this book. Amongst our colleagues and fellow-workers in the field of African studies, we would like to thank A. W. Bradley, Cherry Gertzel, D. Greer, L. L. Kato, J. M. Lonsdale, A. A. Mazrui, H. S. Morris, J. Okumu, J. S. Read and W. L. Twining, and those persons who took part in Law Faculty staff seminars in Dar es Salaam and the post-graduate seminar on African Law at the School of Oriental and African Studies where some of the themes in the book were first tried out. None of the above mentioned people is in any way responsible, however, for the errors and defects of this book. We would like to thank the publishers for their help in getting the book ready for publication once the completed manuscript was in their hands. Finally we should like to express our gratitude to Miss Nuvani Jivani and Mrs. Haneefa Kassam who patiently and cheerfully reduced our illegible handwriting to a neat manuscript.

In general, the law is stated as it stood on the fifth anniversary (December 1968) of independence, though we have managed to incorporate into the text and footnotes the revised version of the Constitution of Kenya, established by Act No. 5 of 1969, which is primarily a consolidation of the Constitution enacted at independence with its ten amendment acts.

Dar es Salaam Y. P. Ghai
Coventry J. P. W. B. McAuslan
July 1969

Contents

Tables of Cases and Legislation

CASES

KENYA LEGISLATION

UNITED KINGDOM LEGISLATION

APPLIED INDIAN ACTS

SELECT SUBSIDIARY LEGISLATION

PART I

The Colonial Era

CHAPTER 1

The Legal Origins of Colonial Power in Kenya

INTRODUCTION

The declaration of a protectorate over much of what is now Kenya on 15 June 1895 marked the beginning of official British rule in Kenya, a rule which was to endure until 12 December 1963. But it may also be regarded as marking the end of the first stage in the process whereby Britain acquired control of Kenya, for the initial steps in this process were taken by a favourite Victorian colonial device, the chartered company—in this case, the Imperial British East Africa Company—and the declaration of the protectorate signified the official demise of the Company as an instrument of acquisition and administration. Thus, in order to examine the legal aspects of the process of acquisition, it is necessary to go back to the period in which the Company was formed and began its operations.

Although the scramble for Africa was a continuous process and not something which sprang up overnight in the 1880s, the year of the Berlin Conference—1885—may be taken as the starting date for this historical survey since it coincided with a change in the attitude of the European Powers towards the East African coast. Hitherto, in so far as Britain had any interest in East Africa, it was primarily in connection with the suppression of the slave trade. The concrete expression of this interest took the form of the appointment of a consul-general at Zanzibar, who exercised considerable informal influence over the Sultan of Zanzibar, who was himself seen as having some authority over an undefined portion of the East African coast and interior, and the existence of several treaties and Acts of Parliament permitting the Consul-General and others to exercise jurisdiction within the dominions of the Sultan of Zanzibar (which dominions included the mainland) in order to suppress the slave trade more effectively. Other European countries had little interest in East Africa, though some maintained consuls at Zanzibar and had concluded treaties with the Sultan providing for the privileges of ex-territoriality for their subjects.[1]

[1] Only the United States (1833), France (1844), and Portugal (1879) had concluded agreements relating to consular jurisdictions with the ruling authorities in Zanzibar before 1885. Thereafter came Italy, Belgium and Germany (all 1885), Austria, Hungary (1887). The United States concluded a second agreement in 1886. For details, see E. Hertslet, *Map of Africa by Treaty* (London, Harrison and Sons Ltd., 1909), 3rd edition, volume I, pp. 315–30.

At the beginning of the 1880s this system of influence via the Sultan was on the wane. This was largely because the Sultan himself was losing what influence he had on the mainland, owing to British pressure on him to abolish the slave trade in his dominions, a policy which his 'subjects' were reluctant to accept and which he did not have the physical means to carry out. The collapse of the system was hastened, however, by Germany's bid for colonies and influence in East Africa, which was rapidly undermining the rest of the Sultan's, and therefore the British, power on the mainland by 1885.

The Berlin Conference of 1885 had as one of its main objects the desire 'to obviate the misunderstandings and disputes which might in the future arise from new acts of occupation on the coasts of Africa . . .'[2] The Conference had convened with the immediate aim of dealing with certain disputes which had arisen in West and Central Africa, but its conclusions set out in the General Act of the Conference had a significance for the whole of Africa, for, by purporting to set out the rules of international law relating to the acquisition of, and establishment of authority over territory in Africa, and coupling these with moral injunctions to stop the slave trade and bring 'civilization' to Africa, they gave new impetus to the scramble, and justifications to its protagonists.

It is important to realize, however, that the part of the General Act which dealt with acquisition of territory was confined to the coasts of Africa. Article 35 stated:

> The Signatory Powers of the present Act recognize the obligation to insure the establishment of authority in the regions occupied by them on the coasts of the African Continent sufficient to protect existing rights and as the case may be, freedom of trade and transit . . .

The Conference declined to consider rules relating to the interior because so little was known of it.[3] The effect of this was both to assist the rise of the dubious doctrines of the hinterland, and the principle of contiguity—both designed to ensure an area of unrestricted expansion behind the initial coastal occupation, and, since these doctrines were never fully accepted, to lead to a series of bilateral agreements between rival powers, delimiting their respective 'spheres of influence' in the interior. A sphere of influence had little more to commend itself than did a hinterland or a contiguous area but the concept was acceptable to the powers and so it became the means whereby the interior of Africa was marked out for future expansion.[4]

[2] General Act: Hertslet, volume II, pp. 468–87, preamble.
[3] M. F. Lindley, *The Acquisition and Government of Backward Territory in International Law* (London, Longmans, 1926), p. 145.
[4] 'The term indicates the regions which geographically are adjacent to or politically group themselves with possessions or protectorates but which have not actually been reduced into control. The phrase . . . rather implies a moral claim than a true right.' W. E. Hall, *Treatise on the Foreign Powers and Jurisdiction of the British Crown* (Oxford, Clarendon Press, 1894), pp. 228–9.

An agreement as to spheres of influence, however, did little more than provide a breathing space during which a colonial power could prepare for further acquisitions; it was not an indefinite substitute for acquisition.

The General Act was signed in February 1885, ratified in April 1886. Independently of that, but no doubt influenced by it, Germany was making rapid progress in East Africa, concluding agreements with chiefs which virtually ignored the claims of the Sultan of Zanzibar to sovereignty within the area. In a last effort to preserve some influence short of occupation in East Africa, Britain proposed to Germany and France that a joint commission be established to delimit the Sultan's dominions on the mainland. The two powers agreed. Whatever the intention behind the proposal, the commission was little better than a farce. The Sultan was not represented on it, and Germany continued to make treaties with chiefs in the disputed areas whilst it was in session. The final conclusions represented the highest common factor of agreement amongst the parties—the dominions of the Sultan on the mainland were to be the coast-line and the area for ten miles back, measured from the high-tide mark. This left the interior 'ownerless' and open to German expansion, and the boundary agreement was therefore quickly followed by a demarcation agreement between Germany and Britain which set out their respective spheres of influence in East Africa, the dividing line following the present Kenya-Tanzania border up to Lake Victoria, but not dealing with the area now occupied by Uganda. Again, the Sultan of Zanzibar was not consulted as to his views on the carve-up of his past and present dominions. The Anglo-German Agreement was made at the end of October 1886; the Sultan accepted the Agreement at the beginning of December, being counselled by his British advisers that he had little alternative.[5]

By the end of 1886, therefore, a reasonably definite portion of the coast and mainland of East Africa had been reserved for future British control and occupation by means of various agreements and treaties with other European powers. This had been done without any reference to the desires or views of the people most likely to be affected. It was necessary, however, to consolidate the position obtained by these agreements if they were to be respected by other European powers. For this purpose a convenient body was to hand—the British East Africa Association—founded by William Mackinnon.

THE INTERREGNUM OF THE IBEAC

As far back as 1877, Mackinnon, who had built up a steamship line plying between Britain and India, had been offered a concession by the Sultan

[5] Oliver and Mathew (eds.), *History of East Africa* (Oxford, Clarendon Press, 1963), volume I, chapter 10, pp. 369–74, from which much of the historical material in this chapter is taken. Hertslet, op. cit.

of Zanzibar to run his customs services but, receiving no encouragement from the Foreign Office, had not taken it up. He remained of the opinion, however, that there were commercial possibilities in East Africa, and at the beginning of 1887 formed the BEAA to open up the British portion of East Africa to commerce and civilization. He received encouragement from consular officials in Zanzibar and from politicians and others in England who saw in the Association a cheap and indirect method of carrying out the policy of retaining and, if possible, expanding British influence in East Africa to which the Government appeared to be committing itself. But the Foreign Office was less enthusiastic as it did not wish to be involved in expense or direct responsibility in East Africa; it did not, however, discourage the new initiative and was soon to lend it its support. The Sultan of Zanzibar needed little prompting to re-open negotiations for a concession, and the Association needed to produce evidence sufficient to convince the British Government of its viability in order to obtain a charter of incorporation, and the best evidence would be an agreement for a concession. Such a mutuality of interests produced quick agreement, and in May 1887 a Provisional Concession Agreement was concluded by which the Sultan made over to the Association for a period of fifty years all the power he possessed on the mainland, together with the rights of administration, which were, however, to be carried out in the Sultan's name, and subiect to his sovereign rights.[6]

This Concession Agreement was to last only fifteen months, being replaced by one in somewhat similar terms when the Association obtained its charter. Little effort was made to begin organizing administration in the Coastal Strip, but the Association's agents were active in concluding agreements with chiefs both in the coastal area and outside, agreements of which it has been said that 'most of the tribes cannot have been aware of [their] real meaning; the stack of treaty forms collected in the Foreign Office files in London represented to the chiefs and elders, who agreeably inscribed them with their X-marks, considerably less than the familiar ceremony of blood-brotherhood'.[7] But to the Government of the day, they represented evidence that the Association was a body worth giving more formal support to, and in September 1888, impelled partly by such evidence and partly by events in other parts of Africa, a Royal Charter of Incorporation was granted to the Association which henceforth became known as the Imperial British East Africa Company.

The chartered company carrying on the purposes and policies of European

[6] Hertslet, op. cit., pp. 339–45, especially articles 1, 11 and 12.

[7] Oliver and Mathew, op. cit., volume I, p. 397. Hertslet lists eighty-four treaties concluded between 1887–1891, the first twenty-two of which were concluded prior to the charter. See volume I, pp. 374–8. Those concluded with chiefs outside the Sultan's dominions were *ultra vires* the company but the charter which it obtained the following year permitted it to retain the benefits of all previous agreements.

governments in Africa was a familiar disguise in the late nineteenth century; thus the grant of the royal charter 'was an announcement to the powers of Europe that the company was henceforth not merely an agent of the Sultan of Zanzibar but an arm of British imperial policy'.[8] In legal terms this meant that whereas the Association had derived its powers solely from the agreement with the Sultan, the Company derived its powers first and foremost from the British Government, and then from agreements with the Sultan and other local rulers. A reference to the charter shows how this was achieved.[9]

The Company was permitted to retain the benefit of all previous grants and treaties but fresh treaties with chiefs had first to be approved by the Foreign Secretary before the Company could take any rights thereunder. If there were disputes between the Company and the Sultan or any chief, the matter had to be taken to the Foreign Secretary for his decision. The Company was subject to, and had to carry out, all the obligations undertaken by the British Government under any treaty or agreement made with another state, and in connection with that obligation as well as with any general dealings with a foreign power, the Foreign Secretary was empowered to give directions or make suggestions to the Company, both of which it was required to follow. The Company was also obliged to defer to the objections of the Foreign Secretary in respect of the exercise of its authority on the basis of treaties concluded with chiefs. Finally, if the terms of the charter were not observed, it could be revoked.

It can be seen that the Government reserved sufficient power to itself to ensure that it could influence and control every move of a governmental nature which the Company might wish to make. A parallel may be drawn with modern statutes governing the relations between a Minister and a public corporation which puts the latter under a considerable degree of political control by the government, although regarded in law as being independent of government. If then the Company appeared to some extent to be uncontrolled, this was due more to lack of communication between East Africa and England and the ambivalent attitude adopted by successive governments in England towards its activities, than to any absence of legal power to control.

Armed with the charter, the Company proceeded to re-negotiate the concession with the Sultan, in effect, taking over that of the Association and expanding its terms. The concession of October 1888 extended from Wanga, on the boundary between the British and German spheres of

[8] Oliver and Mathew, op. cit., volume I, pp. 380–1.
[9] McDermott, *British East Africa or IBEA* (London, Chapman and Hall, 1893), appendix II, articles 2–4, 7–9 and 22. The full text of the Charter is in McDermott, *IBEA*, appendix II.

influence, to Kipini. It was to last for fifty years, but this was extended to perpetuity in 1891. By it the Sultan made over

> all the powers and authority to which he is entitled on the mainland, the whole administration of which is placed in the hands of the Imperial British East Africa Company to be carried out in his name under his flag and subject to his sovereign rights.[10]

In pursuance of the power of administration the Company could appoint commissioners to administer districts, promulgate laws, and establish and operate courts of justice; it was empowered further to acquire or regulate land which had not yet been occupied, and all public lands were to be purchased either by it or through it. A reservation was made that the Articles of Concession were not to infringe or lessen 'the rights accorded by His Highness to the subjects or citizens of Great Britain, the United States of America, France, Germany or any other foreign powers having treaty relations with His Highness or the obligations which are imposed on him by his adhesion to the Berlin General Act'.[11] The effect of this reservation was that rights of ex-territoriality in the dominions of the Sultan obtained by many European powers continued in force in the Coastal Strip and that, at a later date, 1891, the Sultan was able to extend to his mainland dominions the provisions of the Berlin General Act concerning free trade, a decision which led to a certain amount of friction between the Company and the British Government—the latter having by then declared a protectorate over Zanzibar—since the revenues of the Company came from customs dues which it levied on the mainland, and these were reduced by that action.

The reservation makes clear the legal effect of the concession. As Lindley[12] has said, it represents a reversal of the normal method of acquiring sovereignty or control over another territory. The normal method was to encroach gradually on the power of the ruler to conduct his foreign affairs; this culminated in a protectorate being declared, the essential element of which, as far as the outside world was concerned, was that henceforth it would have to deal with the protected state through the protector. As regards the conduct of internal administration, however, the declaration of a protectorate would not necessarily mean any changes, although this often occurred—Zanzibar being a good example of this. With a concession agreement, however, it was the power to conduct internal administration which was lost, the power to conduct foreign affairs remaining intact. Thus in theory the state concerned would still be responsible for acts of maladministration which affected the nationals of foreign powers. In respect of this particular conces-

[10] Hertslet, op. cit., pp. 350–9, article 1. See, too, Supplementary Agreement 1891, pp. 365–6.
[11] Article I.
[12] Hertslet, op. cit., pp. 237–9.

sion, the difference was more apparent than real since the British Consul at Zanzibar was in effective control of the Sultan's foreign affairs at the time, although a protectorate was not formally declared until 1890.

The concession related only to the dominions of the Sultan, but the Company's operational area extended throughout the whole of the British sphere of influence and beyond, covering much of present day Kenya and Uganda. We are not concerned with its activities in Uganda other than to point out how much they influenced events in Kenya, directly and indirectly, both at the time and for the future.[13] Initially it affected the priorities of further 'opening up' of the Company's domains. As the coast was the base from which expeditions went out to Uganda, it was essential to secure it against possible rivals. To this end, the Company worked to extend its jurisdiction over the remainder of the Sultan's dominions at the coast and obtain jurisdiction over the Sultanate of Witu. In 1889 it procured a lease from the Sultan of Zanzibar of all his possessions from Kipini to Mruti (less the Sultanate of Witu) and to Mogadishu. The initial lease was on the terms that the Company would hold the area as the *wakil* of the Sultan, administer it in accordance with the *sheria*, with a power of veto reserved to the Sultan in matters of public policy in so far as this concerned his own subjects. Less than six months later, however, in March 1890, the lease was turned into a concession to be administered and held for the same period and on the same terms and conditions as the original concession. A year later the concession was 'modified' so as to last in perpetuity. This modification did not, however, apply to the Benadir ports, which had been transferred by the Company to Italy in 1889 on the same terms as it had obtained them from the Sultan.[14]

The Sultanate of Witu remained a thorn in the side of the Company since Germany was claiming a protectorate over it and encouraging the Sultan to reject the overtures of the Company. However, by the Anglo-German Agreement of 1890,[15] which settled outstanding questions between the two countries in East Africa, Germany renounced all claims to Witu as she did to Uganda, and a British protectorate was declared over it.[16] The British Government was still unwilling to be directly involved in administration on the mainland and agreed with the Company that it should administer it under the terms of the charter, which it began to do the following year.[17] Thus by the middle of 1891 the Company was responsible

[13] See particularly the comments in Oliver and Mathew, op. cit., volume I, pp. 393; 407–8.
[14] Hertslet, op. cit., pp. 359–64, for details of this series of transactions.
[15] Hertslet, op. cit., volume III, p. 899, especially article 2.
[16] Hertslet, op. cit., volume I, p.364. The Protectorate included all territory north of the River Tana, to the River Juba.
[17] Hertslet, op. cit., p. 367.

for the administration of the coastal area from Wanga to Kismayu, a distance of approximately 500 miles.

The Anglo-German Agreement of 1890, ending a period of rivalry for the Kingdom of Uganda and the Sultanate of Witu, was of great benefit to the Company. The General Act of the Brussels Conference, signed the same year, was not, according to the Company, beneficial, as it imposed fresh obligations on it. The Brussels Conference was convened 'to give fresh sanctions to decisions already taken in the same sense and at different periods by the powers', in relation to the effective occupation and control of Africa. To this end the powers agreed in the General Act that they were under an obligation to end the slave trade and open up Africa to 'legitimate' commerce; that this could be done most effectively by the 'progressive organization of administrative, judicial, religious and military services in the African territories placed under the sovereignty or protection of civilized nations', and particularly by the establishment of fortified stations in the interior.[18] Article IV of the General Act provided that:

> The powers exercising sovereignty or protection in Africa may, however, delegate to Chartered Companies all or a portion of the engagements which they assume by virtue of Article III [which dealt with the suppression of the slave trade]. They remain nonetheless directly responsible for the engagements which they contract by the present General Act and they guarantee the execution thereof.

This gave an international legal sanction to the operations of the chartered companies which were to be assisted to carry out their tasks where possible. At the same time it seems to show that whatever the position in English constitutional law, the British Government was regarded by the other European powers as having a protectorate in East Africa by virtue of the operations of the IBEAC. It can hardly be supposed that the British Government would have been allowed to argue that the provisions of the General Act did not apply to East Africa since neither it nor any other power was 'exercising sovereignty or protection' therein. If the question had been asked, 'to which Power should, for example, Germany look for redress in the event of one of her nationals suffering injury in that part of Africa administered by the IBEAC?', the answer would, and could only have been, 'Great Britain'. What arrangements the British Government made to discharge its obligations or to exact penalties from those who had injured a foreigner was a matter for its own internal law, and the use of a chartered company for these purposes had received the approval of the Powers, but it did not affect Britain's international responsibilities. When it is realized that the charter of the Company referred to the Company's exercise of jurisdiction under the Foreign Jurisdiction Acts, and that juris-

[18] Hertslet, op. cit., volume II, pp. 488–518, preamble, article I.

diction was in fact exercised under the Zanzibar Order in Council 1884[19] and the Africa Order in Council 1889,[20] both made in pursuance of the Foreign Jurisdiction Acts 1843–78, it can be appreciated that the attitude of the international community as set out in the Brussels General Act was a good deal more realistic than that of the English constitutional lawyer who did not accept that the British Government incurred legal obligations in respect of those parts of Africa administered by chartered companies until protection had been assumed directly by the Government itself. The upshot of this is that, whether looked at from the point of view of the European powers or from the point of view of the inhabitants of East Africa, the IBEAC was an irrelevancy which may have served a purpose of obscuring the true position from the British Parliament but did not obscure what was happening from anyone else. In the eyes of international law Britain became responsible for her part of East Africa from the time the IBEAC obtained its charter, the Brussels Conference confirmed that, and the declaration of protectorates, first over Uganda and later over the rest of East Africa, were mere formalities designed to comply with the Brussels General Act, but not altering her international responsibilities.[21]

The IBEAC may have been useful in allowing the British Government to obscure the full implications of its policies, but in the early 1890s it rapidly showed signs of being little use at anything else. It has been called 'ramshackle' and stigmatized as 'poorly conceived, badly managed and grossly undercapitalized';[22] certainly it did not have a successful administrative career but it was in part the victim of the East African policies of successive British Governments to which the same epithets could with equal justice

[19] S.R.O. (revised) volume III, 1890 edition, p. 865.
[20] S.R.O. (revised) volume III, 1890 edition, p. 259.
[21] The question of the liability of the government for the acts of officers of the company arose in relation to some French claims in Uganda. The Lord Chancellor in a memorandum stated that the government had not conferred powers of government upon the company since it had no such powers to confer, and the mere act of incorporation did not of itself render the government responsible to foreign powers for all the acts of the company. But the government had reserved certain powers to itself in the charter and failure to exercise these powers could render it liable. Again, the fact that the company's enterprise had received the blessing of the government imposed some obligation on the government and this could be discharged either by pressing the company to accept the claims, or, if Uganda was abandoned, it would be politic to assume the liability. As a matter of municipal law, however, the government did not become liable for the acts of the company in circumstances where it would not have been liable for the acts of a ruler whose rights had been acquired, and it was municipal law that applied to the situation. See Conf. 6362/1892 in F.O. 84/2275.

The distinction drawn between what it would be politic to do and what, as a matter of municipal law, the government was bound to do, suggests that the Lord Chancellor appreciated that other countries would not accept that the legal obligations of Her Majesty's Government were to be defined solely by reference to English law. On this point see further A. H. Smith, *Great Britain and the Law of Nations*, volume II, part I, p. 83 (London, 1935), and Lindley, op. cit., pp. 99–108, and C. Palley, *The Constitutional History and Law of Southern Rhodesia 1888–1965* (Oxford, Clarendon Press, 1966), chapter 1.
[22] Oliver and Mathew, op. cit., volume I, pp. 393 and 409.

be applied. In May 1893 it withdrew from Buganda following the conclusion of a protection agreement between the Kabaka and the British Government Commissioner, sent out to investigate the question of future British involvement in the area. In July 1893 it withdrew from the administration of the protectorate north of the River Tana with the exception of the territories belonging to the Sultan of Zanzibar; its administration was delegated to the Government of the Sultan of Zanzibar—effectively to British administrators, since Zanzibar was by then a British protectorate, but the delegation had the advantage of avoiding direct British commitment.[23]

By now the writing was on the wall for the Company. It had been severely criticized for its administrative ineffectiveness in East Africa by the Commissioner, and in truth had done little to open up the country. British protectorates had been declared over Uganda to the north west, over the dominions of the Sultan of Zanzibar including the mainland dominions (which had, however, been left within the administrative competence of the Company),[24] and over the Sultanate of Witu, and the territory north of the River Tana.

THE PROTECTORATE: ASSUMPTION OF GENERAL POWERS

In June 1895, the British Government declared a protectorate over the rest of the territory administered by the Company. It was named the East Africa Protectorate a year later. It merely remained to work out the terms on which the Company would surrender its concession at the coast and its charter.

To the last the British Government declined to accept responsibility for what had been done, virtually in its name and certainly on its behalf, over the preceding seven years. In a discreditable transaction, the British Government first induced the Sultan of Zanzibar to pay over to the IBEAC the sum of £200,000 the Sultan had received from the German Government for the sale of his coastal dominions in German East Africa, as compensation for the IBEAC's assets and for all it had done in administering the coast, and secondly informed the Sultan that the Coastal Strip would continue to be administered together with the interior directly by the British Government, thus depriving him of the effective control of the coast, although it was to remain part of his dominions. The reasons given for this were that the affairs of the Ten Mile Strip and of the interior had become so interwoven under the Company that separate administration was impractical, and even if that were not the case, there were customs and transit difficulties in the way of their separate administration. To make this final loss of authority more palatable, the British Government agreed that the sum the Sultan

[23] Hertslet, op. cit., volume I, p. 379. Proclamation of the Consul-General at Zanzibar.
[24] Hertslet, op. cit., pp. 308–10.

had had to pay to the Company would be regarded as a loan to the Government for this purpose, upon which it would pay interest at a fixed rate of 3 per cent, together with an annual rent of £11,000. The Agreement embodying these and other terms was not finally signed until December 1895; besides the financial terms, it provided that the administration of the coast should be entrusted to officers appointed direct by the British Government, who were to have full powers with regard to executive and judicial administration, levying taxes, and over all land and buildings. Neither the sovereignty of the Sultan nor the treaty rights of foreign powers were to be affected.[25]

The Agreement related only to the mainland dominions of Zanzibar but the Company surrendered its charter at the same time, and the Government took over the interior into which the Company had expanded and had the right to expand, and the other portions of the coast. However, the extent of the protectorate was to undergo several changes in the following years as the colonial government began effectively to open up the interior and as boundary changes took place. It will be convenient to deal with these matters here in their chronological order.

In 1896 the Ogaden Somalis agreed to a treaty of protection which resulted in the boundaries of the protectorate being extended to the north.[26] In 1902 the Foreign Office transferred the Eastern Province of Uganda to the protectorate, and the area so transferred became the Kisumu and Naivasha provinces; in 1904 a portion of Lake Victoria around Kisumu was likewise transferred.[27] In 1905 the Benadir Ports were sold to Italy for £144,000, payable to the Government of Zanzibar.[28] In 1907 the boundary with Ethiopia was agreed upon but it was not surveyed on the ground until much later.[29] In 1925 Jubaland was transferred to Italy and became part of

[25] *The Kenya Coastal Strip—Report of the Commissioner,* Cmnd. 1585/1961. For the notification of the protectorate over all the territories under the administration of the IBEAC not being already under British protection, and the full text of statements made by the Consul-General, and the Wazir of the Sultan (Sir Lloyd Mathews) at the Mombasa ceremony of transfer, see Hertslet, op. cit., pp. 380–1.

See, too, the Zanzibar Indemnity Act 1894 dealing with the transfer of the £200,000 from the Bank of England to the Government of Zanzibar. By the Act the bank was authorized to transfer the money which it had held on behalf of the late Sultan to the Government of Zanzibar, and the Treasury was to indemnify the bank against any claims arising in relation thereto. By an agreement scheduled to the Act, the Sultan of Zanzibar agreed that the Zanzibar Government should indemnify the Treasury if the occasion so arose.

[26] Hertslet, op. cit., volume I, p. 387.

[27] East Africa Protectorate Gazette 11/5/02; 24/804. See Hertslet, op. cit., volume I, pp. 385–6.

[28] Italy had administered these ports since 1889 when it acquired the IBEAC concession. There had been a direct Concession Agreement made between the Governments of Zanzibar and Italy in respect of these ports in 1892. Hertslet, op. cit., volume III, pp. 1088–1107.

[29] Treaty Series No. 27 (1908) Cmd. 4318. This Agreement was abrogated and replaced by one in 1947 which 'amended the description' of the boundary without, however, changing the areas actually administered by the two countries. Laws of Kenya, volume XI, Group 2, Boundaries, pp. 80–3.

Italian Somaliland,[30] and in 1926 another portion of Uganda—Rudolph Province (Turkanaland)—was annexed to Kenya Colony.[31]

Internally as well, boundary clarifications took place. In 1899 the boundary between the Coastal Strip and the rest of the protectorate was the subject of an administrative agreement between the protectorate authorities and the Zanzibar Government, which did not, however, give rise to legal rights. This boundary was not finally and conclusively determined until 1921 in consequence of the annexation of the protectorate less the Coastal Strip.[32] Besides this major division which existed for the whole period of Kenya's dependent status, the Sultanate of Witu initially had a special status and boundaries, arising out of the Anglo-German Agreement and the protectorate declared over Witu in 1890. Formally it was treated as a protected state within the East Africa Protectorate (though they were treated as one for administrative purposes), with a Resident in Witu accredited to the Sultan, and with legislative powers vested in the Sultan but delegated to the Resident, who acted under the control of the Commissioner for the protectorate. In practice, as the Commissioner himself stated,[33] legislation in Witu did not differ from the rest of the protectorate, and Witu was effectively controlled by the protectorate authorities. Its special status came to an end when it was annexed in 1920.[34]

The commencement of the protectorate marked the beginning of direct British Government administration in the area hitherto administered and controlled by the IBEAC. It is necessary, therefore, to consider the nature and extent of the powers available to, and the obligations cast upon, the Government by its decision to displace the Company.

More fundamental, however, is the question of whence came the power

[30] Anglo-Italian Treaty (East African Territories) Act 1925. The Treaty, signed in 1924 and providing for the transfer is contained in a schedule to the Act. See further p. 29 below.

[31] Kenya Colony and Protectorate (Boundaries) Order in Council, S.R.O. 1926, No. 1733.

[32] Kenya (Annexation) Order in Council, S.R.O. 1920, No. 2342; Kenya Protectorate Order in Council, S.R.O. 1920, No. 2343; Kenya Colony and Protectorate (Boundaries) Order in Council, S.R.O. 1921, No. 1134. See further on the annexation pp. 50–52, below.

[33] Hardinge: 1899 *J.S.C.L.*, volume I (N.S.) 1.

[34] No separate Order in Council was ever promulgated in respect of the Sultanate of Witu. Apart from the article by Hardinge, the main published sources of information about Witu are those relating to the exercise of jurisdiction over it, and an important proclamation published in The East Africa Protectorate Gazette, 17/10/07 at p. 87: 'The Dominions of H.H. the Sultan of Witu are under the Protection of His Majesty of the United Kingdom, and form part of the East Africa Protectorate, and His Majesty has jurisdiction therein and in pursuance thereof has made laws, and whereas doubts have arisen as to whether laws so made do apply to that part of the Protectorate as is within the dominions of the Sultan of Witu, now I the Sultan of Witu declare and proclaim that all laws in the East Africa Protectorate shall apply to the Sultanate of Witu save in so far as any such law shall apply to the contrary, and shall be enforced by my officers and such officers as His Majesty is pleased to appoint to assist me in administering the said laws in my Dominions'.

of the Crown to exercise jurisdiction in a foreign land either directly, or via a company to which it had given a Royal Charter authorizing it to acquire by purchase, cession or other lawful means foreign lands and to set up a system of government therein. For many years it had been thought that the answer to this lay in the use of the Royal Prerogative, but it was owing to doubts as to powers granted by the use of the prerogative to consuls in the Ottoman Empire that the first Foreign Jurisdiction Act was passed in 1843. This provided for the exercise of jurisdiction by the sovereign in foreign countries.[35] This Act, together with amending legislation, was consolidated into the Foreign Jurisdiction Act 1890. It is this whole scheme of legislation, the Acts and Orders in Council made thereunder, which provided the statutory base for the extent and exercise of jurisdiction by the Company, and afterwards the government, in East Africa.[36]

The 1890 Act provided for the exercise by Her Majesty of any jurisdiction, whether obtained by treaty, capitulation, grant, usage, sufference or any other lawful means, and whether obtained before or after the commencement of the Act, in a foreign country in as ample a manner as if she had acquired that jurisdiction by cession or conquest. It provided also that where a foreign country was not subject to a form of government from which jurisdiction in the above manner could be obtained, Her Majesty should 'by virtue of the Act' have jurisdiction over her subjects in that foreign country.[37] The jurisdiction which might be exercised under the Act, and which was to be specified in Orders in Council, empowered consuls, and later colonial officials, to hold courts, promulgate legislation and carry on an administration in the area to which the Order in Council applied.[38] The relevant Orders in Council here were the Zanzibar Order in Council 1884 and the Africa Order in Council 1889, made under the authority of the Foreign Jurisdiction Acts of 1843–78. The former dealt with the exercise of consular jurisdiction in the dominions of the Sultan of Zanzibar and thus embraced the Coastal Strip, but the latter was a more ambitious piece of

[35] H. Jenkyns, *British Rule and Jurisdiction beyond the Seas* (Oxford, Clarendon Press, 1902), p. 151, and appendix VI (*Report on British Jurisdiction in Foreign States* by Hope Scott, 1843). See, too, *Papayanni* v. *The Russian Steam Navigation and Trading Company 1863*, 2 Moo. P.C. (N.S.) 161 (*The Laconia*).

[36] There is and always has been much dispute amongst writers as to what the Foreign Jurisdiction Acts were designed to accomplish. One view, for which modern authority is to be found in K. Roberts-Wray, *Commonwealth and Colonial Law* (London, Stevens and Sons, 1966), is that the Acts did not create powers of foreign jurisdiction in the Crown but merely 'removed doubts regarding the operation of one branch of the already existing prerogative rights of the Crown' (p. 192). The other view, for which J. E. S. Fawcett, *The British Commonwealth in International Law* (London, Stevens and Sons, 1963), at pp. 124–6, may be quoted is that the Acts conferred powers on the Crown which it did not have before. It is submitted that this latter view is the better one. See, too, the general discussion in Palley, op. cit., chapter 4.

[37] Preamble, sections 1 and 2.

[38] Section 9.

legislation: it created a comprehensive framework of administration, including the power to hold courts and promulgate regulations, to be exercised usually by consuls, and over British subjects, British protected persons and certain classes of indigenous inhabitants and foreigners. It was to be applied in those parts of Africa constituted by the Foreign Secretary as local jurisdictions.[39]

Having summarized the general law, we are now in a position to consider the legal sources of authority for the British Government's administration of the East Africa Protectorate. As originally constituted, the protectorate consisted of three distinct sovereignties: the Sultanate of Witu; the mainland possessions of the Sultan of Zanzibar (the Coastal Strip); and the chartered territory of the IBEAC. This last area may be further subdivided into the part where the Company had begun to organize a system of administration, whether with or without a prior agreement made with a local ruler, and that part into which the Company had not ventured at all, although it was in its legitimate sphere of operation. Enough has already been said of the Sultanate of Witu which was no more than an historical curiosity. As regards the Coastal Strip, legal authority to administer it is to be spelt out from two sources. First, there was the oral agreement between the Sultan of Zanzibar and the British Government of July 1895, which was formally reduced to writing in December 1895. Secondly, there was the Zanzibar Order in Council 1884 as amended from time to time. The original purpose of this piece of legislation was to provide for the exercise of their jurisdiction by the consular courts in the Sultan's dominions, but an amendment of 1888 extended the powers of the consul and provided that he could promulgate legislation, known as Queen's Regulations, binding on all those subject to the Order.[40] When the British Government took over the direct administration of the Coastal Strip, those on whom the Order was binding included subjects of the Sultan as well as British subjects and British protected persons, but did not include the citizens of those powers which had rights of exterritoriality in the Sultan's dominions, for these rights extended to the mainland and were expressly preserved.[41] In respect of the rest of the protectorate, powers were exercisable primarily under the Africa Order in Council 1889, as amended, since the territories administered by the Company had been constituted a local jurisdiction under the Order in 1889, with the exception of the Coastal Strip which, as a part of the Sultan's dominions, was specifically excluded from its operation.[42] Less important as a source of power were the various agreements made by the IBEAC with local rulers

[39] Section 4. A local jurisdiction was distinct from a protectorate and could exist without a protectorate having been declared.

[40] Zanzibar Order in Council 1888, S.R.O. (revised), 1890 edition, volume III, section 2, p. 886.

[41] Zanzibar (Jurisdiction) Order in Council 1893, S.R.O., p. 406, section 2. Concession Agreement, article I.

[42] Section 6 (2).

which the Government inherited; these were not very extensive and the attitude of the new administering authorities towards them can perhaps be gauged from their own practice of extending the area of their effective control without bothering to conclude agreements.[43]

The sources of authority for the two main parts of the protectorate were then initially different but they had this in common; in neither Order in Council was there any specific reference to administrative organization in East Africa; and both were continued unchanged after the assumption of the protectorate. The reason for this was basically that both Orders in Council had been promulgated for one purpose—that of providing for a limited consular jurisdiction in various parts of Africa—and had gradually come to be used for another, at any rate in East Africa—that of being the legal basis for the assumption of general governmental authority to discharge the obligation imposed by the General Acts of the Berlin and Brussels Conferences, first by the IBEAC, and later by the British Government. Such specific extensions of power as were needed were provided for by amendments to the Orders rather than a new Order.

A further and important point may be made. The continuation of the two Orders in Council and the system of administration based on them for the first two years of the protectorate, together with the fact that the East Africa Order in Council 1897[44] did not attempt to provide for a comprehensive system of administration, go some way to show that the assumption of the protectorate as such had less legal significance for the protected area than is sometimes supposed. From the point of view of international law, Britain had had obligations in respect of East Africa imposed upon her for several years past, and the assumption and its public notification may be seen as a belated conforming to Article 34 of the General Act of the Berlin Conference. From the point of view of municipal law, the Government could obtain control over local inhabitants in East Africa without any need to declare that a protectorate was being established, by making use of its power acquired by treaty and usage, and extended under the Foreign Jurisdiction Act. The one possible exception to this control was the power to dispose of land, which will be considered below. Again the declaration of a protectorate did not operate to convert the protected territory into part of the dominions of the Crown; it remained a foreign country. Finally, from the point of view of the inhabitants of East Africa the same administrators continued to exercise the same powers and have the same regard, or lack of it, for their laws and customs as before.

[43] Vincent Harlow and E. M. Chilver (eds.), *History of East Africa* (Oxford, Clarendon Press, 1965), volume II; D. A. Low, 'British East Africa, The Establishment of British Rule 1895–1912', pp. 1–56 in G. H. Mungeam, *British Rule in Kenya 1895–1912* (Oxford, Clarendon Press, 1966).

[44] S.R.O. 1575/1897, p. 134.

In three situations only is it possible that the assumption of a protectorate wrought any significant legal change. First, the status of an inhabitant of East Africa might have been changed in the eyes of English municipal law from an alien to a British protected person, with the rights and obligations that that entailed. It is not possible to be at all certain on this point, for the status of a British protected person was still a hazy one in the late nineteenth century,[45] and it is arguable that those persons whose chiefs had concluded treaties with the IBEAC whereby they were placed 'under' or 'under the protection' of the Company would have been regarded as British protected persons thereafter, by virtue of the treaty, and the fact that East Africa was a local jurisdiction under the Africa Order in Council. The two other situations will be discussed more fully later in this chapter.

We have considered the legal sources of the exercise of power by the British Government in the East Africa Protectorate; and in so doing have touched upon the extent of the power exercised, but we must now consider this matter more fully. It can best be understood by reference to three heads—jurisdiction over the indigenous population, control of the land, and jurisdiction over foreigners. The basic point which must be kept in mind in the ensuing discussion is that a protectorate is, in the eyes of English law, a foreign country, and its inhabitants are not therefore British subjects. This applies to a colonial protectorate as much as to a protected state,[46] and it does not matter that the system of government is indistinguishable from that of a colony. It is, however, a foreign country with this vital difference—that international law does not govern its relations with the protecting power, and the rights and obligations of that power, no less than those of the protectorate and its inhabitants, depend upon the law of the protecting power. This law is set out in the Foreign Jurisdiction Act, and Orders in Council made thereunder, and in the general principles of English constitutional law, particularly the concept of the Act of State.

(a) *Jurisdiction over the Indigenous Population*

Until the late 1880s the general rule, in countries in which the British Crown exercised foreign jurisdiction over its own subjects was that, unless a treaty provided otherwise, subjects of the local ruler remained under his exclusive jurisdiction. This rule was slowly departed from as jurisdictional involvements in Africa increased, and the East Africa Protectorate well illustrates the change, as it was a compound of an Eastern-type protected state where jurisdiction over local inhabitants was usually left at a minimum, and an African protectorate where it slowly grew to full power.

[45] C. Parry, *Nationality and Citizenship Laws of the Commonwealth and of the Republic of Ireland* (London, Stevens and Sons, 1957), volume I, pp. 89–91.
[46] For a discussion of the different classes of protectorates, see M. Wight, *Colonial Constitutions 1947* (Oxford, Clarendon Press, 1952).

At the time the IBEAC began its activities at the coast, British jurisdiction over the subjects of the Sultan derived from the Treaty of Commerce 1886,[47] between Great Britain and Zanzibar and the manner of its operation was set out in the Zanzibar Order in Council 1884. The treaty provided for jurisdiction to be exercised only over those in the service of British subjects. The Company acquired full jurisdiction over the Sultan's subjects through the Concession Agreement, and this position was inherited by the British Government when it took over the administration of the Coastal Strip, in accordance with the Agreement of 1895, but this did not appear clearly from the Order in Council until 1902. It is of interest to note, however, that full jurisdiction was not acquired by virtue of the assumption of a protectorate over the Coastal Strip in 1890.

In the rest of the IBEAC territories the position was more obscure. Jurisdiction over persons whose rulers concluded agreements with the Company may be rested on those agreements, which were phrased in the widest possible language, but there was no provision as to how such jurisdiction should be exercised since at most the Africa Order in Council 1889 only provided for such jurisdiction to be exercised with the consent of the natives concerned. But in respect of persons in relation to whom there were no agreements, it does not appear that the Company had any power to exercise jurisdiction over them legally, for its charter limited it to acquiring jurisdiction bilaterally. There is no evidence, however, that the Company was deterred by this technicality from exercising sporadic though vigorous power at certain stations in the interior.

By 1895, when a protectorate was declared over the rest of East Africa, the British Government's position was that, as against foreigners, as much power as was needed to ensure effective government could be assumed in a protectorate.[48] It might be thought that this same approach would be adopted as against local inhabitants, particularly as full power had been acquired at the coast, but for no very clear reasons this was not the case. The Commissioner appreciated that his administration lacked power to deal with local inhabitants, and that this created particular inconvenience in the exercise of judicial powers, and made recommendations to the Foreign Office accordingly. These resulted in the East Africa Order in Council 1897.[49] The Order dealt mainly with judicial matters and had a restricted application to local inhabitants. The powers conferred were expressed to apply to natives of the protectorate in accordance with the Order but not otherwise, and the only matter of which specific mention was made in the Order was native courts.

[47] Hertslet, op. cit., volume I, p. 302, articles 16 and 17.
[48] McNair, *International Law Opinions* (Cambridge University Press, 1956), volume I, pp. 54–5.
[49] S.R.O. 575. Mungeam, op. cit., pp. 55–8.

In the event, Queen's Regulations on these and other courts and law were made and applied to Africans.[50] There was considerable doubt as to the legality of this and in order to clarify matters the East Africa Order in Council 1899[51] provided, *inter alia*, that unless a contrary intention appeared, Queen's Regulations should apply to natives of the protectorate. Full jurisdiction over these persons was not, however, conferred on the protectorate authorities until the East Africa Order in Council 1902,[52] which empowered the Commissioner to make Ordinances for the peace, order and good government of all persons in the protectorate and established a High Court with full criminal and civil jurisdiction over all persons and matters in the protectorate. It must be noted that the seven year period between the assumption of the protectorate with only limited power over the larger part of it, and the acquisition of full power over the whole of it did not unduly hinder the protectorate administration in opening up the country and controlling its inhabitants, an apt commentary on the rather haphazard attitude evinced towards the law in the early days of the protectorate.

The use of the full powers of government thus acquired may be illustrated by the *Masai Case*.[53] It was early discovered that the traditional grazing grounds of the Masai consisted of rich agricultural land and were therefore eminently suitable for settlers. In 1904, under some pressure, the Laibon of the Masai, together with some other senior members of the tribe, were induced to agree, on behalf of the Masai, to vacating some of this land and being re-grouped in two other areas on the condition, *inter alia*, that the Agreement 'shall be enduring so long as the Masai as a race shall exist, and that Europeans or other settlers shall not be allowed to take up land in the Settlements'.[54] The Agreement lasted seven years, but well before its formal demise and replacement in 1911, the settlers were pressing for it to be abrogated and the Masai to be moved once again. After a period of indecision, the protectorate government finally gave way, concluded another agreement with the Masai whereby they agreed to move from the area the settlers wanted, and after considerable mismanagement, carried out the move. The plaintiff, on behalf of some of the Masai who had been compelled to move in 1911, brought an action for breach of the 1904 Agreement on the ground that that Agreement was a civil contract which was still subsisting, the Agreement of 1911 not having been made with those Masai capable of binding all the tribe. Damages were also claimed in tort for the wrongful confiscation of some cattle. Preliminary objections were raised by the government: the courts had no jurisdiction, since the Agreements of 1904 and 1911

[50] Sections 51 and 52. Native Court Regulations 1897.
[51] S.R.O. 757, section 9.
[52] S.R.O. 661, sections 12 (1) and 15 (1).
[53] *Ol le Njogo and others* v. *A-G of the E.A.P.* (1914), 5 E.A.L.R. 70.
[54] At p. 92.

were treaties not contracts, and the alleged confiscation was an Act of State and neither were therefore cognisable in a municipal court. These contentions were successful both at first instance and in the Court of Appeal for Eastern Africa.

On the treaty point, the E.A.C.A. first decided that as the protectorate was a foreign country, it followed that the Masai were foreigners in relation to the protecting power. They were 'subjects of their chiefs or their local government whatever form that government may in fact take'.[55] But this did not conclude the question of whether a treaty could be made with the tribe. The key to that question was the issue of sovereignty—if the Masai still had some vestigal sovereignty left, after the administering authority had taken over control of their country, then a treaty could be made with them. It was held that the Masai still retained some element of sovereignty and treaties could therefore be made with them, even though they would not be governed by international law but 'by some rules analogous to international law, and [would] have similar force and effect to that held by a treaty, and must be regarded by Municipal Courts in a similar manner'.[56]

Just what sovereign attributes were left to the Masai, however, was not clear. It was admitted that they were entirely subject to the administrative and judicial control of the protectorate government. It was faintly suggested that if there were a sovereign ruler of the Masai he might claim to be exempt from the jurisdiction of the High Court. It is difficult to take this seriously, the more so when it is realized that there were dicta in a case from Zanzibar[57] that it was doubtful whether the Sultan could claim exemption from the jurisdiction of the courts. Reference was made to the Native Court Regulations 1897 which recognized the concurrent jurisdiction by the Masai over native cases, and the Courts Ordinance 1907 which replaced it and provided that nothing in the Ordinance should affect the power of the Governor to recognize the jurisdiction of tribal chiefs.[58] It was suggested 'that this is a recognition of a jurisdiction pre-existent to and apart from jurisdiction conferred by the Order in Council and is a remnant of sovereignty remaining in the Masai . . .'[59] It is more likely, however, that the real basis of this jurisdiction at that point was its recognition by the Governor, and it is significant that the recognition continued after the protectorate became a colony in 1920, which would be difficult to justify on the court's interpretation of it. The court also considered several Indian cases and concluded that they showed 'that where an individual holds his office or

[55] (1914) 5 E.A.L.R. 70 at p. 93.
[56] pp. 91–2.
[57] *Charlesworth Pilling and Co.* v. *Government of H.H. The Sultan of Zanzibar* (1897), 1 Z.L.R. 73 at p. 78 (High Court at Bombay).
[58] No. 13 of 1907, section 10.
[59] p. 93.

territory by way of grant from a sovereign power an agreement made with him is a civil contract but that where the individual is regarded as holding such office or territory as a sovereign, an agreement made between him and a sovereign power is a treaty'.[60] But this conclusion appeared to assume the point that was at issue. There was only one possible ground on which the court could hold that the Masai retained a residual sovereignty—that the ultimate or radical title to their territory was still vested in them, but as will be shown below, it is more than doubtful whether even this was the case. In the final analysis the court's finding here was circular. To the question: can the Masai make a treaty? The answer was: yes, because they retain an element of sovereignty. And to the question: what element of sovereignty do the Masai retain? The answer was, the treaty-making element. It was an unsatisfactory conclusion.

Notwithstanding this conclusion on sovereignty, the court nevertheless went on to consider whether the agreements were in fact civil contracts about land, or treaties. Its major finding here was that there was no provision of law which authorized certain members of a tribe to enter into a civil contract which would bind all the members unless such members formed a central authority in the nature of a government in which it might be presumed some elements of sovereignty would exist, and that was not the case here. The main objection to the court's argument here is that it amounts to saying that the Masai retained sufficient sovereignty to make a treaty but not to make a civil contract about land. A possible explanation for such an extraordinary conclusion is to be found in its further finding that it was not within the province of the court to enquire whether a treaty had been made with the right persons or obtained by duress. Both these factors would have had to be investigated in the case of a contract, and in neither of them would the government have emerged unscathed.

Finally, with regard to the claim to damages for tortious liability, the defence of Act of State was considered and upheld. Since the protectorate was a foreign country, the acts of a British official under orders which resulted in a 'tort' against a foreigner were not actionable. The very broad range of the defence appears from the following statement of the Court:

> . . . if the law as laid down in the case of *Buron* v. *Denman* [(1848) 2 Ex. 167] applies in its entirety to acts committed in East Africa against a native of the Protectorate it would seem that a native has no rights which he can enforce in a court of law in respect of any kind of tortious act committed upon the orders of or subsequently ratified by the Government; he has no remedy against the Crown in tort and if he brings an action against an individual, the latter can plead orders of the Government whereupon the act becomes an act of the Government and one for which the only

[60] pp. 92–3.

> remedy is an appeal to the consideration of the Government; the other remedies of diplomacy and war which might be available to a foreigner the subject of an independent state, not being available to a native of the protectorate.[61]

The use of the defence of Act of State in these circumstances provides an example of arbitrary government which it is hard to parallel. The government could force the agreement on the Masai, could then enforce their obedience to it, and when challenged could decline to allow the matter to be judged in the courts and could prevent or punish any recourse to extra-legal remedies. The aggrieved persons were compelled to rely on the goodwill and sense of fair play of the government by whose actions they had been wronged in the first place. Looked at from the point of view of the natives of the protectorate, the defence of Act of State was the perfect instrument of executive tyranny. It is true that the courts have always reserved the right to investigate whether the circumstances of the case in issue are such that the defence of Act of State may be pleaded but *Buron* v. *Denman* excludes any meaningful investigation in a protectorate where the plaintiff is not a British subject.

Several general points arise from this case, and the preceding discussion on jurisdiction over local inhabitants. They illustrate clearly the great difference between the law made or sanctioned by Whitehall, and the practice on the spot. It is true that the law conferred great power on administrators in East Africa but there were limitations written into these powers. Again, the avowed reasons and objects behind these laws no less than behind international and other treaties were to bring law and order and civilization to East Africa, in modern terminology, the benefits of the Rule of Law. When we examine the implementation of these laws, we find that the limitations contained in them and the local agreements were ignored, the exercise of important governmental powers was unchallengeable by the local inhabitants, and the purposes for which the law was used were different from those for which it was made. The *Masai Case* was a *cause célèbre* which reached the courts but similar or more serious divergence between law and practice occurred many times over in the early history of the East Africa Protectorate, and affected attitudes of both administrators and administered thereafter.

An obvious question which arises then is whether we should regard the legal framework created for the assumption of power in East Africa as an elaborate sham designed to disguise what was really planned to be done. This would be going too far. The politicians, civil servants and lawyers in Whitehall were no doubt sincerely convinced of the importance of getting things legally right, both because that was how they were accustomed to

[61] pp. 96–7.

governing in England, and because they had incurred international obligations in respect of East Africa which good faith required them to make an effort to discharge. But the fatal defects were lack of communication and of control. There was too little control of senior officials by Whitehall, and by senior officials of their juniors. Equally, administrators in the protectorate often did not know what the law allowed or forbade them to do or, if they did, sometimes considered that it was unrealistic and ignored it.

There was, too, a lack of the will to control by the courts. The *Masai Case* highlighted the lack of remedies, but other cases concerned with African protectorates spelt out very clearly the courts' unwillingness to allow challenges to the legal bases of colonialism. Denning L. J. (as he was then) was summing up a succession of cases on jurisdiction in protectorates when he said in *Nyali Ltd.* v. *Attorney-General*,[62] a case concerned with the prerogative of pontage in the Protectorate of Kenya:

> Although the jurisdiction of the Crown in the Protectorate is in law a limited jurisdiction, nevertheless, the limits may in fact be extended indefinitely so as to embrace almost the whole field of government . . . The courts themselves will not mark out the limits. They will not examine the treaty or grant under which the Crown acquired jurisdiction: nor will they inquire into the usage or sufferance or other lawful means by which the Crown may have extended its jurisdiction. The courts rely on the representatives of the Crown to know the limits of its jurisdiction and to keep within it. Once jurisdiction is exercised by the Crown the courts will not permit it to be challenged.

The rationale for such an approach had been provided many years earlier in *R.* v. *Earl of Crewe ex parte Sekgome*,[63] a case from the Bechuanaland Protectorate in a passage quoted with approval in the *Masai Case*:

> The idea that there may be an established system of law to which a man owes obedience and that at any moment he may be deprived of the protection of that law is an idea not easily accepted by English lawyers. It is made less difficult if one remembers that the Protectorate is over a country in which a few dominant civilized men have to control a great multitude of the semi-barbarous.

This is difficult to reconcile with earlier intentions to bring the benefits of civilization to Africa. A system of rules which weighed the balance so heavily against those most in need of its protection must be regarded as a very dubious benefit indeed.

A final point may be made. The *Masai Case* points to a paradox of power in a protectorate, which *Nyali Ltd.* v. *Attorney-General* confirmed. In a protectorate there is a residue of sovereignty left to the protected people or state, and the Crown does not have unlimited jurisdiction therein as is the

[62] [1956] K.B.1 at p. 15.
[63] [1910] 2 K.B.576 at pp. 609–610 quoted at p. 97 of the *Masai Case*.

case in a colony where the Crown has sovereignty, yet the general law relating to the actual operation of this jurisdiction has the effect of conferring a greater immunity on the colonial administration in a protectorate than in a colony. If the limited jurisdiction exercisable in a protectorate is unchallengeable, then the distinction between that and the unlimited jurisdiction exercisable in a colony is virtually meaningless, and lends support for the proposition that a British protected person is protected against everyone except the British. It was only in relation to control over land, and jurisdiction over foreigners, that certain difficulties were experienced in protectorates which would not have been in colonies, and these were largely overcome by the turn of the century.

(b) *Control over the Land*

As far back as 1833, the British Government had been advised by the Law Officers that the exercise of protection over a state did not carry with it power to alienate the land contained therein.[64] This opinion was given in respect of a protected state—the Ionian Islands—where the amount of internal sovereignty acquired by the protecting authority was usually slight, but it was initially adhered to when Britain began to acquire colonial protectorates in Africa, which carried with them far more internal sovereignty. The government was advised that unless a right to deal with waste and unoccupied land was specifically reserved in an agreement or treaty of protection, no such right could be allowed in a protectorate, and even in respect of waste and unoccupied land, it was not clear whether it could be alienated. This position represented a major obstacle to colonial authorities, first, because in Africa no less than in England, he who controls the land is in a good position to influence government and secondly, because if they could not grant parcels of land, they would be unable to attract settlers; this point was of special relevance to East Africa. For immediate governmental purposes in the East Africa Protectorate, the Indian Land Acquisition Act 1894 was extended to the protectorate in 1896[65] and this allowed the administration to acquire land compulsorily for the railway, for government buildings, and for other public purposes.

For the purpose of providing land for settlers the administration promulgated the Land Regulations in 1897. These drew a distinction between

[64] McNair, op. cit., p. 39.

[65] See, too, the East Africa (Acquisition of Lands) Order in Council S.R.O. 551/1898 which provided that land acquired under the Act should vest in the Commissioner in trust for the Crown and permitted him to sell or lease it. The Act was extended to the mainland dominions of the Sultan under the Zanzibar Order in Council 1884 but was not extended to the rest of the protectorate until 1897 under the East Africa Order in Council of that year. The Foreign Office doubted whether that extension was legal. F.O. 7356.

land within the Sultan's dominions and land elsewhere in the protectorate. In the Sultan's dominions, the Commissioner was empowered to sell the freehold of Crown land, not being the private property of the Sultan, a power which the government had obtained through the Agreement of 1895. In the rest of the protectorate, however, the Commissioner could offer only certificates of occupancy, valid for ninety-nine years to those wishing to take up land.[66] But it was in this other part of the protectorate that settlers wished to establish themselves, and there were few applicants for such an interest—a mere licence to use land. Such a situation could not long continue; nor did it. In 1899 the Law Officers vouchsafed a new set of principles to the government. These were, that in protectorates of the African variety, where protection was exercised under treaties which did not specifically grant Her Majesty the right to deal with waste and unoccupied land, the right to deal with that land 'accrued to Her Majesty by virtue of her right to the Protectorate', since protection in these circumstances involved control over all lands not appropriated either by the sovereign or by individuals.[67] Here, then, is one of the occasions when the assumption of a protectorate *per se* operated to confer rights upon the Crown.

The East Africa (Lands) Order in Council 1901,[68] gave effect to the Law Officers' opinion. The Order vested Crown lands in the whole of the protectorate in the Commissioner and Consul-General for the time being, and such other trustees as might be appointed, to be held in trust for Her Majesty. The Commissioner was empowered to make grants or leases of Crown lands on such terms and conditions as he might think fit, subject to the directions of the Secretary of State. Crown lands were defined as 'all public lands within the East Africa Protectorate which for the time being are subject to the control of Her Majesty by virtue of any treaty, convention, Agreement, or of Her Majesty's Protectorate, and all lands which have been or may hereafter be acquired by Her Majesty under the Land Acquisition Act 1894 or otherwise howsoever'.[69] In 1902 the Commissioner promulgated the Crown Lands Ordinance which provided for outright sales of land and leases of ninety-nine years duration, and European settlement in Kenya commenced in earnest the following year.

It is, however, with the jurisdictional and constitutional implications of this legislation and advice of the Law Officers with which we are concerned here. Roberts-Wray has drawn a clear distinction between two kinds of ownership —ownership of the country and ownership of the land. The former is the

[66] Sections 1 and 10. An earlier set of Land Regulations also of 1897, which were replaced, had provided for 21 year certificates of occupancy only.
[67] F.O. 7356.
[68] S.R.O. 661.
[69] Section 1.

essential element of sovereignty that distinguishes a dominion of the Crown from a protectorate, whereas title to land is not *per se* relevant to the constitutional status of a country. However, 'the distinction between these two conceptions has become blurred by the doctrine that the acquisition of jurisdiction in territory which remains outside the British dominions imports Crown Rights in or in relation to the land itself'.[70] What these rights are is unclear, and we must look to the conduct of the Crown to ascertain them and their consequent effect on the rights of indigenous inhabitants. It is our contention that in the East Africa Protectorate such complete sovereign rights were asserted over the land that when title to the country was finally claimed in 1920, it made no difference at all to indigenous rights to land or lack of them.

We may first examine the Crown Lands Ordinance 1902. Freehold estates in the land could be sold by the Commissioner. The rights and requirements of Africans to which regard was to be had in dealing with Crown land were seen in terms of actual occupation only; when land was no longer occupied by Africans it could be sold or leased as if it were waste or unoccupied land.[71] There was no requirement of obtaining the agreement of any chief to any disposition. This would appear to be asserting sovereign ruling powers over the land. This view of the legislation is reinforced by the admission made by the appellants' counsel in the *Masai Case* that the protectorate authorities were under no legal obligation to make an agreement with the Masai; they could have taken away their land by legislation. There can be no fuller exercise of sovereignty over the land than to compel, by legislation, a people to vacate their traditional lands. If it had been considered that a significant element of sovereignty in the land still vested in the Masai after the Order of 1901 and the Ordinance of 1902, the protectorate government would have been obliged to negotiate an agreement with them.

If there was any doubt as to the extent of the power the protectorate government was claiming by the 1902 legislation, they were set at rest by the Crown Lands Ordinance 1915. The Ordinance re-defined Crown lands so as to include land occupied by native tribes, and land reserved by the Governor for the use and support of members of the native tribes. But 'such reservation shall not confer on any tribe or members of any tribe any right to alienate the land so reserved or any part thereof'.[72] Thus not only

[70] Roberts-Wray, op. cit., pp. 625 and 636. See, too, Polak, *The Defence of Act of State in relation to Protectorates* (1963), 26 M.L.R. 138.
[71] No 21 of 1902, sections 30 and 31.
[72] No. 12 of 1915 sections 5, 54 and 56. Miles J. makes an odd mistake in *Gathure* v. *Beverley*, [1965] E.A. 514 at p. 518 where he quotes the definition of Crown land contained in section 5 of the 1915 Ordinance, and takes it to be the definition contained in the 1902 Ordinance. In fact there was no definition of Crown land in that Ordinance. Reference should have been made to the East Africa Order in Council 1902, section 2.

did the protectorate government now have complete control of all land occupied by Africans, but it was made clear that Africans had no right to alienate any of the land, whether they occupied it, or it was reserved for their use. In addition, land reserved for their use could at any time be cancelled and thereafter alienated to settlers. The disinheritance of Africans from their land was complete.

This view of the effect of the 1915 legislation challenges the correctness of the case of *Wainaina* v. *Murito*,[73] where it was held that the effect of the Ordinance and the two Orders in Council which converted the protectorate into a colony was to take away all native rights in the land, vest all land in the Crown, and leave Africans as tenants at will of the Crown in the land actually occupied. The error here is the failure to distinguish between title to the country which is what the Kenya (Annexation) Order in Council was concerned with, and title to the land which had been acquired as far back as 1901, though its implication for African rights in the land had not been clearly spelt out until the Ordinance of 1915.

In respect of control over land then, the protectorate authorities obtained by operation of the general law as complete legal power, at least outside the Sultan of Zanzibar's dominions, as they would have had and were to have in a colony. Was the position any different in the Coastal Strip? Here again we must distinguish between title to the land and title to the country. As regards the former, the power of the protectorate authorities was derived from the Concession Agreement of 1888 between the Sultan and the IBEAC and the Administration Agreement of 1895. By the first, the Sultan agreed to cede all the rights which he himself possessed over the lands in the whole of his territory within the limits of the concession, excepting private lands. The Company was also empowered to acquire and regulate the occupation of all lands not yet occupied. By the second, the British Government was to have control over public lands and regulate all questions affecting land, but the sovereignty of the Sultan in the mainland territories was not to be affected. No distinction was drawn in the laws relating to land between the Coastal Strip and the rest of the protectorate after the Land Regulations. However there was specific legislation, which while asserting sovereign control over the land in the Coastal Strip, conceded greater respect to private rights therein than was the case in the rest of the protectorate.[74]

The major legislation was the Land Title Ordinance[75] which provided for a system of adjudication of rights in the Coastal Strip. It was possible to make a claim to ownership of a plot of land before a Land Registration

[73] (1923), 9 (2) K.L.R. 102.
[74] See, too *H.H. The Sultan of Zanzibar's Government* v. *A-G of the E.A.P.* (1912), E.A.L.R. 142.
[75] No. 11 of 1908.

Court, basing oneself on a pre-protectorate right, and if the claim succeeded, to receive a certificate of ownership valid against the whole world. Thus pre-existing rights were to be recognized, but after recognition would retain their validity through protectorate legislation. The Ordinance further provided that land in respect of which no claim had been made or allowed should be deemed to be Crown land, thus asserting the Crown's claim to the radical title to land.

The other piece of legislation was contained in the Crown Lands Ordinance 1915. This provided that in any action to which the Crown or government was a party, no right or title to possession of land within the dominions of the Sultan claimed under Muslim law should be recognized, unless the claimant should establish his or his predecessor-in-title's possession or right to possession of the land prior to 14 December 1895—the date of the signing of the Administration Agreement.[76] This was a clear indication by the new supreme authority over the land that the old supreme authorities, the Sultan and the IBEAC, had lost all power to grant private rights in land from the given date.

In both halves of the protectorate, therefore, the government asserted and exercised rights of ownership over the land. Were there, then, any circumstances when the absence of title to territory—ownership of the country—affected the powers which the government could exercise in a protectorate? Two good examples from the Coastal Strip show that the answer is in the affirmative.

The first concerns the cession of Jubaland to Italy in 1925,[77] in fulfilment of a pledge made by the Pact of London in 1915. Part of the ceded territory lay in the dominions of the Sultan, the rest in the Colony of Kenya. Article 1 of the Anglo-Italian Convention on the cession of Jubaland acknowledged the Sultan of Zanzibar's interest in the matter, but there was no specific reference to the interests of the Government of the Colony of Kenya; there was no need since the British Government had territorial sovereignty over the colonial part of Jubaland, and could cede it if it wished. More revealing is that when the Colonial Secretary was pressed in the House of Commons to indicate whether the Sultan of Zanzibar, and the Governor and Legislative Council of Kenya had been, or were to be formally consulted, he stated that the Sultan had concurred in the transfer, and the Government of the Sultan had made known formally its concurrence and consent, but that it would be impossible to conduct foreign affairs if the government had to consult a Crown Colony every time action was to be taken which affected them. If the colony was on the verge of self-government it would probably be

[76] Section 134.
[77] Anglo-Italian Treaty (East African Territories) Act 1925. The Convention is contained in a schedule to the Act.

consulted but as a matter of good sense, not constitutional theory.[78] No doubt the consents of the Sultan and the Zanzibar Government were a foregone conclusion, but the indications are that it was appreciated that they had to be obtained, whereas there was no need for this with the Government of Kenya.

The second example is the more recent cession of the Coastal Strip itself to Kenya which took effect at Kenya's independence. The four parties to the agreement signed in October 1963 were the Governments of the United Kingdom, Kenya, Zanzibar, and the Sultan himself.[79] While it was constitutionally necessary to associate the Sultan and Government of Zanzibar with an agreement concerned with abrogation of the protectorate and allied agreements and the cession of Zanzibar territory, the association of the Government of Kenya (at that time only internally self-governing) with the agreement was an example of good sense; it was not a constitutional necessity. It was therefore only in the exceptional circumstances of the transfer of territory from one sovereignty to another that the powers of the protectorate authorities in East Africa (and later Kenya) were insufficient for legal unilateral action.

(c) *Jurisdiction over Foreigners*

To understand this problem, it is necessary to consider also the question of jurisdiction over non-British subjects in the area under the authority, however notional, of the IBEAC.

At the beginning of the Company's activities in East Africa, the British Government's view on jurisdiction over foreigners in Africa was that as against local rulers, the Crown 'can lawfully acquire by Treaty with them the right to exercise civil and criminal jurisdiction over subjects of civilized powers other than Great Britain within the territories of the Chiefs; but as against the subjects of other civilized powers, we think that the jurisdiction (whatever be its theoretical limits) should be exercised with, and cannot safely be exercised without the assent of the Power concerned, given generally or in the particular case'.[80] This opinion must be qualified by the *The*

[78] *Hansard*, House of Commons, volume 179, col. 1361 et seq., 2nd Reading Debate; volume 180, col. 1339 et seq., Committee. Sir R. Hamilton, M.P., Registrar Judge and Chief Justice of the E.A.P. 1897–1920, appreciated the distinction between Protectorate and Colony, 'I must confess that I find it still somewhat difficult to understand how it is that the Sultan of Zanzibar was not made a party to this treaty. Here is a treaty between Great Britain and Italy by which a portion of his possessions are given away . . . I do not intend to argue for one moment that a treaty of this kind cannot be made without consulting the Governor or Legislative Council or governing body of the Colony . . .' Committee, cols. 1342–1343. A different point of view was put forward by Mr. Fisher who deplored the fuss being made over 'this miserable strip of scorching African territory', col. 1351.

[79] Cmnd. 2161/1963, which contains the two agreements. For further details see chapter V, pp. 186–8, below.

[80] McNair, op. cit., p. 42. Law Officers' opinion of 1886.

Laconia[81] where the Privy Council had considered that in Eastern States (and for this purpose Africa may be equated with these) jurisdiction over foreigners could be acquired from the local ruler through mere tacit acquiescence, and from the state of the foreigners concerned, in an informal manner, provided that there was definite evidence of consent from the state concerned.

This position was clearly unsatisfactory. It meant that foreigners could commit crimes in British protectorates or spheres of influence or take refuge there after committing crimes elsewhere and remain unpunished or unextradited if their government declined to concede jurisdiction, or, what is more likely, knew nothing of the matter and could therefore neither decline nor agree. Nevertheless the position was enacted in the two Orders in Council applying to the IBEAC territories—the Zanzibar Order in Council 1884, and the Africa Order in Council 1889. The former applied to British subjects, British protected persons in so far as there was jurisdiction in respect of such persons in Zanzibar, and foreigners in cases specified in the Order. These were mixed cases where a foreigner was involved in a suit with either of the first two classes of persons. The consular court in Zanzibar could take jurisdiction provided that the foreigner had first filed a consent to the jurisdiction from a competent authority of his own state.[82] There was no specific reference to criminal jurisdiction over foreigners but this is to be explained in part by the existence of treaties providing for the privilege of ex-territoriality which several European powers had concluded with the Sultan.

The Africa Order in Council applied to British subjects and protected persons, foreigners who filed both their own consents and the consents of the proper authority of their own government, and foreigners in respect of whom any state of which they were the subjects or by which they were protected, had agreed or consented to the exercise of jurisdiction over them.

The practical operation of these Orders in relation to criminal jurisdiction over foreigners may be seen from two cases, which, although arising in Zanzibar and Uganda respectively, and at a time when British views on jurisdiction over foreigners in a protectorate were undergoing a marked change, illustrate the complications and difficulties which could arise from a narrowly drawn jurisdiction. In *R.* v. *Montopoulo*,[83] the accused was a Greek national who had been sentenced to ten years imprisonment for culpable homicide by the consular court at Zanzibar. He appealed on the ground that, though he was under British protection, he was not subject to the criminal jurisdiction of

[81] (1863), 1 Moo. P.C. (N.S.) 161.
[82] Sections 6 and 33.
[83] (1895), 19 I.L.R. (Bomb.) 741.

the consular court, nor had the Greek authorities consented to that court exercising jurisdiction. The High Court of Bombay, to which appeals from Zanzibar and the East African consular courts went at that time, considered that the evidence showed that the Greek Government was a party to the assumption by the British Government of the protection of Greeks in Zanzibar. Protection connoted jurisdiction and the question of specific consent to criminal jurisdiction by the Greek authorities did not therefore arise. The court noted there was no arrangement for the extradition of Greeks to Greece and stated that it 'would appear that unless the consular courts assume jurisdiction, the foreigner under British protection may slay British subjects with impunity'.[84]

What the court feared in 1895, it helped to bring about three years later by its decision in *Imperatrix* v. *Juma and Urzee.*[85] The accused, German protected persons from German East Africa, were convicted before the consular court at Kampala of offences committed in Bunyoro arising out of the war between Buganda and Bunyoro. At the date of the commission of the offences and the trial, Buganda was part of a British protectorate, but Bunyoro was only within a British sphere of influence. The court accordingly quashed the convictions on the ground that under the Africa Order in Council, foreigners could only be tried without their, and their state's, consents for offences against British laws if those offences took place in a British protectorate. Bunyoro was not a British protectorate and had not been assimilated to one by reason of British military occupation. Nor was the court moved by the fact that there was no extradition arrangement between German and British East Africa so that the alternative to trial was that the accused would go free.

Though this decision disclosed an unfortunate state of affairs in East Africa, it was events in Southern Africa, particularly the influx of miners of all nationalities into areas not under British sovereignty or protection, which had precipitated a modification of British views, and international law and practice that provided a justification for it. It was stated in 1891 that:

> . . . the civilized Powers of the world recognize, as a principle of international law that the protection of an uncivilized territory carries with it many of the most important attributes of a sovereign state, and that the subjects of a civilized power are within such territory to have the benefit of and be subject to all administrative and judicial institutions established by the protecting Power to the same extent as the subjects of that Power.[86]

[84] p. 745. The particular decision was right but the court erred in assuming that, since the Sultan had ceded criminal jurisdiction over Europeans to the British consular court, as a general rule no consent was needed to the exercise of that jurisdiction. This is to confuse foreign jurisdiction as against the local ruler with that as against foreigners.

[85] (1898), 22 I.L.R. (Bomb.) 54. See, too, H. B. Thomas, *7 Uganda Journal*, p. 70.

[86] McNair, op. cit., pp. 49–50. See, too, Palley, op. cit., chapters 3–5.

This jurisdiction, based on implied consents to be found from the signing of the General Acts of the Berlin and Brussels Conferences, was only to apply to territories declared to be under the protection of the Crown, the other occasion when the assumption and declaration of a protectorate *per se* had a considerable legal significance.

Though this new thinking was put into effect by the Africa Order in Council 1892, it was not until the assumption of a protectorate over East Africa in 1895 that the more liberal jurisdictional rules could apply, at least in the possessions outside the Sultan's dominions, by which time British views had modified still further. The true view, apparently not hitherto accepted by Britain, was that the existence of a protectorate in an uncivilized country imported the right to assume whatever jurisdiction over all persons might be needed for its effectual exercise.[87] This new doctrine was acted upon in the East Africa Order in Council 1897, the first to apply to the whole of the East Africa Protectorate. This provided that the power contained therein applied to foreigners who were defined as the subjects or citizens of states in amity with Her Majesty, not being natives. An exception was made for the Coastal Strip, where powers were not to extend to those foreigners, subjects of states that had concluded treaties of ex-territoriality, unless their governments consented to such exercise. This limitation on jurisdiction over foreigners, it should be noted, arose out of the peculiar nature of these treaties and not out of any general limitation on jurisdiction in a protectorate. By 1907 all states with ex-territorial privileges had surrendered them to the British Government, and full jurisdiction over foreigners was thereafter exercisable throughout the protectorate.

CONCLUSION

This detailed study of these three key aspects of power in the East Africa Protectorate show clearly that, by the turn of the century the protectorate authorities had acquired almost as full powers within the protectorate as they would have had if the whole area had been annexed as a colony, and whatever powers were lacking were soon obtained. The British Government appreciated this fact, and not only in relation to East Africa. In 1902 there was a discussion in the Foreign Office as to the desirability of annexing African protectorates. It was pointed out that though jurisdictional problems had existed and caused difficulties in the past, they were now tending to diminish and alterations in English law could virtually remove those that remained. On the other hand, there were political advantages in retaining protectorates. One could withdraw from them more easily, and conversely annexation might cause jealousies and objections from other powers. The

[87] McNair, op. cit., pp. 54–5.

Government thought it would be as well to avoid the possibility of friction, and maintain protectorate status.[88]

These revealing comments suggest a conclusion as to the role of the law in the scramble for Africa. We have shown the lawyers constantly adjusting the law to the needs of the politicians and administrators who were carrying out the forward policy in Africa. Sometimes these persons adjusted the law themselves and left the lawyers to catch up as best they could. In so far as law operated as a check on their activities it did so because there was an inevitable time-lag between the request for reconsideration of basic principles, and the legislative implementation of the new basic principles. Thus neither the lawyers nor the politicians saw the function of the law as standing impartially between two sides, or even leaning in favour of the weaker side, but as making the way smooth for the stronger. Was it impolitic to annexe African protectorates? This did not matter; the law was sufficiently flexible to ensure full governmental powers in a protectorate. Was it politic to break agreements with African rulers? It did not matter; the law would permit an Act of State to be pleaded which would avoid the embarrassment of having to justify one's action in court. It may be unrealistic to expect lawyers to have acted any differently, but then it is also unrealistic and not a little hypocritical to suggest that one of the main benefits of British colonialism was the introduction of the Rule of Law into Africa, for if that concept means anything, it means that the law should help the weak and control the strong, and not *vice versa*. From the African point of view the English law introduced into East Africa was one of the main weapons used for colonial domination, and in several important fields remained so for most of the colonial period, only changing when Africans began to gain political power. The role of the received law then from the beginning of the colonial period in Kenya was to be a tool at the disposal of the dominant political and economic groups.

[88] F.O. Conf. 7716.

CHAPTER II

The Development of the Legislature and the Executive

INTRODUCTION

In the previous chapter we discussed how the colonial authorities initially acquired power and used it to establish their effective presence in Kenya. In this and succeeding chapters we examine how they used the power to establish the main organs of government and administration, and the problems they faced in doing so.

While Kenya's status changed through the various forms of dependencies, the broad outline of its constitutional development was along conventional lines. The legal forms employed and the institutions and structures of government and administration which were established conformed to the pattern elsewhere.[1] Whether a colony or a protectorate, the government in Kenya was based on what Wight has called the two great principles of subordination: '(1) The legislature is subordinate to the executive; (2) the colonial government is subordinate to the imperial government'.[2] Usually, in the earliest stages of a dependency, the legislature is the same as the executive, in the person of the Commissioner or the Governor; and in one sense constitutional progress is measured by the manner in which there is a growing separation of institutions and functions. But it is characteristic of colonial regimes that at the highest levels the separation is never complete; indeed this is little more than a restatement of Wight's second principle of subordination. The Colonial Office remains the supreme legislature and executive. In the colony itself, for daily conduct of policy and administration, separate institutions are established, the most important being the Legislative Council (for making the law) and the Executive Council (for implementing the law). Once these Councils are set up, further progress to independence is reflected in their changing composition and powers, and their relationships with one another and the Governor. The usual practice is an increasing democratization and autonomy of the Councils from imperial control.

While Kenya followed this pattern in constitutional forms, its constitu-

[1] For a general account of constitutional developments in the dependent Empire, see M. Wight, *British Colonial Constitutions, 1947* (Oxford, Clarendon Press, 1952); M. Wight, *The Development of the Legislative Council, 1906–1945* (London, Faber and Faber, 1946) and K. Roberts-Wray, op. cit.
[2] Wight, *British Colonial Constitutions*, p.17.

tional history is unique in several ways. For a long time her eventual destiny was in doubt; unlike many other colonies, uncertainty persisted over the aims of constitutional development—was it to be along the lines of white settlements as in Australia, New Zealand or South Africa; or like the tropical territories of West Africa? The early, frequent change of constitutional forms reflected the conflict between these two goals. Kenya's colonial constitutional history was profoundly influenced by the presence and the claims of her immigrant communities, primarily the Europeans and secondarily the Asians. The small size of these communities[3] bore little relation to their importance, so long as the conflict of eventual goals was not resolved. Once the conflict was resolved in favour of the indigenous people, the balance of power shifted very rapidly and the basis of political activities changed to reflect more accurately the realities of the country.

The constitutional history of Kenya up to independence can be divided into five phases: the establishment of the machinery of government (1897–1905); the attempts by the European settlers to establish their supremacy (1905–23); a long and complicated period when the claims of the various races were balanced and adjusted (1924–54); a phase of multiracial experiments (1954–60); and finally in the few years preceding independence a period of conflict between two and more groups of African leaders (1960–63).

THE ESTABLISHMENT OF THE MACHINERY OF GOVERNMENT

As mentioned in chapter I, it was two years from the assumption of the protectorate before the British Government, acting largely on the recommendations despatched back to England by the first Commissioner for the protectorate, enacted specific legislation under the Foreign Jurisdiction Act for the protectorate. Prior to that legislation, however, the Foreign Office had issued an order in 1896 assimilating the names and powers of administrative officers in the protectorate to those of administrative officers in British India.[4]

The first specific legislation was the East Africa Order in Council 1897,[5]

[3]

Year	*Europeans*	*Asians*	*Arabs*
1911	3,175	11,787	9,100
1921	9,651	25,253	10,102
1926	12,529	29,324	10,557
1931	16,812	43,623	12,166
1948	29,660	97,687	24,174

Source: E.A. Statistical Department and census reports. By 1903, there were less than 100 European settlers, Cd. 1629, p. 19. The first census figures for Africans were in 1948, when they were estimated at 5,251,120.

[4] See footnote 9 below.

[5] East Africa Order in Council 1897, S.R.O. 575. Roberts-Wray has argued that there is no constitutional necessity for an Order in Council and that prerogative forms like Letters Patent could just as lawfully be used, op. cit., p. 25. It would appear from the language of the Act, however, that legislation through Orders in Council was envisaged.

which established the beginnings of the administrative machinery for the region. A striking feature of the Order, however, was its emphasis on judicial power and institutions. Wight has remarked that, 'the Dependent Empire illustrates how in constitutional development the stage of judicial power precedes the stage of legislative power. Early or undeveloped constitutions are concerned with organizing jurisdiction rather than with establishing legislative and executive organs. The Foreign Jurisdiction Act itself is mainly concerned with the establishment and regulation of courts'.[6] The judicial provisions of the Order are discussed elsewhere;[7] but an outline may be given here. A court for the protectorate, normally to sit in Mombasa, was set up, from which appeals would go to the Zanzibar High Court; and authority was given for the establishment of provincial courts. The Commissioner was given extensive powers to establish and regulate native courts, which were to have exclusive criminal jurisdiction over Africans. In addition, specific provisions were made for the application by the courts of certain English and Indian laws.[8]

Despite the preoccupation with the laws and the judicial organization, what emerges most clearly from the Order is the pivotal position of the Commissioner. Appointed by Her Majesty, he was the chief executive officer of the territory. He had the primary responsibility for the establishment of administration, for which purpose he had extensive powers. He also had the responsibility for the maintenance of law and order, for which he had the powers to legislate, to establish courts, and to deport. The Order itself had little to say on the machinery for administration. This was basically a period of experimentation.[9] Although it was known that the first Commissioner was in favour of a provincial system of administration,[10] its establishment was not provided for in the Order, but was left to ordinary legislation. The Commissioner was empowered to legislate by Queen's Regulations and could make laws (i) on matters relating to customs, inland revenue, post offices, land highways, railways, money, agriculture, and public health; (ii) the establishment of a constabulary or other force to be employed in the maintenance of order or (either within or without the limits of the Order) in defence of the protectorate; (iii) securing the observance of any Treaty for the time being in force relating to the protectorate, or of any native or local laws or customs; and (iv) finally the omnibus 'generally for the peace, order and good government of the Protectorate in relation to matters not

[6] Wight, *Constitutions*, op. cit., p. 19.
[7] Chapter IV.
[8] See chapter IV.
[9] Initially the powers and duties of officers were assimilated to similar officers of the Government of India. E.A.P.G. Notice 11/1898.
[10] Mungeam, op. cit., chapter 3.

provided for in the Order'.[11] In addition, he had important powers to legislate a legal system into being for the Africans. Any doubts whether he could legislate for them on other matters were set at rest by an Order in Council two years later.[12] As far as the other courts were concerned, however, their basic provisions were set out in the Orders, and the Protectorate Court was given power to make rules of procedure and the qualifications for practice before it. There was thus some, though far from complete, autonomy for that court. The Commissioner, however, enjoyed personal immunity and the court could not 'exercise any jurisdiction in any proceedings whatsoever over the Commissioner or his official or other residences, or his official or other property'.

It is therefore obvious that the Commissioner had overriding powers in the protectorate. He did not have to act in consultation with any local body, nor was he responsible to a local institution. The legislative and executive functions were combined in him, and there were few limitations on the powers granted to him. The Commissioner, however, did not have a free hand. He was subject to the instruction of the Secretary of State, to whom he was fully accountable. Just as the Commissioner's (or Governor's) dominance within the dependency exemplifies the first of Wight's principles of subordination, so the control over him by Whitehall constitutes the second. Thus, Queen's Regulations did not become law until they were first allowed by the Secretary of State; if urgently necessary, the Commissioner could promulgate them without prior reference to him, but the latter could afterwards disallow them. Similarly, the Commissioner could make rules and orders for the administration of justice in native courts only with the consent of the Secretary of State. He was subject to instructions from London as to the conduct of affairs, and in practice important matters of policy had first to be cleared with London.[13] The Commissioner's general accountability to the Secretary of State was highlighted by a provision in the Order requiring him to make an annual report to the latter on its operation.

[11] Article 45. Strictly speaking, the detailed specification of the purposes for which regulations could be made was redundant since the last category would comprehend the rest. It has been held by the Privy Council that the expression, 'to make laws for peace, order and good government', confers a plenitude of legislative competence. *Croft* v. *Dunphy*, [1933] A.C. 156; *Ibralebbe* v. *R.*, [1946] A.C. 900. The tendency in later Orders was to dispense with the detailed specification and rely on the general clause.

[12] East Africa Order in Council, 1899, No. 757, section 9.

[13] See Mungeam, *passim*, op. cit., for the relationship in the early years between London and the administrators on the spot. In practice the theoretical position as outlined above was not always observed, and the protectorate administration, under pressure from the European settlers, sometimes acted without consultation with London and occasionally in defiance of it. Thus the second Masai Agreement of 1911 was first made by the Governor and only subsequently reported to the Colonial Office. See also footnote 5, chapter III, below.

Before proceeding to an examination of the exercise of the powers in the Order, it may be useful to refer to some other general restrictions on the Commissioner's powers to legislate. The following discussion is pertinent to the competence of the legislature in dependencies generally, and the legislature in Kenya, however constituted, whether a Commissioner as in this period, or an assembly later, suffered from these limitations till independence. First, the Crown's (more accurately, the Crown in Council's)[14] power to legislate, whether under the prerogative or statute, remains unaffected by the delegation to a local legislature, at least if a reservation of this power is made in the instrument of delegation. Locally enacted legislation can be overridden by laws made in this manner. Secondly, the local legislature of a dependency cannot legislate in terms repugnant to the provisions of any Act of Parliament (or regulations thereunder), which extend to that territory.[15] In so far as there is such repugnancy, the local legislation is void, but otherwise it is valid. The rule of invalidation does not extend to the repugnancy with the law of England as such.[16] Thirdly, there is a general, but not clearly defined, limitation that dependent legislatures cannot enact laws with extra-territorial effect, i.e. outside the territory for which the legislature is constituted. This does not prohibit all legislation which might operate outside the territorial jurisdiction, but such legislation must have a close and legitimate connection with the government of the territory.[17] In practice, the limitations of extra-territoriality were overcome by recourse to legislation

[14] Whether the legislation was through the Crown in Council or the Crown alone would depend on the prerogative form used. Thus Letters Patent and Royal Instructions are issued by the Crown acting alone.

[15] The British Parliament's legislative supremacy does not extend beyond the dominions, broadly defined. It therefore did not extend to Kenya till its annexation (1920). A further potential limitation was thus introduced, but in practice direct parliamentary legislation for colonies is rare. 'The intervention of Parliament in colonial affairs during the third quarter of the eighteenth century helped to destroy the first Empire, and re-established the tradition that the colonies are properly left to the executive.' Wight, *Constitutions*, op. cit., p. 91.

[16] The doctrine of repugnancy applies both to colonies and protectorates. For colonies, see the Colonial Laws Validity Act 1865, sections 2 and 3; for protectorates, the Foreign Jurisdiction Act 1890, section 12. Roberts-Wray has argued that the former Act also applies to the protectorates, and therefore the stipulation in the latter Act is redundant, p. 406, op. cit. Legislation by Crown in Council (i.e. Orders in Council) is subject to a similar limitation, p. 210.

[17] See Roberts-Wray, pp. 387–96; Salmon (1917), 33 L.Q.R. 117; and O'Connell (1959), 75 L.Q.R. 318.

It is unnecessary to go into the qualifications to this rule, though it did undoubtedly play an important part in the processes and forms of law making, as far as the Colonial Office was concerned. As O'Connell has written, '(E)xtra-territoriality as a concept was developed more fully in the Colonial Office and in colonial correspondence than it was in court decisions'. For example, the Commissioner was expressly given power by the 1897 Order in Council to make regulations about deportation, which might otherwise be void as involving extra-territoriality, though of *A-G for Canada* v. *Cain*, [1906] A. C. 542, which upheld legislation to deport, *contra Re Gleich* (1879) I.O.B. and F 39 (New Zealand).

through the Crown in Council.[18] Finally, further restrictions on the local legislature are associated with a series of controls exercised by the Imperial Government, like the powers to disallow a bill and require the reservation of a specified category of bills for the signification of Her Majesty's pleasure.[19]

The Commissioner's legislative powers were therefore seriously restricted. Moreover, quite apart from these formal restrictions, most of the legislation he enacted was preceded by consultations with the British Government, whose approval, in practice, was essential.[20] Nevertheless, this was a period of important legislative activity. There was relatively little intrusion of politics, and legislation was largely concerned with administration. There were several laws to deal with public order, under which, for example, police officers were empowered to arrest without warrant a 'vagrant', defined as any person found asking for alms or wandering about without any employment or visible means of subsistence, and such a person could then be ordered by a magistrate to be kept in custody for up to three months;[21] the movements of natives in the protectorate could be controlled, by the institution of a pass system;[22] communal activities like *ngomas* were forbidden after 9 p.m. without a special licence from administrative officers;[23] the sale of native liquor was illegal without licence;[24] and most importantly, the Commissioner could declare any district or part thereof a 'closed district', whereupon entry into that district became illegal without special permission, except for the natives of the district and administrative officers acting under the Commissioner's orders.[25] Regulations were also passed to establish the basic machinery for administration; thus provisions were made for the appointment of village headmen for administration and the maintenance of order,[26] imposition of tax on huts occupied by the indigenous people,[27] and the establishment of armed forces.[28] Other regulations dealt with matters of administration like registration,[29] transactions in land,[30] mining,[31] the

[18] For example many of the laws providing for collaboration and co-operation among the British East African territories—East African Currency, Transport and the Court of Appeal—were enacted through Orders in Council. See chapter XII.

[19] See footnote 72, below, p. 54. This provision was not important in the 1897 Order, since all regulations had to have prior, or exceptionally, subsequent approval of the Secretary of State.

[20] It is interesting to note how the Commissioners were sometimes able to circumvent instructions through administrative action, e.g. in the granting of land on a racial basis, for which there was no basis in law. See chapter III and footnote 13 above.

[21] Regulations No. 3 of 1900 (Vagrancy).

[22] Regulations No. 12 of 1900 (Native Passes).

[23] Regulations No. 15 of 1901 (Preservation of Order by Night).

[24] Regulations No. 32 of 1900 (Sale of Native Liquor).

[25] Regulations No. 31 of 1900 (then 25 of 1902) (Outlying Districts).

[26] Regulations No. 22 of 1902 (Village Headmen).

[27] Regulations No. 18 of 1901 (Hut Tax).

[28] Regulations No. 29 of 1902 (King's African Rifles).

[29] Regulations No. 16 of 1901 and 26 of 1902 (Registration of Documents).

[30] Regulations No. 21 of 1902 (Crown lands).

[31] Regulations No. 9–11 of 1902 (Mining; Mining Rules and Safe Mining Rules).

administration of *wakf* property,[32] the preservation of game[33] and the rudiments of municipality law.[34] Though most of these regulations were eventually repealed, they frequently formed the basis of new legislation and the pattern of administration they established has influenced even the present system.[35]

On the administrative side, the early period was considerably taken up by the extension of British jurisdiction inland and northwards, generally by means of punitive expeditions.[36] An important achievement of this period was the building of the railway from the coast to Lake Victoria, which was completed in 1902.

Before proceeding to the next phase, two events in the present one are worthy of note. Firstly, the 1897 Order was repealed and replaced by a 1902 one.[37] It did not significantly affect the balance of power and responsibilities as established in 1897, but differed from the earlier Order in greater elaboration of specific provisions and a shift of emphasis from courts and jurisdiction to administration. The administration was vested in the Commissioner, subject to imperial instructions; he was given wide discretion to divide the country into provinces and districts for the purposes of administration; his authority over the public servants was defined; and the prerogative of mercy was vested in him. Secondly, his legislative powers were elaborated and expanded, removing many of the previous restrictions; for example there was now no limit as to the fines and penalties he could prescribe. He was, however, now enjoined to 'respect existing native laws and customs, except so far as the same may be opposed to justice or morality in the making of legislation'. The requirement of submission of draft legislation to the Secretary of State prior to its enactment was abolished, as a general rule, though the Secretary of State could require such submission by general or special instructions. The Commissioner had, however, to transmit authenticated copies of all legislation to the Secretary of State who had the power to disallow any legislation in whole or in part. Legislation by the Commissioner was henceforth to be known as Ordinance, and not Regulations. The new Order thus strengthened the Commissioner's position, but since he had been and remained amenable to instructions from London, it can be regarded as an administrative devolution of power. It did not affect any fundamental alteration in the constitutional scheme.

The second event of significance was the transfer of the responsibility

[32] Regulations No. 29 of 1900 (Wakf Commissioners).
[33] Regulations No. 30 of 1900 and 4 of 1903 (Game).
[34] e.g. Regulations No. 31 of 1900 (Street Cleaning and Lighting), No. 33 of 1900 (Nairobi Township), No. 20 of 1900 (Mombasa Streets and Roads).
[35] Regulations No. 25 of 1902 (Outlying Districts), for example, is still in force as Cap. 104, as is No. 26 of 1902 (Registration of documents), Cap. 285.
[36] Mungeam, op. cit., *passim*.
[37] East Africa Order in Council, 1902, No. 661.

for the protectorate from the Foreign Office to the Colonial Office, which took place on 1 April 1905. Since British jurisdiction over the area was acquired through the Foreign Jurisdiction Act as a foreign territory, it was logical that the responsibility had been vested in the Foreign Office. That Office was equally appropriate for another reason: the British interest in the area arose out of considerations of international diplomacy and strategy, and negotiations with other European powers had to be conducted to demarcate spheres of influence and boundaries. But once British jurisdiction was recognized, the Foreign Office was ill-equipped to deal with the task of administration, as it lacked staff and experience. The Colonial Office was better suited to this task. It is important to observe that the transfer did not affect the constitutional status of the territory; it continued as a protectorate, though proposals to declare it a colony were again mooted.[38]

EUROPEAN ATTEMPTS AT SUPREMACY 1905–1923

The period of pacification was not yet over when the young protectorate entered into its second important phase of constitutional development. The most significant factor in this phase was the introduction of settler politics. 1903 is usually regarded as the beginning of an active policy of European settlement, when it received great impetus under the Commissioner, Eliot.[39] The outstanding effect of European settlement was to accelerate constitutional developments; if the country had been allowed to grow as other African protectorates were, initial developments would have been much more leisurely. The Europeans tried to convert the territory into a colony of settlement, with the eventual aim of responsible government under white rule. Their demands were not presented in this stark form at once, but the direction of their aspirations was obvious from the beginning. The early part of this period was marked by important concessions to the Europeans. That they did not achieve more was due to two primary factors: first, the realization in London that an important ingredient of the imperial mission in Africa was the protection of the indigenous peoples, which would be difficult to carry out if control was abandoned to the white settlers; and secondly, the resistance to them from the Indian community, who put up their own competing claims. The period therefore was concerned primarily with the attempts of the Europeans to make good their claims to a settler rule, and the resistance and opposition from the Colonial Office and the Indians.

[38] Mungeam's statement that 'the transfer of April 1905 was the logical, if somewhat tortuous, result of the entry of the first European settlers as early as 1896' (p. 125), is questionable. The Protectorates of Uganda, Central Africa and British Somaliland were transferred to the Colonial Office at the same time—not all of them places of white settlement.

[39] See chapter III.

While there is an element of arbitrariness in it, this period may be said to start in 1905, with the promulgation of a new Order in Council. The Europeans won early victories, and the 1905 Order was a direct response to their demands. The agitation for increased rights came only from the settlers, whose numbers were as yet small,[40] in comparison with the European officials, who were often out of sympathy with the claims of the former. The Indians, on the other hand, had been in East Africa for a much longer period, though their early activity was concentrated on the coast. While the Europeans were basically engaged in agriculture, the Indians were traders, though some were beginning to be employed by the Administration and had helped to build the railway.[41] European pressure ensured that Indians were kept out of agriculture, by preventing alienation of land to them in the fertile regions. Partly as a result of this, the European and the Indian interests remained antagonistic, and the former saw in the latter a threat to the establishment of responsible government under white rule.[42]

The 1905 Order which supplemented the 1902 one marked an important stage in constitutional development. It changed the designation of the protectorate's chief officer from Commissioner to Governor and Commander-in-Chief. His powers were significantly affected, primarily due to the establishment of two key institutions—the Legislative Council and the Executive Council. While its effect was generally to restrict or check his power, there was one respect in which he gained new authority—henceforth all judicial officers, including High Court judges, were to be constituted and appointed by the Governor. The most significant innovation was the Legislative Council, which was invested with the competence to make laws for the peace, order and good government of the protectorate. It was established in response to pressure from the European settlers who, the very same year, had asked for some form of representation on a Legislative Council which, initially, they were prepared to see under official control. The Council was defined to include the Governor and such other persons, not less than two in number, as may be appointed by the Crown; the tenure of the latter was subject to the Crown's pleasure. The Governor lost the competence to make laws on his own, but it is doubtful if there was a real diminution in his power. It was assumed that the majority of the members of the Council would be what is termed 'official', i.e. committed to support the Government, and would therefore take their orders from the Governor. Moreover,

[40] See footnote 3, above.

[41] For a study of the Asians see Delf, *Asians in East Africa* (London, Oxford University Press, 1963); Hollingsworth, *The Asians of East Africa* (London, Macmillan, 1960); Ghai, *Portrait of a Minority* (Nairobi, Oxford University Press, 1965).

[42] The best account of this conflict is still W. K. Hancock, 'Indians in Kenya', in *Survey of British Commonwealth Affairs 1918–1939* (London, Oxford University Press, 1965). See also Dilley, *British Policy in Kenya* (New York, Thomas Nelson and Sons, 1937), chapter I, part 3.

he had a right to veto legislation passed by the Council; and so the Council could not effectively function without his support. The Imperial Government also retained important powers: it reserved the power to disallow any Ordinance passed by the Council, and also the power to legislate directly for the territory through an Order in Council. Further, the Governor and the Council were to observe any directions in relation to the enactment of legislation that might be issued to them through Royal Instructions. Thus while the exercise of legislative power was transferred from the Governor to a Council which included unofficial representation, provisions were included to ensure imperial and gubernatorial control of it.[43] But equally, the Council associated non-officials, albeit nominated by the Government, with its legislative functions and had the potential for development as a more independent body; in this lay its real significance.

The other Council was less significant at this stage. The Executive Council was not one of the demands of the settlers; indeed it would seem that they had hoped to participate in the administration through their representation on the Legislative Council. The Executive Council was the Commissioner's idea. He was anxious to avoid unofficials having a direct executive control, and therefore proposed the establishment of an Executive Council, composed of officials only, to advise him on the application and execution of enactments, the conduct of native affairs and all important matters connected with the administration. The function of the Legislative Council would be to make laws and express public opinion.[44] Neither the composition nor the functions of the Executive Council was set out in the Order. It was merely provided that its members shall be such as may be appointed under Royal Instructions.

The arrangement set up by the 1905 Order is significant for various reasons. It marks the first move away from the autocratic rule of the Governor. It is the beginning of a kind of 'separation of powers', although as we shall see, the Governor in effect retained final legislative and administrative powers for many years to come. Secondly, the Legislative and Executive Councils would eventually ripen into the important institutions of independence—the National Assembly and the Cabinet.[45] Their progressive development became the index of the country's constitutional advance. Thirdly, much of the debate about the great issues of Kenya politics was carried on in these Councils, especially the Legislative. They reflected remarkably well the contemporary tensions and controversies, except for a

[43] It is important, nevertheless, not to underrate the significance of the concession to the settlers. Under their influence, the protectorate gained a council at a remarkably early stage; cf. Uganda, where British presence was older, which did not get a legislative council until 1920.

[44] Mungeam, op. cit., p. 183.

[45] Strictly speaking, it was the Council of Ministers, rather than the Executive Council, which was the immediate predecessor of the Cabinet. See below, p. 72.

period in the fifties, when African agitation was carried on outside the basic constitutional framework.[46] Fourthly, the Councils, with their changing composition, provided a flexible mechanism for accommodating different racial and tribal claims to share in policy and administration. Increased representation in one or the other Council was offered to a group as a palliative, and compromises over numerous controversies were resolved by the allocation of a specific number of seats. So long as an official majority was maintained, the experiments in the allocation of seats could be conducted in the safe knowledge that the basic order of things would remain unaffected. The division of seats only became significant with the establishment of a non-official majority.

Given this basic framework, constitutional issues revolved around it. The outstanding themes were the manner and the size of the unofficial representation. At first, there were six official members, and two unofficials, all of them Europeans. The unofficials were nominated by the government to represent settler interests; and they were not bound to support the government. While the initial settler demand was for nominated representation, they soon began to agitate for elective representation, arguing for it on the ground, *inter alia*, that they paid taxes.[47] This demand met with greater resistance than that for nominated representation; and the European members retaliated by boycotting the Council. Though the Colonial Office had several reservations, particularly that the settlers constituted only a tiny proportion of the protectorate's population and that the others contributed to the revenue greatly in excess of them, the principle of European elective representation was conceded in 1916. A committee of the Council (with unofficials in a majority) was set up to work out the details and in 1919 elective representation was provided for by the Legislative Council Ordinance,[48] having been sanctioned by an Order in Council.[49] The Committee recommended against property qualification and female suffrage; and was 'of the opinion that at this stage of the Protectorate's development when the coloured races outnumber the white it is not desirable that the franchise should be extended to Asiatics or Natives' and instead, proposed a small representation for them through nomination.[50]

[46] For some time concurrently with the Council (from 1911), a great deal of political activity was carried on in the settlers' Convention of Associations, to which officials were invited to answer questions and explain and defend their policy. Hence the association came to be known as the 'Settlers Parliament' or the 'White Parliament'. Its importance declined with the grant to settlers of elective representation on the Council.

[47] Dilley, op. cit., p. 47. In fact a direct tax was not levied on the settlers till 1920. Ordinance No. 23 of 1920.

[48] No. 22 of 1919.

[49] The East Africa Order in Council, 1919. This was promulgated to remove doubts about the competence of the Legislative Council to pass laws about its own Constitution.

[50] Dilley, op. cit., pp. 49–52.

The Ordinance that was in fact passed provided for full adult white suffrage—men and women, the protectorate thus becoming the first place in the Empire (outside Britain) to give the vote to women.[51] The qualifications for franchise were that a person should be an adult (twenty-one years and over), British subject of European origin or descent (the great majority of the settlers), who had ordinarily resided in the protectorate for at least one period of twelve consecutive months prior to the date of his application, and had resided in the electoral area in which the application was made for at least three months. The qualifications for a candidate were slightly more stringent; for example, in addition to the above, the residential requirement was two years' ordinary residence before nomination and the ability to read, write and speak the English language.[52] The vote was to be cast by secret ballot, and provisions were made against corrupt practices, cheating, etc. The successful candidates were to hold their seats for three years, which at that time was also the duration of the Legislative Council. The Governor was given power to nominate a member for an area in which no candidates were duly proposed.

Eleven elected seats were provided for. The electoral areas were specified with the description of the boundaries in a schedule of the Ordinance—the Ordinance indeed contained a great deal of detail, which today would be left to regulations. The demarcation of constituencies did not generate as much heat as other constitutional issues. At this stage, the primary aim was to balance the urban interests with the rural. Later on, with the extension of the franchise to the Indians and Arabs, the really difficult questions of constituency boundaries were avoided by the adoption of the communal rolls. As the Indians were basically urban, and the majority of the Arabs lived on the coast, it was relatively easy to devise constituencies for them. Also, so long as voting was communal, the actual number of seats given to each group was more important than their geographical distribution. The tendency to simplify the problem of constituencies is reflected by the fact that it was enough to provide Indians with some multi-member constituencies rather than undertake a finer and more meticulous balancing of interests through single-member constituencies. The first real difficulties arose with the partial abolition of the communal rolls; and then later with the rise of the importance of the African vote.[53]

[51]There had been considerable opposition to female suffrage among the settlers, but it was accepted eventually as a means of increasing the white vote. Dilley, op. cit., p. 51.

[52] It is interesting to note that the ability to read and write was not a condition of eligibility to vote. Indeed, section 24 of Schedule III of the Ordinance provided for the procedure to vote to be followed by illiterate voters. When later the franchise was extended to Arabs, illiteracy was a bar to the right to vote; the illiterate Indians, however, did not suffer a similar disability. See p. 52 below.

[53] See chapter V.

No sooner had elections been held under the Ordinance than, in typical settler fashion, the Europeans began to ask for more concessions. This time their target was a majority of unofficials in the Council. Even if safeguards were provided to maintain the superiority of the Colonial Office and the Governor, the grant of an unofficial, settler majority would go a long way towards entrenching European influence. The Colonial Office would have serious hesitations before such a development was sanctioned. As it happened, its hand was forced by the Indian opposition to settler demands, and the Indian claim to an equality of rights with the settlers. Tensions between the two communities had developed early, and while the settlers tried sedulously to exclude Indians from any say in policy and administration, the latter opposed most of their claims. The controversy between the two was marked with bitter invective and abuse, mainly from the settlers.[54] It reached a high intensity with the grant of elective representation exclusively to the Europeans; and the Indians' agitation focused imperial attention on the fundamental issue for the development of the protectorate. The Colonial Office responded with the famous Devonshire paper of 1923, known as *Indians in Kenya*.[55] Before the policy of this paper is discussed, it is necessary to trace the growth of Indian representation.

Indian political activity was stimulated by the attempts of the settlers to discriminate against them. They had first collected together to oppose European demands for the reservation of the Highlands. They lost this issue; and suffered a further disadvantage when no one from their community was appointed to the Legislative Council on its establishment. However, in 1909 Mr. A. M. Jeevanjee was nominated, mainly, it is said, at the instigation of Churchill, who on a visit as Colonial Under-Secretary, was much impressed by the qualities of the Indians. His appointment was for two years and under European pressure, he was not reappointed. Indian agitation for representation continued, and support was sought, and was forthcoming, from the India Office. Mass meetings were held and petitions sent to London and India. When elective representation was conceded to the Europeans, the refusal to co-operate by the Indians, combined with the influence of the India Office, forced the issue to a head.

As far as constitutional developments were concerned, Indians had two objectives: an equality of elective representation with Europeans and a common electoral roll of European and Indian voters. In 1919 Indian

[54] See the vivid account in W. McGregor Ross, *Kenya from Within* (London, Allen and Unwin, 1927), part II. An Economic Commission (composed of a majority of settlers) used such intemperate language that Lord Milner was constrained to condemn its performance as 'purely deplorable . . . going quite outside their terms of reference, abusing the Indians, talking about their moral depravity, calling them carriers of disease and inciters to crime and vice, and pronouncing against all Indian immigration into any part of Africa'. House of Lords Debates, 14 July 1920, col. 161.

[55] Cmd. 1922.

representation had been established at two nominated members.[56] This fell far short of their objectives. As a result of their agitation, an inter-departmental committee of the Colonial Office and the India Office was set up to look into the question, which reported in favour of a common roll, 'for all British subjects and British protected persons (male or female) aged twenty-one years and upwards, possessing qualifications which were to be prescribed'.[57] The qualifications were to be so prescribed that approximately ten per cent of the electorate would be Indian. There were to be seven constituencies, three of them returning one European member each, and the other four to return one European and one Indian each, giving a total of seven Europeans and four Indians.

These proposals, known as the Wood-Winterton proposals, were rejected by the Europeans and the Kenya Government, 'mainly on the ground that it gave no sufficient safeguard to the European community against Indian predominance in the future'.[58] After consulting the European and Indian leaders, the British Government declared its policy in what has become a famous document in Kenya's history, *Indians in Kenya*. After considering the pros and cons of the common electoral roll, the British Government rejected it. The arguments that had been made in favour of a common roll were that it would bridge the gap between the Europeans and Indians by giving a candidate of one race an incentive to study the needs and aspirations of the other race, and that it had the strong backing of the Indians. The first of the two arguments was dismissed as invalid; the reactions to the Wood-Winterton proposals in Kenya (which presumably meant the European opposition to it) were cited to illustrate that the common roll would not act as a bridge. It was argued that, given Kenya's conditions, no candidate could stand as an advocate of the interests of the other race without sacrificing the support of his own;[59] a communal franchise, on the other hand, would contract rather than widen the divisions between the races, though it was not elaborated in which way it would do so. More positively in favour of a communal franchise, it was stated that such a franchise secured that every elector would have the opportunity of being represented by a member with sympathies similar to his own. A communal roll would permit Indians a far wider franchise than if a common roll were introduced—on the assumption that in a common roll, European dominance must be preserved

[56] The Council at that time was composed as follows: 10 *ex officio;* 7 nominated officials; 11 elected Europeans; and 2 nominated Indians (Royal Instructions, 1919).
[57] Cmd. 1922, para. 6.
[58] ibid., para. 8.
[59] A former opponent of the common roll has recently written that the effect of the communal roll was that 'it encouraged racialism and tended to emphasize the inherent differences between the various groups in the country to the detriment of a national outlook'. Blundell, *So Rough a Wind* (London :Weidenfeld and Nicolson, 1964), p. 34.

which fact 'alone should render it acceptable to all supporters of the Indians' claims who have at heart the political development of the Indian people'.

One further advantage of the communal system was seen as indicating the lines of future constitutional development. It would allow for the immediate grant of electoral representation with a wide franchise to the other community in Kenya which was 'ripe for such institutions', the Arabs; and a communal franchise provided a framework into which native representation could be fitted in 'due season'. Indian claims of equality of representation with the Europeans were also rejected, though an increase in elective membership was proposed, to bring the total to five.

The White Paper marked the end of the second phase of Kenya's constitutional history. Its importance lay not so much in resolving the dispute between the Indians and the Europeans, as in the recognition of the claims of the Africans. Though both the Europeans and the Indians had tried to set themselves up as defenders of the interests of Africans, there is little evidence that they were genuinely concerned about them. The White Paper, however, was quite emphatic—'[p]rimarily, Kenya is an African territory, and His Majesty's Government think it necessary definitely to record their considered opinion that the interests of the African natives must be paramount, and that if, and when these interests and the interests of the immigrant races should conflict, the former should prevail'. While the existing rights of the immigrants would not be curtailed, 'in the administration of Kenya His Majesty's Government regard themselves as exercising a trust on behalf of the African population, and they are unable to delegate or share this trust, the object of which may be defined as the protection and advancement of the native races'. The Paper helped to put in proper perspective the constitutional issues and controversies till then—a handful of Europeans and Indians fighting for power in a country of overwhelming African majority, whose claim to a share in government neither immigrant community admitted. As has been remarked, the Paper 'rediscovered the vast majority of Kenya's population, namely the native Africans'.[60] It was, however, to be a long time before their full rights were to be accepted.

In retrospect, the real significance of the Paper lies in rejecting the claims of the settlers that Kenya was a white man's country. *Vis-à-vis* Indians, the settlers won a victory in the settlement proposed in the Paper—the rejection of both the common roll and equality of representation. Nor did the Paper put an immediate end to settler aspirations; their ambitions may have suffered a temporary set-back, but they were soon to intensify the agitation for an unofficial majority. They won other important concessions,[61] and the

[60] Hancock, op. cit., p. 224.
[61] e.g. Increased control of the country's finances (see below) and the confirmation of the reservation of the White Highlands.

declaration of African paramountcy was slowly turned into a doctrine of dual policy.[62]

The Paper, however, was not followed by a significant increase in African representation or share in government. This is hardly surprising, as explicit in it was the assumption that Africans were not ready to represent themselves, and their interests should be looked after by others. It was recommended by the election committee of the Legislative Council of 1916 that African interests should be represented by the Chief Native Commissioner. The 1923 Paper stated the policy of nominating a missionary to the Council to advise on African matters, 'until the time comes when the natives are fitted for direct representation'.

Therefore while the 1923 Paper arrested the European march to constitutional dominance, it did not chart a new or clear path for future development. This is evident from the period of constitutional history following the Paper—the Europeans did not give up their claims, and the Colonial Office often lacked the will to resist them; there was an absence of a clear policy, and the developments were *ad hoc*. There was a progressive democratization of the two Councils; at the same time there was a careful balancing of racial interests and claims. It was not till the early fifties that a new philosophy of government known as multi-racialism emerged.

ANNEXATION OF KENYA

Before we discuss the developments in the Legislative and Executive Councils between the 1923 Paper and the emergence of multi-racialism, it is necessary to deal with the change from a protectorate to a colony which took place in 1920. All the protectorate, except the ten mile Coastal Strip, was annexed as a colony;[63] the Strip remained a protectorate administered on behalf of the Sultan of Zanzibar.[64] Two reasons were advanced to justify the annexation of the protectorate; first that it would satisfy the natural desires of the residents in East Africa for closer ties with the British Empire than had previously been possible by living in a protectorate, and secondly, that it would then be possible for the authorities in East Africa to take advantage of the Colonial Stock Acts when they wished to launch a loan on the open market, for those Acts applied only to colonies.

It is difficult to follow these reasons. As to the second it would not have been impossible to change the Act rather than the status of the dependency. As to the first, annexation transformed a foreign territory into a part of the dominions of the Crown. The closer connection with the Crown might

[62] Dilley, op. cit., chapter 11.
[63] Kenya (Annexation) Order in Council, 1920.
[64] Kenya (Protectorate) Order in Council, 1920.

have been seen as setting out a path of constitutional advance more akin to the white dominions than the African protectorates. But in practice the change in status was less significant; as we have seen, the Devonshire paper three years later emphatically rejected any suggestions that Kenya was to develop as a white man's country.

The change in status, however, had legal and constitutional implications. The act of annexation was an Act of State done by virtue of the prerogative. It took the form of the Kenya (Annexation) Order in Council. It applied to that part of the East Africa Protectorate which was outside the dominions of the Sultan of Zanzibar, and thus embraced the Sultanate of Witu which ceased to exist as a separate entity inside the protectorate. The dominions of the Sultan of Zanzibar remained a protectorate. Opportunity was also taken to change the name of the dependency to Kenya and it was henceforth known as the Colony and Protectorate of Kenya.

It is when we look at the manner of providing for the government of this multiple dependency that we can better observe the constitutional implication of annexation. For the protectorate, government was still provided for under the authority of the Foreign Jurisdiction Act, but for the colony the operative act was the British Settlement Act 1887. Kenya fell within the definition of a settlement under the Act which is 'any British possession which has not been acquired by cession or conquest and is not for the time being within the jurisdiction of the Legislature, constituted otherwise than by virtue of the Act or any Act repealed thereby, of any British possession'.

Henceforth, constitutional instruments providing for the government of Kenya had to differentiate between the colony and the protectorate. For the former, prerogative forms replaced the Orders in Council. The basic constitutional framework was set out in Letters Patent under the Great Seal, while the details were supplied in the Royal Instructions under the Sign Manual and Signet. Most of the changes were therefore made through additional Royal Instructions, only the most fundamental alterations requiring amendments of the Patents. The coastal protectorate, however, continued to be provided for by Orders in Council as it fell within the Foreign Jurisdiction Act. No separate constitution was established for the protectorate; the institutions of the colony—the Governor, the Executive and Legislative Councils and the courts of the colony—were deemed to be the same for the protectorate.[65] The Governor was to observe any instructions he received as Governor of the protectorate, but in their absence, he was to observe instructions issued to him as Governor of the colony so far as they were applicable to the protectorate; in practice the former were extremely rare. Thus while the Order followed the Letters Patent very closely, it was careful to preserve

[65] ibid.

the distinction, more theoretical than real though it may have been, between the unlimited power exerciseable in a colony and the limited power exerciseable in a protectorate. It was rare for there to be any difference in practice, but one occasion when doubts arose was over the ability of the legislature of the colony to pass laws affecting the disposition of lands in the protectorate. The East Africa Order in Council 1906 dealing with the position in the East Africa Protectorate had remained in force in the Protectorate of Kenya; it did not specifically provide that the disposition of lands could be regulated by Ordinance, although in practice it had been. The Letters Patent on the other hand which applied only to the colony provided that such disposition could be regulated by Ordinance. The doubts were set at rest by the Kenya Protectorate (Disposition of Lands) Order in Council 1927, which amended the 1906 Order so as to make it clear that it did not curtail the power of the legislature of Kenya to pass laws so as to regulate such disposition in the protectorate. Thus despite the difference in constitutional status of the two parts, their administration was highly integrated, and their constitutional progress was uniform.

CONSTITUTIONAL AND COMMUNAL DISPUTES 1924-1954

The constitution as established by the Letters Patent and the Royal Instructions of 1920 was essentially the same as under the Order. The power and functions of the Legislative Council remained the same; its composition was altered to provide for two Indian elected members and one unofficial nominated member to represent the Arabs.[66] These provisions were in fact not implemented till 1924, when the Legislative Council (Amendment) Ordinance was passed.[67] By this time the recommendations of the 1923 Paper affecting increased Indian representation had been accepted, and five members were to be elected from their community. The Arabs were given one elected member. Separate voters' registers were compiled for each community, and voting was to be on the basis of these communal rolls, so that each community would elect its own representatives. The qualifications for franchise were not uniform for all the communities—those for Europeans remained the same as under the 1919 Ordinance; Indians to register had to be British subjects of Indian origin or descent or an Indian under the suzerainty or protection of His Majesty; as for the Arabs, only *male* Arabs (British subjects or under the protection or suzerainty of His Majesty) who were able to write Arabic or Swahili in Arabic characters, could vote. At the same time, in pursuance of additional Royal Instructions, one unofficial was nominated to represent the interests of the African community,[68] as stated

[66] Section XV of the Royal Instructions, 1920.
[67] No. 1 of 1924.
[68] Additional Royal Instructions, 1925.

in the 1923 Paper. The official representation in 1920 consisted of the Governor as President, ten *ex officio* members and up to seven nominated official members; in 1925 when representation for Indians, Arabs and Africans (through unofficial nomination) was provided for, the number of nominated official members was increased to ten.[69] There was therefore at this time a heavy official majority. The duration of the Council was three years,[70] for which period the elected members held their seat, though the nominated members retained their membership at the pleasure of the Crown.

The Executive Council remained advisory as before. The Governor had to communicate the Royal Instructions to the Council; but the Council could not proceed to business unless summoned by the Governor. He had to consult the Council in the execution of his powers and authorities; there were exceptions to this, however; if he felt that the administration would sustain material prejudice by consultation with the Council, or if the matter was trivial or urgent, he could dispense with the consultation, though in the last mentioned case, he had to communicate, with reasons, this action to the Council at the earliest opportunity. He could act in opposition to the Council, but if he did so, he had to communicate the matter fully to the Colonial Office. He also had to consult the Council when considering the exercise of the prerogative of mercy. The rights of the members were protected to an extent by a provision that they could write their reasoned dissent into the minutes which had to be sent to the Colonial Office periodically.

The Governor retained his central position; as President of both the Councils, he could act in opposition to the Executive Council on the one hand, while on the other, he had the power of veto over legislation. He alone could initiate legislation or motions on finance, and armed as he was with official majorities, his authority was unchallenged. He could suspend and remove members, other than *ex officio*, of either Council, and could prorogue or dissolve the Legislative Council at any time. In turn, there was close imperial control over him: the powers of the Governor and the Councils were subject to the Royal Instructions, the Crown reserved powers of direct legislation and of disallowance of Ordinances, and the Governor was instructed not to assent to a specified category of bills without first obtaining the approval of the Colonial Office.[71]

[69] ibid.

[70] Till 1935, the life of the Council remained at three years, though on occasions provisions were made to extend the period in relation to a Council, e.g. Kenya Council (Amendment) Ordinance, 1923 (No. 4); Legislative Council (Emergency) Ordinance, 1929 (No. 36). It was changed to four years by the Royal Instructions of 1935. Government Notice 537/1935.

[71] The Bills to be so reserved included those for the divorce of persons joined in holy matrimony; affecting the currency of the Colony or relating to the issue of Bank Notes; whose provisions appear to be inconsistent with Treaty obligations; interfering with the discipline or control of land, sea or air forces; and whereby persons not of European birth or descent may be subjected or made liable to any disabilities or

At this time, the Councils were marked by their independence from one another. The executive (that is, the government) had to have the approval of the legislature to translate policy into law. On the other hand, legislation coming from the Legislative Council, if found undesirable by the government, could be vetoed by the Governor. While the officials could be questioned on their policy in the Legislative Council, it had no say in their appointment or removal. Even if there had been any rules determining the relationship between the two Councils, the availability of official majorities to the Governor would probably have made them otiose.

The whole of this period, up to the beginning of multi-racialism, was occupied by agitation over the powers and composition of the Councils. There was much contention over three main issues: the continuing Indian struggle for equality with the settlers and in particular for a common electoral roll; the continuing settler agitation for an unofficial majority in the Legislative Council, and increased European participation in the executive; and the demands of the Africans for greater representation, in particular representation by Africans themselves and on an elective basis. The debates over these issues were intimately connected with the discussions in East Africa over the question of a federation or some other form of closer union. On the part of the settlers, a union involving greater outside influence on the affairs in Kenya had to be compensated for by giving them a majority in Kenya's Legislative Council. On the other hand, the degree of control to be surrendered elsewhere in East Africa to the local Europeans would depend on the adequacy of the safeguards established for the other races.

(a) *The Indian Agitation for the Common Roll*

The Indians did not accept the 1923 awards, and boycotted the Legislative Council in protest against the refusal of a common roll.[72] They urged a common roll on the Hilton Young Commission of 1929–30 which had been set up to advise on closer union in Eastern Africa. In its report, the Commission discussed at length the arguments for and against a common roll. While reiterating the arguments against as outlined in the 1923 Paper, it set up a persuasive case in favour of it—the communal roll, by promoting the election of men of extreme views, emphasized rather than reconciled differences, whereas the surest foundation for a stable constitution was community of interests rather than a nice adjustment of opposing forces.[73] It suggested that the dangers of inter-racial contests

restrictions to which persons of European birth or descent are not also subjected or made liable. This list is substantially similar to that introduced in 1906.

[72] It was provided in various constitutional documents that if a member was not elected from an Indian constituency, the Governor could fill the place by nomination, e.g. Royal Instructions of 1925 and 1927.

[73] Cmd. 3234, p. 208. See pp. 182–211 of the report for an interesting discussion of the policies and principles of representation in Kenya.

on a common roll could be obviated by the reservation of a fixed number of seats for each of the communities—a device that was to be adopted temporarily many years later. It stated that 'in as much as the progress of the territory must depend on co-operation between the races, the ideal to be aimed at is a common roll on an equal franchise with no discrimination between the races'. The Commission's recommendation, from which its Chairman dissented, had as its corollary that universal adult franchise must be abandoned before a common roll could be introduced. Franchise qualifications were necessary in order to ensure that Europeans were not swamped.[74] However, no specific recommendation was made but it was suggested that this question be reviewed later in light of the experience of the working of the new Council.

The British Government gave only a partial endorsement to this recommendation of the Commission, commenting that more evidence was needed before a decision could be made as to how a common roll could be achieved, and promised a further enquiry.[75] This further enquiry was undertaken by the Joint Select Committee on Closer Union in East Africa, which came to the conclusion that it would be impracticable under the existing conditions to advocate the adoption of the system of common roll representation in preference to the current system of election.[76] Though the Indian agitation continued, the question of a common roll was closed till the first steps were taken towards dismantling this racial edifice in 1958. By then the Indians were weakening in their conviction, as a common roll now would include Africans as well. Moreover, the Indian position was considerably shaken by divisions within the community. With the independence of India, and its partition into the sovereign states of India and Pakistan, the Indian Muslims in Kenya began to agitate for separate representation from the other Indians. They were supported by the Europeans 'who considered the Muslims as more friendly to themselves than the Hindus'.[77] The non-Muslim Indians resisted these claims, and were able to convince the Speaker's Committee of the Legislative Council set up to examine the needs of the Muslims that these needs could be met short of another communal roll, by means of reservation of seats on the Indian roll, either through legislation or mutual understanding within the community.[78] The Indian Muslim opinion,

[74] 'If, for example, the Kenya franchise were revised on the lines adopted in Northern Rhodesia, the electoral roll would present a very different picture, and it is not improbable that the number of qualified Indian voters would be found to be far less formidable than the European Community apprehends', p. 210.

[75] Cmd. 3574 (1930), para. 9.

[76] *Report of the Joint Select Committee on Closer Union in East Africa*, para. 100 (London, HMSO, 1931).

[77] G. Bennett, *Kenya, A Political History: The Colonial Period* (London, Oxford University Press, 1963), p. 107.

[78] See, 'Petition of the East African Indian National Congress to the King to Disallow Religious Separate Electorates', Nairobi, 1952.

however, would be satisfied with nothing less and in the end a separate roll, and therefore, representation was allowed them.[79]

Thus the period was marked by a further recession from the principle of a common roll. By the end of the period, the true implications of a wide common roll were becoming clear, with its promise of African dominance. Much of the heated debate on the issue in the twenties and thirties was conducted on the premise of European and Indian franchise. The Indian enthusiasm for it would no doubt have lacked ardour if the question of African admission to the common roll had been raised. Paradoxically, with the increasing democratization of the Councils and the diminution of official majorities, the significance of the communal roll became greater. The immigrant communities held on to it as the only adequate means of representation in a sea of African electors. Yet it was a serious compromise with democratic principles, which clearly had to be resolved before independence could be given.

(b) *Settler Attempts to Control Government*

The second major theme of this period was the settler struggle for increased control, which had as its aim two important objectives—their majority in the Legislative, and greater participation in the Executive Council. The settlers were never to achieve a majority of their own members, though towards the end of the period they shared in an unofficial majority with other races. In fact their elected representation remained at eleven, which they had obtained in 1919, until 1951. The declaration in 1923 that the ultimate responsibility for the protection of the African interest lay with the Imperial Government remained a serious barrier in the way of a settler majority. The Hilton Young Commission reported more favourably on an unofficial majority—it cited the criticism of the official majority as tending to make debate unreal, since the Government always had a majority.[80] Its support for an unofficial majority was tied to its scheme for the institution of a Central Authority for East Africa. It proposed the reduction of official seats by four, to be given to the unofficial side which would mean twenty-two unofficials as against sixteen officials. This recommendation of an unofficial majority did not represent the true aspirations of the settlers, for it was only partly elected (the remainder made up through nomination) and it was not a majority of settlers but of all the races combined. The British Government did not favour any substantial change in the composition of the Council, while at the

[79] The Legislative Council (Temporary Provisions) Ordinance 1951.

[80] *Report*, op. cit., p. 184. The Commission, however, recognized that even with an unofficial majority, problems would remain, for the Government would still be irremovable.

same time approving the proposals for closer union.[81] However, the whole matter was referred to the Joint Select Committee.

The Committee recommended against constitutional proposals for closer union. It also recommended in favour of the maintenance of the official majority. Under such a system, the exact number of representatives of the different communities was unimportant so long as they were able to present the views of their community adequately.[82] To the settlers' argument that an official majority could safely be abandoned provided there were the safeguards of the Governor's veto and power of certification,[83] the Committee replied that 'even with the safeguards suggested, an unofficial majority, whatever may be said to the contrary, does morally and in fact become responsible'.

In return for the rejection of the proposals for closer union by Britain, the Europeans temporarily accepted the maintenance of an official majority and turned their attention to a share in the executive. No changes were made in the composition of the Legislative Council for several years, except for a slight increase in the representation of Africans. But the situation changed after the war; the unofficials had been actively associated with the executive in the prosecution of the war, and the East Africa High Commission was at last to be established. The question of an unofficial majority was raised again and found support from the Governor. The immediate cause for the abandonment of the official majority was the translation of certain *ex officio* members—the General Manager of the Railways, the Commissioner of Customs, the Commissioner of Income Tax and the Postmaster-General—from the Kenya legislature to the Central Legislative Assembly. The Governor advised the Colonial Office that it would not be necessary to replace these officers by Kenya officials solely for the purpose of maintaining the official majority, but his reasons were mainly to relieve the pressure on administrators.[84] The recommendations were accepted, and fresh Royal Instructions were issued in 1948 to implement them. The composition of the Council was now as follows: eighteen officials (Governor as President, Speaker as Vice-President, seven *ex officio* and nine nominated official members) and twenty-two unofficials (seventeen elected—eleven Europeans, up to five Indians and one Arab, and five nominated unofficials—four to represent the interests of the African community and possibly one to represent Arabs).[85] Apart from the unofficial majority, the other innovation

[81] Cmd. 3574.
[82] *Report*, op. cit., p. 41.
[83] For powers of certification, see p. 58 below.
[84] See Sessional Paper No. 1 of 1947 (Kenya), p. 1.
[85] Royal Instructions, April, 1948, sections XV–XIX. It was provided that if none of the nominated official members was appointed to represent the Arabs, the Governor could appoint an extra unofficial for this purpose, bringing the total of

was the institution of the office of Speaker. Up to then the Governor had been the presiding officer, but in 1947 he wrote to the Colonial Office that it appeared to him as 'a necessary corollary' of the changes in the Council, 'that the Governor should no longer sit as President of the Council, although he should no doubt retain his titular position as such, or at any rate the right to attend and address Council on such occasion as he considers necessary'.[86] He therefore suggested that there should be a Speaker, with a casting but not a deliberative vote. In the first instance the Speaker should be nominated, 'but as soon as there is a reasonable prospect of his being elected by the Members of the Council without the introduction of racial controversies, it would have an educative value if the Council were to elect its own Speaker'.

At long last, then, Kenya achieved an unofficial majority. Interestingly, it came with the establishment of institutions of 'closer union'. For the first time, it was possible for the Council to reject government measures. To do so, however, the unofficials of all the races had to vote together, for if the Government could persuade only one group to vote with it, it would have a majority. The probability that all the unofficials of all the different races might vote together was not high in the circumstances of Kenya at that time. In fact as a mechanism for bringing the races together in a working partnership, the 'unofficial majority' was a failure. As a result, it was not necessary to invoke the powers of certification that were given to the Governor simultaneously with the abolition of the official majority. Previously all locally enacted legislation had to be promulgated under the authority of the Council, where the official majority ensured legislative approval of government measures. With the introduction of an unofficial majority, support for the Government could not automatically be assumed, and so long as the executive was to remain supreme, provisions had to be made for the Governor to enact laws despite the opposition of the Council. The powers as granted to him required the introduction of the Bill or motion in the Council; it was only on refusal of the Council to pass it that he could bring it into effect, either in its original form or subject to such amendments as the Governor thought fit, which had been moved or proposed in the Council or any of its committees. Any such action had to be reported forthwith with reasons to the Colonial Office, plus any objections that members of the Council might wish to make. In addition, the Governor retained his power of veto.

The establishment of the unofficial majority did not, therefore, significantly alter the advisory character of the Council. It created an additional cause

unofficials to 22 (Section XV (2)). In fact an Arab unofficial was so nominated. The Arabs had, however, asked for additional representation, which was refused. See Sessional Paper, op. cit., p. 3.

[86] Sessional Paper, op. cit., p. 1.

for tension, both because it sometimes forced the Government to choose allies from one or another racial group, and because of the frustration of an 'irresponsible' majority. It was far from the majority the Europeans had been clamouring for over the years; at best they had achieved a parity with the other races combined on the unofficial side, having eleven members out of a total unofficial representation of twenty-two. Even that parity appeared to represent a passing superiority, and indeed had to be strenuously fought for in the 1951 amendments to the Council which increased the unofficial representatives to twenty-eight, the new European number being fourteen. In 1952, the membership was twenty-six officials versus twenty-eight unofficials (fourteen European elected, six Asians elected [four non-Muslim, two Muslims], two Arabs [one elected, one nominated], and six African 'representatives').[87] This was the last Council of the period under review, and it was clear that European dominance was on the wane.

The European struggle for power was represented not only by agitation for increased membership of the Council, but also by attempts to control its Committees and win more representation on the Executive Council. A considerable degree of success was achieved, and throughout this period their actual influence far exceeded their constitutional power. As early as 1929, only a few years after the 1923 Declaration, the Hilton Young Commission observed that 'unofficial opinion has in practice obtained a much larger influence in the counsels of governments than accords with the strictly constitutional position. The Government still retains an official majority in the Legislative Council. [T]wo of the European elected members of the Legislative Council have been nominated as members of the Executive Council, and have thus been admitted to the inner counsels of the Government . . . A practice has grown up in the Legislative Council of referring all questions of importance to select committees in which the official majority is seldom retained. These committees consist for the most part of a large proportion of unofficial members with only such official members as are directly concerned with the subject in hand. This method of reference to select committees is now established by custom over the whole of the business of the Legislative Council, and results in the exercise of considerable influence by the Legislature in the executive sphere'.[88]

The Legislative Council Committees that the settlers were particularly anxious to control were those dealing with finance. They were anxious to reduce both the imperial and the local executive control over Kenya's finances. In this they met with considerable success;[89] in 1920 it was accepted that no expenditure of public funds derived in Kenya would be

[87] Additional Royal Instructions, 21 November 1951, Government Notice 1395/1951.
[88] *Report*, op. cit., p. 89.
[89] See Dilley, op. cit., chapter 4; Bennett, op. cit., chapter 9.

sanctioned without the approval of the Council; and in 1923 a Finance Committee was set up, consisting of two to three officials and all the unofficials on the Council. It examined the budget proposals after their formal introduction, but before their consideration by the Committee of the whole Council, and was sometimes able to effect significant changes. In 1926 a Select Committee was established to advise on measures proposing the expenditure of public money before their introduction into the Council; it had a majority of European unofficials. In 1934 the Europeans fought for and won the appointment of a Standing Finance Committee, replacing the earlier Select Committee. On it were represented three officials (one to represent African interests), three elected Europeans and one Indian. These committees exercised important influence in modifying financial proposals; but their unofficial members refused to take responsibility for them when they were debated in the Committee of the whole Council, to the great annoyance of the government.[90] Apart from finance, the unofficials played an important part in other Committees, and especially towards the end of this period, were actively associated with the government due to the pressures and needs of the war.

It remains to examine the attempt to control the Executive Council. The settlers had demanded membership in the Executive Council as soon as it was established. It was not until 1919, however, that the first unofficial members were appointed. The Council was initially advisory to the Governor in his executive functions, and its entire membership was made up of senior civil servants. It was not, as we have seen, responsible to the legislature, and it was not easy to imagine how unofficials could be associated with it. Could they, for example, take part in the deliberations of the Executive Council and help to mould policy, and yet to be free to criticize it in the Legislative Council, where they sat more or less as an opposition? They had no particular portfolios, and their main function seems to have been to advise the Governor and his senior officials on policy as it affected their particular communities, and to reach agreement or not as the case might be.[91] Even when unofficials were appointed to the Executive Council, membership was by nomination, not election, and was at the pleasure of the government.

The first unofficial appointees were two Europeans, later an Indian was also nominated. The settlers pressed for greater representation and so in 1938 the Council was reconstituted to provide for parity between the official and the unofficial members—the four official members (Chief Secretary, Attorney-General, Financial Secretary and the Chief Native Commissioner) being balanced by two Europeans, with one Indian and one European

[90] Dilley, op. cit., p. 91.
[91] Blundell, op cit., p. 320.

to represent African interests.[92] In 1952 the membership for African interests was given to an African. The parity in the Executive Council had been established just before the Second World War, but after the war broke out, the unofficial members were very actively involved in government, holding administrative posts, requiring provisions to be made to suspend the rules of disqualification of membership of the Legislative Council for those members employed by the government.[93] There was a clear shift of power to the Executive Council, as, due to emergency powers, most of the regulations could be passed by that Council, without the interposition of the legislature.[94] Important responsibilities were delegated to its unofficial members, and the Europeans were determined to consolidate these gains after the war.

The consolidation came soon, in 1945, with the introduction of the 'Membership' system in the Executive Council.[95] There were two important characteristics of the executive until then. The first was that the chief executive officer and the head of the civil service under the Governor was the Chief Secretary (formerly known as the Colonial Secretary), who was the medium of communication between all departments and the government. The commissioners and the directors of the various departments were merely advisory to him; the most prominent of these were the Commissioner of Local Government, Lands and Settlement who was responsible for 'settled' or European areas, and the Chief Native Commissioner, first appointed in 1918, who advised the Chief Secretary on African affairs. Though these senior officers were members of both the Legislative and Executive Councils by virtue of their office and had certain functions imposed on them by statute, all the decisions in relation to their departments were taken by, or at least in the name of, the Chief Secretary, who in turn was responsible to the Governor.[96] The other, obvious characteristic of this system was that the sole responsibility for the executive was with civil servants. It did not provide for the participation of the representatives of the various communities, for as we have seen, the unofficial representation in the Executive Council,

[92] Additional Royal Instructions, 26 May 1938, Government Notice 441/1938. No mention was made of 'unofficial ministerial' appointments that the Europeans had asked for.

[93] Legislative Council (War Provisions) Ordinance 1941 (No. 29).

[94] The powers were exercised under the Emergency Powers (Defence) Act, 1939 (U.K.) as applied to the Colony by the Emergency Powers (Colonial Defence) Order in Council, 1939. Under the Defence Regulations, Government Notice 635/1939, the Governor assumed wide powers.

[95] *Proposals for the Reorganization of the Administration of Kenya*, Sessional Paper No. 3 of 1945.

[96] For a useful history of the executive and administrative systems, see the report prepared by Pim in 1936, *Report of the Commission Appointed to Enquire into and Report on the Financial Position and System of Taxation of Kenya*, Colonial No. 116, chapters 5, 6, and 7. The reforms of 1945 were foreshadowed by Pim in his recommendations for the improvement of the system, pp. 70–76.

which itself was advisory, had no executive responsibility. It was thus a highly bureaucratic system of executive.

The 'Membership' system was initiated at the instance of the Governor, whose main reason for it was that the unofficial members who deliberated policy in the Executive Council should take responsibility for it in the legislature.[97] Under this system, different departments of the government were grouped in one portfolio under the direction of a member of the Executive Council. It was the beginning of the ministerial system, though there was a long way to go as yet to responsible government.[98] 'Members' were chosen from both officials and unofficials, the government announcing the appointment of two European unofficials, including Cavendish-Bentinck to the controversial portfolio of agriculture. It was at the same time announced that if the appointee happened to be an elected member of the legislature, he would have to resign his seat, since, 'as things are at present, it would be impracticable for an elected member, who is elected to represent a particular community as well as a constituency to retain his elected seat while holding office in the Government as at present constituted'.[99] While the Europeans hailed the new proposals as a great victory, the Indians and the Africans attacked them as a surrender of power to the settlers.[100] If so, this was to be the last surrender to them for a long time.

(c) *African Representation*

We now turn to the third major theme of the period—African representation. We have already seen the early history of African representation.[101] The initial assumption was that the Africans were unable to represent themselves, and it was therefore necessary to appoint a member of another community to speak on their behalf. The assumption in fact went beyond this—not only was the African unable to present his case, but he did not often know what was best for him. Consequently the terms of reference of the appointees made it clear that their function was not necessarily to represent African opinion, but to be guided by what was best for them.[102] There was much

[97] Sessional Paper No. 3 of 1945, op. cit.

[98] The choice of the word 'member' was subsequently explained by the Ag. Chief Secretary in the Legislative Council as being on analogy with the Viceroy's and Presidency Governor's Councils in India, 'as that seems appropriate and is generally understood'. Col. 28, 18 July 1945.

[99] ibid.

[100] See, in particular, A. B. Patel's speech in the Legislative Council. His main point was that it was unwise to transfer responsibility to a member elected on a communal roll, since his interests and loyalties would be exclusively to that community (col. 42). He also regarded the changes as expressly designed to favour the European community, and dubbed the Sessional paper as 'Sectional Paper' (col. 40).

[101] For a historical account up to 1945, see G. Bennett, 'Imperial Paternalism' in *Essays in Imperial Government*, Robinson and Madden (eds.) (Oxford, Blackwell, 1963).

[102] Cmd. 1922. p. 13.

discussion as to who could best represent African interests, and whether only the government members were qualified to do so. The 1923 Paper had recommended the appointment of a missionary,[103] until such time 'as the natives are fitted for representation'; the Governor and the Chief Native Commissioner were of course to continue to be responsible for African welfare. It was, however, inevitable that the views of missionaries and the Africans did not always coincide, nor was the effectiveness of the African cause enhanced by the discretion given to the member to put the African case as he judged best.

The Hilton Young Commission felt that it was unsatisfactory that the government should be an advocate of African interests in the legislature, since this compromised its position as an impartial arbiter holding the balance fairly between the different races.[104] The missionaries were disqualified for lack of adequate knowledge of African affairs, and so were the settlers, for the obvious clash of interests. Retired civil servants, or those nearing retirement, were recommended; their effectiveness was to be increased by the cultivation of local Native Councils with whom the members would consult on issues affecting them. The Colonial Office view was that it was premature to talk of direct African participation in the Council; African opinion should be developed outside it. 'For the native African population, indeed, in so far as the tribal organization is still the basis of its social organization, the most promising line of development for the near future may well lie, not in any direct participation in the Legislative Council, but in the increasing importance to be given to the Native Councils—an importance to be manifested alike in a continuous widening of their functions, and in a constant communication to these Councils, through the District Commissioner or otherwise, of the various proceedings and proposals of the Executive Government, as well as the enactments and Bills of the Colony's Legislature.'[105] It did, however, go on to recommend the increase of nominated members to two (without restriction of race) to be particularly charged with defending the interests and voicing the feelings and opinions of the Africans and other unrepresented persons, and in its reference to 'voicing the feelings and opinions of the Africans', the statement of policy went beyond the existing conventions.

The Africans themselves rejected the various assumptions on which the practices and recommendations in the preceding paragraphs were based. They argued that they were capable of representing themselves; they knew

[103] It was made clear in the legislation that such representation was a temporary expedient, section XV of Additional Royal Instructions, 15 July 1925, Government Notice 320/1925. It was not until the Royal Instructions of 1927 (28 March) that it was stipulated that the nominated unofficial member to represent African interests should be chosen from among the Christian missionaries in Kenya, Government Notice 248/1927.

[104] *Report*, op. cit., pp. 185–9.

[105] Cmd. 3574, para. 1.

what was good for them; no European with the right sympathies and understanding could be found; and they wanted a greater say in the colony's major Councils and not just in the local native institutions. A strong case for direct representation was made by them, and the Kikuyu Central Association in particular demanded nothing less than representation by Africans. The Joint Select Committee, before whom the Africans argued their case, stated that it was 'much impressed by the ability of Africans', and felt 'that the time may well come . . . when the most suitable representation for the African will be by members of their own community'.[106] But due to its doubts whether sufficient educated Africans existed who had the confidence of their tribes, it was unable to recommend more than that 'the nominated representation of native opinion be increased, without prejudice to the power of the Governor at his discretion to nominate for inclusion among them persons of African descent, when he considers suitable representatives are available'. The Governor was urged to consult with the Native Councils before making the nominations.

In 1934, the nominees for African interests were increased to two, without restrictions of race or profession.[107] While the previous members had all been missionaries, a retired civil servant was now appointed. The Africans continued their agitation against being represented by missionaries and retired civil servants; and there is reason to believe that the representation was neither fair nor effective. It was, however, not till 1944 that an African, E. W. Mathu, was nominated to the Council. His performance was highly impressive; and he was joined by another African, F. W. Odede, in 1946 as a temporary member. In 1948, as we have seen, the number was increased to four, and in 1952 to six. Although by now appointments were made from among the Africans, there was no constitutional stipulation for this. A change of terminology also took place—henceforth they were known as representative members.[108]

Thus by the end of the period, Africans had obtained representation through members of their own community. But while other races had enjoyed elective representation since the twenties, the Africans were still represented through nomination. A procedure had, however, grown up for consultation with African opinion before nominations were made.

The procedure was established administratively, not constitutionally. Initially Local Native Councils sent delegates to a provincial meeting to nominate three to five people, from whom the Governor selected one. The procedure became more elaborate when six Africans were to be nominated under the Lyttelton Constitution in 1954. Six constituencies were declared

106 *Report*, op. cit., p. 101.
107 Section XV, Royal Instructions, 29 March 1934, Government Notice 256/1934.
108 Section 11, Additional Royal Instructions, 21 November 1951, Government Notice 1395/1951.

as follows: Nairobi City, Central Province, Coast Province, Rift Valley Province, South Nyanza and North Nyanza. Any African resident in a constituency could stand, regardless of age, income or property, but had to pass a literacy test in English. Though there were variations, especially in the Nairobi constituency, the scheme basically was that each local council sent delegates to sit as members of a District Advisory Nomination Committee, to whom were presented the names of all the candidates in that constituency. While this Committee was free to discuss the candidates, it did not vote, its primary function being to elect delegates to the Constituency Advisory Nomination College. The voting in the College was by secret ballot, each member casting three votes for the candidate of his first choice, two for the second and one for the third. The names of the top three candidates in each constituency were forwarded to the Governor by the Provincial Commissioner, who included his own recommendations. Though the Governor was under no obligation to nominate the top candidate from each constituency, in practice this seems to have been done.[109]

While this procedure ensured some measure of genuine representation, it had several unsatisfactory features, particularly in the effect it had on African electoral and political organization.[110] Political organizations were not integrally tied to the representation in the Council, and much of the political activity was not reflected in the Council. African political groups were becoming active, but there was little opportunity for the expression of their views in the Council.[111] Provisions for African representation had been delayed too long and even now were grossly inadequate; they failed to find a place for such an outstanding leader as Mr. Kenyatta. The situation was aggravated by the intransigency of the Europeans, and the tendency to dismiss African political demands as emanating from a few hotheads and unrepresentative of the mass of the people. It is therefore not surprising that African political expression found other outlets and that the government lost touch with African opinion. Unrest grew while semi-secret societies were organized. The failure of the constitutional system to accommodate the legitimate demands of the Africans was partly responsible for the outbreak of the Mau Mau, which brought about a State of Emergency, declared on 20 October 1952. The normal constitutional processes were partially suspended, enormous powers of legislation being vested in the Governor.[112] There was also a temporary set-back to the constitutional progress. While

[109] For a succinct account of the procedure, see G. F. Engholm, 'African Elections in Kenya, March 1957', in *Five Elections in Africa* (Oxford, Clarendon Press, 1960), Mackenzie and Robinson (eds.), pp. 394–9.
[110] See chapter V.
[111] See Rosberg and Nottingham, *The Myth of Mau Mau* (New York, Praeger, 1967).
[112] The special powers were acquired under the Emergency (Powers) Order in Council, 1939.

the Emergency was being prosecuted, any constitutional change was out of the question, but with the containment of the uprising, the question of future constitutional development had once again to be faced.

It was clear by now that the assumptions of the constitutional arrangements had to be re-examined and a more meaningful place in them had to be found for the Africans. A British Parliamentary delegation visited Kenya and reported to the Colonial Secretary in 1954. It emphasized the necessity to provide an outlet for African politics and urged immediate discussions with representative Africans, with a view to arriving at an acceptable basis for the election of African members to the legislature. At the same time Africans should be encouraged to develop their own political organizations, thus filling the vacuum created by the banning of the Kenya African Union for alleged complicity in the Mau Mau. On the executive side, it was recommended that the Governor should involve the leaders of the main races more actively in the work of the government, and that the Asians and Africans should also be given appropriate portfolios. The keynote of its report, however, was the need to create a new system of race relations. '[T]here should be a declaration once more of the determination on the part of the U.K. that in Kenya the objective is a multi-racial society in which the rights of all men are safeguarded, and not the domination of one race by another, or of the whole country by or for one race.'[113]

MULTI-RACIALISM 1954–1960

Multi-racialism became the keynote of the next period. Multi-racialism was an attempt to bring all the races into a more active participation in the affairs of government. It was based on a recognition of communities as distinct units in society; and therefore in its concern with groups, regardless of numerical strength, rather than individuals, it was in conflict with the basic premise of a true democratic society.

Another characteristic of constitutional developments henceforth was the increasing preoccupation with the powers and composition of the Executive Council. After the 'Membership' system, it ceased, at least in practice, to be an entirely advisory council. More and more, it was an index of the admission to a share in power, for as the executive was not responsible to the legislature, an increase in membership in the legislature was not in itself evidence of progress.

[113] Cmd. 9081. It recommended as a first step that the colour bar should be broken down by legislative and other necessary action. 'At governmental level . . . time is ripe for an examination of laws, with a view to eliminating discrimination. It is also at governmental level that a lead may most appropriately be given in the economic sphere, by payment for the job, rather than the occupant, by the encouragement of a higher standard of living among those who earn it and by leading the way in social and economic reforms', p. 13.

Both these themes were introduced by the Lyttelton Constitution,[114] which was the product of consultation with the political leaders by the Labour and Conservative Colonial Secretaries, after the latter of whom the Constitution was named. It established a Council of Ministers, to whom were transferred most of the functions of the Executive Council. Provisions were now made for a much more meaningful form of ministerial system than under the 'Membership' system. It was announced that the Council of Ministers would be the principal instrument of government and would exercise a collective responsibility for decisions on government policy, but only in the sense that they would be all required to subscribe to fundamental principles of policy.[115] The Colonial Secretary sent out guidance on the behaviour and conduct of Ministers, in particular about their financial affairs, based on the British conventions.[116] But the new Council was still far from being a Cabinet—only part of its members were elected representatives in the legislature, the majority being still official.[117] Nor was it responsible to the legislature, and the Governor's powers remained undiminished—in fact constitutionally his relationship with the Council of Ministers was the same as previously with the Executive Council, and the Ministers held office during his pleasure.

The Executive Council itself was continued in existence, though with greatly reduced functions. All the Ministers were members of it; there were also additional nominated members.[118] There were three basic functions of the Executive Council[119]—it, rather than the Council of Ministers, had to be consulted before the Governor exercised his prerogative of mercy;[120] it had to be consulted by the Governor on any bill which it was proposed that a Minister should introduce in the legislature; and finally, the Governor could refer any other matter to the Executive Council provided he had first consulted the Council of Ministers. It is thus clear that the real executive responsibility had shifted to the Council of Ministers; and one may query why it was necessary to continue the Executive Council. One reason may be that it provided a mechanism for doing the racial balancing act—the compensation to Africans and Arabs for their inadequate involvement in the Ministries being increased representation on the Executive Council.

A significant feature of the representative members of the Council of

[114] Additional Royal Instructions, 13 April 1954, Government Notice 582/1954. See also Despatch to Governor (Government Notice 583/1954).
[115] Cmd. 9103; the principles were outlined in the Annexure.
[116] Government Notice 584/1954.
[117] In addition to the Governor and the Deputy Governor, there were six official members, six unofficial and two nominated. Government Notice 582/1954.
[118] Section V, Royal Instructions, 1954. One Arab and two Africans were appointed under this section. Despatch, op. cit., para. 2.
[119] Section XIII (2), ibid.
[120] No reasons were given for this provision; perhaps it was to emphasize the non-political nature of this power.

Ministers was their racial composition. After much deliberation, it was decided that there should be three Europeans, two Asians and one African.[121] In itself this represented a very hesitant step towards multi-racialism, but its importance lies in assigning executive responsibility for the first time to the Asians and the Africans. No Arab minister was appointed, but the Arab member of the Executive Council was to be permitted to attend meetings of the Council of Ministers when matters relevant to his community were under discussion. One important effect of the appointment of unofficials to the Council of Ministers is worth noticing. As we have seen, six such members were appointed, in addition to the two nominated; since they now had to subscribe to government policy, it meant that the official side of the Legislative Council acquired new votes, for unlike the 1948 arrangements whereby the 'Membership' system was introduced into the Executive Council, the unofficial elected members did not have to give up their constituency seats in the legislature. The effect of this was that although on paper there was still an unofficial majority in the Legislative Council, in practice the Government had a clear voting majority (thirty-four to twenty). This was in fact the end of the unofficial majority, only six years after its introduction. The official majority was not to disappear again until the establishment of self-government in June 1963.

Another executive body was set up at this time, which temporarily affected the importance of the Council of Ministers. A War Council was set up to supervise the conduct of the Emergency and to ensure that action to secure its early end was prosecuted with the utmost vigour. The War Council, which was set up administratively, obviously had no long-term implication. But it did represent an important concession to Europeans, for it was at their insistence that it was established. In its membership also, their influence was felt, for although it was largely official—the Governor, the Commander-in-Chief and the Deputy Governor—there was to be an unofficial Minister as well, nominated by the Governor after consultation with the Council of Ministers,[122] though it was already known that a European would be so appointed.

Finally, a promise of franchise to the African was made as part of the arrangements of the Lyttelton Constitution.[123] It was announced that by 1956 the government would initiate a study, in which Africans would play a prominent part, of the best method of choosing African members of the

[121] Government Notice 583/1954. The portfolios were distributed as follows among them: Europeans: Minister without portfolio, Agriculture, and Local Government and Housing. Asians: Minister without portfolio, and Works. Africans: Community Development.

[122] Cmd. 9103, op. cit., para. 3. The best account of the War Council is in Blundell, op cit., esp. pp. 154–62.

[123] Para. 5 of the Annexure to Cmd. 9103.

Council. Accordingly in 1955 a Commissioner was appointed to advise on the best system of choosing African representatives. He produced a strange and conservative report.[124] His basic assumption was that the vote is a public privilege, not a universal human right. The privilege had to be earned, and the privilege was meted out according to deserts, so that it was possible under his proposals for an African to have as many as six votes, while a great many would not qualify for any. Franchise was made specially difficult for the three 'Mau Mau' tribes, Kikuyu, Meru, and Embu. The government considerably modified his proposals, while still retaining the notion that the ability to vote was a privilege to be earned, and the principle of multiple voting, though the maximum votes an African could have were reduced to three.[125] Under the new law, for an African to get a vote he had to be twenty-one years old or over, and satisfy one of a number of qualifications, getting a vote for each such qualification, up to a maximum of three. The qualifications a potential voter needed were: to have completed intermediate schooling; to have property yielding an income of over a certain amount (£120) or being worth £500 or more; to have been long in government service or the armed forces; to have achieved a higher education; legislative experience or meritorious service; and seniority, i.e. having reached the grade of elder or age of forty-five (women were excluded from qualifying under this last section). African leaders were critical of these provisions, though they did contest elections under them.[126] During the 1960 and 1962 Conferences on Constitutional Developments, decisions were taken to widen the franchise.[127]

Under the new electoral provisions, eight African members were elected.[128] The new members, most of whom had not been in the Council before,

[124] *Report of the Commissioner appointed to Enquire into Methods for the Selection of African Representatives to the Legislative Council* (Nairobi, 1955). An instance of his conservatism is the following remark on universal suffrage. Such franchise had only been exercised in Britain for twenty seven years, and 'I think it would be wise to see the effects of this method of election working, both in the United Kingdom and elsewhere where it has been introduced, for a further period of about fifteen to twenty years, before considering its introduction into the society which now comprises the various races of Africa', para. 20. The Commissioner was Sir Walter Coutts.

[125] The Legislative Council (African Representation) Act, 1956 (No. 10). For a useful summary of Commissioner Coutts's proposals and the Government's modification thereof, see Engholm, op. cit., pp. 402–11.

[126] When these provisions were being consolidated Africans referred the Bill to the Council of State, as being unfairly discriminatory to them. See Ghai (1963) 13, *I.C.L.Q.*, 1089, at pp. 1099–1102.

[127] For the conditions for a vote in 1956, see the schedule to the Act (No. 10), op. cit. The conditions for the candidates were even more stringent; he had, *inter alia*, to be at least twenty-five, have completed studies at an intermediate school, have a minimum income of £120 per annum; be able to read, write and speak the English language with reasonable proficiency, and have taken the oath of allegiance to the Queen (section 16).

[128] Originally there was provision only for six such members—Act No. 10/1956—but by the African Representation (Amendment) Ordinance of the same year, the number was increased to eight. The delay was due to the necessity, as the Government saw it, to consult the leaders of the other races and secure their approval to the increase.

adopted a policy of vigorous opposition to the constitution under which they had been elected. The atmosphere in the Legislative Council was markedly affected by the entry of elected African members; they attacked vigorously the government and its policies; and showed that they were able to learn from the tactics of the Europeans and the Asians in the early days—they adopted a policy of non-cooperation, and threatened a policy of boycott.[129] Almost from the beginning, they began to demand additional reforms, in particular the provision of fifteen new African members, although the Lyttelton Constitution was designed to last until 1960. Their intransigency and refusal to accept a post reserved for them in the Council of Ministers forced the government into fresh consultations on further developments. Typically, the various communities failed to reach agreement, and the Colonial Secretary had to make his own award,[130] which formed the basis of the new constitution, known as the Lennox-Boyd Constitution.[131] Interestingly, this constitution was set up through an Order in Council, repealing the series of Royal Instructions, Letters Patent and Orders in Council which had embodied different parts of the old constitution. There was no juridical significance behind it; it was a political recognition of the fact that Kenya now had an 'advanced' constitution, for even in a colony such a constitution is established through an Order in Council.

Apart from its technical form, the 1958 Constitution was an innovation in other respects as well. First, there was an increase in elected African membership of the Legislative Council, bringing the number of elected Africans to fourteen, the same as of the elected Europeans. As there were elected representatives of other races as well, this marked not only the end of 'parity', a principle much cherished by Europeans, whereby European elected representation would always exceed or equal that of all the other groups put together, but also indicated that further changes would result in increased African representation, bringing them into a majority.

Secondly, there was a move away from the communal rolls. A novel provision of the new constitution was the institution of a special type of membership of the Legislative Council. After the election of members to the Council, they, along with the nominated members, would sit as an electoral college to choose twelve members who were to be known as Specially Elected Members, and who would be able to speak for more than one community, since they had been elected by representatives of all the communities. This was a significant breach in the principle of the communal roll, but as an attempt to get away completely from racial thinking, the scheme was

[129] See Oginga Odinga, *Not yet Uhuru* (London, Heinemann, 1967), chapter 8 for an account of the policy and tactics of African members.
[130] *Proposals for the New Constitutional Arrangements*, Cmnd. 309.
[131] Kenya (Constitution) Order in Council, 1958 (S.I. 600).

somewhat marred by the fact that these seats were communally divided: four each for Europeans, Africans and Asians (including Arabs). However, an announcement was made that in future no further seats would be established for purely communal electorates, thus presaging the growing importance of non-communal voting.[132]

Thirdly, there was the introduction of the concept of safeguards. Talk of safeguards in Kenya is almost as old as British rule there, but the importance of the new feature lies in its being an integral part of the constitution. When the famous 'paramountcy of African interests' declaration was made in 1923, it was also stated that 'obviously the interests of the other communities, European, Indian or Arab, must severally be safeguarded'. Again when Africans were denied direct electoral representation, which the other communities enjoyed, there was much discussion of the need to safeguard 'native interests'. But all this time, it had been assumed that sectional or communal interests would be taken care of by the virtue of imperial control. Thus when discussing the question of the composition of the Legislative Council, in the context of an official majority, the Joint Parliamentary Select Committee said that 'the number of representatives of the different communities is of minor importance provided always that the membership is of sufficient strength and competence adequately to express the views of the community which it represents'. Earlier in its Report, the Committee had emphasized the need for ultimate imperial control. 'The conditions in East Africa, where these widely differing communities exist side by side demand the maintenance of an effective power of intervention by the Crown in all matters of both legislation and administration. The diversity of the interests to be co-ordinated and harmonized require a Government impartial and capable of long views.' This ultimate control by the Crown had diverted attention from the problem of establishing safeguards within the Kenya Constitution itself. Thus the 1958 Constitution marked a clear advance when a safeguard was actually built into the colonial constitution, even though it depended for its efficacy ultimately on imperial control.

Under the constitution, a Council of State was set up in order to protect any one community against discriminatory legislation harmful to its interests.[133] It consisted of a chairman and ten members appointed by the Governor on no particular principle of sectional representation, and held office subject to Her Majesty's pleasure. Its powers were merely advisory and supervisory; it could not make or repeal law, and its purview did not extend to legislation already enacted. Its major function was to examine proposed new legislation to see if it was a 'differentiating measure', which was described as 'any

[132] Cmnd. 309, para. 8.

[133] See Ghai, op. cit., p. 1129. See this article generally for a study of the Council of State.

Bill or instrument any of the provisions of which are, or are likely in their practical application to be, disadvantageous to persons of any racial or religious community and not equally disadvantageous to persons of other communities, either directly, by prejudicing persons of that community, or indirectly, by giving an advantage to persons of another community'. If it was the view of the Council of State that a bill was so discriminatory, it could table an objection before the Legislative Council, followed by a detailed report. If an objection was tabled, the Legislative Council could not go on to enact the bill until the Council's report had been received. It could pass the bill then, but in this case, the Council could ask the Governor to reserve the bill for the signification of Her Majesty's pleasure. Provision was made for the Legislative Council to hold discussions with the Council in order to remove or modify offending provisions. The Council had similar functions in relation to subsidiary legislation.

The Council had two other functions. First, it had the general function of giving assistance to the Governor or the Legislative Council (or a Minister), if so required, particularly in the form of information or advice, in relation to the study of matters affecting persons of any racial or religious community in the country. Secondly, the Governor could not alter the existing regulations prescribing the number of the Specially Elected Members or the manner of their election unless the Council had first considered and approved the terms of the proposed alterations.[134]

Though the Council of State did not provide the model for further development in Kenya, its significance lies in the assumption of the reduction of imperial control and in focusing attention on the methods of protection within the constitution—a matter which later became crucial. Other features of the constitution may be briefly mentioned. It enlarged the Council of Ministers to sixteen, half of whom were to be appointed from the elected members, with the maximum number of officials allowed being eight, though in practice there were only seven officials. The Governor's powers were generally unaffected, though an important innovation was an attempt to separate those functions which he could discharge at his own discretion, and those where he had to consult the Council of Ministers. The Executive Council was abolished, and it was the Council of Ministers, rather than the Executive Council, which was thus the immediate precursor of the Cabinet.

The 1958 Constitution, therefore, while sharing in the multi-racial philosophy of its predecessor, went much further in practice; it provided, for example, a better balance between the races, even though the Europeans were still disproportionately represented.[135] But this was not a philosophy

[134] This function was repealed in 1960. Kenya (Constitution) (Amendment No. 2) Order in Council, S.I. 2201/1960.

[135] See, e.g., T. Mboya, *The Kenya Question, An African Answer* (London, Fabian Colonial Bureau, 1956).

attractive to Africans; they regarded it as a denial of true democracy, and argued that the only valid rights were those of individuals, not communities.[136] They rightly suspected that communal representation was a subterfuge to do them out of their rightful inheritance—the control of government—to which they were entitled because of the preponderance of their numbers. As the new constitution was not the result of agreement, the African members refused to co-operate in its working, and demanded that a constitutional adviser be appointed, to be followed by a conference.

The Secretary of State rejected the demand, and the Africans reacted by boycotting the Legislative Council though remaining in the Council of Ministers. It was only when the Secretary changed his mind, partly as a result of the change of attitude of a section of European opinion led by Blundell, that the African members returned to the Council. A constitutional adviser was appointed, though he was not required to produce a report, and the first of the Kenya Lancaster House Conferences took place early in 1960.

THE LANCASTER HOUSE CONFERENCE 1960 AND THE EMERGENCE OF THE MINORITY PROBLEMS

The decisions taken at the Conference were momentous. All the elected members were invited, plus two nominated members, one to represent Arab interests, and the other to represent the Somalis. The Africans had come demanding 'undiluted democracy', a common roll on a one-man one-vote basis, thus giving them a legislative majority, but were prepared to consider safeguards for the minorities as temporary provisions. They had made clear their stand against permanent safeguards of a communal kind, on the grounds that these tended to perpetuate racial groups and prevented the emergence of democracy.[137] In addition, the Africans wanted control of the Council of Ministers, and a reduction in its numbers.

The Europeans were divided among those who wanted to see another cautious step taken towards responsible government, and those who wanted to put the clock back several decades.[138] The liberal element was committed to the idea of multi-racialism, so that while it was prepared to see a common roll, with a fairly low franchise, it still wanted reservation of seats for minority

[136] ibid.

[137] Mboya, ibid. See, also, Dr. Kiano's speech at the Conference, defining African attitudes to safeguards, *The Times*, 27 January 1960. It was emphasized that the safeguards must not be such as would perpetuate 'the privileged position which the Europeans had built themselves'.

[138] The die-hards, fighting a rear-guard action, agitated for the dissolution of the Legislative Council, and its replacement by an Advisory Council, the real powers of legislation and government to lie with the Governor. In addition they wanted an extension in the powers of the local government authorities, with European control of urban areas. See, *The Times*, 20 April 1959.

communities, preferably on separate rolls. Its policy on the opening of the Highlands and the integration of schools was equivocal, and it was clearly anxious not to alienate too much European support. It wanted safeguards written into the constitution, especially on the sanctity of property. The Asians did not state their policy clearly; and while some came out unreservedly on the side of the Africans, and were prepared to accept a common roll,[139] the official delegates insisted that although abolition of communal rolls was the ultimate objective, it was necessary during the transitional period to continue them on a modified basis; or at least so to arrange the franchise on the proposed common roll that the minorities had a significant voice in the election of members to the Legislative Council. They also wanted other safeguards, and as much legislative and ministerial representation as the Europeans. The Arab member wanted autonomy for the Coastal Strip, while the Somali member wanted to have nothing to do with an independent Kenya, and wanted to be allowed to join the Somali Republic.

The Secretary of State opened the Conference by defining independence as the goal for Kenya. The aim was parliamentary institutions on the Westminster model, in which the right of each community to remain in Kenya and play a part in public life would be recognized.[140] The basic questions to be discussed were the composition of the Legislative Council, and the franchise; the character of the executive; and the question of safeguards, both electoral and property.

No agreement was achieved on these matters, and this compelled the Colonial Secretary to put forth his own proposals on the basis of the discussion that took place. He announced that the Legislative Council would contain sixty-five elected members; in addition, the Governor would retain the right to nominate members to the Council, but whether he would in fact use this power or to what extent would depend on how much support the elected Ministers could command (thus rejecting the African demand for the repeal of the Governor's power of nomination). Of the sixty-five elected members, fifty-three would be elected on a common roll, and twelve would be National Members (formerly known as Specially Elected Members). Although there were considerable reservations about the National Members among the African delegates, they were made more palatable by the fact that only the elected members would vote for them; and so the Africans would be able to control election to them. The fifty-three constituency members were to be elected on a common roll, with low franchise qualifications: (i) ability to read and write own language (or over forty years of age); or (ii) office holder in a wide range of scheduled posts at time of registration; or (iii) income of £75 a

[139] See a letter to the *Guardian* by some Indian leaders, 12 February 1960.
[140] *Report of the Conference*, Cmnd. 960.

year. This would inevitably have meant an overwhelming African majority, and so twenty seats out of the fifty-three were communally reserved, the remainder being open to contest by anyone. It was proposed that ten of these be reserved for Europeans, eight for Asians, and two for Arabs. In order to ensure that the members for these reserved seats had enough support from their own community, and were not 'fellow travellers or extreme left wing',[141] communal primary elections were to be held. It was intended that a candidate, to go to the next stage of common roll elections, had to secure the approval of his own community, expressed by a certain percentage of votes. It was left to a working party of the Chief Secretary and the Attorney-General of Kenya to work out the details of the procedure. Their recommendations,[142] as embodied in the Legislative Council Elections Ordinance, 1960 were that in primary elections, a voter was to delete the names of the candidates he did not support. Every candidate whose percentage of supporting votes was 25 per cent or more was to be declared to be duly nominated. If there was only one such candidate, he was to be declared elected. On the other hand, if no candidate had a percentage of supporting votes of twenty-five or more, every candidate would be declared duly nominated. If in a primary election to nominate candidates for election to more than one seat reserved for the same category of persons, only one candidate had a percentage of supporting votes of twenty-five or more, that candidate was to be declared duly elected, and all the other candidates were to be declared duly nominated for election to other such seat or seats.

The percentage of supporting votes necessary at the primary election was the subject of some debate. The United Party, and its later associate, the Kenya Coalition, wanted a high percentage vote in the primary, and figures of 33⅓ to 50 per cent were suggested. The effect of a high percentage would have been to defeat the purpose of the Conference settlement, which was that the members for the reserved seats should have effective and genuine support within their own community. The community, however, would merely indicate who it wanted to represent it, rather than who it did not want to represent it. Moreover, the high percentage at the primary stage would mean that in all probability only one candidate would have gone on to the next stage—this would have effectively disenfranchised the other voters on the common roll for that constituency, for it has to be remembered that the members for the reserved seats were supposed to represent all the electors of their constituency, regardless of race. The government stood firm on the figure of twenty-five which passed into law.[143]

[141] Blundell, op. cit., p. 275.
[142] Sessional Paper No. 7/1960.
[143] See the interesting debate on this question, Bennett and Rosberg, *The Kenyatta Election: Kenya, 1960–1961* (London, OUP, 1961). The importance of the percentage in the primary became obvious when Blundell just scraped 26.68 per cent against

As to the Council of Ministers, it was proposed that the number of Ministers be reduced to twelve, of whom only four would be officials. Of the eight elected Ministers, four would be Africans, three Europeans, and one Asian. In addition there was to be an Arab representative, who would have the right of attendance. The right to appoint Ministers and to distribute portfolios would remain with the Governor, contrary to the demands of the Africans who had claimed the right of the majority party to nominate Ministers.

Once the above principles had been enunciated, the Conference moved on to the next topic—safeguards—which acquired increased importance due to assumptions underlying these principles of an African majority. There was even less agreement on it. The Africans were anxious to keep safeguards to a minimum. On the other hand, the minorities argued that they had agreed to the principles about the composition of the Legislative Council and the Council of Ministers on the understanding that substantial safeguards would be provided. The main areas of controversy were land and property rights, particularly the right of expropriation. The Africans conceded that for any property or land that might be expropriated, compensation would be given. The dispute centred round the circumstances in which expropriation would be justified. According to the Europeans, expropriation should be permissible only for public purposes, such as building of housing estates, roads or other amenities. The Africans felt that this was too restrictive, and that such appropriation would in particular exclude programmes of land reform and re-distribution which were necessary to provide for the settlement of African farmers in the Highlands.

The Colonial Secretary once again had to announce his award. There was a certain lack of precision in his proposals, which is not surprising, given the deep disagreement among the delegates. He first of all stressed the need for a Bill of Rights, possibly on the Nigerian model. The Bill was to be part of the supreme law of the land, but was not to affect the validity of past legislation. Among the rights to be protected, those of property were important. There was to be no expropriation of property except to fulfil contractual or other legal obligations upon the owner, or for purposes to the benefit of the country (due regard being paid to human needs and individual hardship, confidence and stability, and advantage to the country's economy). Full and fair compensation was to be given to the owner of any property expropriated, together with the right of recourse to the courts for the judicial determination of his rights, and of the amount of compensation to be paid to him. It was also essential to preserve the independence of the judiciary,

his opponent, Sir Ferdinand Cavendish-Bentinck, at that time leader of the die-hard Europeans, who got 76 per cent. In the final common roll election, Blundell overwhelmed Cavendish-Bentinck by 20,009 votes to 2,051.

and for this purpose an independent Judicial Service Commission would be appointed. No other safeguards were mentioned, but the Colonial Secretary gave a hint of one that became later the main plank on the European programme: provision of money to buy out the farms of white farmers who wished to leave Kenya, and to settle Africans on them. Later in 1960 £5,000,000 was given for this and other schemes of settlement.

Important concessions had thus been made to the Africans. They had gained four ministries, and a majority of elected members, with the ability to influence the elections for the other seats. Most importantly of all, a decision had been made that Kenya would progress like Tanganyika and Uganda towards responsible government under African majority. The significance of the decision has been well summed up by Mboya. 'The five weeks of the Lancaster House Conference in January-February 1960 not only brought about the declaration we had sought, that Kenya was to be an African country; it also reversed the whole constitutional process.'[144] The former pretensions of the Europeans and Asians were decisively rejected; and their influence suffered a sharp decline, almost overnight. It merely remained to work out the last stages of the transfer of power. The Conference marked in a very important sense the end of an era.

The remaining part of the journey to independence was not as easy or smooth as might have been imagined. While the claims of the immigrants had been fought off, fresh dissensions appeared in society. The post-Lancaster House period saw the growth of serious rifts among the indigenous peoples. The suspicions and the lack of consensus among them seemed to make the problem of independence as intractable as ever before. The theme of safeguards that had emerged during the Conference dominated politics and negotiations subsequently. The claims of the Arabs and the Somalis had also been foreshadowed in London. Thus the last stages of Kenya's path to independence were characterized not by a vigorous and final onslaught by the Africans, but by a slow and tortuous period of reconciliation of competing claims.

CONCLUSION

The two major institutions of government described above—the executive and the legislature—have remarkable continuity. Introduced early as a result of settler pressure, they helped to influence and qualify official policy and promote political awareness. The settlers had been able to wield considerable influence even before the establishment of these institutions, and it is doubtful if they would have agitated for their establishment if they had foreseen the trends of their future development. For these two institutions—particularly the legislature—soon became one of the few

[144] T. Mboya, *Freedom and After* (London, Andre Deutsch, 1963), p. 128.

'national' institutions. While the dual system operated in several important spheres like the courts, land, local government and administration, the legislature and the executive were too central to develop along segregated or monoracial lines. Attempts were, however, made to encourage African politicians to concentrate their activities in their local councils. Moreover, once the logic of the development of the institutions became obvious, it was urged by the Europeans, unsuccessfully, that they be separated along a white and non-white division.[145]

Given absence of duality, proportions for representation had to be established, and here the institutions proved extremely flexible. The compromise and balancing of interests became the key themes in the development of these institutions. The number of seats, the introduction of communal rolls, and the manipulation of franchise qualifications—all under the control of official majorities—enabled the executive to determine the nature and form of developments and to respond to the changing political circumstances. The institutions quickly grew strong and viable, became the forum for airing grievances and expressing demands, and determined to a certain extent the form and nature of political activity.

These institutions, however, for a long time hid the reality of the power situation. They gave the appearance of democracy and of the association of the people and their representatives with the executive in policy and administration. In practice, power remained with the Governor and the Colonial Office until just before independence, and while the exercise of this power was to a certain degree influenced by pressures resulting from the democratization of institutions, the Governor's discretion was still wide. The impression of popular control and influence but without in practice the substance is their feature which can to some extent be said to characterize their successor institutions.

[145] See, e.g., 'The proposals by Lord Lugard', in Perham and Huxley, *Race and Politics in Kenya* (London, Faber and Faber, 1943).

CHAPTER III

The Development of Agrarian Administration

INTRODUCTION

No part of the law of Kenya has raised stronger emotions over the years than the law relating to land and its administration, and none is of greater importance at present. In chapter I, we showed how the incoming colonial authorities used the law to obtain full governmental control over the land. In this chapter, we seek to show how, starting from a legal *tabula rasa* (in their own eyes), these same colonial authorities created a system of agrarian law and administration which at one and the same time provided the framework for much of the economic development of Kenya in the colonial era, and contributed towards, indeed, was often the root cause of many of the political problems of that time. The political circumstances of an independent Kenya are different from colonial Kenya, but the economic problems of agricultural development are very similar, and many of these lie rooted in the past. Many of the institutions of law and administration being used to deal with them have likewise been inherited from the colonial government, and a second purpose of this chapter therefore is to try and place these problems, and the legal tools available to deal with them, in their historical context.

Once the decision was taken that European settlement should be encouraged in the East Africa Protectorate, certain policy and legal implications inevitably followed. First, the protectorate authorities would have to ensure that they had the necessary legal power to grant land to settlers on sufficiently attractive terms. Secondly, provision would have to be made to regulate where the African inhabitants of the country should be allowed to live, cultivate the land and tend their herds. Thirdly, decisions would have to be taken, and if necessary implemented, as to whether Africans should be encouraged or required to work for the incoming European settlers, and fourthly, some solution would have to be found for the vexed question of Arab and other rights in the land at the coast. With the exception of this last problem, which though intractable, was not politically a burning issue,[1] the decisions on these matters, too often taken under pressure from European

[1] C. K. Meek, *Land Law and Custom in the Colonies* (London, OUP, 1946), second edition, pp. 92–6; Hailey, *Native Administration in the British African Territories* (London, HMSO), part I, pp. 196–7; Lands Department, *Annual Report, 1956*, Nairobi, p. 11.

settlers and with inadequate regard for their long-term implications, shaped the pattern of land ownership and use in Kenya, and set in train those pressures and problems which the independent government was to inherit many years later.

The development of the law on these matters may be seen and discussed in four phases, 1902–21, 1922–39, 1940–60 and 1960 to the present.

THE INAUGURATION OF THE DUAL POLICY 1902–1921

(a) *The Law of European Settlement*

The initial problem of acquiring control over the land has been looked at. The Crown Lands Ordinance 1902[2] provided the more detailed control of grants and other dispositions of land forshadowed in the East Africa (Lands) Order in Council 1901.[3] Although repealed and replaced by the Crown Lands Ordinance 1915,[4] this legislation is significant for several reasons. A considerable area of land was alienated to settlers under it, including many freehold estates. It introduced the principle that ownership of interests in the land was dependent on development of the land, and a residual power must be left to the public authorities to enforce it, though some time was to elapse before the principle was made a reality in practice. Its administration carefully distinguished between Europeans and Asians, though there was nothing in the Ordinance which directly sanctioned that, and it was not until 1908 that the British Government clearly agreed to it. It limited recognition of African rights in the land to that of actual occupation only, but it was popular neither with the settlers nor the Commissioner, Sir Charles Eliot, and where the latter could not circumvent it by rules made thereunder, the former campaigned ceaselessly against it. Whitehall too was dissatisfied with it, but wanted stricter law and administration. The first of many clashes between it and the settlers ensued, with the resulting legislation conceding more of the settlers' demands than Whitehall's.

Salient features of the new Crown Lands Ordinance were that agricultural leases were increased to 999 years, town plots remaining at 99 years, with those who had acquired licences or leases under the 1897 or 1902 legislation being permitted to convert them. Leases could be of up to 5,000 acres. Rents were to be subject to revision every thirty years. The Governor was empowered to veto any transfer of land to a person of a different race from the transferor. An implied covenant in every agricultural lease granted to a European provided that he should not, without the consent of the Governor in Council, allow a non-European to be manager of, to occupy, or be in control of the land. This was the first time explicitly racial provisions had appeared in land legislation, and together with the decision of the Liberal

[2] No. 21 of 1902. [3] S.R.O. 661. [4] No. 12.

Government in 1908 that 'as a matter of administrative convenience grants in the upland area should not be made to Indians',[5] went a long way towards creating a segregated society and the dual system of land law and administration that sustained it. More detailed conditions as to use and development of the land were implied into a lease but as before, little effort was made to ensure that they were complied with. A conspicuous absence from the Ordinance were provisions against dummying, originally wanted by the Colonial Office.

The Ordinance was passed at a time when the first wave of settlement was over; indeed alienation of land to settlers was suspended during the First World War. But immediately it ended, a committee was appointed to consider plans for the allocation of land to ex-soldiers from the United Kingdom, and its report[6] was implemented by the Discharged Soldiers Settlement Ordinance 1919.[7] This Ordinance, with its amendments, provides an interesting example of the role of government and its relations with the settlers in providing and controlling settlement schemes. Approximately two million acres were earmarked for the scheme, a large part of it being excised from the Nandi reserve, without compensation. Two classes of farms were established, A, of three hundred acres or under, B, of more than 300 acres. All settlers had to reside in the protectorate and on their farms for fixed proportions of the first three years of the grant, and were not allowed to engage in general commercial dealings in the land until the purchase price had been paid.

The attempt thus made to prevent speculation and absentee owners and create a class of smallholder farmers was soon abandoned. In 1921 both residence requirements and restrictions on commercial dealings were eased, and the following year the barriers were completely removed.[8] The purchase price was to be remitted if satisfactory improvements were put on the land, and complete freedom of commercial dealings was allowed, whether the purchase price had been paid or any improvement made to the land. In both cases, however, the Crown Lands Ordinance had to be observed. In the result, most of the class A settlers sold up, and those that remained were on average no more energetic in developing their land than the pre-war settlers, though they did eventually make good.

This period also saw the beginnings of agricultural law and administration, devoted primarily to serving the interests of the settlers. 1904 saw the first

[5] Colonial 4117 (1908), *Correspondence relating to the Tenure of Land in the East Africa Protectorate*, p. 33. Administrative restrictions on the granting of land to Indians had been introduced in the East Africa Protectorate in 1902, without the knowledge of the Foreign Office.

[6] *Land Settlement Commission Report*, 1919, Nairobi.

[7] No. 13, as amended by No. 13 of 1920.

[8] Crown Lands (Discharged Soldiers Settlement) Ordinance No. 1 of 1921, as amended by No. 29 of 1922.

recognizably European agricultural legislation with the prohibition of the import of certain coffee plantings to prevent coffee leaf disease.[9] The coffee industry itself was one of the first to be subject to a measure of public control, legislation in 1918 providing for District Commissioners to maintain registers of coffee plantations, and issue certificates of registration to the owners thereof.[10] Although the legislation did not limit registration to European plantations, this result was achieved by the non-issue of certificates to Africans and Asians, and the administrative discouragement of coffee-growing in the reserves.

(b) *The Law of African Reserves*

The development of the law of African reserves was spasmodic and reflected 'indecision and differences of policy as much as shortage of funds and survey staff'.[11] Eliot was against reserves, preferring interpenetration by Europeans, but the creation of the Masai reserve in 1904 heralded a slow policy drift towards them. No general provisions on them appeared in the law, however, until the Crown Lands Ordinance 1915. Until that time, reserves were initially created, either by agreement with the tribe concerned, as with the Masai, or by use of the Outlying Districts Ordinance,[12] under which orders could be issued forbidding entry into a 'closed district'. In addition the administration gazetted some reserves though these were no more than administrative dispositions without legal authority. Policy in favour of reserves had hardened by the beginning of the second decade of this century, however, and this is illustrated by the provision in the Native Authority Ordinance 1912[13] that an administrative officer who found a member of a tribe for whom land had been reserved cultivating unalienated Crown land outside the reserved land might order him back to the reserve.

It was perhaps rather typical of the protectorate administration that such a provision should appear in the law before there were clear legal provisions about reserves, and well before action was taken under those provisions. The provisions appeared in the Crown Lands Ordinance and empowered the Governor to 'reserve . . . any Crown land which in his opinion is required for the use or support of the members of the native tribes of the Colony'.[14] He was also empowered to cancel or exclude land from a reserve. A clear framework for the dual system was thus provided, though it was not for another eleven years that reserves were gazetted, and longer still before any

[9] Coffee Leaf Disease Ordinance, 1904.
[10] Registration of Coffee Plantations and Coffee Dealers Ordinance No. 10 of 1918.
[11] Sorrensen, 'Land Policy in Kenya 1895–1945' in *History of East Africa*, op. cit., volume II, appendix 1, p. 683.
[12] No. 25 of 1902.
[13] No. 22.
[14] Sections 54 and 86.

measure of security of tenure in their lands was restored to Africans. These provisions also made it clear that Africans had no rights in the land, and were at the disposal of the administration. This had considerable significance for the problem of agricultural labour.

(c) *The Law of Agricultural Labour: The Rise of the Squatter*

The settlers considered that the protectorate administration should apply legislative, administrative and financial pressure on the Africans to induce them to go and work on European farms. The administration was ambivalent in its attitude to this question. As early as 1901 a Hut Tax was imposed which was a financial inducement to work, though it was not imposed in order to induce Africans to work on Europeans' farms. The Master and Servant Ordinance 1906[15] imposed penalties of imprisonment or fine for negligent work on those already working. Administrative pressure to work was spasmodically imposed by the use of administrative officers and headmen as recruiting agents. This three pronged attack on the problem of labour, however, fell foul of many administrative officers, who were not prepared to be used as recruiting agents, and the Colonial Office, which objected to the whole manner in which labour was treated. Legislative and administrative changes had to be introduced which had an adverse effect on the supply of labour.

Faced with a shortage of labour, and the impossibility of cultivating all their large holdings, some settlers had adopted—as early as 1904—the practice of 'Kaffir farming' whereby Africans were allowed to squat on the farm on a crop-sharing basis, contributing their labour to that part of the farm which the settler was cultivating. Though condemned by the Native Labour Commission of 1913, this practice contained the seeds of the solution to the problem of agricultural labour. This emerged as the Resident Native (Squatters) Ordinance of 1918,[16] the preamble of which declared that '... it is desirable to encourage resident native labour on farms and to take measures for the regulation of the squatting or living of natives in places other than those appointed for them by the Government of the Protectorate ...'. It introduced a publicly supervised contract of agricultural labour, the basic provision of which was that the labourer had to work for 180 days on a farm in return for which he and his family could live there, and have an area for their own cultivation. Kaffir farming was prohibited.

This legislation was in some ways complementary to earlier land legislation, for one of its objects was to destroy the relationship of landlord and tenant between the European farmer and the African, and so destroy any rights the African might have in the land by reason of the tenancy. A relationship

[15] No. 8.
[16] No. 33.

of employer and employee involving elements of involuntary servitude was substituted, and one of the prime objects of later legislation in this field was to maintain that relationship and to prevent the development of a system of tenancy.

The supply of labourers did not immediately increase after the Ordinance was passed, despite the efforts of settlers to attract Africans to their farms. More settlers were arriving, however, and this led to a revival of the demand that administrative pressure should be brought to bear on Africans in the reserves. This resulted in the 'Ainsworth circular' of 1919 which forcefully stressed the duty of administrative officers to use insistent advocacy to get Africans—women and children included—out of the reserves to work on European farms. The circular produced a storm of missionary and liberal protest which after two years forced the protectorate authorities to climb down. In future administrative officers were not to be used as private recruiters.

By 1921, therefore, a framework of law and administration had been created in which the development of the dual system was clearly discernible. The first priority of this period had been to build up and maintain a European farming community, so that allocations of land, and the terms on which they had been made, were generous, and public control was minimal. The second priority had been to create conditions under which the land could be profitably developed and to this end security of tenure and a plentiful supply of cheap labour were necessary, both of which were provided on the whole, though not entirely to the satisfaction of the settlers. Both these priorities required that Africans be deprived of their security of tenure and confined to reserves and these too were being accomplished by the end of the period. Two problems, the provision of credit and cash crop competition from Africans, were just perceptible by the end of the period. Action on these and other matters to consolidate the positions gained in the early years, remained to be taken in the future.

CONSOLIDATION OF THE DUAL POLICY 1922–1939

(a) *European Settlement*

If the first period of agrarian administration may be seen as one of inauguration, this period may be seen as one of consolidation of the dual system, culminating in the attempt to provide through the law a final and lasting solution, and as one when some of the problems, sown in the early years, began to be reaped. The main thrust of settler pressures, and therefore usually government policies, in this period was to gain increased security and size for their privileged position in the Highlands and elsewhere, adequate supplies of agricultural credit and labour, and to impose restrictions on much African cash crop farming.

In relation to security and size the period brought, on balance, gain, and may be seen largely in terms of the recommendations of the Kenya Land Commission,[17] one of whose terms of reference was to consider the position of the European Highlands. Prior to the implementation of these recommendations, the Highlands had been a European enclave protected from Indian encroachment largely through administrative measures, bolstered by such official declarations of policy as the Elgin pledge of 1908 and the Devonshire declaration of 1923,[18] which whatever else it contained, did endorse the maintenance of the Highlands as a European reserve. Protection from African encroachment had been achieved by more forthright legislative means.

The Kenya Land Commission recommended that the boundaries of the Highlands be finally fixed and legally secured by imperial Order in Council with a board established to look after the interests of Europeans in the Highlands. In addition, they recommended that all native rights outside the reserves be extinguished, the object being to wipe the slate clean and establish unchallengeable European and African rights to separate portions of the land of Kenya.

These recommendations were accepted by the British Government, and after a long delay, implemented by the Crown Lands (Amendment) Ordinance 1938,[19] and the Kenya (Highlands) Order in Council 1939.[20] The Ordinance set out the boundaries of the Highlands and the Order in Council provided that alterations to them were to be reserved for the Royal Assent. The Order in Council also established a Highlands Board, with a majority of unofficials, with the broad functions of protecting and making representations concerning the interests of the inhabitants of the Highlands in the land situate therein, and advising the Governor on the disposition thereof.

Alongside the Highlands Board, the non-statutory Land Advisory Board, established in 1928, continued to function. Composed of even numbers of officials and unofficials, its main functions were to advise the Governor on proposals for alienation and direct grants of Crown land, and schemes for the development and closer settlement of unopened land. Its jurisdiction embraced the whole of Kenya though as might be expected it concentrated its attention on the Highlands.

Security of their privileged land position had been achieved; economic security was much more difficult to achieve but here too, the law was used to create institutions, and, as far as possible, an economic climate sympathetic to European agricultural enterprise. The liberalization of the financial

[17] Cmd. 4556 (1934).
[18] Cmd. 1922 (1923), *Indians in Kenya*.
[19] No. 27.
[20] S.R.O. 517.

provisions of the settlement schemes in the early twenties was one indication of the difficulties the settlers were facing, others being the forcing down of African wages at the time of the currency change and the constant demand for economy in government. Farming was relatively profitable in the twenties, however, and it was not until 1930 that the government came directly to the rescue of the farming community by introducing a system of public agricultural credit and providing relief against the claims of mortgagees, through a series of important Ordinances, the combined effect of which was to give the government an increasingly large direct interest in the agricultural economy, and so lay the foundations of, and provide the justification for, increasing public control of agriculture.

The first such Ordinance was the Agricultural Advances Ordinance of 1930.[21] This established a Central Agricultural Advisory Board and local boards, the latter composed of members of the farming community. Applications for advances were made through the local boards to the Central Board which fixed the details of the advance, and once it was made, was empowered to issue directions as to how all crops, etc., were to be dealt with and disposed of, including directions to the purchaser to pay the price to it. This was an important piece of legislation from the administrative angle as well, as it introduced the system of producer-dominated institutions of public control which was to be a characteristic feature of European agrarian administration.

The following year saw the establishment of the oldest of Kenya's public credit institutions, the Land and Agricultural Bank which put normal farm credit on a sound basis.[22] It was empowered to make advances to farmers on a first mortgage of agricultural or pastoral land of at least ten acres in extent and to a total of not more than 60 per cent of the value of the land. Advances could be for such matters as making permanent improvements in accordance with the Crown Lands Ordinance and discharging existing mortgages. It could refuse to pay any portion of the loan if it was not being economically used or the conditions were not being complied with, which included fulfilling the development conditions of the lease. Thus for the first time some teeth were put into that part of the Crown Lands Ordinance.

In the short space of eight years the Bank became the central institution in a network of law and administration dealing with public and private agricultural credit. Its recovery powers were enlarged in 1933 when it was empowered, on default of repayment, to take possession of land and transfer a good title without need to obtain the sanction of a court.[23] The same legisla-

[21] No. 12.
[22] Land and Agricultural Bank Ordinance No. 3 of 1931.
[23] Land and Agricultural Bank (Amendment) Ordinance No. 4 of 1933.

tion empowered it to act as an agent of the government. The following year, several of the CAAB's powers were transferred to it.[24] It was also given power over advances and payments for crops, including power to agree, and be a party, to arrangements between a debtor and a private firm for anticipatory advances on crops.

As the economic conditions of the settlers continued to worsen, the Bank's powers were increased and for the first time the government intervened directly to provide relief for mortgagors. The Agricultural Mortgagors' Relief Ordinance 1934[25] displaced the powers of a mortgagee under the Indian Transfer of Property Act[26] to realize his security in favour of those in the Ordinance. This permitted mortgagors to seek relief against such realization from the Supreme Court, which, if granted, was to the effect that the mortgagee should not further proceed for at least one year. In deciding whether to grant relief the Court was to consider, *inter alia*, the extent to which the mortgagor's default was caused by the economic crisis in the colony, and whether relief would help him to meet his liabilities within a reasonable time.

This interference with mortgagee's rights was administered by the court, but the Farmers Assistance Ordinance,[27] enacted two years later, established a system of boards and committees to administer a more far-reaching scheme of relief. A judicial aura was maintained by the appointment of a judge to the chairmanship of the Farmers Conciliation Board, the principal board of the new scheme, standing at the apex of a complex system of conciliation and negotiation between, and control of, debtors and creditors. It was assisted by local committees, consisting in part of local farmers, and the Land and Agricultural Bank. A farmer could make an application for assistance to the Board through a local committee, on the grounds that his general financial position made it impossible for him to carry on. Once an application was filed, the local committee issued an interim order which vested all the applicant's property in the Bank, and stopped all actions against him. A temporary supervisor of the property subject to the instructions of the Bank was also appointed. The local committee then called a meeting of creditors and the applicant to try and arrange a voluntary settlement of the latter's liabilities. Any arrangement had to be agreed by the Board and 75 per cent of the creditors by value. Once agreed, the interim nature of the order ceased, and it became effective for twelve months, being annually renewable by the Board for up to five years. Permanent supervision by the Bank was authorized and this gave it complete control of the applicant's

[24] Agricultural Advances (Amendment) Ordinance No. 34 of 1934.
[25] No. 35.
[26] No. 9 of 1882, introduced into Kenya under the East Africa Order in Council 1897.
[27] No. 18.

financial affairs. It provided funds, to the extent considered necessary by the Board to ensure the successful continuance of the applicant as a farmer and to provide a reasonable living allowance for him and his dependants. Three years later, the Bank, which provided the advances and much of the administration of the scheme, was given a more important role in the making of the initial composition arrangement.[28] Applications were in future to go through it to the Board, which considered them together with the Bank's comments before meetings with creditors were arranged.

Several points emerge from this description of the laws regulating the growth of public credit. Seen in historical perspective, it illustrates the speed and size of Government's involvement in the agricultural industry and lends added understanding to the European bid for financial control in Government which reached its maximum intensity in the late thirties. It illustrates too the extent to which Government was, in any event, responsive to the settlers, for despite the great powers that were taken, the main aim of the legislation was to tide the individual farmer over a bad period, and permit him to stand on his own feet again. At this time, Government did not see its function, any more than its function was seen by farmers, to be that of maintaining a continuous supervisory jurisdiction over the manner in which agricultural land was used, though there can be little doubt that the experiences of the thirties considerably influenced later government thinking in this direction. Again government responsiveness to the settlers may be seen in its attempt to associate farmers with the administration of the relief schemes. Finally, it corrects to some extent the rather traditional picture of the Kenya European farmer; from the early thirties onwards he was heavily dependent on direct government action to safeguard his economic no less than his physical position in Kenya and succeeding years only increased this dependence.

Alongside the growth of government involvement in agriculture via the provision of credit, this period also saw a growth in public control of aspects of the growing and marketing of agricultural products. Coffee and maize may be considered here. We have seen that coffee was one of the first industries to be organized on a statutory basis. One of the main reasons for this was the desire of the European planters to keep Africans out of the industry, and in this way they were in the main initially successful through rules made and administrative decisions given under the Ordinance. This was one area, however, where Europeans did not continue their forward momentum. The Coffee Industry Ordinance of 1932[29] increased the types of licences that were required by coffee dealers and established an elected board of planters to issue planters' licences, thereby introducing producer-control into this branch of the agricultural industry. But these licences were not

[28] Farmers Assistance (Amendment) Ordinance No. 2 of 1939.
[29] No. 50, repealed and replaced by the Coffee Industry Ordinance No. 54 of 1934.

necessary for coffee growing in the reserves, and a partial lifting of the administrative ban on African coffee growing followed.

Coffee was a crop grown predominantly by Europeans; maize was grown by both Europeans and Africans, and this posed certain problems for the administration of a dual system of agriculture. Initially, however, maize, without regard to origin, was brought under the Agriculture Produce (Export) and the Crop Production and Livestock, Ordinances,[30] for the purposes of inspection and grading for export, and prohibiting the storage, sale and transport of wet maize. Not until the late thirties were rules made to apply specifically to African grown maize.[31] Marketing of maize was not yet subject to statutory control, but its importance in Kenya's economy was appreciated, and from time to time its growers received special treatment, including interest-free loans from the Kenya and Uganda Railways Administration, to be administered by the Kenya authorities.[32]

(b) *The African Reserves*

The period opened with the Supreme Court decision that the annexation of most of the protectorate had had the effect of destroying all African rights in the land of the new colony;[33] it closed with the apparent entrenchment of the boundaries of the reserves by imperial Order in Council. It might be thought therefore that this period could be seen as one of African advance as well. It was not regarded as such by many Africans, for the entrenchment of the reserves meant the entrenchment of the dual agrarian system with the African part very much the poor relation, and for many of them the seemingly final loss of their rights in their traditional lands. Although it was the avowed intention of the Kenya Land Commission to provide a lasting solution to the pattern of land ownership in Kenya, few Africans were prepared to accept that it had done so.

The principle of reserving land for exclusive African occupation had been written into the Crown Lands Ordinance 1915. Policy on reserves was considered by two post-war settler dominated committees,[34] the first of which opposed, and the second of which accepted, the continuation of reserves, but considered that they should contain relatively little unused land. The Government was reluctant to provide legally secure reserves under the Ordinance and continued to be so until 1926, when the East Africa Commission reported in favour of greater security for Africans on the land.[35]

[30] No. 44 of 1921, No. 3 of 1926.
[31] African Produce Improvement and Inspection Rules, Government Notice 750 of 1937.
[32] Maize Subsidy Repayment Ordinance No. 17 of 1931.
[33] *Wainaina* v. *Murito* (1923), 9 K.L.R. 102.
[34] *Economic Commission* (Final Report, 1919), Nairobi; *Land Tenure Commission* (Report, 1922), Nairobi.
[35] Cmd. 2387, p. 29.

In that year, an amendment to the Crown Lands Ordinance empowered the Governor to declare any area of Crown land to be a Native reserve, though this did not confer any rights of alienation on Africans living therein.[36] Land within the reserve might be leased or set apart for commercial, educational or other purposes beneficial to its inhabitants. Twenty-four reserves delimited on a tribal basis were thereupon established.[37] This did not, however, provide any real security for Africans, since they continued to be denied both rights in the land and control over its administration. They remained tenants at will of a demanding and unsympathetic landlord.

The East Africa Commission had suggested that the problem of security could be met by vesting the reserves in a board of trustees, charged with the duty of administering them in the interests of their inhabitants. Though rejected by the Colonial Office when suggested on other occasions, the idea was now taken up, as the Colonial Secretary saw it as a good way of furthering his policy of associating the settlers with the trusteeship of the Africans. After some delay, an Ordinance embodying the idea was enacted in Kenya.[38]

It established a Native Lands Trust Board composed of the Governor and ten other persons, five official and five unofficial, of whom one was to be an African if a suitable one could be found. Local Advisory Boards were established, consisting of four persons, two officials, one European and one African unofficial. Native tribal reserves, for the use and benefit of the native tribes for ever, were established and placed under the control and management of the Trust Board. The Governor was empowered to grant leases for thirty-three year terms to non-natives but before he did so, the Advisory Boards and the Local Native Council in the reserve in question had to be consulted. If the Council or the African member of the Advisory Board objected, the lease could only be granted with the approval of the Colonial Secretary. In any event the lease had to be of benefit to Africans and could not be of land beneficially occupied by them. If land was excluded from a reserve for public purposes, an equivalent amount had to be added.

Many of the principles and ideas in this Ordinance were to last into the era of African government and it may be regarded as important for that reason. But as an attempt to provide security for Africans, the Ordinance was a broken reed. The basic reason for this was that in the final analysis, neither the Colonial Office nor the administration in Kenya was prepared to support its principles, and the Ordinance may in fact be cited as a classic example of the futility of legislation when those who have to administer it do not believe in it, and those for whose benefit it has been passed have no effective means for ensuring its proper administration.

[36] No. 22.
[37] Gazette Notice 394/1926.
[38] Native Lands Trust Ordinance No. 9 of 1930.

The continued insecurity of Africans notwithstanding the passage of the Ordinance was shown by the Kakamega Goldfield incident in 1932, when gold was discovered in the Kavirondo reserve, and settlers began to mine it. Minerals were reserved to the Crown but it was nevertheless considered necessary to remove the goldfield from the reserve. Special legislation was passed, by-passing the necessity to consult the Local Native Council and to replace the land excised from the reserve.[39] Despite protests from many persons in England, the Colonial Secretary approved the legislation, as did the Kenya Land Commission which was in being at the time.

The Kenya Land Commission was appointed as a result of a recommendation made by the Joint Select Committee of Parliament which had been established to consider the issues arising from the report of the Hilton Young Commission on Closer Union and Native Policy in East Africa.[40] The Commission's terms of reference required it to consider African grievances arising from past alienations of land to non-Africans and how to remedy them; what the present and future African land needs were and how they could be met; and to consider the position of the Highlands. Its report, published in 1934, has been described as marking an epoch in the history of land rights in Kenya,[41] and certainly, of all the reports on land questions in Kenya in the colonial era, it is the most thorough. However, it has been criticized as being too legalistic, and as interpreting its terms of reference so narrowly that it excluded an adequate consideration of the overall economic and social requirements of Africans in relation to the land.[42] Though it looked forward to a time when there could be tribal interpenetration in the reserves and individual tenure of land without regard to tribe or race, its whole approach to the problems was in terms of satisfying each tribe. It did, however, provide the basis for legislation and future policy on land rights which was to last until the sixties.

The Commission's main recommendations were that certain blocks of land should be added to the reserves representing in part what was 'owed' to the Africans and in part an estimation of future needs. Security was to be ensured by entrenching the boundaries of the reserves in Orders in Council, and vesting them in a board of trustees situated in England, the existing Trust Board being criticized as too similar to the Kenya Executive Council to inspire confidence amongst Africans. Finally the designation of the reserves should be changed from Crown lands to Native lands.[43]

[39] Native Lands Trust (Amendment) Ordinance No. 36 of 1934. See Kenya Land Commission, op. cit., pp. 298–301.
[40] Cmd. 3234 (1929). Wrigley, 'Kenya, Patterns of Economic Life 1902–45' in *History of East Africa*, op. cit., volume II, pp. 248–9.
[41] Meek, op. cit., p. 84.
[42] *Report of the East Africa Royal Commission*, Cmd. 9475 (1955), chapter 6 especially paras. 1 to 3.
[43] *Report*, op. cit., paras. 2075-2127, 2144–51.

These recommendations were accepted by the British Government with the exception of the one relating to the composition and location of the Trust Board and after some delay, legislation was enacted to implement them. A Native Lands Trust Board was established by Order in Council,[44] consisting of five persons resident in Kenya with the Chief Native Commissioner as Chairman and one European elected member. It was to protect African interests in their lands, and make representations to the Governor when in its opinion the lands were not being so administered. The Order also provided that the boundaries of the native reserves, set out in Kenya legislation, could only be altered with the sanction of the Colonial Secretary.

The African lands were divided into Native lands and Native reserves.[45] The former were for present use, no longer designated as Crown lands, and vested in the Trust Board. The latter were for future use, remained designated as Crown lands and were not vested in the Trust Board. A hierarchy of bodies was established or empowered to administer the new arrangements based largely on the pattern of the 1930 legislation. The main feature of these bodies was that while Africans were members of them at the local level they were both chaired by and only advisory to, provincial administrators who made the decisions. Final decisions were made by the Governor, not by the Trust Board, though in practice the Chief Native Commissioner had great influence in any decisions that were taken. A very limited class of matters had to be referred to the Colonial Secretary for his decision. In only two situations was this basic pattern of administrative decision-making not adhered to; where the Governor wished to exclude land from a Native Land Unit, he had to be satisfied that a majority of Africans in the area approved and the Local Native Council had to pass a resolution in favour of such exclusion. Secondly, a lease of land set apart could only be forfeited for non-compliance with conditions on the basis of a court order.

While the legislation had gone some way towards securing the boundaries of the Native lands, security against reduction of the area of the lands thus reserved still depended overwhelmingly on administrative decisions made by officers who were in no way accountable to those on whose behalf they were making decisions, but who could, on the contrary, very greatly influence the composition and performance of the advisory body associated with them. In practice, problems tended to arise more over land use and conservation rules than over setting apart and the like, and it is significant in this respect that while rule-making powers were exercisable by the Governor with the advice and consent of the Trust Board, there was no requirement that Local

[44] Kenya (Native Areas) Order in Council, 1939, S.R.O. No. 516.
[45] Native Lands Trust Ordinance No. 28 of 1938.

Boards or Native Councils be consulted, even in respect of rules that applied only to their area.

The aims of the Kenya Land Commission and the legislation which followed it were based primarily on political factors—the desirability of fixing once and for all on a permanent basis the areas of land allocated to Europeans and Africans, and so ensure the maintenance of the dual agrarian system. But economic forces, particularly in the last half of this period, were slowly beginning to move the two systems closer together, as a reference to some of the agricultural legislation applying to Africans will indicate. The Native Grown Coffee Rules 1934[46] empowered the Director of Agriculture to define areas in the reserves where coffee might be grown, and required Africans wishing to grow coffee to obtain a permit from the Director and a licence in respect of their plantation from the District Commissioner. The former had to be satisfied that there would be adequate supervision and development of a plantation, and in order to ensure that he could give orders as to its management and cultivation. Early in 1935 the Director gazetted parts of Nyanza and Central Provinces as being suitable coffee growing areas,[47] but it was some years before a significant number of Africans began to grow coffee.

A most important piece of legislation was the Marketing of African Produce Ordinance 1935.[48] Where the Governor considered that produce would be improved and the inhabitants benefited, he might make an order declaring a district to be one where the purchase and sale of produce should be controlled. The effect of such an order was that produce could only be purchased by a buyer holding a licence to do so from the District Commissioner, and at a place declared to be a market.

It was by means of orders made under this Ordinance that the Kenya Farmers Association was able to maintain and extend its monopoly position as the buyer of maize in Kenya, and compel the African producer to share the burden of the less profitable export market. Until 1934 Africans had sold their maize crop to itinerant traders but rules made in that year required traders to display their prices at all times, and limited trading to the hours between sunrise and sunset which restricted such forms of trading, and gave the KFA a chance to establish itself as a buyer in the reserves. This it was eager to do as African sales on the home market imperilled the profitability of European maize growers and the uniform pool price system operated by the KFA for them. The requirement of sales in a market to licensed buyers only helped complete the process begun in 1934.[49]

Finally, the first efforts to tackle the problem of bad land use may be

[46] Government Notice 516/1934.
[47] Gazette Notice 24/1935.
[48] No. 28.
[49] Wrigley, op. cit., pp. 251–2.

noted. Hitherto, though the problem had been mentioned by the various land commissions, little had been done about it since agricultural administration had been concentrated on the European areas. In much of the African lands, however, the problem of bad use leading to soil erosion was serious by the mid-thirties and prejudiced not only the development of African agriculture, but also the adequacy of the lands to cope with the growing population. No general legislation to deal with the problem was introduced despite a recommendation that that should be done,[50] and it was left to individual administrative and agricultural officers to take action, and individual Local Native Councils to make by-laws to control erosion and repair its worst effects by requiring certain methods of farming to be adopted and permitting the use of communal labour to combat further erosion. In addition, rules made under the Crop Production and Livestock Ordinance empowered administrative officers to limit the number of cattle which could be depastured in certain areas, to confiscate those in excess of the number, and in some cases to authorize compulsory culling.[51]

Though the problem of the Native reserves looked as if it had been solved by the end of the inter-war period, this was to a large extent illusory. Many Africans did not accept the final solutions of the Kenya Land Commission. In addition the problems of bad land use were being accentuated by a growing population, change in traditional patterns of tenure, and the reluctance of Africans to accept the control measures that were introduced for fear that they presaged further inroads upon the land. Law and administration had played a large part in creating this state of affairs. It remained to be seen whether they would be used to correct it.

(c) *Squatters and Resident Labourers*

The 1922–39 period opened with the Resident Natives (Squatters) Ordinance recently enacted, and the possibility that the problem of the squatters could now be brought under control. It ended with the solutions further away than ever. One of the causes of this was the recommendations of the Kenya Land Commission on resident labourers and other African occupiers of land in the Highlands and their attempted legislative implementation. Another cause was the changed situation in agricultural labour, which moved from shortage to surplus during the period, so that, by the end it was considered that there were too many resident labourers and their stock on European farms, and the problems had become how to reduce the labour force and send the surplus back to the reserves.

The settlers and government had been discomforted by the hostile overseas

[50] K.L.C., *Report*, op. cit., para. 1655.
[51] Crop Production and Livestock (Culling of Cattle) Rules, Government Notice 703/1938.

reaction to the Ainsworth circular. A further shock was the decision in *Thathi wa Mbati* v. *R.*[52] where the Supreme Court held that a resident labourer was not a servant under the Master and Servant Ordinance but a tenant, and the criminal penalties attached to desertion did not therefore apply to him. The reaction was predictable; the Master and Servant Ordinance was amended so as to include resident labourers within its scope,[53] but the Colonial Office, still sensitive on labour questions, disallowed the amendments. This set-back was only temporary, however, for a new Resident Natives Ordinance[54] was soon passed which made it a punishable offence for a labourer to fail to carry out his duties or to reside on a farm otherwise than as a resident native under contract. In addition to these penal provisions, it was provided that on a change of ownership of a farm, the contracts should be deemed to be transferred, a provision which clearly indicated the feudal aspects of the relationship. In return for the increased power the settlers were given, they were obliged to provide material for building accommodation in addition to land for cultivation and grazing.

Throughout the twenties when farming was relatively prosperous, the settlers and government continued to encourage migration from the reserves to European farms, despite evidence that numbers of Africans did not go back to the reserves after completing their contracts but stayed on as illegal squatters. By the time the Kenya Land Commission investigated the matter, the pressure was growing for some reduction in numbers. It estimated that 150,000 Africans were living on the farms as resident labourers and the Commission expressed concern on two points—first that the contract should remain one of labour and not become one of tenancy, which would occur if there were no limitations on the number of cattle the labourer could keep, and secondly, that to return all excess stock and labourers to the reserves would exacerbate conditions there, particularly as the majority of the labourers were Kikuyu and theirs was one of the most overcrowded reserves. It nonetheless recommended that reduction of both should take place progressively in the future.[55]

To this end the Resident Natives Ordinance was repealed and replaced in 1937 by a version giving greater powers of control over labourers and their cattle.[56] The employer-occupier might fix the number of cattle the resident labourer could keep and it thereupon became unlawful for him to keep more. A magistrate was empowered to order the removal of labourers from undeveloped farms. District Councils, which were purely European in composi-

[52] (1923), 9 K.L.R. 1.
[53] Master and Servant (Amendment) Ordinance No. 7 of 1924.
[54] No. 5 of 1925. On the disallowance of Ordinance 7 of 1924, the former Resident Natives Ordinance had been revived—No. 19 of 1924.
[55] K.L.C., *Report*, op. cit., paras. 1860–68; 1976, 2038.
[56] Resident Labourers Ordinance No. 30 of 1937.

tion, were empowered to limit the number of labourers which could be employed on a farm, limit or prohibit their keeping stock, and fix the number of days in a year labourers were required to work for their employers. The Ordinance was not brought into effect immediately as the Colonial Secretary wished to be satisfied that there would be land available for the redundant squatters to go to before he would sanction its introduction. Land was not, however, made available for resettlement until 1942, while the Ordinance was ultimately brought into effect in 1940.

Another class of squatters in the European areas were those Africans who had continued to reside on their traditional lands after much of the surrounding land had been alienated to Europeans, and whose right to do so had been expressly preserved by the Crown Lands Ordinance. In pursuance of the recommendations of the Commission,[57] the Native Lands Trust Ordinance extinguished these rights but provided that their erstwhile holders should not be ordered to the reserves until suitable land had been found for them. Once again, legislation had been passed despite the fact that the magnitude of the problem would make the proposed solution impossible to accomplish. There were many more Africans with rights in the Highlands than had been estimated, and they could not all be removed to the reserves straight away. The sole effect of this legislation therefore was to bring into being a class of rightless African occupiers, and so create another African land problem.

The policies and legislation on squatters in this period illustrate most clearly the characteristics of the dual system. Legislation to benefit one community inevitably affected the other adversely. Since the Europeans had an overwhelming say in the direction of government policy, the legislation benefited them, and adversely affected Africans. Economic and political development was looked at from a European perspective, and legislation was designed to further that development with little or no regard to the economic or social effects that such furtherance would have on Africans. As at the beginning of the period, so at the end, Africans were still regarded primarily as the source of labour for European agriculture, with their needs and welfare subordinate to those of the settlers.

The end of this period saw the settlers fully in command of agrarian policy and administration. They had started from a position of strength and had consolidated it. From their point of view the major problems of the period had been resolved satisfactorily. They had been provided with security in the Highlands, a system of public agricultural credit, facilities for controlling the marketing of the major African cash crop at that time, and for reducing the number of resident labourers, and in all these fields they had been granted a fair measure of administrative power themselves, for European agrarian

[57] K.L.C., *Report*, op. cit., chapter 7.

administration was very much a co-operative administration between Government and farmers. From the African point of view the picture was rather different. Security of the land had been obtained, but already it was clear that there were overcrowding problems in many parts of the reserves, and recent legislation had done nothing to alleviate it. If erosion had begun to be tackled, the temptation to use compulsion had not always been resisted, and although Africans had been appointed to local land boards and were allowed to discuss land matters, the decisions were still taken by administrators, and very few opportunities were given to contest them. In only one field was there cause for concern amongst the settlers and for hope amongst the Africans, and this was the growing of cash crops. Events were to show that this was something of an Achilles heel in the development of the dual system.

THE INCREASE IN PUBLIC CONTROL 1940–1960

The Second World War brought about far-reaching changes in the administration and control of Kenya's agriculture which were consolidated rather than dismantled after the war. It was also responsible for bringing about a changed emphasis on the nature of the land problem in Kenya, from ownership to use. The change is shown at its clearest by contrasting the Kenya Land Commission, the major commission of the inter-war period, which was concerned with African and European reserves, and the need to keep them separate, with the East Africa Royal Commission, the major commission of this period, concerned with land utilization and development and looking at the land in Kenya as a whole. Inevitably this way of looking at the land made the dual system more difficult to justify, and political developments equally impelled a reconsideration of long-standing agrarian policies. But the old problems did not disappear, and were to be a major cause of the armed rebellion in the fifties, playing a decisive part in the evolution of new economic policies at the beginning of the sixties, made necessary by the imminence of independence under African majority rule.

(a) *European Settlement and Agriculture*

The settlers may have achieved their aim of security of, and control over, the Highlands, but it was undeniable that a great deal of land therein was underdeveloped, or badly developed, and the government could not accept such a situation in wartime. The pre-war public assistance to the settlers had avoided as far as possible the imposition of public control, but now the price for continued privilege and assistance was to be greatly increased public control over all aspects of the ownership and use of land, made perhaps more palatable by the close association of the settlers with the public bodies established to administer the system.

There were three prongs to the system of control, designed to tackle the effects of bad land use, stimulate agricultural production, and stop speculative dealings in land. The first consisted of the Land and Water Preservation Ordinance 1940,[58] which empowered the Governor to make rules on a wide variety of matters connected with the preservation of agricultural land. Draft rules were to be sent to local authorities in the area concerned and their comments and objections considered before final promulgation. The rules could require action to be taken to the satisfaction of the Director of Agriculture, who was also empowered to issue orders and prohibitions to persons requiring them to take, stopping them from taking, certain action, or imposing conditions on their actions. Appeal lay to area boards constituted by the Governor. Control was increased three years later,[59] when inspectors were appointed to see that required work was carried out, and if it was not the Agricultural Department was permitted to enter and do the work, the owner being debited with the cost. Both the owner, and, where necessary, the Director could apply for an advance from the Land and Agricultural Bank to cover the cost of the work, repayable in both cases, however, by the owner.

The second prong was the Defence (Agricultural Production) Regulations 1940,[60] and the Increased Production of Crops Ordinance 1942[61] which introduced compulsory planting of crops and the system of the guaranteed minimum return in respect of certain essential crops. By the Ordinance, provision was made for Production and Manpower Committees to be formed in local areas. Farmers were to submit programmes of production to their local committee which considered and passed them on to the Agricultural Production and Settlement Board[62] which could approve them as production orders or reject them. If the latter occurred, the Board might issue its own production order to the farmer.

In 1945 the Board was empowered to issue production orders to farmers irrespective of whether they had submitted production programmes.[63] A production order constituted a guarantee by the government that the

[58] Nos. 4 and 33.
[59] Land and Water Preservation Ordinance No. 11 of 1943.
[60] Government Notice 896.
[61] No. 7. Although the Ordinance and the Defence Regulations covered the same grounds, they continued to exist side by side. See Government Notice 122/1943 which conferred powers on the board (see next footnote), and amending Ordinance No. 10 of 1945 which conferred almost identical powers on the board.
[62] Established by the Governor (Gazette Notice 191/1942) with the functions of directing and increasing the colony's agricultural production and exercising such powers as were conferred on it by law. The board had had a previous existence as the Settlement and Production Board, established in September 1939, as a successor to half of the Land and Settlement Board, established in May 1939 as a replacement for the Land Advisory Board (established in 1928), which was reincarnated as the Land Board, the other half successor of the Land and Settlement Board, in September 1939.
[63] Increased Production of Crops (Amendment) Ordinance No. 10 of 1945.

farmer would receive a minimum return per acre on the crops harvested. The Land and Agricultural Bank was to act as the agent for the government in the payment of any differential between the realized return and the guaranteed return. In addition the Bank was empowered to make advances against the guaranteed return to a farmer on receipt of evidence that he had cleared his land and sown the crops, thus ensuring him of sufficient working funds during the course of the growing season, repayable if the value of the crop was above the guaranteed return, and deductible before the proceeds of sale were handed over to the farmer. In any event, the guaranteed return was payable only if the farmer could prove that it was not through his inefficiency that the value of his crops was below it. Furthermore, the Board could issue farming orders which the farmer was required to comply with, and in the event of default, it could enter and cultivate the land.

Increased production required not merely that opened up land be more productively used, but that more land be opened up. Accordingly the Ordinance provided that grants could be made for that purpose, and later,[64] that a farmer given such a grant must keep his land in cultivation for at least three years thereafter.

It was inevitable that such a detailed system of control of, and support for, farming should have, as its corollary, an increased governmental control over the marketing of food crops, though other factors, particularly the need to maintain stable prices in wartime, influenced developments here. Defence Regulations promulgated in 1942 brought maize, oats, barley, beans, butter and coffee under government controlled marketing systems.[65] Maize may be taken as an example of the system. After a certain amount of administrative turmoil,[66] a Maize Controller was established, with the sole right to buy and sell maize produced in or imported into Kenya. The KFA was to be appointed the agent of the Controller in respect of the buying and handling of all European-grown maize. The government fixed the price at which maize was to be bought. All millers were to be registered with the Controller, and receive their supplies from him. He might authorize advances to be made to producers, but these were not to exceed the guaranteed return.

The third prong of control was directed at land transactions and increased settlement. The Land Control Ordinance and Crown Lands (Amendment) Ordinance, both of 1944[67] had, as one of their objects, the introduction of

[64] Increased Production of Crops (Amendment) Ordinance No. 13 of 1943.
[65] Defence Regulations, Government Notice 573 (beans), Government Notice 943 (coffee), Government Notice 1040 (hides), Government Notice 1074 (butter), Government Notice 1139 (oats and barley).
[66] Defence (Control of Maize) Regulations, Government Notice 430, and Government Notice 571, repealed and replaced by Government Notice 877—all of 1942, repealed and replaced by Government Notice 827/1943, repealed and replaced by Government Notice 993/1944. See, too, *History of East Africa*, op. cit., volume II, pp. 252–3.
[67] Nos. 22 and 23 of 1944.

restrictions on, and public control of, alienations of land in the Highlands, and elsewhere. By the first Ordinance a Land Control Board was established consisting of three officials, and six European unofficials. No person might alienate or part with the possession of his land, nor acquire any right nor enter into any sort of agreement relating to land, with the exception of certain mortgages, without the consent of the Board. Transactions taking place without the Board's consent were null and void. The Board might impose conditions as to the development of the land, failure to comply with which could result in forfeiture of the land. The Board was empowered to hold hearings and an appeal lay from a refusal or a conditional consent to a Land Control Appeal Tribunal.

The Crown Lands (Amendment) Ordinance was concerned purely with the Highlands and conferred on the Governor the same powers in respect of dealings with land there as had been conferred on the Board in respect of dealings with land anywhere, with the addition that he could refuse his consent to inter-racial dealings in shares in a company which had interests in the Highlands. The Land Control Board was to advise the Governor in the exercise of these powers.

The great extension of public control over European agriculture and land which the war had made necessary was to prove a Trojan horse. Hitherto, the Europeans had received aid without strings from Government, and one of their strengths was that they were relatively free from dependence on, and control by, Government. Where public financial assistance was necessary, it was channelled through the Land and Agricultural Bank, thus keeping Government in the background. But this approach changed with the war legislation. The justification for the change was that the time had passed when individuals could do what they liked with their land; governments now had a legitimate interest in how land was used.[68] The argument had been used in the past by settlers in relation to the African lands, but it was a novel application for the government to use it in relation to their lands. The legislation itself created a system of financial dependence and administrative control, which the use of the Bank and local committees composed in part of settlers themselves, could not wholly disguise. Perhaps most important of all, the legislation reflected the government's new approach to land—the importance of productive use—and when looked at from this point of view, the rigid division between European and African land was of lesser importance. It was to require a political revolution many years hence before the barriers in the Highlands finally came down, but the wartime stress laid on land use and the public control of agriculture had helped to undermine the rationale of the Highlands.

[68] See *Minority Report of the Land Tenure Committee* (Nairobi, 1942).

These perspectives were not apparent in 1944. By then, European farming had largely recovered from the depression period of the thirties, and the Agricultural Production and Settlement Board, one of whose terms of reference was to encourage and plan for increased white settlement, was working on a soldier settlement scheme.[69] Plans for this scheme were significantly different from that started in 1919. Then, land had been taken from a native reserve; now, it was to be taken from the large amount of unused European-owned land in the Highlands. The Land Control Board was empowered to advise on the suitability of land for settlement, and on its recommendation, the Governor, after consultations with the Highlands Board, might acquire land, compulsorily if necessary, for purposes of settlement.

Settlement began soon after the end of the war and to cope with its administration, the Agricultural Production and Settlement Board was divided into a Board of Agriculture, and a European Settlement Board.[70] It was not until 1948, however, that the latter Board and the schemes were established on a statutory basis. By an Ordinance passed that year,[71] and made retrospective to the beginning of 1946, the Board became the European Agricultural Settlement Board, advisory to the Minister of Agriculture on the settlement schemes. A European Agricultural Settlement Fund, consisting of grants of money and land from the government, and rents from the schemes, ultimately totalling £2,000,000, was established and the Member was empowered to spend it on buying and preparing land for settlement, and making advances to the new settlers. He was also empowered to grant relief in respect of capital and interest repayments, and write off bad debts.

In 1955[72] the Board was transformed from a quasi-governmental advisory body into a statutory executive body in which was vested the Fund and its control and management, and the duty, subject to any specific or general directions of the Minister, to administer the settlement schemes, having for this purpose the same powers as the Member had under the 1948 Ordinance. In addition the Board was empowered to raise or borrow money. Nine settlers were appointed to the Board. The significance of this reform is seen when set alongside African and Asian participation in the Ministerial system introduced in 1954.

Two settlement schemes were introduced in 1946, the Assisted Owner, and the Tenant Farmer Schemes. Under the former, designed for persons with substantial capital, the settler purchased land and, if necessary, received an advance from the Fund to do so. Under the latter, designed for persons

[69] *Settlement Scheme Committee Report* (Nairobi, 1944).
[70] Gazette Notice 52/1946.
[71] European Agricultural Settlement Ordinance No 38 of 1948.
[72] European Agriculture Settlement Ordinance No. 38 of 1955.

with limited capital, the settler leased land from the Minister, provided working capital himself, and had an option to purchase later on. In both cases, loans could be granted for long-term permanent improvements and development. The Minister might exercise all the powers of the Land and Agricultural Bank in respect of the recovery of loans and advances and make rules regulating the crops to be grown and the stock to be kept by the settlers.

By 1960, 493 farmers had been settled on practically half a million acres. The schemes went some way towards transforming the Highlands from low density to high density farming and offsetting the view current since the failure of the first soldier settlement schemes that only large scale farming could profitably succeed there. But they too were something of a Trojan horse, planted in the midst of the settlers, for they and the Board administering them provided the model for the African settlement schemes in the Highlands which began in the sixties.

The first post-war decade saw the maintenance of the system of public control introduced in the war, and the apparent strengthening of the European position in the Highlands through the settlement schemes, although it also saw the slow beginnings of political and constitutional changes which were to undermine that position. The second decade opened with a greatly increased system of public control being introduced to apply to the whole country (though in practice it was not much applied to the African lands) and, as if to provide the justification for it, the publication of the report of the East Africa Royal Commission.[73] This body had been set up in 1953 to consider possible measures to improve the standard of living of a rising East African population, and in particular to consider, *inter alia*, the economic development of land already in occupation, the adaptations and modifications of customary tenure necessary for the full development of the land, and the opening for cultivation and settlement of land not fully used. Many of their recommendations dealt with African lands, and will be looked at later, but their main thrust was the need for governments to play an increasingly active part in bringing about agrarian change and productive land use.

One particular recommendation must be mentioned here. The Commission looked forward to ideals and policies which could command general allegiance and confidence and considered that the maintenance of the privileged European position in the Highlands hindered the emergence of such policies. It advocated a loosening of the restrictions against inter-racial transfers of land in the Highlands.[74] This was the first official suggestion that the Highlands, for so long the ark of the European convenant, might not be so sacrosanct after all. The Government of Kenya rejected the recommendation,[75] but it was an uncomfortable indication to the European

[73] Cmd. 9475. [74] op. cit., p. 385 para. 10. [75] Cmd. 9801 (1956).

community of the danger of their increasing isolation from the mainstream of development in East Africa.

The reorganized system of public control of agricultural land use was established by the Agriculture Ordinance.[76] All agricultural land was divided into Scheduled and Non-scheduled Areas. The former were broadly the Highlands and other areas of predominantly European occupation, the latter were the African reserves. For the Scheduled Areas a Board of Agriculture (Scheduled Areas), Agricultural Committees and Sub-committees were established, and all occupiers and owners of land therein were required to register themselves with the Board. Sub-committees were elected by and from those registered. Agricultural Committees were composed in part of officials or members appointed by the Minister, and in part of the chairmen of sub-committees, and the Board, a direct descendant of the 1946 Board of Agriculture, consisted of officials, Committee chairmen, nominees of certain scheduled agricultural and marketing organizations, and appointees of the Minister. The Committees and Boards were advisory to the one above them (in the case of the Board this was the Minister) and played an important part in the administration of the Ordinance. Their role may be illustrated by considering the example of a land development order.

The Minister might make a land development order against an occupier of land requiring him to carry out a development programme. A sub-committee would inform the occupier that such an order was being considered and a report prepared for submission to the Agricultural Committee. The occupier might appear and make representations and the land be inspected. The Agricultural Committee which received the report was to forward it to the Board, after giving the occupier an opportunity to make further representations. If the Board accepted the report, it required the occupier to submit a development programme to his sub-committee. Once again there was a progression upwards with each body empowered to make modifications to the programme, with or without the occupier's consent, with the Board finally recommending the Minister that he make an order on the basis of the programme approved by it, or, where the occupier failed to submit a programme, drawn up by it. Unless he saw special reasons to the contrary, the Minister was forthwith to make the order in the terms of the programme. As with a land preservation order, the successor to orders made under the Land and Water Preservation Ordinance, an occupier could obtain a loan to carry out the work required by the development order. Application was made to the Board, with the final decision being given by the Minister.

These orders and schemes were novel in their ambit but not entirely in their conception since they were based in part on the Land and Water

[76] No. 8 of 1955.

Preservation Ordinance. An entirely novel administrative institution was, however, introduced to cope with appeals and complaints against the increased powers—the Agricultural Appeal Tribunal. This was to be composed of an experienced lawyer as chairman, and two panels of persons with knowledge of agriculture, one in the Scheduled Areas and the other in the Non-scheduled Areas. Appeals were to be heard by the chairman and two persons drawn from the panel representing the area from which the appeal came. They lay against the making of many of the orders under the Ordinance but not against financial decisions—for instance the refusal of the Board to grant a land development loan. The Tribunal was to determine whether correct procedures had been followed, and if so, whether the order might in all the circumstances of the case reasonably have been made, whether or not the Tribunal would itself have made it. Apart from the possibility of stating a case on a point of law for the Supreme Court, the Tribunal's decision was final and conclusive.

The financial incentives to grow food crops sufficient for Kenya's needs, a declared objective of the Ordinance, were provided for by a reorganized system of the guaranteed minimum return. The Minister was to hold an annual review of the agricultural industry, consulting with such bodies as appeared to him to represent producers—in practice, various producer and marketing boards. The review was to determine which crops and animal products were to be the subject of a guaranteed minimum return, what that return was to be, which crops were to be designated essential crops, and the overall programme for the production of same in the Scheduled Areas. In the light of the review, the Minister was to fix the prices to be paid for the relevant crops and animal products and issue orders to purchasing agents to pay those prices. Producers were required to sell to those agents. Prices could be varied by the Minister during the year, after a special review.

After the annual review, the Minister was to declare what crops were essential. Persons registered with the Board (Scheduled Areas) were thereupon to submit production programmes for those crops to their sub-committee. These were forwarded with recommendations from the sub-committee and the Agricultural Committee to the Board, which might approve, or approve with modifications, or reject, the programme, or prepare one itself if a farmer failed to do so. It then issued a production order on the occupier of land to which the programme applied, which was binding on him, and his successors. A person aggrieved by a production order might appeal to the Agricultural Appeal Tribunal or, where the time limit for such an appeal was passed, he might notify his sub-committee that compliance with the order would entail grave hardship, and, following the usual channels, the Board might permit a variation of the order. All persons to whom a production order applied were required to submit various returns to their sub-committees, and during the currency of the order, no lease or other agreement to use the land could be terminated, notwithstanding its terms, prior to the harvesting of the crop, without the consent of the Board.

As has been mentioned, the Agriculture Ordinance basically extended the system of administration and control introduced by the war-time legislation, and the administration of the payment of the guaranteed return and advances on it followed the earlier system. In indicating how it worked, therefore, we may take the period 1942–60 as a whole. The most striking feature about the system is that, while it was introduced to create and maintain a stable agricultural industry in respect of the crops to which it applied, by providing a form of crop insurance, it was overwhelmingly used by the farmers for the short-term credit facilities which it provided. During this period 16,520 applications for advances were accepted and £9,426,301 paid out; they ranged from 242 applications and £37,137 paid out in 1942 to 1,519 applications and £1,012,133 paid out in 1957. As a contrast to this, only 1,936 claims on the GMR in respect of 247,195 acres were made and £644,173 paid out.[77] The two crops in respect of which most claims were made were maize and wheat. Its stabilizing function therefore was indirect rather than direct, and depended a great deal on the announcement of the support prices in advance, and the proper planning of production by the various Committees and Boards. Hence there was a close connection between the increased control over what the farmer could grow, and the state's guarantee to him of an adequate price for his produce.

The final aspect of public control to be considered is that of controlled marketing. Just as several factors besides control of land use and agricultural production were behind the decision to establish systems of controlled marketing in the war, so extraneous factors contributed to the decision to maintain the system after the war, and gradually put it on a more permanent basis than was provided by Defence Regulations. The marketing of five crops had in fact been the subject of some statutory control since pre-war days,[78] and during this post-war period three of these five systems were reorganized, and were joined by nine others, covering thirteen different crops or types of produce.[79] Each statutory marketing system was different from any other in detail, but all had an underlying common emphasis on producer-control of the system. All systems were continually undergoing

[77] Agricultural Department, *Annual Reports, 1942–60*, Nairobi.
[78] Wheat (1930), Cashew Nuts (1933), Pyrethrum (1935), Passion Fruit (1937), Sisal (1939).
[79] Sisal (1945), Wheat (1952), Pyrethrum (1956), Pigs (1945), Coffee (1946), Tea (1950), Meat (beef, mutton, poultry) (1950), Cotton Lint and Seed (1954), Cereals (wheat, oats, barley, sunflower) (1956), Canning Crops (pineapples) (1957), Dairy Produce (1958), Maize (1959). This excludes produce, the marketing of which was controlled under the Marketing of African Produce Ordinance, Cap. 320 for which see pp. 111–13.

legislative and administrative adjustments. The East Africa Royal Commission queried the whole policy of controlled marketing, preferring a freer system,[80] but control was too well entrenched to be abandoned. A Kenya commission, established in 1959 to investigate whether all the statutory boards were performing their duties in the most efficient possible manner, reached the complacent conclusions that whatever outsiders might think, the system suited Kenya's needs and worked well; there was no need for major alterations.[81]

Two marketing systems, created during this period, and dealing with crops of constant public concern—maize and coffee—may be examined. From 1942 onwards maize marketing was under the control of the Maize Controller, with the growers paid a price fixed in advance of the planting season, under the system of the guaranteed minimum return. Not until 1959 was there any major organizational change, but during the period there were several attacks on the principle of the control of maize marketing, and in 1951 a commission was appointed to consider the marketing of this and similar commodities.[82] It defended maize marketing control on two grounds: that it was the government's duty to ensure stability of the price and quantity of Kenya's food supplies; and that price equalization was necessary in respect of the export market which, whether export prices were high or low, contributed to Kenya's balance of payments, both of which objectives could only be achieved by price fixing in advance of planting and controlled marketing of the crop. It recommended the transfer of the administration of marketing from the Maize Controller to a Board in order to de-politicize it, while accepting that the Board should be responsible to the Minister, since ultimate responsibility for control, so long as prices were guaranteed, must rest with the government.

A Maize Marketing Board was duly established by the Maize Marketing Ordinance 1959.[83] The Board was composed of representatives of Government, the Scheduled and Non-scheduled Areas, commerce and finance. Its functions were to regulate and control the collection, storage, marketing and distribution of maize and its products, to meet the requirements of both producers and consumers by its marketing activities including, where necessary, importing and exporting maize, and to advise the Minister on various aspects of the industry. It was subject to the general or special directions

[80] *Report*, op. cit., pp. 64–76.

[81] *Report of the Committee on the Organization of Agriculture* (The MacGillivray Committee), Nairobi, 1959, para. 329.

[82] Committee on the Marketing of Maize and other Produce (Ibbotson Committee), *Report*, Nairobi, 1952. See, too, the *Report of an Inquiry into the 1951 Maize and Wheat prices* (Troup Report), Nairobi, 1952, and the Sessional Paper No. 6 of 1957-8, Nairobi, which after deploying the arguments for and against control, announced the government's acceptance of a system of control on the lines recommended by the Ibbotson Committee.

[83] No. 6.

of the Minister. With minor exceptions, all maize vested in the Board as soon as it was harvested. Buying and other agents were appointed by the Board, and unless otherwise directed by the Minister, were able to exercise all the powers of the Board, including the appointment of sub-agents. The Board appointed the KFA, and the two general marketing boards established under Marketing of African Produce Ordinance, as its buying agents. In addition, all millers had to be registered with the Board.

The Minister, after consultation with the Board, was to fix the price to be paid for maize. There could be different prices for different grades. He could limit the quantity of maize which the Board was to purchase at the fixed price, apply different limits to different areas of Kenya, and authorize a body representing producers to apply different limits to different producers. Where such a system was in operation, the Board might fix, and later increase, a secondary price for maize delivered after the limit for the area or the producer has been reached. The Board was authorized to administer the guaranteed minimum return. It also managed the import and export of maize although it was the Minister who authorized imports.

Provision was made for appeal from several of the decisions and actions of the Board. For instance, any person aggrieved by a limitation placed upon the amount of maize which he might sell at the primary price, or at any deductions made from the price payable to him on account of advances under the guaranteed minimum return, or at a rejection of maize, might make representations to the Board, and if these were rejected, might appeal to the Agricultural Appeals Tribunal. However, a person aggrieved by a decision of the Board concerning the import or export of maize, or refusing the registration of a miller, was required to appeal to the Minister whose decision was final and conclusive and not questionable in any court. Finally, the whole system was bolstered by a wide range of enforcement powers, and the creation of a considerable number of offences, breaches of which were triable in the ordinary courts.[84]

Coffee growers and dealers had had to be licensed since 1918, but the system had been reorganized and expanded in 1944,[85] when a Coffee Licensing Advisory Committee was established which had to be consulted before coffee dealers' licences were issued. In addition the Coffee Board provided certain extension services to the planters. Marketing of coffee, however, remained unregulated until 1942, when wartime controls were introduced.[86] A controller was empowered to allocate bulk sales, ship-

[84] The creation of a battery of offences has not prevented considerable evasion of the law. See the memorandum of the Kenya Police to the Maize Commission of Inquiry (Nairobi, 1966), *Report*, appendix E, p. 184.
[85] Coffee Industry (Amendment) Ordinance No. 15.
[86] Defence (Control of Marketing and Export of Hard Coffee) Regulations, Gazette Notice 943/1942.

ping and storage space amongst, and to prescribe the terms on which coffee might be exported by, 'The Group', that is, among those coffee exporters who had exported a defined amount of coffee in the preceding three years. Only members of 'The Group' could take part in coffee auctions.

Marketing control was put on a permanent peacetime basis by the Coffee (Marketing) Ordinance 1946.[87] A Coffee Marketing Board was established, consisting of two persons appointed by the Governor, one by the Coffee Board, and six elected by the planters. To assist it in its work, an Advisory Panel of dealers, commission agents and millers was also established. Planters were prohibited, except under permit, from exporting coffee or selling it to any person other than the Board, and no person other than the Board was permitted to buy coffee from a planter. The Board was required to purchase all coffee offered to it. Sale of the coffee was in the first instance to be by auction but the Board could fix a reserve price and bid for the coffee itself. Auction sales were not, however, to be held in respect of coffee sold by the Board to the Ministry of Food in the United Kingdom under bulk-buying agreements, or coffee bought by the Board at an auction. A coffee pool consisting of the moneys derived from the sale of coffee by the Board was established, and planters were paid from this pool at a rate determined by the Board.

The system of marketing and licensing thus provided for, operated with few changes until 1960. The MacGillivray Committee considered that both Boards were functioning effectively and were well co-ordinated[88]—there were in practice several joint committees between them. The Coffee Ordinance 1960[89] was therefore to some extent a consolidation statute, but there were some changes in the direction of tighter control which may be mentioned.

Provision was made for a member of each Board to sit on the other Board. The function of licensing coffee dealers and others was transferred from the Director of Agriculture to the Coffee Marketing Board, and pulping station licences were introduced, issuable by the Coffee Board after consultation with the Director. The Marketing Board was empowered to require planters to cure their coffee and send it samples. Two levies were introduced; an export levy payable by the exporter to the Coffee Board before any coffee might be exported; and a planters' levy, operative for three years and deductible from moneys due to the planter from the Marketing Board. The levies formed a fund for research, publicity and general welfare of the industry.

This period had seen major changes in the administration of the European sector of the agrarian economy, and their root cause was the introduction

[87] No. 6.
[88] op. cit., para. 122.
[89] No. 26.

of the system of the guaranteed minimum return. We have seen that the system necessitated the close control of what farmers could grow, but there was an equally close connection between it and control of land use, transactions, and marketing. In the twenties and thirties, the European farmers had in some respects been no better in conserving their land than had the Africans, though under-utilization of land in the former, and overcrowding in the latter case had served to mask the similarities. But the increased production demanded in wartime followed by settlement schemes after the war both revealed the extent of erosion and farmed-out land, and increased the need to do something about it. The state could hardly be expected to support the farmers to the extent that a system of a guaranteed minimum return entailed, if they continued free to misuse their land.

It was the same with land transactions. If the government was going to give financial support to the farmers, and if the effect of this support was to increase the value of the land, as it did, then the government had a legitimate interest in who was to own interests in the land, how much they were to own, and under what circumstances and when, might they enter into transactions in respect of it. Finally the system was only properly workable if the price and sale of produce was controlled, as this contributed to the stability of prices and the collection of loans and cesses.

These points are important in showing that the controls introduced during the war, and reorganized in 1955, were not only integrated round a common theme, but that their introduction represented something of a revolution in agrarian administration in Kenya, albeit one primarily worked out for, and applied to European agriculture only. The extent of the revolution may be gauged by comparing the legislation and administration of the early forties and thereafter with that of the thirties, when the government had to rescue European farming from almost total collapse. At the risk of a slight over-simplification, the difference may be summed up as public credit with minimum public control in the thirties, as opposed to public credit with maximum public control in the forties and thereafter.

(b) *African Land Tenure and Agriculture*

The period under review saw great changes also in African land tenure and agriculture. Official policy had hitherto appeared to oscillate between taking African land for European settlement and keeping the reserves small and insecure so as to provide a constant flow of labour to European farms, and guaranteeing the security of fair-sized reserves, and reducing the migrant farm labourer population. The one constant theme from early in the century had been the desirability of separating the European on the land from the African on the land, and hence the requirement that a completely separate agrarian administration be applied to each. Much of this was to change in this period.

The war acted as the great catalyst of change. It forced the administration to see the reserves as essential productive units and adopt laws and policies accordingly; once this initial change had been made, the many defects of the reserves could be clearly seen as also could the necessity to take remedial action. The main thrust of the action taken was to attempt to 'Europeanize' the African agrarian economy by increasing the growing of cash crops, providing a controlled marketing system, taking action against bad land use, and finally, by beginning a tenurial revolution through the consolidation and registration of land-holding under a modern statutory system of law. The dual system still existed at the end of this period, but it was crumbling at the edges, and its economic no less than its political rationale was becoming indefensible.

The sporadic attempts to tackle bad land use in the reserves begun in the thirties were almost submerged in the war, when the main efforts of the administration were directed to getting the reserves to produce as much food as possible, irrespective of the long-term consequences. A changed and more urgent approach was heralded in 1945, however, by the Sessional Paper on Land Utilization and Development[90] which stated that vigorous steps would have to be taken to improve African agricultural potential, and that this would inevitably entail bringing about changes in traditional patterns of land tenure and tackling soil erosion which had grown worse with the neglect of the war years. The paper also hinted at the use of direct pressure to get the necessary work done.[91] The Ten Year Development Plan 1946–55 made provision for increased expenditure on agricultural extension work in the African lands, and the African Land Utilization and Settlement Board (ALUS) which became in 1953 the African Land Development Board (ALDEV) was established on a non-statutory basis in 1947 to assist in this and other work in the African lands.[92] It was financed by government grants and an Agricultural Betterment Fund obtained from Local Native Council cesses on African grown maize.

Two characteristics of the role of the law in this first phase of tackling bad land use may be mentioned and illustrated. First, as the E.A.R.C. pointed out[93] it was still based on the tenets of the Kenya Land Commission that African development must be seen in terms of developing specific reserves and areas contiguous to them but not as developing African lands as a national

[90] Sessional Paper No. 8 of 1945–6.
[91] ibid., para. 7.
[92] Gazette Notice 434/1947. Kenyatta was one of the six African members of the seventeen-man board. This board replaced an African Settlement Board, established on an *interim* basis in December 1945.
[93] *Report*, op. cit., pp. 53-6, 366–7.

resource. Perhaps a more important characteristic was that it was used in an essentially coercive role, as opposed to its use in European agrarian administration to create the framework and conditions for co-operation between producers and administrative officials, with coercion very much as a last resort. This inevitably meant that administrative officials themselves saw coercion as a superficially easy and justifiable method of 'getting the people to do what we know is good for them and the land'.[94]

The first characteristic may be seen in the continued resort to land usage by-laws in the reserves rather than taking action on a national scale under national land usage legislation. The second may best be seen in the rules made by central government to control new settlements and major land conservation projects. Thus the Native Settlement Areas (Olenguruone) Rules required the settlers to obey 'all such reasonable orders as may from time to time be issued by the settlement officer for the welfare and good discipline of the inhabitants of the area';[95] their methods and limits of cultivation, extent of depasturing any stock, amount of hospitality and devolution of the plot were all subject to the orders of the settlement officer. Stock could be confiscated for breach of the orders, and conviction and imprisonment for an offence involving moral turpitude could lead to loss of the occupation permit needed to be allowed to live in the settlement. There was no right of appeal against the settlement officer's orders, and his powers were in effect enhanced by his appointment as a magistrate to try offences against the rules. With this framework as a guide it was not perhaps entirely surprising that coercion was increasingly used at this settlement, or that it proved a disastrous failure.[96]

A similar pattern of administration was provided for in the Native Lands (Kimulot Land Utilization) Rules.[97] All occupiers were to be registered with the District Commissioner and only licensed occupiers so registered could use the land. The District Commissioner might require fencing and hedging to be undertaken to his satisfaction, and order stock to be grazed in certain places only. The occupiers were required to develop and maintain the land according to the principles of good husbandry to the satisfaction of an agricultural officer. Failure to comply with these rules, and many other orders, could result in the occupier's licence being cancelled and his name being expunged from the register. Forcible eviction could follow. Appeal lay from orders and decisions of the District Commissioner to the Provincial Commissioner. A rare departure from this pattern was contained in the Native Lands Trust (Reconditioning of Makuene Area) Rules[98]

[94] Agricultural Department, *Annual Report 1954*, Nairobi, p. 2.
[95] Gazette Notices 875/1942 and 699/1945.
[96] Rosberg and Nottingham, op. cit., pp. 249–58.
[97] Government Notice 114/1952.
[98] Government Notices 41 and 407 of 1948.

which required the District Commissioner to appoint an African Advisory Committee to advise him on the exercise of his powers and duties under the rules.

In addition to these powers, administrators made use of the extreme power of forced labour to carry out land preservation measures. Several orders were made under the Compulsory Labour (Regulation) Ordinance[99] during this period compelling, for example, the construction and maintenance of roads, the provision of watering places and the digging of furrows, and the labour of detainees was also used during the Emergency for this purpose.

The attitude of administrative and agricultural officers to their role under the law and the use to which they could put the law is equally revealing. Such officers frequently acknowledged the benefits of the Emergency in enabling them to compel Africans to take conservation measures such as terracing, and to use the courts as part of a drive to ensure that conservation rules were obeyed.[100] While accepting that administrators did good work during this period, the contrast between agricultural law and administration for Europeans and for Africans was striking and deliberate, and betrayed an attitude towards Africans and their land which was long-standing, and was a contributory factor to that State of Emergency which administrators deplored, but were at the same time willing to take advantage of.

The Agriculture Ordinance provided further evidence of different methods between European and African agrarian administration, the former based on democratic co-operation, the latter on administrative paternalism. This ordinance was the first to treat the African lands as one whole rather than as individual tribal reserves, and provided the legislative framework for the plan to develop African agriculture which commenced in 1955. The reserves were designated as the Non-scheduled Areas and a pyramid of committees and boards was established for their administration. District Agricultural Committees were formed in every administrative district, composed of four officials, six Africans appointed by the Provincial Commissioner after consultation with a Local Advisory Council and two other persons appointed by the Provincial Commissioner at his discretion. On top of them were Provincial Agricultural Committees composed of four officials, one African member from each District Agricultural Committee selected by that Committee and two other persons appointed by the Provincial Commissioner. At the top of the pyramid was the Land Development Board (Non-scheduled Areas)—ALDEV restyled—consisting of three officials,

[99] No. 42 of 1932. For an example of its application, see Government Notice 259/1950 (Order applying it to Embu) and Compulsory Labour (Embu) Regulations, Government Notice 358/1950.
[100] Agricultural Department, *Annual Report*, especially 1952 and 1954.

a person nominated by the Minister for African Affairs, a member of the Board (Scheduled Areas), two representatives from each Provincial Agricultural Committee of which one was to be an African, and five other persons nominated by the Minister for Agriculture of which at least two were to be Africans.

The District Committee's main functions were to prepare plans for development, conservation and settlement for submission to the Provincial Committee, and generally advise the latter Committee and the District Commissioner, in the exercise of their executive powers. The Provincial Committee was to prepare similar plans and estimates of expenditure for implementation, and draft rules for submission to the Board, to advise the Provincial Commissioner in the exercise of his executive powers, and be responsible for the implementation of any plans approved by the Minister. The Board was purely advisory to the Minister, in the exercise of his powers to approve plans and make rules.

Detailed provision was made for the preservation of land. The Minister, with the concurrence of the Board and after consultation with the Provincial Commissioner concerned, might make land preservation rules similar to those which he might make for the Scheduled Areas. These might empower a District Commissioner to make land preservation orders, which, except for emergencies, could only be made with the consent of the District Agricultural Committee and the Provincial Commissioner. An appeal lay from the making of an order to the Agricultural Appeal Tribunal, but it was a second appeal, the first one lying to the Provincial Commissioner. Agricultural officials might enter and do the work, and recover the costs thereof from the occupiers. There were, however, no provisions for land preservation loans.

Parallel to the increased regulation of basic land usage went increased regulation of what could be grown and how it could be marketed. Control of coffee growing was tightened in 1949,[101] partly in deference to European fears of the spread of disease from African grown coffee, and partly because agricultural officers needed more powers to cope with the post-war increase in coffee growing amongst Africans. While admitting the necessity for strict control, it may be pointed out that here too, there was a contrast between the method of producer-control created by the Coffee Ordinance and administration-control provided by the rules, where the producer had no say. However, as the number of African coffee planters rose to over 100,000 in 1960[102] and it became apparent that the standard of their coffee was in no way inferior to that of the European planter, the latter became

[101] Native Lands Coffee Rules, Government Notice 1217/1950, replacing the African-grown Coffee Rules, Government Notice 1172/1949, as a result of *Mbiu Koinange v. R.* (1951), 24 (2) K.L.R. 130.

[102] *The Economic Development of Kenya, Report of the IBRD* (Baltimore, Johns Hopkins University, 1963), p. 116.

more ready to concede the former a share in his method of control, and during the fifties, Africans were co-opted on to both coffee boards. One of the objects of the consolidating and amending legislation of 1960 was to provide for full African representation at delegate conferences and on the boards; and in rules made under the Ordinance, the same controls on cultivation and processing were applied to all planters irrespective of racial origin. The long haul for the African coffee grower was over.

Although the marketing of African grown coffee was undertaken by the Coffee Marketing Board, there was a wide range of other produce grown by Africans for which a separate control and marketing system was provided. During the war, much African grown produce was subject to marketing control via a Produce Controller, who had the right to buy any 'native produce' bought at a market and offered for re-sale at a controlled price.[103] In the first decade after the war this system was continued, but in 1955, as part of the plan to increase African productivity, the Marketing of African Produce Ordinance[104] was amended to provide for the establishment of Marketing Boards to handle African grown produce, where the Governor was satisfied that the interests of the producers of a particular produce would be promoted by organized marketing. The Boards were to consist of a chairman, appointed by the Minister of Agriculture, and between six and nine other persons, up to half of whom were to be appointed after consultation with the relevant District and Provincial Agricultural Committees and the remainder from nominations put forward by the relevant producers—the first occasion that legislation provided for direct participation by African producers in a system of control of African producers.

A board was empowered to issue a wide range of orders and directions to producers as to their methods of cultivation, storage, and processing, and the movement of the regulated produce, and make rules on these and other matters. With the approval of the Minister, the board might make a compulsory marketing order in respect of produce under its control which required producers to sell their produce to the board or its order, and impose a levy on all regulated produce. In addition a board might act as the agent of other bodies empowered to control produce in Kenya. In case these wide powers were not enough, the Minister was empowered to confer on any board such additional powers and duties as he might consider necessary for furthering the objects of the boards under the Ordinance. As with other marketing legislation, a battery of offences was created to bolster the system.

The powers given these boards indicated that they were to be much more than marketing organizations, under the control of producers. They

[103] Defence (Controlled Produce) Regulations, Government Notice 805/1943.
[104] No. 39.

were to embrace production, processing, and marketing, and be in effect the institutions through which Government was going to work to increase productivity in the African lands. During the following years, there was a rapid creation of boards; six were established, covering twenty-nine different products in the Nyanza, Central and Rift Valley Provinces. The establishment and early operation of the Nyanza Province Marketing Board, the first board to be established, may briefly be described.[105] Twenty-two products were put under its control including maize, for which it became the agent of the Maize Controller, and later the Maize Marketing Board. It issued a compulsory marketing order in respect of fourteen of these products and, with the approval of the Minister, rules to regulate their movement, under which a licence issued by the Board was required before any such produce could be moved. The Board's operations expanded very quickly and in the third year of its existence it was handling crops with a gross turnover of over £2,000,000. Foremost amongst these was maize; an average of nearly 600,000 bags was marketed by the Board in its first four years of operations.

Hitherto, one of the main differences between African and European agriculture had been the lack of credit available to Africans, principally because banks and other institutions were not prepared to lend money to Africans on such security as they could offer. A committee appointed to consider this matter reported in 1950 in favour of a limited system of individual loans based on the personal character of the borrower, while stressing that the main development of African agricultural credit should come from co-operative credit societies. In any event care should be taken to prevent the growth of a problem of rural indebtedness characteristic of other societies where no control was exercised on the provision of credit to peasant farmers.[106]

A scheme for making loans on the personal security of the borrower, financed and administered by ALDEV, was thereupon introduced and, in addition, money for development was also made available to Africans in the shape of rewards. Those Africans whose land development passed certain tests were rewarded with 'bonuses' which consisted of a return of half the local cess paid towards the Agricultural Betterment Fund.

Credit provided through ALDEV was essentially short-term. The E.A.R.C. considered the question of long-term credit and concluded that it should continue to be provided primarily by specialized lending agencies such as land banks, even though this narrowed the scope for long-term agricultural

[105] Order establishing the board, Government Notice 1745/1955. Regulations to empower the board to make rules, L.N.340/1957. Rules made by the board, L.N. 447/1957. Compulsory Marketing Order, L.N. 504/1956. See, too, Agricultural Department, *Annual Reports 1956–9*, Nairobi.

[106] *Report of the Committee on Agricultural Credit for Africans* (Nairobi, 1950).

loans to Africans, partly because of their inability to offer adequate security, and partly because 'the whole conception of long-term borrowing presupposes a maturity of mind, which, as yet, is only in evidence among a small number of East African cultivators'.[107] Co-operatives might gradually be used for long-term credit but at the present stage of East African agriculture, it was not reasonable to expect that long-term improvements should be financed on the basis of advances to African cultivators. This implied that there should be still greater governmental involvement in African agriculture in order to modernize it more effectively.

In the areas of land preservation, crop production and marketing, the African lands and their occupiers were being slowly brought within a modern market economy, with its inevitable corollary that land began to possess a cash value, and be marketable. This conception of land was directly opposed to that which had inspired the Kenya Land Commission, and the legislation to which its recommendations had given rise, the effect of which had been to hinder Africans from fully utilizing their lands. There were two main reasons for this. First, Africans in overcrowded reserves could not move to other land because it belonged to another tribe. The only 'solution' to overcrowding was to reduce the size of individual plots, reduce the time during which land was allowed to lie fallow, and increase the fragmentation of individual holdings so that the good and the bad land was shared out amongst the community. Secondly, an implication of the legislation of the late thirties was that once Africans were secure in their tribal lands, there would be as little interference as possible with the incidents of their customary tenure, such was the suspicion engendered by previous interferences, despite the realization of the conflict inherent in retaining an unreformed customary tenure and using the land for modern economic purposes.

The E.A.R.C. considered that of all the measures that could be taken to improve the productivity of the African lands, those aimed at modernizing tenure should have the highest priority, and be pursued the most vigorously.[108] In making this general recommendation, however, the Commission seemed to have in mind a picture of customary land tenure which was virtually incapable of change on its own. It must be stressed that this picture was somewhat overdrawn for the programme of land tenure reform that was to start in Kenya in the fifties was based to some extent on changes in the direction of individual tenure which had already taken place with no or very little administrative prompting, and on a desire for change amongst certain sections of the African population.[109] The speed at which, and the

[107] *Report*, op. cit., p. 103 para. 25. See whole chapter on credit for Africans for the general discussion of the problem.
[108] *Report*, op. cit., pp. 346-8, paras. 1–5, p. 394, para. 17.
[109] Sorrenson, *Land Reform in the Kikuyu Country* (Nairobi, OUP, 1967), chapters 3

manner in which the reform programme was initially carried out owed a great deal to the powers conferred on administrative officers by the Emergency Regulations, but the important point is that the programme could never have succeeded to the extent it did if there had not been some measure of approval for it from Africans, which was based upon change and a desire for change in the direction which the programme itself took.

The Government of Kenya was aware of the need to bring about reforms in African land tenure and that some unofficial land consolidation, and individualization of tenure, was taking place. The E.A.R.C. in putting forward the economic arguments for the individualization of tenure had provided one spur to action; the other was the Emergency. By authorizing the round up and detention of thousands of Africans, mainly Kikuyu, by requiring those that remained in the Central and Rift Valley Provinces to be grouped together in fortified villages, by restricting movement, by forfeiting the land of those who joined the rebels, and by increasing the use of forced labour, all actions taken in order to meet the challenge of Mau Mau, the administration at the same time gave itself the opportunity of replanning the holdings, and remoulding the tenure system of much of Central Province on a scale which could not have been, indeed was not by the E.A.R.C., envisaged in normal conditions.[110] Legal backing was, however, required both for the actual implementation of the land reform programme, and to provide security for the holdings of consolidated plots, for hitherto consolidation had rested on unenforceable agreements and was subject to ever enforceable claims. After considerable delays this was provided for by the Native Land Tenure Rules,[111] which established a system of adjudication, consolidation and registration, in many ways a small scale forerunner of the present system, and based to some extent on what administrative officers were doing in the field. The rules marked a step forward both in tenure reform, and the government's role therein, and in African agrarian administration. They were the first official government sponsored attempt at providing control and guidance for reform, and they were based on the principle that the users of the land should play a major part in regulating and controlling its reform, a counsel of perfection which was not always adhered to in practice. The whole system, however, still suffered from the defect that the registered private right created by it was almost certainly repugnant to the rights created by the Kenya (Native Areas) Order in Council and the Native

and 4. P. and I. Mayer, 'Land Law in the Making' in *African Law—Adaptations and Development* (Berkeley, University of California Press, 1965), H. and C. Kuper (eds.).

110 Sorrenson, op. cit., chapter 7. Emergency (Movement of Kikuyu) Regulations, Government Notice 192/1953; Emergency (Kikuyu, Embu and Meru Villages) Regulations, L.N. 185/1956.

111 L.N. 452/1956.

Lands Trust Ordinance, and thus the security of title and marketability of land which it was hoped to confer remained in jeopardy.

Two remedies were forthcoming to deal with this problem. An Ordinance suspended all suits in African lands,[112] and a committee was appointed to draw up a new law which was, if necessary, to depart from the principle of the earlier law.[113] The most important of the recommendations of the committee were that the process of adjudication and consolidation should be based on the pre-existing system with its emphasis on the use of local committees, that the legal title to the consolidated plot was to be derived from the fact of registration rather than conferred by act of the government, that a simple code of modern land law should be introduced to provide a framework for transactions in the registered land, and that it would be most necessary to create a system of control of land transactions to prevent rural indebtedness, and limit the growth of a class of landless peasants.

The committee incorporated their recommendations into two draft bills which eventually became the Native Lands Registration Ordinance,[114] and the Land Control (Native Lands) Ordinance.[115] In addition, the Native Lands Trust Ordinance[116] was amended to embrace the new types of rights created by the other legislation. Between them these Ordinances did for land tenure and transactions what agricultural and marketing legislation had previously done for conservation and productivity—they supplied the framework for administrators to bring about great changes. How this was accomplished may briefly be described.

The Registration Ordinance was applied to any area of the African lands whenever it appeared expedient to the Minister that ascertainment, consolidation and registration of rights and titles to land should take place in that area. An adjudication officer, a Committee of not less than twenty-five, and an Arbitration Board of between six and twenty-five persons with knowledge of local rights, were appointed. The officer appointed a day by which all claims to rights in the land must be submitted. The Committee adjudicated on the claims in accordance with customary law, but if it could not reach agreement, the matter was referred to the Board. Claimants were required to attend before the Committee or Board but both bodies could proceed in their absence. A Record of Existing Rights was prepared in accordance with the decisions of the adjudicating bodies. Objections might be made to it and these were considered by the officer in consultation with

[112] African Courts (Suspension of Land Suits) Ordinance No. 1 of 1957.
[113] Working Party on African Land Tenure in Kenya (Report 1958). Branney, 11, *J.A.A.*, 208–24.
[114] No. 27 of 1959.
[115] No. 28 of 1959.
[116] No. 38 of 1959.

the Board. His decision was final, and after all objections had been dealt with, so was the record.

The second stage of the process then began. The Committee first set aside such land as might in its opinion be required for the needs of the community. It then allocated consolidated plots of land to holders of existing rights. It might require a plot holder to relinquish one piece of land and accept another in lieu, and it might award compensation, to be paid by those who had benefited from exchanges to those who had suffered detriment thereby. The allocated plots were then demarcated, and an Adjudication Register consisting of the names and nature of interests of the holders of the allocated plots was compiled. Objections might be made to it and these were considered by the officer with the Committee; the officer might order the register to be rectified, or he might award compensation in lieu. No appeal lay against such a decision but an objector who was dissatisfied with the compensation awarded might apply to a magistrate's court for revision. After all objections were disposed of, the Adjudication Register became final, and any person named therein as an owner of land was then to be registered as the proprietor of the freehold title to that land.

A crucial requirement of the system was that the first registration should be unchallengeable in any other proceedings. That part of the Ordinance providing for this was put to the test in the case of *The District Commissioner, Kiambu* v. *R. ex parte Ethan Njau*.[117] Njau had been allocated a consolidated plot of land and a certificate of allocation had been issued to him. Munge, who had been allocated a consolidated plot half a mile away, complained to the Committee that the allocation was unfair to him. The Committee considered the objection and reversed its decision in respect of these two plots. Njau complained that by virtue of the certificate of allocation he was the owner of the plot of which he had now been deprived. The Committee rejected this complaint, and confirmed the register. Njau then applied to the Supreme Court for an order of mandamus to the appellant to register him, Njau, as the owner of the first plot. The Supreme Court issued the order but the E.A.C.A. reversed the decision, although admitting that the register contained an erroneous entry, because to issue the order 'would offend against the letter and policy of the Native Lands Registration Ordinance'.[118]

To administer the system of control of transactions in registered land, two classes of boards were established, Divisional and Provincial Native Land Control Boards, consisting of the District Officer and Provincial Commissioner respectively as chairmen with membership divided between officials and nominated and elected unofficials. No person might dispose of or deal with any interest in any land in a division without the consent of a

[117] [1960] E.A. 109. Sorrenson, op. cit., chapter 12, especially pp. 203–6.
[118] [1960] E.A. 109, at p. 129.

Divisional Board, or by virtue of a general consent of a Provincial Board. Every person applying for a consent from a Divisional Board was required to attend before it, and in addition the Board might inspect the land. Its consents were not to infringe the prohibition against the vesting of an interest in land in more than five persons—a prohibition designed to prevent the recurrence of fragmentation and uneconomically sized plots. Dealings to which consent was refused were null and void.

Appeals lay from a Divisional Board to a Provincial Board, the decisions of which were final and conclusive, except that any person refused consent to an inter-tribal or inter-racial transaction might appeal to the Governor whose decision was also final and conclusive. Provincial Boards had general supervisory and directory powers over Divisional Boards, and were in turn subject to directions from the Governor, given after consultation with the Trust Board.

Though last in time of all the legislation designed to tackle the outstanding problems of the African lands, these Ordinances were first in importance. Without the tenure transformation set in motion by them, it is doubtful whether continuing and meaningful progress could have been made in ending the dual agrarian system in all its manifestations; as it was, they provided a most important springboard for vigorous and conscious steps in that direction after 1960. They provided the legislative framework for the implementation of the most important part of the colonial authorities' deliberate policy of creating a stable and, it was hoped, conservative African middle class that would provide a bulwark against nationalism and the radical policies that were thought to go with it.[119] Finally, they represented a substantial change in administrative practices in relation to African agrarian problems, and the close association of the administered with the whole system of administration helped in making the programme acceptable.

The period under review had seen greater and more far-reaching African agrarian changes than in the two preceding periods put together. Whereas policy then had been directed towards putting Africans into reserves, securing them against too much encroachment, and discouraging them from growing cash crops, an essentially negative and repressive policy, in the period under review policy was increasingly directed towards allowing, at times requiring, Africans to use their land properly and productively, culminating in a decision to transform their tenurial system so that they could begin to deal with it as an economic asset. The policy represents a distinct change; its implementation too often continued the paternalistic and coercive approach which characterized previous policies, but even that was changing by the end of the period as Africans were gaining more political power in central and local government, and could make their objections to that type of

[119] Sorrenson, op. cit., chapters 13 and 14.

administration felt.[120] The gap between the European and African agrarian systems had become less wide, and the machinery for reducing it still further was in existence. Perhaps most important, however, was that by the end of this period, the key to future stability and development in Kenya was seen to lie in solving African agrarian problems, and this coloured all future policy and legislative developments in agrarian administration.

(c) *Resident Labourers and Squatters: The Tightening of the Screw*

The Resident Labourers Ordinance had as its main objects a reduction in the number of labourers on European farms, a reduction in the acreage and stock which those labourers could use for their own purposes, and a reassertion of the employment relationship of the contract at the expense of the tenancy relationship. But the onset of war delayed, and in the long run made impossible, their full attainment. The resident labourers were included within the productivity drive, not only in relation to their work as labourers but in relation to their farming activities. Their total production of maize, for instance, was regarded as significant enough for special provisions as to its purchase and sale to be provided by the wartime maize marketing control and maize inspection legislation, and continued by the Maize Marketing Ordinance.

District Councils, however, quickly began to exercise their powers under the Ordinance but initially permitted a fair amount of stock to be kept by resident labourers, and fixed the number of work days they were required to do at 240 per annum. But starting in 1944, there was a drive to increase work days to 270 per annum, and cut down both stock and acreage of the labourers, and generally reduce the number of labourers permitted on a farm. Thus the Trans-Nzoia District Council in 1943 prohibited goats and pigs (this was a common provision) but permitted ten head of cattle and five of sheep per labourer. In 1945, cattle were reduced to five head, and in 1947 a draconian set of rules required the number of labourers employed on farms to be reduced by a third by the end of 1948, and the number of cattle by two-thirds by the end of 1949, and eliminated by the end of 1950. These provisions were, however, impractical as well as harsh, and amendments to the rules in 1948 envisaged a five year run-down of cattle; further amendments in 1955 were bravely envisaging a final elimination in 1959.[121]

The vicissitudes of the Trans-Nzoia District Council amply sum up the whole problem of the resident labourers in these years. Even the 'liberal' provisions of the very early forties represented a drastic reduction on what had

[120] e.g. The debate in the Legislative Council on the application of the consolidation programme. Legislative Council, *Debates*, volume LXXVI (part I) (29 May 1958), col. 1129 et seq. Discussed in Sorrenson, op. cit., pp. 244–8.

[121] See the series of Orders made by the Council; Government Notices 700/1943, 1018/1945, 1027/1947, 92/1948, 853/1955.

previously been permitted or tolerated by occupiers. There was no place where the surplus stock could go, so it tended to remain illegally on the farm. This problem was met by an amendment to the Ordinance in 1949 which permitted surplus stock to be confiscated, and sold, the proceeds being paid to the owner. The same amendment made it an offence to cultivate more than was permitted by one's contract.

The labourers themselves were not so easily disposed of, but the Emergency provided opportunities for remedial action here as it had done in other areas of African agrarian administration. Regulations were promulgated in 1953 under which members of the Kikuyu, Meru and Embu tribes could be removed from their normal place of residence and sent back to the reserves.[122] During the next three years, thousands of resident labourers and their families who were members of these tribes (and the majority were so) were repatriated to the reserves, irrespective of overcrowding, or whether they had any rights to land therein, and few of them did.

By these means the European farmers, with the support of the government, went some way towards solving the squatter problem. The effect of the legislation was summed up by the E.A.R.C. as follows:

> . . . the long-term interests of the farmer, in so far as they were endangered by the uncontrolled activities of resident labourers have been safeguarded by legislation whereas no legislative measures have been taken to protect the resident labourer from a lowering of his real income. This was a serious omission and it has been the cause of much discontent which was avoidable.[123]

The Commission considered that the resident labourer's place in the Highlands should be accepted for what it was—permanent and basically a tenancy—and in doing so deliberately rejected the approach of the Kenya Land Commission. It recommended the separation of the place of work from the place of cultivation, with the creation of rural labourers' villages with proper amenities, with adequate land surrounding them for cultivation purposes of which the labourers could obtain leases. The Highlands, in other words, should be required to make their contribution towards the solution of the problem of overcrowding in the reserves, and the resident labourer should be enabled to 'earn the maximum income which the product of his labour warrants in conditions of security and stability . . .'[124]

Such a set of recommendations was too strong a beer for the government and the settlers, and nothing was done to implement them. The District Councils continued trying to limit the labourers and their stock, but with no greater success than before. Amidst all the ferment of reform in the African lands from 1955 onwards, this failure to do anything towards relieving the

[122] Emergency (Movement of Kikuyu) Regulations, Government Notice 192/1953.
[123] *Report*, op. cit., p. 167, para. 62.
[124] p. 168, para. 65. On the whole question see pp. 162–70.

conditions of the resident labourer can only be regarded as an abdication of responsibilities on the part of the government, and a continuing reminder that rights to land in the Highlands were reserved for Europeans, and there was to be no departure from that ark of the covenant.

Some attempts had, however, been made to resettle redundant and surplus resident labourers in accordance with the recommendations of the Kenya Land Commission and one such attempt may be mentioned. In 1942 34,000 acres were carved out of the Masai Native Land Unit designated the Olenguruone Native Settlement Area,[125] and a settlement of resident labourers amongst others started. Persons might apply to the Chief Native Commissioner for an occupation permit, which could only be issued where the applicant was a resident labourer at the beginning of the Ordinance who had been outside his native land unit for the preceding seven years, and could produce a certificate from a Provincial Commissioner to the effect that he had not and could not obtain any land in that unit. Settlers were subject to the strict regime of land use and settlement rules already described.

The other important class of squatters in the Highlands may be dealt with here. These were the rightless occupiers, those persons deprived of all rights in their traditional lands by the Native Lands Trust Ordinance in accordance with the recommendations of the Kenya Land Commission. For these persons, too, the government was required to provide land, and could not move them until it had done so, a difficult undertaking since the numbers involved were much greater than those given in the estimates of the Kenya Land Commission.[126] However, in 1942 the government announced the setting aside of the Lari and Kerita Uplands in the Kikuyu Forest Reserve for the settlement of these persons, saying that they had all agreed to move, and the movement was under way.[127] The Lari settlement was not a great success; there were already people on the land, some of whom were moved, and this caused bad blood between the two groups of occupiers. As has recently been shown, this long resentment was an important contributory factor in the Lari 'massacre' of 1953.[128]

The problems of the squatters were not therefore resolved during this period, despite attempts to do so. The failure of the attempts is a good illustration of the limitations of the law in dealing with intractable social problems. What the legislation tried to do was to sweep the problem under the carpet, to legislate it out of existence. However, the problem concerned

[125] Crown Lands (Amendment) Ordinance No. 19 of 1942.
[126] The K.L.C. estimated the numbers of Kikuyu involved to be 'two or three hundred inclusive of women and children' (para. 1855). In fact about 4000 Kikuyu had to be moved to give effect to the recommendations, E.A.R.C., op. cit., p. 55, para. 5.
[127] Legislative Council, *Debates*, volume VIII (4 January 1940), cols. 539–541.
[128] Rosberg and Nottingham, op. cit., pp. 286–92.

people, where they were to live and how they were to earn their living, so naturally it remained in existence despite the legislation. There was no proper investigation of the extent of the problem, or the possible alternative solutions before legislation was enacted. Its basic principle was the sanctity of European rights in the Highlands, and the importance of agrarian segregation, and this inevitably limited the possible solutions that could be adopted. Finally, the problem was seen as a European economic one not as an African social one, and this too precluded adequate solutions.

CONCLUSION

For the greater part of the colonial period, agrarian policy was concerned to create and maintain two separate and unequal systems of administration, the African system existing to serve in a subordinate capacity the European one. The dominant economic role of the settlers which this policy was designed to produce was complemented by their dominant political role in the Government of Kenya. Together they dictated not only the substance but the form of the law of agrarian administration, for the settlers were in a position to ensure that they played a major part in administering the law applying to them and that the administration of the law applying to Africans should reflect their assumptions about the place of Africans in Kenya. Only when Africans began to win for themselves a place in the political institutions of government, hitherto dominated by settlers, did both substance and form of law begin to change, substance with the slow movement away from the dual system, form with the uneven progress from a coercive to a co-operative type of administration over Africans. From our perspective, the change in form is as significant as the change in substance, for it was in part a response to African pressure from below channelled up via their political representatives in the Legislative Council to the government, and in part a recognition by that government that once policy on African agriculture and land emphasized its development for its own sake rather than its use as an adjunct of European development, little could be achieved without the co-operation of Africans themselves. We would conclude therefore that there was a correlation between the form of the law, and the method of its administration, and both the wielders of political power and the policies that they adopted which were in turn reflected in the substance of the law. As with the legal origins of the acquisition of Kenya, so here; the law and its administration had no inherent values, but derived both values and form from the predilections of the dominant political and economic groups in society.

CHAPTER IV

The Development of the Administration of Justice

INTRODUCTION

The General Acts of the Berlin and Brussels Conference had imposed an obligation on the signatory powers to establish systems of justice in their African possessions and had stressed the importance of judicial institutions as a civilizing influence. Towards the end of the colonial era, the proud boast was frequently heard that of all the imperial legacies Britain had conferred upon her African possessions, the Rule of Law and British conceptions of justice were the finest and the most important. Thus the object at the beginning and the claim at the end tallied—the creation of a legal system for the administration of justice was to be, and had succeeded in being, one of the foremost civilizing and enlightening institutions which the colonial power had brought to Africa.

How far is this the case in Kenya? What sort of legal system was created by the colonial power and what were its main characteristics? What aspects of the development of the administration of justice seem to have been constant in the past and are therefore most likely to influence developments in the future? These are the questions with which this chapter will attempt to deal. But first, it is necessary to spell out the basic problem facing the colonial authorities in this matter, and the main themes which are apparent in the attempted solutions to this problem. For it is through these themes that we will examine the development of the administration of justice in Kenya in the colonial era. The basic problem was quite simply to develop a legal system embracing the whole country. The problem was aggravated, however, by the presence of different races in Kenya and the existence of conflicting ideas amongst them of the desiderata of a desirable legal system, and the existence of conflicting policies which had to be applied. Thus, colonial policy stressed at one and the same time the civilizing and pacifying influence to be derived from the introduction of systems of justice, and the desirability of maintaining and working through traditional institutions as far as possible. The Muslim population at the coast wanted their legal system preserved, while the incoming British settlers were quickly insistent that they were entitled as of right to the English legal system which they had brought with them from England as part of their heritage of the common law.

The effect of these conflicting pressures on the colonial authorities may be seen through three major themes which between them dominated developments for most of the colonial period. The themes were the confrontation between the indigenous tribal and the incoming colonial systems of justice, the clash between the administrative and the judicial approach to the administration of justice and the function of the courts, particularly in the field of criminal law, and the segregation of the legal systems so that different systems applied to different races. Inevitably in the practical operation of, and disputes over, the system of courts established by the colonial authorities these themes overlap and become blurred, but they are separate and will be treated as such here.

An important limitation on this approach must first be mentioned. To discuss the development of the administration of justice in terms of themes must not be taken as suggesting that there was a continuous or consistent development in any one particular direction or that these themes can be clearly and continuously seen throughout this period. Rather, the pattern is of three underlying themes which manifested themselves in various ways, with first one, and then another, appearing to preoccupy the administration and the judiciary. At most we could say that the early years of the protectorate saw a greater preoccupation with the problem of reconciling colonial and indigenous systems of justice; the clash of judicial and administrative views assumed greater importance in the twenties and thirties; and the problems of the segregated systems were a preoccupation of the fifties.

BRITISH CONSULAR JURISDICTION 1822–1890

As we have seen in Chapter I, the East Africa Protectorate developed out of agreements made with, and control exerted over the dominions of, the Sultan of Zanzibar. The system of courts which began to be developed in the protectorate after 1895 grew out of these same agreements, and so have a long ancestry. A brief outline of this pre-protectorate system of courts may be given as a prelude to the colonial period. There were in effect two strands to this jurisdiction—admiralty, and ordinary civil and criminal, though they often appeared in the same treaty or Order in Council. Admiralty jurisdiction was a product of British efforts to end the slave trade; civil and criminal jurisdiction was to a large extent a product of the efforts of British subjects to expand 'legitimate' trade and commerce in East Africa.

The development of admiralty jurisdiction came first, and it is significant that the early treaties—and the earliest was in 1822 with the Sultan of Muscat[1]—were concluded on the British side by naval officers carrying out the general policy of the British Government to suppress the slave trade wherever it continued. These early treaties were more concerned with

[1] Hertslet, *Commercial Treaties* (London, Butterworth, 1885), volume III, p. 265.

sanctioning the policing activities of the British Navy and the East India Company than establishing a system of admiralty jurisdiction at Zanzibar or elsewhere, though outline provision was made for this latter activity. However, it required legislation in addition to treaties before a consular court could exercise the jurisdiction granted to it by treaty, and legislation was not forthcoming until 1848.[2] From then on, however, a succession of statutes dealing with the East African slave trade and admiralty jurisdiction over it was passed, culminating in the Colonial Courts of Admiralty Act 1890. The 1848 statute is noteworthy for its introduction of Indian courts to the East African scene. It empowered Admiralty courts in the United Kingdom and courts of the Vice-Admiral in British dominions and the territories of the East India Company to exercise jurisdiction over vessels subject to the treaties made with the Sultan of Muscat in 1839 and 1845.[3]

Civil and criminal jurisdiction of the consular court at Zanzibar may be traced to the Convention of Commerce of 1839. This contained provisions dealing with 'mixed' cases between British subjects and subjects of the Sultan or other Muslim powers, and cases between British subjects exclusively, or between them and subjects of other Christian powers. At this stage the ex-territorial privileges conferred upon British subjects, and administered by the consul, were similar to those obtaining during the same period in the Ottoman Empire, and for the same reasons; inhabitants of Christian nations could not be expected to submit themselves to Muslim law. There was no law regulating the exercise of this jurisdiction until the Zanzibar Order in Council 1866[4] but that it was exercised is not to be doubted.[5] That Order in Council conferred civil and criminal jurisdiction over British subjects and British protected persons on the consular court. In respect of civil jurisdiction appeals lay to the High Court at Bombay which had in addition concurrent original civil jurisdiction. In respect of criminal jurisdiction no other provision was made but that no act was to be regarded as criminal in Zanzibar which was not criminal in a British possession. In face of such vague provisions, the consul reasonably enough promulgated rules the following year which stated that the Indian Penal Code was to be the criminal law for those subject to his jurisdiction. Unfortunately, he had no power to make such rules, but his exercise of criminal jurisdiction based on the Code was not retroactively validated until 1882.[6]

[2] Slave Trade (Muscat) Act 1848. See, too, Slave Trade Jurisdiction (Zanzibar) Act 1869, Slave Trade (East African Courts) Act 1873, Slave Trade Act 1877, Slave Trade (East African Courts) Act 1879.

[3] Convention of Commerce 1839; Hertslet, op. cit., volume V, p.611. Agreement of 1845, section 1; Slave Trade (Muscat) Act 1848.

[4] Hertslet, op. cit., volume XII, p. 973.

[5] *Wagji Korji* v *Tharia Topan* (1878), 3 I.L.R. (Bomb.) 58 (Civil appeal from the consul of Zanzibar to the High Court at Bombay).

[6] Zanzibar Order in Council 1882, Hertslet, op. cit., volume XV, p. 495.

Increasing trade from India, and increasing international interests in Zanzibar and the East African coast in the 1880s, brought increased work to the consular court, and a greater need to clarify and expand the consul's powers. This was achieved by the Zanzibar Order in Council 1884,[7] which, with amendments, was, as we have seen, one of the initial legal bases for the exercise of jurisdiction in the East Africa Protectorate. Zanzibar was deemed a District of Bombay, and appeal lay to the High Court of Bombay. The jurisdiction of the court was to be exercised in accordance with Indian and Bombay legislation, particularly the Indian Penal, Criminal and Civil Procedure Codes, the Indian Evidence and Succession Acts, and the Bombay Civil Courts Act. English law was to be applied as the residual law. The importance of these provisions is that they provide the background and understanding to the reliance on Indian administrative and legislative precedents in the East Africa Protectorate. By the time the administration of justice in the protectorate came to be considered, there was nearly fifty years of admiralty, and thirty years of civil and criminal jurisdiction based on Indian law, and sometimes exercised by Indian courts in relation to East Africa. It was this system which the Foreign Office and the first Commissioner for the protectorate, who was also Consul-General for Zanzibar, were familiar with. It was already applied in the Sultan's dominions at the coast, and its extension to the interior was no more than was to be expected.

THE ADMINISTRATION OF JUSTICE UNDER THE IBEAC 1887–1895

The development of consular jurisdiction helps to explain initial Indian influence on the development of the legal system in Kenya. Equally important was the attempt by the IBEAC to provide for the administration of justice for it helped influence early African attitudes to colonial justice, and differentiated between the coast and the interior—a small but important characteristic of the Kenya legal system from that time onwards. At the coast, the Company permitted the Muslim courts to continue, and the Kadhis to be nominated by the Sultan, though a Company judicial official also exercised Muslim jurisdiction. A consular court was established by the Company at Mombasa in 1890 exercising jurisdiction in accordance with the Zanzibar Order in Council 1884. The court was part of the Zanzibar 'District' of Bombay and appeal lay to the High Court at Bombay.[8]

In the interior, the Company's agents were left a good deal of latitude as to what sort of judicial powers they exercised. In theory, they were governed by the Africa Order in Council 1889 (before the promulgation of that Order, they were not governed, even in theory, by any law) and any treaties they concluded with chiefs. In practice, it is very doubtful

[7] S.R.O. (revised) volume III, 1890, edition 865.
[8] Mungeam, op. cit., p. 55. Hamilton, 'Introduction to 1897-1905', 1 *E.A.L.R.*, IV.

whether they had ever heard of the former or paid any attention to the latter source of power, or held anything which resembled a court in either an English or African sense of that term, as Portal's scathing report of 1893 on Company administration in the interior indicated.[9] At best, a certain rough and ready discipline was dispensed within a small radius of the Company station, and traditional methods of settling disputes were left alone.

INDIGENOUS AND COLONIAL SYSTEMS OF JUSTICE: THE PERIOD OF EXPERIMENTATION 1895–1913

The protectorate administration inherited the unsatisfactory position from the Company of a confused system at the coast, and a complete absence of system in the interior. The Commissioner's declaration on taking over the administration in June 1895 made it clear that the system of Muslim courts and law would continue to be preserved at the coast, and this was done through successive legislative and administrative changes. The position in the interior, however, called for something more than a declaration of intent. But before considering the administration's actions, it is necessary to enter a caveat in respect of this whole period. We have called it the period of experimentation; it could equally well be called the period of pacification, for throughout this period military or quasi-military expeditions were constantly having to be used to extend the writ of the administration. In these conditions, it was difficult to evolve a system for the administration of justice, let alone the beginnings of a philosophy or coherent policy about the system, although in later years administrators were to trace their policies back to this period. A series of experiments were tried, some of which were the foundations of later developments, and some of which were discarded almost immediately. Again the systems created by the laws of the protectorate gave the appearance of universality; the fact of military pacification will serve to remind that this was not the case, and it was many years before the systems established by the laws approximated to the systems actually on the ground throughout the protectorate.

The Commissioner followed up his coastal declaration, embodied in the Agreement of December 1895, with a general circular to the administrative officers in the interior (the Company agents who were kept on at their posts in lieu of anybody else to take over) stating that they should exercise their judicial powers in accordance with the Indian Penal Code, pending more formal arrangements.[10] Besides being somewhat impractical, since few, if any, of the officers had copies of, or were acquainted with the Code, this circular was almost certainly *ultra vires* the Commissioner since the interior

[9] Oliver and Mathew, *History of East Africa*, volume I, pp. 416–17.
[10] Mungeam, op. cit., pp. 55–9. See, too, the order issued 1/2/1900 E.A.P.G., volume II, p. 35.

was governed by the Africa Order in Council 1889 which required consuls and other judicial officers to apply the substance of the law of England. Nothing daunted, the Commissioner despatched copies of the Indian Penal Code to the one officer who had written to him stating that he did not know the Code.

If one problem was as to what law to apply, another was to whom should the law be applied. Here the Commissioner was more tentative and recognized the limits of the system he was establishing. British subjects and protected persons were always to be tried or have their disputes settled by administrative officers wherever their acts or disputes arose, but jurisdiction over Africans was to be confined to those within a radius of five miles from the station. The rest were to be left to traditional judicial machinery which was not to be too much interfered with, or undermined. In any event, this formula could only apply to fully pacified areas.

These administrative instructions were confirmed, amplified and given the force of law by the East Africa Order in Council 1897,[11] and Queen's Regulations made thereunder which established an embryo legal system based on a tripartite division of subordinate courts; native, Muslim, and those staffed by administrative officers and magistrates, which may be called colonial, and a dual system of superior courts, one styled Her Majesty's Court for East Africa, from which appeals lay to Her Britannic Majesty's Court at Zanzibar and the Privy Council, the other styled a Chief Native Court from which appeals lay to a High Court. This system lasted in effect only five years but it contained the germ of several later developments and conflicts and may therefore be briefly looked at.

The Order in Council established Her Majesty's Court for East Africa to be presided over by the Judicial Officer of the protectorate. It empowered the Foreign Secretary to establish provincial courts to be held by administrative officers having jurisdiction over British subjects and protected persons and certain classes of foreigners, and equated the powers of these courts and the aforementioned court to various courts in the Presidency of Bombay. Indian legislation applied by the Zanzibar Order in Council 1884 to the coast was now applied to the whole protectorate.

The Native Court Regulations of 1897 established the other types of court. At the top was a High Court consisting of the Commissioner and two senior judges of Her Britannic Majesty's Court at Zanzibar. Below that was a Chief Native Court staffed by the Judicial Officer with power to supervise all inferior native courts in the protectorate. The powers of the Chief Native Court and Her Majesty's Court for East Africa were similar. Below this court were two types of native court—colonial and indigenous. Colonial

[11] S.R.O. 1897 No. 575; Native Courts Regulations 1897. E.A.P.G. Orders and Regulations, volume I, p. 65.

native courts were provincial, district and assistant collector's courts, having the powers of magistrate's courts set out in the Indian Penal and Procedure Codes by which they were to be guided. In the coastal region they were also to be guided by the general principles of Muslim law when deciding a civil case between Muslims, and in the rest of the protectorate they were to have regard to native laws and customs not opposed to natural justice and morality. Most important were the limits put upon their jurisdiction—they were to hear all cases in their jurisdiction within a radius of fifteen miles from their station but beyond that they were not generally obliged to hear cases to the exclusion of tribal authorities. Provision was made for the future extension of jurisdiction beyond the fifteen mile limit, and in any event, a limited supervision of indigenous authorities was to be exercised.

Indigenous native courts were of two main types—those deriving from the old administration of the Sultan, and having jurisdiction in the Coastal Strip only, and those deriving from tribal societies having jurisdiction over the particular tribe alone. The coastal courts were courts of the Liwali and the Mudir—with powers equivalent to the district and assistant collector's court respectively, and with appeals going to the provincial and district court respectively, and the court of the Chief Kadhi[11a] having jurisdiction throughout the coastal region, and Kadhi's courts having jurisdiction within a district only. Kadhi's courts were Muslim religious courts and applied Muslim law identical to that observed in the courts of the Sultan of Zanzibar in all cases affecting the personal status of Muslims. The tribal courts were the courts of local chiefs and elders; the Regulations recognized the jurisdiction of certain named groups of chiefs and elders, and the Commissioner was empowered to recognize any other chiefs 'as exercising . . . legitimate authority over his tribesmen'.[12]

Already at this early date, while the Regulations betrayed both an absence of effective control over the interior, and a lack of a clear policy of development, certain interesting guide-lines are discernible nevertheless. The two different final courts of appeal, a judicial one for non-Africans, a semi-administrative one for Africans, besides introducing a racial division into the legal system, also hinted at different conceptions of the role of courts depending upon whether they were to serve Africans or non-Africans. There was, too, the ambivalence over the use of indigenous tribal authorities—to some extent forced on the administration by its lack of knowledge about the people of the protectorate. On the one hand, the jurisdiction of the 'colonial' native court could be extended in the future; on the other hand,

[11a] There are many different ways of spelling Kadhi. To avoid confusion we have adopted throughout the book the current official Kenyan spelling as evidenced by the Kadhi's Courts Act 1967.
[12] Regulation 46.

the Commissioner could recognize further chiefs, which suggested that an extended use might be made of them.

In the event there was a slow movement away from relying on traditional authorities for much of this period, a movement which was partially reversed towards its close, and it is worth attempting to state why this was the case, since in neighbouring Uganda and Zanzibar, not to mention the Muslim courts at the coast, great reliance was placed on traditional institutions, suitably modified where necessary. Phillips stated the major difficulties in the way of using traditional authorities as follows:

> [I]n most of the tribes of Kenya it appears that the indigenous system of justice was very fluid; that there was no standing judicial body; that disputes were adjudicated upon by *ad hoc* councils of elders, usually within the framework of the lineage system; that the composition of the judicial body was liable to vary with the nature and importance of each individual case; and that the sanction behind its decisions was the solidarity of the group. The only step in the direction of an organized judicial system was the recognition of certain elders as traditionally qualified to participate in adjudication and this recognition was usually based on their seniority as members of the social unit. It needs no argument to show that a system such as this cannot be taken over wholesale as part of the machinery of government by a centralized authority.[13]

Early administrative officers and policy-makers did not know of these defects, or at least not in such detail. They were concerned with administrative convenience, and not anthropology, in deciding what sort of native courts there should be, and what they observed appeared to be both inefficient and not susceptible to very much control. Hence the move towards change instituted by the new Commissioner, who had no great regard for indigenous institutions. With the advantage of hindsight, however, we can the better appreciate the contemporary background against which these decisions were taken, why they were taken and what sort of effect they were likely to have on indigenous institutions, which were later to be resurrected.

If the first Commissioner's policy had been a gradual extension of statutory courts at the expense of traditional institutions, the policy of his successor was to speed up the process. A major reorganisation took place throughout the whole court system in 1902 which had the effect of bringing about a greater measure of unity in the courts, and moving away from traditional bodies. At the top two new courts were established by Orders in Council—Her Britannic Majesty's Court of Appeal for East Africa to act as a court of appeal for Uganda and Nyasaland as well as the East Africa Protectorate,[14] and a High Court for the East Africa Protectorate, the latter with full jurisdiction over all persons and things in the protectorate.[15] Below them,

[13] Phillips, *Report on Native Tribunals in Kenya* (1945), para. 520 (Nairobi, Legal Department).
[14] S.R.O. 1902, No. 661. Appeals Ordinance No. 28 of 1902.
[15] East Africa Order in Council 1902, S.R.O. No. 661.

the East Africa Native Courts Amendment Ordinance 1902[16] introduced special courts, constituted by the collectors or assistant collectors of a district which had been declared a special district, having full criminal and civil jurisdiction over natives in the district. Jurisdiction was to be exercised according to the laws in force in the protectorate at the time, amongst which was the following important provision:

> In all cases civil and criminal to which natives are parties, every Court (a) shall be guided by native law so far as it is applicable and is not repugnant to justice and morality or inconsistent with any Order in Council or Ordinance or any regulation or Rule made under any Order in Council or Ordinance; and (b) shall decide all such cases according to substantial justice without undue regard to technicalities of procedure and without undue delay.[17]

First introduced by the East Africa Order in Council 1902, this provision remained part of the laws of the East Africa Protectorate and Kenya from that time onwards and was to play a significant part in the development of the administration of justice.

Appeal lay from the special courts to the High Court which also had general supervisory powers over them. The Native Court Regulations were no longer to apply to districts declared to be special districts. By the end of 1902, all the districts in five of the seven provinces of the protectorate had been declared to be such and in the following year two districts were added from a sixth province, leaving only the coastal districts governed by the Regulations.[18] The effect of this Ordinance was to extend the jurisdiction of the colonial courts throughout the protectorate. This represented a considerable change of policy, for the Native Court Regulations had envisaged the colonial courts gradually extending their sphere of operations following on after pacification and as administration became a reality, whereas this Ordinance envisaged the courts being used as instruments of pacification.[19] It was as if they had been converted from support into front-line troops, and it was a conversion which was to be permanent.

Displacement of the Native Court Regulations left the question of traditional institutions in the air; here too there were significant changes. The Amendment Ordinance reaffirmed the Commissioner's power to recognize the jurisdiction of tribal chiefs, and the exercise by them of such authority as might be vested in them, and in addition provided for powers to be granted to them by the Commissioner. A collector could transfer cases to them, enforce their orders and exercise a general supervision over their proceedings. More important, however, was the enactment of the Village

[16] No. 31.
[17] Section 20.
[18] Gazette Notices 15/12/02; 30/5/03; 15/12/03.
[19] See the Gazette Notice appointing the officers commanding troops in Jubaland, Kismanu and Yanti as magistrates with jurisdiction under the C.P.C. 11/2/05.

Headman Ordinance[20] in the same year. This was the legislative *fons et origo* of the system of native administration in Kenya, and provided for the Commissioner to appoint official headmen of villages or groups of villages who were to be the representatives of, and charged with the duty of maintaining order within the village. Powers might be conferred on these headmen to hear and determine petty native cases. The importance of this legislation was that these official headmen were not, generally, traditional office-holders but persons chosen by the administration, and therefore owing their authority to the administration. To confer executive and judicial powers on such persons represented at one and the same time a move away from reliance on traditional institutions, and a move towards closely associating native courts with the administration.

Whether the full implications of these changes were appreciated at the time may be doubted. Phillips pointed out that the shift from traditional elders to government-appointed chiefs caused the latter to become dominant even where the former were still used, and drove them 'into an attitude of apathy, of sulky acquiescence or even of hostility. It is probable that during this period [1902–10] were sown unwittingly the seeds of many future difficulties'.[21] The shift in the use of the courts and the relationship between the administration and the native courts were equally important and productive of future clashes. In several respects, the changes of 1902, though later modified or even departed from for varying periods of time, fixed the pattern of development of the administration of justice in Kenya from that time onwards. The salient features of the system thus created should therefore be summarized: the use of non-traditional native courts closely associated with the administration; the use of colonial courts as organs of pacification; the use of the administrative officers acting administratively as the link between the two different kinds of courts.

The system thus created, albeit somewhat tentatively, was put on a firmer base by the Courts Ordinance 1907,[22] and rules made thereunder. Though replaced by the Courts Ordinance 1931,[23] in consequence of major changes in the native courts system the previous year, the basic framework of 'colonial' subordinate courts established by this Ordinance was to last for sixty years. Three classes of subordinate court were established, first-class, to be held by a resident magistrate and Senior (later Provincial) Commissioner, with jurisdiction throughout a province; second-class, to be held by a District Commissioner, and third-class, to be held by an Assistant District Commissioner (later District Officer), both having jurisdiction within the district

[20] No. 22.
[21] *Report*, op. cit., chapter 3, para. 56 (b).
[22] No. 13.
[23] No. 16.

in which they were situated. Three classes of subordinate native courts were established, Liwali, Kadhi and Mudir having jurisdiction in the coastal districts and over natives only. Kadhi's courts had jurisdiction over Muslim natives in matters of personal status. All subordinate courts had both civil and criminal jurisdiction of varying amounts, and were subject to the control, supervision and revisional jurisdiction of the High Court to which, in addition, appeals lay. When sitting to hear an appeal from a Kadhi's Court, the High Court was to have the Chief Kadhi as assessor. All courts could make use of assessors for purposes of ascertaining native law and custom. All courts were to follow the Criminal Procedure Ordinance and the Civil Procedure Code so far as the same might be applicable and suitable, an important limitation which allowed the 'substantial justice without undue regard to technicalities' provision of the East Africa Order in Council 1902, to remain applicable to trials of Africans.

The Ordinance drew a distinction between subordinate native courts and native tribunals. The latter were to consist of any headman or council of elders to whom jurisdiction was granted by the Governor by rules made under the Ordinance, but this jurisdiction was to be confined to members of the tribe of the headman or council of elders. Subordinate courts had the same supervisory, transfer and enforcement powers in relation to the native tribunals as had been introduced by the 1902 legislation. The Ordinance envisaged the use of both traditional and non-traditional persons in these native tribunals for it repeated the 1902 provision as to recognition of chiefs and elders as well as referring to the jurisdiction of village headmen.

The Native Tribunal Rules 1908[24] elaborated some of the provisions of the Ordinance. Only those headmen appointed by the Governor could exercise the powers conferred by the rules but headmen included chiefs and councils of elders. In practice, the tribunals that were constituted were a mixture of government-appointed headmen, and traditional elders who were usually subordinate to the first group. The tribunals were given both civil and petty criminal jurisdiction; in civil, to adjust claims; in criminal, to award compensation according to the custom of the tribe, or to imprison. Their decisions were subject to revision by administrative officers where they saw good reason to do so, but this revision was to take the form of a re-hearing of the case under the provisions of the Courts Ordinance, thus providing a link between the High Court and the native tribunal, for a case which had been re-heard could be appealed to the High Court.

The system of native tribunals thus created lasted for twenty-two years, but not without legislative and administrative changes. The most important legislative change took place in 1911. This was the attempt by Girouard, a Governor who was severely critical of much of the administration he found

[24] E.A.P.G., Orders and Regulations, p. 67.

on his arrival in the protectorate, to re-base the native tribunals purely on the traditional institutions. It was a policy recommended to him by his senior Provincial Commissioners who were also concerned, as we will consider in more detail later, with the amount of judicial interference in the operation of the native tribunals, and its general justification was that associated with the principle of Indirect Rule, with which Girouard was familiar from his service in Northern Nigeria; '. . . we must be prepared to work out the salvation of the natives of this country by the building up of a policy based on their own administrative system'.[25] As we have seen, however, the indigenous administrative systems of the East Africa Protectorate were very different from the administrative systems of the Emirates of Northern Nigeria and had, in addition, taken a battering over the preceding ten years which had not been paralleled in Nigeria. All the king's men could not put Humpty-Dumpty together again, and the back-to-the-pure-indigenous-system experiment was short-lived.

The Native Tribunal Rules 1911[26] provided that the powers conferred, which were considerably increased over the 1908 powers, should only be exercised by such councils of elders as were constituted under, and in accordance with, native law and custom, and were recognized by the Governor. Supervisory powers by administrative officers were enlarged by the interesting provision that they could order a re-trial to take place in their presence. Where traditional courts of appeal existed, they might continue to operate. Traditional procedures were to be followed, and punishments awarded but not those which were inhuman or involved torture and similar practices. Thus, there were inevitable departures from traditional practices even in these Rules and a system of supervision and re-hearing of cases would in time result in even more departures. But two years later, a revised version of the Rules[26a] permitted departures even in the traditional composition of the tribunal to take account of the fact that some Provincial Commissioners had 'in some cases induced native communities to alter the constitution of Native Councils',[27] which suggests that the 1911 Rules were never strictly followed on this point. In addition, administrative officers were given power to revise cases from these tribunals administratively—that is without being controlled by the High Court—a most important legislative innovation though one which again reflected current practices. To these legislative departures from traditional institutions we may add Phillips' comment that 'the headmen still retained their executive power and were inclined to resent the curtailment of their authority in regard to

[25] *Memorandum on Native Policy* by Ainsworth and Hobley 1909, quoted in Mungeam, op. cit., p. 214.
[26] E.A.P.G., Orders and Regulations, p. 53.
[26a] E.A.P.G., 1913 Orders and Regulations, p. 54.
[27] Phillips, *Report*, op. cit., para. 43.

judicial matters. The result was that the tribunals still tended to be subservient to the headmen and if they did try to assert their independence they found themselves powerless to enforce their judgements'.[28] The departures from previous policy trends introduced in 1911 had, in the final analysis therefore, little positive but considerable negative effect on the development of the tribunal system, and paved the way for greater administrative control.

By 1913, therefore, different policies and successive changes of legislation had finally produced a recognizable legal system covering the whole country which was to remain the same in broad outline for most of the next two decades. Legislation in this early period had reflected the preoccupation of the protectorate administration with the creation of a system for the administration of justice for Africans, and the difficulties of reconciling the need for a system which could be fitted into a hierarchy of courts and administrative bodies and was sufficiently formal to be susceptible to some sort of judicial and administrative control, with the need for a system which bore some resemblance to traditional methods of dispute-settlement and so would stand a chance of being acceptable to the people for whom it was created. The position at the end of the period showed that on balance the first alternative had been chosen, but a forlorn attempt was being made to combine traditional composition with non-traditional powers, functions, and supervision—an attempt which was to continue intermittently in different parts of Kenya for more than thirty years thereafter. In opting for the first alternative, the administration was adopting the same approach to native tribunals as to native administration—direct administration via government-appointed headmen, and ensuring that there would be a close link between the two, and that the orientation of the first would be as a handmaiden to the second.

In later years, administrative officers were wont to justify this close connection between tribunal and administration as being traditional; separation of powers was not something, they averred, that Africans understood or wanted. (It should be pointed out, however, that at the same time as they spoke thus, they were endeavouring to bring about a separation of personnel between the two bodies.) Quite apart from the fact that Africans in the Legislative Council when speaking on the native tribunals were unanimous in criticizing the connection between them and the administration, this argument overlooks the very great change in the function of a statutory native tribunal from a traditional judicial body. The function of the latter was broadly to establish or re-establish the social equilibrium of the group and adjust the rival claims which had led to the dispute. Because the group was involved, it took part in the reconciliation process, and the traditional

[28] *Report*, op. cit., para. 56 (c).

judges were therefore in the nature of mouthpieces of the group supervising the settlement procedures and pronouncing the final decision. But a statutory native tribunal did not have the same intimate connection with the group over which it was set. In a civil case it gave a judgment which represented victory for one side and defeat for the other. In a criminal case, it had to enforce a law external to the group. In both cases it was doing something alien to a traditional body, and at all times owed allegiance to the colonial power rather than the tribal group. It by no means followed therefore that Africans continued to approve or desire the close connection between the new tribunals and the administration. If the close connection persisted, as it did, it was for reasons other than, or at the very least, in addition to African pressure.

THE ADMINISTRATION OF JUSTICE AND ADMINISTRATIVE AND JUDICIAL ATTITUDES THERETO

What sort of legal system had been created by 1913? This may be looked at from two points of view: judicial and administrative. The judicial would turn to the legislation and would find that it had created a legal system rather similar in many ways to the one the holders of this view—primarily judges but also other professional lawyers in government service—were most familiar with, the English legal system. There was a hierarchy of superior and appellate courts leading up to the Judicial Committee of the Privy Council. Below the High Court, which had all the jurisdiction, criminal, civil, common law and equity, probate and admiralty of the English High Court, there was a hierarchy of subordinate courts, which while making concessions to different social systems, were all under the ultimate control of the High Court to which appeals lay and which had revisional jurisdiction over them. This last power was admittedly rather un-English since it permitted the court to revise a decision on its own motion without hearing the parties but it was given the High Court precisely in order to ensure that all these rather strange subordinate courts did themselves broadly conform to British standards of justice which it was the High Court's duty to uphold and inculcate.

The judicial parallel with England could be carried further. The administrative officer, the village headman and the Muslim officials could be seen as Justices of the Peace, and the administrative-cum-judicial régime established by the law as equivalent to the seventeenth to early nineteenth century English system of local government. The essence of this system, from the judicial point of view, was that in East Africa no less than in England the administrator-judge was bound by the law; what he could or could not do was fully set out in a statute or judicial decision, and procedures were available to ensure that he kept within the law. This picture was, of course, a mixture of the actual and the ideal; in respect of England the picture overlooked the inevitable class bias of Justices of the Peace and the manner in which they in fact carried out their judicial duties in times of political and industrial unrest, particularly in the nineteenth century, supported by the judiciary,[29] and in East Africa it overlooked the fact that the superior courts no less than the inferior administrator-judges were organs of colonialism, and in the last analysis were required to support the order of which they were an important part. British conceptions of justice in other words included the use of the courts by the dominant political forces to maintain the political and social *status quo*.

The administrative point of view was rather different. It disregarded the hierarchy of courts—indeed considered them to be an impediment to the administration of justice, and took its stand on the provision in the relevant Order in Council that:

> In all cases civil and criminal to which natives are parties, every court . . . shall decide all such cases according to substantial justice without undue regard to technicalities of procedure and without undue delay.[30]

and saw in this both the requirement and the justification for entrusting the administration of justice for Africans to administrative officers, free from overmuch judicial control and untrammelled by too many legal rules. They were better able to administer and supervise the administration of justice for the Africans because they knew more about them than the judges and in the last resort that knowledge mattered more than following procedural rules. Moreover they were in a better position to judge the effect on the maintenance of law and order and the regard in which the administration was held, of an acquittal, or a severe punishment, and these factors should properly be taken into account when considering the case of a particular individual or group of individuals, and could only be taken into account if the administrators had unfettered powers to administer justice themselves, and supervise its administration by the native tribunals. Had administrators looked to England for parallels, they would have seized not on the ideal picture of judicial control posited by the judges, but the actual picture of magisterial vigour in administering the criminal law which characterized the inferior courts in England in the eighteenth and nineteenth century.

The gap between these two points of view was wide, and affected policy and practice in the colonial era. We will consider it in connection with various facets of the development of the administration of justice, and the Bushe Commission[31] which provided the opportunity for a major and most vigorous confrontation of views.

[29] Mather, *Public Order in the Age of the Chartists* (Manchester University Press 1959).
[30] Section 20, East Africa Order in Council 1902.
[31] *Report of the Commission of Enquiry into the Administration of Justice in Kenya, Uganda*

(i) *Punishment*

From the first, corporal punishment was permitted, initially up to fifty lashes with the *kiboko* or the 'cat'; later no more than twenty-four with a cane, and from the first there were differences between the judiciary and the administrative officer on its use. The first two High Court 'Circulars to Magistrates' in 1904 and 1905 were about flogging; the former insisting that sentences of maximum flogging must receive prior confirmation from the High Court and such extensive jurisdiction as was exercisable under the East Africa Native Courts (Amendment) Ordinance should be exercised with care and attention;[32] the latter recommending that more discretion should be used in awarding the punishment of flogging. It should be used for brutal offences but not, as magistrates' monthly returns showed, for comparatively trivial offences.[33] From that time onwards there were repeated circulars to magistrates calling their attention to the need to limit their use of flogging, to keep within the law on this matter, and to send proper returns concerning it to the High Court. Apparently so little regard was paid to the first circulars that in 1911 a circular drew the attention of magistrates to the Colonial Secretary's desire 'that magistrates should be instructed that they must not regard flogging as an everyday occurrence to be freely administered but as a serious and exceptional form of punishment to be employed only in special cases'.[34] Thirty-seven years later, in 1948, the Supreme Court was still reminding magistrates that flogging should only be used in cases of serious personal violence, and then not of necessity.[35] In between those dates the Bushe Commission had considered the whole question of corporal punishment and after hearing much administrative and settler evidence in favour of it concluded that it should be used as sparingly as possible.[36] However, like so many other of their criticisms of the administration of justice in East Africa in general and Kenya in particular, this fell on stony ground.

Secondly, the question of punishments for stock theft may be mentioned. Stock theft was often a euphemism for inter-tribal raiding and warfare, and in an effort to stamp it out the law at one time required a fine of ten times the value of the stolen stock to be paid in addition to any other punishment.[37] Punishments given by administrative officers were severe and one of the

and the Tanganyika Territory in Criminal Matters 1933 and correspondence arising out of the report, Cmd. 4623 (1934).

32 No.1 of (1904) 1 E.A.L.R. 146. See section 11, East Africa Native Courts (Amendment) Ordinance 1902.

33 No. 1 of (1905) 1 E.A.L.R. 156.

34 No. 6 of (1911) 4 E.A.L.R. xvi. See, too, circulars No. 7 of (1913) 5 E.A.L.R. 224. 3 of (1921) 9 (2) K.L.R. 186, 10 of (1932) 14 K.L.R. 181, 15 of (1933) 15 K.L.R. 157.

35 No. 1 of 1948 (1949) 23 (2) K.L.R. 113.

36 *Report*, op. cit., p. 63, para. 178.

37 Stock and Produce Theft Ordinance No. 8 of 1913, section 3, repealed by the Stock and Produce (Levy of Fines) Ordinance No. 17 of 1933.

major complaints by administrators to the Bushe Commission concerned the Supreme Court's reduction of sentences for stock theft, the bad effect this had on the maintenance of law and order, and the importance of this consideration in meting out punishment. The Commission considered the administrative sentencing policy in Kenya on this matter to be severe and the Attorney-General, a member of the Commission, went so far as to describe it as 'too severe, at times almost savage'.[38] In his capacity as Attorney-General, he took the opportunity in a criminal revision case on stock theft with the obvious approval and support of the court, to restate the principles of punishment which magistrates should follow.[39] The principles were drawn from decisions in English cases and the court queried whether they could apply where the magistrates were dealing with uncivilized people in unsettled districts. With the instant case in mind, where the prisoner had been sentenced to two years' imprisonment and a thirty shilling fine or four more months in lieu for stealing a goat worth three shillings in broad daylight from a fellow Nandi tribesman, the Attorney-General agreed that the position was not exactly similar but in that case the legislature was woefully backward in fixing maximum punishments, and it was therefore for the court to do so and 'two years is just as long a time in the life of an illiterate African as it is in the life of anyone else'.[40] The sentence was reduced and a circular sent to all magistrates impressing upon them the importance of reading and acting upon the Attorney-General's submissions to the court. Further circulars, however, suggested that this too was largely ignored.

(ii) *The Conduct of Criminal Proceedings*

A continuous battle was waged between the two sides on the basic question of the proper manner of conducting criminal cases, and the necessity to keep within the law and follow procedural requirements. Time and again judgments in criminal revision cases would commence with such statements as: 'this trial was unsatisfactory'; 'there are many defects here'; 'this cannot be supported'; 'there is no such offence as'. Circular after circular cajoled, advised and pleaded with magistrates to observe the Criminal Procedure Ordinance and its amendments, to submit accurate returns of cases and to give only lawful punishments. Some examples from the cases and circulars will highlight the two attitudes to the judicial function.

In *R.* v. *Lohira wa Esondyi*[41] a collector holding a Special Native Court sentenced the prisoner to eighteen months' imprisonment and twenty-five lashes for an offence for which the Indian Criminal Procedure Code fixed

[38] Bushe, *Report*, op. cit., p. 112.
[39] *R.* v. *Malakwen arap Kogo* (1933), 15 K.L.R. 115.
[40] 15 K.L.R. 115 at p. 125.
[41] (1903) 1 E.A.L.R. 57.

a maximum punishment of three months. The High Court conceded that 'special circumstances' might justify a departure from the law but there were no special circumstances here and generally magistrates should try to keep within the laws of the protectorate. A circular in 1913 warned against the practice of trying large groups of Africans on the same charge of failing to pay hut and poll tax pointing out that A's failure to pay the tax had nothing to do with B's alleged failure.[42] A stiff circular in 1920 drew magistrates' attention to two cases where persons sentenced to imprisonment and a fine or more imprisonment in lieu had been kept in prison after completing their substantive sentence notwithstanding that they had paid their fine because no notification of the payment had been sent to the prison authorities.[43]

One area of particular sensitivity was the criminal part of the employment relationship governed by the Master and Servant, Resident Labourers, and Employment of Natives Ordinances, for here administrative attitudes towards the administration of justice were outflanked by settler attitudes with the result that there were even greater departures from judicial standards. Several circulars reminded the magistrates that they should first investigate whether a contract of employment existed before punishing a person for alleged breach of it. Some cases went even further in their disregard of the law and the case of *R. through Major Luxford* v. *Waibenga wa Rori*[44] is a classic of this genre. The accused had been convicted of failing to take proper care of Major Luxford's cattle while the latter was in England, contrary to the Employment of Natives Ordinance,[45] which imposed a criminal liability for neglect of duty. An extract from the judgment of Sheridan J. on criminal revision may be left to speak for itself:

> It is manifest that the sentence of fine with imprisonment in default cannot stand; the sole object of that sentence was to bring compulsion on the accused person to compensate the complainant for loss said to have been caused. The Court has had occasion to point out in more than one Judgment that a fine imposed in such circumstances must be set aside . . . The charge put to the accused contained no particulars whatever whether as regards time or place or the character of the act. It was framed as a result of a letter stating that the heifers had been found in a particular condition by the complainant after the discharge of the accused. In effect what was said to the accused by the Magistrate was: "The complainant's heifers have been interfered with during his absence in England and you are called upon to explain satisfactorily the circumstances under penalty". The impropriety of such a method of charging a prisoner quite apart from specific legislation to which we will refer must be obvious.[46]

[42] No. 7 of (1913) 5 E.A.L.R. 224.
[43] No. 2 of (1920) 9 (2) K.L.R. 180.
[44] (1927) 11 K.L.R. 100.
[45] Cap. 139, Laws of Kenya (1926 edition).
[46] p. 101.

The case might be extreme but the magisterial attitude was not exceptional and continued decisions of that ilk in all fields of crime prompted an even stronger judicial condemnation by Thomas J., in 1933:

> In the appendix of 1 K.L.R. appears the following: "The valuable provisions of Article 20 of the Order in Council of 1920 are not to be misconstrued into an authority for administering justice to the native in the rough and ready style of which some affect to think highly but which is generally but the sign of lack of experience or of sympathy and patience and not infrequently results in what is in reality rough and ready injustice". These words meet with my entire approval and I repeat them here and give them even greater force if possible than they had in the early history of the Colony. This I deem necessary for some would still seem to think that the language of the Order in Council is to be treated as a charter of liberty to allow any breach of regularity in the administration of justice and more especially to excuse errors in the proper conduct of trials on the part of authority.[47]

It is sometimes suggested in defence of the administrative officer and his attitudes towards his judicial functions that the judges needlessly insisted on rigid adherence to procedure and the correct filling in of forms—matters which did not go to the essential fairness of a trial. It is certainly true that there is always a danger that lawyers are inclined to believe that strict adherence to procedure will automatically produce a fair result in a trial, and departures will conversely automatically produce injustice, and that this is an attitude with which most administrators would disagree, since often it is only a judicious bending or ignoring of the rules that produces a fair result. These examples, however, show that such an attitude did not generally animate the judges. Essentially, what they wanted administrative officers to do was to keep within the law and observe those rules of evidence and procedure evolved over the years with the express purpose of protecting the accused person, without which it was not possible to conduct a fair trial as understood by lawyers. It was this which administrative officers were clearly reluctant to do, not so much because they did not accept the relevance of fair trial for Africans—indeed they spent a great deal of their time trying to ensure that native tribunals conducted trials fairly—but because their notions of what a fair trial was were far removed from judicial notions. An early articulation of their notions had been made in 1909 when senior Provincial Commissioners had complained to a sympathetic Governor that the general confusion in native administration was in part due to 'judicial rules and regulations creeping in';[48] what was needed was considerable discretion given to the Provincial Commissioners in their administration

[47] Confirmation Case No. 97 of 1933 (unreported). This extract, is quoted with approval in the Report of the Bushe Commission, para. 156. 1 K.L.R. is a misnomer, as the correct designation is 1 E.A.L.R.
[48] Ainsworth and Hobley, op. cit., in Mungeam, op. cit., p. 214.

of local African law. The clearest and most forthright expression of administrative attitudes, however, came in their reaction to, and virtual rejection of, the Bushe Commission.

(iii) *The Commission of Inquiry into the Administration of Justice in Kenya, Uganda and Tanganyika Territory in Criminal Matters*[49]

The Commission, consisting of five persons, of whom three were lawyers, investigated the system of criminal justice in East Africa in 1933. It adopted the judicial viewpoint on the administration of justice, declared that the British system had been introduced into East Africa, but was very critical of its resultant operation, particularly its rough and ready nature in Kenya. Its general conclusion, stated at the beginning of the report, was that 'the machinery of the administration of justice as apparently set up by law in these territories does not work, and as at present constituted cannot work'.[50] Three general defects were pinpointed; the conferring of excessive jurisdiction on magistrate's courts; the excessive use of the power of investing magistrates with the powers of the High Court; and the infrequent circuits of the High Courts owing to their understaffing.[51]

The Commission's major criticisms in detail, however, were reserved for the administrative conception of the function of the courts on which they received much evidence. They rejected the administrative approach *tout court*.[52] Suggestions had been made that magisterial powers of administrative officers should be increased as they knew the Africans, and it would increase their prestige. The Commission considered that a District Officer was first and foremost an administrative officer charged with the maintenance of law and order in his district, having to police it and investigate crimes. In these circumstances it was not always easy 'to assume the judicial role and to proceed calmly and dispassionately to apportion responsibility and arrive at the proper sentence'.[53] It did not consider that 'knowing the native' and 'knowing the circumstances of the district' were acceptable substitutes for knowing the Criminal Procedure Code, the Indian Evidence Act and acting on the basis of evidence given in open court; the first approach was parental correction, the second was justice according to law, and it was the second which should be administered in East Africa. Nor was it impressed by the argument about prestige; it considered that this was overdone and that in any event personality and not the power to punish should determine an officer's prestige. Its general conclusions on this point were that while administrative officers must for some time be retained as magistrates, their

[49] Cmd. 4623 (1934), *Report*.
[50] *Report*, op. cit., p. 8, para. 18.
[51] *Report*, op. cit., p. 9, para. 19.
[52] *Report*, op. cit., pp. 17–25, paras. 44–67.
[53] *Report*, op. cit., para. 45.

powers should be reduced, the High Courts' valuable powers of revision of criminal cases must be retained, more judges should be appointed to the High Court so that there could be more circuits, and the aim should be to replace administrative officers with legally qualified professional magistrates.

There was, too, the inevitable dispute between the Commission and administrative officers on 'technicalities'. The latter's point of view was that judicial reversal of convictions on the basis of technicalities meant that people who were clearly guilty went free, and law and order consequently suffered. The former's view was that there were no technicalities where injustice to the individual was involved, and a perusal of court records on criminal revision showed that convictions were only quashed on serious irregularities.

The administrative view having been rejected by the Commission, it was waged with redoubled vigour and sharpness by administrators in their official comments on the report. This was especially true as to the comments from two senior Kenya administrators, the Acting Governor and the Chief Native Commissioner. The Attorney-General, who had been a member of the Commission, and the Chief Justice agreed with the Commission's approach, its strictures and its recommendations.[54] The administrators rejected its approach, its 'condemnatory generalizations' and many of its recommendations. The Acting Governor claimed that the evidence did not support the strictures, and defended the role of the administrative officer in the administration of justice.[55] The Chief Native Commissioner rejected the Commission's assumption that a British system of justice had been introduced into Kenya; on the contrary, there had been a deliberate and consistent policy since 1907 to create a different system for Kenya suited to local conditions in which magistrates were given wide powers and required to exercise them 'without undue regard to technicalities'. That was the root of the present system. The administration of justice to the Africans had been entrusted to those who knew about them because only with their background knowledge could magistrates get at the truth.

He reserved his strongest comment, however, for the Commission's criticism of taking political considerations into account in trying and sentencing accused persons which it claimed District Officers were in the habit of doing especially in stock theft cases in Kenya. After forcefully expressing his disagreement with the Commission over the facts, he then proceeded to defend the practice of administrative officers, which the Commission had criticized, of taking into account the effect of their decisions on public order.[56] The prevention of stock theft was of the highest public

[54] *Report*, op. cit., annex, pp. 109–13.
[55] *Report*, op. cit., annex, pp. 104–8.
[56] *Report*, op. cit., p. 17, paras. 45–6.

importance. The only practical method of prevention was by the infliction of severe punishment on those who were caught and convicted. Failure to check such outbreaks promptly and firmly was fraught with the gravest dangers, as it could lead to a serious outbreak of lawlessness and bloodshed. It was these factors which actuated administrative officers, but would not be understood by judges whose knowledge of local conditions might be very imperfect.[57]

It is not possible to see these two views, articulated so clearly and forcefully by the Commission and its administrative critics, as merely a difference of degree. They represented a fundamental division of attitudes as to the nature and function of courts and law enforcement. The administrators believed that their conception of the administration of justice was rightly different from the British conception. It had to be seen as an essential part of native administration, and as contributing wholeheartedly to the overriding necessity to maintain law and order. The individual's claim to justice had to be subordinated to the welfare of society as a whole and short-cuts, or failures to observe procedural and substantive laws, could be justified not solely on the narrow technical ground of an article in an Order in Council but on the broader ground that until order and respect for order had been established, law and justice were irrelevant and obstructive. Force, not justice, was respected and the courts must be used for the first objective before they could be used for the second.

This was anathema to the judiciary and most lawyers. Their point of view was perhaps summed up by the Bushe Commission when it stated: 'It is the duty of the Government to civilize and maintain peace and good order and this can only be done by the introduction of British conceptions of wrong-doing'.[58] Here the duty to civilize and the introduction of a British judicial system are correlated, and the fundamentals of this system were the need for the judge to comply with the law, the notion of individual criminal responsibility, and a procedure which would prevent one innocent person from being convicted even if it meant that nine guilty men went free.

The conflict came to a head in, but was not resolved by, the Bushe Commission. That had provided an arena for the exchange of views, but when the dust had settled matters continued much as before. By judgment and circulars, the Supreme Court continued to try and inculcate judicial standards of administration of justice into the magistrates, and they in turn, knowing that they had the support of senior administrators, continued to try and avoid the imposition of such standards. As the Commission perceived, it was

[57] *Report*, op. cit., annex, p. 117, para. 13.
[58] *Report*, p. 57.

only through the replacement of administrative officers as magistrates with a professional magistracy that the judicial point of view was likely to prevail and that did not take place on a significant scale until the sixties.

(iv) *The Native Tribunals*

The controversy over the place and function of the native tribunals in the system of the administration of justice provides further illustrations both of the theme under examination, and of the first theme, of the conflict between the indigenous and the colonial systems of justice, and how the two interacted. As we have seen, the Native Tribunal Rules 1913 were an uneasy compromise between indigenous and colonial, administrative and judicial systems. Composition and procedure were to be indigenous, with colonial variations, but the powers reflected more the colonial system. Administrative officers had power to revise cases administratively but appeals took the form of a re-hearing in a subordinate court with an eventual appeal to the High Court. Tribunals were therefore nominally at least under the control of the High Court.

This system was to last for seventeen years. It was a period which was characterized by little supervision and control by the administration, and much inefficiency and corruption in the tribunals, according to Phillips who obtained his information from files and administrative officers.[59] The amalgamation of native administration and native tribunals via the headmen or other government officials gave rise to opportunities for abuse of power which were not always resisted. The tribunals were increasingly being used for non-traditional purposes, particularly enforcing the rules and orders of headmen made under the Native Authority Ordinance, an area where even subordinate courts did not always appreciate the distinction between *intra* and *ultra vires* rules and orders,[60] and various sections of the Penal Code, though no statutory authority permitted them to do this. As their non-traditional functions increased, so did the power of the non-traditional members, as also did the lack of respect of the community for them.

This led to two somewhat opposite developments. On the one hand, unofficial bodies, what might be termed 'real traditional' bodies, flourished in many parts of the country dispensing traditional justice and using traditional procedures relying on community pressure to ensure compliance with their decisions. On the other hand, since the subordinate court system was open to African litigants, a fair amount of use was made of it, the appellate jurisdiction of the Supreme Court, and the assistance of advocates to prepare and argue cases there. In the eyes of the administration, some lawyers and some African litigants, this in turn created abuses and difficulties. Large

[59] *Report*, op. cit., para. 56 (c) and (d).

[60] e.g. *Mathendu* v. *Masenti* (1906–8), 2 E.A.L.R. 134.

sums of money were spent in litigating over small matters, especially about land; decisions displaying a lamentable ignorance of customary law were handed down by the Supreme Court; certain advocates fomented or employed touts to seek out or foment litigation in the reserves, and the whole process of civil justice was inordinately delayed.[61]

Administrators saw the cause of this as being too much judicial and too little administrative control of the tribunals. They failed to appreciate that the root cause of the state of disarray was the policy of the administration in using the tribunals as the enforcement part of the system of native administration, rather than as dispute settlement machinery amongst Africans as the Native Tribunal Regulations 1897 had envisaged their role. Since, however, the needs of the colonial system rather than any inherent defects in African judges or judicial control were to blame, there was little chance that the administration would go back on its policies; tribunals were an integral part of the system of native administration, and were their functions to be radically changed and separated from that system, it would break down.

If fundamental policies could not be changed, the superficial causes of disarray could be tackled by a reversal of current methods of control. In the twenties, action began to be taken and suggestions put forward to this effect. Administrative officers began to increase their supervision of tribunals though this could not of itself prevent judicial control as well. In addition, however, suggestions were made that the native tribunal system be completely separated from the judicial system of the colony, and be made subject solely to the control of administrative officers answerable only to the Governor. Besides increasing their efficiency, it was said that this would be more in keeping with African conceptions of the place of a tribunal in the governmental system, since it would completely eliminate the separation of the executive and judicial functions. As might be expected, this suggestion was opposed by the then Chief Justice and Attorney-General on the traditional ground that the administration of justice should not be subordinated to the executive.[62] They realized that to give the administration complete control would inevitably increase the administrative, and decrease the judicial, features of the tribunals. The movement towards complete separation, however, received a powerful impetus from the Committee on Kikuyu Land Tenure in 1929 which stressed African preference for final decisions by a District Commissioner in land tenure cases and objections to the jurisdiction of the Supreme Court in those matters.[63] Additional support could be adduced from Tanganyika where the Native Courts Ordinance[64],

[61] Phillips, *Report*, op. cit., paras. 47, 49, 53 and, 56 (d).
[62] Phillips, *Report*, op. cit., para. 48.
[63] *Report of the (Maxwell) Committee on Kikuyu Land Tenure 1929*, Nairobi, pp. 40–1.
[64] No. 5 of 1929.

which effected a complete separation between native courts and the judicial system, was passed the same year.

These two events probably clinched the matter for, in 1930, the Native Tribunals Ordinance,[65] modelled closely on the Tanganyikan statute, effected the desired separation in Kenya. The salient features of the Ordinance were as follows: Provincial Commissioners were empowered to establish, by warrant, such native tribunals in their province as they thought fit. The warrants, which were subject to the approval of the Governor, were the constitutions of the court and contained provisions as to their composition and jurisdiction. Tribunals were to be constituted in accordance with native law and custom but any tribunals purporting to be so constituted were to be deemed lawfully constituted unless the contrary could be shown. In addition, Provincial Commissioners, with the approval of the Governor, might prescribe the constitution of any tribunal. They also had the power of suspension and dismissal of members of a tribunal.

The jurisdiction of the tribunals was to be over all Africans in the area for which they were constituted, a change from the previous system where jurisdiction was tribal, in respect of all civil and criminal matters arising within the area. Limitations on their jurisdiction were of two sorts. The first arose from the nature of the subject matter; cases where death was involved, cases concerning marriage unless the claim concerned a customary marriage, and cognizable offences committed in a municipality or township, were not to be dealt with by tribunals. The second limitation arose from the law which the tribunals were to apply. This was native law and custom not repugnant to justice and morality, rules and orders issued under the Native Authority Ordinance, and such other statute law as set out in the warrant or permitted by the Governor. Practice, procedure and punishment were to be in accordance with native law and custom, but the latter could also include fines and imprisonment.

From a first instance tribunal, an appeal lay either to a Native Court of Appeal, established by a Provincial Commissioner, or to a District Commissioner, and from there to a Provincial Commissioner. With leave of this officer, a case could thereafter be stated to the Supreme Court. This represented a concession to the judicial point of view but it turned out to be a somewhat half-hearted one since the facility was rarely, if ever, made use of. A more important variation of the purely administrative appeal structure was the requirement that the records of all criminal cases decided by the tribunals be sent monthly to the Attorney-General, which would operate as an automatic appeal. Besides their appellate powers, administrative officers had extensive powers of control. They had access to all records, might revise cases or transfer them between tribunals or to a subordinate

[65] No. 39.

court (in which they sat as magistrates), might order a re-hearing of a case and might sit in the tribunal during its hearing of cases as an adviser. No advocates were allowed in any part of the tribunal system but litigants could be represented by their relatives.

The system introduced by the Ordinance was to last with variations until 1951. Even after the major reorganization of that year, the essential aspects of the system, its dissociation from the judicial system and association with the administration, continued unchanged for a further decade. The system represented a considerable victory for the administrative approach, for it meant that henceforth the developments of the native tribunals would depend on administrative requirements first and foremost, as opposed to judicial requirements. It also represented the clearest support that the administrative approach had received in legislation; not merely the operation but the very organization and framework of the system reflected administrative requirements, for in essence it gave administrators complete power to create any sort of tribunals they wanted, and use them as they saw fit.

How did administrators exercise their great powers and what sort of system did they create? We are fortunate in having as our guide in attempting to answer that question the exhaustive and classic *Report on Native Tribunals* compiled by A. Phillips in 1944.[66] Phillips was appointed, partly as a result of the comments by Hailey in 1938 on the lack of any coherent policy on native tribunals in Kenya, and partly as a result of the appointment of a Judicial Adviser to the native courts in Buganda in 1940, whose function it was to keep the courts under review and plan future policy.[67] He was to inquire into the native tribunal system and make recommendations on the possible functions of a Judicial Adviser in Kenya. The great merit of his Report is the detailed description of how the tribunals were actually operating at that time, and how administrative officers saw their own and the tribunals' functions, based as much as possible on first-hand observation or on the *ipsissima verba* of the administrators themselves.

On the basis of this report, we would say that there were four salient features about the tribunal system as it had been developed by the mid-forties. The first and most important was that, for what were no doubt the best motives of improving efficiency and incorruptibility, administrative officers regarded the tribunals as fair game for any and every experiment they wanted to carry out. In district after district the greater part of the 139 tribunals existing in Kenya had been subjected to perpetual and radical change in the fourteen years since the system was inaugurated. Often a new system would last no longer than a tour of a District Commissioner and fundamental alterations in composition, procedure, relations with indigenous

[66] 1945, Nairobi, Legal Department.
[67] *Report*, op. cit., para 2.

institutions or the local Native Authority were quite common every two or three years. What one District Commissioner put forward as a panacea, the next found to be anathema; what worked well in one area was exported to another without much regard to whether social and other relevant conditions were broadly similar. On several occasions the original warrant which was the constitution of the court, non-compliance with which caused the court to become illegal, was disregarded in these experiments, or had been otherwise forgotten about and not brought up to date as members had been dismissed from or dropped out of the tribunal. Despite the general opinion that corruption and inefficiency were being contained, many officers admitted that they had had to dismiss tribunal members and reorganize their local system for those very reasons. One fairly consistent development had been the gradual separation of the personnel of the tribunal and the Local Native Council, but this was by no means uniform, and there was still a close and continuing connection between the two organs of native administration, the latter of which promulgated rules and orders, while the former enforced them, both being subject to the control and sypervision of an administrative officer. No official attempt had been made to acquaint officers with developments in areas other than their own, and the result of handing the tribunals over to the administration had been that each district had gone its own way, the unifying supervision of the Supreme Court not being replaced by any unifying supervision of the Governor or the Chief Native Commissioner.

The second salient feature was that, with one idiosyncratic exception,[68] most of the experiments with tribunals had, as one underlying theme, a gradual movement away from traditional forms, methods, and personnel—a movement which was in fact under way before 1930—so that tribunals increasingly took on the outward trappings of an English-type court. This does not mean that the procedures and functions of the native tribunals began to approximate to those of the Supreme Court which, as we have seen, administrative officers rejected when there was an attempt to apply them to their own subordinate courts, but rather that the informal, often long-drawn out, reconciliation procedures which characterized indigenous institutions were replaced by a form of trial in which there was sufficient procedure to mark off plaintiff from defendant, prosecution from accused, and the various stages of a trial from one another. In addition, some sort of records had to be kept for appellate and review purposes. All this required some literate tribunal members, and so they replaced the traditional members who were often somewhat out of place in the new style tribunals. This trend

[68] H. E. Lambert, a D.C. in the Kikuyu Reserve in the thirties and forties. His views are set out and discussed by Phillips in chapter 5, paras. 182–216 and postscript; and chapters 13 and 14, paras. 502–4, 522–9 and postscript. Lambert's reply is in appendix F.

was to a very large extent inevitable in view of the changed role of the tribunal referred to above, but the accelerated if erratic progress made in this period illustrates the importance in the eyes of the administrators of the criminal and public order side of the tribunals' work. Civil work could have continued to be conducted much as in the old style—the community adjusting rival claims with the *wazee* playing the most important part. But this would not do for criminal work. A criminal trial had to produce a definite answer—guilty or not guilty—and procedures therefore had to be adopted that would produce in a minimum of time, a clear-cut decision that could be understood both by those involved in the case, and by those looking at the records. The imposition of English-type procedure on the tribunals, however, placed the administrative officer in a paradoxical situation; as an administrator he insisted on some sort of procedural form in the tribunals, as a magistrate he resented and rejected the insistence of the Supreme Court that he follow procedural forms. The paradox would have been regarded by administrators, however, as more apparent than real, for administrative procedure was common-sense designed to ensure that substantial justice was done, while judicial procedure was technicalities which quite often let the guilty go free.

The third salient feature follows from this. By the mid-forties the tribunals were enforcing a large amount of statutory criminal law; Native Authority Rules and Orders; parts of the Penal Code and other general 'administrative' criminal law, in addition to customary criminal law. Their powers of punishment had increased in some cases to imprisonment for up to one year. The picture which emerged of this criminal jurisdiction was far from reassuring. Phillips described it as follows:

> . . . The fact remains that the tribunals possess and not infrequently use, the power to try a variety of statutory offences of a specialized nature, and that they have neither the requisite legal knowledge nor the opportunity of acquiring that knowledge. On the whole, therefore, I think it is an illusion to suppose the tribunals are administering statutory law. What they are administering is a form of paternal or "public school" justice. The elders, in the light of such instructions as may be given them by the District Commissioner, measure the conduct of each accused person by what they conceive to be the appropriate standards. To each case is attached, usually by the clerk, one of the "labels" supplied by the District Commissioner. Sometimes this label is attached before the case is tried, sometimes afterwards. It may even be left for the District Commissioner when confirming the judgement to decide on the most suitable label.[69]

In these circumstances there was a grave risk of administrative pressure to convict being brought to bear on tribunals which, left on their own, would have acquitted because neither the members of the tribunal, nor the community at large, approved of the legislation. Such pressure was not the less likely because it was exerted in indirect forms, for example, a tribunal

[69] *Report*, op. cit., para 773.

convicting a person because it feared the disapproval of the District Commissioner if it did not.

Nor was customary criminal law any better administered. What it amounted to was either 'the application of non-indigenous penal sanctions to infringements of native law which were formerly settled by the payment of compensation'[70] or 'a sort of "contingencies vote" on which a tribunal can always fall back to justify a conviction in circumstances which were not foreseen or provided for by any other law'.[71] This latter use of customary criminal law was advocated by at least one administrative officer who considered that one of its advantages would be to cut the tribunals off entirely from 'the machinations of the Supreme Court and the Attorney-General'[72] but rejected by Phillips as being inconsistent with the basic idea of law itself. Certainly such an amorphous criminal law was open to abuse by the tribunals and the administration, and the catalogue of customary criminal 'offences' listed by Phillips suggests that it was used to punish any conduct of which a tribunal or an administrative officer happened to disapprove.[73]

This widespread increase in criminal jurisdiction was a clear example of far-reaching changes being made without much thought for their full implications. Phillips' conclusion was that the step was taken 'largely for reasons of convenience, and in particular by the desire to relieve administrative officers of magisterial work'.[74] This was a significant conclusion, for it highlighted both the administrative role of the tribunals, and the administrators' attitudes towards their judicial work. The tribunals were there first and foremost to help out the administration irrespective of whether in so doing they were able to administer justice to their community. The administrative officer's judicial work, though occupying a large proportion of his time was not so highly regarded that it could not be devolved on to bodies unsuited and unable to exercise it properly. A side-effect of such devolution was that the enforcement of this criminal law ceased to be a matter over which the Supreme Court had any jurisdiction. Phillips considered that with careful supervision, a reasonable measure of substantial justice was usually done in these criminal cases, but as we have already seen, there was a wide divergence between judicial and administrative notions of what that phrase meant and it is not clear in what sense he was using the term.[75] From his description quoted above, however, it is to be doubted whether the Supreme Court would have accepted that substantial justice was being done.

[70] *Report*, op. cit., para. 794.
[71] *Report*, op. cit., para. 799.
[72] *Report*, op. cit., para. 777.
[73] *Report*, op. cit., para. 792. Included amongst these was illegally returning an aged stepmother to her relations (Meru, 1943).
[74] *Report*, para. 765.
[75] *Report*, para. 772. The context suggests the administrative sense.

It was basically because the tribunals were so obviously used for administrative and criminal law enforcement purposes that they were regarded by the Africans as government institutions notwithstanding that they had evolved out of indigenous institutions, and still bore traces of their origins. Those uses and attitudes lead on to the fourth salient feature—the continued existence of unofficial and indigenous bodies, notwithstanding their illegality under the Ordinance, to settle disputes. While the tribunals certainly dealt with a large amount of civil business, a fair amount was settled 'out of court' by these bodies which, in the rural areas, approximated closely to indigenous institutions and in the settled or urban areas were based on various tribal or social units. Even where a case went to a tribunal that was often the second stage of the proceedings, the first having been before the unofficial body.

This phenomenon suggests that while the administration relied on the native tribunals extensively, they were not looked on quite so favourably by the persons for whom they had been created. Administrative officers generally assumed that the tribunals were performing a much appreciated social service, and as evidence they pointed to the large number of civil cases which they handled. It is certainly true that in some areas there were exceptionally heavy demands upon the tribunals but this is not necessarily evidence that they were doing a good job. Repeated resort to a tribunal by a community may well indicate that there are deep-seated social and economic problems within that community which the tribunal is unable to solve, but which the legal and governmental framework within which that community lives does not allow to be solved in any other way; for example, overcrowding in a reserve contributing to a multiplicity of suits over land when the land problem could have been solved only by planned migration from the reserve, and resettlement elsewhere. In such circumstances one is driven to use the court again and again despite its inability to provide satisfaction. At most, we could say that the tribunals were providing an outlet for the airing of some of the problems and tensions of development which traditional institutions could no longer handle on their own, but whether they were contributing significantly to their solution is more open to question. The first is an important function to perform but it is surely only when the second function is performed that one can argue that a tribunal is providing an effective social service.

It is opportune here to mention a fifth salient feature of the tribunal system, although it does not occupy a central part in the Phillips Report. We have seen that the native tribunals formed an essential part of the system of native administration. Native administration was in turn based on the system of native reserves, and the native tribunals played an essential part in maintaining that system. The essence of the policy of reserves was that each tribal group in Kenya should be given its own block of land on which it could develop in its own way, and the Native Lands Trust Ordinance of 1930 was a milestone in the development of this policy which received its fullest justification in the Kenya Land Commission. The Native Tribunals Ordinance of 1930, by removing any central judicial control of the tribunals, permitted administrative officers to ensure that their development dovetailed in with the requirements of the reserves, and prevented their decisions, even on appeal, from having any other than local application. The tribunal system could not be used as an institution of national integration, or even to make a start at creating a common law of Kenya. The two policies of reserves and native tribunals were essentially complementary, and it was no accident that after a long period when neither were looked at from a national point of view, the mid-forties saw the production of reports on both matters which urged the need for a national policy and made suggestions as to what it should be and how it should be carried out.[76]

There are some significant indications in the Phillips Report of the close and essential connection between the reserves and the tribunals. Phillips investigated the state of tribunals in the two municipalities of Nairobi and Mombasa, and in the Highlands, and found tribunals very different from those in the reserves. In the two municipalities they were of a tribally mixed composition, functioning very much as magistrate's courts, and applying a mixture of customary laws moving towards a Nairobi or Mombasa customary law.[77] In the Highlands they were much less satisfactory, for while the rural environment was somewhat similar to the reserves, they could not draw upon the same facilities in terms of personnel to man them, law to apply or social system to fit into, from the communities of resident labourers and other African inhabitants of those areas.[78] Designed with the native reserves in mind, the tribunals fitted uneasily or changed their nature completely in any other environment.

It may be said by way of summary that by the mid-forties the general administrative attitude towards the native tribunal system was that its primary purpose was and should remain the law enforcement agency of native administration, but within that context, there was a great need for some overall planning and policy for future development. Attitudes towards the courts having anything to do with the system had not changed, and indeed had hardened. The Ordinance of 1930 had not given the native tribunals exclusive jurisdiction in civil matters over Africans and the Supreme Court had held in *Kahahu* v. *Anderea*[79] that it had jurisdiction in suits and matters relating to rights to land in the reserves, basing itself on the provisions

[76] Phillips, *Report on Native Tribunals 1944*, Nairobi, op. cit.; Sessional Paper No. 8 on *Land Utilization and Settlement, 1945*, Nairobi; Humphrey, *et al.*, *The Kikuyu Lands 1945*, Nairobi.
[77] *Report*, op. cit., paras. 435–54.
[78] *Report*, op. cit., paras. 455–60.
[79] (1938), 18 K.L.R. 5.

of the Kenya Colony Order in Council 1921. An amendment to the Ordinance in 1942[80] had closed this loop-hole by providing that suits in respect of immovable property in the reserves should be commenced only in the native tribunals. The amendment was justified on practical grounds; the procedures and requirements of the Supreme Court did not make it a convenient forum for such cases.[81]

The recommendations of the Phillips Report[82] did not entirely conform to the administrative approach; it accepted that the style and manner of the dispensing of justice in native tribunals were different from a British court system, but the aim should be to foster the evolution of a modernized system of law and justice which would be part of the normal judicial system of the country. Steps should be taken as soon as possible to establish a token link with the Supreme Court and well-educated Africans with a professional legal training should be appointed to the tribunals. If these were the more long-term aims, in the short-term the Report called for the appointment of administrative officers having full-time specialized duties in relation to the tribunals, supervising, hearing appeals, and encouraging and guiding research into the problems of the tribunals and customary law. More specialized and centralized appellate courts should be established and the hierarchy of appeals reduced. Fewer appointees, but with greater security of tenure, should be introduced in the tribunals.

The recommendations as to the appointment of specialized administrative officers were accepted immediately, and Phillips himself was appointed Judicial Adviser in 1945 with the duty of co-ordinating and supervising the development of the tribunals. A Provincial Judicial Adviser was appointed to Nyanza Province in 1948 in view of the high incidence of litigation there to provide more localized and intensive supervision.[83] Other recommendations took longer to digest and when legislation based on them was finally produced, it was found that some had been rejected as unpalatable. One thrust of the recommendations had undoubtedly been directed at loosening the tight administrative control, via supervision, appellate jurisdiction, and appointment and dismissal of members which had existed and been widely used. These recommendations were significantly rejected.

The African Courts Ordinance 1951[84] which repealed and replaced the Native Tribunals Ordinance followed the main outlines of that Ordinance very closely. Provincial Commissioners retained the power to establish the courts, and, together with District Commissioners, retained supervisory

[80] Native Tribunal (Amendment) Ordinance No. 17 of 1942.
[81] Legislative Council, *Debates,* volume 14 (20 August 1942), cols. 272–276 (Attorney-General introducing the Bill on the 2nd Reading).
[82] *Report,* op. cit., chapter 30, 'Summary of Conclusions and Recommendations'. Hailey, op. cit., part I, chapter 2, deals with developments in the tribunals in the late forties.
[83] Barnett, *A Report on Local Courts in East Africa,* 1965, p. 35 (mimeo).
[84] No. 65.

and dismissal powers. In respect of dismissal and suspension powers, the government specifically rejected a suggestion that tribunal members ought to be given due notice and a hearing before the powers were exercised; it was essential that administrative officers should be able to act first and inquire later.[85] The law, practice and procedures to be applied remained the same, but the remedies which the courts could award were spelt out in more detail, as was their pre-trial criminal jurisdiction—the granting of bail, or remanding in custody. Jurisdiction over persons and things, including exclusive jurisdiction over land in the reserves, was unchanged.

The major changes concerned transfer powers, the appellate system, and the appointment and powers of the African Courts Officer and Provincial African Courts Officers. These were administrative officers who were to have general supervision over the African courts. The former could sit in and inspect the records of any African court and exercise all the statutory supervisory powers. All monthly criminal records were to be sent to him rather than the Attorney-General, though this would still act as an automatic appeal. This was done in the interests of centralized supervision and control but it represented a somewhat retrograde step for it substituted an administrator's examination of the records for a lawyer's, an interesting decision in view of Phillips' strictures on the criminal work of the native tribunals. Provincial African Courts Officers had the powers of District Commissioners in relation to courts in the province in which they were stationed, though they could have delegated to them the Provincial Commissioner's appellate powers, which in practice represented a major part of their work for some of them.

The appellate system was reorganized. African Courts of Appeal were, if possible, to be established in each province and they were to be the first appellate court in the hierarchy. From them there was a limited liberty of appeal to a District Commissioner (if there was no such appeal court, there was an unrestricted first appeal to the District Commissioner). From the District Commissioner an aggrieved person could apply to the Provincial Commissioner for a certificate to go to a new final appellate court—the Court of Review, consisting of one person of high potential or actual judicial standing appointed by the Chief Justice, the Chief Native Commissioner, the African Courts Officers, and one African appointed by the Governor. The Provincial Commissioner had extensive powers, from which there was no appeal, to refuse a certificate, or order a case to be reheard. Phillips had recommended that Provincial Commissioners should be removed from the hierarchy of appeals because they did not have sufficient time to give

[85] Legislative Council, *Debates*, volume XLI (21 February 1951), cols. 207–208 (Chief Native Commissioner in 2nd Reading Debate on Native Courts Bill [as it was originally called]).

proper consideration to this side of their work, but the government retained them as such work assisted them in getting to know what was going on in their provinces.[86] The Court of Review had full powers of an appeal court to confirm, vary or reverse a decision or order a re-hearing. The new system was a tentative step in the direction of a centralized case law evolution of customary law and of providing African litigants with a more professional appellate structure. It could only be regarded, however, as tentative because at the same time as providing such a system, the right of appeal beyond the African Court of Appeal was severely restricted. On a par with the reorganized appellate structure may be put the reorganized transfer system. For the first time, a case could be transferred from a subordinate court to an African court as well as vice versa; previously only the latter transfer had been possible.

The basic system and the basic attitudes towards it had thus remained unchanged. Co-ordinated centralized supervision and future planning was now possible but moves towards integration of the African courts with the judicial system appeared to be as far away as ever. Administrative control remained entrenched. The debate in the Legislative Council on the Bill was the first occasion on which African members had had an opportunity to express their views on this type of courts system and they are worth recording here. Those who spoke considered that the African courts system represented a desirable advance on the native tribunals system but seized on two points which were at the core of the administrative position—administrative control of the courts, and the ban on advocates in the courts. They urged that there ought to be a separation of functions in the African courts system and that administrative officers ought not to continue their supervisory and control tasks. Further, that advocates ought to be allowed as of right at the appellate stage and when the courts were applying statute law. These arguments received short shrift from the government. Africans, the African Members of the Legislative Council were told, do not understand or like the separation of powers and advocates should not be allowed in the African courts because they were administering customary law and a person trained in another system could not give them any help.[87] The point about the administration of statute law went unanswered, and indeed on this line of reasoning was not only unanswerable but distinctly embarrassing.

Although the African Courts Ordinance had made few concessions to the judicial point of view, an overview of the whole system of the administration of justice at the beginning of the 1950s would have provided slightly more cause for optimism amongst adherents of that view. Negative evidence

[86] ibid., col. 211.
[87] ibid., col. 210. The African members who spoke were Mr. Mathu (cols. 183–188) and Mr. Ohanga (cols. 195–198).

in the form of fewer circulars and criminal revision cases critical of magistrates' exercise of their judicial powers suggested that they were being exercised with more care and regard for proper procedures. The existence of an African Courts officer, and a Court of Review would go some way towards ensuring that the development of the African courts system and the law that it applied was conducted on orderly lines, and in the general direction suggested by the Phillips Report. Generally, there appeared to be a narrowing of the gap between the two points of view on the function of a judicial system; the judicial accepted that for the time being African courts should continue as part of the administration; the administrative that in time there would be integration of the two systems and the creation of a system basing itself on British conceptions of justice. At this point, the Emergency overtook Kenya, and transformed the situation. At once, there was a regression to older attitudes and views, and clashes between the administrative and judicial viewpoints as to the functions of the courts reappeared.

(v) *The Emergency*

Although the Emergency was an exceptional period and so arguably too much attention should not be paid to it in the context of the development of the administration of justice over the colonial period, some consideration must be given to laws made and views expressed on it for three reasons. First, they indicate the continued conflict of views lying just beneath the surface even this late in the colonial period. Secondly, some of the laws, repealed for the most part in 1960, have since been resurrected by the independent Government of Kenya to deal with the *shifta* in the North Eastern Province,[88] and it seems right that their historical origins should be mentioned. Thirdly, government under emergency powers or their equivalent has become the rule rather than the exception in Kenya, and though this has not affected the system of courts other than in the North Eastern Province and contiguous districts, it is instructive to consider earlier arguments, put forward against a backcloth of an Emergency, for a reorganization of courts and law to deal with such a state of affairs, for the authorities in Kenya are not slow to justify their measures of the present with arguments drawn from their past.

Attention will be concentrated on views expressed but a reference to legislation and case law may first be made. It is not possible to examine here the overwhelming amount of repressive legislation which the administration enacted in pursuance of its powers under the State of Emergency, declared in October 1952. Their total effect was to place the person and property of the inhabitants of the Central Province utterly at the mercy of the administration, and during the early years of the Emergency the admi-

[88] See chapter XI, below.

nistration showed little mercy. Many of these Emergency regulations and rules affected the operation of the legal system, and it is these with which we are especially concerned. The legislation may be classified into two groups; that which in effect ousted the jurisdiction of the courts by extending the public order and disciplinary powers of the administration to deal with conduct or to take action which otherwise would have come before the courts, and that which reduced the procedural and other safeguards surrounding a criminal trial on a serious charge, and took away judicial discretion as to the sentences that could be given.

The second group may be considered briefly. The general effect of a series of emergency regulations was to decrease the safeguards associated with a criminal trial in order to speed up the trials and increase the rate of convictions at the same time as there was an extension of crimes and severe punishments, including in many cases a mandatory death sentence. The two most important regulations were the Emergency (Criminal Trial) Regulations 1952[89] and the Emergency (Emergency Assizes) Regulations 1953.[90] These permitted trials to take place without preliminary inquiry or committal proceedings. The former were directed at magistrates who were required to comply with an order from the Attorney-General dispensing with a preliminary hearing; the latter applied to judges and commissioners of assize trying emergency offences. A special emergency procedure was also introduced by these Regulations. There was an increased power of joinder of charges; the judge was required to make only a shortened and simplified record of the proceedings, and if there was an appeal, it could be dismissed by one judge of the Eastern Africa Court of Appeal. In considering whether an offence should be tried by the emergency or ordinary procedure, the judge had to take into account the circumstances of the offence and its relation to public order generally. The rules of evidence relating to confessions made to police and administrative officers were relaxed, and inducements to confess were held out.

The judiciary could not but accept this assault upon the safeguards of the criminal trial. In addition, it is reasonable to suppose that they shared the horror of the administrators and settlers at what they conceived to be the bestiality of Mau Mau. But within the narrow confines left to them they endeavoured to see that justice was done according to the law, and in one case delivered a broadside at administrative methods during the Emergency and vigorously reasserted the importance of administration according to

[89] Government Notice 1403/1952.
[90] Government Notice 931/1953. For an example of an introduction of a mandatory death sentence, see Emergency (Amendment No. 17) Regulations, Government Notice 760/1953; and of inducements to confess, see Emergency (Amendment No. 8) Regulations, Government Notice 262/1953.

law, and the court's role in ensuring it. In *Githinji & Mwangi* v. *R.*[91] the appellant had been arrested and charged with consorting with a person who had in his possession a home-made gun without lawful authority, and handed over to a screening team for questioning. At his trial he alleged that he had been beaten up and forced to confess, an allegation that was left unanswered. He was nevertheless convicted of the offence which carried a mandatory death sentence. On appeal, the E.A.C.A. considered from the other evidence available that he was clearly guilty but they had this to say of his treatment by the screening team:

> As we have said, in the absence of any rebutting evidence there seems no good reason to doubt that the appellant's allegations of ill-treatment were substantially true . . . What legal powers of detention these teams have or under whose authority they act we do not know . . . It has certainly been made clear to us by the disclaimer made by Mr. Brooks for the Crown/respondent that the Attorney-General is not in any way responsible for screening teams and there are some indications that they are not under the control of the police but are under administrative officers. But whatever be the authority responsible it is difficult for us to believe that these teams could continue to use methods of unlawful violence without the knowledge and condonation of that authority. Such methods are the negation of the rule of law which it is the duty of the courts to uphold and when instances come before the courts of allegations that prisoners have been subjected to unlawful and criminal violence, it is the duty of such courts to insist on the fullest inquiry with a view to their verification or refutation.[92]

The upholding of the conviction was as significant as the criticism of the lower court and the administration, for it suggests that while the judges were prepared if necessary to bark, they felt considerable hesitation over biting during this period.

Despite the judiciary's willingness to move with the times, their efforts were not regarded as adequate by many administrators. The latter's point of view found expression in a judiciously phrased condemnation of British justice as administered by the courts written by Mr. Corfield in the course of his official *Historical Survey of the Origins and Growth of Mau Mau.*[93] After citing two important pre-Emergency cases to illustrate how the administration's task of keeping order amongst the Africans was hampered and made much more difficult by judicial decisions,[94] he launched into a general discussion of the deficiencies of the law relating to public security in Kenya.[95]

[91] (1954), 21 E.A.C.A. 410. [92] At p. 414.

[93] Cmnd. 1030/1960. We would agree with Rosberg and Nottingham (op. cit., p. 378, footnote 60) that this publication is useful as a source of the European myth of 'Mau Mau' rather than for what it claims to be, but as such it contains most interesting insights into European attitudes towards the enforcement of law on Africans. See particularly chapters 5, 8, 12 and 13.

[94] *R.* v. *Gikungu* (1947), 22 K.L.R. 129. Existence of common law right of peaceable meeting in Kenya (Corfield, op. cit., pp. 69–71), *Mabrougi* v. *R.*, 1950 (unreported), incorrectly framed charge of unlawful oath-taking (Corfield pp. 85–7).

[95] op. cit., chapter 13, 'The Law and Public Security', pp. 242–54, from which all the quotations in this paragraph are taken.

He considered that there were two areas of deficiency—first, the lack of legislation which would empower the government to take strong and effective action in the 'twilight period' which occurred between the beginning of a period of disorder and subversion, and the complete breakdown of public order which would permit a State of Emergency to be declared, and drastic action taken.

Secondly, the processes of the law—particularly, as was made clear, the judicial process. The complaint here was that while British justice—the concept of equality before the law—'may well prove to be one of their greatest contributions to the advancement of civilization in this world', the British had imposed this system with too little modification on the subject peoples they had become responsible for, in circumstances which were entirely different from those in which the system had evolved. In doing this had there not been a mistaken tendency to equate judicial procedure with the administration of justice? The basic difference between British and African conceptions of justice was the relationship between the individual and the community—the former being based on the concept of the individual and individual responsibility, the latter being based on the protection of the community with the individual therefore subservient to the community. This conflict posed a great dilemma for those responsible for the administration of justice in colonial territories but 'there are, however, signs that the times are changing and there is a growing body of opinion both lay and judicial which realizes what so many living in Africa have for some time realized—that the processes evolved in the United Kingdom for the conduct of the state and the administration of the law do not function so effectively in the still primitive conditions of so much of Africa'. What was necessary above all was to put an end to 'the failure of the processes of law to obtain a conviction *when the law is broken*' which had 'happened so often in the years before the Emergency'.

Despite his disclaimer of involvement, there is little doubt how Corfield would have solved the dilemma which he saw underlying the administration of justice in Kenya and elsewhere in Africa. Debates in the Legislative Council during the Emergency revealed less inhibitions. One referred to by Corfield may be mentioned here.[96] It arose out of settler disquiet that six months after the Lari incident, not one African had been hanged although 109 had been convicted, of whom 105 had appealed, and 81 awaited the completion of their cases. Demands were made for more speed, and less safeguards in trying emergency cases. One proposal put forward in all seriousness was that laymen's courts, with lawyers kept in the background, should administer

[96] Legislative Council, *Debates*, volume LVII (8 October 1953), cols. 67–111 (debate on a motion to speed up the trial of capital charges by the introduction of special emergency procedures. The motion was carried unanimously).

a species of natural justice, from which there should be no appeal, to those captured by the forces of law and order, so that those forces should have confidence that when they had captured a criminal, he would be quickly brought to justice.[97] There was a general feeling that appeals could well be sacrificed. Only the Acting Solicitor-General and Mr. Ohanga were prepared to speak out against this point of view. The former recited the many inroads already permitted by emergency legislation on the safeguards of criminal trials in order to speed up the administration of justice, but conceded that the appellate system could and would be further streamlined. However, he queried the belief that more speed always meant more justice, and insisted that the principles of justice and the Rule of Law in the strictest form that they had inherited them should be adhered to, otherwise people would cease to respect the law.[98] Mr. Ohanga protested that the Council was being asked to sanction rough justice and thought that it would be out of order to depart from British justice, and get rough justice rather than sure justice.[99]

Debates in the Legislative Council were revealing of attitudes rather than practice; a brief description of the development of the African courts written by the African Courts Officer in 1958 gives us a good indication of the practice at that humble level during the Emergency years.[100] Integration between the African courts and the subordinate courts was increasing owing to the amount of statutory criminal, particularly emergency work, that the African courts did, and increased punishment that they could give. The Emergency had helped to streamline many of the courts particularly in the Central Province where the courts had 'borne a heavy share of the emergency and are today [1958] more closely linked with the police than any other courts in the country with the exception of those in the Nairobi Extra-Provincial District. In some courts of the Central Province all the accused are finger-printed for previous convictions before being brought before the elders'.[101] The general pattern of development was that the African courts had acted more and more to relieve the magistrate's courts of the petty crime connected with the Emergency, though the degree to which this had occurred varied from province to province. The stress on the role of the African courts, in the eyes of the administration as basically criminal courts, had been re-emphasized by the Emergency.

THE SEGREGATED SYSTEM

Our discussion of the development of the administration of justice so far has done no more than indicate that that development was based on the

[97] ibid., cols. 94–95.
[98] ibid., cols. 83–90.
[99] ibid., cols. 81–83.
[100] Carson, 'Further Notes on the African Courts System in Kenya', 10 *J.A.A.* 34.
[101] p. 36.

principle of segregation—different systems of courts or procedure for different races or classes of people in Kenya. In this section we will bring together in summary form the main legislative provisions for this system and consider in a little more detail some of its aspects and implications.

From the date of the first local legislation on courts in 1897, there was a triple system of courts in Kenya. This consisted of, first, the colonial or English system of the High, later the Supreme Court, and the courts of appeal above it, which exercised a general though rather spasmodic supervisory jurisdiction over the whole system, and the subordinate courts, staffed by administrative officers and applying an English-type law and procedure. Second, the Muslim system, primarily at the coast, in the dominions of the Sultan of Zanzibar, staffed by traditional Arab officials applying both Muslim and English-type law. Third, the native tribunal system, staffed by Africans, both traditional court-holders and colonial nominees, and administrative officers, applying primarily customary law, and a 'common sense' approximation of English-type law and procedure. As can be seen there was overlapping of personnel and the law that was applied, and in addition there was overlapping of jurisdictions over Africans, for they were subject to the jurisdiction of the first and third systems, and if they were Muslims residing in the Coastal Strip, they might also be subject to the jurisdiction of the second system. Despite these overlappings, however, the three systems were distinct and during most of the colonial period, there existed pressures to keep them apart.

An important difference in the pressures to keep the systems separate must, however, be noted, as it had a bearing on post-colonial reforms. Separation of the Muslim system from the other two was at the behest of the Muslim community and derived from the Protectorate Agreement of 1895; in so far as the colonial authorities had any policy on this system, it was in the direction of integration into the English system of courts as will be shown below. Separation of the native tribunal system from the rest, on the other hand, was the declared policy of the colonial authorities for the greater part of the colonial period, and it was African politicians who pressed for integration. The Muslim community regarded their own system as separate but equal, and a guarantee of their special status in Kenya; Africans increasingly regarded their own system as an overt indication of the second class justice meted out to them by the colonial authorities, and the English system available to the immigrant communities as another unjustified privilege for the immigrants. The desire to end racial discrimination in Kenya was therefore an important driving force behind reform of the courts in the sixties just as the desire to retain a separate identity and status in Kenya was a driving force behind the Muslim community's policy of obtaining special safeguards in the independence constitution for the continued existence of their courts.

The native tribunal system has been considered in previous parts of this chapter. Consideration will be given here to the Muslim and English court systems.

(i) *The Muslim Courts*

Muslim courts were always classified as subordinate native courts rather than native tribunals.[102] As such, appeal lay from them to the Supreme Court and they were at all times subject to the supervisory jurisdiction of that court. There were, however, several clear differences in the manner in which these powers of appeal and supervision were exercised from that of the ordinary or English subordinate courts. On an appeal from a Kadhi's court, the Supreme Court sat with the Chief Kadhi as an assessor to assist the court in its application of Muslim law. Much of the supervision of the Muslim courts was carried out by the Liwali for the coast who was empowered to inspect all books, records and proceedings of all courts presided over by Liwalis, Kadhis and Mudirs, and render reports on them to the Supreme Court.[103]

The Liwali's and Mudir's courts were courts of general civil and criminal jurisdiction over Arabs, Africans and Baluchis staffed by Arab administrative officials and deriving from similar courts in existence prior to the intrusion of the IBEAC and the establishment of the protectorate. The extent of the jurisdiction of the Liwali's courts was equivalent to the ordinary jurisdiction of a first class subordinate court in the English system in civil matters, and second class in criminal matters and *mutatis mutandis* the Mudir's courts and the third class English subordinate courts, though neither Liwalis nor Mudirs were legally qualified to the extent that their colonial counterparts were. The Kadhi's courts may be regarded as the Muslim courts properly so called, their main jurisdiction being over Muslim Arabs, Africans and Baluchis in matters relating to personal status, marriage and divorce and their composition being of persons who were proficient in Muslim law.

The operation of the courts and the problems arising therefrom in the colonial period have been described in great detail by Anderson,[104] and it is not proposed to try and cover the same ground. However, from the perspective we are looking at these courts, it is relevant to deal briefly with one constant problem—that of the procedure and evidence to be applied in them—for this highlights the conflicting views and policies on the courts as displayed

[102] Courts Ordinance No. 13 of 1907, section 4, and Courts Ordinance No. 16 of 1931, section 2.
[103] Liwali's Courts Ordinance No. 28 of 1921 and Liwali's Courts (Amendment) Ordinance No. 26 of 1923.
[104] Anderson, *Islamic Law in Africa*, London, HMSO, 1954, pp. 81–121.

by the Muslim community and the colonial authorities.[105] As subordinate courts, the Muslim courts were required to follow the ordinary territorial laws on these matters rather than Muslim law. The Muslim judges of these courts, however, did not know the territorial law, and, in the case of the Kadhis in particular, declined as a matter of religious principle to apply a non-Muslim law of evidence to matters as personal to Muslims as family law, where so to apply such a law would produce a decision contrary to the tenets of Muslim law. Hence territorial procedure and evidence law was not applied in these courts.

In the early years of the protectorate, the Supreme Court and the E.A.C.A., whether by accident or design, were tolerant of this departure from the law by the Kadhi's courts in matters of family law, being prepared either to state boldly that in such a matter Muslim rules of evidence should apply,[106] or to interpret important Muslim rules of evidence as rules of substantive family law and thus correctly applicable by the courts.[107] This approach was confirmed as late as 1936,[108] but shortly thereafter two cases, of which one was an E.A.C.A. decision, reversed this approach and held that all Muslim courts were bound by the territorial laws of procedure and evidence.[109] When Anderson investigated the situation in 1950 he found that Liwalis and Mudirs did attempt to follow such rules for they understood English, and handled cases where the rules could more easily be applied, but Kadhis continued to refuse to apply them. He stigmatized the situation as making a farce of the law, and proposed solutions,[110] but nothing was done, and the conflict between the law in the books with its emphasis on integrated procedure and the law as applied with its emphasis on separation continued.

(ii) *The 'English' Courts and Justice for Europeans*

The English colonial courts had a tripartite jurisdiction, over Africans, Asians and Europeans in the sense that the powers and procedures of the courts varied depending upon the race of the person before them. This may be illustrated by reference to the general civil and criminal jurisdiction of the subordinate courts, and the special provisions relating to the criminal trial of Europeans. In civil matters a characteristic feature of jurisdiction from the time of the Courts Ordinance 1907 onwards was that, generally, the monetary limit of jurisdiction over Africans was twice that of jurisdiction over non-Africans. Thus under the Courts Ordinance 1931 the civil juris-

[105] Anderson, op. cit., pp. 99–101.
[106] *Athman bin Mohamed* v. *Ali bin Salim* (1916), 6 E.A.L.R. 91.
[107] *Sheriff Abdulla* v. *Zuena binti Abedi* (1912), 4 E.A.L.R. 86.
[108] *Hussein* v. *Abdulla* (1936), 17 (2) K.L.R. 95.
[109] *Baraka binti Bahmishi* v. *Salim bin Abed Busawadi* (1939), 20 (1) K.L.R. 34; *Said bin Salim* v. *Masood bin Said* (1947), 14 E.A.C.A. 32.
[110] Anderson, op. cit., pp. 100–1.

diction of a second class subordinate court, generally held by a District Commissioner, was up to sh. 1,000 for non-Africans and up to sh. 2,000 for Africans.

The rules as to criminal jurisdiction varied considerably over the years, and tended to give an appearance of greater racial equality as time went on, but such appearances were deceptive, as a reference to procedural provisions will show. The move towards equality in jurisdiction may be illustrated by contrasting provisions of 1914[111] as to imprisonment with those of 1959.[112] In 1914, where the accused was a non-African, a first class subordinate court might sentence him to two years' imprisonment, a second class subordinate court might sentence him to six months' imprisonment, while a third class subordinate court had no jurisdiction over Europeans but might sentence Asians to one month's imprisonment. Where the accused was an African, first and second class courts might pass any sentence authorized by law, and third class courts might sentence him to six months' imprisonment.

By 1959 such overt racial distinction had disappeared from the general provisions as to jurisdiction in the Criminal Procedure Code. A first class subordinate court presided over by a Resident Magistrate might then apparently sentence any accused person to seven years' imprisonment; other first class subordinate courts might pass sentence of up to three years' imprisonment. Second class subordinate courts might pass sentence of up to twelve months, and third class up to three months' imprisonment. The discriminatory nature of criminal jurisdiction still continued however.

First, third class subordinate courts did not yet have jurisdiction over Europeans. Secondly, while subordinate courts were required to follow the Criminal Procedure Code and the Indian Evidence Act in trials of non-Africans, criminal jurisdiction over Africans continued to be governed by a more informal system free from the 'technicalities of procedure', the practical operation of which we have examined in another part of this chapter. Thirdly, the special provisions governing the trial of Europeans, in operation in 1914,[113] remained in full force and effect in 1959,[114] and rendered the general provisions as to jurisdiction somewhat misleading. The general rule was that a European accused of an offence for which the punishment exceeded six months' imprisonment must be tried by the Supreme Court. There were several exceptions to this general rule of which the most important was that a court might try a European for an offence the maximum punishment for which was three years, if the court considered that a punishment of less than six months was adequate, and the accused consented to be so

[111] Criminal Procedure Ordinance, No. 6 of 1914.
[112] Criminal Procedure Code, Cap. 27 Laws of Kenya (1948 edition).
[113] Criminal Procedure Ordinance, part VIII—Trial of Europeans.
[114] Criminal Procedure Code, part VII—Special provisions for trial of Europeans.

tried, or if the evidence did not disclose the greater offence, but disclosed a lesser one the maximum punishment for which was less than six months.

It was not, however, at the subordinate court level that the most notorious discriminatory practice in the administration of justice in Kenya existed. This practice was trial by jury in the Supreme Court, available to Europeans only in respect of offences carrying a maximum punishment of more than six months' imprisonment, and it must be contrasted with trial with the aid of assessors in the Supreme Court for non-Europeans in the relatively few number of major crimes which had to be tried in that court. One or two salient points must be made about the institution of assessors so as to highlight the contrasts between it and the jury.[115]

A panel of three assessors, until recently always of the same race, and often, where relevant, of the same tribe as the accused, is an integral part of the court in a trial with the aid of assessors. The assessors have a twofold function. First, to give their opinion upon the guilt or innocence of the accused. This opinion need not be unanimous, and should be accompanied by a brief statement of reasons given in open court. The opinions, even where unanimous, do not bind the trial judge, though in such a case he should indicate his reasons for not following them. As a general rule, the judge should sum up to the assessors, though failure to do so does not necessarily vitiate the trial. Secondly, assessors act as a kind of expert witness, assisting the judge to evaluate local customs and customary law where relevant. In this guise, they might give evidence of local customs, and be subject to cross-examination as are other expert witnesses, and other evidence on the same customs may be called.

Such positive reasons as have been advanced for the use of assessors seem to be more concerned with the second function than with the first, though in practice the functions are not always clearly distinguishable. The most commonly advanced reason is that assessors, being local people, assist the alien judge to understand the local laws, customs and people, and apply the alien law accordingly.[116] The reasons advanced to justify the first function were couched in more negative terms, as follows: juries give verdicts which are binding, members of the jury must therefore have a certain level of education and intelligence so as to be able to follow the trial and summing up, and thus offer some guarantee that their verdict is based on the evidence

[115] Allot, *Essays in African Law* (London, Butterworths, 1960), pp. 78–81; Gray (1958) 2 *J.A.L.* 5; Jeary (1960) 4 *J.A.L.* 133 and (1961) 5 *J.A.L.* 36, 82; Knox-Mawer (1958) 2 *J.A.L.* (1962) 10 *I.C.L.Q.* 892. See, too, *Vesta* v. *R.* (1934), 1 E.A.C.A. 191; *R.* v. *Mutwiwa* (1935), 2 E.A.C.A. 66; *R.* v. *Ndembera* (1947), 13 E.A.C.A. 65; *Benjimini Panda* v. *R.* (1951), 18 E.A.C.A. 263; *Washington* v. *R.* (1954), 21 E.A.C.A. 392; *Bansel* v. *R.*, [1959] E.A. 813; *R.* v. *Wilken*, [1965] E.A. 286. On the last case see chapter XI, below.

[116] *King Emperor* v. *Tirumal Reddi* (1901), 24 I.L.R. (Mad. 523, quoted with approval in *R.* v. *Mutwiwa*).

and the law and not on their own feelings and prejudices, and they must be in basic agreement with the laws they are required to enforce.[117] There were considered to be few such persons amongst the non-Europeans in Kenya, so the jury could not be used for their trials. The association of laymen with the administration of criminal justice was, however, a valuable feature of British justice, and could be achieved by the use of the assessor who, not being so well educated or intelligent as the European juryman, would give only a non-binding opinion.

Whatever the validity of the reasons given for the use of assessors, the assumptions behind the use of the jury for trials of Europeans in Kenya were always clearly erroneous, and the contrast between the two systems of trial as they operated in practice reveals the essentially discriminatory nature of jury trial. The views and opinions of African and Asian assessors had to be stated and could then be, and often were, dismissed by the trial judge as worthless through bias or prejudice, or as irrelevant for the purpose of ameliorating the rigours of the alien criminal law. But the views and opinions of the European jury did not have to be stated, while their conclusions founded on those views and opinions, often as much as on the evidence and the law, had to be accepted by the judge.

It was in respect of serious offences against Africans that trial by jury operated most frequently to defeat the ends of justice. Because the jury was all European and had to be unanimous, it was difficult to obtain a verdict of guilty when a European was charged with murdering an African, even when the evidence was overwhelming. The colonial authorities had to resort to the expedient of trying a European for a lesser offence as well as for murder in the hope of obtaining a verdict of guilty at least for that lesser offence.[118] For the same reason, not until 1960 did a European convicted of murder suffer the death penalty;[119] previously they had always had their death sentences commuted to life imprisonment by the Governor. On at least one occasion commutation took place before an appeal to the Judicial Committee of the Privy Council was heard.[120] Perversion of justice was not confined to capital charges. Where a European was alleged to have beaten or otherwise severely maltreated an African, he was often charged with an offence which could be dealt with by a subordinate court in order to try and avoid the necessity of a jury trial.[121] While this might ensure a conviction where the evidence warranted it, the punishment was inevitably far less than the offence warranted.

[117] Jeary, op. cit., p. 46.
[118] N. Leys, *Kenya* (London, Hogarth Press, 1924), chapter 7 and Ross, *Kenya from Within*, op. cit., pp. 178, 434.
[119] *Poole* v. *R.*, [1960] E.A. 62 (E.A.C.A.) 644 (J.C.P.C.).
[120] *Wehner* v. *R.* 1905 (unreported).
[121] The most notorious examples of this were *R.* v. *Gray* (1907), 2 E.A.L.R. 40, and *R.* v. *Grogan* (1907), 2 E.A.L.R. 46. Both the accused had been concerned with the

Some of the more outrageous cases drew forth protests in the United Kingdom and official remonstrances from the Government of the day to the colonial authorities in Kenya, but despite the occasional hint as to its possible abolition, the root cause of the unequal application of the criminal law—trial by jury—was allowed to remain. Two questions accordingly present themselves: why was trial by jury introduced into Kenya in the first place, and why was it allowed to remain when the evidence showed that it was leading to miscarriages of justice?

In attempting to answer these questions one possible misconception may be cleared up. Trial by jury did not come to Kenya automatically as part of the common law brought by the English settlers; Kenya was initially a protectorate and therefore a foreign country to which the principles as to the automatic application of the common law did not apply, and the Judicial Committee of the Privy Council in *R.* v. *Staples*,[122] an appeal from Southern Rhodesia, had ruled against the contention that Magna Carta entitled a British subject to a jury trial in a foreign country. Thus jury trial depended initially on legislation introduced by the colonial power. Nor was the position any different after Kenya became a colony; jury trial might then have become part of the common law automatically received in Kenya as a settled colony, but that fact did not preclude alteration of that law by local or imperial legislation.[123] The most likely explanation for its introduction and maintenance was that this was regarded as a cheap concession to the settlers; it would mean a great deal to them, but it would in no way alter the balance of political power between them and the colonial authorities in Kenya.

Whether this was the approach of the colonial authorities or not, the introduction of trial by jury may be criticized on two grounds. First, it paid insufficient attention to the fact that jury trial would inevitably alter the balance of power between the settlers and the legal system, for the settlers would in effect have a veto power over whether they should be convicted and punished for serious offences, particularly against Africans. Secondly, too little attention was paid to the effect such an institution and its workings would have on African opinion and increasingly, though never an object of strife and political tension to the extent that the incidents of land ownership were, trial by jury figured high on the list of discriminatory practices which African politicians were concerned to eliminate.

thrashing of an African before the court-house in Nairobi. They were charged with a minor offence so that the trial could take place before a Magistrate only; they were convicted and appealed on the ground that a magistrate had no jurisdiction to try a lesser offence when the evidence disclosed a greater. The appeal succeeded! The law was changed thereafter.

[122] 1899 (unreported); Palley, op. cit., pp. 54–5.

[123] British Settlements Act 1887, section 2.

It was not until the 1950s, however, that the colonial authorities began to address themselves to the question of the elimination of the segregated legal system which in varying degrees was a characteristic feature of British colonial administration in East and Central Africa. Integration of the courts became official policy, but this was concerned more with the creation of a unified system of appeals to the local High or Supreme Court, and the elimination of the administrator-judge, than with the elimination of racial distinctions in the jurisdiction and procedure of the courts.[124] Even in the former two matters, integration proceeded very slowly in Kenya, and the beginning of the 1960s saw no change in the basic racial divisions of the system and very few changes in the other aspects of the segregated system.

We have concentrated on the subordinate courts and jury trial as being the most obvious examples of the segregated system, but the role and influence of the Supreme Court and the E.A.C.A. in maintaining such a system must be mentioned. These courts were avowedly based on the English High Court and Court of Appeal. Their trappings were those of those courts, wigs, robes and assize courts held on circuit. Their practice and procedure was governed by the Indian codes of procedure but the residual procedural law was English, and the English education and background of the judges ensured that an English flavour was given to the Indian codes. Indeed this phenomenon was not confined to the application of Indian rules of procedure. The reception clause,[125] which imposed a statutory obligation on the courts to apply English law as the residual law in Kenya, was the golden thread which was held to bind the courts to the English hierarchy, and its precedents,[126] and this meant that English cases were referred to and followed even where the basic law was an Indian Act,—the Indian Contract Act, which was part of the law of Kenya until 1960, being the worst example of that tendency.

The judicial insistence on a rigid adherence to English precedents became more pronounced as the colonial period went on. Until about 1930, there were occasions when the Supreme Court appeared to realize that the law to be applied in Kenya need not necessarily be the same as the law which was applied in England, but in the thirties and thereafter the judges became increasingly English orientated. Among the reasons which may be advanced for this are that some of the early judges served for very much longer periods

[124] See chapter IX.
[125] See chapter IX.
[126] *Trimble* v. *Hill* (1879), 5 App. Cas. 342; *Robins* v. *National Trust*, [1927] A.C. 515; *Cooray* v. *R.*, [1933] A.C. 407 (all J.C.P.C. on authority of English decisions in Colonial and Commonwealth courts). *Ageni s/o George* v. *R.*, [1960] E.A. 663 (E.A.C.A. held that it should follow English C.C.A. decision in preference to its own, which it considered was given *per incuriam* because the English decision had not been cited to the court).

in Kenya than did those in the latter half of the colonial period,[127] and had more opportunity and perhaps more inclination to think in terms of Kenyan law rather than the law applied in Kenya, and that after 1930 the Supreme Court was completely cut off from contact with civil litigation amongst Africans and customary law, so that there was no need to try and understand local laws and customs. In addition, the influence of the two supra-national courts of appeal, the E.A.C.A. and the Judicial Committee of the Privy Council, must be noted, particularly the latter court, for throughout the whole of the colonial period, it conceived its duty as being the maintenance of the unity of the common law throughout the Empire, and this meant, more often than not, the extension of the rules of the English common law throughout the Empire. Thus the jurisprudence of the superior courts in Kenya reinforced the legislation which provided for the segregated system, prevented the development of a common law of Kenya via the decisions of the courts, and emphasized that the superior courts catered primarily for the immigrant communities who regarded English law as their law.[128]

CONCLUSION

It was clear by 1960 that the basic problem of developing a legal system for the whole country had not been satisfactorily solved. The conflict between indigenous and colonial systems of justice had been resolved in favour of the latter and such a decision was irreversible, but the other two themes of development, though still almost wholly institutionalized in the courts' system, were coming under increasing attack from African politicians and appeared to be more and more indefensible in the new political climate which was unfolding in Kenya. Some kind of summing up, however, particularly on the clash between the administrative and judicial approaches

[127] Hamilton, the first C.J., served in one capacity or another from 1897 to 1920. Barth, the second C.J., from 1903 to 1934. The careers of the other C.J.s offer an interesting contrast. Sheridan C.J., from 1934–46, had served previously in Nyasaland (1908–13), Kenya (1913–29) both as R.M. and puisne judge, Tanganyika (1929–34). Nihill C.J., from 1946–50, had served previously in Hong Kong (1921–7), Baghdad (1927-33), Uganda (1934–6), British Guiana (1936–8), Ceylon (1938–46). He was President of the E.A.C.A. from 1950 to 1955. Hearne C.J., from 1951–4, had served previously in Uganda (1916–33), Tanganyika (1933–6), Ceylon (1936–45), Jamaica (1945–51). He later became J.A. and Acting President of the West African Court of Appeal (1954–5, 1958). O'Connor C.J., from 1954–7, had served previously in India (Indian Army, 1915–18, Government of India, 1920–22), Mesopotamia (1919), and has practised at the bar in London and Singapore (1924–41), served in Nyasaland (1944–5), Malaya (1946–8), Kenya (A.-G., 1948–51), Jamaica (1951–4). He was President of the E.A.C.A. (1957–61). Sinclair C.J., from 1957–62, was called to the bar in New Zealand, and served previously in Nigeria (1931–8), Northern Rhodesia (1938), Tanganyika (1946–53), Nyasaland (1953–5).

[128] For a discussion of the authority of English decisions in other countries in the Commonwealth, see Allott, op. cit., chapter 2, and 12 *J.A.L.* 3. Roberts-Wray, op. cit., chapter 11, pp. 563–79, Elias, 18 M.L.R. 356. Superior courts in East Africa generally made very little use of the proviso to the reception clause to fashion a local variant of the common law. On occasions they had to be corrected in this by the J.C.P.C.

is relevant both because this dispute went to the heart of the problem of developing a new legal system, and because, with the advantage of hindsight, we can now see that it was the one issue out of the three which has continued to be important in the era of African government in Kenya.

The fairest summing up that can be made of both points of view is that judges and administrators were victims of their own propaganda. Both put forward idealized pictures of their work which failed to take account of the defects and conflicts inherent in it, and both points of view were tinged in practice and discussion with a hostility for the other side which exaggerated their weak points. Administrators were more eclectic than they were prepared to admit. For instance, they relied on British conceptions of justice to alter the composition, power and functions of traditional institutions, until they were no longer recognizable as such and had become wholly a part of the colonial system, yet relied on African conceptions of justice, or what they conceived them to be, to justify their own departures from that British conception of justice espoused by the judiciary.

The judiciary, on the other hand, were less humane and impartial than they thought. The courts, no less than the administration, were part of the new colonial order, and had to and were prepared to support that order when it was essential to do so. The British system of justice as operated in the Supreme Court was not geared to the needs and requirements of the African population. An African on trial for a serious offence would find himself before a court in which proceedings were conducted both in a manner and in a language which he did not understand. Facilities for interpretation were often inadequate. Defence counsel would be assigned on a capital charge but not otherwise.[129] The judge could dismiss as irrelevant or unimportant such customs as the accused had followed in doing what he did. However such a trial might have appeared in the eyes of the English-trained lawyer, and not all of them were happy with such a system, it would not be unfair to stigmatize it as being just as productive of injustice and hardship as the more rough and ready methods of the administrative officer.

In sum, both points of view suffered from the fatal defect that they represented what the colonial authorities thought was best for the African, and only when African opinion coincided with the prevailing viewpoint was much attention paid to it. Towards the end of this period, this defect and the system which had resulted from it were beginning to be appreciated by some colonial officials, and the trenchantly expressed viewpoint of one such official who had helped operate the system, made in 1956 may stand as a fitting commentary on sixty years of colonial justice. 'I am not sure that the average African [in Kenya] has quite the same confidence that British

[129] There is no statutory basis for legal aid for the poor accused, and the courts would only assign a lawyer in a capital charge.

justice is there in order—not only to punish him—but to protect him. He is more likely to regard the whole system just as another government department that is there to join in the general power of coercion. This may be to some extent because from the start the white population has been in a position of economic and social superiority and as a result expected this superiority to extend into the field of law as well . . . What we should try to do in Kenya with regard to the administration of justice generally is to get away from the view that may be prevalent in certain circles that you cannot put the African into the legal system except in one place, that is the dock.'[130]

In the final decade of this period Africans were able to contribute to, and comment on, the long-standing debate on the development of the legal system via the African members of the Legislative Council. As we have seen, their views approximated to that of the judiciary, though they were by no means hostile to the work of the administrative officers in developing the African courts. By 1960, when Africans were increasingly in a position to influence policy as Ministers, the pressures to integrate the African courts with the subordinate courts and move away from the racial divisions in the system were growing, but this did not conclude the question of what sort of unified system it was going to be—administrative or judicial? Perhaps the key to the future development of the administration of justice lay in the fact that the Africans in broadly supporting the judicial point of view had done so as members opposing the Government. As such, it was natural to be critical of government institutions and policies. But when members of the opposition inherit those institutions and realize the power that they confer, they tend to look at them afresh and perceive the advantages of using them for governmental purposes, as well as the great difficulty of creating a completely new system. On this analysis, the problem of which approach the legal system would in future aim towards depended, to a large extent, on whether an African government would continue the policies and attitudes of its predecessor on finding them politically and administratively advantageous, or whether it would endeavour to bring about a complete separation of the judicial from the administrative system and introduce throughout the system all the safeguards and procedures generally associated with the British conception of justice which Africans had called for when in opposition.

[130] Sir Barclay Nihill, at Africa Bureau Conference on Kenya and Britain, May 1956, London (mimeo).

PART II

The Era of Independent Government

CHAPTER V

Transition and Interlude: from Lancaster House to The Republic

INTRODUCTION

In 1960 at the London Conference, the official aim was to direct progress towards a constitution based on the principles of the Westminster parliamentary system which at the same time incorporated special provisions for the protection of minorities.[1] The first of these purposes was generally accepted, without debate, though not unanimously, but there was great controversy about the principle and the form of the second. The 1960 Conference was followed by long and protracted negotiations in Nairobi, followed by another bitter and marathon Lancaster House Conference in 1962,[2] where the outlines of the independence Constitution were drawn up. The details of the proposals were worked out in numerous meetings in Nairobi over a period of several months among the leaders of the various political parties, though the personal intervention of the Colonial Secretary was necessary to resolve certain deadlocks. During this period Kenya was governed under the 1960 Constitution, where the Governor retained ultimate authority, though in 1962 there was an important delegation of it to the Council of Ministers, where, except for the portfolios of Legal Affairs and Defence, the membership was divided between leaders of the Kenya African Democratic Union and the Kenya African National Union in the form of a coalition government. Due to the rivalry between the two parties and the need to give each equal representation and status in the coalition government, Mr. Kenyatta and Mr. Ngala were given comparable seniority and Kenya therefore missed the stage of a Chief Ministership, which is conventionally the stage before full internal self-government. As a result of the 1962 Conference and the subsequent meetings in Nairobi, Kenya was granted internal self-government on 1 June 1963.

The self-government Constitution was extremely important;[3] it was the product of vigorous bargaining on various sides and, with minor modifications, formed the basis of the independence Constitution. Its outstanding characteristics were a form of Westminster government and an extensive system of regionalism. As to the first, the office of the Prime Minister, to be appointed to by the Governor from amongst the members of the House of

[1] Cmnd. 960. [2] Cmnd. 1700. [3] Statutory Instrument 791/1963.

Representatives most likely to command the support of the majority, was established for the first time for Kenya. The Governor was to act on the advice of the Cabinet, but the Constitution fell short of a full Westminster system in that the Colonial Office retained important powers: the Governor, acting under its instructions in these matters continued to be responsible for defence, external affairs and internal security, in respect of which he had extensive legislative and executive competence;[4] the Governor's veto over legislation was retained and there remained limited powers of disallowance.[5] The name and the form of the legislature was changed—it was now called the Central Legislature (to be renamed Parliament at independence), consisting of the National Assembly and the Queen (replacing the former reference to the Governor). The National Assembly became bicameral, with the House of Representatives as the lower house, and the Senate as the upper house.

The other characteristic of the Constitution, regionalism, referred to as *majimbo*,[6] was the division of the country into seven regions, each with its own legislative and executive powers.[7] In the performance of certain important functions, the centre could act only with the approval of the Regions. Thus the unitary character of Kenya's government, which had persisted throughout its colonial history, was discarded towards its end. The introduction of this Constitution was preceded by a general election to the two legislative houses—for the first time based on universal adult suffrage without a communal franchise—in which KANU was victorious and won the right to form the Government. Further talks in Nairobi and another conference in London in September were necessary before the constitutional arrangements for the granting of independence were finalized.[8] Apart from some dilution of regional powers, important matters like citizenship provisions, the amendment procedure, and the decision to declare Kenya a dominion rather than a republic at independence, were concluded. On 12 December 1963, Kenya became independent.

TRANSFER OF POWER

There were two important instruments in the transfer of sovereignty from Britain. First, the Kenya Independence Act 1963, was passed by the British Parliament, which renounced Britain's rights of government and legislation in Kenya and repealed all the limitations on the competence of Kenya's

[4] Section 68.
[5] Section 49.
[6] *Majimbo* is a Swahili word which means an 'administrative unit' or 'region', and is generally used to refer to those provisions of the Constitution which established the regional structure.
[7] See chapter 5 of the Self-government Constitution.
[8] Cmnd. 2156.

legislature. As we have seen in earlier chapters, the marks of dependency of a colony are the ability of the imperial parliament and the Crown to legislate directly for it and the limitations of its own legislature to pass laws either with extra-territorial effect or inconsistent with imperial legislation applicable to the colony. In addition, the Crown has the power of veto and disallowance; and the local executive has to perform its functions in accordance with Royal Instructions. Legally, as has been said, 'to give independence means no more or less than erasing marks of dependence'.[9] The Independence Act removed the marks of dependence. The first section provides that on or after 12 December 1963 Her Majesty's Government in the United Kingdom shall have no responsibility for the Government of Kenya and the second that no Act of Parliament of the United Kingdom passed on or after independence shall extend or be deemed to extend to Kenya. The more specific limitations on Kenya's legislature were removed by the provisions of the First Schedule, which disapplied the Colonial Laws Validity Act 1865 to legislation passed in Kenya after independence and provided that no such legislation shall be void or inoperative on the ground of repugnancy to the law of England, including the Independence Act itself. There was, however, one exception to the last provision. As we shall see, the independence Constitution was highly entrenched through a complex procedure for its amendment, and in its unqualified form, the last mentioned provision of the Schedule might be interpreted to remove the entrenchment. It was therefore made clear that the Act did not confer on the Kenya legislature any power to repeal, amend or modify the constitutional provisions—defined as the Act and the Independence Order in Council—otherwise than in such manner as may be provided for in those provisions. Finally, the legislature of Kenya was given full power to make laws having extra-territorial operation (the word 'full' suggesting that the legislature in Kenya always had some such power). No mention was made of the royal powers of disallowance, but since these were generally provided for in Orders in Council or other prerogative instruments, they were indirectly dealt with in the Order in Council, by their total omission. Most of the external and internal limitations on Kenya's sovereignty were therefore removed by the Act, but before we go on to discuss the second instrument for the transfer of power, it is interesting to observe that the protectorate over the Coastal Strip was included within the territory of Kenya which was given independence. Normally a British possession outside Her Majesty's dominions is annexed as a colony just before independence is given, so that it can become a dominion within the Commonwealth.[10] In relation to the Coastal Strip, there appears to have been no

[9] Roberts-Wray in Anderson (ed.), *Changing Law in Developing Countries* (London, Allen and Unwin 1963), p. 45.
[10] ibid., p. 58.

explicit act of annexation, unless it is deemed to have been done somewhat indirectly through the Independence Act or as a result of the agreements between the Sultan of Zanzibar, the British and the Kenya Governments, which are discussed later. If so, it can be said that the Coastal Strip Protectorate was annexed and made a part of the Colony of Kenya before independence, and the two parts emerged as a unified dominion on 12 December 1963.

The other constitutional instrument was the Independence Order in Council,[11] which provided for transitional matters, including the continuance in force of the existing laws, but whose Second Schedule was its most important part—it contained the Constitution for the independent Kenya. It would have been possible for Parliament to have enacted the Constitution either in the Independence Act or as separate legislation, as was indeed done in relation to the older members of the Commonwealth. The procedure for Kenya, however, was in keeping with the practice for other parts of former British Africa. The constitutions of African dependencies were generally provided through prerogative instruments and it was therefore not unnatural or illogical that the independence Constitution should also be provided likewise. Professor de Smith has suggested two further reasons for enacting the constitution through an Order—the independence constitution is generally the product of delicate compromises reached through long negotiations, which might be upset if it had to go through the legislative processes of the British Parliament, and normally, the final stages of independence are hurried, leaving insufficient parliamentary time for a long and detailed Bill.[12]

The independence Constitution was long, detailed and complex. As indicated above, it was based on two important principles—parliamentary government and minority protection. To an extent, the two principles are inconsistent, for the parliamentary system is generally unitary, highly centralized and powerful. In Kenya, therefore, the parliamentary system was modified by the provisions designed to protect minorities. The powers of the state, for example, were divided among a central and regional governments. The essentials of the parliamentary system were, however, maintained in relation to the Central Government. The Governor-General appointed as Prime Minister a member of the lower house who in his opinion was likely to command the support of a majority of its members; the rest of the Cabinet was appointed on the advice of the Prime Minister. Though the executive power was vested in the Queen and delegated to the Governor-General, he was to exercise it according to the advice of the Cabinet. The Cabinet was collectively responsible to both houses of the legislature, and

[11] Statutory Instrument 1968/1963.
[12] 20 M.L.R. (1957) 355–6.

could be removed by the lower house through a vote of no confidence. Conversely, the Prime Minister could ask the Governor-General to dissolve the lower house. These parliamentary conventions were incorporated into the Constitution through express provisions, defining the relationship between the Governor-General and the Cabinet in a detailed and precise manner.

The provisions of the Constitution which had aroused the deepest controversy and fundamentally affected its scheme were those for minority protection.[13] To understand the Constitution, it is necessary to deal briefly with the history of minority fears and agitation. We have already seen how up to the 1960 Conference, constitutional developments were determined by racial conflicts. Once it was obvious, however, as it was after the Conference, that Africans were going to gain steadily in power, heat was taken out of interracial politics. Though a group of Europeans fought a rearguard action, the Asians and the Europeans confined their activity to protecting their specific interests, rather than attempting to claim a share in political power. For the most part the Europeans concentrated their efforts on establishing the principles of compensation for white farmers and civil servants who wanted to leave Kenya, and of the security of the property of those who might wish to stay on. The Asians had similar interests to protect, though as they were a much larger and less mobile community, they were more concerned to establish their right to reside and work in the country in favourable conditions. The issues of the Asians and the Europeans, though they continued occasionally to generate heat, were henceforth peripheral to the main constitutional developments.

The last stages of independence, however, were complicated by disputes among the indigenous people. There arose two secessionist movements, of Somalis in the North Frontier District and of Arabs in the Coastal Strip. The Arabs live mainly in the Coastal Strip. Among them were many landowners, with African labourers living on their land as squatters. They are Muslims, a fact which coloured their view of life and their cultural traditions. The British had treated them as a separate community, initially with rights superior to the Africans, and the impression grew that Arabs were constantly trying to curry favour with the British, and were always willing to support them. Thus the Arabs, as much as the Europeans or the Asians, stood outside, and often in hostility to, the stream of African nationalism.[14]

The Somali situation is even more complex. They live in the North Frontier Province (formerly known as the Northern Frontier District—

[13] See, generally, Y. P. Ghai, 'Independence and Safeguards in Kenya', in 3 *East African Law Journal* (1967), pp. 177–217.

[14] See the *Report of the Commissioner on the Kenya Coastal Strip,* Cmnd. 1585, for a discussion of Arab-African relations.

NFD), an area which was never fully integrated into the rest of Kenya. It was an area difficult to administer, due to tribal fighting over grazing land, remoteness from the capital, bad communications, and the nomadic habits of the people. The administration felt that the ordinary laws and techniques were not suitable; and no development of local institutions was undertaken. Entry into, and movement within, the province were restricted, under the Outlying Districts Act, 1902. The result of this insulation was that the major African parties failed to penetrate the area. The majority of the inhabitants, Somali or allied groups, were keenly aware of their differences from the Africans; apart from the racial, there were also the cultural and religious differences, the Somalis being Muslims. Another factor which militated against their integration into the political system of Kenya was the presence of the State of Somalia across the frontier, with which they shared many characteristics and a strong feeling of kinship.[15]

Among the Africans in the south, a serious split occurred between the smaller, mainly pastoral and relatively backward tribes, on the one hand, and the bigger, largely cultivating, progressive and urbanized tribes, Kikuyu, Luo and Kamba, on the other. The history of tribal animosities goes back a long time, and it has been argued that the British policy had the effect of accentuating these.[16] While there was no thoroughgoing system of indirect rule, the tribe was generally the unit of administration, and inter-tribal contacts were minimal. Even when African political activity spread through the greater part of the country, the emergence of a common nationalism was hindered by restrictions on movement and communication and of the formation of other than district political parties. Attempts were, however, made by the leaders to preserve a common policy, but in 1957 the first cracks appeared in their ranks, with the election of African members for the first time to the Legislative Council. At that time there were prohibitions on colony-wide political parties, and so the African elected members were not under the discipline of a national party and were unable to accept the leadership of one of themselves.[17] At the important 1960 Lancaster House Conference, they were able to patch up their incipient disunity, but disintegration soon followed, paradoxically with the lifting of the ban on nation-wide organizations. With the ban lifted, attempts were made to create a national party, and a series of meetings were held, culminating in the formation of the Kenya African National Union (KANU), which was envisaged as a mass, radical party. Partly this projected policy of radicalism, and partly

[15] See the *Report of the North Frontier District Commission*, Cmnd. 1900; A. A. Castagno, 'The Somali–Kenya Controversy', 2 *Journal of Modern African Studies*, p. 165.

[16] T. Mboya, *Freedom and After*, op. cit., p. 75, and O. Odinga, *Not Yet Uhuru*, op. cit., p. 146.

[17] An interesting account of the problems of unity in this period appears in Odinga, op. cit., pp. 146–71.

the fact that most, though by no means all, of the leaders came from the two big tribes, the Kikuyu and the Luo, aroused the apprehensions of the smaller, more rural and conservative tribes, who began to form their own associations, the chief of them being the Kenya African People's Party, the Kalenjin Political Alliance, the Masai United Front, the Coast People's Union, and the Somali National Association. A further step in the polarization of politics was taken when these minority parties merged to increase their effectiveness. From their union was born the Kenya African Democratic Union (KADU), which claimed to speak for the smaller, basically rural, tradition bound tribes, and one of the causes of whose strength was the mutual fear of the Kikuyu-Luo domination.[18]

The situation of extreme disunity in which Kenya found herself in 1963 was not without parallel in colonial experience elsewhere. It has been a common feature of decolonization that the imminence of independence is accompanied by the emergence of ethnic or minority problems. In the scramble for colonies, the European powers demarcated the boundaries of their overseas possessions with scant respect for the facts of tribal distribution of population, with the result that a colony would be proclaimed over an area with different, often warring tribes; and equally, one particular tribe would find itself divided between two or more colonies. The encouragement given to immigration from other continents, notably Europe and Asia, created further complications. As long as the colonial power remains in control, racial and tribal conflicts are resolved within a constitutional framework in which the imperial power acts as the often partial umpire, and the worst forms of tyranny of one group over another are avoided. Indeed, the very presence of foreign domination provides a motive for co-operation among the different groups. With the prospect of independence, the racial or tribal conflicts, or as more often, the potential conflicts, become obvious; competition for political power, with its many rewards, becomes acute; and the minority groups, aware of their vulnerability and remoteness from power in unitary-type constitutions, start to agitate for safeguards. These safeguards range from an outright secession, through federalism, to Bills of Rights and the insulation of certain sensitive areas of administration from political control.[19] The minorities get a patient, indeed an encouraging, hearing from the colonial power. Their intransigence is increased by the fact that the colonial power often makes the acceptance of the constitution by them a pre-condition of independence. This leads to exaggerated claims, many of which are conceded. A complicated constitution results, but the sanctioning authority of the imperial power has disappeared.

[18] See Bennett and Rosberg, op. cit., chapter 2.

[19] For a useful account of the various forms of safeguards, see S. A. de Smith, *The New Commonwealth and its Constitutions* (London, Stevens and Sons, 1964), chapter 4.

The agitation for safeguards in Kenya was of two kinds, first, for safeguards outside the constitutional framework. This could have been achieved in two ways: secession, or the involvement of outside powers in an international system of minority guarantees. The other was for safeguards within the Constitution. The non-African minorities were mainly occupied with the first of these, the Africans were content with the second, if they could be sure that they would wield substantial powers in their own tribal or regional areas and surrender as little as possible to a Kikuyu-Luo dominated central government. We shall first consider the attempts to secure safeguards outside the constitutional framework.

SAFEGUARDS OUTSIDE THE CONSTITUTION

The most important claims in this respect were for secession, made by the Somalis and the Arabs. Both the claims were resisted by the African parties, and were the subject of study by independent commissions.

(a) *The Somali Demands for Secession*

At all the constitutional conferences leading to independence, the Somalis refused to participate in the discussions on the future framework of government, insisting that nothing less than secession, with eventual merger with the Republic of Somalia, would satisfy them. The British Government refused to commit itself for a long time, and more as a means of postponing a decision than anything else, announced at the 1962 London Conference that 'an investigation should be undertaken in order to ascertain public opinion in the area regarding its future'. No change in the status or arrangement of the NFD would be made pending the findings of the commission, and a decision on the findings would be taken before an independence constitution for Kenya was brought into operation.[20] The commission was duly appointed, and after touring the NFD and talking with the people there and in Nairobi, it issued its report in December 1962.[21] As the commission itself observed, it was purely fact finding and was not required to make any recommendations as to the future government of the region. Six districts were involved in the enquiry: Garissa, Wajir, Mandera, Moyale, Marsabit and Isiolo. The commission found basically two kinds of opinion: the Kenya opinion which favoured remaining within Kenya, and the Somali opinion, which favoured secession. After discussing in detail the support for each opinion district by district, the commission came to the following conclusions. It found opinion within a tribe was often unanimous, and as

[20] Cmnd. 1700, p. 11. See generally on this problem, J. Drysdale, *The Somali Dispute* (London and Dunmow, Pall Mall Press, 1964); I. M. Lewis, *The Modern History of Somaliland* (London, Weidenfeld and Nicolson, 1965); and Castagno, op. cit., p. 178.
[21] Cmnd. 1900.

tribes by and large occupy separate areas, it was possible to achieve unanimity of opinion within particular areas. Thus the Somali opinion areas 'extend from the Somali frontier to the Somali-Galla Line and beyond, to include the grazing lands of the Adjuran'. The areas of Kenya opinion were the 'grazing lands of the Gabbra, in the Marsabit District, of the non-Moslem Boran in Moyale District, and the Riverine Tribes on the banks of the Tana in the Garissa District'. There were some areas of mixed opinion; these comprised 'Moyale township, and the grazing areas of the Sakuye to the east as far as the Boran-Adjuran Line, Marsabit Township, Isiolo District, Garissa Township, and the grazing area of the Orma south and west of the Tana River'. The Gelubba the commission found to lack 'a coherent opinion'. The Rendile had expressed themselves in favour of secession, but the commission doubted whether this represented their true opinion 'since they have more in common with . . . the Samburu and the Masai'.

The commission noted that 'opinions were influenced by religion, ethnic affiliation and way of life', and the 'division of opinion almost exactly corresponds to the division between Moslem and non-Moslem'. In sum, the people favouring the secession were in a very clear majority, and also occupied the largest area of land. While the findings led the Somalis to believe that secession was about to be granted, and though the British press urged that a settlement of the dispute must be made before independence, recommending a referendum under the UN,[22] the British Government refused to take any decision for a long time, and then later argued that the matter was one to be settled by the Governments of Somalia and Kenya, and indeed tripartite talks were held in Rome (the reason for the venue would seem to be that by this time the Somalia Republic had broken off diplomatic relations with Britain) which, predictably enough, resulted in a deadlock. The issue was more or less closed, as far as the British and Kenya Governments were concerned, when the Colonial Secretary announced in Nairobi in March 1963 that a new Region was to be established, called the North-Eastern Region, to consist of predominantly Somali areas.[23] The rest of the North Frontier District had already been excised to form part of the Eastern Region, which had followed the recommendation of the Regional Boundaries

[22] *The Times*, 9 March 1963; *Observer*, 10 March 1963.

[23] He said, 'We are not so foolish as to imagine that the creation of a seventh region will be hailed as providing complete satisfaction, but I do trust that it will be received by the Somali as an expression of sincere goodwill not only from the British, but also from the Kenya Government . . . We, not only the British Government, but both parties here in Kenya, understand the desire of Somali people to express their own identities particularly when you get people of one race living in a country with people of another. But Kenya is a country which depends for its future on being able to recognize people of different races and prove it is capable of providing a home where people of different races can live honourably and amicably together.' *The Times*, 9 March 1963.

Commission.[24] Thus the Marsabit District, the Western part of the Moyale District, and most of the Isiolo District had been included in the Eastern Region.

This did not satisfy the Somali; they boycotted the general elections of March 1963, though they did contest the re-election in October of the same year. The agitation for secession continued and terrorist activity was mounted. At independence, the Kenya Government was given wide emergency powers over the North-Eastern Region, for an indefinite length of time;[25] the Government extended these emergency powers to the Districts of Marsabit, Isiolo, Tana River and Lamu by a constitutional amendment in 1966,[26] and has continued to govern these areas through emergency regulations.[27]

(b) *The Arab Claims for Autonomy for the Coastal Strip*

As we have seen, the Strip had been leased by the Sultan of Zanzibar to the British Government in 1895, which had the rights of administration over it, in return for an annual payment. The future of the 1895 Agreement had to be decided before independence, and the coastal Arabs, led by the Mwambao United Front, began to agitate for some form of autonomy for the Strip. The discussion of the issue was excluded at the 1960 conference, but the agitation continued, and as a result a decision to hold an enquiry was announced, and soon afterwards Sir James Robertson, former Governor-General of Nigeria, was appointed to 'report to the Sultan of Zanzibar and Her Majesty's Government jointly on the changes which are considered to be advisable in the 1895 Agreement relating to the Coastal Strip of Kenya, as a result of the course of constitutional development in East Africa'.[28]

The Commissioner found that the issue of autonomy was complicated by the fact that Mombasa is Kenya's chief port, serves as Uganda's main port, and handles sizeable amounts of Tanzania's and the Congo's exports and imports. Moreover, the Strip had always been administered as an integral part of Kenya, the boundary between the Colony and the Protectorate not having been 'followed or observed in any administrative context by the Government or local authorities'. The Sultan's sovereignty was purely nominal, 'the only manifestation of it on the coast of Kenya is his flag, which flies everywhere in the Strip . . .' However, the sovereignty, though 'nebulous' was 'emotionally . . . a factor that cannot be lightly dismissed'.

The autonomists were not agreed among themselves as to the form auto-

[24] Cmd. 1899.
[25] Section 19, S. I. 1968 of 1963. Now Constitution section 127.
[26] Act 16 of 1966.
[27] See chapter XI. On 28 October 1967 an agreement was reached between the Governments of Kenya and Somalia to stop hostile activity and to allow for the normalization of conditions and regulations—*Memorandum of Understanding*. In February 1969 the Kenya Government announced its intention to lift the emergency regulations.
[28] Cmnd. 1585 (Report of the Commissioner).

nomy should take, and it was for this reason that the Commissioner felt unable to recommend a referendum to decide the future: 'should the autonomists win, no clear cut answer would be obtained'. After considering and rejecting various possible solutions, like the independence of the Strip, or its independence after the addition to it of part of its hinterland, or federation or other association with Zanzibar, or a Monaco-type status for Mombasa, the Commissioner recommended that the Strip should be administratively integrated with Kenya just before Kenya became self-governing and that the 1895 Agreement be abrogated. Whether the Kenya Government would then negotiate a similar agreement with the Sultan or the Sultan would make a final renunciation of his sovereignty, was a matter left for future discussion. This recommendation was subject to two qualifications.

First, suitable financial provisions ought to be made for the Sultan and the Zanzibar Government. Secondly, certain safeguards should be entrenched in Kenya's Constitution to 'meet the legitimate and very real anxieties of the Coastal minorities'. He made a number of suggestions for this purpose, including guarantees of religious freedom in a Bill of Rights. The *sheria*—the law dealing with marriage, divorce, alimony, trusts and inheritance—should be retained, and with it the system of courts—the Khadi's courts—hitherto used for its enforcement. He also made proposals to retain the system of Arab administrative officers—Liwalis and Mudirs—on the coast. He made elaborate recommendations about land; he found that 'one of the greatest fears of the Coastal minorities is that unless their land titles are acknowledged and preserved their lands will be invaded and taken from them by squatters and invaders from upcountry'. To allay these fears, he suggested the establishment of a Coast Land Board, with advisory and executive functions in relation to disputes about land, its disposal and transfer, etc., which would be entrenched in the Constitution. Finally, he made recommendations to safeguard Arab education and particularly the teaching of Arabic script. He went on to say that if the ideas about regionalism which were then being discussed were adopted, the solution to the coastal problem might well be found within such a regional devolution of powers.

The report formed the basis of discussions in London in 1962 at the time of the Kenya Constitutional Conference, between delegates from Zanzibar, Kenya and the British Government, with an observer from Uganda. The representatives of the Sultan said that they were not concerned with his abstract juridical rights, and would be satisfied if he could be assured that the institutions and way of life of his subjects would be safeguarded along the lines set out in the report. As the details of the future Kenya Constitution had yet to be finalized (the principle of regionalism had, however, been accepted), it was decided that further talks should be held when the Constitution had been drafted to see if the Sultan was then satisfied with the safeguards. The Mwambao United Front did not subscribe to this agreement.[29] When the details of the Constitution had been settled after talks in Kenya, the Colonial Secretary visited Zanzibar, when the Sultan noted with satisfaction the assurance about protection of Muslim law and religion and the rights of the minorities, and accordingly agreed that after the introduction of the self-governing Constitution, the Coastal Strip would continue to be administered as part of Kenya. It was decided that further talks would be held before independence.[30] These were held in October 1963, when Kenya's independence Constitution was being finalized. An agreement was reached on the merger of the Strip with Kenya and the 1895 Agreement was abrogated, the Sultan renouncing his sovereignty. To do this, an Agreement was made between the Government of the United Kingdom, His Highness the Sultan of Zanzibar, the Government of Kenya and the Government of Zanzibar. The Agreement recited an exchange of letters between the Prime Ministers of Kenya and Zanzibar, which contain undertakings from Kenya to Zanzibar in relation to the treatment of the Sultan's former subjects.[31]

These related to the safeguards which had been recommended in the Commissioner's report—religion, *sheria*, education—but did not include a Coastal Land Board, though it was stipulated that the freehold titles to land in the Coast that were registered would be recognized at all times and that steps would be taken to ensure the continuation of the procedure for the registration of new freehold titles. Some of these rights were also guaranteed in the Constitution and will be discussed below.

To complete the picture, it should be mentioned that after it had been decided that Kenya should be divided into semi-autonomous Regions, a Regional Boundaries Commission was appointed to implement the decision and placed the Strip in the Coast Region, which included the former Coast Province and, initially, parts of the NFD, but these were later excised to form a separate North-Eastern Region. Thus, even in the Coast Region, the Arabs remain a minority.[32]

(c) *European and Masai Demands*

Two other attempts to seek solutions to minorities' problems outside the constitutional framework must be briefly mentioned. The Masai had sought to obtain guarantees from the British Government arising out of the Masai

[29] Cmnd. 1701.
[30] Cmnd. 1971.
[31] Cmnd. 2161.
[32] The total population of the Region was estimated at 741,000, of the Arabs and related groups, 37,000—from estimates prepared by the census officers, 1962. See the *Preliminary Report*, Ministry of Commerce, Nairobi, 1964.

Agreements of 1904 and 1911. The British agreed to entrench some Masai land rights in the Constitution but repudiated liability for others.[33] The Masai subsequently at a meeting in Kenya requested the British Government to stay on in Masailand after other parts of Kenya had obtained independence. The Governor declined the invitation.[34]

Some European leaders had urged that Britain should act as a guarantor of the independence Constitution, and should reserve to herself the right to intervene militarily if any of the terms of the Constitution were violated.[35] But most Europeans realized that this was a non-starter and pursued instead with great pertinacity demands that the European civil servants be given compensation on leaving their service and that the British Government should ensure that those white farmers who wanted to leave the country should be enabled to sell their farms to a Central Land Board with its finances guaranteed by the British Government. The case for the white civil servants was easily won, since the principle had already been conceded in Nigeria, Ghana, Tanganyika and Uganda.[36] Under section 14 of the Independence Order in Council, the Government was given power compulsorily to retire expatriate civil servants, if suitable local candidates were available. Elaborate provisions were made for compensation to such officers, and for their right to appeal against the amount of compensation. They were also successful in their demands for a Land Board to buy their farms; by this time, the interests of the Europeans and Africans had converged on the issue of security and control of land, and this, in addition to a very effective lobby in London, ensured the success of their efforts. A Central Land Board was set up, entrenched firmly in the Constitution.[37]

Finally, the Europeans won important concessions in relation to citizenship. Having failed in their demands that they should have more than two years to make up their minds whether or not to opt for Kenya citizenship they urged the British Government to pass legislation enabling those Europeans who gave up their British citizenship to become Kenyans to resume their British nationality, should they decide at a later stage to do so, without having to go through the normal naturalization process, and without having to live in Britain. The British Nationality Act, 1964, was passed to meet their cases.[38]

[33] Cmnd. 1700, pp. 9–11.
[34] *Guardian*, 12 July 1960.
[35] See letter by Mr. H. B. W. MacAllan to *The Times*, 22 March 1960.
[36] See A. L. Adu, *The Civil Service in New States* (Allen and Unwin, 1965). See also Kenya (Compensation and Retiring Benefits) Order in Council, S.I. 1969 of 1963.
[37] See below, pp. 197–8 et seq.
[38] See Ghai, *E.A.L.J.*, op. cit., pp. 188–9 for an analysis of the Act. Its terms would cover a majority of the Europeans and Asians.

SAFEGUARDS IN THE CONSTITUTION

Paradoxically, the final stages of the constitutional developments were taken up with the removal of overt forms of safeguards. Thus the special electoral laws, with communal rolls, and the Council of State were abolished. But other forms of safeguards were introduced. The constitutional document that finally led Kenya to independence showed a remarkable distrust of power. The basis of the new constitutional system was the scheme of regionalism, which had been advocated by KADU. It was urged that Kenya should be divided into several regions, and that considerable powers should be devolved to them. KADU's plans matured over a period of two years; and there is little evidence of clear or coherent thought behind the plans. For example, it said at first that there would be five to six regions,[39] then when some time later its representative came to London and for the first time the party gave some details of its thinking, he announced that there would be four regions.[40] Then, at first it was said that each region would be demarcated on the basis of tribal homogeneity; later it was said that each region would contain a number of different tribes, so that the regions could provide a training ground for people of diverse tribes to live together.[41] Furthermore, it was suggested initially that the executive should be outside and independent of the legislature, on the American pattern, with the upper house reflecting the regional principle, and having powers to veto the appointment of all judges, diplomatic representatives, senior military commanders, and also having the right to remove them.[42] It was subsequently suggested that the executive should be part of the legislature, on the Swiss model, so that the MPs would vote for members of the Council of Ministers, who in turn would elect the Prime Minister.

The details of the scheme, which was eventually adopted, were worked out at a series of meetings and conferences in 1962 and 1963. Once the framework had been agreed on, a commission was appointed to mark the boundaries of the Regions, at that time intended to be six in number. KANU wanted minimal interference with the existing provincial boundaries, but as the Commission went round the country taking evidence, it discovered much dissatisfaction with the provincial boundaries.[43] Accordingly, the Commission recommended major boundary revisions. A number of groups were still dissatisfied. This shows the limitation of any scheme of minority protection based on the geographical distribution of power: it is almost impossible to establish new regions or states without creating fresh minorities.

[39] *Guardian*, 3 October 1961.
[40] *The Times*, 6 October 1961.
[41] *The Times*, 14 March 1962.
[42] *Guardian*, 7 March 1962. These were the plans as presented at the 1962 London Conference.
[43] Cmnd. 1899, p. 5.

Before considering in detail the *majimbo* provisions and some other provisions designed expressly as safeguards, brief mention must be made of the general provisions to regulate the exercise of power and to prevent abuse and corruption. Such provisions have become standard form for new Commonwealth constitutions.[44] They provide, for example, for an independent judiciary: this is done by insulating the appointment of judges from political influence, and by guaranteeing them a high degree of tenure. The appointments are made by the Judicial Service Commission, whose members are themselves largely appointed from and by the judiciary. A judge cannot be dismissed except for inability to perform the functions of his office or for misbehaviour, and then only if the question of his dismissal has been referred to an independent judicial tribunal of senior judges from the Commonwealth.[45]

Provisions are similarly made to insulate the recruitment to and promotion within the Civil Service by the establishment of an independent Public Service Commission, whose members are appointed by the Judicial Service Commission. The Commission also has powers of dismissal over public servants. In Kenya the Constitution gave directions to the Commission in regard to appointments, primarily in order to ensure that each Region had an adequate representation in the central establishment.[46] The same Commission appointed to the regional public services; the original scheme had provided for separate regional public service commissions.[47] In the appointment of very senior civil servants, the Commission had to consult the Prime Minister or the Regional President, as the case might be. Certain civil servants had a high degree of security of tenure, and were not dismissable by the Commission. These included the Attorney-General and the Controller and Auditor-General.[48] It is the responsibility of the Auditor-General to ensure that the Government observes probity in its finances, that is, to ensure that the money withdrawn from the Consolidated Fund has actually been voted for the purpose by Parliament, and that the money is actually so spent. Because of the delicate nature of his task, it is important to ensure that he performs it without fear, and so it provided that he could not be dismissed except by a procedure similar to that for the dismissal of a judge.

There was also a separate appointments commission for the police, which consisted of the Chairman of the Public Service Commission, a judge appointed by the Chief Justice, and three other members appointed by these two members after consultation with the Inspector-General. The Police

[44] See de Smith, op. cit., chapter 4.
[45] Sections 172 and 173.
[46] Chapter XI of the Constitution.
[47] Cmnd. 1700.
[48] Sections 188, 189 (5)-(8), 190 (4)-(7).

Service Commission performed functions in relation to the police similar to those of the Public Service Commission in relation to the civil service, including the appointment of the Inspector-General.[49]

Provisions were also made to ensure impartiality and honesty in elections to the legislative bodies, and for this purpose an independent Electoral Commission was established, consisting of the Speakers of the two houses of the National Assembly, and a nominee of the Prime Minister and each Regional President. The Commission was responsible for the drawing of constituency boundaries, to obviate the dangers of gerrymandering, and for the actual conduct of the elections.[50] As one of the basic safeguards of the constitutional order is vigorous and vigilant parliamentary institutions, the Electoral Commission was extremely important.

Another general device was the Bill of Rights, which will be discussed in a subsequent chapter. Mention, however, must be made of the specific guarantees for the coastal minorities. These concerned the judiciary and the civil service. The Kadhi court system was entrenched, and it was provided that no part of the former protectorate should be outside the jurisdiction of the court of a Kahdi. The jurisdiction of such a court would extend to the determination of questions of Muslim law relating to personal status, marriage, divorce or inheritance in proceedings in which all the parties profess the Muslim religion. It was provided that only a Muslim who possessed some knowledge of Islam would be eligible for appointment by the Judicial Service Commission as a Kadhi.[51] This did not, however, entrench the *sheria* as such, though the Agreement between the two Prime Ministers had contained the undertaking; the freedom of religion might, however, be implied to have entrenched the *sheria*. As far as the civil service is concerned, section 194 provided for the appointment of Liwalis and Mudirs on the establishment of the Coast Region, the power of appointment being vested in the Public Service Commission, but only Muslims could be so appointed. The Commission could consult anyone it wished who knew about the needs of the Muslim residents of the former protectorate before making its appointments; if the Regional Assembly set up an advisory board for this purpose then it became obligatory for the Commission to consult it.

Finally, provisions for citizenship must be discussed before we turn to regionalism. The Constitution provided extensively for citizenship. While attempts were made to ensure as wide a protection as possible for the rights of all the residents, regardless of citizenship, the question of citizenship was of the utmost importance. Even though the Constitution tried to prohibit the deportation of non-citizens, it was evident that sooner or later, the right of non-citizens to reside would be curtailed. Moreover, the exercise of political

[49] Sections 160, 161 and 162 (1). [50] Section 48. [51] Section 179.

rights, like the franchise, was to be tied to citizenship, even though certain classes of non-citizens might be given these rights for a transitional period.[52] Finally, it was to be expected that the Government would discriminate in its treatment of non-citizens, especially in employment in the civil service. For these reasons, it was important to determine who would become or be eligible to become citizens. As far as the African population was concerned, it was assumed that they would all be citizens. The real importance of the issue lay in the future of the immigrant communities.

The issue was complicated by several factors. First, until independence, there was no Kenya citizenship, and political or other rights were not therefore connected with such citizenship. Secondly, the immigrant communities were far from clear in their minds what they wanted. In a sense, they wanted both to have their cake and eat it. Ideally, they would have wished for provisions allowing dual citizenship, so they could acquire Kenyan citizenship without losing the safety of a British, or less significantly, Indian citizenship. But the African leaders opposed dual nationality, for they were suspicious of divided loyalties. On the other hand, it was conceded that it would be unfair to expect the members of the immigrant communities to make up their minds immediately on independence. A certain period following independence would be allowed for such people to make up their minds; some debate on the precise length of this period took place, a few Europeans demanding three years or more. However, the two year precedent of Tanganyika and Uganda was followed. Finally, there were some people who might not want to become citizens. There is little evidence of thought being given to the problem of such people, and, in the event, certain categories of people automatically became citizens who might have preferred to retain their former British nationality.[53]

In framing the provisions on citizenship, there were two kinds of problems to answer. First, what was to be the position of people living in Kenya, or having connections with Kenya, at the time of independence? Secondly, what were to be the provisions for those born after independence? The first problem was the more immediately acute as far as the immigrants were concerned; and also the more complex as the provisions for the second were more 'standardized'. In relation to the first, a distinction was made between those who would become citizens automatically by the operation of law on independence, and those who would have a right to be registered as citizens

[52] Under section 10 (3), residents of Kenya who were British citizens or protected persons or citizens of Ireland on the date of independence, and persons naturalized as British in Kenya before independence, were given the rights of citizens till 12 December 1965.

[53] Under the Kenya Independence Act, 1963, passed by the British Parliament, all those British subjects who became Kenyans automatically on independence lost their British status.

if they so desired. The result of this distinction would be to ascribe different nationalities to the different members of the same family.

The actual provisions followed the pattern set by Tanganyika and Uganda; they were, however, more liberal to the immigrants than in the other two countries.[54] Of those living at the time of independence, a certain category of persons became citizens by the automatic operation of the law on independence.[55] This group included almost all the indigenous people and a certain percentage of the immigrant communities. A person became a citizen under this provision if he was born in Kenya, was on 12 December 1963 (day of independence) a citizen of the United Kingdom and Colonies or a British protected person, and if one of his parents was also born in Kenya. To confer a similar right on persons who had equally strong links with Kenya but happened to be born outside the country, an additional provision was made which said that every person who, having been born outside Kenya, was a British citizen or protected person, on independence, would become a citizen of Kenya if his father became an automatic citizen, or, if his father was dead, then would but for his death have so become.

In addition to the first category of persons who became citizens automatically, there were several categories of persons who had the right to be registered as citizens if they so wished. Under these provisions, the great majority of the residents of Kenya, provided they were British citizens or British protected persons, could qualify to become citizens. Thus the following persons could become citizens: a person born in Kenya but neither of whose parents was born there, a lawfully and ordinarily resident person at independence, otherwise than on temporary pass; a person naturalized or registered in Kenya before independence as a citizen of the United Kingdom and Colonies either before or after the British Nationality Act of 1948; a woman who has been married to a person who becomes a citizen by the automatic operation of the law, or but for his death, would have so become; a person one of whose parents on the date of application is a citizen; and finally, a woman who has been married on or before independence to a person entitled to citizenship by registration due to his birth or registration as a British citizen in the country but whose marriage has been terminated due to death or dissolution before independence, or after independence but before the former husband has exercised his right to registration. Presumably, if he had himself exercised the right, she would be entitled to registration under section 5, which gives the right to any woman who has been married to a citizen of Kenya; though not expressly covering a divorced wife, the expression

[54] For Uganda, see Morris and Read, *Uganda* (London, Stevens and Sons, 1966), pp. 177–82. For Tanganyika, see Cole and Denison, *Tanganyika* (London, Stevens and Sons, 1964), pp. 16–17.
[55] See chapter 1 of the Constitution.

'has been married' would seem to include such a person. It is likely, from its position in the Constitution, that section 5 refers to marriages that take place after independence, but again there is nothing in the language to warrant such a restriction.

A person who was entitled to registration had to make his application within a specified time; in most cases, the period allowed was two years after independence, but Parliament was authorized to prescribe a longer period. Secondly, he had to renounce whatever other nationality he might have had when he became Kenyan, and take an oath of allegiance within a specified time, which in the case of a person over twenty-one years was three months after the registration, and in other cases, two years after reaching that age. The provision about renunciation also applies to citizens by the automatic operation of the law, and a citizen loses his citizenship if he acquires some other nationality by a voluntary act other than marriage.

The Constitution also provides for citizenship for those born after independence. Anyone born in Kenya after independence shall become a citizen, with the usual exception of children born of foreign parents who enjoy diplomatic immunities, or of enemy aliens, or born in a part of Kenya under enemy occupation. A child born to a citizen father outside the country becomes a citizen. Thus Kenya allows citizenship both by birth and descent; and it means that children of non-citizens born in Kenya become citizens. Such children may of course have another nationality; it is possible for them to renounce Kenyan citizenship or just wait till they are twenty-three, when their Kenyan citizenship would automatically lapse, unless before then they have taken steps to renounce their other nationality.

In addition, the Constitution authorizes Parliament to make rules about further registration and naturalization as citizens, the former word being used in relation to citizens of Commonwealth and certain African countries, 'naturalization' for others. Another distinction is that once a person in the first category had satisfied the conditions laid down by Parliament, he was entitled to registration, whereas a person in the second category, even though he had satisfied the requisite conditions, was merely eligible.[56] The conditions for such eligibility are actually spelt out in the Constitution; in the case of registration, it is left to Parliament to decide on the conditions.

The Constitution also contains provisions for the deprivation of citizenship. It is not possible to take away the citizenship of a person who has acquired it by the automatic operation of law. Therefore the Government can take away the citizenship only of those persons who have acquired it through registration or naturalization. Even in these cases, the Government

[56] But this right of citizens of the Commonwealth and African countries was removed by Act No. 16 of 1966; they are now merely eligible for Kenya citizenship. Now Constitution section 92.

can only exercise this power on one of the five grounds allowed by the Constitution. The grounds are: disloyalty, by speech or act, to Kenya; association with the enemy during war; a conviction and sentence of twelve months within five years of registration or naturalization; obtaining of registration by fraud, false representation or concealment of any material fact; and the residence by the citizen abroad for a continuous period of seven years, unless his absence is due to service in an international organization of which Kenya is a member, or he has registered annually his intention with a Kenya consulate to retain his citizenship. Thus, though the grounds for deprivation are specified, nevertheless, the first one is so widely phrased that the Government is given extensive powers of deprivation. The deprivation of citizenship is of course a very serious matter, and because Kenya does not allow dual nationality, it means that a person deprived of his citizenship becomes stateless. The Hague Conventions on Nationality have recommended that no country should be allowed to deprive a citizen of his nationality, if the effect is to render him stateless. Perhaps there was a case for allowing the Government less freedom to deprive citizens of their status.

REGIONALISM

While many of the preceding provisions were designed to protect the minorities from abuses of power, the establishment of regionalism was to provide for the sharing of power. It is not enough to be protected from tyrannical rule; it is also important to participate in the processes of government. Regionalism would make such participation possible on the part of even the minority tribes.

As we have seen, seven Regions were created. In each Region there was a Regional Assembly, with elected and specially elected members.[57] The qualifications for voters were such as to ensure that only those persons who had a genuine connection with the Region had a vote;[58] and no candidate for elections to the Regional Assembly could be validly nominated unless he was registered in the Region as a voter.[59] The boundaries of the Regions could not be altered unilaterally by the central legislature; this could only be done through a complex procedure which included the consent of the Regions affected by the changes.[60]

The Constitution did not provide for a proper party government in the Regions. The executive functions of the Regions were vested in a committee

[57] See generally chapter 7 of the Constitution. The Regions were: Coast, Eastern, Central, Rift Valley, Nyanza, Western and North-Eastern. According to the 1962 census, the breakdown of major tribes was as shown in the appendix, p. 525.
[58] Schedule 5, part 111.
[59] Section 95.
[60] Section 239.

of the Assembly, the Finance and Establishment Committee, and could be exercised on its behalf by other committees of the Assembly. It was, however, possible for the Assembly to confer functions on persons or authorities other than the Finance and Establishment Committee. The administration was carried on through a system of committees, all of which were elected by the Assembly, but no one could be a member of more than one committee, except the President, who was an *ex officio* member of all. The President of the Region was thus the link between the various committees. He was elected to that office by the elected members of the Assembly, either from among themselves or from those qualified to be elected as such and could only be removed by an adverse vote of three-fourths of all the members. The chief executive officer of the Region was the Civil Secretary, who was appointed by the Public Service Commission, after consultation with the Regional President.[61] Each Region had its own separate establishment, whose size and composition were determined by its Finance and Establishments Committee, though the actual appointments were made by the Public Service Commission.[62]

The allocation of powers between the Centre and the Regions was provided for in great detail—greater than in any other Commonwealth constitution. In this, it reflects the lack of consensus and lack of careful thinking as to the functions appropriate to each government; fears could only be allayed by a detailed allocation of functions—down to the determination as to which legislature could provide for public lavatories and refuse and effluent disposal, and which executive was responsible for implementing the law on these subjects. The division of powers was complex, elaborate and confusing. The first schedule set out the division of legislative and executive powers. In Part I were listed matters which were within the exclusive legislative competence of the Regional Assemblies; in Part II, those within the concurrent competence of Parliament and the Regional Assemblies; and finally, in Part III those matters which were within the legislative competence of Parliament, but to which the executive authority of the Regions extended. The residual legislative powers were with the central legislature.[63] The matters on which the Regional Assemblies alone could legislate included agricultural matters (elementary training centres, and branding of livestock), archives (other than records of the Government of Kenya), auction sales, primary, intermediate and secondary education (with the exception of certain important educational institutes and schools), housing, medical facilities and institutions (again with the exception of a list of important hospitals), the protection and control of nomadic people, common minerals, barbers

[61] Section 193. The system bore strong resemblance to the English local government.
[62] Section 187 (3).
[63] Section 66.

and hair-dressers, disorderly houses, wash houses and laundries. The concurrent legislative powers (where the validly enacted central legislation prevailed in case of conflict), included certain other agricultural matters, antiquities, civil aerodromes, land settlement, libraries, public examinations at primary, intermediate and secondary levels of education, public health and slaughter houses.

By and large, the executive authority of the Regions extended to areas of their legislative authority, but in some respects the executive authority went beyond the legislative, as in relation to items on Part III of Schedule I, where the legislative authority over matters like adulteration of food, liquor licensing, probation services, rent control and town and country planning was with Parliament, but the executive with the Regions. It was expressly provided that where in relation to a matter the legislative and executive responsibilities were so divided, it should not prejudice the power of the Central Government to decide whether or not to introduce legislation with regard to that matter and to determine the contents of such legislation.[64] The Regions also had exclusive executive authority over subjects of concurrent legislative competence.[65]

The relatively neat division of powers was seriously upset by Schedule II. This Schedule carried in even greater detail special provisions relating to the legislative powers and executive authority of the Centre and the Regions. Its effect in many cases was to vest such powers in the Centre when Schedule I would have excluded it. Thus while Schedule I purported to vest the exclusive executive authority over libraries in the Regions, Schedule II vested it also in the Central Government. Similar provisions existed in relation to the marketing of agricultural produce, education, antiquities, and others. Schedule II also affected the distribution of legislative powers as provided for in Schedule I. For example, though the legislative authority over civil aerodromes was concurrent under the later Schedule, the former provided that in certain aspects, the central legislature would have exclusive competence. This was also true for agricultural and veterinary education and research. Schedule II makes long and tedious reading in a long and tedious document. It sought to divide important subjects like education, agriculture and planning at various levels, vesting authority over them in different governments.[66]

[64] Section 120 (6).
[65] Section 106 (1).
[66] As an example, primary, intermediate and secondary education was with the Regions exclusively, but a few educational institutions were expressly excluded; also excluded were any secondary technical schools that provided boarding facilities for pupils. Within the concurrent list was public examinations at primary, intermediate and secondary schools; while the maintenance of educational standards at these schools

There were two other important powers. Local government fell within the competence of the Regions. The basic structure of local government was provided in the Constitution, including the electoral law,[67] but considerable legislative and executive powers were vested in the Regional Assemblies. For example, the Regional Assembly had the general power to make laws with respect to local government within the Region.[68] In particular, the Assembly had the power to determine which areas within the Region should constitute local government authority areas, what category of local authority they should constitute, and how they should be divided into electoral areas. However, these functions were to be exercised in accordance with the recommendations of Commissions of Inquiry set up to examine the draft orders made by the Assembly.[69] The Assembly also had certain functions in relation to local government finance.[70] It had some executive functions in relation to the local authorities as well in certain cases of default or maladministration by the council—it could remove all the councillors (or other members) of the local authority and appoint a commission in their place, with all the powers and duties of that authority.[71]

Secondly, the Regions shared in certain police functions, through their representation on the National Security Council, which exercised important control over the disposal of the police forces, their size and organization. Moreover, in each Region there was a Regional Police Contingent, control over which was divided between the Region and the Inspector-General, a reference being made to the National Security Council in case of dispute between them.[72]

The legislative and executive powers of the Regions were, however, subject to various rights of intervention on the part of the Centre. As far as legislation was concerned, Parliament could provide grants and loans from the central finances for any purpose even though that purpose was outside its legislative competence;[73] it could legislate to implement international agreements, even on Regional subjects;[74] during an emergency Parliament

was within the executive authority of the Regions but the legislative competence of the Centre. Though higher education was a central subject, the Regions were authorized to make laws with respect to the grant of scholarships for higher education. In relation to agriculture and planning, the confusion was even more confounded.

[67] Chapter 13 of the Constitution.

[68] Section 237.

[69] Section 236.

[70] Section 143; see below, pp. 203–4.

[71] Section 235.

[72] See chapter 9 of the Constitution for the complex provisions for the control of the police.

[73] Section 67. The ability to raise vast sums of money and to grant them to the Region on conditions is, of course, a classic way to increase the *de facto* powers of the Centre in federations.

[74] Section 68.

could make laws on any subject for any part of the country,[75] and finally, when Parliament decided by 65 per cent of the votes in both its houses that the executive authority of a Region was being exercised in contravention of section 106(2), Parliament could make laws for any part of that Region on any matter.[76]

As to executive authority, the Central Government was authorized to give such directions to a Regional Assembly as appeared to it necessary or expedient in order to ensure that the executive authority of the Region was exercised in accordance with the provisions of section 106(2) or for the performance of any function over which the executive authority of the Central Government extended, but which had to be performed within the Region. If these directions were not complied with, the Central Government had powers of direct administration. The Central Government might, moreover, bypass the Regional Assembly, and address directions directly to regional officers or authorities if it was reasonably satisfied that such a course was necessary to avert a serious threat to the public welfare caused by an outbreak of disease or some other calamity. During an emergency, the central executive responsibility extended to all matters in the Regions, and if Parliament so provided, to the exclusion of the authority of the Regions. Similar provisions applied when Parliament was exercising functions in relation to a Region for non-compliance with section 106(2).[77]

It is obvious from an examination of the powers of the Regions that they were not very important, and were in any case somewhat precarious, for the Centre could take over regional powers in a number of instances. There was very little true autonomy. The regional executives were so designed as not to lead to strong regional governments; they were clumsy and unwieldy; there was a wide dispersion of authority, and no clear lines of responsibility. This was likely to result in weak regional structures, and to promote occasions for outside interference. To guard against the abandonment of regional functions to the Centre, no provisions were made for their delegation to the Centre. While this would prevent KANU dominated Assemblies from surrendering their powers to the Centre, there were several constitutional provisions which would enable the Centre to move in. It is important to remember that the regional structure was a new one, and there had to be a devolution of powers from the Centre before it could begin to function. Thus it lacked a tradition of government, no vested interests had yet been created, and the machinery for administration had to be established, often

[75] Section 69.
[76] Section 106 (2) read: 'The executive authority of a Region shall be so exercised as . . . (a) not to impede or prejudice the exercise of the executive authority of the Government of Kenya; and (b) to ensure compliance with any provision made by or under any Act of Parliament applying to that Region'.
[77] See section 72.

by transferring personnel from the central establishment to the regional. Under these circumstances, the odds against the success of the regional system were many and great.

LAND

It remains to consider the provisions about land—the most touchy question before independence. To a large extent, KADU was able to muster its support by playing on the fears of the smaller tribes that their land would be taken over by the Kikuyu and the Luo. The Arabs were apprehensive of their titles on the coast, and the Europeans were also anxious to secure good prices for their farms. KADU had proposed that land should become entirely a regional matter. However, on this one issue, the interests of the Europeans coincided with those of KANU—both wanted land to be left with the Centre, the Europeans for the reason that they thought it preferable to deal with one authority rather than a plethora, and also because they realized that the chances of securing foreign loans to buy out their farms were better if land was vested in the more reliable Central Government than in the new and untried Regions.

The Constitution confirmed the existing titles and interests in land, and where land was subject to an unadjudicated claim under the Land Titles Act, subject to such adjudication.[78] The confirmation was important at a time when there was a slight uncertainty as to the continued validity of titles due to demands from certain sections of the population that those titles should not be recognized after independence. A Central Land Board was set up to purchase land in the Scheduled Areas and to resell or convey for settlement purposes.[79] The Board was also to assess the fair price for such land; the purchase was to be made by agreement with the owners. In the discharge of these functions, the Board was to be independent of the direction or control of any other person or authority, though in order to assist in the formulation and implementation of land settlement schemes, it was to consult a Central Settlement Committee from time to time.

The Board was less independent in its function to convey the land—its independence in powers of purchase was to safeguard the interests of the European settlers; the control over its powers of disposition was to safeguard tribal or regional interests. The Board was to convey the land to persons nominated by the President of the Region in which the land was situated after consultation with the Minister in the Centre.

Most of what used to be Crown land was vested in the Regions.[80] The

[78] Section 203.
[79] See part I of chapter XII. The market price in 1959 was accepted as the criteria for the buying of farms, as was urged by the settlers.
[80] Section 204. See generally parts II and III of chapter XII.

Central Government was given public and Trust land in the Nairobi area, and such of the Crown lands as the Governor had designated for that purpose under powers given to him by the self-government Constitution.[81] The power of disposal of these lands was given to the respective Governments, though the Central Government had certain narrow powers to acquire compulsorily land vested in the Regions. The most sensitive of all—the Trust land—was vested in the county council within whose area of jurisdiction it was situated. The county council held the Trust land for the benefit of the persons ordinarily resident on that land and had to give effect to such rights, interests or other benefits vested in any tribe, group, family or individual under the African customary law for the time being in force and applicable to it. There were provisions for the central or regional authorities to take over Trust land for public purposes, but important safeguards were provided for the councils; and full compensation had to be paid. The regional authorities had precedence over the central in this respect and both had to offer the land back to the council if it was no longer required for the specified public purposes. If land was thus acquired, the customary rights were extinguished. The county council could also extinguish customary rights by setting apart the Trust land for specified purposes, under the laws made by the Regional Assembly; again, compensation had to be paid to those whose customary rights were thus affected. It was also possible for a county council to request that the Land Adjudication Act apply to any area of Trust land, which would then cease to be Trust land, the customary rights and interests being ascertained and recorded.

The control of the Trust land was vested in the county council, though certain legislative powers were given to the Regional Assemblies. It was possible for the councils to set up an elaborate machinery of Divisional Land Control Boards and appellate committees to exercise the control; the consent of the Boards was necessary for certain transactions affecting agricultural land. This control was extended to the Scheduled land, but in this case, an appeal against refusal of consent could be taken to an independent Appeals Tribunal.

The control of non-public land was thus firmly vested in the local authorities. Nothing less than this would have allayed the fears of the people in relation to their tribal lands. It is important to note, however, that the Regional Assemblies themselves had very little power in relation to such land. It is, therefore, not so much the regional as the local government system which was used for the settlement of the more controversial land issues.

[81] Section 205. For the relevant powers of the Governor under the self-government constitution, see section 195 (2), Schedule 2 of the Kenya Order in Council, S.I. No. 791 of 1963.

FINANCE

Provisions were designed which, it was hoped, would ensure the success of the system of regionalism, of which two were finances and the Senate. A commission was appointed to advise on the fiscal structure, in order, *inter alia*, to provide that the Regions should have adequate sources of revenue secured to them in the Constitution, so that the regional authorities 'should be capable of a life and significance of their own'.[82] The Commission found that the regional authorities, after the assumption of their new responsibilities, would 'between them become responsible for recurrent expenditure of about the same order as that remaining to the Central Government after the changes'. It was on this estimate that the Commission made its recommendations, most of which were incorporated into the Constitution.

Most of the important powers to raise revenue were given to the Centre; the right to fixed amounts of the revenue was assigned to the Regions on the principle of derivation from revenue on specified items, and that of population on others.[83] The rates of duty or taxation were determined by Parliament, on the recommendation of the Central Government, but since the revenue from them affected the Regions so closely, it was provided that before the Government submitted a Bill for this purpose to Parliament, it should consult with the Regional Presidents, if the likely effect was that the revenue which would accrue to the Regions would be lower than the sum from that source in the previous financial year.[84] The taxation from the licensing of motor vehicles and drivers, though determined by Parliament, was collected by the regional authorities and formed part of their revenue.[85] The regional authorities had certain independent powers of taxation—graduated personal tax, and poll tax (up to a maximum decided by Parliament), land tax, entertainment tax and royalties in respect of common minerals.[86] The collection of these taxes was the responsibility of the local government authorities within the Region (to whom they also belonged), except that the Regional Assembly had powers of preception in relation to this revenue.[87]

According to the Fiscal Commission, the revenue thus accruing to the Regions would have been adequate for them to discharge their functions. But, though the Regions had constitutional rights to this revenue, they had only small taxation or collecting powers. Moreover, even when the Regions had independent taxing powers, they were really exercised on behalf of the local authorities. Even here, two of the most productive of these, the graduated personal tax and the poll tax, were subject to the maxima deter-

[82] *Report of the Fiscal Commission*, Nairobi, 1963.
[83] e.g. Section 138.
[84] Section 150.
[85] Section 139.
[86] Section 142.
[87] Section 145.

mined by the Centre; the Commission's reason for this was that it was necessary to have safeguards to 'prevent its competitive overlapping with the EACSO-operated income tax'. The Commission felt unable to recommend greater taxation or collecting powers for the Regions. In its view, within Kenya's fiscal structure, 'all the taxes yielding large sums are not effectively autonomous even on a national basis, but only within a structure the boundaries of which are East Africa'. Due to the fact that Kenya co-operated with the other East African countries through the EACSO on tax matters, it would have been impracticable to vest taxing powers in authorities other than the central. Therefore the Commission tried to devise measures to increase the 'relative autonomy' of the Regions by assigning them fixed amounts of revenue raised by the Centre, and hoped that the collective interests of the Regions would help to reinforce this autonomy. But the point remains that to an important degree, the Regions were dependent on the Centre, and short of a court order, there was no machinery for the enforcement of the fiscal provisions. Thus, financially, the Regions were far from autonomous, and without strong finances, there was not much hope of viability for them.

SENATE

The Senate was intended to act as a political safeguard for *majimbo*. KADU at first asked for a more powerful Senate than it got; it would consist of five members from each Region, chosen by the Regional Assembly; its legislative power would be equal to that of the lower house; conflicts between them would be resolved by a joint committee. The Cabinet would be responsible to the entire National Assembly; its members would be elected by both houses sitting together. In addition, the Senate would have a crucial role in the procedure for constitutional amendment.[88] The proposals were, however, rejected.

The basic provisions about the Senate were as follows: there was direct election to it, from forty districts and the Nairobi Area;[89] the districts were the old administrative units, with the revision that was necessary after the recommendations of the Boundaries Commission, due to the fact that no district could be in more than one Region;[90] the result of the revision was to make Senate constituencies more tribally homogeneous and thus provide more nearly—although still not perfectly—for the representation of tribes as such in the upper chamber.[91] The qualifications for the voters

[88] See J. H. Proctor, 'The Role of the Senate in the Kenya Political System', *Parliamentary Affairs*, volume XVIII, No. 4, pp. 389–415.
[89] Section 35.
[90] Section 240 (1) (d).
[91] According to Proctor, op. cit., p. 393, in thirty-five of the forty-one constituencies, one tribe constituted an absolute majority of the population, and in seventeen constituencies over 90 per cent were of the same tribe.

and the candidates were similar to those for elections to the Regional Assemblies to ensure that the local interests were dominant.[92] The Senate was a continuous body, as one third of its members resigned every two years; the total length of a member's tenure was six years.[93]

The Senate was clearly subordinate to the House of Representatives; its powers were similar to those of the House of Lords, except for its part in constitutional amendments. It had no power in relation to financial legislation; if it did not pass a financial Bill sent to it from the lower house without amendment, then after one month that Bill could be presented to the Governor-General for his assent. However, it could delay such a Bill, for it was possible for the Senate to refer any Bill certified as financial by the Speaker of the lower house to the High Court for a ruling on whether it was really financial. The Senate had to make the reference within twenty-one days of receiving the Bill; the court had to decide within one month of the reference, otherwise the Bill was presumed financial. Thus the Senate could delay a financial Bill for nearly two months. In relation to other Bills, the Senate had greater and more explicit powers of delay, and could hold up legislation for up to at least a year.[94]

The Government was not responsible to it in the sense of being removable by it, though Ministers (except for the Prime Minister) could be appointed from either house, and all had the right to speak in both houses.[95] Two important functions served by the Senate were in relation to the amendment of the Constitution, and the declaration of an emergency. We have already seen the effect of a declaration of emergency on the distribution of legislative and executive powers between the Centre and the Regions; in addition, certain provisions of the Bill of Rights were suspended when such a declaration was in force. A declaration could only be made without the prior authorization of Parliament when it was prorogued or adjourned. Even in this event, it lasted only for seven days, after which it had to be approved by a resolution supported by a 65 per cent vote of all the members of the two houses. If Parliament was dissolved, then the Senate had to be recalled to secure the resolution. Therefore the approval of the Senate was always necessary if the declaration was to last more than a week. No declaration could last more than two months, though it could be extended for similar periods at a time by similar resolutions of the two houses, or of the Senate alone, if the lower house was dissolved.[96]

Commenting on the powers of the Senate, it has been said that 'the Senate retained the power to prevent assaults on constitutionally defined minority

[92] Part I, Schedule 5.
[93] Section 42 (3).
[94] Section 61.
[95] Section 57.
[96] Sections 29 and 69.

rights, but its capacity to defend the substance of the regional system itself was severely reduced'.[97] The Senate, however, did give a significant representation to the smaller tribes in the central legislature. But it failed to attract people of high calibre, and due to this and other reasons, it failed to establish itself as the protector of regionalism and other safeguards.

THE SANCTITY OF THE CONSTITUTIONAL ARRANGEMENTS

Since most of the important compromises and concessions of the various groups were embodied in the Constitution, and since the sanctioning authority of the British Government would disappear on independence, it was necessary to ensure both that there were adequate sanctions behind the Constitution and that the compromises would not be unilaterally upset or altered. The achievement of the first of these objectives was attempted through provisions for judicial review. Though, unlike the Uganda Independence Constitution,[98] there was no express declaration as to its supremacy, it was intended that the Constitution should be supreme over ordinary legislation and the institutions it established. This was clearly stated in relation to Chapter II, which dealt with fundamental rights. The corollary of the supremacy of the Constitution is the jurisdiction of the courts to see that no laws or executive action violate its terms. It was provided that if any question as to the interpretation of the Constitution arose in any proceedings in any subordinate court which in the opinion of the court involved a substantial question of law, the court could, and should, if any party to the proceedings so requested, refer the question to the High Court. For the purposes of this jurisdiction, the High Court would consist of an uneven number of judges, being not less than three.[99] In relation to certain parts of the Constitution, the High Court had, and has, special jurisdiction. If any person alleges that any of the provisions of the Bill of Rights has been, is being, or is likely to be, infringed in relation to him, he can make an application to the High Court, which has original jurisdiction in this respect. If the court finds that there has indeed been such a contravention, it may 'make such orders, issue such writs and give such directions as it may consider appropriate for the purpose of enforcing or securing the enforcement of any of the provisions'. The Court also had special jurisdiction to examine the validity of, and disputes arising from, the expropriation of property, which we shall discuss in another chapter.[100] In addition, the courts had important functions in relation to the elections to and the functioning of legislative

[97] Proctor, op. cit., p. 396.
[98] Section 1 of Uganda's Independence Constitution (contained in S.I. No. 2175 of 1962), provided that the Constitution was the supreme law of Uganda and any other law inconsistent with it was void to the extent of the inconsistency.
[99] Section 175.
[100] See below, chapter XI.

bodies. The High Court had jurisdiction to decide whether any person had been validly elected a member of a legislative body, and whether the seat of a member had become vacant.[101] In case of a dispute between the Senate and the House of Representatives as to the character of a Bill which had been certified by the Speaker of the latter as a financial Bill, a reference could be made to the High Court by the Senate.[102]

The primary responsibility for the maintenance of the Constitution was thus given to the courts. How were the courts equipped to discharge this responsibility? First of all, as we have seen, provisions were made to ensure the complete independence of the judiciary. Secondly, the ultimate responsibility for judicial decisions on the Constitution was given to the Privy Council.[103] As a court of great stature, entirely independent of local pressures, much reliance was placed on its role in umpiring the constitutional agreements which formed the basis of independence.

The object of securing the constitutional agreements from unilateral alteration was intended to be achieved by providing for a rigid and stringent method of amendment of the Constitution. Normally provisions for amendments are not discussed until quite near independence, for the constitutional position is that until that time the Queen in Council retains the power to make changes and the power of amendment is seldom delegated to local institutions until then. But in Kenya political arguments were conducted with such bitterness and concessions were granted with such reluctance that the provisions for amendments assumed great importance early in 1962. Initially KADU wanted high majorities in the two chambers of the central legislature and the agreement of all the Regional Assemblies.[104] However, the agreement reached at the 1962 Constitutional Conference was a modification of the KADU demand. It was decided that changes would require a majority of 75 per cent of each house, except that with regard to particular changes which affected the entrenched rights of individuals, Regions, tribal authorities, or districts, the majority in the Senate would be 90 per cent.[105] KANU continued its opposition to the high degree of entrenchment, and in the final Constitutional Conference in 1963 further modifications

[101] Sections 50 (1) and 101 (1).
[102] Section 61 (3)-(4).
[103] Section 180. The Privy Council has often been looked to as the guardian of constitutional rights (see Bentwich, 'The Judicial Committee of the Privy Council as a Model of an International Court for Human Rights', 2 *International Law Quarterly* 392), and has been regarded as giving rise to the doctrine of judicial review. See Thayer, 'The Origin and Scope of the American Doctrine of Constitutional Law', 7 *Harvard Law Review* 17. Recently doubts have been cast on the ability of the Privy Council to act as a watchdog. See Claire Palley, 'The Judicial Committee of the Privy Council as Appellate Court—The Southern Rhodesian Experience' (1967) *Public Law* 8.
[104] *The Times*, 14 February 1962.
[105] Cmnd. 1700, p. 18.

were made. In the absence of agreement between the political parties, the Colonial Secretary gave his award. He warned against too great entrenchment for this might lead to unconstitutional action. While accepting the need for high entrenchment in the case of certain provisions, he suggested a simpler procedure for others. He removed the high entrenchment for the powers of the Regions. His reason was that the allocation of powers between the Regions and the Centre was the product of inter-party bargaining rather than of objective planning. Therefore certain features of it might prove unworkable; and so a flexible procedure must be provided for their alteration.[106]

The provisions of the Constitution, therefore, could be divided into two from the point of amendment.[107] First, there were the specially entrenched provisions.[108] Such provisions could not be altered except by a Bill which secured three-fourths of the votes of all the members on the second and third readings in the House of Representatives and nine-tenths in the Senate on similar readings. The provisions thus entrenched included the whole of the chapters on citizenship and fundamental rights, provisions about the composition of, elections to, and the powers of the Senate, the structure of the Regions, including their financial powers, judiciary, transactions in tribal land, provisions to alter the regional boundaries, and the amendment procedure itself. It is important to note that Schedule 1, which deals with the exclusive legislative and executive authority of the Regions, was not similarly entrenched; thus while the whole elaborate structure of regionalism was highly safeguarded, its powers were not—a situation which could lead to the attrition of these powers, leaving white elephants behind—which is what happened in fact.

The remainder of the provisions of the Constitution could be altered more easily. The normal requirement was a positive vote of three-fourths of all the members in both the houses on the second and third readings. If such a vote was not forthcoming in either house, then the provisions of the Bill could be presented to the electorate in a referendum, and if two-thirds of the votes cast were in favour, the Bill could be reintroduced in Parliament and would become law if passed as ordinary legislation—i.e. by simple majorities in both houses. Thus, even though the ordinary provisions were well safeguarded, the provision of the alternative method of referendum diminished the importance of the Senate. The system was cumbersome and expensive, and it was doubtful how far the electorate could be made to appreciate the real issues in such a vote. Another point that may be made in relation to the amendment procedure is that once a Bill

[106] Cmnd. 2156.
[107] See section 71.
[108] See Schedule 4.

for amendment had been introduced in Parliament, no changes in it could be made before it was presented to the Governor-General for his assent. The rule introduced an additional element of rigidity. Its effect, however, would probably have been to force the Government into consultation with the opposition before introducing a constitutional Bill. But as far as its own back-benchers are concerned, the effect was likely to be—and has been—to force them into a wholesale acceptance of the Bill. Thus the Government could push through unpopular alterations by putting them together with popular proposals.

From the examination of the provisions about judicial review and the amendment procedure, one may say that as much as possible was done within the Constitution to preserve its terms. As for judicial review, however, it is important to remember that the courts in Kenya had not previously been engaged in the task of umpiring a constitutional system; they had no experience in this matter, nor was there any tradition among the people or the parties to take political disputes to court.[109] Thus while the actual provisions were quite impressive, doubts remained as to their practical value. As far as the amendment procedure was concerned, one great weakness was the omission to safeguard the powers of the Regions. The prospects of maintaining the regional structure lay in their powers, with attendant benefits of patronage and the like. But once the powers were removed, the empty structure would collapse. While the Colonial Secretary was right to point out that the Centre-Region allocation was arbitrary, ways of gaining flexibility could have been achieved without jeopardizing the whole system—such as an independent commission to examine the position after a specified number of years, and a more critical study to see whether some regional powers were not so fundamental to the success of the system that they, at least, ought to have been especially entrenched.

THE ESTABLISHMENT OF THE REPUBLIC

Whatever the assumptions of the permanence of the independence Constitution, it was unlikely in practice to last for long. It had failed to satisfy anyone—the highwater mark of *majimbo* was the self-government Constitution and the recession from it in the independence Constitution was

[109] It was theoretically possible before this Constitution to seek judicial review, but there were few standards to appeal to. For example, the Income Tax Ordinance of 1937 was attacked on the ground that the enactment was not necessary for the peace, order and good government of the Colony and since the Legislative Council did not contain a majority of elected members, it had no powers of direct taxation. The court held that the power to make laws for the peace, order and government which had been validly delegated to the Kenya Legislature by the King in Council included the powers of taxation and that there was no repugnancy with the law of England, *Hay* v. *Commissioner of Income Tax* (1940), 7 E.A.C.A. 7. By the Kenya (Constitution) (Amendment) Order in Council, 1962 (S.I. No. 2599) express provisions were made for questions of interpretation of the then Constitution and appeal to the Privy Council.

bitterly resented by KADU. KANU was equally dissatisfied—but for the opposite reason—it contained too much *majimbo*.[110] The KANU case against regionalism was that it was expensive in terms of money and personnel, would prevent the growth of nationhood, and retard economic development. It was also argued with some justification, that the Constitution was based on artificially engendered fears, for it is obvious that the European settlers and the British Government helped KADU and accorded it an importance out of proportion to its popular support.

It was unrealistic to expect that government could be carried on within the framework of the new Constitution. A *Times* leader commenting on the Constitution—'a formidable instrument of government'—remarked that the first requirement was a skilled corps of lawyers and clerks in the Centre and the Regions to explain to legislators what they were required, permitted, or forbidden to do under scores of legally worded clauses.[111] It is doubtful if anyone really fully understood the division of powers and responsibilities. KANU had never believed in this Constitution, and it is therefore not surprising that no serious attempt was made to implement it, despite an assurance by Prime Minister Kenyatta in October 1963 that powers would be devolved to the Regions, as specified in the Constitution, before independence.[112]

One of the most important ways in which a purposeful implementation of the Constitution was frustrated was by denying the regional authorities an effective and independent secretariat.[113] Most of the officials who previously administered the services devolved to the Regions were retained in the employment of the Centre and were temporarily seconded to the Regions. The chief regional executive officer, the Civil Secretary, was at the same time the chief administrative officer of the Centre in the Region. As most of the salaries came from the Centre, the officials were heavily dependent on it. Moreover, in relation to them, the final authority for the purposes of recall, transfer and dismissal was the Centre. Consequently the primary loyalty of the regional officers was to the Centre rather than to the Regions. Another factor which affected adversely the powers of the Regions was a directive from the Central Government that the Regions should refer all drafts of legislation to it for advice before their introduction in the Regional Assembly. Nor did the Central Government hand over to the Regions the revenue which belonged to them under the Constitution; and although at one time KADU threatened legal action on this issue, the financial provisions of the Constitution were never implemented.

[110] Ngala (KADU) called the Constitution a 'breach of faith', *Sunday Times*, November 1963. Mboya (KANU) described it as 'an experiment . . . and it is obvious that it contains a number of unworkable and unfair provisions', *E.A. Standard*, 15 May 1963.
[111] Quoted in Odinga, op. cit., p. 233.
[112] Cmnd. 2156, annex C.
[113] Odinga, op. cit., p. 242.

While the Central Government was anxious to weaken the Regions, the Regions made matters worse for themselves. The regional institutions had been established overnight by the self-government Constitution on 1 June 1963; they had not evolved over a period of time. Moreover, they were complicated; and so it is not surprising that they did not work well. The Regional Assemblies thought that as the executive authority was vested in them, they should do more than lay guidelines; as was noted by a colonial official, this resulted in their committees discussing every detail of administration at length so that in many cases no decision was reached for the public officials to follow; sometimes the officials were forbidden to take any action without their prior approval; and occasionally resolutions were adopted on matters within the exclusive responsibility of the Centre.[114] The Regional Assemblies lost some sympathy by their solicitude for their own pockets; one of the first acts of most of the Assemblies was to enact legislation to give themselves remuneration and allowances while school teachers employed by the Regions were not paid their salaries and were dismissed for lack of money.

While the Regions were suffering from these difficulties, the Centre was planning full scale constitutional changes. The central feature of the changes was to be the establishment of a Republic. In this, Kenya was following the pattern of constitutional developments set by other East African countries, which abandoned their dominion status on the first anniversary of their independence. The KANU Government was also planning other important changes. On 14 August 1964, Prime Minister Kenyatta announced his Government's proposals to the House of Representatives.[115] On regionalism, he said that the Regional Assemblies should have no exclusive executive authority in any matter which should be planned and directed on a national scale—education, agriculture, health, the economic and social development and the utilization of land—though the Centre would delegate authority on its own terms. Regional establishments were to be abolished, and the public service was to be centralized with regard to such matters as appointments, transfers, discipline, postings and promotion, though the Public Service Commission was to remain executive. The land vested in the Regions was to be transferred to the Centre, but the Trust land was to remain vested in the local councils. The Central Government would assume direct responsibility for local government and the police.

In October 1964 the Government introduced a Bill in the House of Representatives to give effect to these proposals. It was very carefully drafted,

[114] See G.O./G.O. 7A, volume III (Kenya Archives, Nairobi). Part of the reason for this confusion, and the general weakness of the Regions, was that they did not have their own legal advisers, who had been provided for in one of the drafts of the constitution but were removed before the final draft, ibid., volume II.

[115] House of Representatives, *Debates*, volume III, part II (14 August 1964), cols. 1707–1710.

in order not to encroach on the specially entrenched provisions, which required a 90 per cent vote in the Senate, where KADU held fifteen of the forty-one seats; it was indeed expressly provided in the Bill that nothing in it was to affect the specially entrenched provisions. But as we have seen, few of the substantive powers of the Regions were so entrenched, and were therefore listed for deletion. The Bill had been preceded by an Act to provide for the holding of a referendum on the constitutional proposals if they failed to secure the 75 per cent vote in either House of Parliament, in accordance with section 71. The supervision of the referendum was vested not in the Electoral Commission, as was urged by the opposition, and required by the Constitution, but in the officers appointed by the Government.[116] In the event, no referendum was necessary.

While the House was debating the constitutional proposals, several members of the opposition in both Houses had crossed the floor to join the Government party; and on 10 November 1964 the dissolution of KADU was announced in Parliament; its members later joined KANU. Henceforth the requirements of the process for constitutional amendments ceased to operate as real barriers, and the Government launched on an extensive legislative programme to dismantle the regional structure and to modify other important provisions of the independence Constitution. In this chapter we shall discuss briefly the abolition of the regional institutions and the Senate, but first we must examine the provisions for the establishment of the Republic.

By the first Amendment Act of 1964, Kenya was declared a sovereign Republic on 12 December 1964 and hence ceased to form part of Her Majesty's Dominions.[117] The office of the President, who was to be the Head of both the State and the Government, was established. Provisions for his election were set out, though the first President was not to be elected through them; the person holding the office of the Prime Minister immediately before the declaration of the Republic was automatically to become the first President.[118] The privileges and prerogatives of the Queen in relation to Kenya were transferred to the new Republican Government, to be exercised on its behalf by the President.[119] In 1965 appeals to the Judicial Committee of the Privy Council were abolished.[120]

[116] Act 26 of 1964.
[117] Act 28 of 1964.
[118] Section 8.
[119] Section 16.
[120] Act 14 of 1965, section 15. At independence appeals on constitutional matters to the East African Court of Appeal were prohibited (sections 176 (3) and 180). These sections or subsections have now been repealed (Act 14 of 1965) and it would appear that under the ordinary rules for appeal to that Court, appeals on constitutional questions can go to it. (Criminal Procedure Code, Cap. 27 (1948 Revised Laws), sections 378 and 360, and the Civil Procedure Act, Cap. 5 (1948 Revised Laws), sections 66 and 72–77).

Turning now to regionalism, we have seen how the first amendment Act stripped the Regions of most of their substantive powers. In addition, the control and operation of the police were centralized; its Service Commission was abolished, the functions being transferred to the Public Service Commission, whose members were now to be appointed by the President. By the second Act, the provisions for the independent revenue of the Regions were likewise repealed, so that in future they were dependent entirely on grants from the Centre.[121]

By the Amendment Act of 1965, whose operation was backdated to the inauguration of the Republic, the inferior status of the Regions and their Assemblies was emphasized by the change of their names to Provinces and Councils. The exclusive legislative competence of the Regional Assemblies was displaced by a rule which vested a concurrent competence in these matters in Parliament; the Regions' exclusive executive authority was also removed. The schedule dealing with the specially entrenched provisions was repealed *in toto*. All these changes reduced the regional system to a purely nominal one; it became at best a glorified system of local government, deriving its legislative and executive authority from delegation from the Centre. In practice, it ceased to perform any functions or have any significance early in 1965, though it was not until 1968 that it was legislated out of the Constitution.[122]

We have seen that great emphasis was laid on the Senate and the rigidity of the amendment procedure to ensure the viability of regionalism. The amendment procedure was an effective protection so long as the opposition had an adequate representation in the Senate, but with the dissolution of KADU and its merger with KANU, constitutional change was easy to bring about. The amendment procedures as established in December 1963 were, however, themselves a casualty of change—by the 1965 amendment a new procedure was established, which did not distinguish between the different provisions of the Constitution. Henceforth any section could be amended by a Bill which was supported in each House on its second and third readings by 65 per cent of all its members. At the time the new procedure was adopted, Kenya was a *de facto* one party state, and so the exact voting percentage might have appeared unimportant, but the position could change in the future. The other aspect of the old procedure—that a constitutional amendment Bill could not be altered once it had been introduced in Parliament except for changes certified by the Speaker to be necessary due to the lapse of time between its introduction and promulgation—was, however, retained.

It had been the Government's intention all along to abolish the Senate—it had been established over the strong objections of KANU. But whereas it was possible to persuade the Senators to repeal several provisions of the

[121] Act 38 of 1964. [122] Act 16 of 1968.

Constitution which it was expected they would safeguard, it was clearly going to be extremely difficult to get their support for the abolition of their own house. The Government did not tackle this issue until it had removed most of the other features of regionalism. It had, however, consistently undermined the importance of the Senate—no Minister was ever appointed from it and the decision was taken early that all legislation would first be introduced in the lower house.[123] To abolish the Senate required its own consent, but as it became obvious that its members were not deeply committed to the institution as such, being mainly anxious to retain the privileges they acquired from their membership, a way out was possible.

In July 1966 the Government announced its proposal to abolish the Senate. As a preliminary, an Act was passed requiring the Electoral Commission to review the constituencies (of the lower house) and to increase their number to not less than 160 and not more than 175, the revision to be carried out in such a way as to create an additional constituency in each senatorial district and the Nairobi Area.[124] The aim behind this was to absorb the Senators in the lower house; in this way they would retain the privileges of the membership of Parliament and be willing to vote for the abolition of the Senate. The Electoral Commission carried out the revision and recommended the establishment of 175 constituencies.[125] The effect of the recommendation would have been that even after the absorption of the Senators, there would have been 13 seats to be contested at elections. The Government therefore changed its mind and introduced new legislation to repeal the former Act and to ask the Commission to divide the country into 158 constituencies.[126] The Government stated that at this stage it was only interested in the establishment of a unicameral legislature and that 'any other changes in the composition of the National Assembly, including changes in the number of Elected Members, and in the number and manner of election or appointment of Special Members, should not be introduced before the next General Election (which will not occur later than June 1968) and should then be the subject of further study'.[127]

On 20 December 1966 legislation was introduced in the Senate for the merger of the two houses.[128] The elected members of the House of Representatives and the Senators were declared elected members of the new

[123] G.O./G.O./11, Constitution 1/8/11/27/12 (Kenya Archives, Nairobi). Ironically, the only Bill to be first introduced in the Senate was the last one it dealt with—providing for its own abolition.

[124] Act 27 of 1966. [125] Legal Notice 302/1966. [126] Act 35 of 1966.

[127] Memorandum of Reasons and Objects, Parliamentary Constituencies (Preparatory Review) Bill, 1966, Gazette Supplement 92.

[128] Act No. 40 of 1966. When introducing the Bill for the Act in the Senate, the Attorney-General deplored the reference to the 'abolition' of the Senate, for what was proposed was a merger of the two Houses. However, it is of interest to note that the specific functions and procedures of the Senate were abolished.

National Assembly, and each was assigned to a new constituency (as drawn up by the Commission) by the schedules in the amendment Act. The specially elected members of the House of Representatives were declared the specially elected members of the new Assembly, and their number was fixed at 12. The Speaker and the Deputy Speaker of the House of Representatives were to hold similar positions in the new Assembly, but only until such time as it held its first meeting, when there would be elections for these positions. The law and the rules of privileges, etc., and the Standing Orders of the lower house were to govern the new Assembly, subject to appropriate modifications.

The amendment Act went beyond the merger of the houses. It prolonged the life of Parliament for a further two years until 7 June 1970 although the Government had earlier pledged a general election by June 1968, the time stipulated by the Constitution. The reasons given for this were that elections were tiresome, expensive and a waste of money, and secondly that it would otherwise have been unfair to those Senators whose terms of office would not have come to an end until 1970 if the Senate had not been abolished.[129] The recently formed opposition put up a spirited resistance, but the Bill was overwhelmingly supported in both the chambers, taking no more than four days from its first publication to its final approval through the legislative processes of the Senate and the House of Representatives.

AUTOCHTHONY

Thus by the end of 1966 the Constitution had changed fundamentally. Apart from the removal of *majimbo*, several other amendments had been made, and the effect of most of these (which are discussed elsewhere) was to strengthen the executive. The Constitution became more streamlined and compact, though perhaps not necessarily completely coherent in its basic assumptions. All the changes were carried out according to the letter of the law; at no time was there a break in legal continuity, so much so that until the end of 1968 the Constitution was formally a 'British' document whose interpretation was governed by the English Interpretation Act, 1889, 'as it applies for the purpose of interpretation and in relation to the Acts of the Parliament of the United Kingdom'.[130] Nor, unlike Tanzania and Uganda, has there been a Constituent Assembly to enact the new constitutional provisions, and the legislation providing for the Republic had to have the assent of the Governor-General.

Kenya does not, therefore—to use the jargon of some academics—have an autochthonous Constitution, which for this purpose is defined as a consti-

[129] House of Representatives, *Debates*, volume X, part II (3 November 1966), col. 1671; (21 December 1966), col. 3028 et seq.

[130] Section 247 (15). The reference to the English Interpretation Act has been omitted in the Constitution Act (1969) and so the constitution will be construed according to Kenya's Interpretation and General Provisions Act (Cap. 2).

tution which does not trace its validity to any British legislation, but is 'home grown', 'rooted' in the country itself.[131] But there is another, less formal, sense in which autochthony may be understood; and for this purpose the content rather than the origin of the new Constitution is more important. The criterion here is the manner in which it conforms to the 'national form' and reflects local traditional values.[132] There is yet a third sense in which autochthony can be relevant—and this is to examine the impact of local leadership and policies on the *independence* Constitution. We have seen that in Kenya the independence Constitution was hammered out during an interminable series of meetings between KANU and KADU, under the admittedly not completely impartial chairmanship of the British, and to a large measure represented a compromise between their positions. In this sense, could the independence Constitution not be regarded as autochthonous, the product of local politics as it was? The KANU case, however, was that it was an imposed Constitution, and this was seen as providing one justification for its modifications.

In its various proposals for constitutional alterations, the Government has made much use of the second sense of autochthony, without actually using the expression. They have been justified on the grounds that they will bring the Constitution more into line with traditional African values and customs. Introducing the Republican proposals, the Government spokesman said, 'We are an independent African state within the African family of nations. This fact must be reflected both in the forms and reality of our government'.[133] On the actual establishment of a Republic it was said, 'Our country was never at any time a monarchy. Colonialism imposed monarchical rule on us and as part of the process towards our full independence and the regaining of our complete status, the declaration of a republic restores the historical reality of our freedom'.[134] It was argued in favour of the merger of the positions of the Head of State and Government in one person that the division was 'an illusory arrangement' which 'people do not understand'.[135] The case for the rules for presidential elections which tied them to those for Parliament was that 'here again, our approach to these matters is one of directness and simplicity. When our people go to the polls, they will elect at one time a body which will make the law, that is Parliament, and the man who—with his Ministers—will rule by and under those laws. This is the best way to simplify this matter as far as our people

[131] K. C. Wheare, *Constitutional Structure of the Commonwealth* (Oxford, Clarendon Press, 1960), chapter 4.
[132] Robinson, 'Constitutional Autochthony in Ghana', 1 *Journal of Commonwealth Political Studies* (1961), 41.
[133] House of Representatives, *Debates*, volume III, part III (27 October 1964), col. 3880.
[134] ibid., col. 3879.
[135] ibid., col. 3881.

are concerned, and we believe it to be a true reflection of African thought and tradition that the chosen leader of the nation should have his home and roots in a locality where, also, he is the chosen leader of his kinsmen and his neighbours'.[136] In defence of Cabinet responsibility to Parliament, it was stated to be 'suited to traditional needs . . . Our people have always governed their affairs by looking to a council of elders elected and headed by their own chosen leader, giving them strong and wise leadership. That tradition—which is an Africanism—will be preserved in this new Constitution'.[137] On another occasion it was said that 'Our whole constitutional structure is rooted in our African traditions. These give our people the right to select and to strengthen our council of elders, that is today called the Kenya Parliament'.[138] In favour of the abolition of the Senate, it was argued that there was no example of African traditional society with a 'two tier system'; it was part of the Westminster system, which was unsuitable for Africa.[139]

The Government has not, however, been consistent in the use of this line of argument. It has sometimes sought a justification for its proposals in the practice or the law of foreign countries. The Preservation of Public Security Act, under which the Government acquires extensive power, including that of preventive detention, was justified by reference to the emergency powers in India and other places.[140] The vesting in the President of powers of civil service appointment and dismissal was urged on the analogy of similar powers in the British Crown.[141] The amendment requiring MPs who cross the floor to resign was said to be based on the law or conventions in Western countries. When the accuracy of this statement was challenged, it was abandoned in favour of pride in the originality of the Government's thinking, '. . . the most important thing about Kenya is that we think for ourselves. The Constitution that we now have in Kenya is a product of our own thoughts, imagination and philosophy . . . .'[142]

It is not proposed to examine the authenticity of claims that the Constitution is based on African traditions,[143] except to make a few observations. The Government's position shows sensitivity to the political popularity of arguments based on 'autochthony'. It is generally regarded as strengthening a case if it could be shown to be, or argued to be, inspired by African tradi-

[136] ibid., col. 3882.
[137] ibid., col. 3883.
[138] House of Representatives, *Debates*, volume X, part II (21 December 1966), col. 3036.
[139] House of Representatives, *Debates*, volume VII (2 November 1965), col. 8.
[140] House of Representatives, *Debates*, volume IX, part I (2 June 1966), col. 291.
[141] House of Representatives, *Debates*, volume VIII (2 March 1966), col. 1658.
[142] House of Representatives, *Debates*, volume VIII (28 April 1966), cols. 2022 and 2025.
[143] cf. KADU's case which argued that decentralization with powers devolved to the elders, was an African way of government. Similar justifications were made in favour of an Upper Chamber. House of Representatives, *Debates*, volume III, part III (27 October 1964), col. 3908.

tions—in this, the reaction is part of the wider phenomenon of liberation from the 'cultural imperialism' of colonialism. But in Kenya's constitutional changes, genuine concern for rediscovering and preserving African traditions is not so clear. Several points may be briefly mentioned here. First, there is no evidence of a thoroughgoing review of the Constitution to examine how far it is laden with alien concepts and how African ideas of government could be incorporated in it. Secondly, as we have attempted to show and as we argue in the last chapter, there is a remarkable continuity of law and institutions from the colonial era, which was the period when many of these were deliberately modelled on Western ideas. Thirdly, the government position assumes the existence of certain traditions common to all African societies. It has been argued elsewhere that generalizations in this area are not possible, given the range of variations in social, political and economic systems among the different tribes. Fourthly, it is doubtful how far reliance on traditional ways is compatible with the goal of rapid economic and social development. The other official justification for constitutional changes has been the need to produce a workable system, which is simple and inexpensive to maintain and is capable of overcoming the obstacles to modernization. It is not always clear that resort to traditional ways might not retard this objective.

Indeed, it might be argued that the ability of a constitution to solve problems of development is more valuable than its consonance with tradition. In this sense, the alterations to the Constitution since independence have been positive. The rigidity and complexity of the *majimbo* provisions would have acted as a constraint on planning and development and would have interfered seriously with coherence in administration. A complicated constitution may work if conventions for co-operation exist between different governments and institutions. Given the immediate pre-independence history in Kenya, it was naive to expect co-operation between KANU dominated Central and Regional Governments on the one hand and KADU Regions on the other. The system also made heavy demands on personnel and money. After the alterations, however, central planning is possible, as is a coherent administration. The new system is more flexible and more able to respond to changing circumstances. The potentiality of sharp and permanent divisions manifest in the independence Constitution has been mitigated.[144]

The *majimbo* provision and some others to safeguard against abuse of power did not therefore last long, and in conclusion it may be asked whether

[144] These comments refer only to amendments for the abolition of *majimbo*. Extensive changes were also made in other areas (e.g. the abolition of the offices of Mudirs and Liwalis by Act 28 of 1964), including the relationship between the executive and the legislature; it is doubtful if all of the latter are beneficial and will be discussed in subsequent chapters. For these, see Ghai, 'The Government and the Constitution in Kenya', *E.A.J.*, 1967.

it was wise to have devised such a complicated Constitution for Kenya in 1963. Experience elsewhere has shown that such provisions are resented and got rid of soon after independence, and it has indeed been argued that it would be better if dependencies were established immediately on independence as republics rather than as dominions, still nominally under the sovereignty of the Crown.[145] There are two separate issues here: first, is it necessary or wise that residues of the imperial past should continue to operate after independence; secondly, how effective are provisions in restraint of power likely to be? As to the first, if the local leaders evince strong desire to move at once to a republican status, the British Government would consent to it. There may, however, be arguments in favour of a dominion—when the leaders of the new country embark on the novel experience of running a government, it is useful to have an experienced person as Governor-General, who can advise and guide. Also, a year's experience as a dominion may help to put the national problems in a better perspective and to indicate what constitutional arrangements are best suited for them—a consideration which often gets overlooked in the preoccupation with negotiations for independence, which are more concerned with accommodating existing demands. Thus, when the country does move to a republican status, it is also able to make other appropriate changes in its system.

As to the second, the restraints on power are regarded as evidence of lack of confidence in the ability of the new government to rule fairly and impartially—all the more so since in the Westminster system there are few such restraints, except through conventions. But the ease with which it has been possible to remove these restraints gives an air of unreality to all the constitutional haggling in the period preceding independence. It is doubtful if any of the parties really believed that the 1963 constitutional arrangements would be other than short-lived, despite the heat generated during the negotiations for them. It may be argued that the arrangements were a convenient device for the grant of independence; on the part of the British Government, it could be seen as fulfilling its pledges to the minority groups, and so could be seen to leave with a good conscience; on the part of KANU, it would enable them to achieve power, which could later be used to upset the arrangements; and on the part of the minorities, the recognition that this was the most they could expect anyway. If this somewhat cynical interpretation is valid, then the criticisms made of the complicated constitutions that bring independence are misplaced, for they misconstrue their true purpose.

[145] Robinson, in *Essays in Imperial Government*, op. cit., pp. 283–97.

CHAPTER VI

The Executive

INTRODUCTION

A study of the Executive in Kenya is a study of presidential power. This emerges both from the Constitution itself and from evolving practice. This chapter must therefore be related round the office and powers of the President, but inevitably it will branch out and consider other institutions and their relationship to the President. Foremost among these matters to be discussed is the relationship between the Executive and the Legislature including the vexed problem of the responsibility of the former to the latter. Though the distinction is not always a clear one, we are concerned here with the more political aspects of the Executive; the administrative aspects will be looked at in chapter VII.

In common with several African States, Kenya moved to a presidential form of government shortly after independence, but unlike some of these states, she has tried to secure the advantages of a strong Executive in conjunction with the principles of parliamentary government. When constitutional amendments in Africa are proposed, arguments are often advanced to the effect that the parliamentary system does not produce an effective Executive, that this is Africa's great need, so as to establish and maintain stability and order in the country, and that an executive presidential system in which the President is no longer a member of the National Assembly is best for this purpose. Such a line of argument shows an inadequate appreciation of the mechanism of the parliamentary system, for the growth of strong parties, the evolution of the rules of parliamentary procedure in favour of the Executive, and the accretion of power in the hands of the Prime Minister ensures that the parliamentary system provides for an extremely powerful executive. In such a situation, the active association of the Government with Parliament is a source of strength.

The Government of Kenya rejected the model of the executive Presidency which both English and French-speaking African states had, up to that point, favoured, and adopted instead a system of a parliamentary presidency in which the President, while combining in his person the offices of both Head of State and Head of Government is at the same time an MP, and the whole Government can in law be dismissed from office by an adverse vote in the National Assembly, however remote a possibility that might be in practice. This form of government is a variant of, rather than a departure from, the Westminster model inherited at independence, but there are good reasons why such a variant should be adopted. In a developing political system which depends so greatly on the charisma of one person, such a division at the top is confusing and weakening, invites clashes of personalities, and fails to provide a clear focal point for loyalty and support. In addition, it tends to lead to difficulties at the time of elections, or succession of governments, particularly when the Governor-General is a local citizen only recently retired from an active life in politics as tends to be the case, at the very time when it is essential that the operation of the Constitution leaves no room for dispute, or abuse of power. Combining the two posts obviates some of these difficulties, though it in turn creates some constitutional problems, not all of which have received satisfactory solutions.

When announcing the Government's intention to introduce a Republican Constitution, Mr. Kenyatta, then Prime Minister, outlined the aims of the new Constitution as follows:[1] 'It should embody the fact of national leadership as seen in the eyes of the people, the concept of collective Ministerial responsibility and also guarantee the supremacy of Parliament.' The first two aims will be discussed, *inter alia*, in this chapter, the third falls more naturally to be discussed in chapter VIII.

THE ELECTION OF THE PRESIDENT

The aim of the system of presidential elections created in 1964 was to combine a popular election to the office with a general election to the National Assembly in such a way that the President was virtually certain to have a majority of his supporters in the National Assembly and thus be able to form a government and carry on with the task of governing. In the event of it becoming necessary to elect a President at a time other than at a general election, the system provided that the National Assembly would elect one, thus ensuring continuity of majority government. This system was not foolproof in theory, though it probably would have been in practice. It was, however, extensively changed in 1968. The new system has the same aim as the old one, but goes about it in such a way that it is reasonable to infer that it has other aims as well, namely to take away power from a National Assembly that has shown itself at times to have a mind of its own, and increase the power of the Cabinet, and the central organs of KANU over both presidential and parliamentary candidates, and to reduce the chances of an opposition party obtaining a significant number of seats in the National Assembly. These points may best be illustrated by outlining in brief the former system before looking at the new system.

[1] House of Representatives, *Debates*, volume III, part II (14 August 1964), col. 1708.

Under the old system, there were two methods of electing the President. The first method was to be used only upon a dissolution of Parliament. The procedure was as follows.[2] To stand in the presidential election, a person had to be a citizen of at least 35 years of age, and be registered in some constituency as a voter in elections to the National Assembly. Nominations of presidential candidates had to be supported by not less than one thousand persons registered as voters in elections to the National Assembly. Such candidates had also to be candidates for election to the National Assembly from a constituency, for a person could not be President unless he was also a constituency member of the Assembly. All the candidates for parliamentary election had to declare before the polling day their support for one of the presidential candidates; in the absence of such a declaration their own nomination as a parliamentary candidate was void. Where the election was contested in any constituency, the ballot papers were to be in such a form as to disclose both the names of the candidates for election to the Assembly, and the name of the candidate for the President which each of the candidates for election to the Assembly supported. Where a candidate for President was elected to the Assembly and received the declared support of a number of members elected to the Assembly (including himself) exceeding one half of the number of constituencies into which the country was divided, he became President, but if there was no such candidate, no one was declared elected.

In such a case, resort was made to the second procedure for electing the President.[3] That procedure was also employed in the following other instances: when the President died; or resigned his office without having first dissolved Parliament; or it was determined that the election of the President was invalid; or the President ceased to be a member of the Assembly otherwise than by reason of a dissolution of Parliament; or retirement of the President due to his inability to perform his functions due to physical or mental infirmity for a period of over three months. In any one of these events, the Assembly acted as an electoral college; the Speaker summoned a meeting as soon as practicable of all the members of the Assembly (in the case of the election just after the general election, before the election of the specially elected members). Any of the elected members of the Assembly was eligible to stand for election for President; in addition, such a nomination was only valid if it was supported by at least 20 other members of the Assembly qualified to vote, at each sitting at which the ballot is taken. All the members of the Assembly who were entitled to vote on any question before the Assembly, and who were entitled to attend the election meeting, other than the

[2] Constitution of Kenya (Amendment) Act No. 28 of 1964, Schedule 1, adding sections 33 A-G to the independence Constitution.
[3] ibid., section 33 A (6)–(10).

Speaker or the Deputy Speaker, were allowed to vote at the election. The election was by secret ballot, and to be successful a candidate had to have the votes of more than one-half of the total number of persons entitled to vote. If no such clear majority was obtained by a candidate at the first ballot, two further ballots were to be taken; another two might be taken if the Speaker, who presided at the meeting, considered that a result might be achieved thereby. Only one ballot could be taken at one sitting, and the Speaker might adjourn the meeting between the taking of any two successive ballots for such period as he thought fit, being not less than two hours and not more than two days. If there was no nomination for the first ballot, or if the successive ballots failed to yield a result, then Parliament stood dissolved, or if the ballots followed a general election, the general election was voided and another general election took place.

That system represented an uneasy compromise between popular choice and the assurance of majority support; between democratic choice and certainty in the succession. The presidential candidate did not have to approve of a parliamentary candidate who declared a preference for him, so that he was not guaranteed a clear majority in the National Assembly. Indeed as the rules stood there was nothing to stop a parliamentary candidate for one party declaring a preference for a presidential candidate from another. There was the conflict between the system at the general election and at any other time; on the former occasion the electorate voted for the President, on the latter only the National Assembly; and there was the long-drawn out method of election if the general election failed to produce a President, at a time inevitably of great uncertainty. These compromises and conflicts were not seen, or were ignored, in 1964, because no Presidential election in Kenya was envisaged without President Kenyatta being a candidate and sweeping the board, and because Kenya was at that time a *de facto* one-party state in which all supported the President with varying degrees of enthusiasm. But the events of April 1966 when twenty MPs left KANU to found the KPU and 'The Little General Election'[4] which followed indicated that the KPU had a good measure of popular support, albeit they failed to win many seats, showed that these assumptions might be somewhat optimistic. Again, the President was getting old, it could not be assumed without question that he would contest a presidential election, there was no obvious successor to him, nor would he designate one. Added to these factors is the general tendency of constitutional developments in Kenya since independence which has been to alter the balance of the Constitution in favour of increased executive power, and the maintenance of the present Government in office.

This is the background against which the 1968 amendments to the system, and the struggle in and out of the National Assembly that they produced,

[4] Bennett, 'Kenya's Little General Election', *World Today*, 1966, p. 336.

must be seen. One further previous amendment to the Constitution must be mentioned, however, for the 1968 amendments are to some extent a corollary of them. This is the amendment in 1966 which required those MPs who crossed the floor of the National Assembly to resign their seats, and fight an election.[5] Both that amendment, and the one under discussion have as one of their primary aims a tightening of discipline over MPs and an increase in the certainty that the President will have a stable, even a docile, majority in the National Assembly.

The system as amended still distinguishes between a presidential election at the time of a general election, and at any other time. In the former election,[6] each political party taking part in the general election must nominate a presidential candidate, who must also be a parliamentary candidate, and to be valid that nomination must be supported by 1,000 registered voters. Assuming that there are two or more validly nominated presidential candidates, a poll takes place in each constituency at the general election for the President. In each constituency only one ballot paper is to be used and it is to be in such a form as to pair the presidential candidate with the candidate nominated by the same political party for the National Assembly (and only candidates nominated by political parties may in future stand for the National Assembly)[7] so as to permit one vote to be cast for one of the pairs of candidates, and that vote shall be taken to be a vote for each member of the pair. A candidate for the presidency who is elected to the National Assembly and who receives a greater number of votes than any other candidate elected to the National Assembly shall be declared elected the President. Thus independents and hangers-on to the presidential band-wagon are eliminated. The voter is compelled to support the same party for both presidential and parliamentary elections, neither splitting the vote nor voting only for a presidential or parliamentary candidate being possible.

In the latter election,[8] which occurs on all those occasions where previously the National Assembly elected the President, other than where a general election fails to produce a clear result, a presidential election must take place within ninety days of the office of President becoming vacant. Candidates for the presidency must be nominated by political parties (though no party is obliged to nominate a candidate) and the candidates must be elected members of the National Assembly and supported by 1,000 registered voters. A poll is taken in each constituency, and the candidate with the highest number of votes is declared the President.

[5] Constitution of Kenya (Amendment) (No. 2) Act No. 17 of 1966. See pp. 320–2, below.

[6] Section 33 A (1)-(3), added by Constitution of Kenya (Amendment) (No. 2) Act No. 45 of 1968. Now Constitution section 5 (3).

[7] Constitution section 34 (d). It would appear, however, that parties are not required to put up candidates for Parliament.

[8] Section 33 A (4)-(5). Now Constitution section 5 (5).

Any evaluation of this new system must be tentative since it has yet to be put to the test, and it must also take account of the political context of Kenya. One or two apparent gaps in the rules may first be mentioned. It is not made clear whether a political party is disqualified from contesting the elections to the National Assembly if its presidential candidate fails to be validly nominated, e.g. fails to obtain 1,000 valid supporting declarations from registered voters. It would seem a very drastic penalty, if, for lack of ten valid voters' declarations for a presidential candidate, a political party and its 150 or more parliamentary candidates were disqualified from contesting a general election.[9] It is not immediately clear why a political party must nominate a presidential candidate at a general election but is not required to at any other time. If the object is to present the electorate with a clear choice, they should have that choice at each presidential election. If, on the other hand, the object is to ensure that the President has a majority in the National Assembly, then logically only the majority party should put up a presidential candidate other than at a general election, lest the opposition candidate win, and government breaks down. Even after a general election it is possible for the President to be of one party and the majority in the National Assembly to be of another, for he is President who receives the greatest number of votes *and* obtains a seat in the National Assembly; receiving the greatest number of votes is not sufficient by itself. Thus a candidate, popular in the country at large, but unpopular in his constituency, could fail to become President, while his popularity has been sufficient to ensure that a majority of his supporters win seats in the National Assembly.

These points may never be put to the test though it is no answer to them to say that they have deliberately not been dealt with so that the Constitution can be kept flexible, and common sense will ensure adequate solutions.[10] More important perhaps is to consider the new rules in the political situation as it was in Kenya in the middle of 1968. The ruling party, KANU, despite attempts at organizational reform in the period during and after the ousting of Mr. Oginga Odinga and his supporters, still remained much more of a collection of local party bosses than a unified centralized party. As such, the central organs had little control over candidates for elections, whether party, national or local, and over the performance of MPs in the National Assembly, where, irrespective of Government office or party affiliation, MPs were wont to speak out against the Government as they saw fit. The Government and Party had to depend very much upon the personality of the President to maintain order and unity and, on occasions, get govern-

[9] cf. The disqualification, on technical grounds connected with nomination, of all opposition KPU candidates at the 1968 local government elections.
[10] National Assembly, *Debates*, volume XV (28 May 1968), col. 90 et seq. (Attorney-General introducing the amendments).

ment measures through the National Assembly. These amendments may be seen in part as an attempt to substitute constitutional rules for the personality of the President in an endeavour to keep the ruling party together if and when the President vacates his office and retires, and to transfer the inevitable succession struggle from the floor of the National Assembly where it would take place in public and with the opposition able to influence events, to the Cabinet and Party organs where it would be in private, and confined to KANU alone. Whether they will succeed in this aim depends to some extent on the method adopted by KANU to decide who will be its presidential and parliamentary candidates, for the elimination of differences by constitutional rules does not necessarily mean that those differences will disappear. If the Party does not allow differences to have an airing, the rules may prove as fallible as others in Africa.

The other political factor which must be considered is the strength of the main opposition party, the KPU, and the likely effect of the new rules on it. One aim of the rules has been to devalue the local influence and personality of an MP, but, paradoxically, standing on their own, they could help the KPU considerably. It must put up a presidential candidate at a general election and may do so at other times, so that it will attract a national vote, and not just a local vote in those areas where it puts up parliamentary candidates.[11] Dissident KANU officials who can no longer stand as independent KANU candidates may be tempted to join the KPU if they can thereby stand for the National Assembly. The obligation to vote for presidential and parliamentary candidates together will help an opposition party with a good presidential candidate, and the present leader of the KPU cannot be underrated on that score. Electoral rules are not, it must be admitted, the only guide to the chances of an opposition party in an election. The fair administration of such laws as those relating to the licensing of public meetings, the registration of political parties and their branches, and preventive detention are equally important, and here the opposition is not so well served in Kenya. Indeed, to the extent that the electoral rules improve the chances of the KPU, these other rules will no doubt be administered so as to 'redress the balance' so that in the final analysis the KPU may not gain.

In sum, the new rules, though introduced as being an important innovation, are not a significant improvement on the old. They still leave open the possibility that the President and the National Assembly may be of different parties, and they contain important omissions. Under the guise of giving more power to the electorate, they give increased power to the Executive

[11] Since it is not required to put up a full slate of parliamentary candidates, it follows that its presidential candidate could win the presidential election and yet find himself faced with a majority of the National Assembly of a different political persuasion.

and the central Party organs in the conduct of the elections. Perhaps most important of all, their successful operation will still, in the final analysis, depend on personality—the personality of President Kenyatta or the person who is to replace him.

TENURE OF OFFICE

It is intended that the term of the President will be coterminous with the life of a Parliament. Parliament is elected for five years, though it is possible that a dissolution may take place before that, just as it is possible that Parliament may decide to prolong its own life for further periods of twelve months to a maximum of five years. So in normal circumstances, a President would hold office for five years. There is no prohibition against eligibility to stand for a second or subsequent terms of office.

However, there can be several factors which could lead to the termination of office before the five years. It is possible for the President to resign at at any time before then. His term also comes to an end if he ceases to be a member of the National Assembly, otherwise than by reason of a dissolution of Parliament. A person can cease to be a member of the Assembly for a variety of reasons. Some of these reasons, however, are adverse judgments in criminal or civil proceedings, and since the President has immunity from all legal suits they cannot operate in his case. A member also loses his seat if he has been absent from eight consecutive meetings of the Assembly in any session without the permission of the Speaker.[12] As a member of the National Assembly, the President would be covered by this rule. But the Constitution also provides that when a member is due to lose his seat for such absence, the President may direct that he should not so vacate his seat if he thinks fit. Presumably he could use this discretion in his own favour; and thus the rule is no real disqualification in his case.

The President can be removed for inability to perform the functions of his office due to mental or physical infirmity.[13] The procedure for removal, which also applies in relation to any other person discharging the functions of the President for the time being, is as follows. The question whether the President is unfit can generally only be raised by the Cabinet; a resolution that an enquiry be held is given to the Speaker of the National Assembly to be forwarded to the Chief Justice. In exceptional circumstances, the Speaker can make the request to the Chief Justice on his own initiative, if there is no member of the Cabinet in the country, other than the person in respect of whom the enquiry is to be made, and the Speaker considers that it is in the interests of Kenya that the question should be determined

[12] Constitution section 39 (c).
[13] Section 33 E as revised by Act No. 45 of 1968. Now Constitution section 12.

without delay. The Chief Justice refers the matter to a medical tribunal of not less than five persons, two of whom, oddly enough, can be nominated by the President who is suspected to be infirm. The tribunal reports on the matter to the Chief Justice who certifies accordingly to the Speaker. The whole procedure must be gone through again when the Cabinet wishes to know whether the President has recovered from his infirmity, if the first certificate was to the effect that he was suffering from infirmity. The President himself can request such a review. If the tribunal then concludes within three months of the original examination that the infirmity has not ceased, or if no review within this period is requested, the President automatically ceases to hold office.

Two points may be made about these provisions. First, they appear to allow a President who is declared to be unable to exercise his office nonetheless to do so for at least three months. The wisdom of this is difficult to understand. An automatic delegation of power to the Vice-President on receipt of an unfavourable report of the tribunal would make more sense of the elaborate provisions.[14] Secondly, it is by no means clear who may convene the Cabinet if the President is unable to exercise his functions, and has not delegated them to the Vice-President. It would be a strange argument which said that any majority of Cabinet Ministers constituted a Cabinet sufficient to set these procedures in motion, yet short of such an argument it does not seem that they could be set in motion. Could the President then be overruled by his Cabinet on this matter? The answer to this depends on the precise relationship between the President and the Cabinet in general which is discussed below, but difficulties can be perceived from either possibility. Perhaps this is an occasion when common sense would prevail, though how much common sense would be shown by a President, alleged by his colleagues to be too infirm to carry out his duties, is a moot point.

VICE-PRESIDENT AND ACTING PRESIDENT

The President ceases to hold office immediately if he resigns, ceases to be a member of the National Assembly, remains infirm for a period exceeding three months, or has his election declared invalid. In such instances the Constitution provides in great detail for persons who are to exercise the functions of the President, and attempts to make radical alterations to these provisions in 1968 provoked great controversy in the National Assembly. To understand why this was so requires a consideration of the position of the Vice-President. The Vice-President's position differs from those of the other Ministers in several important respects. The office of Vice-President is

[14] The President may, however, delegate his powers to the Vice-President if he is ill (section 11). The old section (33 D), replaced in 1969, provided for automatic delegation of power in case of declared infirmity. No reason was given for the change.

established by the Constitution, and its holder is described as the principal assistant of the President in the discharge of his functions.[15] He must be appointed from the elected members of the National Assembly, unlike Ministers who may be nominated members. No person can be appointed to the vice-presidency when the functions of the President are being exercised by some other person. All the Ministers, including the Vice-President, are removable by the President, but while the other Ministers can be removed by the acting President, with the concurrence of the Cabinet, the Vice-President can only be removed by the substantive holder of the Presidency.

These provisions suggest that the framers of the Constitution thought of the office of the Vice-President as being one whose holder could carry out many of the President's administrative functions, leaving him to be primarily concerned with the political and ceremonial sides of his office. Since the office was so intimately connected with that of the President, it was only proper that the President alone could appoint and remove the holder. Likewise it was desirable that the Vice-President should be an elected member of the National Assembly so that he could the more convincingly be a leader of the House should the President decide not to be an active member of the House, as has turned out to be the case. This relationship is made clear by a provision empowering the President to appoint the Vice-President to exercise his functions, subject to certain constitutional restrictions, when he is to be absent from Kenya, is ill, or for any other cause.[16]

In all these circumstances, it was natural that it should be the Vice-President who generally was to act as the President when the substantive holder of that office had vacated it. Prior to the 1969 amendments to the Constitution, there were a series of detailed rules to deal with the possibility that the Vice-President or some other Cabinet Minister might be unable to act as the President, which had the effect of conferring great power on the Speaker, but which were deficient to the extent that they did not indicate clearly how long an acting President could remain in that position. One thing which was clear, however, was that he could not exercise, except in accordance with a resolution of the Cabinet, certain important presidential powers relating to the composition of the Cabinet, the dissolution of Parliament, and the bringing into force of the Preservation of Public Security Act.[17] The acting President in other words was to head a caretaker Government until such time as a new President was elected to office.

In 1968 there were two attempts made by the Government to alter these

[15] Section 15 (3).
[16] Constitution section 11.
[17] Constitution of Kenya (Amendment) Act No. 28 of 1964, first schedule, section 33 D (6).

provisions fundamentally, by separating the temporary exercise of presidential power by the Vice-President, when the President delegates his functions for some cause, from its permanent exercise by the Vice-President when the presidential office becomes vacant. The temporary exercise of presidential power was to be on the same terms as before, but when the presidential office had been vacated it was proposed that the Vice-President should assume the office of President and exercise all the powers of a President, in the first proposal for the rest of the former President's term,[18] in the second proposal for six months until elections for a new President were held.[19] Whatever the merits of these proposals from the point of view of continuity of government—the main reason put forward by the Government for their introduction[20]—and this is a very crucial matter for which the Constitution had not hitherto made adequate provision, they met with very strong opposition in the National Assembly. MPs, and even Ministers, spoke out against them on the grounds that such a person thus elevated to the Presidency would be neither the people's nor the National Assembly's choice, that he would be tempted to use his full powers to perpetuate himself in office by, for example, detaining his likely principal opponents in the forthcoming presidential elections, and that this represented a further accretion of power to the Cabinet which was undesirable. The Government, or those members of it who supported the amendments, ultimately and, for whatever reason, to its credit, backed down and produced a third draft which in effect repeated the main provision of the 1964 rules. These were passed by the National Assembly. The position now is that when the office of President is vacated for some cause, the Vice-President, or where there is none, or he considers that he is for any reason unable to do so, some other Minister appointed by the Cabinet, exercises the functions of the office of President, subject to the same exceptions and limitations as before, for up to ninety days.[21] During this period a presidential election must be held.

Since the inauguration of the Republic there have been three Vice-Presidents, and a consideration of the development of the office under them may help explain in part the objections of MPs to the proposed amendments discussed above. When Mr. Oginga Odinga was appointed Vice-President in 1964, the President made it clear that there was no automatic right of succession to the office of Presidency, and indeed the Vice-Presidency has in practice been very much what the President wanted it to be. By the time Mr. Oginga Odinga resigned in 1966, the office was a name only. He had lost all administrative powers and on a crucial occasion had been bypassed by

[18] Constitution of Kenya (Amendment No. 2) Bill, 29/3/1968—later withdrawn.
[19] Constitution of Kenya (Amendment No. 2) Bill, 10/5/1968—later withdrawn.
[20] *Debates*, op. cit., (A-G).
[21] Section 33AB added by Act No. 45 of 1968. Now Constitution section 6.

the rest of the Government as Leader of Government Business in the National Assembly.[22] His successor, Mr. Murumbi, was never a serious contender for the succession to the Presidency, and was not a particularly powerful political figure in his own right. He was, however, an old and close confidant of the President, and during his tenure of office the Vice-Presidency approximated more closely to the original conception of the office, being an important adjunct of the President's office. The third Vice-President, Daniel Arap Moi, has slowly emerged as a more powerful political figure than Mr. Murumbi, and a more powerful administrative one than Mr. Oginga Odinga. He has retained the office of Minister for Home Affairs, he is Leader of Government Business in the National Assembly, he makes more trips abroad than, and as many round Kenya as, the President, and retains a powerful political base in the Rift Valley. More than any other Vice-President he has the appearance of being a possible successor to President Kenyatta. But that this should occur without a vote of any sort was contrary to the expectations of all MPs, and would radically alter the nature of the Vice-President's office. It was this that was appreciated, and objected to, by MPs.

POWERS AND IMMUNITIES OF THE PRESIDENT PECULIAR TO HIS STATUS AS HEAD OF STATE

The President is both the Head of State and the Head of Government. His powers and immunities, therefore, reflect the need to ensure the dignity of a Head of State and the participation of the Head of Government in political controversy, and his responsiveness to political pressures. There is some contradiction in these two positions. This contradiction is reflected in the rules about the President's participation in the National Assembly.[23] He can participate in the Assembly in two different capacities—as the President or Head of State and as the Leader of the Government and a constituency member. When he participates as the Head of State, he sits on a special seat of honour provided for him beside the Speaker. In this capacity, he cannot take part in the debate or vote; nor can he be interrupted. It is in this capacity that he would deliver presidential addresses, and outline governmental policy, in the manner of the British speech from the throne. In his other capacity, however, he is able to take a full part in the proceedings of the Assembly, vote, and be interrupted and questioned. This is likely to lead to a certain amount of confusion, and fears have also been expressed that the President may use the more favourable rules regarding his participation as Head of State to make controversial announcements from the presidential chair, and avoid debate on them.[24] A member of Parliament made a helpful sugges-

[22] House of Representatives, *Debates*, volume VIII (15 February 1966), cols. 900–902.
[23] Constitution section 52. See, too, House of Representatives, *Debates*, volume VII (10 December 1965), col. 1052.
[24] House of Representatives, *Debates*, volume III, part III (28 October 1964), col. 4018.

tion that when the President wanted to resume his seat as an ordinary member after his participation as the President, there should be a short adjournment of the House so that people might appreciate the change of role.[25] It is rather unsatisfactory that a person should participate in the House in this dual way, and it is a little artificial to think that if a person takes part in the rough and tumble of the Assembly as the Leader of Government, he is likely suddenly to be invested with respect and dignity when he appears as the Head of State. One of the points made in favour of this kind of merger of the offices of Head of State and Government was that it had the merit of simplicity and directness, but the preceding discussion shows that this may not be the case in the National Assembly. In practice, confusion has not arisen because the President comes to the National Assembly only in his capacity as Head of State leaving the role of Head of Government to the Vice-President in his capacity as Leader of Government Business. Another source of confusion, however, which may be mentioned here, which does arise in practice, is the rule concerning criticism of the President in the National Assembly. The Speaker has ruled that Standing Orders prevent any criticism of the President or his conduct except on a substantive motion, even when he exercises a power such as the prerogative of mercy. The only exception appears to be the ill-defined area of where the President does an administrative act.[26] The implications of this ruling will be discussed below.

The President has been given wide immunity from legal process—no criminal or civil proceedings can be instituted against him in respect of anything he has done or omitted to do.[27] The immunity lasts only so long as he is President, and the period of limitations does not run when he is enjoying this procedural immunity. The substantive rights, therefore, are preserved, and the rule of immunity enables the President to discharge better his functions and to maintain the dignity of his office. There was, however, much disquiet about this legal immunity, though it is not unusual in other systems. The Government defence of it was one which has become typical in cases of provisions strengthening the Executive, that the 'main safeguard of the good conduct of future Presidents is that they will depend on the people for their election and on the support of Parliament for their continuance in office'.[28] This argument is hardly valid when the question of the President's liability to an individual is concerned. Such personal,

[25] The Standing Orders in fact provide for a Chair of State in the Assembly; when he sits on that he is head of state and becomes head of government only when he moves to the front bench (Standing Orders 11–16). He uses the Speaker's Chair for ceremonial occasions.
[26] National Assembly, *Debates*, volume XI (7 April 1967), cols. 2208–2209; volume XIV (12 March 1968), col. 713.
[27] Constitution section 14.
[28] House of Representatives, *Debates*, volume III, part III (27 October 1964), col. 3893.

individual liability is unlikely to assume political dimensions, and the rule of parliamentary accountability is a poor remedy for an aggrieved individual; the President's official and personal liabilities could have been distinguished, legal immunity being granted only for the former.

Finally, the President's emoluments may be mentioned. The National Assembly determines his salary and allowances, and, on retirement, the gratuities and allowances payable to him. The salary and allowances cannot be altered to the disadvantage of a President during his tenure of office; and all his emoluments are charged by the Constitution on the Consolidated Fund.[29]

SUBSTANTIVE PRESIDENTIAL POWERS

The substantive presidential powers can be divided into various categories: powers in relation to the Cabinet and the Ministers; powers in relation to the Civil Service, the Police and Armed Forces; powers in relation to Parliament; powers in relation to the judiciary, and other miscellaneous powers. It is also possible to divide the powers according to the manner of their exercise; whether they can be exercised by the President at his own discretion, or on the advice of, or after consultation with, the Cabinet or some other body, or whether they are merely nominal. At one time the latter would have been a fruitful way of discussing the presidential powers, but the trend in the recent amendments to the Constitution has been to make powers exercisable at the discretion of the President. Therefore they will be discussed in relation to other institutions.

(a) *The Cabinet and the Ministers*

Executive authority is vested in the President of Kenya.[30] He may, subject to the Constitution, exercise this power either directly or through officers subordinate to him. Apart from the office of Vice-President, specifically established by the Constitution, there are such offices as Minister of the Government of Kenya which may be established by Parliament, or subject to any provisions made by Parliament, by the President.[31] Ministers and Assistant Ministers must be appointed from the National Assembly but need not be elected members.[32] The President has sole responsibility for the appointment, and dismissal, of the Vice-President, the Ministers and Assistant Ministers, the allocation to them of responsibility for a department of Government, and the granting to them of permission to be absent from the country.[33] Where a Minister is charged with responsibility for a department

[29] Constitution section 13.
[30] Constitution section 23.
[31] Constitution section 16 (1).
[32] Constitution sections 16 (2); 19 (1).
[33] Constitution sections 77; 81 (2) (a); 82; 16 (3) (a); 18; 19 (2) (a); 20.

of Government, he is required to exercise a general direction and control over it. It is clear from these provisions that the general provision vesting executive power in the President is bolstered by the specific provisions dealing with his power over, and relationship with, his Ministers. A person stays in the Government only so long as he enjoys the confidence of the President. This must be borne in mind when we consider the function of the Cabinet and its relationship to the President.

The function of the Cabinet is to aid and advise the President in the Government of Kenya.[34] Since the President is Head of State as well as of Government, it is not immediately clear what meaning to attribute to this provision. If the President's position were similar to that of the Governor-General before the Republic, the interpretation would be that the Governor-General was bound to act as advised by the Cabinet. In the present context, it may be that when the Constitution vests the executive authority in the President, it does so in the President as the Head of State, and he is bound to follow the advice of the Cabinet, which happens to contain the President, as Head of the Government. It is perhaps a fanciful interpretation, but one that was put on the section by the Government at the time it was promulgated.[35] If one accepts it, then the President is no more than *primus inter pares*.

Such an interpretation is bolstered by the fact that there is a list of powers in respect of which the Cabinet has no function before the President exercises them, yet it is expressly given a function in relation to them when an acting President is in office. It is arguable that it would be strange if it were only in respect of those matters that an acting President had to comply with a resolution of the Cabinet, so the implication of these provisions is that the President may act only on advice on all matters other than those specified, and on those matters the acting President must act on advice also.

The Constitution will, however, support an alternative interpretation. There is no express provision requiring the President to act on the advice of the Cabinet as there is in relation to his power to appoint judges when he is required to act on the advice of the Judicial Service Commission.[36] There is no indication that a distinction is being made, in the section vesting executive power in the President, between the President as Head of State and Head of Government, as one might expect to find if the same person holds both offices yet is to act differently in each of them, and as there is in the section dealing with the President's power to address the National Assembly in his two capacities. The exemption of certain exercises of power from Cabinet advice does not necessarily imply that on all other matters Cabinet advice must be accepted, and the inclusion of a provision that on the exempted matters

[34] Constitution section 17 (2).
[35] House of Representatives, *Debates*, volume III, part III (3 November 1964), col. 4193.
[36] Constitution section 61 (2).

the acting President must act 'in accordance with' a resolution of the Cabinet is consistent with the view that were that section not phrased thus but merely as 'aid and advice', the acting President would be free to disregard the views of the Cabinet.

It is therefore doubtful if the phrase 'aid and advice of the Cabinet' introduces the principle of collective decision-making at the summit of the Executive into Kenya. It is true that the Constitution refers to the collective responsibility of the Cabinet to the National Assembly. The implications of that provision will be considered below, but it may be remarked here that the rule of collective responsibility does not necessarily import the rule of collective decision. If anything, it is a rule which strengthens the position of the President, for it requires that the Cabinet must present a united front to the world once a decision is taken in its name, whatever the processes whereby it was taken, and if some Minister disagrees with the decision and wishes to carry his opposition into the open, he should, or can be asked to, resign.

It is more than probable that the rules of the Constitution are based on what is conceived to be the British position, and so the interpretation put upon them by government spokesmen would reflect what they understood British practice to be. But it is to be doubted whether Kenya can be equated with the United Kingdom here. In the case of Kenya, the President, as the Head both of the State and the Cabinet, has greater pre-eminence than the Prime Minister as head of the Cabinet. Whatever the constitutional significance of the coalescence of the offices of the Prime Minister and the President, in practice it has led to the gravitation of power into the hands of the President. In Britain the Prime Minister is not directly elected by the people; in Kenya he would be, a factor which tends to strengthen his position. In Britain, the responsibility of the Government has by convention become vested in the Cabinet; in Kenya it is the President who has been vested with the authority to govern, and the primary responsibility therefore is his. In particular, the rules of practice that have emerged in relation to the principle of collective responsibility emphasize the primary responsibility of the President, to the dilution of the individual responsibility of the Ministers. Moreover, the Kenyan President has unfettered powers to dissolve Parliament, the exercise of which power is a matter of his personal discretion, whereas the British Prime Minister's powers in this respect, while not free from controversy, are not as extensive.

Such clear evidence of practice as there is indicates that the President is a great deal more than *primus inter pares*. Where two Ministers disagreed in the National Assembly as to whether a motion was official government business, the Speaker ruled that it was the President who had the decisive say, and rejected suggestions that the National Assembly be adjourned so that the Cabinet could discuss the matter.[37] There was no government objection to that statement of the position of the President and the Cabinet. There have been several occasions when the President has issued a directive on a matter of policy and administration concerning a particular ministerial field, in which no indication is given that that is the result of a Cabinet decision.[38] Rather, it has been his personal decision, though no doubt influenced by advice received from his Ministers. There have been occasions—the constitutional amendments of 1968 being the latest one—when important matters were decided upon, and Bills introduced into Parliament, without a full Cabinet discussion beforehand. In an area such as this, the rules of the Constitution alone are an unsafe guide, for they are soon filled out and sometimes altered by practice, which is unlikely to be overturned by a judicial decision, but it would seem that the practice here is in conformity with the tenor of the rules in that the rules do not require, nor does the practice show, the Cabinet to be the major executive instrument of the Government of Kenya.

(b) *The Legislature*

For convenience of discussion it will be best to deal with this subject before considering the question of collective responsibility and the relationship between the Executive and the Legislature. Five heads of power may be looked at. First, the President has general powers of dissolution,[39] and not merely at the time of a vote of no confidence, which adds a great deal to his strength. Besides acting as a threat to restive MPs, it enables the President to choose the most propitious time to seek a fresh term of office. He also has the power to summon and prorogue Parliament,[40] valuable powers for he can decide when to call Parliament, and may want to use that of prorogation to bring an unruly or critical session to an end. It is not, however, possible for the President to postpone indefinitely the calling of a session of Parliament; he has to summon it into session not later than twelve months from the end of the preceding session if Parliament has been prorogued, or three months from the end of that session if Parliament has been dissolved. The President will also have to call a session to get approval of his budget, since only Parliament can authorize the levying and collection of taxation, though the Government has extensive powers of borrowing which would enable it to survive an appreciable time without the collection of taxes.[41]

[37] House of Representatives, *Debates*, volume VIII (15 February 1966), cols. 900–902.
[38] e.g. Legal Notice 179/1967. Prohibition of consent to certain land transactions. The President issued the prohibition but the regulations under which he purported to act conferred power so to do on the Minister for Lands and Settlement.
[39] Constitution section 59 (2).
[40] Constitution sections 58 (1) and 59 (1).
[41] See chapter VIII for a discussion of this matter.

Secondly, the President may nominate up to twelve MPs.[42] This power was conferred upon him by the constitutional amendments of 1968, and replaced the provisions for the specially elected members. These members are now deemed to be nominated members.[43]

Thirdly, the President can waive, in relation to any MP, the rule that he loses his seat if he is absent for eight consecutive days in any session without the permission of the Speaker.[44] It is no doubt necessary if such a rule exists to provide an 'equity jurisdiction', but it is difficult to justify its vesting in the President; it gives him unnecessary powers in connection with the conduct of the MPs, and constitutes a potentially serious interference with the functions and procedures of Parliament.

Fourthly, the President is a member of the National Assembly and can take a full part in its proceedings, using its debates to persuade the members to his point of view. In addition, he can choose to address the Assembly, not as an ordinary member, but as the Head of State. Though some doubts were expressed that an active participation by the President in the affairs of the Assembly would lead to a diminution of his prestige and importance, it is clear that the rules provide an astute President with an opportunity to exert great influence on the members. Mr. Kenyatta, however, has not played an active part in the proceedings of the National Assembly, and where it has been necessary to persuade the back-benchers to an official point of view, he has done it in private meetings of parliamentarians.

Fifthly, he appoints the members of the Electoral Commission, including the Chairman (which position under the previous rules was filled by the Speaker, as *ex officio*); he cannot, however, dismiss them at will for their tenure is secured in the same manner as is that of a judge of the High Court.[45]

These powers must be taken into account when considering how far Parliament is supreme over the Executive as is claimed, or how far in reality the Executive closely controls Parliament, a question which will be considered below, and in chapter VIII.

(c) *Collective Responsibility*

There is much confusion, both in the Executive and in the Legislature, as to just what collective responsibility entails in Kenya. The confusion arises from the following factors: first, an imperfect understanding of the British practice which in any event has been developed in relation to a different political system; secondly, a lack of consideration as to how far that practice has been imported into Kenya by reference to the term 'collective

[42] Constitution section 33.
[43] For further discussion see chapter VIII.
[44] Constitution section 39 (1) (c).
[45] Constitution section 41. For further discussion see chapter VIII.

responsibility' in the Constitution; thirdly, a change brought about by practice in the Constitution since 1964 which may have affected the operation of the concept; and fourthly, the rulings of the Speaker of the National Assembly who has striven to bring order out of chaos, but owing at times to a legalistic approach to the Constitution, has not always succeeded.

It will be as well to have the British principles in front of us before looking at the rules and practice in Kenya, but it should be realized that these are not wrong or inferior because they are different to the British ones. We look at the British rules because these are the base-lines from which developments in the Kenyan Constitution can be traced.

The British doctrine has been succinctly stated as follows:[46]

> The substance of the Government's collective responsibility could be defined as its duty to submit its policy to and defend its policy before the House of Commons, and to resign if defeated on an issue of confidence.

This doctrine was evolved over the years, first as a means of defeating the rival doctrine of successive monarchs that Ministers were only individually responsible for their departments, with no reference to their colleagues, and had direct access to the monarch, thus allowing the monarch to play one off against the other, and later as a means of maintaining the position of the Government in Parliament, by preventing Ministers who disagreed with policy from remaining in the Government, yet encouraging the majority party to vote for Government policies. As party Government grew in strength, the principle became essential for its maintenance, for serious breaches in collective responsibility would 'let the other side in'. Today the convention has lost some of its force, for it is a long time since a Government fell because the House of Commons withdrew its confidence from it. But it still retains some importance. Ministers do resign when they no longer agree with policy, and realize that they cannot defend it in and out of Parliament; the convention explains much of the daily give and take in the House of Commons, particularly the use of the motion of censure either on the Government or on an individual Minister, and the reaction of the Government to it, and the whole business of the Whips, and their reactions to dissident back-benchers. In sum, the modern operation of the principle in Britain can only be understood in the context of the constitutional monarchy, the two-party system, and the conventional basis of its Constitution.

The principle has never been precisely formulated in Britain but it has been exported, in whole or in part, still on occasions unformulated, to other Commonwealth countries, and Kenya is no exception. At independence, Kenya became a constitutional monarchy and the rules relating to the

[46] Marshall and Moodie, *Some Problems of the Constitution* (London, Hutchinson, third edition, 1964), p. 72.

exercise of executive power and collective ministerial responsibility followed the outlines of the position in Britain, the major omission being any reference to political parties, or how they interacted on the constitutional rules. The Governor-General had to act on the advice of the Cabinet, except for certain stated matters mainly relating to the dissolution of Parliament when he acted either on the advice of the Prime Minister or at his discretion, and the appointment of Ministers, when he acted solely on the Prime Minister's advice.[47] The Prime Minister was required to keep the Governor-General informed of the business of government.[48] The Cabinet, which was separate from the Governor-General, was collectively responsible to both Houses of the National Assembly for the advice which it gave the Governor-General, but only an adverse vote on a motion of no confidence in the lower house—the House of Representatives—resulted in the fall of the Government, according to the rules of the Constitution.[49]

The amendments to the Constitution which brought into being the Republic clearly attempted to preserve as much of this outline as possible, but without perhaps fully realizing that rules evolved for a constitutional monarchy might not be entirely satisfactory for an executive presidency, albeit one of the parliamentary variety. We have already discussed one of the difficulties arising out of the transition, and have seen that whatever the rules may have said prior to the Republic in relation to the Governor-General, neither the rules nor the practice now require the President to act only in accordance with, or on, the advice of the Cabinet. How this affects the doctrine of collective responsibility in relation to the legislature will be examined here.

A fundamental point to understand is that the Constitution seeks to draw a distinction between what may be called the two branches of the rule of collective responsibility, that of resignation following defeat on a motion of no confidence, and that of submission of policy to, and its defence before, the National Assembly. On the first branch of the rule a clear procedure has been established. Seven days' notice must be given of a motion of no confidence in accordance with the procedure of the Assembly, and for that motion to be successful, it must be supported by a majority of all members of the Assembly, not just of those present and voting.[50] It was argued that unless there was an express stipulation of this voting requirement, a handful only of the members, just enough to constitute a majority of a quorum, could overthrow the Government, which would amount to an overthrow by a minority.[51] One reason for requiring an overall majority is to offset

[47] Independence Constitution, S.I. 1968/1963, sections 79 and 75.
[48] ibid., section 80.
[49] Sections 76 (2); 65 (2) (a).
[50] Constitution section 59 (3).
[51] House of Representatives, *Debates*, volume III, part III (27 October 1964), cols. 3895–3896.

the ill-effects of a snap vote, but since the Constitution insists on a week's notice, there can be little possibility of that. The real object of the rule is to ensure as far as possible a stable Executive and to avoid quick changes of government. An absolute majority is the most that can be required; to ask for a bigger vote would be patently undemocratic. Another rule discouraging the application of the no confidence motion procedure is that if such a motion is successful, the President has a choice of action. He can either resign or dissolve Parliament; if he decides on the latter, the members stand to lose their seats; the reflection may produce circumspection. If within three days of a successful motion of no confidence the President neither resigns nor dissolves Parliament, then on the fourth day Parliament shall stand dissolved automatically. Since the procedure for the removal of the Government is set out so clearly, it means that there is no legal obligation on it to resign if it receives an adverse vote on some other important motion or Bill. The rule is obviously preferable to one which requires resignation on a defeat on any vote. The Kenyan rule allows more flexibility in voting; enables more freedom to be given to the back-benchers; and makes it possible for the members to express their disapproval of individual governmental policies, without jeopardizing its existence.

It would, however, be mistaken to assume that there would be no other occasions when a government might resign because of an adverse vote in the National Assembly. A ruling of the Speaker on this issue is pertinent.[52] When a motion of confidence in the Government was being debated in 1966, he explained to MPs the significance of an adverse vote. Such a vote would not result in the automatic fall of the Government for that could only occur when the exact terms of the Constitution were followed, but it might lead to the President dissolving Parliament and calling for fresh elections, which he could do at his own discretion. There was, in other words, a clear distinction between dissolution because the President willed it, and dissolution because the Constitution ordained it. It may be remarked that automatic dissolution appears to be one area where the attempt to apply the Westminster doctrines to an executive President has resulted in the President having less power than the Prime Minister, for the President has no discretion in the matter at all.

The second branch of the rule is provided for in the Constitution as follows:[53]

> The Cabinet shall be collectively responsible to the National Assembly for all things done by or under the authority of the President or the Vice-President or any other Minister in the execution of his office.

It might be thought that such a vague formula was not meant to be subject

[52] House of Representatives, *Debates*, volume VIII (15 February 1966), cols. 937–938.
[53] Constitution section 17 (3).

to a close legal analysis but that is what it has received from the Speaker, and his rulings on this section are giving rise to conventions of the Kenyan Constitution more binding and more important than the conventions of the British Constitution on which the original wording of the section is based. Three matters may be examined here which have arisen several times; speeches by Ministers and Assistant Ministers in the National Assembly attacking government policy, attempts to censure individual Ministers, and attempts to discuss the President's exercise of power, specifically exempted from Cabinet discussion by the Constitution.

Attacks on government policy and Bills by Ministers, and more especially Assistant Ministers, have been a feature of debates in the National Assembly, and the practice which is emerging from the Speaker's rulings is that while the rules of procedure of the House allow anyone to speak as they will, subject to rules such as relevancy, unparliamentary language, bogus points of order, Ministers and Assistant Ministers should observe rules of practice derived from the principles of collective responsibility and when they speak, indicate in what capacity they are speaking—as Ministers or as constituency members. In addition, Cabinet Ministers to whom alone section 17(3) applies cannot repudiate the actions and the speeches of another Minister in the House whether the matter has been discussed in the Cabinet or not, though they can apparently vote as their conscience dictates. Furthermore, it is not a matter for the House what rules of government discipline are applied to Ministers and Assistant Ministers who speak against the Government, and the Vice-President could not therefore issue an instruction from the President as part of the rules of the House that Ministers and Assistant Ministers should speak only in support of the Government.[54]

These rulings raise several issues of importance and controversy. The distinction which appears to be drawn on occasions between Cabinet and Assistant Ministers confuses the responsibility for making a decision with the responsibility for defending it. When we are concerned, as we are in the National Assembly, with attacking or defending government policy, it should not matter whether a member of the Government actually played a significant part in making that policy. Assistant Ministers are required to assist Ministers in the performance of their duties, and assistance must surely include supporting the policies and actions of the Ministers in the National Assembly. The moral blameworthiness of the Assistant Minister might be less if he played no part in shaping policy, but that is for posterity to determine. The confusion in the National Assembly is in the present, and is the

[54] National Assembly, *Debates*, volume XI (7 March 1967), cols. 798–799; volume XII, part I (7 June 1967), cols. 687–688; volume XIII, part I (4 October 1967), col. 129; volume XIV (29 February 1968), cols. 191–193; volume XV (28 May 1968), cols. 115–116, 122.

same whether the Vice-President, or an Assistant Minister attacks the Government. The second branch of the rule of collective responsibility is designed to prevent confusion in the Legislature, and to present to it and the general public a stable and united administration. This it is not always doing at the moment. In fairness to the Speaker, however, it must be mentioned that Assistant Ministers have proved much more difficult to call to order in this respect than Ministers, since, though they are members of the Government, they rarely take part in any collective decision-making.

The second aspect of these rulings to which attention may be drawn is the differing degrees of strictness between the rules of the House and the rules of government discipline outside the House. The relatively liberal rulings of the Speaker seem to miss an essential point about collective responsibility as set out in the Constitution. No doubt the Speaker cannot discipline Ministers who speak out against the Government in the National Assembly, and in the final analysis the Government must (and does) take action, but the rule of collective responsibility does not exist in a vacuum; the Cabinet is collectively responsible to the National Assembly and this must mean that the Cabinet, and, as suggested above, the Assistant Ministers as well, should speak with one voice, should be 'prepared to submit its policy to, and defend its policy before' the National Assembly. This is a rule of the Constitution, and as such overrides procedural or any other rules of the National Assembly. The Speaker is usually very quick to pull up MPs whose speeches appear to infringe the Constitution, but his rulings here do not seem to give sufficient effect to the provisions of the Constitution relating to collective responsibility. In a recent ruling on these matters the Speaker appeared to see the difficulty that he was in, for he said that Ministers may say what they like but may not repudiate the actions of a colleague in the House, and cannot by their speeches escape responsibility for Cabinet colleagues. This leaves the matter unclear. Granted he is in an extremely difficult position when Cabinet colleagues disagree in public, if only because he may not know which is government policy, and which opposition to it, it would seem that his best refuge is the Constitution, and he would be going no further than he has done on other occasions if he ruled that an oath to uphold the Constitution requires the taker to uphold the rule of collective responsibility, and that this entails that Ministers and Assistant Ministers should support the Government in the National Assembly or not speak. If differing ministerial opinions continued to be voiced he could adjourn the Assembly to allow the conflict of views to be resolved outside the chamber. This would in fact be better than attempting to adjudicate upon the dispute himself as has happened in the past.

The second matter—motions of censure against Ministers—concerns the relationship of individual to collective responsibility. On this the Speaker has ruled as out of order opposition attempts to give notice of a motion censuring an individual Minister for what he has done or not done as a Minister, on the ground that section 17(3) of the Constitution provides that the President and all the Ministers are collectively responsible for what any Minister does in the course of his duty so that only a motion critical of the whole Government can be accepted. Motions attacking Ministers individually must be directed against them in their personal, not their official, capacities.[55] Thus the rule of collective responsibility has been held to oust the rule of individual responsibility not only in the sense that the Minister cannot be compelled by the National Assembly to resign through failures in his department, but in the sense that his conduct as head of a department cannot be discussed on a substantive motion of censure.

This ruling reflects a very strict and narrow interpretation of the Constitution, seems to conflict with many practices in the National Assembly accepted by the Speaker, and is open to question. The rule of collective responsibility as set out in the Constitution means that the Cabinet cannot publicly disown what a Minister has done in his capacity as a Minister yet allow his actions to continue, but it is difficult to construe it to mean that the National Assembly cannot debate a motion of censure on that Minister. The rule in other words presents the Cabinet with a choice: defend or sacrifice the Minister and his policies; it does not present the National Assembly with a choice: censure the Government (which in effect means the President), or keep quiet.

As to the practices in the Assembly, several show that the Speaker accepts that Ministers are individually answerable for their departments. First, MPs ask questions of individual Ministers, and while the Speaker has ruled that the question may be transferred to and answered by a Minister other than the one to whom it was addressed, because the organization of government business is for the Government to determine, he has never suggested that any Minister could answer all parliamentary questions on a particular day regardless of their subject-matter, and his portfolio, because the matters concerned the Cabinet as a whole and not the individual Minister. Indeed he has criticized the absence of individual Ministers when a parliamentary question by private notice is addressed to them, and has further stated that when an individual Minister undertakes to answer a question, he is expected to know about it.[56]

Secondly, during debates on the second reading of Bills and at the Committee stage, the Speaker has accepted as proper a motion for adjournment because

[55] National Assembly, *Debates*, volume XII, part II (6 July 1967), col. 1853; (19 July 1967), col. 2410.
[56] National Assembly, *Debates*, volume XII (9 June 1967), col. 806; (21 June 1967), col. 1258.

the relevant Minister was not in the House listening to the debate, so the House could not properly do its work.[57] But if there is no individual responsibility of Ministers, it matters not which Minister introduces a Bill and attends the debate, so long as one, representing the Cabinet, is present—it need not be the same one all through the debate. Thirdly, the Speaker has expressly ruled that it is in order to criticize an individual Minister for inefficiency in the running of his department during the course of a debate.[58]

In view of these practices, sanctioned by the Speaker, it is not possible to argue that all a Minister is doing when he comes to the National Assembly is 'performing as a kind of parliamentary press and information officer' and that MPs are no more than 'curious or interested bystanders'.[59] He is, and the Speaker has made it clear in his comments that he acts on this assumption, answering to a body, which has some vaguely defined authority over him, for the manner in which he is discharging his responsibilities. What the Speaker has done by his ruling on censure motions coupled with his other rulings outlined above is to say that Ministers do have a political obligation to appear before and answer to the National Assembly, but if they decline to do so, or do not do so to the satisfaction of MPs, the National Assembly has no effective weapon at its disposal to try and compel the performance of that political obligation. He has indeed spelt this out in relation to MPs' dissatisfaction with answers received to parliamentary questions; MPs may say they are dissatisfied, they may try and raise the matter on a motion for the adjournment, they can remind the Minister to come to the House the next day, but that is all they may do. They may not put down a motion criticizing the Minister.[60]

It may be that the Speaker considers that to allow a censure motion on a Minister would be to introduce the notion that the National Assembly can criticize the President's choice of Minister, and that as this is not a matter for the collective concern of the Cabinet, it cannot be a matter for debate in the House. Again he may consider that such a motion would in some way outflank the provision in the Constitution that only a motion of no confidence in the Government can bring the Government down. But these fears, if they exist, arise from a failure to distinguish myth from reality. The myth may be that Ministers can be compelled to resign after an adverse vote on a motion of censure, and that this in some way reflects on the competence of the person who selected the Minister in the first place; the reality, however, is very different. The real value of a censure motion lies not in the remote possibility of its being successful, in the sense of resulting in a defeat for the

[57] National Assembly, *Debates*, volume XII, part I (31 May 1967), cols. 472–473 (Committee stage of Kadhi's Courts Bill).
[58] National Assembly, *Debates*, volume XI (8 March 1967), col. 874.
[59] Marshall and Moodie, op. cit., p. 81.
[60] National Assembly, *Debates*, volume XI (7 April 1967), col. 2208.

Government, but in its securing the attendance of the Minister, and an explanation and justification for his policies and his actions, and its absence in Kenya has seriously weakened the ability of the National Assembly to ensure that Ministers are responsible to the Assembly, a fact of which both MPs and Ministers are only too well aware, to judge from the latter's rather cavalier approach to attendance and answering parliamentary questions, and the former's continual and ineffectual complaints about this.

The basic fallacy of the Speaker's ruling is that it adopts too legalistic an approach to the business of government, and its accountability to the Legislature. His approach seems to be to say that because the Constitution mentions only collective and not individual responsibility, a motion seeking to censure an individual Minister cannot be allowed. But the Constitution is concerned to provide a framework for a form of government in which there is a close relationship between Executive and Legislature. That framework has to be filled in by the day to day operation of government in which political factors and obligations play an important part. No ruling designed to provide guidelines for that operation, least of all one not given in a court of law, where the peculiar rules of evidence sometimes operate to exclude relevant facts, should ignore these political factors, as has happened here.

Thirdly, the President's exercise of powers may be looked at. The Speaker has ruled that neither the President's conduct nor his exercise of power personal to him, for example, the prerogative of mercy, may be criticized in the National Assembly other than on a substantive motion.[61] This ruling appears to be based on the President's status as Head of State, and to be an attempt to prevent the Head of State from being dragged into the political arena. The ruling may have some affinities with similar ones in the British House of Commons which seek to keep the Sovereign from being attacked. But it is here that the distinction between a constitutional monarch and an executive President is crucial. A constitutional monarch is by definition above the political battle and the ruling would merely reinforce an already well-established position. An executive President, especially a parliamentary one, is not above the political battle for he is his own Prime Minister, and by law entitled to take part in the debates in the National Assembly. It is not possible to argue that the President exercises some executive powers as Head of State and some as Head of Government; he exercises them all as President, an office which combines both roles, though in respect of some of these powers no person or authority is constitutionally entitled to give him advice before he exercises them. To exclude these exercises of power from the purview of the National Assembly other than on a substantive motion further handicaps MPs in their attempts to call the Government to account, for

[61] National Assembly, *Debates*, volume XI (7 April 1967), cols. 2208–2209; volume XIV (21 March 1968), col. 713.

they are naturally inhibited in putting down a motion specifically critical of President Kenyatta. It also opens the door to the possibility of a widening area of virtually non-responsible government action which could be brought about by conferring on the President powers in many fields which he might exercise at his own discretion.

Whatever the intentions of the draftsmen of section 17(3) of the Constitution, practice in Kenya has left the form but virtually destroyed the substance of the second branch of the rule of collective responsibility. It has transformed a rule designed to ensure that government presents a united front to the National Assembly into one which allows Ministers and Assistant Ministers both to affirm and deny their support for government policy. It has transformed a rule which gave the National Assembly an opportunity to call the government to account into one which enables the government to pick and choose what it will be responsible for, even to the extent of declining to be responsible for its actions. If the National Assembly is still able to check the government, which it can, this is in spite of, and not because of, the practice of collective responsibility, and is due to political factors outside, rather than within, the National Assembly.[62]

(d) *The Public Service*

The powers of the President in relation to the public service are somewhat obscure. At the time of independence an executive Public Service Commission was established by, and entrenched in, the Constitution.[63] It was not subject to the directions or authority of any other person. Strong provisions existed to ensure that neither serving nor ex-politicians nor public officers could be members of the Commission nor could members of the Commission hold public office for three years after leaving the Commission. Equally strong provisions existed to isolate it from politics, for its members were appointed on the advice of the Judicial Service Commission and could only be removed after a judicial inquiry had investigated allegations of incompetence or inability and reported adversely on the member complained of. The only concession made to the political wing of the Executive was that certain senior officials, mainly Permanent Secretaries, and the Law Officers were not subject to the jurisdiction of the Public Service Commission, but were appointed on the advice of the Prime Minister.[64]

Since the inauguration of the Republic there have been several significant changes in the law relating to the Public Service Commission, and the public service, all of them designed to bring the service more under the control of the President, and close the gap between the Public Service Com-

[62] For further discussion of the effectiveness of Parliament, see chapter VIII.
[63] Independence Constitution, S.I. 1968/1963, sections 186–188.
[64] ibid., sections 188(15)–192.

mission and the service it helps control. In 1964, the President, rather than the judges, was empowered to appoint the members of the Commission, and the Commission was empowered to delegate its functions and impose duties on public officers for the purpose of carrying out its functions, but only with the consent of the President.[65] In 1968, the prohibitions on public officers being members of the Commission, and members of the Commission being public officers within three years of leaving the Commission, were removed.[66]

It is in relation to appointments to and dismissal from the public service that difficulties exist as to what the division of responsibilities between the President and the Commission are, as a matter of law, though it is more than probable that presidential power has been increased. Subject to the provisions of the Constitution, the Commission has power to appoint persons to hold or act in offices in the public service (including the power to confirm appointments), the power to exercise disciplinary control over persons holding or acting in such offices, and the power to remove such persons from office.[67] The provisions relevant to the presidential powers are as follows:[68]

> Subject to the provisions of this Constitution, and of any other law, the powers of constituting and abolishing offices for the Republic of Kenya, of making appointments to any such office and terminating any such appointment, shall vest in the President.
> Save in so far as may be otherwise provided by this Constitution or by any other law, every person who holds office in the service of the Republic of Kenya shall hold such office during the pleasure of the President.

From these provisions it is a little difficult to know which of the two has the superior powers. It could be argued that since section 25 was an amendment of the Constitution, it must be intended to overrule earlier provisions in case of conflict. Unless section 25 is taken to mean that all offices in the public service are held at the pleasure of the President, it is difficult to see the point of the amendment. Government statements at the time of the enactment of the section do not help to find the legislative intention, for it was stated both that its purpose was to ensure that public servants cannot claim a right to serve the Government, thus preventing it from cutting its staff as and when necessary, and that it did not mean that the President had obtained power to dismiss public servants, as they were all still governed by the Commission; it was just bringing the post-Republican law into line

[65] Constitution (Amendment) Act No. 28 of 1964 amending Constitution sections 186 (2) and 188 (1).
[66] Constitution (Amendment No. 2) Act. No. 45 of 1968 deleting Constitution section 186 (3) (d), (4).
[67] Constitution section 107.
[68] Constitution sections 24 and 25. Section 25 was first introduced by the Constitution (Amendment) Act No. 16 of 1966 as 87A.

with the pre-Republican law.[69] These reasons do at least suggest that the law was being altered, and, just as M. Jourdain spoke prose without realizing it, so it is possible that the Constitution has been changed through that alteration without the legislators realizing it.

A possible reconciliation of the conflicting provisions is to distinguish between offices and officers as is hinted at in the first of the two government explanations of section 25. The President may constitute and abolish offices, and as a logical corollary of this, appoint persons to, and remove them from, these offices. Since the exigencies of government cannot be predicted in advance, all public servants hold office at the pleasure of the President to facilitate his constituting and abolishing offices. The Commission on the other hand deals with established officers and established posts. Thus the President could create and staff a new Ministry and abolish an existing one, but could not interfere with the day to day management of the public service—new appointments to existing posts, cross-postings, promotion, discipline, etc.—the responsibility for which is vested in the Commission. If this analysis is correct, the Commission has, despite the retention of its powers and position in the Constitution, been seriously undermined as a matter of law. In practice, however, the Commission still exercises the functions with which it is vested by the Constitution, though it has delegated many of these functions in relation to junior and subordinate staff to senior officers of the service which suggests that a likely explanation of the provisions relating to the powers of the President is that it was felt that they conferred powers which an executive President ought to have, though there was no immediate plan to use them. The position remains, however, that the powers are there should they be wanted.

In addition to these general powers over the public service, the President has been given important specific powers over it for the purpose of Kenyanization, or localization. If, on his request, the authorities responsible for making appointments to the public service (i.e. the Public Service and the Judicial Service Commissions) report that there are more local candidates qualified for appointment or promotion to a public office, which is held by an expatriate officer, the President can direct the authorities compulsorily to retire the expatriate officer and to appoint a local candidate in his place.[70] The power is expressly extended to judicial officers. The President can, however, only give directions to provide for localization; he cannot in law direct the Commission to appoint any particular candidate.

It was mentioned above that certain senior posts in the public service were placed outside the jurisdiction of the Public Service Commission at

[69] House of Representatives, *Debates*, volume VIII (22 February 1966), cols. 1279–1280.
[70] Kenya Independence Order in Council S.I. 1968/1963, section 14. Now Constitution section 126.

independence. This is still the position, and the President has important powers in relation to such officers. Thus, the Attorney-General, the Controller and Auditor-General, the Commissioner of Police, the Permanent Secretaries, including the Secretary to the Cabinet, the Solicitor-General, the Director of Personnel and the senior diplomatic envoys are all appointed by him. Once they are appointed, however, he does not exercise an equal degree of control over them. The Attorney-General, the Auditor-General and the Commissioner of Police are not dismissable except in accordance with the same procedure as for judges and members of the Service Commissions. No express provision is made for the dismissal of other officials appointed by the President. As mentioned above, applying section 25, we would infer that the President can dismiss them at will. The justification for this set of rules is that it is important that the President should have the power to appoint to the senior administrative posts; the whole success of his Government could depend on the efficient and loyal execution of his policy. It is a necessary corollary of his primary responsibility for good government that he should control these senior appointments. At the same time, some of these officials have functions of much delicacy or potential political controversy, and if they are to perform these functions efficiently and impartially, they need to have some security of tenure. The functions of these officials are insulated from governmental control, in that neither the President nor anyone else can give them directions about how they should conduct their functions. Thus the Auditor-General uses his own discretion in the discharge of his duties, as does the Attorney-General in discharging some of his functions.

The office of Attorney-General merits special attention in this connection, however. He has a dual role in law, one impartial, the other more partisan. In the former role he has the following special duties: to decide whether to institute or undertake criminal proceedings;[71] to apply to the High Court when the need arises to determine any question of the validity of elections to the National Assembly or the vacation of seats therein;[72] to institute proceedings against a person suspected of having voted in the Legislature knowing or believing that he had no such right;[73] and to require the Commissioner of Police to investigate any matter which in his opinion relates to any offence or alleged offence or suspected offence.[74] In carrying out all these duties, he is free from directions from anyone else. His other role is that of chief legal adviser to the Government, and in this position he is very closely concerned with the policies of the Government. He is a member of the Cabinet, and has a seat in the Legislature, though without a vote, and helps to steer many Bills through Parliament. Apart from the lack of a vote,

[71] Constitution section 44 (2).
[72] Constitution section 44 (2).
[73] Constitution section 55.
[74] Constitution section 26 (4).

he is indistinguishable from a Minister in the House. He is thus deeply involved in political matters, and the wisdom of making him irremovable by the Executive may be questioned. The one argument in favour of the present rules of tenure is to safeguard his independence in matters of prosecution, so as to prevent the political abuse of criminal proceedings. But this purpose can be more satisfactorily safeguarded by the establishment of an independent Director of Public Prosecutions, who does not have any political responsibilities. To paraphrase, a director of prosecutions must not only be fair, but must be seen to be fair. It is doubtful if any Attorney-General can satisfy this requirement in the Kenya constitutional system. The fallacy of these provisions is that they are based on the colonial assumption that the Attorney-General is merely a super government draftsman called in to advise the policy-makers on the legal implications of what they are doing. It is doubtful whether this assumption was correct in the colonial period, but in a popular government inspired by political principles, policy and law cannot be so easily divorced, and it is no criticism of the present Attorney-General to say that he takes as active a part in the Government as does any Minister. His terms and conditions of service should therefore be the same as theirs.

From this discussion, it is clear that the President's powers in relation to the public service may not be as extensive as in some other countries, e.g. Tanzania.[75] But it is doubtful if in practice this means that the Government has less control over the public service than in Tanzania. Despite its formal independence, the Public Service Commission is responsive to government needs and wishes; there is a large amount of delegation of the functions of the Commission to the Permanent Secretaries, who, though theoretically responsible to the Commission for the performance of these functions, do carry out the wishes of their Ministers. The Government has been able to carry out its policy of Africanization of the public services through the Commission. It may be suggested that had the Government faced any serious difficulties in its attempts to control the public service, the powers and composition of the Commission would have been more qualified in the Constitution than they have been.[76]

(e) *The Judiciary*

Let us now turn to the powers of the President in relation to the Judiciary. An independent Judiciary is an important principle of the Constitution, and in the various amendments of the Constitution that have been enacted

[75] As to which see, McAuslan, 'The Republican Constitution of Tanganyika' (1964) 13 *I.C.L.Q.*, pp. 519–29.
[76] See further on the public service in chapter VII.

since independence, the Judiciary has been little affected. The main power that the President has in relation to the Judiciary is in the appointment of judges, and members of the Judicial Service Commission. The President appoints the Chief Justice, the puisne judges and the Judges of Appeal (when an appeal court is established by Parliament), but—except in the case of the Chief Justice—when exercising the power of appointment in relation to them, he has to act on the advice of the Judicial Service Commission.[77] This is a constitutional body, with executive power, in whose appointment the President plays a major part. Directly or indirectly, he appoints all five members. The Chief Justice is the Chairman; other members are the Attorney-General, two High Court judges, formerly appointed by the President on the advice of the Chief Justice, but, since 1968, appointed by the President at his discretion, and the Chairman of the Public Service Commission.[78] These provisions represent a definite though justifiable change from the independence Constitution which conferred upon the Judiciary the status of a self-perpetuating body, a status which few, if any, body of judges enjoyed in the rest of the world.

Apart from the exceptions to be noted below, the President has no independent power of removal over the Chief Justice or puisne judges. They can only be removed for inability to perform the functions of their office (whether arising from infirmity of body or mind or any other cause), or for misbehaviour, and then only after the case against them has been referred to a judicial tribunal, which finds against them. In the case of the Chief Justice, the tribunal can be appointed if the President thinks that the question of his removal ought to be investigated; the members of the tribunal are appointed by the President but acting on the recommendations of the Chairman of the Public Service Commission. In the case of the other judges, the tribunal can be appointed if the Chief Justice thinks that the question of removal ought to be investigated; the President has no right to initiate an inquiry on his own. The tribunal is appointed by the President, in his own discretion, though the Constitution rules previously required him to do so with the advice of the Chief Justice. It is possible for the President to suspend the Chief Justice or any other judges pending the result of an inquiry, but the suspension ceases to have any effect if the result of the inquiry is in favour of the judges.[79] Thus, except in the case of the appointment of the Chief Justice, the President has very little direct control over the Judiciary.

[77] Constitution sections 61 and 64 (2). The latter section merely provides for the appointment of the President and members of the Appeal Court in the same way as those of the High Court. Does this mean that its president is to be appointed by the President at his own discretion, but the other members only on the recommendation of the Judicial Service Commission?

[78] Constitution section 68.

[79] Constitution section 62.

A possible derogation from the security of tenure of the Judiciary must now be considered. This is the question of the appointment of a judge for a specified period of time. The President has power to ask for the retirement of overseas officers in the public and judicial services to make room for local candidates. Can he not for the same reason appoint them for a term of years only? It may be doubted whether this would be constitutional. Expatriate judges can, under the relevant provisions, be removed only for one reason—to Kenyanize their offices. An appointment for a term of years, however, which can be renewed, is not within the purpose of the provisions for premature retirement. The Executive would be in a position to exercise an important influence over the Chief Justice and other judges if the latter were employed on short term, renewable contracts, a form of employment which has occurred since independence. It is true that the provisions authorizing the President to seek a premature retirement weaken the security of the tenure of expatriate judges, but the chances of governmental pressure being applied are much greater in the case of contractual appointments than when there is a once and for all termination of office, in order to appoint a Kenyan. It may be stressed in this connection that legislative pressure to Africanize the Judiciary has been stoutly resisted by the Government;[80] indeed, by the middle of 1968, it had appointed only two non-African citizens to the High Court.

Can it not be argued, however, on a more general ground that the members of the Judiciary, whether local or expatriate, can be appointed for a term of years? The Constitution provides that judges shall vacate their office on reaching the retirement age fixed by Parliament (which Parliament has fixed at 68);[81] before that, a judge can only be removed for misbehaviour or inability, in accordance with the procedure already discussed. Nothing in this section expressly forbids an appointment for a term of years; it merely fixes the upper retirement age beyond which no judge may continue in office, and rules out arbitrary dismissal. While this is true, the intention behind the section, and other provisions dealing with the Judiciary, is to safeguard in as ample a manner as possible the independence of the Judiciary. It assumes that once a citizen is appointed to the bench, he shall be immune from the possibility of all undue influence from the Executive and the Legislature; and the security of his tenure is essential to make this intention a reality. If it were allowed that judges, even though citizens, could be appointed

[80] e.g. House of Representatives, *Debates*, volume XI (1 March 1967), cols. 598–608 (Adjournment debate on Kenyanization of Senior Judicial Posts).

[81] Judicature Act No. 16 of 1967, section 9. Until the passage of that Act it was unclear at what age judges retired. The Kenya Constitution Order in Council, S.I. 600/1958 fixed the age limit at 62, and there had been no legislation on the matter since then. There was some criticism in the National Assembly at the retiring age fixed by the Act. National Assembly, *Debates*, volume XII, part I (25 May 1967), cols. 211–235.

for short term, renewable contracts, it would subvert the whole scheme for an impartial upright Judiciary.

For these reasons, it is clear that judges cannot be appointed for a term of years. The only important direct influence the Constitution allows the Executive in relation to the Judiciary is in the appointment of the Chief Justice. At this stage political considerations may enter into the decision, and perhaps should,[82] but once the appointment has been made, the Executive must respect the intent of the Constitution. It is, however, not an undue limitation on the powers of the President; unless the Judiciary deliberately sets out to sabotage governmental policies, the President can function quite effectively within the framework of the Constitution. It is no doubt for this reason that the Judicial Service Commission has been retained through successive constitutional changes.

A final point which may conveniently be discussed here is whether the Executive could outflank the spirit of the provisions of the Constitution relating to an independent Judiciary by creating special tribunals or courts for the trial of criminal or civil matters, and appointing to them persons without the necessary, or indeed any, legal qualifications. Chapter IV of the Constitution permits Parliament to create subordinate courts and courts-martial, and gives the High Court jurisdiction over such courts to supervise civil and criminal proceedings therein.[83] Chapter V of the Constitution—the Bill of Rights—strengthens these bare provisions by providing that a person accused of a crime shall be afforded a fair trial before an independent and impartial court established by law, and spelling out what is entailed in that right.[84] As with other rights in the Bill of Rights, the High Court is empowered to issue the necessary orders and writs at the behest of a person who considers that it has been infringed in relation to him. Thus it would appear that any criminal trial could ultimately be brought before the High Court, either on appeal or by way of an application for an order such as *certiorari*, if the accused considered that his trial had not been conducted before an impartial and independent court. The continuation of provisions for the use of District Officers and District Commissioners as magistrates since independence is difficult to reconcile with these provisions, for though they may be impartial, they can hardly be regarded as independent.

Would these provisions also cover the appointment of unqualified persons to preside over trials? The difficulty here is that both at and after independence, legally unqualified persons administered much of the criminal law in Kenya, as they do in England, including sitting in a final court of

[82] cf. The appointment of the Solicitor-General, Mr. M. K. Mwendwa, to the post of Chief Justice in August 1968.
[83] Constitution section 65.
[84] Constitution section 77.

appeal in all customary criminal and civil cases, and as an intermediate court of appeal in all criminal cases, whether arising from breach of statute or customary law, originating in African courts. The Constitution provides only for the qualifications to be possessed by a person who is to be appointed a judge of the High Court—he must be, or have been, a judge of a court having unlimited civil and criminal jurisdiction in any country in the Commonwealth, or the Republic of Ireland, or of a court hearing appeals from such a court, or hold, and have held for at least seven years, one of the professional qualifications required for admission to practise as an advocate in Kenya[85]—and it is significant that the Judicial Service Commission has not laid down in its regulations any minimum qualifications which persons must have before being appointed to the magistracy.[86] In practice, advertisements specify, and appointees are required to possess, certain professional qualifications as Resident Magistrates, and other magistrates have to pass a law examination prior to their appointment. The absence of provisions in the Constitution dealing with magisterial qualifications suggests that it does not prevent the appointment of legally unqualified persons to try criminal and civil cases in the subordinate courts. The safeguard against such persons abusing their powers through ignorance or malice lies in the provisions relating to the jurisdiction and composition of the High Court—the court may supervise all criminal proceedings and the judges of the court must be experienced and professionally qualified in law, independent, and secure in their tenure of office.

(f) *Special Presidential Powers*

To complete an account of executive authority, reference must be made to three instances of special powers. First the Government has inherited all the prerogative powers that the Queen could exercise in relation to Kenya in 1964.[87] It is not immediately clear what additional powers are bestowed by this provision. It has been held that since the prerogative is part of common law, and Kenya, during her dependent status had received the common law, the Queen's prerogative powers were in some respects as extensive as in Britain, with minor exceptions, though in other respects they were even wider.[88] But the prerogatives that the President can exercise

[85] Constitution section 61 (3).
[86] Legal Notice 163/1966. It is slightly surprising that these regulations were only published in June 1966, three years after an executive Judicial Service Commission had been established. They are dated May 27th 1966, and repeal no previous regulations. It is not known what regulations, if any, governed the judicial service until then.
[87] Constitution of Kenya (Amendment) Act No. 28 of 1964, section 16. The Constitution Act of 1969 makes no mention of prerogative powers, except the prerogative of mercy.
[88] *Nyali Ltd.* v. *Attorney-General*, [1956] 1 Q.B.1. (C.A.); reversed on another ground in [1957] A.C. 253.

on behalf of the Government are those that belonged to the Queen in relation to an independent Kenya, which were not as extensive. It is, for instance, clear that the Queen could no longer have claimed to legislate by Orders in Council. Again, the prerogative, being part of the common law, is liable to be displaced or repealed by written law. Thus, many of the former prerogatives are either regulated by law, or have been repealed. An example of the former is the exercise of the prerogative of mercy.[89] The President may remit or reduce the punishment, including a term of imprisonment, or a forfeiture, on conviction for any offence. An Advisory Committee on the Prerogative of Mercy has been provided for, which consists of the Attorney-General, and not less than three nor more than five other members, including at least two Ministers, and at least one medical practitioner. Apart from the Attorney-General, the members are appointed by, and can be dismissed at the will of, the President. He is required to refer any sentence of death (otherwise than at a court martial) to the Committee; he can only exercise the prerogative after receiving its advice, though he is not bound to follow it. In all other instances, he may consult the Committee if he wishes, but is not obliged to follow its recommendations. The exercise of the prerogative is therefore ultimately the responsibility of the President; furthermore, its exercise is a matter for his personal discretion, and is not a subject of collective responsibility.[90]

An instance where a prerogative has been displaced is the abolition of the right of appeal to the Judicial Committee of the Privy Council. The Crown has the prerogative, confirmed and regulated by imperial legislation, to grant special leave to appeal to the Judicial Committee from British Dominions and possessions overseas. It is doubtful if this prerogative can pass on to a Republican Government, for it is connected with the Crown's association with its overseas possessions. In any case, a constitutional amendment has expressly abolished all appeals to the Judicial Committee, thus repealing the prerogative even if it did exist.[91]

What powers then does the President have under this provision? Most of the ordinary prerogatives are now regulated or provided for by the law—legislative, judicial, governmental immunities,[92] tenure of holders of public office, dissolution of Parliament and the formation of Government, escheat,[93] right to take property during emergencies,[94] and control of the armed forces.[95] Of the remaining prerogatives, it is arguable that many are, by their very

[89] Constitution sections 27, 28 and 29.
[90] See p. 245 above.
[91] Constitution of Kenya (Amendment) Act No. 14 of 1965, section 15.
[92] Government Proceedings Act, Cap. 40.
[93] Act No. 14 of 1965, section 18.
[94] Preservation of Public Security Act, Cap. 57, section 4 (2) (g).
[95] Constitution section 4. Kenya Military Forces Act, Cap. 198, sections 166–167; Kenya Military Forces (Military Council) Act, Cap. 198A, sections 3–5.

nature, inapplicable in Kenya. If the prerogatives operate in Kenya by virtue of the reception of the common law, then they have to be suitably modified. It would therefore seem, for example, that the sole right to print or licence others to print the Bible would be excluded. So would the other prerogatives arising from the Queen's position as head of the official Church. The scope of prerogative powers is thus narrow. One possible area is the conduct of foreign affairs. But it is equally arguable that the power to conduct foreign affairs is part of the executive powers that are expressly vested in the President. The Government is free to negotiate treaty and other relations with foreign nations, though the common law rule requiring incorporation by Parliament into the domestic law applies, if such incorporation is necessary. Nevertheless, there are wide and important areas in foreign affairs where the Government is free of legal, as opposed to political, controls; these include the declaration of war and the making of peace, and the recognition of foreign governments or countries. Indeed, if a war is declared, the Government *ipso facto* gets vastly increased powers. Can the Government or its agents plead an Act of State as a defence in a legal suit? The defence, in the common law, is applicable only in relation to suits by subjects of a foreign state, for acts committed abroad. Though there is nothing in the ordinary laws which confers an immunity in such a case, it is probable that it would be available under the provision for the transfer of prerogative powers to the Government of Kenya.

The only instance so far where the prerogative has been used is in the institution of honours and awards. The conferment of these honours is also a matter for the prerogative. But here again the Proclamation establishing the honours and awards refers not only to the provisions about the prerogative, but also to section 24 of the Constitution dealing with the constitution of offices.[96] It is doubtful if honours can be regarded as public offices; their establishment is better regarded as emanating from the prerogative powers.

The full import of the prerogative powers is therefore unclear but unlikely to be of much significance. But the two remaining special powers of the Government are much more important.

First, the Government has wide and unfettered powers in the North-Eastern Province, which were authorized at independence,[97] and which were subsequently extended to the contiguous districts of Marsabit, Isiolo, Tana River and Lamu.[98] These powers enable the Government to administer these parts without any constitutional constraints—the President can make

[96] Legal Notice 114/1966. Later proclamations amending the first one, or setting out rules governing the awards, do not specifically refer to the President's power under a section of the Constitution. Legal Notices 97–105/1967.
[97] Kenya (Independence) Order in Council, section 19. Now Constitution section 127.
[98] Act No. 16 of 1966.

any law by regulations, his legislative competence in this respect not being bound by any constitutional or other legal restrictions; he can thus authorize any administrative action that he feels necessary or expedient for the purpose of ensuring effective government. Though these powers were given for the specific purpose of dealing with the security problem created by the secessionist movement among the Somali, they are of indefinite duration, and it is for the President to decide when they shall cease. In relation to these parts of Kenya, therefore, the Government's powers are complete and unfettered, since there is no requirement of a reference to, or approval by, Parliament.

The powers of the Executive as discussed so far are those that it is intended that it should have in normal times. However, its powers are vastly increased in times of crises. Though these increased powers are meant to be exceptional, extensive use has been made of them; realistically, therefore, one should regard them as an important adjunct to the presidential powers. Many of these special powers override important provisions of the Constitution, and the Constitution can to that extent be looked on as embodying aspirations or defining desirable standards of conduct and relationships rather than governing the present exercise of power. That it is intended that these powers are to be used fairly frequently is shown by substituting the expression 'public security powers' for 'emergency powers'. Also, parliamentary control on the exercise of these powers has been considerably reduced; the Government can assume these powers indefinitely without obligatory public accountability.

The extraordinary powers of the President are provided for in the Preservation of Public Security Act.[99] The Act provides for two kinds of powers—Public Security Measures and Special Public Security Measures; no authorization of Parliament, before or after, is necessary for the exercise of the powers in the first category; it is for the second. Under the first, the President gets important legislative powers, though his legislative competence is circumscribed by that of Parliament; nor can his regulations contravene the existing law. Neither of these two limitations applies to his legislative competence under the second category, though some constitutional limitations remain. The details of these powers are discussed elsewhere,[100] but it is pertinent to point out here the wide range of action, including severe curtailment of basic human rights, open to the Government. Whatever the justification for them, there is little doubt that they strengthen the hands of the Government enormously, and since the checks on their exercise are minimal, one cannot be sure of the *bona fides* of the Government in their use. The

[99] Cap. 57. Extensively amended by Constitution of Kenya (Amendment No. 3) Act No. 18 of 1966. That part providing for preventive detention *inter alia* was brought into force throughout Kenya by the Constitution (Public Security) Order, Legal Notice 211/1966.

[100] Chapter XI.

very existence of these powers has an unhealthy and inhibiting effect on the assertion of democratic rights, and their prolonged use is clearly inimical to the growth of democratic institutions.

CONCLUSION

This consideration of the evolution of the law of presidential power shows that the original aims of the Government in introducing the Republican Constitution have been added to, and in some respects superceded. The further alterations to the electoral machinery, the attrition of the doctrine of collective responsibility, and the increase in presidential power over the civil service, the Judicial Service Commission and human rights suggest that executive dominance of the Constitution has become a major aim of Government. What are being sought for are fool-proof legal formulae which can ensure a smooth succession, not merely to the office of the President, but to the whole dominating position—legal, administrative and political—which has been built up during the term of office of the present President and around which now rotates the rest of the Executive. Experience, however, suggests that fool-proof legal formulae crumble in the face of changing political circumstances and he would be a bold man who would conclude that constitutional changes in this area in Kenya are now complete.

CHAPTER VII

The Administrative Process

INTRODUCTION

In chapter III we examined agrarian administration as a case study of the role of law in the creation and operation of Kenya's dual economy. In this chapter we shall examine the administrative process, the machinery by which the policies of the President and his Ministers, approved or enacted into law by the Legislature, are carried into effect, within the context primarily of agrarian administration. Our reasons for this approach are as follows: by the time of the Lancaster House Conference in 1960 many aspects of the dual system had begun to disappear partly because political circumstances were changing, but more because increasing numbers of Africans were growing cash crops and were therefore subject to the same administrative regime as their European counterparts. In the crucial matter of land ownership, however, there were still differences, but these were the subject of priority action in the sixties, which in turn contributed to an increase in laws and institutions in this area. At the same time other political influences were causing a break-up of the central administration, and the growth of regionalism which, on paper at least, had a profound effect on administration in this area. Since independence, over and above the reversal of regionalism, there has been a constant restlessness about agrarian administration; new institutions have been created, old ones rejuvenated, committees have investigated and sometimes reported, laws have been threatened and enacted. Any attempt therefore to consider the administrative process not just as a static phenomenon, but as one in which decisions are taken, institutions play a particular role and the total performance influences the political and economic development of the country, is drawn inevitably to agrarian administration. We do not claim that this is the only part of the administrative process which will tell us something about political change in Kenya, but what remains true today as of old is that land and agriculture are the staple diet of politicians, and the root of economic development in Kenya. A consideration of the more important laws and institutions governing these matters is therefore an essential part of this study.

It is important too at the outset of this chapter to indicate some general political matters in Kenya on which a study of the administrative process might throw some light. Three may briefly be mentioned. A significant fact in political upheavals in many new states is the extent to which the new authorities make use of the existing administration with very few changes. This suggests that the administration plays an important role in preserving political stability in a new state. On the other hand it may have materially contributed to the breakdown of the old order through its actions, and the expense required to maintain it. It must be seen then as an independent factor in political development capable of exerting great influence on its own. There are signs that the administration in Kenya is at something of a cross-roads from this point of view.

Secondly, running through much of the agricultural development that has taken place or is planned to take place in Kenya in this era is the conflict between political and economic objectives—seen most clearly in the settlement schemes—and a question which inevitably arises is: how far has this been reflected in the institutions and laws created to implement development? Thirdly, the element of continuity in Kenya's political development comes through very clearly in the area of agrarian administration so that at times it is almost a misnomer to talk of new policies or new laws—rather they are old policies and laws given a face-lift in the interests of political expediency.

THE CENTRAL ADMINISTRATION: ORGANIZATION AND POWERS

Before examining the operation of the administration in agrarian development, the organization and powers of the central administration must first be surveyed. As seen above, executive authority is vested in the President and is exercised by the President, Ministers appointed by him, and civil servants, the majority of whom are appointed by the Public Service Commission, and other governmental institutions. There are two classes of Minister in Kenya, those that are in the Cabinet, whether they have specific portfolios or are designated Ministers of State, and Assistant Ministers. Since independence the number of both classes of Ministers has steadily risen, and had topped the fifty mark by the middle of 1967. Of these, twenty-one including the President were in the Cabinet, the rest being Assistant Ministers. The Cabinet formally operates both as a whole and via standing and *ad hoc* Committees, one of the most important of the former being the Development Committee which concerns itself particularly with the land reform and settlement programme.[1]

The Cabinet and its Committees are served by a Secretariat under a Permanent Secretary, who is responsible 'in accordance with such instructions as may be given to him by the President for arranging the business for and

[1] *Development Plan of Kenya 1966–70*, Nairobi, p. 5, para. 13, and pp. 10–11. The Development Committee has given birth to its own Committees (Gazette Notice 329/1967), establishing the Inter-Ministerial Committee on an Accelerated Land Reform Programme which implements directives of the Development Committee.

keeping the minutes of the Cabinet and for conveying the decisions of the Cabinet to the appropriate person or authority'.[2]

The bulk of the Ministers' work, however, is done in their Ministries under the authority of a multitude of statutory powers and duties conferred by Acts of Parliament, either by the Ministers themselves, or by civil servants within the Ministry. Kenya is no exception to the general rule that in practice much of the work of the Ministries is carried out by civil servants, including a fair amount of policy-making. The civil service has therefore a central role to play in the implementation of the Government's development plans. In addition to its task of implementation, however, the civil service, in Kenya, via the provincial administration branch of it, retains the task of explaining government policy to the people, and urging their co-operation with the Government, part of the traditional duties of the provincial administration though now the cause of some friction with MPs who consider that their role in this matter is being usurped by civil servants. These three governmental functions of policy-making, implementation, and explaining place the civil service *qua* institution of government in a powerful position in Kenya. It is also in a powerful position *qua* pressure group on the Government. Its governmental position, its size, and organization, and in the administrative class at any rate its general level of administrative competence and intellectual ability, all combine to make it an institution to which the political side of the Executive must have special regard when planning its policies, and these points must be borne in mind when considering certain organizational aspects of the civil service.

(a) *The Civil Service*

Three matters may be considered: methods of appointment and internal management, discipline, and staff and industrial relations. The power of appointment of civil servants is divided between the President,[3] the Public Service Commission in whom certain powers are vested by the Constitution,[4] and Permanent Secretaries and heads of departments to whom certain powers have been delegated.[5] The President appoints the Commission itself, all Permanent Secretaries, and certain other named officials. The Commission appoints the administrative and professional classes, and the higher grades of secretarial, executive and technical classes. Permanent Secretaries and others have had delegated to them the power to appoint and exercise general administration over the lower grades of the last three classes,

[2] Independence Constitution section 85 (2). This section was repealed in the Constitution Act, 1969 as being unnecessary. The functions of the office remained unaffected.
[3] Constitution section 24, 25, 106 (2), 108–111.
[4] Constitution section 107.
[5] Public Service Commission Regulations, Legal Notice 48/1965.

and the subordinate staff. In respect of those officers whom the Commission appoints, however, a Permanent Secretary must give it information, and a recommendation as to whom he considers should fill the post, from amongst established officers, or full details of why he does not consider any such officer should fill it. While the Commission will usually act on such information, it would be within its legal rights if it declined to do so.[6]

The Commission is in charge of any examinations that are run both for entry into, and for promotion within, the service. Where, as in the case of the administrative and professional classes, promotions are decided on criteria other than examinations, both the Commission and Permanent Secretaries are to have regard to merit and seniority with the former taking priority. The Constitution also provides for localization to be a relevant criterion in promotion, as it is in entrance into the service, expatriates being required to retire to facilitate these processes.[7]

Information on how these legal provisions operate in practice is difficult to obtain. Two points may, however, be made. First, though there was a general speeding up of the process of localization after independence, there were still in 1967 a considerable number of expatriates in the administrative and professional classes, in both middle and senior positions, the pressures for localization being met to some extent by an increase in the size of the service. Secondly, the Salaries Review Commission admitted that there may have been a certain amount of political interference in the selection and promotion of civil servants immediately after independence, but considered that that period was now past.[8] Not everybody would agree with that assessment but it is certainly the case that there is a greater formal separation between political and other considerations in appointment and promotion in the Kenya public service than in either Tanzania or Uganda, and this may influence the practice.

Internal management of the service is divided between the President's and Vice-President's offices and the Ministry of Finance. The first two deal with all personnel, establishment and training questions, the last with pay and pensions. Thus questions concerning the creation of new posts, or the establishment as permanent and pensionable of those which have hitherto been temporary or contract posts, are the concern of the Director of Personnel in the President's office, who will seek information from the Directorate, located in the Vice-President's office and liaise on salary

[6] Apart from the legislation referred to in the above three footnotes, a useful source of information on these and other matters connected with the public service is the *Report of the Salaries Review Commission* (Nairobi, Government Printer 1967). See, too, McAuslan, 'Administrative Law in Kenya—A General Survey' in *East African Law Today* (London, British Institute of International & Comparative Law, 1966), at pp. 26–32.

[7] Kenya Order in Council, S.I. 1968/1963, section 14, now Constitution section 126.

[8] *Report*, op. cit., p. 88, para. 298.

questions with the Treasury. This division of responsibilities stems ultimately from the Constitution which vests the power of constituting offices in the President, and while it may work well enough within the administration, it hinders staff relations as it makes it difficult for the official side of the Whitley Council to be brought together for meetings of the Council.[9]

The powers of discipline and compulsory retirement are again shared between the Commission and senior civil servants[10]—usually heads of departments—to whom the Commission has delegated its powers, and in relation to teachers, a specialized branch of the public service, the Teachers Service Commission.[11] Disciplinary powers vary from reprimand to dismissal or termination of appointment. Disciplinary procedures vary in their formality and safeguards for the accused officer depending (a) on the nature of the charge—alleged offences which could lead to dismissal being the subject of an inquiry with greater procedural safeguards than those leading to other punishments and (b) on the status of the accused officer, officers being divided according to their salary and grade with those in the highest grades receiving on a charge carrying dismissal all the procedural safeguards of the best disciplinary tribunals, including an inquiry presided over by an officer with legal or judicial experience, while for those in the lowest grades (members of the subordinate staff) a Permanent Secretary or head of department is permitted to award any punishment, including dismissal, with a bare minimum of safeguards which may in certain circumstances be dispensed with. In between these two extremes the pattern is more akin to that provided for the most senior grade with the important proviso that the decision to hold an inquiry is left to the discretion of the Commission. In all cases an appeal lies to the Commission, with, in exceptional circumstances, a second appeal being entertained within one year of the decision being communicated to the officer concerned.

The stock justification put forward for this pattern is that the subordinate staff do not understand or appreciate elaborate procedures and provided a right of appeal is preserved summary justice will be perfectly fair in their case. On the other hand, the efficiency and morale of the higher civil service is so important that elaborate procedures are necessary to ensure that groundless charges are not made and carried through, and those that have substance are properly pressed and pursued.[12] We can admit the strength of the latter argument while querying the former. Subordinate staff are just as likely to feel aggrieved by an inadequate investigation and hearing of a disciplinary charge as are senior staff. Moreover very little time is, in the end, likely to be

[9] For the Whitley Council see p. 265, below.
[10] Public Service Commission Regulations 34–39; McAuslan, op. cit., pp. 27–9.
[11] Teachers Service Commission Act No. 2 of 1967.
[12] Adu, *The Civil Service in New African States*, op. cit., pp. 143–4.

saved by a summary proceeding for an aggrieved person will complain to his union, and the matter will continue to be pursued in the new context of an industrial dispute.

A very good illustration of this situation occurring is provided by the Industrial Court case of *Kenya Civil Service Union* v. *Ministry of Works.*[13] Nizamdin, a member of the union, was employed as a driver by the Ministry. His services were abruptly terminated after the last of a series of disciplinary charges, extending over a two-year period, had been considered and found proved by a Regional Engineer. Termination meant that he failed to qualify for a gratuity. On his request his union took the matter up. There were meetings between officials of the union and various senior engineers and an appeal to the Civil Secretary of the Region. At these meetings, the Administration put forward as an additional reason for termination that Nizamdin was over fifty-five and it was not its policy to retain people over that age. The union challenged the question of age and a Medical Board was appointed which examined Nizamdin, pronounced him to be about fifty years of age and fit for work. Agreement still not being reached, a conciliator was appointed. His conclusions were rejected by both sides, and the matter was referred to the Industrial Court. The Court found the termination in order, and upheld the original decision given more than three years previously. It is not unreasonable to suppose that had the original decision been preceded by a formal hearing at which Nizamdin had had the assistance of a union official, and by greater care in explaining it to Nizamdin and his union much of the time and expense of negotiations, appeals, and hearings over that three year period would have been saved.

This case is also instructive as illustrating the use of the power of compulsory termination of appointment. This may be exercised either to retire a person who has reached the minimum retirement age, in which case he will be retired with a pension, or to retire a person in circumstances in which disciplinary proceedings are not appropriate, or in the public interest. In all cases the officer concerned must be informed of the matters under consideration and given an opportunity to comment upon them. In Nizamdin's case this appears to have been done at best only indirectly. The facts disclosed that the administration considered that his general inefficient performance over the previous two years, characterized by individual acts of insubordination and careless driving, warranted termination while no individual act would warrant dismissal. However, Nizamdin was never given an opportunity to make representations on the general question of termination, only on each individual disciplinary charge. While the charges may be accumulated so as to amount eventually to good cause for termination,

[13] Gazette Notice 375/1967.

it may be doubted whether the representations can be, so that representation before termination can be dispensed with.

In staff and industrial relations, a division is made between those civil servants who may and those who may not belong to unions. For those junior civil servants, subordinate staff and teachers who may, the general trades disputes law and machinery applies, as *KCSU* v. *Ministry of Works* indicates. This means that, besides the machinery of disputes settlement, which both unions and Government can make use of, the Government has power to declare a strike of civil servants illegal if they have not exhausted the use of that machinery.[14] A strike called by the Kenya National Teachers' Union in 1967 was so declared twenty-four hours after it had commenced.

Those civil servants who may not belong to trade unions have their staff associations which negotiate on terms of service and allied matters with the Government on a Central Whitley Council, first established in 1952. As originally established, the Council operated on the English pattern with decisions becoming operative on being reported to the Council of Ministers, but this position was changed after independence, and the Government now reserves the final decision to itself. Indeed at the annual meeting of the Senior Civil Servants' Association in July 1967, the President of the Association complained that Government representatives saw Whitley Council meetings not as a place for negotiation, but as a place to present a set of proposals on a take it or leave it basis. The Salaries Review Commission also considered that there was insufficient consultation at the Council, and recommended a reduction in numbers from eighteen to eight members on both staff and official sides, and the appointment of standing committees of the Council at which most of the detailed discussions would take place, as a means of reviving the Council. It stressed the need for the official side to be in a position to negotiate although accepting that the final decision would have to rest with the Cabinet or the relevant Minister.[15]

A further and final matter which may be considered here is that part of the criminal law which applies particularly to civil servants and Ministers, and their exercise of power.[16] An offence is committed by a person who deals with property in which he has acquired a personal interest in the exercise of his administrative or judicial duties, or by one who, while employed in the public service, and in discharge of the duties of his office, commits a fraud or breach of trust affecting the public, whether such would have been criminal or not if committed against a private person. It is an offence to submit a false return in respect of sums payable to the claimant or others. A public

[14] Trades Disputes Act No. 15 of 1965, sections 19, 20 and 25. These provisions apply to all strikes.
[15] *Report*, op. cit., pp. 88-9, paras. 299–304. See, too, *East African Standard*, 15 July 1967.
[16] Penal Code Cap. 63, chapter 10, 'Abuse of Office', sections 99–107.

officer who does, or directs to be done, in an abuse of the authority of his office, an arbitrary act prejudicial to the rights of others, whether this is done for gain or not, commits an offence. A very wide net is cast by the Prevention of Corruption Act[17] to trap any corrupt practice or attempt thereat whether done or solicited for consideration or not. The Act permits special investigations to be made of bank accounts of suspected persons, and the possession by an accused of sums or property disproportionate to his known sources of income which he cannot satisfactorily explain may be proved and regarded as corroborative evidence of corruption at his trial. Penalties include disqualification from public office for life, and from being a elector for seven years. Finally the Official Secrets Act,[18] modelled on the English legislation, makes it an offence to obtain or retain official documents and papers which one should not have, to communicate or attempt to communicate them to a foreign power, or in addition, to any unauthorized person.

(b) *Some General Administrative Powers*

The matters to be considered here are the transfer and delegation of powers, the exercise of the power of making subsidiary legislation, and controls over it, consultation, and formal inquiries. The President may transfer any power or duty conferred on him by Act of Parliament, to any Minister.[19] An Order providing for such a transfer must be laid before, and approved by, the National Assembly. The power is not very often used, for an alternative method of achieving the same end with perhaps less publicity is to use Acts of Parliament or Presidential Regulations[20] to amend a variety of Acts of Parliament by substituting the word 'Minister' for the words 'Governor', 'Governor-General' or 'President' as the case might be wherever the latter words appear in the Acts, and by amending the definition section to indicate which Minister is being referred to.

A more frequently used power permits the President in the case of a Minister, and a Minister in the case of a public officer upon whom certain powers and duties are imposed, temporarily to transfer those powers and duties to other named Ministers and public officers who may then exercise them to the fullest extent. The power is usually used when a Minister is to be absent from the country for any appreciable length of time. In addition to

[17] Cap. 65.
[18] No. 11 of 1968.
[19] Interpretation and General Clauses Provisions Act, Cap. 2, sections 36–39.
[20] Under section 4 (4) of the Kenya Order in Council the Governor-General had power for one year to make amendments to the laws to bring them into conformity with the Constitution. This power was continued for a further two years by section 6 (4), Constitution of Kenya (Amendment) Act No. 14 of 1965, as amended by Constitution of Kenya (Amendment No. 2) Act No. 17 of 1966, and became exercisable by the President by the first Act. See chapter VIII.

these powers of transfer, the President, the Attorney-General, and all Ministers may delegate the exercise of powers and performance of duties conferred upon them by an Act unless that Act expressly forbids it, or the powers conferred are legislative or judicial, in respect of which there is a general prohibition of delegation.

These wide powers do not draw a distinction between the delegation of discretionary, and non-discretionary or ministerial, powers and duties; both sorts may be delegated. In respect of the civil service, however, this distinction exists and discretionary powers may not be delegated by a civil servant to whom they have been delegated unless there is express authorization for such delegation. The general rule of *delegatus non potest delegare* applies. A good example of the distinction between discretionary and ministerial powers in relation to the civil service is provided by *Odendaal* v. *Gray*[21] where the E.A.C.A. considered that it was in order for the Commissioner of Lands to delegate the notification of consent to a land transaction to a subordinate, provided that he had himself given the consent, as he was empowered to do by a delegation from the Governor under the Government Lands Act. The latter power could not be delegated as it was discretionary, but the former was no more than a piece of administrative machinery, and involved no exercise of discretion at all.

Transfer and delegation of powers are the lubricants of the administrative machine. Powers are conferred by statute on the President or a Minister and if they could not delegate them, the civil service would have no legal authority to administer the country, and implement government policy. To confer a specific power on a named civil servant would bring to a halt either the organization of the civil service or its work, as duties could not be reorganized and civil servants transferred, or half the civil service would be constantly employed preparing new laws to take account of such changes in the other half. Equally, without the power of transfer, the President would be handicapped in reorganizing his Government since it would be difficult without a special Act of Parliament to amalgamate or divide Ministries or reallocate duties of Ministers. At the same time a knowledge of the extent and operation of these powers highlights the limitations of ministerial responsibility as a method of legislative control of the Executive. Ministers do not exercise all powers conferred on them, and these provisions exist to facilitate that. Though they are required to answer for the acts of their officials, they may not be fully or at all conversant with what has been done in their name, and a meaningless dialogue on the matter takes place in Parliament while the actual exercisers of power remain virtually uncontrolled by Parliament.

The exercise of the power of making subsidiary legislation may be regarded

[21] [1960] E.A. 263.

as part of a Minister's power for, although other bodies such as commodity boards are empowered to make such legislation, the bulk of subsidiary legislation in Kenya is made by Ministers in the exercise of powers conferred upon them by Act of Parliament. In any event the following general rules apply to all subsidiary legislation of Central Government, whether made by a Minister or some statutory public body. Such legislation comes into force when published in the Gazette unless stated otherwise and it must be so published; it may be retrospective in effect but not so as to take effect before the parent Act comes into force. Equally the power to make such legislation may be exercised before the Act comes into force but rules and regulations so made cannot come into force before the parent Act does. Penalties for breach may be annexed to such legislation.[22]

The above provisions apply to the exercise of power. What of the actual powers themselves? The general pattern is to confer very wide powers of making subsidiary legislation. Acts may confer powers for specific purposes but there is always a general power and it is expressly provided, as a general rule of interpretation, that when powers are conferred for general and special purposes, the special purposes shall not be deemed to derogate from the general. General powers are conferred in such terms as: 'generally for carrying this Act into effect' or 'for the better carrying out of the objects and purposes of this Act' or 'for prescribing anything which this Act enables or requires to be prescribed'. Occasionally these powers are widened by being couched in subjective terms. Thus the National Social Security Fund Act provides as follows:

> Without prejudice to any specific power conferred by any of the foregoing provisions of this Act, regulations may be made for facilitating the implementation of this Act . . . Any regulations made under this Act may make different provisions with respect to different cases or classes of case, and for different purposes of this Act may impose conditions and make exceptions and may contain such incidental or supplementary provisions as appear to the Minister to be expedient for the purpose of the regulations.[23]

Such wide powers are generally accepted as necessary nowadays to permit governments to act with speed and flexibility, and meet changing political and economic circumstances as effectively as possible. In addition legislatures do not generally possess sufficient expertise to examine all the legal and technical minutiae of a detailed Bill. This latter argument is of special relevance to Kenya where the National Assembly spends the greater part of its time debating motions on general issues, or Second Readings of Bills and comparatively little time on Committee or Report stages of Bills or on other matters which require a certain amount of technical expertise.

[22] Cap. 2, sections 27–35.
[23] No. 28 of 1965. See, too, section 44 (1).

Less generally accepted, but equally necessary, is the possibility of some control over the exercise of the power, so as to try and ensure that governments' exercise of the power remains responsive to the needs and demands of the electorate, and within the law. Such control may take one of three forms: a requirement that the Minister, prior to making rules, consults with some advisory body, or makes rules only with the approval of some other body; a requirement that the legislature should have an opportunity to examine and reject the rules; and the possibility that the courts may examine and decline to give effect to the rules on the grounds that the Minister does not have the power to make them, or has not followed the correct procedure in making them—*ultra vires* the Minister. All three forms of control exist in Kenya with varying degrees of effectiveness. Consultation will be examined later; legislative and judicial control may be examined here.

Unless otherwise provided, all subsidiary legislation when made must be laid before the National Assembly, where it is subject to annulment within the next twenty sitting days thereafter. This provision has been in existence since 1956,[24] but there is no record of the National Assembly having used the power given to it, even for the purposes of raising a debate on some rules without proceeding to a vote. More rarely a positive vetting procedure is provided with the National Assembly being required to approve draft subsidiary legislation before it comes into effect. For example, an order made under section 12 of the Agriculture Act adding a crop to the first schedule of the Act which has the effect of empowering the Minister to fix the price to be paid to the grower, must be so laid and approved before it comes into effect.[25] The opportunity thus provided for a debate is not, however, extensively used, though the responsible Minister is obliged to provide some sort of justification for his exercise of the power which would not otherwise occur. On the whole, however, legislative control is a formality, the motions are gone through but the substance is missing. It is perhaps unrealistic to expect anything more from a legislature disinclined to examine the texts of Bills too closely, and belonging overwhelmingly to the party which forms the Government. Nor, in practice, has the Government taken undue advantage of legislative indifference; though wide general powers are delegated, matters of fundamental importance, such as the taxing power, are still generally provided for only by Acts of Parliament. Again a reasonable ratio is maintained between the amount of legislation produced by Parliament and the amount of subsidiary legislation excluding by-laws, produced in any one year.[26]

[24] Rules and Regulations (Laying) Act No. 39 of 1956. Now Cap. 2, section 34 (1).
[25] For an example, see National Assembly, *Debates*, volume X (22 November 1966), cols. 1834–1838—sugar-cane was added to the first schedule.
[26] e.g. In 1966, there were 39 Acts of Parliament occupying 385 pages in the statute book, and 359 Legal Notices (which include by-laws, and notifications of Acts

Judicial control tends to arise out of a criminal prosecution for breach of a provision of subsidiary legislation where the defence is put forward that the instant rule is *ultra vires* the Minister, and, notwithstanding the wide terms in which most delegated legislative powers are conferred, there are several instances in which this defence has succeeded. In *R.* v. *Juma bin Mwalimu*[27] the High Court quashed a conviction for breach of a rule made under the Native Hut and Poll Tax Act on the ground that the Act conferred powers to make rules imposing duties of collection on headmen, but the instant rule had imposed a duty to answer questions on the taxpayer. Another example of misuse of powers is provided by *Koinange Mbiu* v. *R.*[28] where powers conferred to limit the area within which certain crops could be grown were used to limit the classes of people who could grow the crops. Again in *R.* v. *Jan Mohammed*[29] a conviction was quashed on the ground that while the Crop Production and Livestock Act empowered the Governor to make rules applicable to the areas specified therein, the rules under which the charge was made had empowered the Director of Agriculture to specify the areas to which they should relate. Finally *Mwangi* v. *R.*[30] provides an example of a conviction being quashed because the regulation, admitted to have been broken, had not been published as provided by the general law.

Ministers are required or empowered to consult or obtain the approval or advice of various bodies before exercising both their legislative and their executive powers in many fields of administration and examples of both may be given. In the agricultural field, the Agriculture Act[31] alone establishes a plethora of consultative and advisory bodies and imposes a duty on the Minister to consult with them in various exercises of his power; for instance he is required to consult with organizations representing producers in conducting his annual review of the agricultural industry.

The Central Agricultural Board, composed of both official and unofficial members, has a key advisory role in the industry. For a start it advises the Minister on national agricultural policy. Again the Minister is required to

coming into force), occupying 674 pages. In 1967 totals were 36 Acts, 669 pages, 228 Legal Notices, 508 pages. By-laws are published in the Gazette, and numbered in the same series as other subsidiary legislation. They must be open to inspection and objection in the offices of the local authority concerned, which must consider all objections received. The Minister must approve all by-laws before they come into force—Local Government Regulations Legal Notice 256/1963, part XIV. See, too, *Chhaganlal* v. *Kericho U.D.C.*, [1965] E.A. 370.

[27] (1916), 6 E.A.L.R. 175. (Rule 7 *ultra vires*). The administration attempted to exercise the same power under rule 5, but this was declared *ultra vires* the ordinance in *R.* v. *Mgeni bin Juma* (1917), 7 E.A.L.R. 2.

[28] (1951), 24 (2), K.L.R. 130.

[29] (1937, 17 K.L.R. 108.

[30] (1950), 24 (1), K.L.R. 72.

[31] Cap. 218, sections 5, 37 and 186.

consult with it before exercising his powers to acquire land to facilitate the growing of a particular crop which he may do, so as to promote the public benefit, and again before exercising his powers to zone an area within which a particular crop must be delivered to a particular factory. The Water Act[32] establishes a Water Resources Authority, consisting in equal numbers of officials and unofficials whose duties include advising and making recommendations to the Minister on such matters as present consumption and estimated future needs. In consultation with the Authority the Minister may appoint Regional Water Boards with advisory functions. A final example is provided by the Wheat Industry Act[33] which establishes a Wheat Board which is advisory to the Minister in the exercise of his powers under the Act, for instance his granting of permission to expand an existing mill or acquire a new mill.

More far-reaching consultative provisions exist in the field of social welfare. The National Social Security Fund Act[34] establishes a National Social Security Advisory Committee consisting of fifteen persons representing in equal parts the Government, employers and employees. The Minister appoints all members but in appointing those representing employees and employers he is obliged to consult organizations appearing to him to represent those two groups of persons. The function of the Committee is to give advice and assistance to the Minister in connection with his implementation of the Act which establishes a system of national insurance in Kenya. The Minister may refer to the Committee such matters as he sees fit including the question of amending the Act. When the Minister makes regulations he may submit a draft of them to the Committee. The Committee is then required to bring the purport of the regulations to the attention of people most likely to be affected by them so that they have an opportunity to make objections to them. The Committee is to consider the draft regulations and the objections thereto and submit a report to the Minister. When such regulations are laid before the National Assembly by the Minister he must also lay the report of the Committee and a statement showing what effect has been given to its recommendations, and if no effect has been given, why not. It is difficult to be enthusiastic about such an elaborate procedure; the Minister is not obliged to make use of it, and indeed may be inhibited from doing so because of the delays and complications which may ensue. It appears to have been lifted rather uncritically from the English National Insurance Act, which, however, imposes a duty on the Minister to consult the equivalent Committee.[35]

[32] Cap. 372, sections 19–23.
[33] Cap. 344, sections 4, 9 and 10.
[34] Sections 4 and 47, first schedule.
[35] National Insurance Act 1946, section 77.

The final example of consultation comes from the administration of the National Parks and illustrates both that Ministers may be required to consult with bodies other than statutory advisory or consultative bodies and that consultation can have teeth put into it. Before the Minister may declare an area to be a national park, he must consult with the competent authority which may be another Minister in the case of State land, a county council in the case of Trust land, or a person entitled to the rents and profits in the case of privately owned land. If the competent authority does not consent to the declaration, it may not be made unless the National Assembly by resolution approves a draft order, and if the park is to be in Trust land, the land has been set aside. Such a procedure of consultation, introduced in 1967,[36] is to be explained by the great political importance of land in Kenya, and the widespread feelings of apprehension that arise whenever land ceases to be available for settlement or cultivation.

Somewhat comparable to consultation is the procedure of an inquiry in that both are designed to ensure that all possible facts and views are put before a Minister before he makes a decision. Provisions for public inquiries into individual applications to do something—for example, build an explosives factory[37]—do exist in the law but such inquiries rarely take place. More important are provisions for inquiries at large into matters of public importance, for these have been and remain a constant feature of the administrative process in Kenya. Such inquiries may take one of three forms: an inquiry under the Commissions of Inquiry Act;[38] an inquiry carried out by an *ad hoc* Committee; and an inquiry carried out by a Select Committee of Parliament.[39]

The Act provides for the setting up of a Commission of Inquiry to investigate the conduct of a public officer or any other matter on which, in the opinion of the President, it would be in the public interest to have such an inquiry. The Commissioners, of whom there can be any number, must sit in public except where for some good reason they direct otherwise. They are empowered to call for papers and summon witnesses, and the inquiry is a judicial proceeding for purposes of the criminal law relating to judicial proceedings which covers such matters as perjury, suborning witnesses, destroying and fabricating evidence. Witnesses have the privilege of witnesses in a court of law. Persons whose conduct may directly or indirectly be called into question at the inquiry may be allowed representation thereat and

[36] National Parks of Kenya Act, Cap. 377, section 3 (1) as amended by the Statute Law (Miscellaneous Amendments) Act No. 9 of 1967.
[37] Explosives Act, Cap. 115. For details, see McAuslan, op. cit., pp. 45–6.
[38] Cap. 102. For a general review of this type of inquiry see the English *Report of the Royal Commission on Tribunals of Enquiry 1966*, Cmnd. 3121.
[39] As to which, see chapter VIII, pp. 330–1.

must be given due warning of the matters which involve them. The Commissioners report to the President. The report is usually published but there is no obligation to do so.

The procedure tends to be used for two quite distinct types of inquiry, of each of which there have been examples since independence. There is the inquiry into an alleged administrative scandal such as was appointed in 1965 to inquire into the maize position in Kenya following allegations of inefficiency, corruption and unfair dealing by the Ministry of Co-operatives and Marketing and the Maize Marketing Board. Secondly, there is the inquiry into the possibility or necessity for some new policy or reform to be introduced; two such inquiries were appointed in 1967 to investigate and propose reforms which would institute unified laws of succession, and marriage and divorce in Kenya. The procedure to be followed by a Commission varies depending upon the nature of the inquiry. In the former type of inquiry, the procedure at a hearing is akin to the adversary, in the latter it is inquisitorial. Thus at the Maize Commission of Inquiry, State Counsel questioned witnesses and persons whose conduct was under investigation on behalf of the Commission, and counsel representing those persons and other institutions were allowed the right of cross-examination. In addition the police assisted the Commission by obtaining statements from relevant persons.[40] The two law reform Commissions, on the other hand, did not make use of counsel but questioned witnesses themselves. Both types of Commission, however, called for, and received, written submissions.

Ad hoc committees established either by the President or a Minister, are used for the second of the two purposes outlined above, and differ from an inquiry under the Act in that they have no power to compel the attendance of witnesses or call for papers. Since, however, they are used to investigate matters of current importance, they usually have little difficulty in obtaining such evidence as they need, which is both written and oral. Matters which have been the subject of investigation by such committees include the organization of agriculture, with particular reference to the system of consultation, and the boards and committees within the industry; rent control; and the whole field of statutory organizations, public corporations, commodity boards and tribunals.[41]

STATUTORY ORGANIZATIONS

We have concentrated so far on Ministers, the civil service, their executive and legislative powers, and the various advisory and information-gathering

[40] *Report of the Maize Commission of Inquiry*, op. cit., pp. iii–v, paras. 11–17.
[41] The reports of the first two Committees were published as *Report of the Committee on the Organization of Agriculture* (Nairobi, 1960) and *Report of the Working Party on Rent Control* (Nairobi, 1965); that of the third was not published.

aids which have been established to assist them in their task of administering. But the administration in Kenya is notable for the very great number of bodies, legally separate from the Government, which have important nation-wide decision-making powers, and must therefore be regarded as an integral part of the administration. The variety of these bodies is very great but they may be broadly classified into three main functional groups, though there are inevitable sub-divisions within each group: Public Corporations, Regulatory Agencies and Managerial Boards.

(*a*) *Public Corporations*[42]

The public corporation is used by government to participate in some important economic or social activity which it is considered private enterprise cannot or should not be allowed to provide either at all or without a public alternative, and in respect of which there should be some public control. In a developing country such as Kenya an additional reason for the use of a public corporation, particularly of the developmental type, is that such a corporation is often the only way in which economic development, planned in accordance with government policy, can take place; private enterprise on its own being unwilling to take the commercial risks involved in developing a new industry, or in starting operations in a less well developed part of the country.[43]

There are twelve public corporations established by or under the law of Kenya, operating within Kenya, and between them, they illustrate all the above reasons for the establishment of public corporations. They are as follows: Land and Agricultural Bank of Kenya,[44] Agricultural Finance Corporation,[45] Agricultural Development Corporation,[46] Cereal and Sugar Finance Corporation,[47] Kenya Meat Commission,[48] Industrial and Commercial Development Corporation,[49] Kenya National Trading Corporation,[50] Kenya National Properties Ltd.,[50] Kenya Tourist Development Corporation,[51] National Housing Corporation,[52] National Irrigation Board,[53] and

[42] Bradley and McAuslan, 'The Public Corporation in East Africa' in Friedmann and Garner, *The Public Corporation* (forthcoming).
[43] *Development Plan, 1966–70*, Nairobi, p. 58.
[44] Agricultural Credit Act, Cap. 323 (until 1963 it was entitled the Land and Agricultural Bank Act).
[45] Agricultural Credit Act.
[46] Agricultural Development Corporation Act No. 7 of 1965.
[47] Cereal and Sugar Finance Corporation Act, Cap. 329. Originally established only in respect of cereals, its operations were extended to cover sugar in 1959.
[48] Kenya Meat Commission Act, Cap. 363.
[49] Industrial and Commercial Development Corporation Act, Cap. 517.
[50] These two corporations are wholly owned subsidiaries of the I.C.D.C., concernde primarily to assist in the Africanization of the economy.
[51] Kenya Tourist Development Corporation Act, No. 25 of 1965.
[52] Housing Act, Cap. 117. Formerly the Central Housing Board, the corporation received its present name and powers in 1967.
[53] Irrigation Act No. 13 of 1966.

Central Bank of Kenya.[54] All but the last three may be regarded as basically commercial public corporations, that is corporations established to carry out commercial operations similar to those carried out by ordinary commercial companies, and with the same obligation to conduct these operations without incurring a loss. We will concentrate on those corporations operating in the agrarian field.

Most of these corporations operate primarily as lending agencies. Thus the Land and Agricultural Bank established in 1931 makes loans on mortgage to farmers for such things as the purchase of land, permanent improvements to land or buildings, the establishment of agricultural and rural industries, and the construction of irrigation works. The Agricultural Finance Corporation established in 1963 assists in the development and promotion of the agricultural industry by making loans to farmers, co-operative societies, and private and public corporate bodies. The Agricultural Development Corporation was established in 1965 to promote and execute schemes for the agricultural development and reconstruction of Kenya by the initiation, assistance or expansion of agricultural undertakings or enterprises. It obtains funds from overseas sources, and owns, and provides credit for the operation of, large scale farms. The Cereal and Sugar Finance Corporation established in 1955 provides finance to the Government and its agencies for the purchase of and advance payment for cereals and sugar and to meet the expense of making sugar available to the public at a uniform price. The Kenya Meat Commission established in 1950 has a monopoly position in the wholesale meat trade and allied products as a buyer, seller and exporter, and in the slaughter of cattle, though it may licence others to undertake this last activity.

The National Irrigation Board, established in 1966, is responsible for the development, control and improvement of national irrigation schemes. An area is designated by the Minister to be a national irrigation scheme, and the land within that area is then vested in, or leased to, the Board. The Board in conjunction with the Water Resources Authority is to formulate and be responsible for the execution of policy in relation to such schemes, and in pursuance of this function it may raise funds, co-ordinate, plan, and administer settlement schemes in the irrigated areas, promote the marketing of crops and produce grown in the schemes, and provide for their processing.

There are certain common characteristics in the relationship between the corporations and their responsible Minister. The Minister may give them general or special directions which they are required to follow; alternatively they may only take certain action, for example, raise a loan, with the approval of the Minister. They must all have their accounts audited annually, and produce an annual report and set of accounts for their Minister, which he is

[54] Central Bank of Kenya Act No. 15 of 1966.

then required to lay before the National Assembly. The Ministers appoint most of the members of the corporations, though here there are some statutory limitations on their powers. Thus out of the twelve members of the Agricultural Development Corporation, the Minister appoints the chairman and eight members; of these eight at least one must be an accountant, one have knowledge of international finance, one have knowledge of the marketing of agricultural produce, one is to represent the interest of the lenders of funds and two are to be appointed from a panel of five names submitted by the Central Agricultural Board. This Board also features in the appointment of members of the Kenya Meat Commission, five being appointed by the Minister from a panel of stock producers submitted by it; four others being appointed by the Minister from amongst those who possess qualifications which in his opinion are likely to benefit the work of the Commission. This provision or variants of it appear in other statutes. Thus the Minister may appoint up to three members to the National Irrigation Board from amongst persons whom he considers can benefit the Board, in addition to the chairman whom he also appoints.

The operation of some of these public corporations will be considered in more detail below but some general comments on them may be offered here. There would seem to be a good administrative case for some rationalizations and amalgamations among them. Despite a recommendation by the MacGillivray Committee that an Agricultural Finance Corporation be established as a separate institution from the Land and Agricultural Bank, it is difficult to see what advantages are now derived from such an arrangement, since both perform the same functions. As it is, the same legislation establishes the two corporations and places the Land and Agricultural Bank in a subordinate position to the Agricultural Finance Corporation in that it must in certain circumstances obey instructions received from it. At the beginning of 1967, the same persons were appointed to both Boards, so that it is reasonable to suppose that their policies will henceforth be co-ordinated. The maintenance of a separate legal personality and administrative structure thereafter became even less understandable.[55]

It is arguable that the Agricultural Development Corporation should also be amalgamated with the above two corporations but it does have the slightly different function and mode of operation of owning and operating farms itself, and relying to a great extent on overseas sources for its funds.

[55] See Gazette Notices 71 and 72/1967 for appointment of members of the two boards. The Report of the IBRD, *The Economic Development of Kenya* (Baltimore, Johns Hopkins University Press, 1963), recommended the establishment of an Agricultural Credit Corporation to take over most agricultural credit responsibilities of government bodies and their assets and liabilities, including those of the L.A.B.K. (pp. 266–7). It considered that Kenya had too many agricultural boards (p. 110). See, too, House of Representatives, *Debates*, volume IV (23 March 1965), cols. 648–690.

It could, however, be amalgamated with the Industrial and Commercial Development Corporation to form a Kenya Development Corporation on the lines of the Ugandan and Tanzanian development corporations. Both the Kenya development corporations operate by attracting foreign capital and starting joint ventures, and the advantages of co-ordinating all forms of development with which they are concerned would be considerable. Foreign capital might well be more attracted to a strong multi-purpose corporation, and planned balanced development in rural and the smaller urban areas could be the more easily accomplished. Again it would be possible for the Government to ensure that all development projects were vetted and co-ordinated by, and all development specialists concentrated in, the one development organization of the state. Both efficiency and accountability would also be increased. The Kenya Tourist Development Corporation might also with advantage be amalgamated into such a development corporation. Many of its activities will inevitably be economic, commercial, and promotional, and it could therefore take advantage of the presence of these skills in a multi-purpose development corporation. Alternatively the Agricultural Development Corporation and the National Irrigation Board could be amalgamated since both look to funds from overseas, own, and are responsible for developing agricultural land, and have to engage in experiments and research in so doing. There will inevitably be close co-ordination between the two. This would leave the ICDC and the KTDC to amalgamate, and allow the latter to draw on the expertise and financial goodwill built up by the former in its thirteen years' existence.

A second point which follows on from suggestions for amalgamations, is that there would appear to be a tendency to establish a public corporation (or other statutory body for that matter) as if the establishment was itself evidence of development, or the solution to an administrative problem. But the proliferation of statutory corporate bodies may well impede development and the solution of administrative problems, by the creation of a bigger, more complex and more expensive bureaucracy to do exactly the same job as was previously being done by a smaller and cheaper one. The dangers of a proliferation of corporate bodies, legally separate from government, are compounded by the pressures and requirements of foreign aid donors, who often feel that their investments will be more secure if they are channelled into, and administered by, a body separate from government, yet enjoying some of its freedoms, on which they can have some representation or influence. It is to be doubted whether aid which results in a multiplicity of administrative institutions is wholly desirable.

A third point is that it is clear both from law and practice that Ministers tend to keep the public corporations, particularly the more newly established ones, on a very tight rein, and do not always give them that freedom of action that is their main justification. Appointments to the corporations and boards are used for the purposes of politics and patronage; membership is frequently changed, with many members appointed for a period fixed by the appointing Minister; often the constitution of the corporation or board is reorganized by statute. All these factors have an inevitably unsettling effect on the members of these bodies and make them less able and willing to resist formal ministerial directives, and minimize informal ministerial pressure. When to this is added the financial control that Ministers legally exert over the corporations, the result is that they are reluctant to take even quite minor policy decisions, before ministerial opinion has been sounded out. It is perfectly legitimate for government to retain some control over the corporations both because it is usually required to guarantee any loans made to them, and foot any losses they incur, and because otherwise public accountability in relation to them would be meaningless, but control which results in the corporations being virtually indistinguishable in independent initiative and decision-making from ordinary government departments renders the whole institution useless. The outward form of independence is retained while the substance disappears. To some extent this has happened in Kenya.

(*b*) *Regulatory Agencies*

The regulatory agencies comprise a heterogeneous collection of bodies, whose common characteristics are that they exist to regulate and control, rather than participate in, a particular activity, though to do that, they may have to participate to some extent, and that some part of their functions must be discharged in a judicial manner, for example, the grant of a licence or the extension of a tenancy. The most important agencies are the statutory commodity boards and development authorities within the agricultural industry whose function is to regulate and control the growing, marketing, and processing of Kenya's main agricultural crops, the land control boards, the rent tribunals, the Transport Licensing Board, the Industrial Court and the Agricultural Appeal Tribunal. We consider here the first three of these regulatory agencies.[56]

A survey of the agricultural bodies, which by the middle of 1967 numbered fifteen, reveals a very diverse pattern of composition, and manner of exercise of powers and appeals therefrom, even if the ends being aimed at are the

[56] For Transport Licensing Board, see McAuslan, op. cit., pp. 47–50; Hazelwood, *Road and Rail in East Africa* (Oxford, Blackwell, 1964), pp. 43–51. For Industrial Court, see Cockar, 'The Industrial Court and Labour Relations in Kenya', 2 *E.A.L.J.* 257; Musch, 'The Kenya Industrial Court', 2 *E.A.L.J.* 266; Livingstone, 'The Government, the Worker and the Law in Kenya', 3 *E.A.L.J.* 282.

same.[57] As a generalization it may be said that in respect of composition, there has been a movement away from election of board members by producers which was a feature of these boards when they catered primarily for the European sector of the agricultural industry, and towards appointment by the relevant Minister, with or without consultation with organizations representing producers. Thus by the middle of 1967, only the Kenya Tea Development Authority and the Coffee Board had constitutions which provided for a certain proportion of their members to be elected, via a system of election through district and regional committees in the case of tea, and via an annual conference of delegates in the case of coffee. The constitutions of the Pyrethrum Board and the Sisal Industry Board provided for some of their members to be appointed by the Minister from a panel of producers, which panel is not, however, elected. Yet others provide for members to be appointed from a panel submitted by the Central Agricultural Board, this is the case with eight members of the Kenya Dairy Board, five members of the Maize and Produce Board and three members of the Sisal Industry Board, or after consultation with the Central Agricultural Board, as is the case with five members of the Cotton Lint and Seed Marketing Board. The constitution of the Tea Board provides for the Minister to appoint nine members after consultations with organizations representing both small holders and large scale tea planters, while the constitution of the Pig Industry Board provides for two members to be appointed by the Minister on a recommendation of a pig producers' association. Only in the constitutions of the Pineapple and Coffee Development Authorities is there no provision for producers to be consulted or to make recommendations before appointments are made. In addition to this power of appointment of producer representatives the Minister has also in respect of most boards a power to appoint two or three persons whose special qualities or abilities would in his opinion benefit the board concerned. It is under this provision that the power of political patronage is often exercised. Finally on most boards there are some *ex officio* members—usually the Directors of Agriculture and Veterinary Services or their representatives.

The boards and authorities are empowered to issue licences for a variety

[57] Maize and Produce Board (Marketing of Agricultural Products Act, Cap. 320); Kenya Dairy Board (Dairy Industry Act, Cap. 336); Coffee Board and Coffee Marketing Board (Coffee Act, Cap. 333); Cotton Lint and Seed Marketing Board (Cotton Lint and Seed Marketing Act, Cap. 335); Canning Crops Board (Canning Crops Act, Cap. 328); Pyrethrum Board of Kenya and Pyrethrum Marketing Board (Pyrethrum Act, Cap. 340); Sisal Industry Board (Sisal Industry Act, Cap. 341); Pig Industry Board (Pig Industry Act, Cap. 361); Tea Board of Kenya (Tea Act, Cap. 343); Kenya Tea Development Authority (KTDA Order, Legal Notice 42/1964); Coffee Development Authority (CDA Order, Legal Notice 279/1966); Pineapple Development Authority (PDA Order, Legal Notice 33/1967); Horticultural Crops Development Authority (HCDA Order, Legal Notice 229/1967). The four Authorities are established under section 190 of the Agriculture Act.

of purposes and in a variety of ways. The Pig Industry Board is empowered to license butchers and bacon factories. It might issue a licence with conditions, vary it, or cancel it without notice in the event of the licensee committing an offence under the Pig Industry Act or a breach of the conditions of the licence, or cancel it at three months' notice on the ground that cancellation is desirable in the interests of the pig industry or the public. An appeal lies from the exercise of these powers to the Agricultural Appeal Tribunal. A grower of pyrethrum must obtain a licence from the Pyrethrum Board, and no licence may permit him to grow more flowers than his annual quota fixed each year by the Pyrethrum Marketing Board. The Pyrethrum Board may grant or refuse an application for a licence at its discretion and in granting a licence may impose such conditions as it thinks fit. Appeal lies to the Agricultural Appeal Tribunal. A miller of wheat who wishes to construct premises for milling is required to obtain a permit from the Minister who gives a decision at his discretion after consulting the Wheat Board. No appeal lies against a refusal of a permit. In the field of maize marketing the Maize and Produce Board acts as a final appeal tribunal, whose decision is not to be questioned in any court, for any person aggrieved by a revocation of his appointment as a sub-agent of the board for buying purposes, but where the board gives a decision on such questions as when maize is to be delivered to its sub-agent or what deductions of price are to be imposed on the produce for various reasons, an appeal lies to the Agricultural Appeal Tribunal. The Coffee Marketing Board is required to consult the Coffee Licensing Advisory Committee, a body composed of members of the Marketing Board and licence holders elected by the two coffee trade associations of East Africa, before issuing a dealer's licence, and the Coffee Board is required to consult the Director of Agriculture before issuing a planter's licence, a provision which also applies to the licensing of tea planters by the Tea Board. Appeals from both classes of decisions lie to the Agricultural Appeal Tribunal, but an appeal against a classification of coffee by the Marketing Board lies to a special Appeals Board nominated in equal parts by the Board and the appellant. A final contrast is provided by the Canning Crops Board which cannot make a final issue of a crop grower's licence; it makes a provisional grant which is to be referred to the Director of Agriculture who may at his discretion approve or refuse the issue or refer the matter back to the board.

There are several provisions which are common to all boards and authorities. They are all subject to the general or special directions of the Minister, who also appoints the chairmen. In addition the Minister is empowered to make rules, after consultation with or on the advice of the boards, on all matters with which the boards deal, but the development authorities may themselves make rules. All boards and authorities may employ persons to assist them in their work, amongst whom are inspectors who are empowered to enter the land and premises of licensees to ensure that they are complying with the legislative and administrative directions applying or issued to them, and the terms and conditions of their licences. All boards and authorities are empowered to charge fees for licences, impose cesses on produce delivered to them, and establish funds into which their income is to be paid. Where they are empowered to raise loans they may do this only with the sanction of the Minister.

Some general comments in addition to those made on public corporations, which apply to these bodies—for example, the use of political patronage, and ministerial directions and pressures on the decision-making abilities of the boards—may be offered. One original purpose behind the establishment of these bodies was to try and combine the interests of producers of agricultural crops in a stable well-priced market, and in the provision of various extension and research services, with the wider interests of the country as a whole in the adequate provision of food at reasonable prices, and in the export potential of high-quality primary produce efficiently marketed. To this end the boards combined producer representatives chosen for the most part by producers themselves or their organizations, with ministerial nominees or *ex officio* public figures, but thereafter, in an effort to isolate the boards from politics, their relations with the Ministry of Agriculture were kept largely at the level of informal liaison and consultation, and with the legislature, to an annual report and questions to the Minister.[58]

From about the middle of 1963 this operational framework began to be changed by the Government, which wished to increase its control over them. The following reasons contributed to this: first the Government had become much more openly involved in managing the economy and planning its future development, and wished to ensure that these boards fitted into its plans. Secondly, there was the feeling and in some cases, the experience, that the boards could not be trusted to co-operate with a KANU Government,[59] and thirdly they were important institutions of political and economic power which were taken over as part of the broad policy of Africanization. Hence the increase in the ministerial power of appointment of board members and of the creation of the power to give general and special directions to the boards. The effect of these changes has been to put the boards into the political arena, tie them more closely to government, and so to some extent alter the purposes for which they exist. They are now specialist extensions of the Ministry of Agriculture and Animal Husbandry, exercising the Government's administrative and licensing power in respect of

[58] Development Plan, 1966–70, op. cit., pp. 1–8, 67, 166–7. Sessional Paper No. 10/1965, para. 109 (Nairobi).
[59] House of Representatives, *Debates*, volume III (4 March 1964), cols. 462–463.

particular crops. Policy in respect of all these crops is made by the Ministry. It seeks specialist advice from the boards both via its representatives on them and through exchanges of views and information between senior officials, but the relationship is now superior to subordinates whereas six years ago it was at most *primus inter pares*.

It may be asked why the boards and authorities are not amalgamated with the Ministry if they now have little more than an administrative function, especially as it is government policy to streamline their organization and operation and produce some common approach both *inter se*, and with the civil service, in the conditions of employment for both members and staff. There would appear to be a number of reasons for their retention. Politically they provide a very useful outlet for patronage. By the middle of 1967 twenty-one MPs alone had positions on the boards,[59a] to say nothing of other party stalwarts and government supporters. Administratively they had built up considerable expertise over the years—some have been in existence in one form or another for more than twenty years—and little would be gained by scrapping them. Internationally they have established links with equivalent boards in Uganda and Tanzania, and contacts with overseas buyers, which might not be retained, or might not be so close, if a board became no more than a department in a large ministry. Again, as is the case with some public corporations, foreign aid is more forthcoming if it is channelled via a separate body on which the donor organization can have representation.

All these factors suggest that the boards will remain and may even increase in number. It is essential therefore that the implications of the Government's policy which has been implemented in a rather piecemeal fashion should be appreciated and acted upon. The implications are that a division has now been made as far as possible between policy and administration. The Ministry makes the policy and plans for agricultural development as a whole; the boards execute the policy in relation to their particular crop dealing with both its internal and its international aspects. It follows therefore that there must be adequate co-ordination between the boards as a group and the Ministry, and between the boards and other ministries with whose sphere of operations they are likely to come into contact. Such organized co-ordination is not clearly provided for at present. Furthermore any decisions which are likely to affect policy in a significant way should be taken in the Ministry; the rest which are merely concerned with the detailed application of the policy should always be left to the boards to take, with an appeal to the Agricultural Appeal Tribunal. If it is considered that the boards have too much discretion to grant or refuse applications for

[59a] National Assembly, *Debates*, volume XII (31 May 1967), cols. 485–486.

licences, they could be provided with statutory policy guides, as is already the case in relation to pulping station licences with the Coffee Board. This would be better than reserving a final decision to the Minister, giving the boards unpublished and vague policy directives, or a seemingly unfettered direction to grant or refuse licences.[60] The first wastes the time of busy policy-makers, or, if the final decision is taken by a junior official, means that there is an appeal from an expert to a non-expert body; the second will not act to reduce the numbers of applications to the boards, as might be the case if policy on applications were published in advance.

A final point may be made on a matter common to public corporations, boards, and authorities. They are all required to produce annual reports and accounts which the Minister is required to lay before the National Assembly. This is the traditional link between the legislature and any parastatal body, and provides an opportunity for the legislature critically to examine their performance. In Kenya annual reports are produced, though not always with regularity by some bodies, but a follow-up debate in the National Assembly is rare. In effect, public accountability, in so far as it refers to the legislature calling a public body and the responsible Minister to account for the performance of that body, hardly exists in Kenya. In part, the edge of the National Assembly is blunted by the growing number of MPs who as Ministers or members of the boards have too great a stake in the system to wish to probe it or be critical of it; in part, the National Assembly is generally disinclined to engage in many detailed examinations of the administration and its offshoots. While this might not matter were the offshoots small in number and importance, it clearly does where as in Kenya they form such a large part of the administration even if their policy-making functions have been reduced. The use of these public bodies has had an opposite effect to their use in England; there, many of them have taken the place of private bodies and have led to an increase in public scrutiny over areas of economic activity; in Kenya they have been created, for the most part, instead of additional ministries, and have led to a slight decrease in public scrutiny, never very effective even in the case of ministries, over areas of economic activity.

Turning to control over transactions in land, this has existed in the former Scheduled Areas since 1944, and in the former Non-scheduled Areas since 1959. Both systems of control were brought closer together and entrenched in the Constitution for the first year of independence, but from the commencement of the Republic, they led a precarious existence, being

[60] For a vague policy directive from a Minister, see House of Representatives, *Debates*, volume II (4 March 1964), cols. 463–464; for an unfettered discretion, see section 4 (2) of the Crop Production and Livestock Act, Cap. 321, added by Statute Law (Miscellaneous Amendments) Act No. 21 of 1966.

extended from year to year, until in 1967, the systems were unified and put on a more permanent basis by the Land Control Act.[61]

The Act is to be applied to any area of the country if the Minister considers it expedient to do so. Where it is so applied, a three tier system of boards is established from which permission to engage in any transaction in agricultural land must be obtained. At first instance a Land Control Board is established, composed so that half of the members represent the local landowners, the remainder being public officials and nominees of the County Councils with the District Commissioner as chairman. From this board an appeal lies to a Provincial Land Control Board composed of the same classes of persons as the first instance board but with the Provincial Commissioner as chairman. From there a final appeal lies to the Central Land Control Appeal Board which consists of four Ministers and the Attorney-General. All boards may require the applicant and other interested parties to appear, produce documents and other relevant evidence before them, and are empowered to visit and inspect the land. They must give reasons for a refusal of consent or a dismissal of an appeal. Their decisions are final and conclusive, and may not be questioned in any court.

The composition of the final appeal board together with the exclusion of judicial review emphasize the political as opposed to the judicial side of the control function, and represent a change both from previous systems of control and an earlier draft of the Bill. That had proposed an appellate tribunal of a lawyer and two assessors, repeating provisions from earlier legislation on the same topic, but had been criticized for so doing by the Mission on Land Consolidation and Registration,[62] which considered that control was a paternalistic process requiring local administrative knowledge and discretion rather than the application of judicial principles. Indeed the Mission regarded a central appellate authority as impractical for the same reasons, considering that a ministerial power to issue directives similar to that used in the original Non-scheduled Areas system of control sufficient to ensure uniformity of administration. Such directives could also have required local boards to take into account relevant political considerations. As it is, the system which has been established may to some extent divorce the consideration of general political from local agricultural factors, despite provisions in the Act designed to offset this, because these will be the respective areas of competence of the central and local boards. From the point of view of those wishing to make use of the machinery of control, this is not an entirely satisfactory position.

[61] No. 34 of 1967. For earlier systems of control, see chapter III, pp. 99–100, 119–20; and McAuslan, 'Control of Land and Agricultural Development in Kenya and Tanzania' in Sawyerr (ed.), *East African Law and Social Change* (Nairobi, East African Publishing House, 1967), pp. 194–6.

[62] *Report* (Nairobi 1967), p. 82, para. 293. (Under the Chairmanship of J.S.D. Lawrence).

The Act confers an absolute discretion on the boards to grant or refuse consent to a transaction. In the exercise of this discretion, however, all boards must have regard to, take into account, or act on, certain specific matters which would in practice cut down its absolute nature. These matters may be broadly divided into agricultural, economic, social and political. Under the first head come the effects of a grant or refusal on the economic development of the land and the standards of good husbandry in the land control area, and the principle that consent should generally be refused if the applicant is unlikely to develop the farm adequately, the nature of the land will prevent its intended use being profitable or the transfer or subdivision of land will lower its productivity. Under the second head comes the principle that consent should generally be refused where the applicant already has sufficient agricultural land or the terms and conditions of the sale are markedly unfair or disadvantageous to one party. Under the third head comes the rule that consent is to be refused to transfers of land to persons who are not either citizens or declared by the President to be an approved enterprise for the purposes of the Act.

The first two heads repeat long-standing principles of control; the third was introduced into the former system of control in the latter half of 1967 after repeated criticisms by MPs of a situation which had permitted more than a thousand non-citizens to acquire agricultural land in Kenya since independence while Africans remained landless.[62a] Its value remains to be tested for, not for the first time, a legal concession apparently made to political pressure is rendered virtually meaningless through the power given to some senior official to make unfettered exceptions to it. As to the first two heads, the comment of the Lawrence Mission may be repeated, that they more closely resemble those originally applied in the Scheduled rather than the Non-scheduled Areas—a comment made the more significant by the fact that the Mission's specific suggestions for protecting the 'unsophisticated landowner in the early days of ownership'—the primary purpose of the Non-scheduled Area controls—by writing into the Bill provisions to that effect have not been acted upon.[63] Thus neither the principles to be applied, nor the composition of the boards to apply them, offer any real guarantee that this new system of control will prevent the slow growth of a landless or indebted peasantry which so often accompanies newly-acquired individual tenure, and to prevent which, successive committees in Kenya have recommended control of land transactions.

Systems of control of land transactions have been in operation in Kenya for more than twenty years now, but their effect on the property market

[62a] National Assembly, *Debates*, volume XII (23 May 1967), cols. 10–13; (31 May 1967), cols. 474–483.
[63] *Report*, op. cit., p. 80, para. 287.

has never been adequately investigated. The overwhelming majority of transactions in the former Scheduled Areas were always approved, and at one time consideration was given to abolishing the whole system.[64] Such investigations as have taken place of the system introduced for the Non-scheduled Areas show that a very rigid conception of an economic minimum size of plot prevails to counteract sub-division leading to possible refragmentation without at the same time preventing such sub-divisions from occurring on the ground, and that family considerations are often taken into account by the boards in reaching their decisions.[65] Furthermore, decisions have been delayed owing to the existence of a long-standing dispute between landowner members of boards and the Government as to whether the former should receive expenses, which has resulted in some boards not meeting for long periods. On the basis of this evidence it may be hazarded that control has not had a very significant effect on the property market in the past. It may be doubted too whether it will have much effect on the pattern of transactions, official and unofficial, in the future which are much more likely to be determined by factors such as the provision of agricultural credit and family obligations. Despite the fact that control appears to have come to stay, its likely effectiveness in achieving its avowed purpose of securing the efficient and economic use of agricultural land remains in doubt.

Rent control was introduced in Kenya in 1940, and, with the exception of one brief period in respect of business premises, has continued ever since. Successive committees that have considered the matter in the last decade have recommended in the case of residential premises its retention and in the case of business premises its re-introduction.[66] It is surprising therefore that even the latest amendment to the Rent Restriction Act preserved the fiction that it is basically temporary legislation, due to expire at the end of 1969.[67] But the conditions which give rise to the need for some public control of residential landlord-tenant relationships, a general shortage of low-cost accommodation in the main urban areas, particularly Nairobi and Mombasa, grow worse rather than better with each succeeding year. Equally the growth of the small African trader for whom business is new, and who is therefore open to exploitation by a landlord, a class of trader whom the latest committee found to be particularly in need of protection,[68]

[64] *Annual Report of Department of Lands 1952,* Nairobi. In that year, 936 applications were received by the Land Control Board of which only 32 were refused. The number refused was usually between 1 per cent to 5 per cent.

[65] *Land Consolidation and Registration Report,* op. cit., chapter 16, pp. 78–82.

[66] Rent Restriction Inquiry, Gazette Notice 3288/1957; *Report,* 1958 (Madan Committee); Rent Restrictions Inquiry, Gazette Notice 5837/1962; *Report,* 1963 (Konchellah Committee); Working Party on Rent Control 1964; *Report,* 1965 (Waruhiu Committee). The first two committees were concerned with residential premises, the last with business premises.

[67] Rent Restriction (Amendment) Act No. 37 of 1966, section 2.

[68] Waruhiu Committee, op. cit., pp. 8–9.

requires a continuance of the public control of business landlord-tenant relationships. The present Acts extend the ambit of control beyond that formerly in existence and it is reasonable to suppose that they are as much a permanent feature of the Kenya legal landscape as is legislation relating to land registration. There are, however, some respects in which they are unsatisfactory and could with advantage be amended. We consider these below.

Control of business premises is provided for by the Landlord and Tenant (Shops, Hotels and Catering Establishments) Act.[69] A landlord wishing to alter or terminate a tenancy, which he may generally do only on certain stated grounds, must give at least two months' notice, with reasons, to the tenant. A tenant who wishes to oppose the notice must refer it to a tribunal. Tribunals, composed of such persons as the Minister for Commerce and Industry shall appoint, and having jurisdiction in such cases as are specified in the appointment, have wide powers themselves and may in addition employ valuers and inspectors and other officials to assist them in their work.

Where a notice of termination is referred to a tribunal, it may permit the landlord to put forward grounds other than those specified in the Act to support it. After an inquiry, which may include an inspection of the premises, it may approve the termination on terms, or refuse it. Where a notice of alteration is referred to it, it may, after a similar inquiry, approve it or make an order altering the terms of the tenancy itself. Its orders may go right outside the terms, by being made applicable to any person, whether or not a tenant, who is in occupation of the premises comprised in the tenancy, or by permitting the landlord to excise vacant land out of the premises for the purpose of erecting additional buildings when it considers such a course desirable in the public interest. It may also investigate any complaint relating to a tenancy made to it by a landlord or tenant and make such order thereon as it thinks fit, and make orders for compensation payable by the offending party to the party suffering damage or loss where it has been induced to make orders as a result of misrepresentations made to it. An appeal lies from any determination or order of a tribunal to a Senior Resident, or Resident Magistrate's court, and from there, an appeal on a question of law, or mixed law and fact, lies to the High Court.

Control of residential premises is provided for in two Acts, the Rent Restriction Act,[70] and the Eviction of Tenants (Control) (Mombasa) Act,[71]

[69] No. 13 of 1965.
[70] Cap. 296.
[71] Cap. 298. The Act dating from 1943 purports to deal with the problems posed by the case of *Said bin Seif* v. *Shariff Mohammed Shatry* (1938), 19 K.L.R. 9, where the Supreme Court, applying the Indian Transfer of Property Act to a relationship created on the basis that Muslim law would apply to it, held that a house owner permitted to build temporary accommodation on another's land could be evicted by the landowner without compensation or the option to purchase the land on which the

of which the first is the more comprehensive and important. It applies to practically all dwelling houses in Kenya let at a rent of eight hundred shillings and below per month if unfurnished and eleven hundred shillings and below per month if furnished. Rent Tribunals consisting of lawyer-chairmen and between two and four others are appointed by the Minister responsible for housing, and established by the Minister in such areas as he thinks fit. They have two main functions; first, to determine the standard rent of any premises to which the Act applies in pursuance of a reference, which a landlord is under a duty to make to them in respect of premises for which a standard rent has not been determined. Secondly, to make orders for the landlord's recovery of possession of the premises in the event of certain circumstances where it considers it reasonable to make such orders. The circumstances include the breach of the terms and conditions of the tenancy by the tenant, the landlord's requiring possession of the premises for a variety of purposes, and the fact that in the opinion of the tribunal the premises are overcrowded and constitute a danger.

In addition to these functions, the tribunals may investigate any complaints relating to the tenancy brought to them by landlord or tenant and take cognizance of any infringement of the Act, or any dispute or matter likely to lead to a dispute between landlord and tenant of which no complaint has been made to them and make such orders in respect thereof as the justice of the case may require. To carry out all these functions, tribunals have wide powers conferred upon them amongst which are to fix the date from which the standard rent is payable and apportion it if necessary, to order the landlord to carry out repairs, permit excision of land for additional building, to reopen any proceedings of its own motion or for good cause shown by landlord or tenant, and revoke, vary, or amend its previous orders, and generally to exercise all the civil jurisdiction and powers of the High Court.

An unusual, though in the circumstances of Kenya, sensible provision permits a tribunal to delegate some of its powers to an administrative officer or other person, in cases where there is no standard rent or the standard rent does not exceed two hundred shillings per month. Such delegation does not authorize the delegate to fix or increase the standard rent so that it exceeds two hundred shillings, but it may be made in respect of any particular class or description of premises which in the opinion of the delegate is unlikely to have a standard rent exceeding two hundred shillings. Notwithstanding such delegation, a tribunal may still exercise its powers in

house stood. The decision affected many people on Mombasa Island, and the Act was designed to give them a measure of security by forbidding eviction of house owners or their tenants or raising of the house owners' rent by the landowner, without the permission of a board. The Konchellah Committee reported that the Act provided much needed protection but the board established to administer it had not met since its establishment! *Report*, op. cit., pp. 5–6, paras. 29–34.

respect of the matters delegated. A person aggrieved by any decision of a delegate may apply to a tribunal for a review of it, and the tribunal may then make such order as it thinks fit. There is no appeal from such an order, but appeal lies to a Senior Resident Magistrate's court in certain other cases—from an order made after investigating complaints, infringements and disputes, on a point of law, or where the standard rent exceeds two hundred shillings per month, on a point of mixed law and fact. There is no further appeal.

The legislation gives the appearance of a wide and effective public control of all landlord-tenant relations. In few parts of the administrative process, however, is there a greater separation between the formal and the effective, between what the law says, and what happens on the ground. The law is based on the premise that its main function is to ensure equality of safeguards for landlords and tenants, and to keep an even hand between them. It is not to ensure the advantage of one group in society by subsidizing the housing costs of the urban poor and placing the burden of this subsidy upon the landlord.[72] As such it provides a facility—a tribunal—which parties may, and in some circumstances must, use to order their relations *inter se*. Although this tribunal is empowered to act of its own motion, the whole framework of the legislation presupposes that the normal pattern will be that it will act only on the application of a party, and the legal personnel who play an important part in its operation will also be accustomed to working in this manner.[73]

The premise, and its practical application, presuppose an equality of urban sophistication on the part of landlord and tenant, that is, equal participation in urban culture and all its ramifications, particularly an awareness of the civil role of lawyers, and a knowledge of the content of the law and how one can use it. Whatever may be the case in England, from where the broad pattern of Kenya's rent control legislation derives, this most certainly does not exist in Kenya. The urban poor have little knowledge of the content of rent control legislation, though they may be vaguely aware of its existence, and they have practically no contact with the legal profession in its civil capacity. They are therefore totally unable to make use of the facilities provided for them. Landlords are well aware of this, and thus despite the existence of criminal penalties attached to breaches of the legislation, they are able to disregard it with virtual impunity.[74] This is not to say that the legislation is a dead letter, but that as it exists at present, it is, and can only be, used by those tenants who come from the same broad class or social

[72] Madan Committee, op. cit., pp. 2–3, para. 13, adopted with approval by the Konchellah Committee, op. cit., p. 4, paras. 20–21.
[73] All Rent Control Boards and Tribunals have advocates as chairmen, and usually amongst the membership. Advocates may also appear before them.
[74] Madan Committee, op. cit., p. 2, para. 11.

culture as landlords and who are familiar with law, lawyers and urban life. Those tenants who are relatively new to urban life and are most in need of protection cannot obtain it under the present legislation and its administration.

If rent control legislation is to be effective, even on its own premises, there must be alterations in the manner in which it is administered. Administration must change from a passive to an active role. Instead of the tribunals waiting for applications to be made to them, they should be under a duty to seek out infringements of the Act, and ensure that it is complied with. The officials which they are empowered to employ should be used for this purpose. They should be more vigorous in using their power to compel people to attend before them, and be empowered to fix standard rents without having to wait for the landlord to apply, or if necessary give him a hearing. Once fixed, rents should be safeguarded by being registered in a public register under the jurisdiction of the tribunal, and not left to be entered in a rent book, a dubious protection for an illiterate tenant. It should be an offence for a landlord to grant an unregistered letting. As a general rule no fees should be charged to a tenant, as it is not he who will be commencing an action in the tribunal, and where the landlord is represented by an advocate, some form of representation should be made available to the tenant. No more than one appeal should be allowed.

There is some recognition in Kenya of the need for some such reformed system as is outlined here. In the second reading debate on the Landlord and Tenant (Shops, Hotels and Catering Establishments) Bill, several speakers in the National Assembly showed a real understanding of the futility of creating a legal superstructure of tribunals, references, appeals and other formalities which depended upon the tenant taking the initiative, when the problems tenants were facing were hardly legal problems at all, and in any event, they would be ignorant of their rights, unable to afford to assert them because of the expense, and unwilling to because of possible reprisals from the landlord.[75] It is unfortunate that though the most eloquent plea for government to take the initiative in fixing fair rents was voiced by a Minister, his views clearly do not represent government policy. However, the constant tinkering with the legislation, and appointment of committees to report on the matter, suggests that even those who shy away from radical reform are aware that all is not well. Until it is realized that this particular housing problem of the urban poor cannot be solved in the English manner with its emphasis on traditional judicial forms and their role in protecting the sanctity of private property, it is unlikely that any reforms will be

[75] House of Representatives, *Debates*, volume IV (22 April 1965), col. 1421 et seq., especially speeches by M. Kibaki (Minister for Commerce and Industry), J. M. Kariuki and J. Wariithi.

much use or that much progress will be made in bringing together the formal and the effective.

It would be misleading to leave a consideration of those regulatory powers of the administration which must be exercised in a judicial manner, without making the point that beside bodies specifically established to exercise this power either exclusively or in conjunction with other powers, Ministers, civil servants, and local authorities are also empowered to deal with a variety of individual applications or in the case of a Minister, is often the final appellants' authority from some inferior licensing body, which may require them to act in a judicial manner. Examples of these powers of Ministers and civil servants in the agrarian field have already been referred to in this chapter.[76]

(c) Managerial Boards

The third main group of administrative bodies, the managerial group, may be dealt with more briefly. These are statutory bodies having no judicial and few legislative powers, whose function it is to manage some institution of a comparatively small or local nature on behalf of the Government. These bodies are perhaps to be distinguished from those in the second group as much by reason of the small scale of their operations as by their different nature. The best examples come from the educational and cultural fields, the Kenya Cultural Centre,[77] the National Museum,[78] and Egerton Agricultural College[79] for instance. All these institutions have governing bodies—in the case of the museum they are trustees—appointed in whole or in part by the Government, and all have the duty to manage their institutions so as to promote their aims, be it the provision of a centre for cultural entertainments, for research into natural history, or for agricultural education. In the exercise of their powers of management, they may appoint staff, raise money and incur expenditure, and in the case of the college make decrees regulating its operations. There is no power given to a Minister by any of the statutes to give directions to the governing bodies, which are generally left alone in their management of these institutions, though no doubt ministerial wishes can be made known if necessary through their appointees.

DEVELOPMENTS IN AGRARIAN ADMINISTRATION

We have considered the administrative process so far in terms of institutions and their powers. This is a static conception of a process which in

[76] For further examples of these powers of the central government, see McAuslan in *East African Law Today*, op. cit., pp. 47, 53. For an example of local government licensing powers see Kericho Urban Council (Drainage and Sewerage) By-Laws, Legal Notice 16/1967.
[77] Kenya Cultural Centre Act, Cap. 218.
[78] Museum Trustees Act, Cap. 216.
[79] Egerton Agricultural College Act, Cap. 214.

fact is active and changing all the time as new demands are put upon it, and the political context in which it operates itself changes. This aspect of the process may be considered in terms of developments in agrarian administration, of which two matters may be singled out for study both because they provide continuity from the historical chapter, and because they throw light on the interaction of political developments and the administrative process in this era: the settlement schemes, and the development of tea-growing.

(*a*) *Administrative Aspects of the Settlement Schemes*[80]

In the colonial era, a national policy on settlement was prevented by the continued adherence to the principles of segregation laid down by the Kenya Land Commission. This did not, however, prevent settlement schemes for Africans and Europeans, the former usually being contiguous to a reserve and taking one of three forms, unplanned, planned, and planned irrigation, the latter being within the European reserve and taking the form of closer settlement. Changes in this communal approach to settlement had been called for by the East Africa Royal Commission in 1955, and while rejected at the time, had been generally accepted by the Kenyan and British authorities by the end of that decade. Two sessional papers put forward proposals to break down tribal barriers, to open up the Highlands to all races, and at the same time confer greater security of tenure on Europeans by allowing them to convert their long leases to freehold[81]—a concession extracted by the settlers for their agreement that Africans should receive a similar title to their plots of land once they had been consolidated, and clearly of great importance once it became clear that Kenya was to have an African government.

The principles of these papers were agreed at the Lancaster House Conference in 1960, as also was a decision to begin a settlement scheme for Africans in the Highlands. Imperial and local legislation implemented these decisions and provided a framework for settlement. The Kenya (Land) Order in Council[82] repealed the Highland and Native Areas Orders in Council, declared racially restrictive covenants and similar provisions void, and empowered the Governor to make regulations providing for the conversion of estates from leasehold to freehold. The Agriculture (Amendment) Act[83] established a Land Development and Settlement

[80] Nottidge and Goldsack, *The Million Acre Settlement Scheme 1962–66* (Department of Lands and Settlement, Kenya 1967). Ruthenberg, *African Agricultural Production Development Policy in Kenya 1962–65* (Berlin, Springer-Verlag, 1966), pp. 52–86.
[81] Sessional Papers No. 10 of 1958–9 and No. 6 of 1959–60 (Nairobi).
[82] S.I. 1960. No 2202 (Legal Notice 589). See, too, Conversion of Leases Regulations (Legal Notice 631/960), Conversion of Leases Rules (Legal Notice 632/1960), and Kenya (Land) Order in Council, section 1, 1830/1961.
[83] No. 47 of 1960.

Board composed of members of both Boards of Agriculture, and officials from the Treasury and the Ministry of Agriculture, with the primary functions of acquiring land for settlement, and preparing and administering settlement schemes for all races. An Agricultural Settlement Fund was established under the control of the Board, but subject also to the control and audit of the Ministry, which could be expended on agricultural business, particularly purchasing land, and giving mortgages to settlers. The Board had all the powers of the Land and Agricultural Bank to recover loans and in addition could write off bad debts.

The model for this Board was clearly the European Agricultural Settlement Board, and the model for the original settlement schemes which this Board devised was likewise the post-war European settlement schemes, the Assisted Owner and Tenant Farmer schemes, the rules governing them being adapted for use by African settlers. These administrative arrangements taken in conjunction with the increased security conceded to European settlers indicate that the political pressures and feelings on the land question were still not being fully faced up to, even in the early sixties. What was being attempted was an 'in-filling' in the Highlands; the unused land was to be settled with African peasant farmers who had already proved their capabilities as such. There was, too, perhaps an expectation that such persons would provide an additional bulwark against African nationalism, a role in which the colonial administration had previously cast the consolidated plot-holders in the former Trust lands.

When dissatisfaction was shown with the initial schemes, a 'new' scheme was introduced which envisaged a doubling of the acreage to be transferred, and of the families to be settled, but a reduction in the planned annual income. This, too, failed to make any real impact on the problem of land hunger which was at the root of political instability. By the beginning of 1962 it was accepted that nothing short of a massive land transfer plan would cope with the problem, and the Million Acre Scheme was launched envisaging the settlement of approximately 34,000 African families on former European owned land in the Highlands within five years, and the conferring on those families of a freehold title to their plot. Such a programme dictated by political expediency needed more forceful handling than could be achieved by the Board; accordingly a Ministry of Lands and Settlements was created to administer the programme on its behalf. The Board, however, retained legal control; land was purchased in its name and vested in it; settlers derived their title from the Board and any legal action was taken in its name.

The smallholder schemes which formed the backbone of the Million Acre Scheme were normally reserved for specific tribes and as far as possible the areas to be settled were therefore contiguous to an erstwhile reserve. The tribal nature of the Scheme, however, meant that its administration was an obvious target for the protagonists of regionalism who feared that if left under central control it would unduly favour one tribe at the expense of others. At the same time some central direction was needed as the money for the schemes came from there, and central purchasing of land and uniformity of administration would ensure that it was properly spent. Finally, European fears of political interference with the purchasing side of the programme had also to be taken into account.

The reconciliation of these three requirements produced one of the more complex parts of the regional Constitutions which existed for eighteen months during 1963–4. The aim was to retain central administrative control, reduce central political influence, and increase regional political influence. To this end a Central Land Board was established by, and entrenched in, the Constitution,[84] consisting of representatives of the Central and Regional Governments, the owners of agricultural land to be purchased for the schemes, and a Chairman and Deputy Chairman, removable from office only on the basis of an adverse finding by a judicial tribunal as to their inability or misbehaviour. In the exercise of its functions the Board was not subject to the direction or control of any person or authority.

The Board had a four-fold function;[85] to select land for settlement, to assess its fair purchase price, to purchase it by agreement with the owners, and to convey it or interests in it to settlers. In the exercise of its first function the Board was required to consult with the Central Settlement Committee consisting of political and administrative representatives of the Central and Regional Governments concerned with settlement and agriculture, in order to plan future purchasing programmes, so as to fit in with future implementation of the settlement schemes. It also in practice consulted with the Kenya and United Kingdom Governments, which provided the money for the purchasing programme in the exercise of its second and third functions, which were to some extent circumscribed by the prior agreements of the two Governments on the basic price to be paid for the land. The Board acted as a final appellate authority for landowners dissatisfied with the valuation put on their land by its valuers.

Once the land was purchased, the major work of the Board was done. The function of preparing and executing settlement schemes was transferred to another new body[86]—the Settlement Fund Trustees, who were three Ministers of the Central Government, in whom the Agricultural Settlement Fund was vested, as were all the 'settlement' powers of the Land Development and Settlement Board. The trustees consulted with the regional authorities as to the implementation of schemes in their regions, while the

[84] See, too, second schedule heading 12. See chapter V, p. 200.
[85] *Annual Reports* of the Central Land Board, 1963–5.
[86] Agriculture (Amendment) Regulations (Legal Notice 352/1963).

actual administration of the schemes continued to be carried out by officials from the Ministry of Lands and Settlement.

A crucial element in the whole programme was the choice of settlers, and here the regional authorities had the executive responsibility.[87] Settlers were nominated by the President of the relevant Regional Assembly who could exercise this power only after consultation with the Minister responsible for settlement. Once selected, these settlers received their initial letter of allotment, and the final title from the Board, in which their land was vested until that time.

The new arrangements thus split the executive functions of the Land Development and Settlement Board three ways between the Central Land Board, the Settlement Fund Trustees and the Presidents of Regional Assemblies, and endeavoured to ensure co-ordination by consultative and advisory arrangement between these bodies. At the same time legislative powers as to land settlement were placed on the concurrent list, and the Constitution made it clear that the regions could initiate their own settlement schemes. In their endeavours to satisfy tribal and communal fears therefore, the constitution-makers had been forced to create a top-heavy administrative machine with a built-in potential for collapse since no part of the machine was legally superior to the others, able to provide central direction, and require co-ordination and co-operation in the legislative and administrative fields.

No such collapse in fact occurred. In part this was because the political fears which gave rise to it proved groundless, so that there was a sufficient underlying basis of trust in the political arena to make co-operation in the administrative arena possible, but in part it was because the Government never really relinquished its control over the settlement programme, any more than it did over other areas of agrarian administration which constitutionally should have been shared with, or devolved on to, regional authorities. The key institution was the Settlement Fund Trustees, and this consisted of Ministers. Day to day administration of the schemes was carried out by a Central Government Ministry, and the annual reports of the Central Land Board indicate how closely that institution unavoidably worked with the Government on joint co-ordinating committees. The establishment of the machinery may have been necessary to allay tribal fears but the other major fear—political upheaval following independence—was paradoxically allayed by the virtual side-stepping of that machinery by the Government, so that the settlement schemes could go on as fast as possible, thus alleviating land hunger, the root cause of that fear.

Regionalism was swept away at the end of 1964, all executive and legislative functions revesting in the Government. Henceforth the Ministry of

[87] Independence Constitution section 198 (1) (d).

Lands and Settlement was to be the final authority in the selection of settlers, working through District Commissioners who in turn established selection committees to vet and recommend applicants for plots. The Central Land Board continued to discharge its functions for a further year but it had now become little more than an appendage of the Government. It was no longer entrenched in the Constitution and it had a majority of government members. An indication of its changed status in practice is provided by the fact that the Minister now gave it directives about its valuation and pricing policy. At the beginning of 1966 it was wound up,[88] and its powers and duties transferred to the Settlement Fund Trustees who were to exercise them subject to the instruction of the Minister. The wheel had come full circle for the arrangements at the beginning of 1966 were an exact replica of those current before the changes imposed by regionalism—a Ministry undertaking the administration of the schemes on behalf of an 'independent' body outside the Ministry, in which all the land and finances were vested, and from whom the settler received his title. Perhaps more important, the successive formal changes to which the administrative machine was subjected over this period had not seriously interfered with the increasingly rapid implementation of the schemes, as they had never been put fully into practice, so that administrators had been able to continue at their same jobs.

We have so far been concerned with the central administrative organization of settlement programme, as opposed to the powers of the administrators on the ground. This latter aspect may be considered in the context of loan-defaulting settlers. This has been one of the most tricky problems which the Government has had to face. On the one hand, the schemes are financed to a large extent by foreign loans making it imperative that settlers repay the advances that they receive: on the other, the pressures to settle the landless irrespective of whether they are capable of farming make it impolitic to remove them for failure to repay. The Land Development and Settlement Board had the same power as the Land and Agriculture Bank to foreclose without recourse to a court, but this power was not passed on to other bodies. By 1965, loan-defaulting had reached serious proportions, and the Government decided to act by conferring summary re-entry powers on the trustees, exercisable without recourse to any court. In the face of considerable opposition, the necessary legislation was put through Parliament,[89] and as a concession to that opposition, a Loan-Defaulters Sifting Committee containing a majority of MPs was established to advise the Minister of Lands and Settlement, one of the trustees, on how to exercise these powers in relation

[88] Constitution of Kenya (Winding up of the Central Land Board) Regulations (Legal Notice 97/1966).

[89] Agriculture (Amendment) Act No. 16 of 1965. House of Representatives, *Debates* (22 April 1965), volume IV (3 March 1965), cols. 487–497, 522-550; (4 March 1965), cols, 1418–1421.

to chronic defaulters. The powers have since been exercised without great outcry. While the legislation might be necessary, it provides a revealing contrast with that dealing with somewhat similar problems in the thirties. Then, the emphasis in the legislation had been to exert power on behalf of the settlers to provide relief from the claims of their private creditors, and to keep them on the land; now that the Government is both creditor to the settlers and debtor to foreign aid donors, the emphasis in the legislation is to exert public power on behalf of public creditors, and provide a means of removing settlers from the land. Differences in administrative arrangements are equally revealing. Then, the use of quasi-judicial bodies and committees of debtors invested the proceedings with an air of respectability and equity; now the Government retains full control but makes use of a political advisory committee to soften that fact.

(b) *The Development of Smallholder Tea-growing*

It was only in the fifties that smallholder tea-growing began to develop in Kenya, previous policy having been based on the belief that such development would be uneconomic. The drive to develop cash crops in the reserves caused a reversal of this policy, however, and provincial tea-marketing boards established under the Marketing of African Produce Act, together with agricultural officers, were the main administrative organs used to effect such a reversal. This piecemeal approach was radically reorganized following the report of a mission which stressed the importance of integrated development, in order to enable long-term plans to be made, and long-term finance to be attracted.[90] The institution that has been established to provide for these matters—the Kenya Tea Development Authority—is one of the most interesting administrative devices to emerge in this era, and is worth examining.

The Authority was originally created as the Special Crops Development Authority in 1960, receiving its present name and powers in early 1964.[91] Its establishment is provided for in the Agriculture Act which permits the Minister to declare any crop to be a special crop for development purposes, and by an order establish an authority as a corporate body for the promotion of that development. Such an order is also used to confer all necessary powers and duties on the Authority to enable it to carry out its functions. The

[90] *Kenya Tea Development Authority, The Operations and Development Plans* (Nairobi, 1964). Ruthenberg op. cit., pp. 39–47.

[91] Agriculture (Local Land Development Board) Order, Legal Notice 458/1960; Agriculture (Special Crops Development Authority) Order, Legal Notice 243/1961; Kenya Tea Development Authority Order, Legal Notice 42/1964. The Authority was originally established as a Local Land Development Board under Part X of the Agriculture Act, as the power to declare a crop to be a special crop was not at that time part of the Act. It was introduced as a new Part—XD—by the Agriculture (Amendment) Act No. 47 of 1960, in force in 1961.

KTDA consists of officials from the Ministry of Agriculture, the Commonwealth Development Corporation (so long as the authority remains in debt to it), the Chairman of the Tea Board, and elected tea-growers from the areas over which the Authority has jurisdiction. It is empowered to prepare and carry out schemes for tea-growing, to supervise the tea-growing, to purchase, transport, process in factories which it may establish, and market the tea. It may deduct levies from the growers, raise loans and fix prices. It may make rules, but in this and other matters it is subject to the general or special directions of the Minister.

Though responsible to the Minister, it is designed to be a self-contained financing and administrative entity. The loan agreement to finance the second phase of development indicates how these principles are reconciled. There were four parties to a complex of agreements, the International Development Association, the Commonwealth Development Corporation, the Kenyan Government and the Authority. The first agreement was a Development Credit Agreement governing the IDA's loan to the Government; this was for 40 years at a service charge of three-quarters of a per cent. The second was a Project Agreement between the IDA and the Authority which placed certain development covenants on the Authority. The third was a Subsidiary Loan Agreement between the Government, the CDC, and the Authority, which provided for the terms of a CDC loan to the Authority guaranteed by the Government, and the on-lending of the IDA loan to the Authority by the Government, at five and a half per cent interest. The Authority in turn obtains its revenue to repay the loans from the sale of stumps to the growers, cesses on the sale of the tea by the growers, and initially a capital levy from those growers who do not produce a reasonable quantity of tea within five years of the date of purchasing stumps. Thus, the lenders look to the Government for the repayment of their loans, and the Government looks to the Authority. Though notionally free to arrange its finances as it will to discharge its responsibility, the Authority inevitably consults closely with the Government since their responsibilities are in practice inextricably mixed.

The self-contained administration of the Authority may best be seen in its relations with the Tea Board, which is responsible for the licensing of tea growers and tea factories. The Board issues block planting licences to the Authority to cover its areas of operation, and has agreed that it will not issue licences to individuals from those areas without reference to the Authority. For its part, the Authority is required by its rules to issue licences to growers within its jurisdiction specifying how much tea they may plant, so that the total of plantings by individuals does not exceed the total specified in the block licences issued to the Authority by the Board.

The success of the Authority's operations depend upon its being able to control the speed at which tea-growing expands, and these arrangements are designed to achieve that. It must be remarked, however, that in some respects they fall short of complying with the law. There is no legal authority for the agreement between the Board and the Authority, and it contravenes two well known principles of law. First, that a licensing authority may not fetter the exercise of its discretion in individual cases by laying down in advance general rules which will have the effect of preventing some applications being given full consideration.[92] Secondly that in the absence of express statutory authority, a licensing authority may not share the exercise of its discretion with other bodies.[93] Again, for a long period the Authority did not comply with its own rules to issue individual licences; instead, stump receipts were regarded as the legal authority to plant tea up to the number of stumps shown on the receipt.

The final aspect of the Authority's work which may be examined is its supervision and control over the growers. It determines the areas in which tea may be grown and fixes the amount of tea each grower may plant. Before stumps are issued, it must approve the land and may require soil conservation and basic cultivation to be carried out. Tea-growers must comply with the directions of officers of the Authority, which may include putting in wind-breaks and artificial shade, plucking, pruning, and uprooting the bushes, and generally complying with the principles of good husbandry. All tea must be sold to the Authority, or to its order, and it has an absolute discretion to reject tea offered to it. The tea is processed in factories owned by the Authority or commercial companies associated with the whole operation, though it is planned that eventually the growers themselves will own most of the factories. Despite this detailed control over the growers, the layout of the plantations stresses the individual nature of the enterprise at the growers' level, and the importance they attach to landownership; each tea plantation is part of an individually owned plot of land, a method of planting chosen in preference to the administratively more convenient one of block plantations in which each grower would have his individual 'garden', because of the opposition of the growers to this latter method.

The development of smallholder tea-growing is one of the successes of agricultural development in this era, and an important factor in this success is the Authority. It is designed to be an institution which allows the lenders of funds to be closely associated, together with the Government, with their detailed disbursement, and permits the public authorities to engage in a joint venture with commercial organizations. Furthermore, its constitution is extremely flexible, being alterable by the Minister in the exercise of his

[92] *Singh* v. *Municipal Council of Nairobi* (1946), 22 (1) K.L.R. 8. *R.* v. *Port of London Authority, ex parte Kynoch Ltd.*, [1919] 1 K.B. 176.
[93] *Birkdale District Electricity Supply Co.* v. *Southport Corporation*, [1926] A.C. 355 at 364. Mitchell, *Contracts of Public Authorities* (London, University of London, G. Bell, 1954), p. 59.

subordinate law-making powers. Perhaps its greatest asset, however, is that it has been able to combine the advantages of large-scale administration with those of the retention of individual ownership and initiative, regarded as important by the peasant. These factors have no doubt contributed to the Government's decision to establish three similar authorities to develop the growing of coffee, pineapples and horticultural products.[94] But it may be questioned how far the Authority as such ought to be regarded as a *sine qua non* of development as appears to be the case here. Equally, if not more important factors in tea-growing, were the rising market in tea prices, the intensive supervision of growers, and the comparative simplicity of tending tea bushes. Not all these factors will necessarily be present in the development of these other products. One is left with the feeling that an administrative device found to work satisfactorily in one situation is being applied too uncritically to other and dissimilar situations.

JUDICIAL CONTROL OF ADMINISTRATIVE ACTION[95]

No survey of the administrative process would be complete without a consideration of the place of judicial control of administrative action therein. We will consider first the law, and then its effectiveness. The commonest methods of controlling the administration are by means of the prerogative orders of certiorari, mandamus and prohibition,[96] and the equitable remedies of injunction and declaration though these last remedies are not very frequently used in Kenya.[97] The Criminal Procedure Code contains a remedy known as directions in the nature of habeas corpus,[98] which is in lieu of the prerogative writ of habeas corpus, but the powers of the High Court in issuing such a direction and the procedure to be followed in applying for it are similar to those appertaining to the writ.[99] In addition to these methods of reviewing administrative action, the High Court is vested by the Constitution with original jurisdiction to make such orders, issue such writs and give such directions as it may consider appropriate for enforcing the provisions of the Constitution relating to fundamental rights and freedoms.[100] Such protection as these provisions afford embrace administrative as well as legislative action,

[94] Footnote 57 for details.
[95] McAuslan in *East African Law Today*, pp. 55–65. The courts in Kenya have closely followed the principles evolved in England on this subject, on which see de Smith, *Judicial Review of Administrative Action* (London, Stevens and Sons, 1968, second edition).
[96] Law Reform (Miscellaneous Provisions) Act No. 48 of 1956, section 8. *R.* v. *Chairman and members of Central Rent Control Board ex parte Corbett Ltd.* (1955), 28 K.L.R. 137 (certiorari), *D. C. Kiambu* v. *R. ex parte Njau*, [1960] E.A. 109 (mandamus), *Re an application by the A-G of Kenya*, [1958] E.A. 529 (prohibition).
[97] *A-G of Kenya* v. *Block*, [1959] E.A. 180 (injunction), *Ramji* v. *A-G of Kenya* (1956), 23 E.A.C.A. 20 (declaration).
[98] Cap. 75, section 389.
[99] *Re an application for Habeas Corpus, Shah* v. *A-G of Kenya* (1955), 22 E.A.C.A. 216.
[100] Constitution section 84 (2).

thereby considerably extending the scope of judicial review. Finally, the courts also have occasion to consider the decisions and the actions of the administration when hearing an appeal from the decision of an administrative tribunal—e.g. a tribunal established under rent control legislation, or a case stated on a point of law from the Agricultural Appeal Tribunal—and when hearing a suit brought against the Government in accordance with the provisions of the Government Proceedings Act.[101]

There are several examples of the use of the power of judicial control by the High Court and its predecessors since 1898 when the first such case[102] —wrongful dismissal of a railway employee through failure to give him a hearing—was decided. Since then, the decisions of administrative tribunals and officials such as immigration officers have been upset on a wide variety of grounds including failure to observe the *audi alteram partem* rule,[103] presence of bias,[104] excess of jurisdiction,[105] insufficient evidence on which to base a decision,[106] wrongful delegation of power,[107] informality,[108] and something akin to abuse of power.[109] Cases where decisions have not been upset include, first, the decision of a District Officer sitting as a magistrate in a criminal matter which he had been responsible for investigating because the element of bias in his position was created by law.[110] Secondly, the decision of a rent tribunal made in the absence of the parties was upheld because it was a justifiable assumption on the part of the tribunal that failure to attend indicated lack of a desire to attend.[111] Thirdly, the decision of the Transport Appeal Tribunal where the tribunal had looked at a document circulated by the chairman of the Transport Licensing Board to the members thereof, without showing it to the appellants, was held not to contravene the *audi alteram partem* rule.[112] Fourthly, relief was denied to an applicant for an entry permit who had been refused one and declared a prohibited immigrant by an immigration officer and the Minister on appeal, as, on the grounds that the entry permit was a privilege not a right, both the immigration officer and the Minister could rightly take into account policy considerations in deciding whether to issue one, which they were not obliged to disclose to the applicant, so that there was no *lis* between the applicant and the adminis-

[101] Cap. 40, *A-G of Kenya* v. *Shah*, [1959] E.A. 575, *Gohil* v. *A-G*, [1967] E.A. 570.
[102] *Postwalla* v. *Secretary of State* (1898), 1 E.A.L.R. 8.
[103] *Patel* v. *Plateau Licensing Court* (1954), 27 K.L.R. 147.
[104] *Ndegwa* v. *President and members of the Nairobi Liquor Licensing Court*, [1957] E.A. 709.
[105] *Sheikh Brothers* v. *Members of the Control of Hotels Authority* (1949), 23 (2) K.L.R. 1.
[106] *Singh* v. *Municipal Council of Nairobi* (1946), 22 (1) K.L.R. 8.
[107] *Municipal Board of Mombasa* v. *Kala* (1955), 22 E.A.C.A. 319.
[108] *Desai* v. *Ali* (1952), 20 E.A.C.A. 1.
[109] *R.* v. *Kabuga* (1906), 2 E.A.L.R. 61.
[110] *R.* v. *Eman* (1945), 21 (1) K.L.R. 47.
[111] *Rehman* v. *Gudka*, [1957] E.A. 4.
[112] *Muringan and Sons* v. *Transport Appeal Tribunal*, [1959] E.A. 449.

tration and no denial of natural justice, in respect of which orders for certiorari and mandamus would lie.[113] This case also provides an illustration of the statutory exclusion of judicial control by means of a section in the Immigration Act providing that the Minister's decision should be final and conclusive, and not questionable in any court, which the instant court considered apt to exclude its jurisdiction.

The picture which emerges from this brief survey is of a constant tussle between the courts and the administration in which both are reasonably circumspect in the exercise of their powers. When we consider the effectiveness of the courts' role here, however, this picture appears to be slightly misleading in so far as it suggests that there are no particular problems in this area of the law. The traditional role of the courts here, and particularly the High Court in which this review jurisdiction is vested, is to uphold legality, to ensure that the administration acts according to law, and that the rights of the individual are safeguarded during any administrative action. This traditional role for which traditional weapons are provided has been reinforced by the constitutional jurisdiction of the High Court to enforce fundamental rights and freedoms. But the reality of this role depends to a large extent upon its being accepted and acted upon by society at large, and it is here that one of the problems of the present position appears.

The dual system of administration which characterized most of the colonial period of Kenya's development has had the inevitable effect of making judicial control of the administration much more of a reality for the non-African than the African. There was to all intents and purposes no judicial control of native and African administration in practice, other than the somewhat ineffective control of the magisterial powers of administrative officers. Prior to 1930 it was possible to challenge the decisions of native tribunals, and thus of other organs of native administration, in the High Court via a criminal appeal. After that date it was not, and administrative officers who resented judicial control of their own decisions could in effect evade it, by increasing the criminal and quasi-criminal jurisdiction of the native tribunals and African courts, and thus their own administrative supervision of criminal trials, none of which was subject to the supervision of the High Court. Though there was no express prohibition of the use of the prerogative writs to challenge the actions of administrative and agricultural officers, village headmen and the like, it would have required the combination of a bold African and an unusual advocate, both with knowledge of each other's predicament, before such a case could have been brought, and such a combination was rare. Perhaps the strongest indication of this state of affairs is that there is not one reported case of judicial control arising out

[113] *Re Marles' Application*, [1958] E.A. 153 (the Immigration Act at issue in that case was replaced by the Immigration Act No. 25 of 1967).

of a challenge by an African to any of the extensive and harsh legislative and administrative measures introduced into Kenya during the Emergency, yet even the most fervent admirers of the administration during that period do not claim that it kept within the law at all times.

The non-African on the other hand has always been accustomed to using the courts for this purpose. The major areas in which the courts have been used here are rent control, immigration, transport licensing, liquor licensing and the powers of local authorities, yet only in the penultimate one have Africans had anything more than a peripheral interest for much of the time. The non-African had easy access to lawyers, and the courts with which he had contact in other matters were not obviously a part of the administration, as was the case with African courts. These factors were important in any consideration of whether to use the courts to challenge some administrative action or decision which had adversely affected one. Thus the High Court has in the past performed its traditional role for a very limited section of the population, and the position has not changed appreciably since the advent of an African Government. The court cannot therefore rely on the understanding and support of society at large for a role which may at times give the impression that it is opposing or obstructing the Government, nor can it alone create the necessary climate of acceptance for its work in this field. It must rely to a great extent on the support of the Government which it is controlling, and it is here that the second of the problems of the present position arises.

On the surface the courts' power of review of administrative action is greater under an African Government than ever it was under the colonial authorities, and this power remains relatively unmolested. But it is not beyond the bounds of possibility that the reason for the immensity of the court's control powers is that they are very infrequently exercised and when they are, it is rarely in the crucial areas—the courts' powers in other words do not really affect the administrative process. When they do, or might, they are whittled down. Thus in the area of fundamental rights, the phraseology of the Preservation of Public Security Act virtually precludes judicial control of the great powers available to the Government thereunder. Colonial administrators were insistent that the whole operation of African land consolidation and registration should be judge-proof, and so it has remained since 1956, despite attempts to involve the courts in the process.[114] Each succeeding Immigration

[114] *D. C. Kiambu* v. *R. ex parte Njau*, [1960] E.A. 109. The Mission on Land Consolidation and Registration strongly recommended that the High Court should have power to revise the first registration of land on the application of a person aggrieved by an entry in the final adjudication record, and that this power should operate retroactively to enable any first registration to be rectified (*Report*, op. cit., paras. 176, 273–274; appendix E, Draft Land Adjudication Bill, clause 32). This recommendation was not accepted by the Government, whose own Land Adjudication Bill (published in March

Act confers wider powers on the Minister and his officials and provides less opportunities for appeals to, or review by, the court. The discretion whether to foreclose on a settler in one of the settlement schemes has been transferred from the High Court to a political-cum-administrative body. When to these individual diminutions of the control power of the High Court we add the great quantity of illegal administration that has necessitated so many retrospective validating Acts since independence in respect of which no challenge was commenced in the courts, we can see that there is no need for the Government to introduce any general restriction on the control powers of the court, and no reason for not adopting a tolerant attitude towards them.

We may say then that formally the courts appear as an institution of control performing a function similar to that which they perform in England; effectively, their influence on the administration is small, because there are relatively few people who think of them or use them for this purpose compared to the number of people who could, and the number of occasions when the circumstances warrant it, and because there is little political impediment in the way of the administration reducing their control function to a very small ambit. Both these factors in turn mean that there is very little external pressure on the administration to act at all times in accordance with the law, and this external pressure—public opinion in effect—is vital if the courts' function is to be effective, and ensure that the administration observes both the letter and the spirit of the law. No doubt the administration will usually try to do so, but as we have seen, it does not always succeed and this is not thought particularly reprehensible. So long as it remains necessary for the courts to have to rely primarily on the support of the Government to control the Government, so long will their control function be relatively ineffective.

CONCLUSION

SOME GENERAL ASPECTS OF THE ADMINISTRATIVE PROCESS

One characteristic of the two examples of agrarian administration is that in both there was at some time a divergence between what the law authorized or permitted and what administrators actually did. This is not a phenomenon peculiar to agrarian administration and its extent and implications generally require more consideration. Consideration may also be given to other general aspects of the functioning of the administration in Kenya in the era of African government and this may be put under three heads: administrative illegality and the use of retrospective legislation; the Maize Commission of Inquiry and its implications; and the proliferation of the administration.

1968) provided for an appeal to the Minister by a person aggrieved by the adjudication register

(a) Administrative Illegality and Retrospective Legislation

Since independence, and up to the middle of 1967, when the fifth session of the first independent Parliament ended, there had been no less than twenty-two Acts of Parliament passed which were, in whole or in part, retrospective in effect. They ranged across the whole field of administration, and represented a formidable total of erstwhile illegal administrative action. While a few were concerned to validate action first taken in the colonial period, the vast majority were concerned with actions taken since independence. It is clear that such a state of affairs suggests an administration either ignorant of the processes of law, and the general desirability of keeping one's actions within the law, or a situation where the divergence between the formal and the effective within the administration has become almost uncontrollable. Two examples of this exercise of governmental power may be given. An Act passed early in 1966 retrospectively raised vehicle licence fees, and provided that those who had obtained licences for the old fee should not be provided with another licence when they came for renewal until they paid the increased amount in respect of the old licence.[115] Also early in 1966, an order made under the Marketing of Agricultural Produce Act purported to establish a Maize and Produce Board to take over the powers, functions and staff of the Maize Marketing Board established by the Maize Marketing Act.[116] Only in 1967 was an amendment to the latter Act passed which regularized this administrative action.[117] The Second Reading debate on this Bill is interesting and revealing of attitudes towards retrospective legislation.[118] The Assistant Minister introducing the Bill explained that it was to legalize the working of the new Board, the matter being presented as a rather minor technicality. Objection was taken that the Board itself was illegal as a Minister could not by an order dissolve a board established by an Act of Parliament. The Deputy Speaker assured members that there was nothing unusual about the procedure; governments often did something administratively, and then sought the permission of Parliament to legalize retrospectively what they had done; this was always happening in Kenya. Thus the Government regards, and Parliament is told to regard, illegal administration and retrospective validation thereof as something normal and acceptable.

It is a not uncommon situation for governments in developing countries

[115] Traffic (Vehicle Licences) (Duration, Fees and Refund) (Amendment) (Rules) Validation Act No. 12 of 1966.

[116] Marketing of Agricultural Produce (Maize and Produce Board) Order, Legal Notice 76/1966. The Marketing of Agricultural Produce Act had previously been known as the Marketing of African Produce Act, Cap. 320. Its name was changed and its ambit extended by the Constitution of Kenya (Amendment of Laws—Marketing of Agricultural Produce) Order, Legal Notice 321/1965.

[117] Maize Marketing (Amendment) Act No. 8 of 1967.

[118] National Assembly, *Debates,* volume XI (22 March 1967), col. 1486 et seq.

to find that the law, passed by the legislature and drafted by lawyers trained in a different legal *milieu* to that in which the law is to be applied, does not meet the requirements of administrators on the spot, or the approval of the administered, and so is either not applied, misapplied or half-applied. The result is that conduct which is acceptable to ordinary people, and perhaps condoned by administrators, is illegal when judged by the formal rules. To talk of 'illegal administration' with its connotation of abuse of executive power in these circumstances is a misnomer, for the administrator is doing only what the public will tolerate. So too with retrospective legislation. Generally it is condemned, but in this situation it might have the desirable aim of bringing the law into line with what has always been administratively possible, so confirming, rather than disturbing, vested interests.

Such situations do exist in Kenya. They appeared to some extent in the two examples of agrarian administration given above, but are most prevalent in transactions in land and their registration, where the law is being used to try and steer people away from the obligations imposed by customary law, and the limitations of subsistence agriculture and as such, is ahead of consumers' opinion, and urban housing, and in public health where a shortage of administrators renders impossible the proper enforcement of sanitary, building and town-planning laws in the shanty towns growing up on the outskirts of the main urban centres.

But in addition to these situations there are those where the processes of the law are disregarded as being irrelevant or time-consuming, and in the knowledge that challenges to, or criticism of, such conduct will be negligible and can be disregarded with impunity. Here it is correct to speak of abuse of executive power. These situations too occur in Kenya as the above facts and examples indicate, and cannot be so easily condoned. Credit may be given for eventually passing legislation validating administrative action, but it suggests an attitude that the law can be used, or not, as suits the Government, rather than the more desirable one that Government must comply with the law, that the law must be changed in advance of, rather than after, new administrative action, so that the legislature, and through it the public may have the opportunity to comment on government plans and their projected implementation. There is a tradition, as old as Kenya itself, of administration based on the former attitude, which may help explain but hardly justify the present, for a Government which claims to be based on consent should not adopt the administrative practices of one which it claims was not so based.

(*b*) *The Maize Commission of Inquiry*

The Maize Commission of Inquiry was appointed towards the end of 1965 to investigate the organization of the industry and allegations that there had been corruption and profiteering in its operation, following widespread maize shortages in 1964–5. The Commission's report painted an unflattering picture of the administration under pressure, and the activities of the responsible Minister.[119] The Ministry of Co-operatives and Marketing, and the Maize Marketing Board, though appreciating that there would be a large shortfall of home-produced maize so that imports would be needed, were slow to do anything about getting those imports once the full extent of the shortfall revealed itself. There was confusion between the Ministry, the Board, the Ministry of Finance, and the Kenya Embassy in Washington as to how the American maize, which was to be imported, was to be bought and shipped to Kenya. Contradictory instructions and directions were issued from different Ministries, various officials were only too eager to 'pass the buck' or do nothing to expedite matters even when they were aware of the urgency of the situation. There appeared to be little order, regularity, and co-ordination in the administration. Recommendations were made to increase co-ordination both at the policy-making and senior administrative levels, but clearly to avoid the near-chaos described in the report something more than some committees is required. Experienced administrators (and every month increases the reservoir of that type of talent) would no doubt have helped, but as important is an ethos of dedicated public service, a willingness to shoulder responsibility and work long hours which was too much absent from the actions of the civil service as described in the report.

The extra-ministerial activities of the Minister, as described in the report, showed a definite departure from what one had hitherto supposed to be acceptable canons of ministerial conduct in Kenya.[120] Prior to becoming the Minister, the individual concerned had been Chairman of the Maize Marketing Board, and he continued to maintain close contact both officially and unofficially with the Board after leaving it. Both as chairman and as Minister, the Committee found that he had allowed his private interests to come into conflict with his public duty to the detriment of the latter, in that he had shown undue preferences to firms with which he was closely connected, or to individuals for whom he had a 'soft corner'.[121] He had also interfered too much in the day to day administration of the Board. The recommendations of the Commission on these matters were that politicians should not be appointed to any board dealing with maize marketing, and

[119] *Report of the Maize Commission of Inquiry*, op. cit., see particularly chapter 6, part 7 (paras. 179–248), and part 12 (paras. 440–514).

[120] Apart from the laws referred to above, at pp. 265–6, the principles governing ministerial conduct in Kenya had been laid down in a despatch from the Colonial Secretary in 1954, printed as Gazette Notice 584/1954. There was no indication that these principles had been formally changed by the independent Government and the Maize Commmission appeared to assume that they were still in force (paras. 512–513).

[121] *Report*, op. cit., para. 505.

that the rule requiring Ministers to disclose their business interests and put public duty before private interest should be applied more stringently.

In so far as the Government accepted these recommendations it did so in the narrowest possible manner. The Minister was not required to resign. He was relieved of his duties, but not of his office, for a short while, before being transferred to the Ministry of Housing. The political situation in Kenya at the time made it difficult to do more. Politicians were appointed to the new Maize and Produce Board, and have continued to be appointed to other boards in all areas of administration, including in some cases to the chairmanship thereof. There are, in short, uncomfortable signs that the clear implications of the Maize Commission of Inquiry—the demoralizing effect that unethical conduct can have upon the public service, the inefficiency to which it can give rise in the administrative process, and the need therefore to adopt policies and practices which will eliminate it—have been shrugged aside with no more than lip-service paid to them.[122]

(*c*) *Proliferation of the Administration*

We have remarked upon the proliferation of public corporations since independence. There has been a similar growth of all types of administrative bodies from ministries downwards in all departments of government. Even at independence, Kenya had a more complex administrative system than many African countries, arising out of the fact that it had originally been built up to serve the European community. It has now expanded in size without any noticeable increase in efficiency. The Salaries Review Commission noticed two tendencies within the central administration which arise out of the increased size and complexity of the machine, and which connote inefficiency.[123] First, the reluctance of senior officers to delegate any substantial measure of authority to their subordinates, and secondly, the tendency to hold too many inter- and intra-departmental meetings, and invite too many officers to them, some of whom do not adequately brief themselves before attending.

Inefficiency within the governmental machine, serious though it is, is outweighed by other implications of the growth of government. An increasingly large slice of government's recurrent expenditure is having to be spent on the salaries and allowances of the public service—approximately 40 per cent being the figure in the 1965/6 financial year.[124] As the Government continues to grow, so will this figure, and there will be less and less money drawn from internal sources available for development expenditure

[122] Another possible area of conflicting interests in the circumstances of Kenya arises from the fact that civil servants and Ministers are allowed to purchase land, one of the less desirable practices carried over from the colonial period.
[123] *Report*, op. cit., p. 95, paras. 319–20.
[124] *Report*, op. cit., p. 9, para. 33.

and running government services. A burgeoning bureaucracy and a slowing economy is a classic recipe for political instability. Again, the bigger the governmental machine, the more difficult it is for Parliament to exert any sort of control over it, particularly as more and more MPs are sucked into it on their appointment to various Ministries and boards. This too is potentially dangerous for the stability of the system.

Finally, the growth of the administration is a synonym for the growth of governmental power. When civil servants license political meetings, run local and other elections, co-ordinate the distribution of maize during shortages, oversee the land consolidation programme, and administer the other laws through which the Government seeks to implement its policies, it is obvious that the Government is in a position to control directly and in great detail most of what goes on in the country in the political, economic, and social spheres, and ensure that developments in all these spheres contribute towards the consolidation of its position. While there need not be anything particularly reprehensible about this, it is not easy for a civil servant in such circumstances to continue to be an impartial administrator, and this could in time lead to a loss of confidence in the bona fides of the administration.

In sum, while on the surface the administrative system appears to be in good shape, having successfully come through a period of rapid Africanization in the middle sixties, the direction and nature of its continuing development do not give rise to such optimism.

CHAPTER VIII
Parliament

INTRODUCTION

In the modern process of decolonization, independence has usually meant more than just the removal of external sovereignty. It has also included the establishment of a democratic system of government. While the latter often took the form of a parliamentary executive, this has perhaps been less important than provisions for an elected, democratic legislature, which is regarded as the linchpin of the new constitutional order. In a multi-racial Kenya, in particular, the progress towards increasingly wide franchise and the common roll was an index of her constitutional advance to independence. It was mainly the advances in the Legislature which preceded and were a necessary condition for advances in the Executive. The campaign for independence was conducted on an important moral basis, which revolved round the inherent right of a democratic franchise. It was partly this factor, and partly the general folklore of legislatures, that has invested Parliament with a high moral authority. Much of the discussion of its role and functions is implicitly or explicitly based on it; this point is important in an assessment of its role, and we shall return to it later.

Parliament, or its predecessor, the Legislative Council, has been an important body for debating major policies. During the colonial régime, the Legislative Council was a forum to air grievances and to criticize the Government or its officials, but in relation to legislation, however, its role was unimportant. It is true that from quite early times the Council obtained the power to make laws, but the Government majority ensured that all government proposals got through; the Governor also had a veto over Bills passed by it and the power of law-making through certification. As a forum for debate and criticism, the Council had a vigorous record. Even before the first African elected members injected a new militancy into the Legislative Council after 1957, it had been the centre of strong clashes between the Government and the unofficial members. It had also witnessed the clash between the races, at first between the Europeans and the Indians, then the Europeans and the Africans. Thus while the Council had not lacked in vigour, it had lacked in responsibility, which inevitably produced frustration and bred a certain amount of recklessness.

It was only with independence that Parliament became the supreme law-making body. But the Legislature that was established for independence was quite different from its colonial predecessor. Apart from the fact that it consisted overwhelmingly of directly elected members, it was now bicameral, with the Senate in some senses, rather than the more democratic lower house, in the direct line of succession to the old legislature—it incorporated the principle of special representation and was more of a debating than a policy making body, with no real control over the Government. It had more important powers in relation to legislation, but these were inferior to those of the lower house. The other important respect in which the new legislature was different from the old one was that its legislative competence was restricted by the Constitution. The old legislature had the restrictions associated with a colonial legislature, in particular with respect to extra-territorial effect and repugnance to English law. These were removed at independence, but new restrictions were then imposed—certain important areas were excluded from alteration by the ordinary legislative process. This limitation was imposed by two different sets of provisions.

First, certain subjects were assigned to the Regional Assemblies exclusively, and the Central Legislature had no power to make laws in regard to them in the ordinary circumstances. Secondly, certain basic human rights were placed beyond the reach of any legislature, central or regional. It was not possible for Parliament to remove those restrictions except through a difficult and complicated procedure. This constituted a serious derogation from the principle of parliamentary supremacy as understood in the English doctrine, and to which the new leaders thought themselves entitled.

Much resentment was therefore directed at the form and limitations of the new legislature. The Senate was seen as a divisive factor, retarding the growth of nationhood. President Kenyatta saw new evidence of unity in its abolition, and said that 'the unification of this Parliament is the culmination of our constitutional struggle'.[1] The division of legislative powers between the Regional Assemblies and Parliament was regarded as impeding the implementation of coherent policies and slowing down the process of change and reform. The entrenchment of human rights was resented for two reasons; it placed serious limitations on the scope of legislative and executive action, and it implied lack of confidence in the good sense and fairness of the leaders. In a sense complete independence had not been achieved until such restrictions were removed; the reasoning here is reminiscent of the great South African constitutional debates in the 1950s. In Kenya, however, there were no doubts on the legal effects of these limitations; and so the Government embarked on a careful plan to remove these restrictions. As we have seen, most of these restrictions have been removed; some of those

[1] National Assembly, *Debates*, volume XI (15 February 1967), col. 9.

associated with human rights remain, but their import is insignificant and at best unclear.[2]

While the legislative competence of Parliament has enlarged since independence, in other respects its authority has declined, especially in its control over the Executive. Important changes have been made in the composition and the powers of Parliament, but what effect the amendments of the provisions for Parliament have had on its role in the constitutional and political system can be assessed only after we have a clear idea of the functions of a legislature. There is a great deal of misunderstanding of these, which in part accounts for the mood of disillusionment with legislatures that is prevalent in many parts of the world. The role of a legislature can differ from one country to another, but the two commonest of its functions are the making of laws and the control of government.[3] It may also help to formulate the policy for the administration of the country, offering both new ideas and criticism of governmental plans. In addition, a legislature can have particular functions like the election (or sometimes dismissal) of a government or president or other officers, and in most Commonwealth countries it has a special role in the raising and expenditure of public money. The claim of a legislature to discharge these responsibilities is supposed to arise from another of its important functions—the representational—giving expression to the views of various national or parochial interests and providing a forum for the articulation of grievances. It expresses the will of the nation, and it is also sometimes thought that it ought to be a place where conflicting interests are balanced or reconciled and a national consensus achieved. It serves to form and demonstrate the 'conscience of the nation'.

The above view of a legislature has to be qualified in various ways. It contains bald statements which need greater elaboration, for the 'making of laws' is often a formal process of giving a legal sanction to executive policy and the 'control of government' can mean little more than its ability to ask the government embarrassing questions. Secondly, it overlooks the effect on the working of a legislature of one of the key developments in this century—political parties—which distorts both its representational and control functions. Thirdly, it takes no account of the control exercised over the legislature by the executive, which sometimes reduces the former to the role of the handmaiden of the latter. All these factors result in a legislature's function being in practice mainly related to the legitimation of government policy, and in this respect it takes a secondary place to the executive.

[2] See chapter XI.
[3] See, generally, Wheare, *Legislatures* (London, OUP, 1963). For other references, see footnote 129.

When opening the first session of the Legislature on 14 December 1964 under the Republic, President Kenyatta described its functions as follows:

> What this House must contribute to the Republic is something far more than just machinery which can give the plans or requirements of the Government their lawful status. This must be our forum, for discussions and proposals, for question, objection or advice. It must give full modern expression to the traditional African custom, by serving as the place where the elders and the spokesmen of the people are expected and enabled to confer . . . Let me emphasize to the members of this House that theirs is a two-way obligation; to represent fairly to the Government the views of their constituents and then to interpret fairly to their people the policies and decisions of the Government. Members of Parliament must serve as a bridge between Government and people. They stand astride the national stream of activity and thought. Unless this bridge is maintained, the national well-being suffers, through lack of access to, a lack of contribution from, some portion of our land . . . To carry out this task requires the discipline that is normally described as the dignity of Parliament. And while we will be giving further thought to the symbols and the procedures of this House, a foundation of dignity is something we will always preserve.[4]

To what extent Parliament has performed or is enabled to perform its functions according to the expectations of the President and to the general beliefs about legislatures is the theme of this chapter.

COMPOSITION

Parliament consists of the President and the National Assembly.[5] The President is also a member of the National Assembly. The inclusion of the President in the definition of Parliament has significance in particular to his role in law making; his assent is necessary for the validity of Bills passed by the National Assembly, even though he does not have a veto.[6] For most other practical purposes, Parliament means the National Assembly, and indeed in many important contexts, apart from, or in conflict with, the President.

There are three types of membership of the National Assembly. The most important group is that of the elected members, each of whom represents a single-member constituency. At independence, the number of constituencies was set as being between 110 and 130, while the actual figure was to be determined by the Electoral Commission and was fixed at 117. Now, the number is 158, though Parliament can prescribe a number up to 168.[7] The principle of representation through single-member constituencies was

[4] House of Representatives, *Debates*, volume IV (14 December 1964), col. 4.
[5] Constitution section 30.
[6] Constitution section 46 (2), Sub. (3) reads, 'Upon a Bill that has been passed by the National Assembly being presented to the President for assent, it shall become law and shall thereupon be published in the Kenya Gazette as a law'.
[7] Independence Constitution sections 37, 38 and 49. Now Constitution sections 31, 32 and 52.

accepted without controversy; in such a system each constituency can return only one member and the candidate with the highest votes ('first past the post') is declared elected. It is generally agreed that elections under this system do not always reflect most accurately the wishes of the people, as it is possible to win on a plurality of votes, there being no provision for the redistribution of preferences if no candidate emerges with an absolute majority. Also, the system favours the bigger parties unduly at the expense of the minority parties, and in a pluralistic society a system of proportional representation is often considered more equitable.[8] It might be argued that the latter would have been more desirable in Kenya on the basis of its political divisions in 1963. The lack of discussion at that time of its suitability may be explained by at least two factors—the absence of British or Kenyan experience of it (though Kenya has had one or more instances of two member constituencies) and the establishment of the Senate, which was supposed to take care of minority representation and interests. The creation of the Senate made it possible to remove the principle of special representation from the House of Representatives, and it was the basis of representation in the House which is now adopted in the new unicameral legislature. The Constitution provides that all constituencies shall be of equal size in population; the principle of equal size may, however, in certain cases, be qualified to take account of the density of population, and in particular the need to ensure adequate representation of urban and sparsely populated rural areas; the means of communication; geographical features; community of interest and the boundaries of existing administrative areas.[9] Since the rationale of special representation in Kenya had always been that the country lacked homogeneity in ideals and aspirations among its various people, the removal of such representation amounts to an assertion that the country has achieved a unity of purpose and trust; and is also at the same time a means of strengthening that unity.

The second category of members is that of nominated members, who replaced the specially elected members, first introduced in 1958, by an amendment in 1968.[10] The specially elected members, whose number originally under the Constitution was to be in the proportion of one for every ten elected members,[11] but was fixed at 12 in 1966,[12] were chosen by the elected members acting as an electoral college. Originally this category of members was created to introduce an element of non-racialism or multi-racialism in a legislature dominated by the communal representation; its

[8] See W.T.W. Mackenzie, *Free Elections* (London, Allen and Unwin, 1958).
[9] Constitution section 42 (3). The 1969 Constitution Act added a further criterion, 'population trends'.
[10] Act No. 45 of 1968.
[11] Independence Constitution section 39.
[12] The Constitution of Kenya (Amendment) (No. 4) Act No. 40. of 1966.

continuance in the new conditions of a common roll was not explained, but could be justified as a means to provide representation for either minority or intellectual or professional interests or skills. In fact the element of politics predominated in their election (though certain members of the minority groups were so elected), and this was one of the justifications offered for its substitution by the system of nomination. The new provision provides that there shall be 12 nominated members, who will be appointed by the President.[13] Among the points argued in its defence was that it would enable the House to secure interests and talents not so far provided, particularly the representation of women. It was at the same time mentioned that it would ensure an official majority of at least 12[14]—a dubious point since a government with a considerable minority is possible as we have seen. But it is clear that one of its primary purposes is to strengthen the government side. It can also be argued that nomination was substituted for elections in order to secure candidates supported by the Government for in the past the backbenchers had often rejected its candidates in favour of those of their own choice. No rules are laid down for the nomination; when the new provisions were being debated in the Assembly, some members fearing a capricious use of this power by a president, recommended that the President should nominate only from a list submitted by his party.[15] The President has, however, no power to remove a person once he is nominated, but that he is to be subject to political discipline is made clear by applying to him the rule, discussed below, that a member loses his seat if he changes his party.

The final category of members is those *ex officio*, which includes the Speaker and the Attorney-General only. A Speaker may be elected from among the existing members of the Assembly; if so elected, his seat becomes vacant. The Speaker has a casting vote only while the Attorney-General does not have a vote.

THE FRANCHISE AND ELECTIONS

The elections for the elected members are held on a wide franchise.[16] All citizens of the age of twenty-one or over are entitled to register as voters; and no one can vote in an election unless he has been so registered. In addition to citizenship and age, certain residential conditions have to be satisfied before registration can be obtained. First, the applicant must have been resident in Kenya either for a period of not less than one year imme-

[13] As amended by Act No. 45 of 1968. By the same Act, all the specially elected members are declared to be deemed to be nominated under section 39 (section 4 (1) of Act). Now see Constitution section 33.

[14] National Assembly, *Debates*, volume XV (28 May 1968), col. 90 et seq.

[15] ibid., col. 130.

[16] Constitution sections 32 and 43.

diately preceding the date of application or for a period of, or periods amounting in the aggregate to, not less than four years in the eight years immediately preceding that date. Secondly, he must have resided for five months in the previous twelve in the constituency in which he applies to be registered; alternatively, he must for a similar period have been employed, possessed property, or conducted business in the constituency. A person is disqualified from registration for a number of factors—if he has been adjudged to be of unsound mind, is an undischarged bankrupt, is under a sentence of death, or lawful custody, and finally, if Parliament so prescribes, due to an election offence.[17] No person can be registered in more than one constituency; it is an offence to try to seek registration in more than one constituency.[18]

There is no requirement that a fresh register be drawn up before an election; it can therefore sometimes happen that between the time when the register was drawn up and the elections, there has been a significant movement of population, so that not only are many new residents denied a say in choosing their representative but also those registered voters who have moved to a different constituency are often effectively disenfranchised as there is no provision for a postal ballot and one can only vote in the constituency where one is registered. The Electoral Commission has the power to direct the registration of voters in a constituency where by-elections may have become necessary, before holding those elections. While this power is exercisable at the discretion of the Commission, it is desirable that there should be a requirement of revision of the register not less than four nor more than five years since the previous general election.

To qualify either as a parliamentary candidate or for nomination to the Assembly, a person must be a registered voter in a constituency (though he is not restricted to contesting elections in that constituency only). A candidate therefore would have satisfied all the conditions for such registration; but if between registration and nomination he incurs any of the disqualifications connected with bankruptcy, insanity or a sentence of death or imprisonment for six months or more, he cannot stand for election. The last provision is a little curious, for, as we have seen, to be disqualified from registering to vote, it is enough if a person is in custody at the time, but for disqualification from candidature, a much graver offence seems necessary—the consequence perhaps of the piecemeal manner in which the

[17] Constitution section 43 (2). 'Lawful custody' is not defined; this disqualification replaced an earlier one in 1968 of being under a term of imprisonment of twelve months; the new disqualification would appear to be unduly wide and would cover, for example, a person in custody pending trial or in preventive detention, at the time when registration is carried out. Parliament has also imposed a further disqualification for an offence under the Corruption Act section 3 (3), Cap. 65. *Quaere*, whether this is valid now since the Constitution does not provide for or authorize Parliament to provide for such a disqualification.

[18] See, generally, National Assembly Elections Act, Cap. 7.

Constitution has been amended. There are, however, certain additional requirements for the valid nomination of a candidate. A candidate must show proficiency in the speaking and reading of the English language, since English is the official language of Parliament. He must not be under allegiance to a foreign power. He must not be a public officer or on the staff of a local government authority; it is, however, open to Parliament to exempt specified officers from this disability. Parliament can prescribe further disqualifications—it is thus open to it to provide for the disqualification of persons with an interest in a government contract, or those connected with the conduct of elections or of those found guilty of an election offence, for a maximum of five years.[19]

Finally, it has recently been provided that no candidature is valid unless it has been nominated by a political party in the prescribed manner.[20] What the 'prescribed manner' is, has not been set out in the Constitution, but proposed amendments to the National Assembly Elections Act provide some details:[21] the party selects the candidates and its leader nominates them. The proposed amendments require the constitution of a party to provide for nomination forms to be available to all its members seeking nomination, and for their right to address the selection body, and for the convening of conferences to select the candidates for nomination, at least two weeks before the beginning of the month in which nominations are to be made. In addition, the right to vote in the selecting conference is to be secured to all members of all committees of that party for that constituency or any part thereof. The party has to provide for appeals against decisions of the committees to a higher authority within the party, and in any case if the appeal is dismissed or not disposed of within seven days, an appeal can be lodged with a magistrate whose ruling will be final. The definition of a 'political party' in the Constitution ensures that no organization will be so certified unless it has made provisions for these rules.

Most of these rules for qualification as a voter and as a candidate are obviously designed to ensure that the franchise is only granted to those who have not shown themselves unfitted for this right; and that the right to represent others is withheld from those who show a lack of maturity or sense of responsibility. It is interesting that the age of franchise is twenty-one, though for most of the population the age of majority is eighteen.[22] Some of the disqualifications on candidature have been attacked on the ground

[19] Constitution section 35.
[20] Act 45 of 1968. Now Constitution section 34(d).
[21] National Assembly Elections (Amendment) Bill, 1968, Gazette Supplement, p. 605.
[22] Age of Majority Act, Cap. 33. The Commission on the Law of Marriage and Divorce has recommended a uniform age of majority at 18. See appendix VII of its *Report* (Govt. Printer, Kenya, 1968).

that they restrict the rights of constituents to choose their representatives;[23] but if the political and constitutional system is not to fall into disrepute, such qualifications may be important. A disqualification which has come under attack as being unsuitable in a country where English is a foreign language, is the requirement of proficiency in that language. There is little doubt that the language test has an important effect on the quality of leadership. It restricts the class of persons from which parliamentarians can be chosen, excluding some people with genuine qualities of leadership, and perhaps also produces a certain barrier between the people and their representatives. It has also been suggested that the language test not only affects the choice of candidates, but also their behaviour once they have been elected. It has been said that

> those who were launched on a parliamentary career were an élite of the educated for only those proficient in English could qualify for the Legislative Council. This group was easily seduced by the trappings of power, overwhelmed by parliamentary traditions.[24]

It would surely be in keeping with Kenya's emphasis both on grass roots democracy and the Swahili language to prescribe proficiency in that language as an alternative to knowledge of English.

Of even greater importance is the requirement of nomination by a party. Many of the provisions about Parliament in Kenya were based on the rules and conventions of Westminster, where there is almost no regulation by law of the role of political parties in the electoral or legislative process but a considerable emphasis on the rather special relationship between a member and his constituency. While political parties do put up their official candidates, there is nothing to prevent an independent candidate from contesting elections; moreover the endorsement by a party of a candidate is its domestic matter and can differ as from one party to another. A similar system applied in Kenya until 1965, but in practice it worked differently from Britain. In particular, there tended to be a large number of independent candidates, many of whom were successful—a reflection both of the weak party organization and often of the unrepresentative character of its committees, no

[23] See, for example, the debate on the second reading of the Constitution of Kenya (Amendment) Bill in the House of Representatives, volume VIII (22–25 February and 2 March, 1966).

[24] Odinga, op. cit., p. 250. On 23 April 1965 (House of Representatives, *Debates*, volume IV), a private member introduced a motion in the House of Representatives urging the Government to introduce constitutional amendments to adopt Swahili as the language of the House 'in view of the fact that Swahili is the indigenous common African language in Kenya', col. 1460. There was general support for it, though the Government was successfully able to move an amendment that the Government should introduce the constitutional amendment 'when the time comes, to adopt Swahili as one of the languages of this house and to hasten the date upon which the use of Swahili would commence in the National Assembly', col. 1485. Constitution section 53 continues English as the sole official language.

doubt due to the absence of regular elections to them. The success of the independents had a further adverse effect on the party organizations, for generally these independents were candidates who had failed to secure the party endorsement but joined the party parliamentary group once elected. In the circumstances party discipline was never strong, and there was a considerable friction between the local party organizations on the one hand and the headquarters and often the local MP on the other. In 1966 KANU made a serious attempt to revitalize the party through various changes in its organization, including the appointment of eight vice-presidents, one from each Province and Nairobi—thus to some extent incorporating in its own constitution the principle of 'regionalism' removed from the Constitution—but without total success. The amendment of 1968 can, therefore, be seen as an attempt through the law to achieve what had not been achieved by political controls: the strengthening of the party. The amendment can, however, be set in another context: the establishment of the KPU, whose party organization was weak (partly because of the difficulties placed in its way by the administration) but whose support, though unascertained, was reckoned to be considerable. It may have been hoped that this amendment, which makes crucial the factor of a strong party organization, would place the KPU at a greater disadvantage than KANU.[25]

These rules bear some resemblance to the Tanzanian electoral system and might be thought an improvement on the previous system. But there are significant differences. In Tanzania the party nominates two candidates and is neutral in the electoral campaign, whereas in Kenya the uneven power and authority of the parties may prevent the electorate exercising real choice between candidates selected by the parties. Secondly, the party in Tanzania has regular elections in which there is a turnover of personnel. Do the parties in Kenya? Regular party elections become much more important in Kenya now, since fundamental franchise rights hinge on them.

Thirdly, it is doubtful if the effect of the new rules would be what was alleged to be their aim—the strengthening of the parties. The possibility of independent candidates has a salutary effect on the parties, ensuring attention to local problems and grievances. In the new system some of the incentives disappear, and a great deal depends on the strength of the rival party or parties. In Kenya's experience since independence, it is obvious that one of the factors helping a party's responsiveness has been its own 'rebels' and 'independents'. There is danger in trying to make a party viable through this form of constitutional provision. The strength of a party depends on its own constitution, the ability to promote and maintain a consensus, and

[25]In 1968 when similar rules were applied to local authorities (Local Government Regulations (Amendment) (No. 2) Act No. 31), all the KPU candidates were disqualified as having failed to fill the nomination forms correctly.

the loyalty that the leadership inspires and deserves. A parliamentary democracy works best when the coherence and the policies of the parties depend on their own organization; if a restrictive law is brought in aid, the form of the party may be preserved, but its substance may atrophy.

Fourthly, the new rule could lead to a proliferation of short-lived electoral alliances in the guise of political parties for the sake of conformity with the new rules. Above all, however, one should not overlook the possibility of political abuse to which the new rule might lend itself; the registration of political parties—and no party can nominate candidates unless it has been registered under the law—is basically an executive decision, and could therefore be refused unfairly. There is also the possibility that pressures may build up within the ruling party to ban a strong rival party, thus disqualifying all its prospective candidates and leaving no room for the electors to exercise any sort of choice.[26]

TENURE OF SEATS

As a general rule, when a person is elected or nominated to Parliament, he retains his seat until its dissolution.[27] It is, however, possible for him to lose his seat before then for a variety of reasons.

A member loses his seat if he incurs any of the disqualifications that would prevent him from standing for Parliament.[28] There are, however, some additional factors of disqualification—all of them introduced subsequent to independence. If a member is elected Speaker, he vacates his seat, since the Speaker is now a member *ex officio*.[29] Secondly, if a member is absent from the Assembly for eight consecutive meetings without the Speaker's permission, he loses his seat, but it is possible for the President to waive this rule in relation to any member.[30] Thirdly, a member who contested elections with the support of or as a supporter of a political party, vacates his seat if he resigns from that party at a time when that party is a parliamentary party. A nominated member loses his seat in similar circumstances if he has accepted nomination as a member or supporter of a political party.[31] If the party with which he was thus associated is dissolved (and it may be queried whether there is any difference between 'dissolution' and 'ceasing to be a

[26] In March 1968 some KANU back-benchers introduced a motion in the National Assembly on an adjournment debate to outlaw KPU, National Assembly, *Debates*, vol. XIV (1 March 1968), col. 267 et seq.

[27] The normal life of Parliament is five years, but the President can bring it to an end earlier by dissolution or it can be extended up to a further period of five years, though not more than one year at a time, when the country is at war. Constitution section 59.

[28] Constitution section 39. The Attorney-General's membership is unaffected by these and following provisions.

[29] Constitution section 37 (4).

[30] Constitution section 39 (1) (c).

[31] Constitution section 40. *Quaere*, whether a nominated member could be nominated without a party attachment.

parliamentary party'), and he joins another parliamentary party, he cannot leave that second party without resigning his seat. The vacation takes effect at the expiration of the session of Parliament then in being, or if the resignation from the party took place during a recess, the end of the next session. If, however, before the end of the session, the party ceases to function as a parliamentary party, he can continue as a member of Parliament. The certificate of the Speaker as to whether a political party is or is not at any time a parliamentary party or as to whether a specially elected member stood at his election with the support of a political party is conclusive, and binds the courts in the determination of the questions of membership of the National Assembly. This power of the Speaker was justified on the basis that 'matters within this House are normally outside the jurisdiction of the courts'.[32] However, the Constitution does expressly grant the courts certain jurisdiction in relation to the House, and the determination of elections to and vacation of seats has traditionally been within such jurisdiction. Nevertheless, it may be that since the questions posed by this provision are eminently political, they are best left to the determination of the Speaker, though it could be argued that this is precisely the reason why the determination should not left to him but to the courts.

Members have resisted the introduction of some of these further rules of disqualification. Their opposition has been based less on the threats to the independence of the National Assembly than to their own tenure of the seat. Thus they opposed the Bill which provided for disqualification on a sentence of six months or more, with the reason that it was unfair to members since there was no guarantee against a wrong or biased judgment of the court.[33] The rule of vacation after absence from eight consecutive meetings was attacked on the grounds of bad roads and communications, and the priority of constituency over parliamentary affairs,[34] but there was little opposition to the 'equity' jurisdiction of the President. In determining questions of parliamentary parties, the Government was anxious to preserve the autonomy of the House; the members could have argued that autonomy is equally important in other contexts; and if there was a need for an equity jurisdiction, it should have been vested in the Speaker or a parliamentary committee rather than the Executive. There was, moreover, remarkably little opposition from the government back-benchers to the provision of resignation for leaving a parliamentary party—a real threat to the autonomy of the House.

The Government has justified these rules of disqualification on its 'faithful desire to ensure democratic practice and the preservation of democratic

[32] House of Representatives, *Debates*, volume VIII (3 March 1966), col. 2029.
[33] ibid. (23 February 1966), col. 1344.
[34] ibid. (24 February 1966), col. 1424.

institutions in this country'.[35] Despite the strenuous opposition of many members, the first two are defensible, so as to protect the interests of the constituents to be represented in the Assembly. The third is more controversial. It has been the experience in most African countries that after independence, the opposition parties lose a lot of adherents to the ruling party. It is also true to say that changes of allegiance are determined more often by considerations of personal or political gain than ideological conviction. A considerable crossing of the floor thus takes place, and the party system remains fluid and unpredictable. A rule which tries to strengthen the party system, in a constitutional framework which assumes such a system, may not be without some justification—as a member, himself known for a shift of allegiance, remarked—'this will stop these political acrobats from fooling about with the public'. But the circumstances in which the rule was introduced, plus its own inner inconsistencies, induce some scepticism about the Government's motives. In April 1966 the Vice-President, Oginga Odinga, resigned his office and left KANU. He carried about twenty other KANU members with him across the floor and on 28th April the Speaker accepted their request to be recognized as the official opposition under the name of the Kenya Peoples' Union (KPU). Alarmed by the possibility of further defection, the Government introduced the amendment and secured its passage through the National Assembly in one day by suspending the Standing Orders and thus dispensing with the rules requiring fourteen days' notice of the Bill, and the lapse of time between its various stages. After the ensuing elections for these vacancies—known as the 'Little General Election'—two of the unsuccessful candidates who were formerly MPs applied to the High Court for a declaration that they were still MPs as they had left KANU before the amendment was passed, and its provisions did not purport to apply retrospectively. While their petition was still before the court, the Government introduced a further amendment to 'clarify' that the original provisions were to apply retrospectively,[36] thus rendering the court's decision otiose.

Implicit in the rule is the rejection of Edmund Burke's views set out in his famous *Address to the Bristol Electors* on the role of a member of Parliament. He is to be regarded less as a representative who acts according to the way which in his opinion would best promote the interests of his electors, than as a delegate who must carry out their instructions—the instructions being the policies on which he fought and won elections. A change of political party is regarded necessarily as a departure from the mandate given to him; and so the right to represent is forfeited. The rule, however, does not remain true to its own logic. If the

[35] ibid. (28 April 1966), col. 2015.
[36] Act No. 4 of 1967.

party on whose support a member was elected is dissolved during the same session (either before or after his resignation from it), he continues to represent his constituency; so do all the other member supporters of the erstwhile party. Now it can be argued that the decision to dissolve a political party affects the mandate of the delegates in such fundamental respects that a reference to the electors would be necessary. The law does nothing to protect the interests of the electors in this situation. Nor is it easy to understand why a member who leaves a party (on or before its dissolution) should be free to join another without first securing a fresh mandate to do so from his constituents. Such a mandate, however, seems to be automatically assumed, for if he then leaves the second party (which he may have joined contrary to the wishes of his electors), he is deemed to have broken a pact with the electors, and loses his seat.

The difficulties about the rule discussed above indicate its unsuitability as applied at present. There are other unsatisfactory aspects as well. It assumes that people vote for policies and not personalities, and that they understand policies—a doubtful assumption in most countries at the best of times, and very questionable in a country with a large percentage of illiteracy and the politics of charisma. Secondly, even if the assumption is valid, how is one to determine who remains true to the party creed and who betrays it—the dissidents or the remnant? The case of the KPU has been that the present KANU leadership has broken that party's electoral pledges, and that that leadership, and not the KPU, are the real deviationists. The present Government has successfully initiated drastic changes in the constitutional structure which they were elected to rule under, increased the life of Parliament, and assigned constituencies to members for whom they were not necessarily elected—all this was done without reference to the people. Moreover, in a young country which is engaged on important tasks of national integration and economic development, dependent on so many outside influences and a rapidly changing domestic scene, the spirit of a rule of this kind is probably unwise, attempting to tie the hands of the parties and their members in advance of new and often unforeseeable contingencies. Flexibility is necessary to meet changed conditions: a conscientious application of the rule would exclude it. However, it is important to note that the real import of the rule is not to preserve the pact of a member with his electors, but to provide disincentives for the attrition of parties. As stated above, the rule may help to produce some stability in the political scene; but it is equally important to note that if the rule had been in the Constitution at independence, it may well have hindered the increased national unity since then, following at first the trickle and later the flood of KADU members to KANU.

THE ELECTORAL MACHINERY

The central role devised for Parliament by the Constitution would be frustrated unless there were sufficient guarantees that its composition would not be determined directly or indirectly by the Government. The Government could abuse the process for elections in various ways—by a skilful delimitation of constituency boundaries to give its party an unfair advantage (gerrymandering), in the preparation of the register of voters, and in the actual conduct of elections, including the counting of the votes. To safeguard against these abuses, the Constitution has provided for voting by secret ballot and an electoral machinery, central to which is an independent Electoral Commission. It used to consist of the Speaker of the National Assembly as chairman, two members appointed by the President, and one member to represent each Province (or such other area as may be substituted by Parliament), also appointed by the President. By the 1969 Constitution Act, however, the President has been given power to appoint the chairman and its other members, whose number must not fall below four. Appointments are made for five-year periods, and dismissal before then can take place only through a procedure similar to that for the dismissal of judges.[37] This is in order to ensure that the Commission does its job fairly and honestly. It is not subject to the direction or control of any other person or authority in the discharge of its functions; and may regulate its own procedure.

The Commission serves two important functions: it draws up the boundaries of the constituencies for elections and is responsible for the conduct and supervision of the elections, though in regard to the latter, it is doubtful if the implementing legislation[38] gives full effect to the constitutional provisions. As we have seen, the Commission no longer decides on the exact number of constituencies (which is done by Parliament) but it divides the country into the prescribed number, on the basis of the principles outlined previously. It undertakes a review of the division at intervals of not less than eight or more than ten years, or at such time as Parliament may prescribe; and may also do so after a census of the population has been held. In 1966, however, as already noticed, the Commission was required by Parliament to create additional constituencies on principles laid down by Parliament itself—the conversion of senatorial districts into constituencies within roughly the same geographical area—as a preliminary to the amalgamation of the two houses of the Legislature.[39]

[37] It would appear that the Speaker cannot be appointed the chairman, since a member of Parliament cannot be appointed to the Commission. Constitution section 41. For the functions of the Commission, see Constitution section 32 (3) (direction and supervision of registration of voters and the conduct of elections) and 42 (the demarcation into constituencies).

[38] National Assembly Elections Act, chapter V, Cap. 7.

[39] It is interesting to note that the instructions to the Commission were given through

The second function of the Commission is to direct and supervise the registration of voters and the conduct of the constituency elections. According to the National Assembly Elections Act, however, 'direct' is rather narrowly interpreted and the Commission's role is small. It can order the preparation or revision of the registration, but it is the Government which provides the machinery for such registration.[40] Again, when elections are due, it is the Speaker who issues writs to the returning officers—for a general election, within eight weeks of the dissolution of Parliament; in case of a vacancy as a result of a successful election petition, within one month of the vacancy; and in all other cases, within four months.[41] The appointment of returning officers and the designation of polling stations are done by the Government.[42] The practice is to appoint civil servants for this purpose, and though it is true that in this capacity they act according to their duties under the law, direct or indirect influence by the Government cannot be ruled out, and has indeed been complained of by the opposition on various occasions. So despite the intention in the Constitution to vest the responsibility for elections in the independent Electoral Commission, the Government plays an important role.

It is arguable that the Constitution envisages a greater role for the Commission than is given it under the Act. It ought to be given greater responsibility; in particular it, rather than the Government, should designate officers to prepare the voters' register and act as returning officers, otherwise the essential democratic character of Parliament might be imperilled, or be thought to be imperilled. In a constitutional system where the Government has pointed to Parliament as the linchpin, it is essential to preserve fairness and honesty in elections to it.

The High Court has been given jurisdiction to determine questions as to the membership of the National Assembly.[43] The declaration of the results by the returning officer in each constituency names the successful candidate and he is thereby elected; the vacation of a member's seat, otherwise than at a dissolution of Parliament, is determined by the Speaker. Both of these determinations are appealable to the High Court, under a procedure established by Parliament. In the former case, that of election, an application to the High Court may be made by any person entitled to vote in the election to which the application relates or by the Attorney-General; as to the second, amendments were introduced by the 1969 Constitution Act

an ordinary act of Parliament, but a constitutional amendment was necessary to give effect to its results.

[40] Section 30 of the Act.

[41] ibid., section 12.

[42] ibid., section 30; see also Legal Notice 742/1963.

[43] Constitution sections 44 and 50, and part V of the National Assembly Elections Act.

so that while previously the application could be made by the Attorney-General or by any elected member or any person who was a registered voter, now where the Speaker has declared that a member's seat has become vacant by reason of any provision of the Constitution, only that member can apply; in all other cases, the application can also be made by the Attorney-General or any registered voter. The determination by the High Court is final and not appealable elsewhere. For the exercise of this jurisdiction, the application has to be presented in the form of a petition, and the election court is constituted by two High Court judges. If the judges are divided, then the election is confirmed. The procedure is very similar to the normal procedures of the Court; but in this case, the findings of the Court are certified to the Speaker, who then takes appropriate action—thus preserving, technically, the autonomy of the Assembly. The court may also report to the Speaker if an election offence has been committed.

The elections to the Assembly are thus well secured by law through the participation of the Electoral Commission, the Speaker, and, in the case of disputes, the courts. Abuses of the electoral process cannot, however, be ruled out; the dangers of it, or at least the suspicions thereof, are present in the wide powers of administration vested in the Government by the ordinary laws. Nor is there enough knowledge of the procedure for a petition to the courts, and the courts have recently shown an inclination to dismiss petitions for technical reasons.[44]

PROCEDURES AND PRIVILEGES

Before we proceed to a discussion of the role of Parliament, it is essential to examine the procedure for the conduct of its proceedings and the special privileges allowed to it under the law to discharge its functions more efficiently. Though very few of those are provided for in the Constitution, they are of primary importance for the success or failure of the work of Parliament. The procedure inside the National Assembly can determine to a significant degree how effectively the Government is to be held accountable to it, the role of the Opposition and the speed and volume of parliamentary work, but as with so many other aspects of recent constitutional developments, the rules have tended to be used for definite partisan political objectives rather than to maximize the efficiency of the Assembly.

Within a few rules of procedure prescribed in the Constitution, the Assembly is free to determine its own procedure.[45] The Speaker (or in his absence, the Deputy Speaker) presides at its meetings and plays a key role in its proceedings. The Speaker is elected by the Assembly from among

[44] One case was dismissed in 1967 on the ground that the petitioner had failed to leave a deposit with the court, the applicant's offer of late payment was not accepted.
[45] Constitution sections 46–56.

persons who are elected members, except for a Minister or an Assistant Minister, or are qualified to be elected as such. The Deputy Speaker, on the other hand, has to be elected from among the elected members, other than Ministers or Assistant Ministers. The rules for their election are a little elaborate, in order to ensure that persons elevated to these delicate and difficult jobs enjoy wide acceptance in the Assembly.[46] A person shall not be elected as Speaker (or Deputy Speaker) unless he is supported by the votes of two-thirds of all the members of the Assembly. If no candidate achieves this support on the first ballot, a second ballot takes place. If the second ballot is also abortive, the two top candidates only in that ballot proceed to the third, where the candidate with the higher votes is elected. These rules may be necessary in case of a contest, but as they stand at present, they also apply even if only one candidate for the Speaker or the Deputy Speaker, as the case may be, has been validly nominated. Since such a candidate would in any case be elected on the third ballot (unless of course he fails to obtain even a single vote), much harm might be done to his reputation, and hence partially to his ability to discharge his duties, if on the first two ballots he suffers a low vote. The Speaker or the Deputy Speaker can be removed from office by a resolution of the Assembly supported by the votes of three-quarters of all the members thereof. He also loses office if he incurs a disqualification from being a member of the Assembly, and when Parliament first meets after a dissolution.

The Speaker symbolizes in himself the dignity and autonomy of Parliament, and has to ensure that proceedings in the House are orderly and fruitful. He also performs other functions.[47] In this chapter, we shall examine his role as the presiding officer of Parliament. The present Speaker defined his responsibilities to the members as follows:

> It will be my duty to all of you to enforce strict compliance with your own rules of procedure, and to ensure that the voice of the minority is always given a fair hearing; but, in doing so, I shall only be giving effect to what you yourselves really desire. In all other respects, I shall always consult and bow to the will of the majority, or such special majority as the Constitution may require for special occasions.[48]

He has to hold an even hand between the Government and the opposition, and afford to all a fair hearing. His rulings are final, and his conduct can only be debated on a substantive motion[49]— rules which are essential for orderly

[46] These rules are now no longer set out in the Constitution but are to be found in the Standing Orders. (Constitution sections 37(1) and 38(1)). The relevant Standing Orders are 4 and 8 (Standing Orders, 6 December 1967).

[47] His role as Chairman of the Electoral Commission has disappeared, but see chapter VI for his role in relation to the procedure for the removal of the President for inability to perform his functions.

[48] House of Representatives, *Debates*, volume I (7 June 1963), col. 2.

[49] Standing Order 73. (References are to Standing Orders as amended up to and including 6 December 1967.)

proceedings. The powers of the Speaker and the manner of their exercise are set out in the Standing Orders. In the matters not provided for in the Orders, the Speaker has to decide them at his discretion;[50] previously it was provided that in such instances he was to be guided by the rules, forms and usages of the British House of Commons.

The Speaker also exercises an important influence on the development of constitutional practices and understandings. During the course of parliamentary proceedings, several questions arise about the interpretation of the Constitution; the Speaker has to rule on them. In the absence of court decisions on the Constitution, his rulings become quite authoritative, and in any case, for certain domestic purposes, they cannot be challenged elsewhere. Among the important issues on which the Speaker's rulings have been influential are the meaning and application of the doctrine of collective and ministerial responsibility, the right of the members to vote, and the permissible scope of debate. As we shall see, the effect has generally been restrictive; the members have often been reminded of their oath 'to preserve, protect and defend the Constitution', and the Speaker has said that as long as it stands, he 'cannot allow any argument—let alone resolution—which ignores its implications, other than a substantive motion for its amendment or repeal'.[51]

Classically, legislatures have been seen as checks on the executive; at present the antagonism implied in the contrast is no longer true in parliamentary systems, but it is nevertheless the responsibility of the Speaker to preserve the autonomy of the House against executive arbitrariness. In particular, he must make his own evaluations on points of law and procedure. Unfortunately a tendency seems to be developing for the Speaker to rely on governmental interpretations. The Speaker has looked to the Attorney-General, for example, for authoritative rulings on points of law, when it might have been better had he sought independent advice on them—and despite the protests of the opposition.[52] On one important occasion, however, he did overrule the opinion of the Attorney-General, on the question of the right to vote, which we discuss below. Any impression of too close a relationship between the Speaker and the Government could do irreparable harm to the office of the Speaker, and to the fairness of parliamentary procedures.

The Constitution prescribes the procedures and rules for voting. The quorum for the Assembly is thirty; and unless it is provided otherwise,

[50] Standing Order 1.

[51] House of Representatives, *Debates*, volume XII, part II (11 July 1967), col. 1989. Standing Order 40 (3) (6) permits the Speaker to rule as inadmissible any motion which is contrary to the Constitution without expressly proposing appropriate amendment of the Constitution. The Speaker's earlier rulings were made before such a provision was part of the Standing Orders.

[52] National Assembly, *Debates*, volume XI (9 March 1967), col. 914; House of Representatives, *Debates*, volume XII, part II (11 July 1967), col. 1987.

any question proposed for its decision shall be determined by a majority of the votes of the members present and voting.[53] Where special majorities are necessary, difficulties have been experienced in obtaining enough MPs when a division took place on those motions;[54] the Speaker had indeed indicated that when a special majority was not obtained, though the majority of those present voted affirmatively, the vote would be abortive rather than the motion defeated—a sensible but incorrect interpretation of the Standing Orders as they were at that time.[55] Subsequently this problem was expressly taken care of by a provision in the Orders which enables the Speaker in similar circumstances to hold another division within a week. As far as constitutional amendments requiring special majorities are concerned, the 1969 Constitution Act itself enables a further vote to be taken within the terms of the Standing Orders, so long as the Bill is not opposed by 35 per cent or more of all the members.[56] Even apart from cases of special majorities, a quorum is often a problem; the Speaker has allowed a debate on one adjournment motion to continue despite its lack, on the ground that in such a debate, no question has to be resolved.[57]

The Speaker has a casting but not an original vote; if, however, some other member is presiding, he has both an original and a casting vote.[58] However, it is possible on a particular motion that a member may be disqualified from voting. The Constitution enables the Assembly by its rules of procedure to provide that a member who votes upon a question in which he has a direct pecuniary interest shall be deemed not to have voted, though the present Standing Orders do not contain such rule.[59] There is no other express rule of disqualification, but an interesting question of the right to vote arose during the debate on the Constitution Amendment Bill 1967 which sought to make the operation of an earlier amendment, vacating the seats of members who leave their parliamentary parties, retrospective; at the same time there were election petitions before the High Court challenging the right of the persons newly 'elected' after the amend-

[53] Constitution sections 51 and 54.
[54] e.g. House of Representatives, *Debates*, volume III (26 November 1964), col. 5656, voting on Constitution Amendment Bill, 1964, was twice postponed; House of Representatives, *Debates*, volume IV (22 April 1965), col. 1417, second reading on the Constitution Amendment Bill, 1965, was postponed; House of Representatives, *Debates*, volume VIII (2 March 1966), col. 1663 and (3 March 1966), col. 1719, voting postponed on second and third readings respectively of Constitution Amendment Bill, 1966.
[55] e.g. National Assembly, *Debates*, volume XI (8 March 1967), col. 880.
[56] Constitution section 47 (3). The relevant Standing Order is 61. Under this Order, the Speaker may in his own discretion direct one further division within seven days, otherwise the motion is lost. The motion is also lost unless at the further division, the requisite majority is obtained. There is thus a discrepancy between Constitution section 47 (3) and Standing Order 61.
[57] National Assembly, *Debates*, volume XIV (10 April 1968), col. 1894.
[58] Constitution section 54 (2).
[59] Constitution section 54 (3). Such disqualification was previously in the orders.

ment to sit as MPs. The question arose whether these MPs should be allowed to vote on a motion which would legalize their position as members.

The Speaker found no express provision in the Constitution or the Standing Orders to guide him; the Attorney-General, on behalf of the Government, strongly urged that they be allowed to vote, since the rules provided for no disqualification. Another Minister contended that they were members until declared otherwise as a result of the petition. The Speaker, however, ruled that they had no right to vote; he felt that the fact that those whose personal interest was involved should not vote was a matter of fundamental principle, 'going to the root of the Constitution and stability of this National Assembly'.[60]

In certain instances the Constitution requires a special majority for or a specified manner of expressing the parliamentary will. The approval of a proclamation under the Preservation of Public Security Act is by a resolution,[61] while the legislative power can only be exercised through Bills passed by the National Assembly and assented to by the President.[62] The different stages of a Bill are prescribed in the Standing Orders. The Bill must be published fourteen days before its introduction; it then has its First Reading, which is very formal, followed by the Second Reading, which is an occasion for a debate on the general principles of the Bill, after which it is referred to the Committee of the whole House for debate and discussion on the detailed provisions. If the Committee reports favourably to the Assembly, it then has its final and Third Reading, where the debate, if any, is restricted to a general statement or reiteration of objections. If approved the Bill is ready for the Presidential Assent. Not more than one stage of a Bill can be taken at one sitting. For financial Bills, the procedure is more elaborate and is described below.

Certain other features of the procedure will be briefly mentioned. The Assembly has an official verbatim report of its proceedings, known as *Hansard*, though the Speaker can order the exclusion of any matter which in his opinion is 'secret or purely domestic'.[63] The Standing Orders establish various committees, either of the whole House or select.[64] Of the former, there are the Committees of Supply, and Ways and Means, apart from the general; of the latter, there is the Sessional Committee, and the Estimates and the Public Accounts Committees. The Sessional Committee is extremely important, for it determines the business of the Assembly and appoints to the other Select Committees. Committees can also be established under

[60] National Assembly, *Debates*, volume XI (8 March 1967), cols. 828–829.
[61] Constitution section 85 (2).
[62] Constitution section 46 (1). Section 123 (2) provides that except where the context otherwise requires, any powers conferred upon Parliament by the Constitution to establish, provide for or prescribe any matter or thing shall be exercisable by Act of Parliament.
[63] Standing Order 29. See Standing Orders 26–29.
[64] Standing Orders 126–157.

legislation, such as the Privileges Committee,[65] and the Assembly is free to establish any other committee it wishes for the conduct of its business. Many of the Standing Orders can be waived with the leave of the Assembly; 'leave of the Assembly' was previously deemed to be denied even if one member objected—now an objecting member must have the support of either the Speaker or two other members.[66] Some other provisions can, however, be waived on an ordinary motion.[67]

Parliament is also authorized to make provisions for its own powers, privileges and immunities for the purpose of the orderly and effective discharge of its business, which it has done through the National Assembly (Powers and Privileges) Act. Members have immunity from legal proceedings for words spoken before, or written in a report to, the Assembly or its committees including motions and resolutions introduced in the Assembly.[68] There is also freedom from arrest for civil debt during session; and court process for civil jurisdiction cannot be served on a member within the precincts of the Assembly.[69] The official publications of the Assembly are absolutely privileged, while unofficial reports or extracts therefrom enjoy only qualified privilege rebuttable if the publication is malicious and *mala fide*.[70] Despite the wide immunity granted by the Act from legal suit for conduct in the Assembly, the members are not exempt from detention under the Preservation of Public Security Act. At one stage the Speaker thought that there was complete immunity, but it is now accepted that this is not the case.[71]

[65] The National Assembly (Powers and Privileges) Act, Cap. 6 as amended by Act No. 14 of 1966.
[66] Standing Order 2 (a).
[67] Standing Order 166.
[68] Section 3.
[69] Section 4.
[70] Section 24.
[71] In May, 1967 a Kenya member of the Central Legislative Assembly, Mr. Keen, was detained under the Act. No reasons for his detention were given, but it was widely believed that he was being detained for his criticism in the C.L.A. of the failure of the East African governments to bring about a federation (despite a denial by the Vice-President, National Assembly, *Debates*, volume XII, part II (26 May 1967), col. 293). An MP concerned with the freedom of speech in the National Assembly asked the Speaker to explain the protection available to members in respect of their speeches in Parliament. The Speaker assured the Assembly that its members were protected from detention by the Privileges Act (National Assembly, *Debates*, volume XII, part II (26 May 1967), col. 258). One of the authors (McAuslan) pointed out in a letter to the *East African Standard* that MPs were liable to detention under section 7 (3) of the Public Security Act, not withstanding the Privileges Act (2 June 1967). When the issue was raised in Parliament subsequently, the Speaker assured the Assembly that he had asked the Government to clarify the position (volume XII, part II (28 June 1967), col. 1503). On 20 November 1967, the Vice President in a debate on a motion to extend the Public Security Order under the Act said that while the MPs had no immunity from arrest under it, the government 'recognizes the principle that no Member of Parliament may be detained on account of anything said by him in the House'. He also said that the Government expected the Members 'to behave responsibly', volume XIII, part II, col. 2159.

There have been accusations that some of the members tend to abuse their privileges. Too many allegations are made, which they fail to substantiate, even within the broad definition of 'substantiation' for this purpose.[72] There have also been incidents of unseemly and unruly behaviour.[73] These were serious enough to lead to an important amendment of the Act early in 1966, which empowered the Speaker to issue a Code of Conduct regulating the conduct of members within the precincts of the Assembly (outside the Chamber itself, the Speaker, as presiding officer, has some disciplinary power). A Committee of Privileges was also set up under the chairmanship of the Speaker, with power, either on its own motion or reference by any person, to inquire into any alleged breach by a member of the Code, 'which is alleged to have been intended or likely to reflect adversely on the dignity or integrity of the Assembly or the member thereof or to be contrary to the best interests of the Assembly, or the member thereof'. The Committee makes a recommendation to the Assembly, which can take any disciplinary action against the defaulting member which is provided in the regulations, including suspension from the service of the Assembly and exclusion from its precincts.[74]

The Speaker has also been given power to make regulations for the better conduct of the Assembly, including the entry and the exclusion of strangers from its precincts.[75] The House and its committees can order the attendance of witnesses, who may be examined on oath. The witnesses have the same privileges as a witness in a court of law. The rules about the production or disclosure of documents and other evidence are specified—the Government has wide immunities, whereas for others, reference must be made to the usage and practice of the House of Commons in Britain, to determine whether production or disclosure can be compelled. The Speaker or other officials of the Assembly are not subject to the jurisdiction of any court in respect of the exercise of their powers under the Act or the Standing Orders. But the Assembly itself has no power to punish strangers for breaches of the Act or the regulations thereunder; only a court can do that, after a written sanction of the Attorney-General to institute the prosecution. The Assembly,

[72] '. . . hon. members are too free with offensive allegations, not only against each other but against defenceless members of the public, without being able to substantiate', Speaker, National Assembly, *Debates*, volume XI (30 March 1967), col. 1769. The Speakers have ruled that it is not necessary to prove the truth of the allegations, it is sufficient to indicate the source of the report or allegation.

[73] See, for example, the first Report of the Committee of Privileges, 5 April 1967 (mimeo., Nairobi); debate on it, volume XI (5 April 1967), cols. 2002–2027. See, also, the second Report of the Committee (mimeo), and the debate on it in the National Assembly (National Assembly, *Debates*, volume XII, part II (27 July 1967), cols. 2774–2780).

[74] Act No. 14 of 1966. The Standing Orders have also been amended to vest new disciplinary powers in the Speaker, see Standing Orders 88–92.

[75] See, generally, National Assembly (Powers and Privileges) Act; also Standing Orders 163–165.

however, has a sanction in the Standing Orders against a newspaper whose reporter persistently misrepresents its proceedings or refuses to publish satisfactory corrections—it can exclude a reporter of such a paper from the Press gallery.[76] Among the offences made punishable by the Act are disobedience to a lawful order of the Assembly or a committee to appear before it, answer questions or produce documents, obstruct officials in the course of their duties, commit slander or libel on the Assembly or its proceedings, and bribe or attempt to bribe a member to support or oppose a bill, motions, etc., in the Assembly.

To facilitate their work and to enable them to devote more time to constituency and parliamentary matters, the MPs have been secured financial independence. Each MP gets £1200 per annum, which is supplemented by a £120 constituency allowance and attendance and subsistence allowances when the Assembly or its committees are sitting. The Speaker gets £2000, plus £500 allowance and housing, while the Deputy Speaker, in addition to his parliamentary salary, gets an allowance of £400. The Chief Whip and the Deputy Chief Whip also get allowances of £400 and £150 respectively. Ministers get a salary of £3200 plus an allowance of £350 and housing; the Deputy Ministers £2200 plus housing. An allowance of £400 is also provided for the leader of the opposition, but only so long as the number of the opposition party equals the quorum in the Assembly, which at present excludes the opposition leader from the benefit of this provision.[77]

President Kenyatta once called Parliament 'our Council of elders', when he was claiming that 'our whole constitutional structure is rooted in our African traditions'.[78] A study of the procedures and proceedings of the National Assembly makes it difficult to support such a claim for Parliament. The language of Parliament, English, is not understood by the vast majority of the nation. The difficulties are compounded by the fact that the reading of speeches is not allowed; the Speaker has justified the prohibition on the grounds that such speeches are dull to listen to and 'there is always the possibility that the Hon. Member who reads it does not know the meaning of its content'.[79] It is true that some Ministers rely overmuch on the speeches written by their advisers, and the rule may have the salutary effect of helping

[76] Standing Order 165.
[77] The National Assembly Remuneration Act No. 20 of 1968. The Act also provides attendance and subsistence allowances for meetings of parliamentary groups, again with the proviso that the group's membership should equal or exceed the quorum of the Assembly. The Attorney-General's remuneration is set out in the Constitutional Offices (Remuneration) Act, No. 64 of 1968. He gets £3,200, plus housing and other benefits available to public officers.
[78] See above, chapter V.
[79] National Assembly, *Debates*, volume XII, part II (23 May 1967), col. 20. Standing Order 65 prohibits the reading of speeches.

them to understand their own policies. But it also affects the back-benchers adversely; and the use of a foreign language takes the edge off the procedure for supplementary questions and adjournment motions. It is, however, not just the language which is foreign; even more so are the procedural rules. The Standing Orders are by and large a faithful reproduction of the practice of the House of Commons—the paraphernalia of the mace and wigs, the restrictions on the points of order and the motions for adjournment, the notional conversion of the Assembly into the Committees of the whole House (with the change of presiding officers)—most of which are beyond the comprehension of the members. In an Assembly where the general educational level is not high, and few members possess legal qualifications, the written rules acquire an added mystique and become a hindrance to effective debate. The artificiality of the rules induces in the members a feeling of participating in a game. When the Speaker administered one of the most severe of the penalties the House can administer on an erring member—an open reprimand—there was much confusion as to the procedure, and considerable amusement and laughter among the members, so much so that the Speaker felt compelled to ask 'the Hon. Members not to treat it as a very funny matter'![80] Moreover, not many members fully understand the Constitution, and this also affects their performance, though they can hardly be blamed for this since only from the beginning of 1969 has there been an up to date edition of the Constitution in which it is possible to find what its provisions are.[81] A simplification of the procedural rules would seem desirable, even though in their favour it has been said that they help to preserve decorum and discipline, and reinforce the necessary authority of the Speaker.

FUNCTIONS OF PARLIAMENT

We now turn to the functions of Parliament, which may be divided into legislative and the formulation of policy, the control of finance, and the control of the Executive and the representation of the people. At one stage it had important electoral functions—it could in certain circumstances be called upon to elect the President; under the EACSO Agreement, it elected nine national (or 'territorial') members to the Central Legislative Assembly; and finally its elected members constituted an electoral college for the specially elected members. All these electoral functions have, however, now been abolished.

[80] National Assembly, *Debates*, volume XI (5 April 1967), col. 2026.

[81] Till the 1969 Constitution Act, by which time there had been eleven wide-ranging and important amendments acts, it was very difficult to find out what the constitutional provisions were. The Speaker had on several occasions criticized the lack of a clear, up to date edition of the Constitution, e.g. National Assembly, *Debates*, volume XII, part II (6 July 1967), col. 1974; volume IX (16 February 1967), col. 38.

(a) *Legislative*

Subject only to the provisions of the Constitution, Parliament has the power to make laws for the peace, order and good government of Kenya or any part thereof[82]—a formula which confers a plenitude of powers—and no other authority has a competing power. It has the power to make laws with retrospective effect (and often does)[83] but such effect cannot be given to a law which makes an act or omission a criminal offence, or increases the penalty for a crime, retrospectively.[84] There are certain provisions of the Constitution which restrict the competence of Parliament in its ordinary law making capacity; these include the basic constitutional structure itself, the independence of the judiciary, and human rights and citizenship provisions. However, even these provisions are alterable by Parliament when acting in its 'constituent capacity'. For an alteration of the Constitution, a Bill must be supported on the Second and Third Readings by the votes of at least 65 per cent of all the members of the National Assembly (excluding *ex officio* members).[85] The amendment procedure has thus been greatly simplified since independence, but one curious provision remains in force. When a Bill for a constitutional amendment has been introduced in the National Assembly, no alterations to the Bill can be made before its presentation to the President for his assent. If during the course of the debate it is decided to introduce a change, then the Bill has to be withdrawn and a new one introduced. It is a cumbersome procedure and its deletion has been urged.

The initiative for a Bill can come from any member of the Assembly, except in relation to finance, when only the Government can propose legislation. But how realistically can one say that Parliament makes law? The argument is often made that the role of the Legislature in law making is a small one; that the legislative process comes into it only in its advanced stage.[86] Proposals for legislation originate with the Government, which formulates its policy, sometimes after discussions with interests outside Parliament, reduces it to a draft Bill which is then for the first time presented to Parliament—often months after work began on it and generally by which time the Government's views have been crystallized. Under the circumstances, therefore, Parliament's role is sometimes little more than rubber stamping.

The above view can with some justification be applied to Parliament in

[82] Independence Constitution section 66. The Constitution no longer uses this phrase and merely vests the 'legislative power of the Republic' in Parliament (Constitution section 30). The competence of Parliament was not intended, nor would seem, to be affected by this change.

[83] See the Deputy Speaker's comments during the debate on the Maize Marketing Amendment Bill that retrospective legislation of government's administrative acts was 'quite normal' and he gave several examples of it. National Assembly, *Debates*, volume XI (22 March 1967), col. 1490. See, also, chapter VII, p. 305.

[84] Constitution section 77 (4).

[85] Constitution section 47.

[86] Griffith, 14 M.L.R. (1951), pp. 279–96 and pp. 425–36.

Kenya. Only once in the last fifteen years or so, has there been a private member's Bill, but it was on an important topic—hire purchase—and it was passed.[87] Until recently, it appeared that not all MPs knew of their right to propose legislation; moreover, the Standing Orders impose more stringent rules for Bills privately introduced than for those by the Government; in the former case the leave of the House to introduce the Bill, supported by an explanatory statement of its objects and reasons, is first necessary.[88] Furthermore, considerable expense is incurred by a private member who wishes to introduce a Bill, including fees for legal and drafting assistance, and there are few effective lobbies. It may help to encourage private initiative in this matter if services by the Government draftsmen could be made available to members who have obtained leave of the House to introduce legislation on a specific topic. It is, however, unlikely that private member's legislation will become important in the near future. An alternative to a private member's Bill is for the Government to take up a recommendation of a member to introduce particular legislation. It is unlikely that an individual member will be able to persuade the Government to adopt his proposals, but if a significant number agitate for it, the Government may respond by initiating legislative proposals. It is possible to regard the recent laws to accelerate Africanization of trade and commerce as a response of this kind.

The bulk of the National Assembly's legislative work is in connection with government measures. How effective is it? The Standing Orders provide ample scope for the discussion in the Assembly of the Government's proposals. The major stage for its criticism and discussion is the committee stage, at which vigorous and instructive debates have seldom taken place. It is also possible to refer a Bill to a Select Committee, if it is particularly controversial. It is seldom that a Bill is passed without considerable discussion of its principles. Nor is this discussion always without consequence. Members have been able to secure amendments to Bills and on occasions, when the opposition has been directed at the basic principles of a Bill, the

[87] Act No. 42 of 1968. The leave to introduce the Bill was first sought on 6 December 1967 (National Assembly, *Debates*, volume XIII, part II, col. 2903). At the same time the Speaker elaborated on the provisions of the Standing Orders. He explained that the motion appears as the Order Paper at the discretion of the Sessional Committee as to time, and if the House grants leave, it is then published like any other Bill but is in charge of the private member rather than the Government. It is important to distinguish a public Bill introduced by a private member, and a private Bill. A private Bill is defined as a Bill, introduced other than by a Minister, which is intended to affect or benefit some particular persons, association or corporate body. It can only be introduced after a petition for leave by its promoters has been first presented to the Assembly. The promoters have also to defray the cost of printing the Bill and certain other fees. See Standing Orders 116–125. See, also, Erskine May, *Parliamentary Practice* (London, Butterworths, 1957), 16th edition, chapter XXXI.

[88] Standing Order 95 (2).

Bill itself has been withdrawn. In 1966 a Dairy Industry Bill was introduced, but the widespread opposition to it led to its withdrawal by the Government.[89] Further discussion then took place on its provision and a revised draft was prepared, taking into account criticisms made in Parliament, which was subsequently passed by the Assembly. We have also seen that the constitutional proposals to provide for the automatic succession of the Vice-President to the Presidency in certain circumstances were withdrawn more than once due to opposition from back-benchers (and some front-benchers) and were finally abandoned.

Despite these instances when the Assembly has been able to exert its influence, its total impact on the substance of the legislation has not been significant. There are several reasons for this. First, the trend is towards increasingly complex legislation, often full of technical terminology; and the general style of drafting is by amendments to existing legislation, so that radical changes are made by a clause which says, for example, 'in section 2, for "14 days", substitute "3 months" '. Though the Standing Orders now provide that where a Bill seeks to amend a provision of an existing Act, the text of the original provision must be printed,[90] this is often not enough for the appreciation of the implications of the amendment. It is obvious from the debates that many members find difficulty with the technicalities of the language, nor are there more than three or four legally qualified members to provide the legal expertise which is so valuable in the work of a legislature. The result is that the members' criticism often lacks sharp thrust and precision and is the more liable to be ignored or to be deflected by verbal dexterity.

Secondly, the Government commands majority support in the Assembly, which, if effectively mobilized, enables it to disregard criticisms and counter-proposals. However, the price of this support is sometimes concession to its own back-benchers; this is generally arranged at a private meeting of the members of the party, but there have been occasions when it appeared that this procedure was not followed, and then if the back-benchers proved recalcitrant, the debate in the Assembly was adjourned to convene a private meeting to iron out the difficulties.[91] This process of informal consultation perhaps hides the real influence of the members of the Assembly, albeit the members of the ruling party. However, it is not always obvious who has made the concession; it is quite likely that in some cases the back-benchers are disciplined,

[89] The Dairy Industry Bill, 1966, was withdrawn and referred to a committee of enquiry—House of Representatives, *Debates*, volume X, part II (23 November 1966), cols. 1902–1931; (24 November), col. 1965; (8 December), col. 2545. See, generally, C. Gertzel, 'The Role of Parliament in Kenya', *East Africa Journal*, October 1968.

[90] Standing Order 96.

[91] e.g. House of Representatives, *Debates*, volume IV (18 February 1965), cols. 131–136. See, too, Gertzel, 'Parliament in Independent Kenya', *Parliamentary Affairs*, XIX, 4, 1966.

exhorted or cajoled. In assessing the role of Parliament in law-making, we can conclude that it is seldom passive, is sometimes able to mount effective pressure to amend provisions of a Bill, but that on the whole its criticisms do not result in changes in the legislative proposals. Generally, when a substantial number of members are opposed to a measure, the Government induces them to vote for the measure even though they may continue to criticize it.

We began this section by saying that Parliament has no competitor. This statement, however, does not mean that legislative powers cannot be exercised by any other body. Though there are no express provisions for the delegation of its legislative powers by Parliament, it can, and has, in fact, delegated them, but the authority with the delegated powers can only make laws within the terms of the delegation. Apart from subordinate law-making bodies like local government and ministerial authorities, the East African Legislative Assembly of the East African Community performs important legislative functions in relation to Kenya. The competence of the East African Legislature is wide and includes subjects like railways and harbours, postal telecommunications, aviation, statistics, university and specified research institutions and the machinery for revenue collection. The laws of the Community apply directly in Kenya; we shall examine later the legislation providing for it, when we also look at its implications.[92] Though the general rules of interpretation provide for a presumption in favour of the Community legislation in case of conflict with Kenya legislation, the Kenya Parliament can override the Community laws by express terms. Thus theoretically Parliament's powers have not been fettered by the Treaty of East African Co-operation, but in practice it involves an important surrender of its competence.

The President has also at various times held legislative power, some of it directly under the Constitution. The self-government Constitution as well as the independence Constitution gave the Governor-General certain law-making powers for limited periods.[93] The purpose defined the scope of the powers: he could make amendments to the existing laws necessary or expedient in his view for bringing that law into conformity with the provisions of the Constitution, or otherwise for giving effect or enabling effect to be given to those provisions; and he could make only such amendments as were within the competence of Parliament. These powers were thus narrowly circumscribed, and were to last until 12 December 1964. The first constitutional amendment Act continued these powers in the President in wider terms, for another year.[94] While the powers given at independence were

[92] Chapter XII.
[93] S.I. 791/1968, section 11; S.I. 1968/1963, section 4 (4).
[94] Section 14 (4), Act No. 28 of 1964; see, also, section 6, Act No. 14 of 1965.

restricted to bringing the law into conformity with the Constitution, in 1964 they extended to changes considered necessary or *expedient* in consequence of the amendment of the Constitution. The President also got limited powers to repeal the legislation already enacted by the Regional Assemblies.

Extensive use has been made of these powers, often to achieve purposes perhaps not explicitly warranted by the constitutional provisions.[95] Thus a large amount of legislative activity has taken place outside the precincts of the National Assembly. Finally, mention must be made of the wide legislative competence the President enjoys in relation to the North Eastern Province and contiguous districts.[96] Not only does the National Assembly not participate in the enactment of laws which can (and do) affect the vital interests, including the life, of the inhabitants of these sections of the country, but has in practice little control.

(b) *Financial Control*

The provisions for financial control of the Government are complex; Parliament plays an important but not exclusive role. The outlines of the provisions are found in the Constitution, and there is much detail in ordinary legislation and the Standing Orders. The system of financial control antedates the Constitution, which, however, entrenches the basic principles. The rules are modelled on the British system, and except for a few modifications, have been in operation since 1955. Before 1945, the machinery for the control of public expenditure was generally similar to that in other colonies and was designed to meet the requirements of an administration under which the Governor was responsible to the Secretary of State for the control of public expenditure, the Colony's estimates being approved by the Secretary of State and the Accounts of the Colony certified by the Director of Colonial Audit in Britain.[97] The Financial Secretary was responsible for financial policy, while the Accountant-General was the chief accounting officer at the head of a separate and self-contained department, thus leading to what was considered an undesirable divorce between the policy of finance and the machinery of finance, that is, the accounts. Under this system, the local legislature had only a tenuous control over expenditure and not much more over supply, especially in relation to the supplementary estimates, where the recommendations of the Standing Finance Committee were often not placed before the Legislative Council till long after the expenditure had been

[95] e.g. By Legal Notice 521/1963 members of Divisional Land Control Board were appointed, so bypassing the County Councils; Legal Notice 602/1963 amended National Assembly (Powers and Privileges) Act; Legal Notice 193/1965 the Entertainment Tax Act; Legal Notice 153/1965, the Public Order Act, and it would seem, going to the substance of the legislation.

[96] See chapter XI.

[97] See, generally, *A Summary of Events leading to the Introduction of the Exchequer System in 1955* (Nairobi, Government Printer, 1955).

incurred. The separation of policy and accounts also made legislative control more difficult since it was not easy to place responsibility for expenditure where it should properly lie.

The defects of the system were highlighted by two major constitutional changes—the devolution of financial responsibility by the Secretary of State to the Legislative Council in 1948; and the introduction of the membership system in 1945 which developed into the ministerial system in 1954 when individual Ministers became directly responsible to the Governor for the porfolios assigned to them. In 1948 a new budgetary procedure was adopted, and the procedure for the supplementary estimates was amended in 1952, so that all expenditure would in future be approved by the Legislative Council, either in the original or supplementary estimates, before being undertaken. In 1948 the Public Accounts Committee was set up for the examination of the accounts showing the appropriation of the sums granted for the public expenditure and any other accounts laid before the Council as the Committee deemed fit. In 1953 the Estimates Committee was established to investigate expenditure in the departments. Due to the tightening up of the supply system, it was realized that excess expenditure might have to be incurred in the public interest when there was insufficient time to obtain prior approval. As a result, a Civil Contingencies Fund was established in 1952.[98] The position and duties of the Auditor were placed on a statutory footing in 1952.[99] Finally, in the same year, the accounting machinery was placed under the control of the Treasury, so that both the financial policy and the accounting system became co-ordinated in one department. A review of all these developments was undertaken by a committee, which recommended the adoption of the British system. The recommendation was accepted and the Exchequer and Audit Ordinance was passed in 1955. The system thus created was continued under the Constitution, which entrenched the basic principles, and the office and functions of the Controller and Auditor-General, which had been first established under the 1955 Ordinance. In 1955 when the Ordinance was passed, the Minister for Finance remarked that the powers of the Kenya legislature of financial control were the same as those of the House of Commons and that it had been granted 'full parliamentary responsibility and control over expenditure as much as lies within the power of a government'.[100] What is the reality of control?

The Constitution lays down three basic principles.[101] First, no taxation or revenue can be levied without parliamentary authority. Secondly, no

[98] *Summary*, op. cit.
[99] Ordinance No. 14 of 1952. The position established was designated The Director of Audit.
[100] Legislative Council, *Debates*, volume 65 (19 May 1955), col. 687.
[101] Constitution sections 99 (1) and 48.

public money can be expended without the same authority. Thirdly, the initiative for financial legislation lies only with the Government. Much of the legislation on finance and many rules of the Standing Orders are intended to give effect to these three basic principles. The parliamentary control over revenue and expenditure is secured by the establishment of the Consolidated Fund, into which all revenue of the Government must be paid.[102] There are two general exceptions to this rule: [103] Parliament may authorize the establishment of other funds for specified purposes; and secondly, Parliament may provide that some of the revenue need not be paid into any established fund but may be retained by the authority which received it for defraying the expenses of that authority; this sum, however, is offset against the appropriations voted to the authority—neither of these exceptions compromises the principle. However, Parliament may establish a Contingencies Fund and authorize the Minister for Finance to make advances from that fund if he is satisfied that there has arisen an urgent and unforeseen need for expenditure for which no provision exists. In this instance there are two safeguards against executive disregard of Parliament. Parliament can fix the amount of the fund and the Government is obliged to present supplementary estimates to Parliament as soon as possible for the replacement of the sum borrowed.[104]

Parliament may prescribe the procedure whereby money may be withdrawn from the funds; it has done so through the Exchequer and Audit Act,[105] the Paymaster-General Act,[106] and the Civil Contingencies Fund.[107] The Exchequer and Audit Act vests the primary responsibility for the management of the Consolidated Fund in the Treasury, which in turn appoints accounting officers for the various votes appropriated by Parliament. The Paymaster-General is subordinate to the Treasury, and the Treasury controls the issue of money to the various Ministries and departments of the Government through him. Though the primary responsibility for financial policy is with the Treasury, each accounting officer is responsible for probity in relation to his own vote.

An essential part of the machinery for parliamentary control is the Controller and Auditor-General. Before we discuss his functions, and the other procedures for control, it is necessary to look at the third basic principle mentioned above—the initiative of the Government in introducing financial legislation and associated rules. Except on the recommendation of the President signified by a Minister, the National Assembly shall not proceed upon any Bill or any amendment to a Bill that in the opinion of the person presiding makes provisions for the imposition of taxation or the alteration of taxation otherwise than by reduction; for the imposition of any charge

[102] Constitution section 99 (1). [103] Constitution section 99 (2).
[104] Constitution section 102. [105] Cap. 412. [106] Cap. 413. [107] Cap. 425.

upon the Consolidated Fund or any other fund of the Government or the alteration of any such charge except by reduction; for the payment, issue or withdrawal from the Consolidated or other fund of any moneys not charged thereupon or any increase in the amount of such a payment, issue or withdrawal; or for the composition or remission of any debt due to the Government; nor can the Assembly proceed upon any motion or amendment to a motion, the effect of which is to make provision for any of those purposes.[108] Whatever the historical reasons for these restrictive rules (which have been taken from Britain),[109] they can today be justified on the grounds that the provision of finance is intimately connected with plans for social and economic development, for which the Government has the primary responsibility. The government monopoly of the policy of revenue and expenditure is also considered necessary to ensure economic and monetary stability. However justified the argument, the effect is to put serious restrictions on the control by Parliament, and to reduce its role to one of scrutiny and criticism.

The Minister for Finance prepares and lays before the National Assembly in each financial year estimates of revenue and expenditure of the Government for the following financial year.[110] It is important to distinguish between the procedures for revenue and expenditure. It has been provided by the Standing Orders that both sets of proposals are considered by Committees of the whole House—the Committee of Ways and Means for revenue and Supply for expenditure.[111] When the proposals have been approved by the Committee, they are embodied in two separate Bills, known as the Finance Bill and the Appropriation Bill respectively, and their passage into Acts constitutes authority for the collection and expenditure of revenue. As regards the collection of revenue, annual approval by Parliament is not required unless new or altered rates or taxes are introduced; whereas appropriations require such approval except for those charged to the Consolidated Fund by the Constitution or any other law, and Parliament has even provided that unless an Appropriation Act declares to the contrary, any moneys appropriated but not spent at the end of the financial year shall be surrendered to the exchequer account, that is, the Consolidated Fund.[112] The Appropriation Act specifies, under separate votes for the several services,

[108] Constitution section 48.
[109] See G. Reid, *The Politics of Financial Control* (London, Hutchinson, 1966), pp. 35–45. It is said that the Commons, aware of the unpopularity of levying taxes, were traditionally in favour of royal economy and, 'abstained from taking the initiative in offering money to the Crown'. Later the Commons, inundated by petitions from individuals for pecuniary relief, found the restriction on its competence useful and wrote it in its Standing Orders.
[110] Constitution section 100 (1).
[111] Part XVIII of the Standing Orders.
[112] Cap. 412, section 27.

the purposes for which the money is granted; and if the need for unforeseen or excess expenditure arises later, then supplementary estimates have to be introduced by the Government for a Supplementary Appropriations Act.[113]

Since the legislative process may delay the authority for collection and expenditure, and since it may be important to acquire the authority quickly to prevent the avoidance of payment, provisional measures have been provided for. Under the Provisional Collection of Taxes and Duties Act, as soon as a Bill is published in the Gazette providing for a new or altered duty or rate, the Minister can make an order for collection under the proposed terms.[114] Such an order ceases to be in force if the Bill is not introduced into the National Assembly within eight weeks of the order; or on the rejection or withdrawal of the Bill; or at the expiration of six months of the order (though Parliament may by resolution authorize its operation beyond the six months); or when the Bill becomes law. More stringent conditions exist for prior expenditure which are stipulated in the Constitution. If the Appropriation Act for any financial year has not come into operation, or is not likely to come into operation, by the beginning of the year, the National Assembly may, by a vote on account, authorize the withdrawal from the Consolidated Fund of moneys (not exceeding in total one-half of the sums included in the estimates of expenditure for that year that have been laid before the Assembly) for the purpose of meeting expenditure necessary to carry on the services of the Government during that year until such time as the Appropriation Act comes into operation (subject to being offset against the appropriation).[115]

We must now turn to the functions of the Controller and Auditor-General, for though appointed by the President, he is usually considered an officer of the National Assembly and helps in securing parliamentary control over finance. Nevertheless, in the actual performance of his duties, he is not subject to the direction or control of any person or body. In order to enable him to perform his functions, he has been given access to all the documents which he considers relevant.[116] His salary and tenure are well secured.[117] The function of the Auditor-General, as defined in the Constitution, is restricted to the expenditure of public money, but the Exchequer and Audit Act also vests him with responsibility in relation to the collection.[118] He is to satisfy himself that all reasonable precautions have been taken to safeguard the collection of revenue and to see that all lawful directions are obeyed—and thus to ensure that unless expressly excluded, it must all be paid into a

[113] Constitution section 100 (3).
[114] Cap. 415.
[115] Constitution section 101.
[116] Constitution section 105 (3).
[117] Constitution sections 104 (salary) and 110 (tenure).
[118] Section 11 (2) (a).

fund. Under the Constitution, withdrawals from the Consolidated Fund are possible only after this authorization, which he gives on satisfying himself that the proposed withdrawal is authorized by law. Further, he has to satisfy himself that all moneys that have been appropriated by Parliament and disbursed have been applied to the purposes for which they were appropriated, and that the expenditure is generally in conformity with the law. At least once in every year he has to audit and report on the public accounts of the Government, the National Assembly and the Commissions established by the Constitution. He may also report if at any time he feels an irregularity has been committed. The Constitution provides for him to audit governmental accounts, but it is possible for Parliament by resolution to direct that the accounts of any statutory board, commission or body shall be so audited as well. His reports have to be laid before the Assembly within seven days of their submission to the Minister.[119] If the Minister fails to do so, the Auditor-General can present the report direct to the Speaker.[120] Since Parliament itself is ill-adapted to exercise a continuous control and check on governmental expenditure, the role of the Auditor-General is extremely crucial, and his reports provide indispensable means whereby the Government can be called to account by the Legislature.

His reports are particularly useful for one of the two select committees specifically concerned with finance—the Public Accounts Committee.[121] When the Assembly has an official opposition party, the chairman and the majority of its members shall be from those not on the Government side; traditionally, the chairman would be the leader of the opposition. Its function is to examine the accounts showing the appropriation of the sum voted by the Assembly to meet the public expenditure and other accounts laid before the Assembly as it may think fit. Its primary concern is to see that the money has been spent for the appropriate purpose, rather than to examine how efficiently it has been used. Thus, while the Committee has a history of vigorous and searching scrutiny, its function is narrowly limited. The other select committee on finance—the Estimates Committee—has a greater 'policy' function.[122] It may examine such annual or supplementary estimates as it shall think fit or as are referred to it with a view to recommending what economies or improvements of form should be made in such estimates for the future, consistent, however, with the proper carrying into effect of the policies implied in or by such estimates. The number of items that can be looked at in this way is necessarily limited and as selection is somewhat random no overall assessment is possible, nor, as the estimates are only for one year, is it feasible to comment on the long term planning of particular projects.

[119] Constitution section 105 (4). [120] Cap. 412, section 23 (4).
[121] Standing Order 147. [122] Standing Order 146.

From this brief sketch of the financial provisions, it is obvious that Parliament does not exercise as much control as is often suggested. The initiative lies entirely with the Executive. At best the legislature has a power of veto, and the procedural rules are such that the outcome is weighted in favour of the Government. The Standing Orders provide that as a rule financial business has priority over other business, and if the estimates have not been approved by the allotted time, they shall be immediately put to a vote, without further debate.[123] The estimates are long and complex; it is doubtful if there is enough time for a thorough debate and only a few items get selected for detailed discussion. Because the estimates are yearly, the Assembly has little opportunity for control over long term expenditure and planning. In an age of five year (or longer) plans, this is a serious defect.

A vast amount of governmental policy is carried out through parastatal institutions, over whose finance Parliament has only limited control. Much of the public money is involved in the operation of railways and harbours, research facilities, postal services, and so on which do not at present come under the jurisdiction of the National Assembly. A large proportion of official activity is financed by loans or grants from foreign countries and institutions; there would seem to be no reason why Parliament should be consulted over grants, though in the case of loans, since their servicing is likely to be a charge on the Consolidated Fund, parliamentary approval would be needed. Even here, Parliament has tended to authorize the Government in the most general and broad terms to raise loans, thus abandoning any possibilities of control.[124] And once money has been raised, apparently painlessly, there is correspondingly less concern about its expenditure.

Finally, even if there are financial irregularities, there are no effective sanctions. In 1964 the Central Government refused to hand over the money that was claimed by the regions; there was no effective means of challenging its refusal. It is unusual for the supplementary estimates for the replacement of the Contingencies Fund to be rejected.[125] The ineffectiveness of parliamentary control is illustrated by the attempt of the opposition in 1964 to censure the Government for breach of the constitutional provisions. The Government had exhausted the Contingencies Fund by the end of 1963, but had not introduced supplementary estimates to replenish it. Early the next year, when the Government wanted money for further urgent and unforeseen expenditure, instead of going to Parliament for authorization, it asked the Treasury to make funds available by administrative action,

[123] Standing Orders 138 and 142.
[124] e.g. Loans Act No. 25 of 1966. cf. External Loans (Credit Purchases) Act, No. 23 of 1964, and Loans and Credit Facilities Act No. 12 of 1968.
[125] See, generally, Reid, op. cit., for the rhetoric and reality of parliamentary control over finance in Britain. The Kenyan procedures are similar to those in Britain.

from the money appropriated for other purposes, despite the objection of the Auditor-General and the opinion of the government lawyers that such a procedure was illegal.[126] The Auditor-General therefore reported the illegality to the National Assembly in accordance with the Exchequer and Audit Act, and the opposition moved a motion to censure the Government. The Government, while clearly in the wrong, successfully moved an amendment to the motion which took away all taint of criticism, and urged an increase in the Contingencies Fund.[127] Similarly, in 1967 the attempt of the Government back-benchers to prevent the reduction in a married person's tax allowance was frustrated by the pressure of whips.[128]

(c) *Criticism and Control of the Government*

Parliament's ultimate power of control over the Government lies, as we have previously seen, in the provisions of a vote of no confidence, which, if passed, can lead, depending on the decision of the President, either to the dissolution of Parliament or the resignation of the Government. This is a clear proof of the rule of executive accountability to the legislature and illustrates the principle that a government can stay in power only so long as it enjoys the confidence and support of the majority of the nation's representatives. Not all legislatures have this power, and the vesting of it in Parliament in Kenya points to the central position that was intended to be established for Parliament. In practice, however, these provisions have seldom acted as a threat to the Government, and while on several occasions it has made concessions to the back-benchers, it is likely that the motives have been other than the fear of a vote of no confidence. The power of removal of the Government is residual and is an extreme sanction. It is likely to be employed very rarely and only in the event of a fundamental alienation of the majority of the MPs from the politics of the Government. We shall see later why it is improbable that it will become a significant factor in the constitutional and political system, though its theoretical possibility must enhance the morale of the members.

At this point it would be apposite to state the position adopted by some writers who contend that it is not the function of a legislature to control the executive. The tasks of government are complex and require initiative and flexibility which are incompatible with parliamentary control.

[126] See the Auditor-General's special report to the National Assembly, appendix A in *Annual Report of the Controller and Auditor-General for the year 1963/64* (Nairobi, Govt. Printer).

[127] House of Representatives, *Debates*, volume III, part I (25 June 1964), cols. 616–634.

[128] Volume XII, part II (29 June 1967), cols. 1613–1626. The Government came under heavy attack for its proposals and lost on a motion to adjourn the debate. The motion for the proposals was then voted on and the Government lost. The Minister for Finance had said he would resign if defeated, but in fact no resignation took place.

A power of removal may be conceded, but only as a drastic way out in a drastic situation. Otherwise, Parliament discharges its responsibilities when it criticizes and proposes. How far can and does Parliament do this in Kenya?[129]

There are several rules which facilitate the function of criticism. We have already seen the opportunities provided for criticism in the debate on legislative and financial proposals. Secondly, it is usual at the opening of a session for the President to deliver an address, outlining the policy and the legislative programme of his Government. The address is followed by a motion to thank the President for his address, when a general and wide-ranging debate takes place on government policy.

Thirdly, questions may be put to the Ministers on matters of administration or policy, and each sitting of the Assembly normally begins by oral replies to the questions, though a member can request a written answer. Supplementary questions are allowed but only for the purpose of elucidating the answer to the original question. While the provisions for questions are very valuable, they do restrict rather narrowly the purposes for which they may be employed—in particular, a question cannot raise a matter of policy too large to be dealt with within the limits of an answer, and it cannot be made the occasion for a debate.[130] Fourthly, it is possible to move for the adjournment of the Assembly for a debate on a matter of government policy or administration. There are two kinds of adjournment motions for this purpose—adjournment on a matter of administration, which is generally a half hour debate at the end of a day's sitting, notice for which has previously been given and accepted;[131] and adjournment on a definite matter of urgent national importance, on acceptance by the Speaker that the matter is of such a nature and with support from at least fifteen members, when the Speaker nominates a time the same day for the debate.[132] Fifthly, it is possible to move a specific motion with the aim of raising issues of government policy,[133] though the Speaker has ruled that it is not possible to bring a motion of censure against an individual Minister in respect of the administration or policy of his Ministry.[134] This procedure can, however, also be used by the Government to rally support similar to the motion mentioned elsewhere moved by the Government that the House had confidence in it.

All these devices have been exploited by the members to criticize the Government and to try to make it accountable to the Assembly. We have

[129] e.g. Wheare, op. cit., and Griffith, op. cit.; Jennings, *Parliament Must Be Reformed* (London, Kegan Paul, 1941), p. 42; A. H. Hanson, 'Purpose of Parliament', *Parliamentary Affairs* (1964), volume XVII, No. 3; *Political Quarterly*, volume 36, No. 3.
[130] Standing Orders 35–39. [131] Standing Orders 17 (4) and 18.
[132] Standing Order 20. [133] Standing Order 40.
[134] National Assembly, *Debates*, volume XII, part II (19 July 1967), col. 2410.

already seen that the majority of legislative proposals are widely debated. The debate on the presidential address is generally thorough. Numerous questions are put to the Ministers and it is usual to follow up with supplementaries.[135] The procedure for adjournment motions is widely used, particularly the adjournment on administration, often as a follow up of an unsatisfactory answer to a question. The nation's major controversial issues have been discussed in this way—racial discrimination and Africanization policies,[136] the ban on political meetings of the opposition,[137] police brutality,[138] squatters and land settlement,[139] conduct of political parties and the civil service.[140]

[135] In the first session of Parliament (7 June 1963–29 November 1963), 208 questions were submitted and 158 answered in the House of Representatives; the figures for the Senate were 38 and 33. The figures for the second session (13 December 1964–22 October 1965) were House of Representatives 1917 and 1533; Senate 492 and 450; for the third session (12 November 1965–30 April 1966) House of Representatives 612 and 406; Senate 160 and 108; for the fifth session (15 February 1967–22 December 1967) notice of 1828 questions was given, out of which 126 received oral and 287 written answers; 75 were withdrawn by members.

[136] e.g. Volume X, part II (14 December 1966), cols. 2782–2799 (Eviction of Non-Africans from Municipal Market Stalls, debate under Standing Order 20); (16 December 1966), cols. 2897–2924 (Africanization of Kenya Army); cols. 2934–2944 (Africanization of the Kenya Police Force); volume XII, part I (30 May 1967), cols. 391–400 (Africanization in the Nairobi County Council); ibid. (23 May 1967), cols. 71–80 (Removal of Pumwani Asian Crematorium); volume XIV (29 March 1968), cols. 1303–1329 (Select Committee on Tribalism); volume XII, part II (7 July 1967), cols. 1962–1988 (Africanization in the country).

[137] Volume III, part III (21 October 1964), cols. 3739–3750 (Cancellation of Licence for Public Meeting); volume XIV (28 February 1968), cols. 153–161 (Members' Public Meetings in Constituencies); volume X, part I (7 October 1966), cols. 580–606 (Removal of Ban on Political Meetings); volume XIII, part I (3 November 1967), cols. 1655–1684 (Public Meetings by Party Leaders).

[138] Volume X, part II (22 November 1966), cols. 1803–1834 (Report of the Select Committee; Makupa Police Station Incident); volume XII, part I (7 June 1967) cols. 710-721 (Police Arrests at Riosori Market); volume XII, part I (13 October 1967) cols. 631–670 (Alleged Police Brutality).

[139] Volume XII, part II (23 November 1967), cols. 2383–2402 (Ceiling on Property Ownership by Foreigners); volume XIII, part I (6 October 1967), cols. 249–274 (Control on Ministerial Land Deals); volume XIII, part II (15 December 1967), cols. 3359–3382 (Select Committee to Investigate Ownership of Settlement Scheme Plots); volume XI (7 April 1967) cols. 2172–2189 and volume XII, part I (2 June 1967) cols. 498–511 (Settlement of State Lands); volume XI (28 February 1967), cols. 514–522 (Coastal Squatters: Land Ownership), (29 March 1967), cols. 1734–1745 (Van Arkadie Mission Report on Land Settlement); volume X, part II (2 December 1966), cols. 2316–2344 (Land Ownership: Compensation and Acreage Limitation); volume XIV (28 March 1968), cols. 1285–1293 (Alleged Illegal Occupation of Engoshura Farm by Freedom Fighters).

[140] Civil Servants: e.g. volume XI (5 March 1968), cols. 428–437 (Frequent Transfer of Civil Servants); volume X, part I (14 October 1966), cols. 870–900, (28 October 1966), cols. 1382–1399 (Irregularities in Employment and Tribalism); volume XII, part I (16 June 1967) col. 1062 (Appointment of Civil Service); volume XXII, part II (11 July 1967) cols. 2061–2072 (Politicians Addressing District Commissioners' *Barazas*); volume XV (7 June 1968) cols. 649–675 (Status of Provincial Commissioners); volume XII, part II (21 July 1967), col. 2576 (Appointment of Chairmen to Statutory Boards).

For political parties, see footnote 137 above; House of Representatives, *Debates*, Volume X, part I (28 September 1966), cols. 158–168 (Threats to KPU supporters); House of Representatives, *Debates*, volume VIII (3 March 1966), col. 1693 (forthcoming KANU elections).

On occasions the members have pushed their concern on a matter further, as when they were dissatisfied with the action taken by the Government to deal with police officers at Makupa police station in Mombasa alleged to have beaten up innocent persons. The Assembly set up a select committee to inquire into the incidents and to report to it.[141] The Committee found the allegations of brutality justified.[142] A further debate was held in the Assembly, and while these proceedings show the possibilities of action open to the Assembly in examining and exposing maladministration, they also highlight its inability to do more; the Government may have been chastened by the proceedings and warned that its maladministration would not pass unnoticed or unquestioned, but it could not be forced into a specific course of action which it was unwilling to take.[143]

The debating function of the Assembly should not, however, be underestimated. Its debates are free and uninhibited, and the convention that even the most serious and sensitive matters can be raised in the Assembly helps to keep Kenya's political system remarkably open. While the members of the opposition may have difficulty in obtaining permission to hold meetings, they are free to use the Assembly to air their views, and in the latter half of 1968 at any rate the Assembly has been the major forum for the projection of their policies. A careful perusal of the debates gives a clear and accurate picture of the political problems and trends in the country. MPs are generally concerned with their popularity in their own constituencies and so important local grievances with the administration get raised in the Assembly. The Assembly is still the place whose membership of and performance in are crucial for political advancement. Both the President and the Ministers have to be members of Parliament, and a person who has political aspirations has to look to Parliament and prove his ability there.

[141] House of Representatives, *Debates*, volume IX, part I (31 May 1966), col. 183. Matter first raised under a question. Due to the unsatisfactory nature of the reply, the matter was debated on an adjournment motion, cols. 509–524 (9 June). It was raised again and the Select Committee appointed, volume IX, part II, col. 1299. One important reason why the MPs pursued the matter with such vigour was their feeling that the Government had tried to mislead the Assembly. One of its specific terms of reference was to investigate whether the misinformation by the Assistant Minister for Home Affairs was deliberate.

[142] House of Representative, *Debates*, volume X, part II (22 November 1966), cols. 1803–1834.

[143] ibid., col. 1834. For a detailed account of the episode, see Gertzel in *Parliamentary Affairs*, op. cit. Adopting the report of the Committee, the MPs urged legal action against the police officers. The Speaker pointed out that the House could not direct the Government to prosecute or take executive action, since in this respect the Government was supreme. Asked what implications this ruling had for the supremacy of Parliament, the Speaker explained that the ultimate supremacy of Parliament lies in that 'if Government too frequently, with too little reason, ignores the recommendations of this House, it is liable to a vote of no-confidence'—col. 1883.

The representational functions of an MP, however, tend to get confused due to the position and behaviour of the local administrative officer, to whom complaints still tend to be taken, rather than the MP. There has been considerable hostility between the politicians and the civil servants, especially the district and provincial administrators who have been accused of continuing the colonial mentality of regarding politicians as enemies. The KANU Government inherited a strong system of provincial administration and the MPs have repeatedly complained that the Government has employed the administrators to undermine the position of the politicians, particularly those belonging to the opposition, whose applications to hold public meetings are almost always turned down. The local administrators have been used both for executive and exhortative functions; power is seen to reside in the administrators, so their appeal is often more effective than that of the politicians. Recently the government has urged a closer identification between the administrators and KANU, striking at the root of the principle of civil service neutrality in a multi-party system. The vexed question of the relationship between the local administrators, and the politicians and the party was discussed at the KANU conference in Nakuru in 1968, which the Provincial Commissioners were invited to attend and where they were allegedly urged to identify themselves with and serve the ruling party, since it constituted the government to which they had pledged loyalty. The relationship between the provincial administrators and the local party officials was discussed, and it was recommended that when the District Commissioner held a *baraza*, he should invite the party officials to share the platform with him; further, a code of behaviour was to be drawn up on this matter. The conflict, however, appears to have been unresolved, and in June 1968 a motion was introduced and debated in Parliament that either the Provincial Commissioners should be *ex officio* members of Parliament and thus accountable to Parliament, or that political commissioners should be appointed in the provinces to deputize for the President; the majority support tended to be for the latter alternative. The debate revealed a wide degree of resentment on the part of the MPs against the administrators for the latter's lack of respect for the former, and at what they regarded the usurpation of their function of representation.[144]

[144] e.g. National Assembly, *Debates*, vol XIII, part II (3 November 1967), col. 1656 (allegations that District Commissioners are instructed not to license meetings), also volume XIII, part I (16 June 1967), col. 1064; volume XII, part II (11 July 1967), col. 206 (allegations that Ministers use administrators to attack opponents); volume X, part I, cols. 256–257 (a debate on the lack of co-operation between the civil servants and politicians). An MP complained, 'These days, the Voice of Kenya is trying to give much more publicity to civil servants than to politicians who are the actual leaders of the people. So a district officer all of a sudden becomes the leader of the people, the Provincial Commissioner is more or less the chief of the whole area, and so forth . . . A politician must be given due recognition and a civil servant kept in his place', col. 261; volume XV (7 June 1968), cols. 649–674 (debate that Provincial Commissioners

The effect of the activities of the Assembly is difficult to quantify. There is value for a political system in the articulation of views and grievances. It is useful that the Government should realize that its actions are watched and policies scrutinized. Doubts, however, remain of the real influence of the members. There are issues, like electoral laws, land and Africanization, where the back-bench opinion does appear to have influenced policy, but on many other issues the impression is gained that the Government ignores the views expressed in the Assembly. It has also shown little support for the ministerial committees which were set up in 1967 to enable MPs to be conversant with the policies of various Ministries, so that they may discharge more efficiently their function of review and constructive criticism. Despite the vigour of the debates, the Government has all too often been easily able to get its way in respect of controversial or unpopular policies and the Assembly has seemed to be impotent. The Government has ignored the persistent pressure by it to Africanize the judiciary and other public legal offices. Despite agitation to put a ceiling on landholding and a resolution that a Committee be set up to advise on it, no action has been taken in this direction. The Government has likewise not responded to a resolution to bring about greater political union among the three East African countries.[145] Allegations have been made that the Sessional Committee, which has a majority of the ruling party with considerable ministerial representation, has disregarded the wishes of the back-benchers.[146] There have also been accusations that the Government has deliberately misled members.[147] The attendance of the Ministers in the Assembly is poor, not least at question time, and on at least one occasion the Assembly adjourned its sitting due to the absence of ministers.[148] All too often, the Government has come with retrospective bills, to legalize actions deliberately undertaken by it knowing them to be against the law. Therefore, while it is important to make the point that Kenya's Parliament is perhaps the most vigorous in independent Africa, it is also a fact that its influence on the Government has been determined less by its own pressure

should be *ex officio* members, etc.). On 4 November 1968, the Vice President, addressing an inter-African public administration seminar in Nairobi, urged the politicians and the civil servants to co-operate and attempted a delineation of their respective functions, see *East African Standard*, 5 November 1968.

[145] National Assembly, *Debates*, volume XI (16 February 1967), cols. 36–38 (judiciary); House of Representatives, *Debates*, volume III, part I (18 June 1964), col. 322 (E.A.Federation).

[146] House of Representatives *Debates*, volume IV (17 February 1965), col. 82.

[147] National Assembly, *Debates*, volume XI (21 March 1967), col. 1357. See also footnote 141.

[148] e.g. House of Representatives, *Debates*, volume VIII (4 March 1966), cols. 1743–1746; National Assembly, *Debates*, volume XI (21 February 1967), col. 190. On another occasion, the Speaker did not allow a motion for postponement of debate due to the absence of Ministers, on the grounds that the back-benchers had themselves hardly shown the kind of interest 'which is being expected of the Ministers'—volume XII, part I (21 June 1967), col. 1216.

than by the Government's volition. In sum, the impression which is given from observing relations between the Government and the National Assembly is that there is great activity and excitement in the latter which impinge but rarely on the former, and then only when and to the extent that that body wants it to. The gradual withering away of collective responsibility, described in an earlier chapter, has contributed to this state of affairs, and may be re-emphasized in the context of the present discussion. Other factors have, however, contributed and may now be discussed.

Much of the discussion of the role of the National Assembly assumes a certain degree of tension, if not hostility, between it and the Government. In most modern parliamentary systems of government this assumption is no longer valid due to the development of the political parties; and in any case in Kenya we have seen how the rules for the election of the President and the Assembly aim to remove the tension. Again, a large proportion of the members are part of the Government—about one third, who do in fact support the Government by vote, albeit sometimes rather reluctantly. Now the presidential power of nomination will ensure further support for it. A further number are also rendered ineffective by their appointment to statutory boards and corporations, which carry rich financial rewards.[149] The Government's control of patronage has been fundamental in the attrition of the influence of the Assembly, as it was of the opposition.

What is the position of a parliamentary opposition party now? The Constitution does not explicitly recognize an opposition, but the cumulative effect of its Bill of Rights is to prohibit a one party state. Nor was there any provision in the Standing Orders at independence, though initially the practices of the British House of Commons were applied. Kenya began its independence with opposition parties, but less than a year later it had become a *de facto* one party state. The group of MPs who broke away from KANU in April 1966 sought the recognition of their status as a formal opposition from the Speaker. He found that the breakaway members:

> intend to function not merely as a group of independent individuals, but as a definite Opposition in the true sense; that is to say, offering to the House and to the nation an alternative Government with a definite alternative policy, and with their leader as alternative President of the Republic.

He then elaborated the principles governing the recognition as an opposition:

> there can be a Parliamentary group or party, whether or not supported by any external or country-wide political party. Therefore, although no country-wide

[149] In answer to a question the Government stated on 31 May 1967 that there were 20 MPs, other than Ministers and Assistant Ministers, who held positions of members, directors or chairmen on statutory boards, which carried pecuniary benefits in the form of allowances, stipends or salaries (National Assembly, *Debates*, volume XII, part I (31 May 1967), col. 487). The number of Ministers is 22 and of Assistant Ministers 29.

> political party other than the Kenya African National Union has yet been registered, this group of Members is entitled to be recognised in this House as a separate Parliamentary party. Moreover, since this Parliamentary party is offering an alternative Government, and is prepared in the event of the resignation of the present Government, to assume office, it is entitled to recognition in this House as an official Opposition.[150]

The recognition ensured the KPU certain rights—its motions had precedence over any other business on alternative Fridays, its leader became the Chairman of the Public Accounts Committee, and also became entitled to a special salary as Leader of the Opposition. At the end of 1967, however, new Standing Orders were introduced which deal expressly with the position of opposition parties. The Orders define a party as a 'parliamentary party consisting of not less than seven members'.[151] A distinction is made between an opposition party, which presumably must have at least seven members, and an 'Official Opposition Party', which could be a coalition of parties, but whose membership must be a minimum of thirty.[152] At this time the strength of KPU was below this figure. The difference between the rights of an opposition and an official opposition is that only the leader of the latter is entitled to the chairmanship of the Public Accounts Committee and to a special salary. The right to precedence of business and the convention that it should have fair representation on the committees of the Assembly are equally available.[153] The stipulation of a minimum of seven members, however, does mean that an opposition group could have no special rights—the present opposition, the KPU, has for some time carried on with a precarious number of seven members. The Speaker has been careful to safeguard the rights of the opposition and constantly urged that minority views be heard, but recently the members of the majority party have shown impatience with parliamentary convention which supports this position.[154]

The members of the opposition have played an active part in the proceedings of the Assembly and made a full contribution to its debates. They have asked questions, criticized policy, moved adjournment motions and proposed new policies. Its leader, as chairman of the Public Accounts Committee, has a record of careful and constructive scrutiny of expenditure. But inevitably the small size of the opposition has meant that too much work falls on a few persons, who also have to shoulder more than their fair burden of committee work. The influence of the opposition on official policy has, naturally, been negligible. Even if its size were bigger, it is doubtful if it

[150] House of Representatives, *Debates*, volume VIII (28 April 1966). (The African People's Party had joined KANU in September 1963.)
[151] Standing Order 2.
[152] ibid.
[153] Standing Order 33 (a). See also Speaker's ruling, National Assembly, *Debates*, volume XIV (29 February 1968), col. 163.
[154] National Assembly, *Debates*, volume XIV (27 February 1968), cols. 26–35.

would command greater influence. While the concept of a parliamentary opposition is accepted in Kenya's constitutional system, the Government accepts it only grudgingly and subjects its members to considerable harassment, and its legitimacy has still to be established. Unless that happens, the role and prestige of the opposition is unlikely to be significant.

As is often the case, the Government has had to pay more attention to its own back-benchers than to the opposition. Normally the control of the majority party by the Government ensures its supremacy, and is regarded as the single most important factor in the decline of legislatures. In Kenya the majority party has never been tightly organized and it is primarily the lack of the Government's control over its back-benchers which has made Parliament a lively institution. The Government majority has, however, always been a comfortable one and except for questions of constitutional amendments in the early days of independence with KADU still in the opposition, the back-benchers have not been crucial. In any case, despite all the criticism they may make of a government policy, they rarely vote against it. Nevertheless the Government has tried to curb the exuberance of its back-benchers. It was during the period when Kenya was a *de facto* one party state—end of 1964 to early 1966—that the back-benchers were most critical—they felt that in a one party system, this was their primary function.[155] Apart from the KANU parliamentary group, which included all the MPs, the back-benchers had their own KANU group, which amounted almost to an organized opposition and caused considerable embarrassment to the Government. Pressure was brought on them to disband this group and it was argued that all that was needed was a KANU parliamentary group.[156] After considerable initial resistance, it was agreed to dissolve the back-benchers' organization.[157]

Control over back-benchers may now be exercised through the parliamentary group. KANU's constitution provides that its President shall be the leader of the parliamentary group, which consists of all its members in the legislature and other MPs who accept the party's whip and are admitted by the group. It is provided that the parliamentary group shall be under the direct supervision of the President of the party, who shall report to the Governing Council and the National Executive Committee on its work, activities and general behaviour. The group is responsible for tactics and programmes within Parliament but has no power to initiate policy. Members have to accept the control of whips and the President or the National Executive Committee can expel any member for disregard of policy. If it functioned according to these rules, the group could be an important factor in controlling

[155] House of Representatives, *Debates*, volume IV (17 February 1965), col. 82 et seq.
[156] See, *East African Standard*, Nairobi, 14 July 1965.
[157] *East African Standard*, 22 July 1965.

the back-benchers. But the party has never succeeded in maintaining this control. It has been suggested that the reason for it is the weak organization of the party—its meetings and elections have been infrequent and irregular and there has not been an adequate machinery for any debate on policy or articulation of grievances.[158] Nor is the group always consulted on the proposed legislation. Consequently dissatisfied members have used the forum of the Assembly for this purpose, highlighted by a debate in 1966 on the organization of the party under an adjournment motion.[159]

Under these circumstances, it has been the President who has imposed some cohesion and discipline on the group. When there is deadlock between the front- and back-benchers, the President's personal intervention is necessary to resolve it. He himself does not take an active part in the proceedings of the Assembly, rarely attending it, but a kind of convention has emerged that if the back-benchers persist in their opposition, a meeting with the President would be arranged, and the Assembly has on occasions adjourned expressly for this purpose.[160] The present President's hold upon the back-benchers arises in large part from his own charisma, but it is arguable that the presidency itself is inherently a powerful position for the performance of this function. It could indeed be argued that one of the reasons for the relative unimportance of the Assembly is the powerful position established for the President. We have already seen his relationship with the Assembly, but two points may be made which are relevant to our present discussion. Preferment to high political office depends on the President and an ambitious back-bencher will seek to avoid defiance of official policy. Secondly, the President has the power to dissolve Parliament, the threat of which would often be effective to overcome the recalcitrance of back-benchers.

The Speaker's rulings may be mentioned here. While they have been helpful in some areas, they have sometimes inhibited parliamentary control. His interpretation of collective responsibility has prevented attacks on individual Ministers for their policy.[161] As a result, the pre-eminence of President Kenyatta provides a shelter for too many, and debate is unnecessarily stifled. The Speaker has also ruled that the Government has no obligation to answer questions from the members.[162] He has also disallowed debates on important matters on the ground of the members' oath of loyalty to the Constitution. Thus members have been prevented from discussing the desirability of separate Kadhi's courts for the enforcement of Muslim law since the Constitution provides for their establishment;[163] and debate on

[158] See J. Okumu, 'Charisma and Politics in Kenya', *E.A.J.*, February 1968.
[159] House of Representatives, *Debates*, volume VIII (3 March 1966), col. 1693 and cols. 1727–1740.
[160] See footnote 91.
[161] See chapter VI.
[162] National Assembly, *Debates*, volume XI (February 1967), col. 1974.
[163] See chapter IX, footnote 26.

Africanization has been curbed, unless this is understood to mean Kenyanization.[164] Except on one occasion, he has ruled out of order debates on matters concerning political parties (even at a time when the country was a *de facto* one party state) unless they relate to the question of administration by the Government.[165]

There is a significant delegation of legislative and administrative responsibilities to the East African Community. The Government remains responsible to the Assembly for its role in the Community and for its policies. But in the very nature of things, such responsibility is tenuous and difficult to enforce. The Government can too easily shift responsibility onto its partners,[166] and in any case does not normally depend on the Assembly for legislation in these matters. Similarly, a large amount of official activity, carried on through parastatal institutions, is excluded from effective parliamentary scrutiny; the occasions for debate on their affairs are few, and even when offered, for example, on presentation of an annual report, are rarely taken up by the MPs.

Finally, a measure of blame must be ascribed to the members themselves. They do not always do the necessary home-work, and therefore, while the debates are vigorous, they are not always equally informed and debates at the committee stage are particularly poor. They have displayed a considerable degree of selfishness; the two issues on which they have been most agitated are those concerning their own position and privileges, and the alleged slowness in Africanizing the public and private sectors, when they have given expression to extreme racialism. On other, more fundamental issues, they have been quite compliant; thus they have been prepared to vote the Government wide powers under the Preservation of Public Security Act without satisfying themselves of the need for them;

[164] e.g. National Assembly, *Debates*, volume XII, part II (7 July 1967) col. 1973 and (11 July 1967), cols. 1989–1991.

[165] The Speaker ruled that only matters of administration could be raised under an adjournment motion, and disallowed the discussion of the party's internal organization. '[I]n spite of having only one party, internal party affairs are not the responsibility of Government as such. The party leaders and the Government are not always the the same . . . . You may have one person with two functions, a party leader who is also a Minister. But you have to distinguish between the functions, and we are only free to discuss, under this procedure, something which concerns the Government of the country.' He conceded, nevertheless, in this case that 'where you have only one party, to which all the members are supposed to belong, and where the President is also the head of that party, and the declared purpose of the meetings is to hear from Government what government policy is, then I think that it is difficult to say that it is not connected with the administration of this country'. National Assembly, *Debates*, volume XIII (3 March 1966) col. 1993 et seq.

[166] cf. The budget debate in 1967 when the Minister of Finance argued that the reduction in the married persons tax allowance was a joint decision of the three East African governments, though he offered to take responsibility and resign if the reduction was rejected. National Assembly, *Debates*, volume XII, part II (29 June 1967), cols. 1608 and 1616. See also col. 1613, and see footnote 128, above.

and were all too willing to extend their own life as members of Parliament. Even allowing for the unnecessary complexity of rules of procedure, they have made little effort to master them, or exploit them to their own benefit.

CONCLUSION

In the kind of parliamentary system that Kenya has, the role that the National Assembly plays depends largely on the Government. The official rhetoric is full of the supremacy of Parliament and its control over the Executive. It is true that the Government has promoted several constitutional changes to increase its legislative powers. While the increased legislative power of Parliament can be justified on the ground of its democratic nature, it is important to notice that in practice such increased powers do not necessarily have the effect of heightening its stature. The executive control of Parliament means that the enlarged competence of the Legislature has merely resulted in the Executive becoming more powerful. The effect of many of the earlier restrictions on Parliament was to prevent its authorization of the Executive doing certain things. The removal of the restrictions has meant that the Government has been able to get the authorization from Parliament.

It is significant that while Parliament's legislative competence has increased, its control over the Executive has decreased. The weakening of control can be seen in the modifications that have taken place in the procedure for the removal of the Government, and in its role in the operation of emergency powers. At independence, the House of Representatives could pass a resolution of no confidence in the Government, and if within three days the Prime Minister did not resign or advise a dissolution, the Governor-General could dissolve Parliament. No special notice of the resolution had to be given, nor was any special majority required for its passage. At present the rule is that seven days' notice of the motion must be given, and for the passage of the motion there must be a majority of all the members of the House. Secondly, the Executive did not have unfettered powers of dissolution, as it does now. The Governor-General could refuse the request of the Prime Minister for a dissolution if he considered that government could be carried on without a dissolution and that a dissolution would not be in the interests of Kenya.

In relation to emergencies, no declaration of emergency could be made by the Executive without the prior authority of Parliament if it was then sitting; if it was not sitting, then a meeting had to be summoned and the declaration ratified within a week of its announcement. Today, there is no requirement of previous parliamentary authorization; and the period within which approval must be obtained is twenty-eight days. There is no obligation to recall Parliament if it is not sitting, and indeed the twenty-eight days do not begin to run till Parliament meets, and stop running if Parliament adjourns—thus enabling a presidential declaration to operate for conceivably several months before Parliament has a chance to pronounce on it. After independence, the two houses of Parliament had to approve of the declaration by votes of 65 per cent of all their members; while it was always open to either house to revoke the declaration by a majority of all the members. Now a simple majority is sufficient for approval, while for the revocation, an absolute majority is required, thus making it easier to grant, than to control, the extensive powers that are thus given to the Executive. Initially, a resolution approving the declaration was in force for only two months; later the period was extended to eight months, and now it remains in force indefinitely.

It might be argued that the Government has seen fit to increase the powers of Parliament in order that Parliament may in turn give the Government more powers. Even the amendment which the Government put through Parliament to force the resignation of those members who leave their parliamentary party, though purportedly to strengthen the electorate and Parliament, had the effect of strengthening the Government. Similar comments can be made on the electoral changes requiring the nomination of a party, and the President's power to nominate twelve members to Parliament. The changes in the Standing Orders, especially in respect of the opposition, discussed in this chapter, are also hardly consistent with the aim of strengthening Parliament. Likewise the extension of the life of the present Parliament indicates little concern for its democratic and representational functions.

An active and vigorous legislature was one of the institutions which Kenya inherited at independence. Combined at that time with its newly acquired democratic character, it had a potentially important role as an instrument of legitimation of the new political and constitutional order. Since independence, the thrust of the Government's constitutional changes, and administrative and political practices has been to whittle down the controlling function of the legislature, and curb its political effectiveness. While they have to some extent succeeded in the former aim, they have not yet managed to bring MPs to heel and thus reduce the Legislature to a greater degree of conformity. Kenya can still boast an active and energetic legislature, and it may well be in the interests of the Government that it should allow Parliament to perform the role which was assigned to it by the makers of the Constitution.

CHAPTER IX

The Administration of Justice: 1. Courts and Law

INTRODUCTION

The administration of justice in the colonial era had been characterized, as had all administration in that era, by the dual system. There was one system of justice for non-Africans and another for Africans. The African system had in turn been characterized by the use of the courts as an integral branch of the administration rather than as institutions independent of the administration. The courts had also, inevitably, been used as 'agents of modernization', introducing into the reserves, concepts, ideas, and rules alien to the traditional pattern of life there, and displacing customary rules and procedures in the process. It was to be expected that an African government would wish to abolish the dual system, and at the very least loosen the ties between the provincial administration and the courts, but short of attempting to revert to traditional judicial institutions, the use of the courts as agents of modernization would continue. The important question was, what specific modern values and ideas would an African government try and introduce via its reformed courts and laws?

The main thrust of development in colonial times was to displace African courts and laws with courts and laws owing their inspiration to the English legal system and common law, but with variations to take account of local circumstances, and the necessities of colonial rule. Since 1960, the thrust of development has been in the same direction, but the tempo has been slightly stepped up, and in some areas there has been an attempt to introduce a less diluted version of the English legal system. In several significant places, however, some of the characteristics of the colonial legal system have been retained. What has not occurred is an attempt to create a more African legal system for Kenya—to blend together African and English legal ideas and rules such as was sometimes rather half-heartedly attempted in the colonial period. The Government seems to have decided that such attempts were still-born, and a modern unified legal system can only be built on the imported English base. In this chapter we will examine how far this has been achieved in courts and law reform in the 'sixties.

REFORM OF THE COURTS

In 1960, while the administrative role of courts for Africans was perhaps more muted than previously, there were still many obvious signs of the differences between justice for Africans and non-Africans. Some courts had greater civil and criminal jurisdiction over Africans than non-Africans. An African could not appeal to the Supreme Court from any decision, civil or criminal, given in an African court, though the criminal jurisdiction of some African courts was greater than that of a third class magistrate, from whose decision an appeal could be taken to the Supreme Court. Only Africans were subject to the jurisdiction of the African courts. The African courts were still under the control of the provincial administration whereas other courts were under the control of the Supreme Court.

It was clear that such a system would not last long under an African government. In addition, increasing outside interest was being shown in the development of law in Africa, and one of the first matters which it was felt should be reformed was the dual system of courts; integration of courts was the order of the day. The colonial authorities had always envisaged that ultimately integration would take place so that the advent of an African government might have been expected to alter the tempo, but not the direction, of change in Kenya. The reforms that took place, together with changes consequent upon constitutional developments in Kenya and East Africa, fall into four parts: administrative reforms up to the end of 1962; legislative reforms of 1962–3; administrative reforms 1963–7; and finally legislative reforms of 1967.

(a) *Administrative reforms to the end of 1962*

It is a feature of the reform of the courts in Kenya in this period that administrative changes preceded major legislative changes rather than vice versa, legislation being to confirm what the administrators had done, as much as to provide the framework for future administrative changes. This is justified on the ground that it prevents chaos during the introduction of a new system by allowing administrators to pace the changes in a realistic manner. It would not, however, have been impossible to do this if legislation had come before administration, and perhaps a more accurate reason for the procedure adopted was that it was the traditional way of reforming the inferior courts in Kenya, and in the new political atmosphere of the 1960s it had the additional merit of presenting the legislature with a *fait accompli*. It stands also as a reminder of the great control the administration retained over the African courts in this period, that many far-reaching reforms could take place without the need for legislation.

The administrative reforms of the period up to the end of 1962 concentrated on the creation of new posts in the African courts' system, the consequent rearrangement of the composition and jurisdiction of the courts, and the institution of training programmes to equip African court holders with sufficient legal knowledge to justify giving them increased responsibilities.[1] (It should not be forgotten, however, that even before the introduction of these training programmes at the beginning of 1961, African courts had a considerable statutory criminal jurisdiction, that was continually being extended, notwithstanding the criticisms of the Phillips Report of 1944.[2]) The new posts which were created were Senior District and District Registrars (African Courts) staffed by members of the African courts' service whose function it was to take over the supervisory role which administrative officers had previously exercised over African courts. The composition of the courts was standardized; in future they were to consist of two or three panels, each panel having three members with a quorum of two. The panels were composed of both old experienced members and younger less experienced, but more formally educated, members and it was these members who in 1962 were appointed to the new post of recording member of the court, if they had passed the relevant law examination. As their name implies, they were required to keep a record of the proceedings. The jurisdiction of the courts was also rearranged; some were given both appellate and district-wide jurisdiction while others remained first instance and divisional courts only.

All these changes had taken place while the African courts were still controlled by officers of the provincial administration. The figures of the number of cases heard by them show too that they were still regarded and used primarily by the administration as police courts; indeed the figures suggest that this trend had been accentuated over the years since the Phillips Report. In 1959 the courts dealt with 180,000 criminal, tax and rate cases, and 48,000 civil cases. In 1962 the first class of cases rose to 306,000, the second fell to 38,700.[3] Clearly it would require more than formal rearrangements of control and composition before the image of the courts as organs of the administration changed.

(b) *Legislative reforms, 1962-3*

1962 saw important reforms in the African courts' system brought about by legislation which marked a definite step towards the integration of the courts. By the African Courts (Amendment) Act,[4] changes were introduced into the system of appeals, representation, and responsibility for the courts. Appeals on statutory criminal law matters could in future go up to the Supreme Court, though the powers of that court might be, and in practice

[1] *African Conference on Local Courts and Customary Law (1963)*, Report (n.d.) (published by Faculty of Law, Dar es Salaam), appendix C. Background Papers, No. 6, Review of Developments in Kenya since 1959, pp. 87–91. T. E. Barnett, *A Report on Local Courts in East Africa* (1965) (mimeo.), pp. 31–57 and 133–44.
[2] See chapter IV. For extensions, see *African Conference*, op. cit., pp. 88–9.
[3] ibid., p. 89.
[4] No. 50 of 1962.

were, exercised by a magistrate with first class powers. Appeals on civil and customary criminal matters still lay to the Court of Review as the final court of appeal, but the composition of that court was changed. The Chief Native Commissioner and the lawyer-chairman disappeared, a judge of the Supreme Court becoming the new chairman. The African Courts Officer remained a member, though, as a result of other changes introduced by the Act, his office in future came under the jurisdiction of the Supreme Court. The two African members of the court were to be appointed by the Chief Justice. Representation was still not permitted in the African Courts but in a statutory criminal case an accused might apply to a magistrate for a transfer to a subordinate court on the grounds that he wished to be represented by an advocate, and the magistrate, on being satisfied that he would be so represented, was to transfer the case.

The most important change, however, was that the whole system of African courts was transferred from the administration to the judiciary and henceforth became the responsibility of that branch of government. Thus it was the Chief Justice who was to appoint African court members, though only after consultation with the Provincial Commissioner of the province in which the court had jurisdiction, and dismiss them, and appoint African court officers; the supervisory and revision powers were now to be exercised by magistrates. In practice District Registrars, upon whom third class magisterial powers were conferred, and administrative officer-magistrates exercised these powers, but they were subject to the control of the Supreme Court. In addition, the financial and administrative sides of the system were transferred to the judiciary. Though the step was an important one, the change was in some respects more apparent than real, for the same officials as previously continued to supervise the courts and be in day to day charge of their administration and reform. In one respect indeed the reform had an adverse effect on the system; the Court of Review was unable to sit until May 1965 owing to the pressure of other work on the Supreme Court.

The amending legislation provided an opportunity for the legislature to give its views on the African courts and the reform programme.[5] Few members of the legislature availed themselves of the opportunity, but those who did were hostile to the continued existence of the African courts system. They condemned the changes as illusory, since administrators still had powers over the courts, and demanded an immediate move to a fully integrated system. One of the more interesting detailed criticisms was that against the continuance of the 'no technicalities' section in the Act;[6] in effect,

[5] Legislative Council, *Debates*, volume 90, cols. 592–610.

[6] 'No proceedings under this Act in the Supreme Court, the Court of Review, a Magistrate's court or any African court, and no summons, warrant, process order or decree issued or made thereby, shall be varied or declared void upon appeal, revision or review solely by reason of any defect in procedure or want of form, but all matters

it was alleged, Africans were being deprived of important safeguards available to non-Africans in the conduct and hearing of their cases by this section and this was especially regrettable when both the civil and criminal jurisdiction of the African courts was being increased, the increase in civil jurisdiction being in such a technical and commercial matter as partnerships. Exception was also taken to the stress laid by the main government spokesman on the revenue-earning capacity of the African courts; it was asked whether they were there to earn revenue or administer justice. The Government defended the record of the courts, the reforms it was introducing and rejected out of hand attempts at the committee stage to amend the Bill so as to remove all criminal jurisdiction from the courts. Though ineffective, the criticisms were in line with previous criticisms of the African courts and may be borne in mind when the debates on the 1967 reforming legislation are considered.

1962 saw also a definitive change in the status, though not in the powers, of the Eastern Africa Court of Appeal which may be considered here. From 1902, when it was first created, until the end of 1962, the E.A.C.A. was a creature of imperial legislation, and administration. The judges of the Court were appointed by the Crown and the administrative staffing was undertaken by the Kenya Government, which was reimbursed by the Governments of the other states using the court.[7] This arrangement had survived Tanganyika's independence in 1961 and the creation of the East African Common Services Organization in the same year, but it could not survive Tanganyika's move to a republican status in December 1962. A new arrangement was worked out whereby the E.A.C.A. would become one of the constituent parts of the EACSO being provided for in the constitution of the Organization, and established by an Act of the Central Legislative Assembly. This was duly done,[8] the legislation providing that the judges of the court should be appointed by the Authority of the Organization, the constitution of the court could only be altered by a two-thirds majority of the Central Legislative Assembly, and the staff of the court should be employed by the court and paid by the EACSO. As before, what use an East African state made of the court was dependent upon its own legislation, and in the case of Kenya its existing appellate jurisdiction was confirmed, together with its position and powers as a superior court of record in and for Kenya, whose process was to run throughout Kenya.[9]

shall be decided according to substantial justice without undue regard to technicalities.' Section 54, Cap. 11.

[7] Appeals from Uganda had lain to the E.A.C.A. from 1904, Tanganyika from 1922, and Zanzibar from 1914.

[8] EACSO (Amendment) (No. 2) Agreement, Legal Notice 95/1962 EACSO Gazette; East Africa Court of Appeal Act No. 13 of 1962.

[9] Appellate Jurisdiction Act No. 38 of 1962, Cap. 9.

Internal self-government and independence in 1963 brought further changes to the laws relating to the organization of the courts, some of them of far-reaching importance, but the actual system of courts was not disturbed by the constitutional changes associated with regionalism, though the provisions relating to the judges were tainted with regionalism. Two most important changes in the procedure of the courts, however, which removed a long-standing African grievance occurred directly after internal self-government; jury trial for Europeans was abolished and trial by assessors in serious criminal cases became universal for everybody in Kenya, and the special provisions relating to trial of Europeans in subordinate courts were likewise abolished.[10]

The chapters in the two constitutions of 1963 on the judiciary and the courts were very similar and may be dealt with briefly and as one.[11] A Supreme Court was established with unlimited criminal and civil jurisdiction over all persons and things. In addition it had jurisdiction in various constitutional matters.[12] The judges of the court were to be appointed by the Governor-General, acting on the advice of the Judicial Service Commission, with the exception of the Chief Justice, who was to be appointed by the Governor-General acting on the advice of the Prime Minister, who in turn was required to consult the Presidents of the Regional Assemblies, and only make a recommendation in which at least four of them concurred. Presidents of Regional Assemblies were placed in an even stronger position in relation to the removal of judges, for any one of them had the same power as the Prime Minister to initiate moves for the removal of a judge. Removal could only be effected, however, by the Governor-General on a recommendation to that effect by the Judicial Committee of the Privy Council following a judicial inquiry into the matter. A surprising omission from the constitutions was a retiring age for the judges; that was to be prescribed by Parliament.[13]

The Judicial Service Commission itself consisted of the Chief Justice, two puisne judges designated by the Governor-General, on the advice of the Chief Justice, and two members of the Public Service Commission (all of whom were appointed on the advice of the Judicial Service Commission). The members of the Judicial Service Commission appeared to be irremovable as such. In addition to its function in relation to the judges

[10] Criminal Procedure (Amendment) Act No. 33 of 1963.

[11] Kenya Order in Council, S.I. 791/1963, chapter XI (Internal Self-government); Kenya Independence Order in Council, S.I. 1968/1963, chapter X (Independence). The text is based on the latter constitution.

[12] As to which see chapters V and XI.

[13] The Judicature Act No. 16 of 1967 fixed the retiring age at 68 (section 9). There was considerable criticism of this age in the second reading debate on the Bill, but the Attorney-General who introduced the Bill and wound up the debate neither referred to it, nor offered any justification for it in his two short speeches. National Assembly, *Debates*, volume XII, part I (25 May 1967), cols 211–235; (6 June 1967), cols. 604–611.

of the Supreme Court, it also had vested in it the power to appoint, discipline and remove all judicial and magisterial personnel in Kenya, other than magistrates who were such by virtue of their administrative office, but including members of African courts.

The constitutions specifically provided for two other courts. The first was a Court of Appeal for Kenya which Parliament might, if it thought fit, establish. Such a court would have replaced the E.A.C.A., for appeals from it would have gone to the Judicial Committee of the Privy Council. It would have had to be staffed by justices of appeal, and the judges of the Supreme Court. It is interesting to note that while this provision has not yet been acted upon, it has remained in the current Constitution through successive constitutional changes.

The other courts provided for were Kadhi's courts in the former protectorate. From the time of the first British penetration into Kenya in the 1880s, the Muslims in the Sultan of Zanzibar's dominions had received special consideration in relation to their religion, and one of the matters for which special provision had always been made was the system of courts. As Muslim law and courts had received preferential treatment in the colonial period, so the inhabitants of the protectorate were correspondingly worried that the transfer of the protectorate to an independent Kenya would see the end of these privileges. Thus the maintenance of Kadhi's courts and Muslim law were two of the salient features of the quadripartite agreement, and the exchange of letters between the Prime Ministers of Kenya and Zanzibar which provided for the accession of the protectorate to the rest of Kenya, subject to certain undertakings and safeguards designed to protect the way of life of the Muslims of the coast.[14] The constitutions carried out this undertaking by providing that there should be a Chief Kadhi and not less than three other Kadhis, all of whom must profess the Muslim religion and be proficient in Muslim law, empowered to hold a court of a Kadhi having jurisdiction within the former protectorate, so that no part of that area should be outside such jurisdiction. The jurisdiction was to 'extend to the determination of questions of Muslim law relating to personal status, marriage, divorce or inheritance in proceedings in which all the parties profess the Muslim religion'.[15] These provisions were entrenched in the independence Constitution, other provisions on the Kadhi's courts, and all the provisions about Liwali's and Mudir's courts being left in the Courts Act, and being the subject of legislation and controversy in the reforms of 1967.

It is convenient here to deal with the changes introduced into the courts system, consequent upon Kenya's becoming a republic in 1964. First, the hierarchy of appeals, and thus of precedent, was altered by the elimination

[14] Cmnd. 2161/1963. See chapter V.
[15] Independence Constitution section 179 (5).

of the Judicial Committee of the Privy Council, with the usual savings for pending appeals.[16] More use had been made of the Judicial Committee by Kenya over the years than by the other two East African countries—indeed, an appeal from Kenya was both the first East African appeal the board heard,[17] and the first in which a member of the board exercised the newly given right to deliver a dissenting judgment[18]—but its abolition as a final court of appeal was an inevitable accompaniment of republican status, for the decision whether to use it or not is always a political one, and once the main decision to cease to be part of Her Majesty's dominions had been taken, it would have been difficult to justify continuing the judicial link with the United Kingdom. Secondly, the Supreme Court was renamed the High Court, but its jurisdiction remained unchanged, apart from the elimination of that part of it dependent upon the regional provisions of the Constitution.[19]

(c) *Administrative reforms 1963-7*

On balance, the constitutional changes had remarkably little direct effect on the system of courts,[20] but indirectly every change made more anomalous the dual system of subordinate courts inherited from the colonial period. The habit of administration before legislation was, however, adhered to, and thus while the system remained a dual one in the statute book, the period after the passing of the African Courts (Amendment) Act was one of administrative activity which continued progress towards complete integration. Some African court members were appointed third class magistrates with jurisdiction over everybody, to be exercised in accordance with the Civil and Criminal Procedure Codes, while retaining their position as members of African courts where they had a wider jurisdiction freer from procedural rules. The District Registrars were given greater administrative and appellate powers over the African courts in their district, though a sympathetic observer at the time doubted whether these persons had adequate experience to be given the latter powers.[21]

It was, however, in the area of appeals that the greatest changes were made in this period. African courts of appeal were eliminated, and customary, criminal and all civil appeals went to eight specially selected magistrates who were either District Registrars or administrative officers specially

[16] Constitution of Kenya (Amendment) Act No. 14 of 1965 (retrospective to 12 December 1964).

[17] *Secretary of State* v. *Charlesworth Pilling and Co.* (1901), I E.A.L.R. 24.

[18] *National and Grindlays Bank Ltd.* v. *Vallabhji*, [1966] E.A. 186.

[19] Constitution of Kenya (Amendment) Act No. 14 of 1965. See, too, Constitution of Kenya (Amendment No. 4) Act No. 40 of 1966 which abolished the Senate, and the High Court's jurisdiction to adjudicate on disputes between the two Houses of the National Assembly.

[20] There was more effect on the manner of appointment of judges, as to which see chapter VI.

[21] Barnett, op. cit., p. 48.

selected for their knowledge of customary law, who were seconded to the judiciary. This change illustrates well the wide discretionary powers conferred on the controllers of the African courts by the Act. The Act referred to appeals going to an African court of appeal, or, if there was none, to a magistrate. Until the 'sixties, the policy had been to create African courts of appeal and fall back on a magistrate, that is, an administrative officer, only in the last resort. Now, without any significant alteration of the Act, this policy was completely reversed and a new one implemented by administrative fiat.

Changes in composition and powers were introduced at the first instance level as well. Composition was at first reduced to benches of two, of whom the more formally and legally educated member kept the record. The policy was to rely more and more on the educated member, and towards the end of this period of administrative reform, increasing numbers of African court elders were retired and courts were composed of one member only, approximating closely to the projected new third class magistrate's court of the integrated system of magistrate's courts, the major differences being that advocates could still not appear before the African courts, nor was the court member bound to follow the codes of procedure. Even here, however, there was a steady progression towards more procedural formality.

(d) *Legislative reform 1967*

The culmination of the period of reform came with the passage of three interrelated Acts in the middle of 1967—the Kadhi's Courts Act, the Judicature Act, and the Magistrate's Courts Act, which between them repealed and replaced all legislation relating to subordinate courts, other than the provisions of the Constitution, and the law all courts were to apply. The Kadhi's Courts Act[22] establishes six Kadhi's courts, subordinate to the High Court, four having jurisdiction within the area of the former protectorate—this was in accordance with the Constitution—one having jurisdiction in Nyanza, Western, and parts of the Rift Valley Provinces, and one having jurisdiction within Garissa, Wajir, and Mandera Districts, the Muslim parts of the North Eastern Province. The Act thus goes further than the Constitution in its establishment of these courts, but no further than actual practice, for these other Kadhi's courts were already in existence, the Act putting them on a more formal basis. The jurisdiction of the courts in Muslim personal matters was set out in the same terms as in the Constitution, so finally settling the vexed question of the juridical basis for the application of Muslim law by such courts outside the protectorate,[23] but the Act makes clear that this is not an exclusive jurisdiction. The High

[22] No. 14.
[23] Anderson, op. cit., pp. 81–5.

Court and all subordinate courts are not excluded from exercising jurisdiction over Muslim personal matters, and in the exercise of such jurisdiction, they would not necessarily apply Muslim law;[24] nor are there any provisions requiring them to transfer such a case to a Kadhi's court. On the other hand, the Kadhi's courts are limited in that they have no jurisdiction over mixed cases, that is, cases between Muslims and non-Muslims. If these provisions are from the Muslim community's point of view slightly unsatisfactory, a concession has been made to it by the provision that the Kadhi's courts shall apply the Muslim law of evidence, with two important limitations—there shall be no discrimination against witnesses on the ground of sex or religion, and issues shall be decided upon the credibility of the evidence and not upon the number of witnesses giving evidence. These limitations in fact strike at the heart of the traditional Muslim law of evidence so the concession is to some extent more apparent than real, but it does represent a partial victory for the Kadhis.[25] Procedure and practice, however, are to be in accordance with those prescribed for other subordinate courts, or with rules of court which may be made by the Chief Justice. Appeals from the Kadhi's courts lie to the High Court, which sits with a Kadhi as assessor to hear the same.

The bare outline of the Act conceals the controversy which it engendered, and some of the assumptions behind it. Despite strenuous efforts by the Speaker to prevent MPs from discussing the desirability or otherwise of Kadhi's courts, it was clear that there was some opposition to the whole principle of separate courts and laws for Muslims.[26] There was objection to institutionalizing diversity instead of encouraging unity, and it was argued that it was illogical to establish special Muslim courts to deal with just those matters which were the subject of two Commissions expressly charged with drafting unified non-denominational codes. Muslim MPs and sympathizers on the other hand defended the Bill on the ground that it would give

[24] The Act does not require them to apply Muslim law, nor would they be bound by the application of the rules of the conflict of laws. On this latter point, see Sawyerr, 'Internal Conflict of Laws' in *East African Law and Social Change*, op. cit., pp. 110–71.

[25] For past disputes, see Anderson, op. cit., pp. 99–101.

[26] National Assembly, *Debates*, volume XII, part I (23 May 1967), cols. 66–71; (29 May 1967), cols. 143–169; (25 May 1967), col. 211 (second reading); (31 May 1967), cols. 469–473, and 579–599; (6 June 1967) (Committee) cols. 599–603; (6 June 1967) (Report and third reading). The Speaker's grounds for objecting to debate on the principle of Kadhi's courts were as follows: 'Members cannot discuss on this Bill whether or not it is desirable to have separate Kadhi's courts because it is in the Constitution that we shall have them, and until someone moves a motion for an amendment to the Constitution it is not open to us to debate that provision of the Constitution . . . One of the oaths which is taken by hon. Members is to uphold the Constitution, so you cannot speak freely contrary to your oath' (col. 155). This may be regarded as one of the conventions of the Kenyan Constitution for there is no provision to this effect in the actual text of the Constitution. Standing Orders now provide for the exclusion of motions contrary to the Constitution, unless for its amendment (No. 40 (3) (6)).

the lie to Somali propaganda that Muslims were not properly treated in Kenya, and that Muslim law was a special religious law which could not be treated as an ordinary secular law. They took objection to the provision of appeals to the High Court since they considered that it was illogical to allow non-Muslims who might not apply Muslim law to give the final decision on Muslim legal matters.

The attitude of the Government, however, was most interesting. It would be fair to say that while the Bill confirmed and in some respects extended the special position of Muslim law and courts, the Government was not very enthusiastic about the whole business. The Attorney-General, who introduced the Bill into the National Assembly, denied that Muslim law was in any way special; he stressed those aspects of it which needed reform and made it clear that he considered that one of the functions of the High Court in its appellate capacity would be to introduce reforms into Muslim law; indeed he did not seem to think that it would be obliged to apply Muslim law at all on appeal.[27] The general tone and content of his remarks on Muslim law were such that strong exception was taken to them by Muslim leaders at the coast,[28] who seem to have overlooked that it was he who was responsible for introducing the Bill which confirmed their legal privileges.

The controversy over the Kadhi's courts is but a prelude to the controversy over the reform of Muslim family and succession law which has been set in train. It is hard not to sympathize with the Government which is facing a difficult dilemma here. The more predominantly Muslim parts of the country, the coast, and the old Northern Frontier District, were, for over seventy years of British colonial rule, treated differently and apart from the rest of the country, and the Government started off its independent existence saddled with a treaty in respect of one, and an armed secession struggle in respect of the other area, as legacies from Britain. In these circumstances giving some special treatment and privileges to Muslims is unavoidable. On the other hand, the Government's policy is to create an integrated modern legal system in the belief that such a system is both more efficient, and a contributory factor in building a united nation, and Kadhi's courts and Muslim law are serious obstacles in the way of implementing such a policy. It will not be easy to eliminate these obstacles, but a prerequisite is surely that greater tolerance and tact be shown towards them, and those for whom they represent a way of life. Failure to do this in respect of the Kadhi's Courts Act has not helped the cause of modernization.

The main piece of reforming legislation is the Magistrate's Courts Act,[29] which also produced the major controversy. The Act establishes two Magistrate's Courts, the Resident Magistrate's Court, constituted by a Senior

[27] Cols. 66–67, 583, 602–603. [28] Cols. 472 and 585. [29] No. 17.

Resident or Resident Magistrate, having civil and criminal jurisdiction throughout Kenya, and the District Magistrate's Court constituted by a District Magistrate, of the first, second or third class, and having civil and criminal jurisdiction throughout a district. The Resident Magistrate's and first class District Magistrate's Courts are equated, in that both are regarded as magistrate's courts of the first class, but this has reference mainly to supervisory, revisory, and appellate powers and not original criminal and civil powers.

The criminal jurisdiction of all magistrate's courts is extensive; in effect, the new third class magistrate's court has had its jurisdiction increased compared to the old court of the same class, and second class magistrate's courts are empowered to try the same offences as first class magistrate's courts. Their powers of punishment are, however, different. Senior Resident Magistrates, and Resident Magistrates upon whom special powers have been conferred, may pass sentences of up to ten years' imprisonment, fines not exceeding sh. 10,000/-, and corporal punishment not exceeding twenty-four strokes. Other first class magistrates have the same fining and whipping powers but may only pass sentence of up to five years' imprisonment. A second class magistrate may pass sentences of up to one year's imprisonment, up to sh. 2,000/- fine, and up to twelve strokes of corporal punishment, while a third class magistrate is confined to sentences of up to six months' imprisonment, or fines not exceeding sh. 1,000/-, these being the powers of the old African courts.

From a decision of a third class magistrate's court both the accused and the Attorney-General may appeal to a Resident Magistrate's Court, the accused against both conviction and sentence, the Attorney-General against an acquittal. The appellate court has wide power to deal with the appeal but may not make an order adverse to the accused or convicted person unless he has first been given an opportunity of being heard, nor make one in excess of the jurisdiction of the lower court. From the Resident Magistrate's Court, the convicted person may appeal to the High Court, with the leave of that court. From a first or second class magistrate's court the convicted person may appeal to the High Court, and from all three classes of courts, the Attorney-General may appeal to the High Court against an acquittal. No explanation was given in the National Assembly or elsewhere of this dual right of appeal vested in the Attorney-General in respect of acquittals in third class magistrate's courts.[30]

A significant amendment to the provisions relating to appeal, which was

[30] It is possible that it is an oversight. Appeals to the Resident Magistrate's court are provided for in the Magistrate's Courts Act, section 11. Appeals to the High Court are provided for in the Criminal Procedure Code, section 348A, introduced by the Criminal Procedure Code (Amendment) Act No. 13 of 1967.

introduced at the committee stage of the Bill, was to eliminate the old rule, which had found a place in the Bill as published, that there could be no appeal where the sentence was a fine of sh. 100/- or less. MPs had objected to this provision on the grounds that it had been much abused by administrative officers in the past, and the Government conceded the point. In addition to appeals, a first class magistrate's court has powers to examine the records of the criminal proceedings of any court subordinate to it within the local limits of its jurisdiction, to satisfy itself of the regularity of those proceedings. If it considers that such proceedings are irregular or improper, it forwards the record, with its remarks, to the High Court.

The extent of civil jurisdiction depends both on the class of magistrate holding the court, and the nature of the claim. Senior Resident Magistrates may exercise jurisdiction where the nature of the claim does not exceed sh. 6,000/-, Resident Magistrates where it does not exceed sh. 3,000/-, while the Chief Justice may increase the limit of either class up to sh. 10,000/-. Neither class of magistrate, however, has jurisdiction in claims arising under customary law. A District Magistrate's court of any class has unlimited customary law jurisdiction, and limited jurisdiction in other civil cases, sh. 1,000/- for second and third class magistrates, sh. 2,000/- for first class magistrates. It is difficult to support the continued division between customary and non-customary civil jurisdiction. It has undertones of the old racial divisions in the jurisdiction of the subordinate courts. It stems from the days when customary law was not regarded as law at all, and claims were subject to a process more akin to arbitration than adjudication by the traditional elders. The differing non-customary civil jurisdiction of magistrates is based on the principle that the greater the value of the subject-matter in dispute, the more experienced should be the court that is seized of the case; there is no reason why a similar rule should not be applied to customary matters many of which are quantifiable in monetary terms. It seems strange that a court which has no jurisdiction over a simple claim for repayment of a debt of sh. 1,200/- may deal with a case of succession under customary law worth ten times as much, both the value and subject matter of which are outside the limits of the jurisdiction of the Senior Resident Magistrate. This anomaly can only be explained by the decision, as a matter of deliberate policy, not to accord customary law a status equal to the other laws which all courts are required to apply, a matter dealt with in more detail below.

Appeals from a third class magistrate's court lie to a first class magistrate's court, and from there, on a question of law only, to the High Court. Appeals from other decrees and orders of all other subordinate courts lie, on a question of law or fact, direct to the High Court. A judge of the High Court may summarily dismiss any appeal. Since there is no provision requiring a certain type of case to be started in a third class magistrate's court, the appellate system which a litigant will be able to make use of, will depend on the class of magistrate stationed in his district, notwithstanding that the civil jurisdiction of the second and third class magistrate's courts are exactly comparable. This too is a provision for which it is difficult to see the justification.

Though the jurisdiction for the new system of courts has been spelt out in some detail, it was not that which aroused the major controversy over the Bill when it was debated in the National Assembly.[31] Controversy blew up over the composition of the magistracy. It had been envisaged by some of those planning the new system, and assumed by those waiting for it, that amongst other reforms it would bring about, would be a complete separation of the judiciary from the administration at district level, the amalgamation of which had been the key to the administrative conception of justice in the colonial period. There was, therefore, considerable surprise when the Magistrate's Courts Bill as published, provided for all provincial and district administrators to be District Magistrates *ex officio*, the particular class being left to be designated by the Judicial Service Commission. Many MPs, including both Ministers and Assistant Ministers, strongly attacked this provision, claiming that it had led to much hardship and abuse of power in the past, and that too much power was being given to civil servants at present, who were on the whole hostile to politicians. The Government defended the provision on the grounds that there were not enough qualified persons available to have a full-time professional and lay magistracy, though this was the ultimate aim. MPs were not placated and the Government accordingly purported to bow to the storm. The provision was withdrawn, and it was stated that it would be left to the Judicial Service Commission to select as magistrates only those administrative officers who were suitable to hold such a post. In effect, instead of the legislation providing that administrative officers would continue to be magistrates, the legislation was silent and administrative dispositions were to be used to achieve the same result. One or two MPs complained that this amendment did not meet the objections, but it was of no avail. The first lists of District Magistrates appointed by the Judicial Service Commission contained many District Commissioners who were appointed first class magistrates, and District Officers who were appointed third class magistrates, besides many ex-African court members who were appointed second and third class magistrates.

This decision is clear evidence that the modernization of the legal system is stopping short of the full British conception of justice, demanded by both the judiciary and African politicians in the colonial period. As in that period, it is to be tempered by the necessities of executive power, notwithstanding

[31] National Assembly, *Debates*, volume XII, part 1 (6 June 1967), cols. 612–613; (8 June 1967), cols. 745–766 (second reading); (13 June 1967), cols. 878–898 (Committee) and cols. 908–919 (Report and third reading).

that the arrangement gave rise to well-documented abuses of power in the past. It is not possible to support, and hardly possible to justify, the decision. As far back as 1956, Lord Hailey pointed out that it would be necessary to move away from the administrative magistrate as government in Africa became more 'political'—the administrative officer would increasingly be seen as a political figure and as such no longer properly impartial in the administration of justice.[32] It may be doubted whether it was easy or possible for him ever to be as impartial as a magistrate should be, but certainly the necessity to function in a political atmosphere is an added disqualification. To continue the system is to ignore the principle that justice must not only be done, it must be seen to be done, even if we assume in its favour that justice will in fact be done.

There are two other significant provisions in the Act and its operation that may be mentioned. The Attorney-General is empowered to give orders, where it appears to him to be necessary in the interests of public safety, or for the maintenance of public order, and after consultation with the Chief Justice, as to where a case is to be tried. These orders prevail over any order, direction, or process issued by any court to the extent of any inconsistency between them, and shall not be questioned in any legal proceeding whatsoever. The need for this power, the giving of it to the Attorney-General rather than the Chief Justice, and the absence of any sort of judicial control over it, was neither explained nor criticized in the National Assembly, yet in some respects it gives the Government greater administrative control over the legal system than exists via administrative magistrates, who are subject to the control of the High Court.

The Chief Justice is given a wide discretion to take such steps as may be necessary for the supervision and inspection of magistrate's courts. To assist him in this task, the Judicial Service Commission created a new post, that of Administrative Registrar of the High Court, with first class magisterial powers exerciseable throughout Kenya. He is charged with the responsibility of supervising magistrate's courts, particularly those third class magistrate's courts staffed by ex-members of the now defunct African courts.[33]

Finally, an important omission must be mentioned. The African Courts Act prohibited the usurpation of judicial powers, but exempted from that the customary arbitration or settlement by tribal elders of issues concerned with customary law. No such provision exists in the new Act, notwithstanding that such customary arbitration still plays an important role in the administration of justice. For instance, research has shown that the decisions of

[32] Hailey, *An African Survey Revised* (London, Oxford University Press, 1956), p. 616.

[33] The first appointee to the post was the last holder of the post of African Courts Officer.

tribal elders were sometimes deferred to by, and could frustrate the implementation of the decisions of, the African courts in the rural areas, and informal dispute settlement is widespread in the urban areas, particularly Mombasa.[34] It must be doubted whether such arbitration will cease, but the lack of any official recognition of it is further evidence of the 'anglicization' of the legal system, and the reduced role of traditional elements therein.

The Magistrate's Courts Act is a curious hybrid. In its creation of a unified courts' system in place of the dual colonial system it represents a move towards modernization long called for by African politicians. In its distinction between customary and non-customary civil matters, it represents the traditional colonial lawyer's approach to African customary law. In its maintenance of the administrative magistracy, and other administrative controls over the courts, it represents a continuance of the British colonial pattern. It represents the culmination of a whole period of reform from 1960 which shows a remarkable continuity of development with the colonial period. Modernization has been tempered by colonial traditions and practices, so much so that it would appear that neither the advent of an African government, nor independence, seriously affected even the pace of reform.

THE REFORM OF THE LAW

If the trumpets of modernization sound uncertain notes in the reform of the courts, they blow more clearly in the reform of the law. We may consider first the Judicature Act.[35] The main purpose of this statute is to set out the various categories of legal rules, in conformity with which the jurisdiction of all courts must be exercised. These rules consist of the Constitution, all other written laws, including various named Acts of the United Kingdom Parliament, and subject thereto, the substance of the common law, the doctrines of equity and the statutes of general application in force in England on 12 August 1897, provided, however, that this latter category shall apply so far only as the circumstance of Kenya and its inhabitants permit, and subject to such qualifications as those circumstances render necessary. This is a modernized version of the original reception clause which first appeared in the law of Kenya in 1897, and one would not generally expect to find any changes in such a clause. It would, however, have been conducive to certainty and publicity in the law, if an attempt had been made to extract from the many hundreds of pre-reception date English statutes, those which were regarded as being both of general application in England, and suitable to the circumstances of Kenya, making specific reference to those in the

[34] Research by I. S. Gichuru amongst the Meru, and R. E. S. Tanner in Mombasa.
[35] No. 16 of 1967.

Judicature Act or enacting them as Kenyan Acts of Parliament, and abolishing all reference to the troublesome concept of a statute of general application.[36]

It is in the reference or non-reference to other laws that the Judicature springs surprises and marks a clear development in the direction of English modernization. In many African countries, independence has brought an upgrading of the status of customary law in the legal system; it is put on a par with the other laws that all courts are required to apply, and its status as law is confirmed by the fact that judicial notice may be taken of it. This has not happened in Kenya, and in one respect, customary law seems to have been to some extent downgraded. Under the old system, the African courts were required to 'administer and enforce African customary law . . .'[37] Under the new system, all courts are required to 'be guided by African customary law in civil cases in which one or more of the parties is subject to it or affected by it . . .'[38] The provision that courts shall be guided by, rather than apply or administer, customary law, confers the same discretion on all courts to depart from the rules of customary law as was formerly conferred only on courts in the British colonial system. The courts already have discretion to decline to be guided by customary law if it is repugnant to justice or morality—this repeats the old rule—but this new discretion might permit a court to depart from customary law on the grounds that it considered the particular rule old fashioned or out of date.[39] Whatever the merits of that provision, a considerable change is that a non-African can now find his actions governed by customary law, if a court decides to be so guided in a dispute between an African and a non-African, and this represents a distinct advance from the previous position which was that a non-African could only be bound by customary law if he so chose to be.

The Magistrate's Courts Act extends to the whole of the new courts system the rules relating to proof of customary law used in the non-African courts in the colonial era, and in doing so, confirms a decision of the E.A.C.A. in 1965 that such rules still applied in Kenya, notwithstanding the Evidence Act.[40] The rules provide that a party wishing to rely on a rule of customary

[36] This has been done in Western Nigeria. See Park, *The Sources of Nigerian Law* (London, Sweet and Maxwell, 1963), pp. 40–2, 146–7. There is no satisfactory description of what a statute of general application is, and no clear test for determining whether it applies in Kenya, or any other country in which the phrase is in use. The result is that it is still, more than seventy years after the introduction of English law into Kenya, impossible to say with any certainty just how much of that law applies, and therefore what the law of Kenya is on many points. See, further, Sawyerr, op. cit., pp. 120–4; Macneil, 'Research in East African Law', 3 *E.A.L.J.*, pp. 47–78 at footnote 27, p. 71; Morris and Read, *Uganda, The Development of its Laws and Constitutions*, op. cit., pp. 237–44, 250–3.

[37] Section 18 (a) African Courts Act.

[38] Section 3 (2) Judicature Act.

[39] See *Talibu* v. *Executors of Siwa Haji* (1907), 2 E.A.L.R. 33 especially at p. 38.

[40] *Kimani* v. *Gikanga*, [1965] E.A. 735.

law must plead and prove it through witnesses to the satisfaction of the court. Only after a rule of customary law has become notorious in the courts may judicial notice be taken of it. It is unrealistic to expect all magistrates to know all of the customary laws of Kenya, as would be deemed to be the case if judicial notice had to be taken of customary law, but it is strange that there is no statutory reference to the recordations of customary law of which a fair number now exist at a semi-official level in Kenya. These could be published and given the status of prima facie evidence of the customary law of which they are a record. As it is, the general reference to evidence, coupled with the general provisions that courts are merely to be guided by customary law, suggests that the Government is set on a policy of moving right away from customary law, and does not therefore find it necessary to enact detailed rules as to its application. Evidence from other actions, mentioned below, would support this conclusion.

Provisions for the application of customary law do exist even if they herald its eclipse; provisions for the application of Muslim law by non-Muslim courts are entirely absent. Anderson[41] long ago pointed out the shaky foundations for the application of Muslim law in the protectorate, and the failure to clarify the position in an independent Kenya means that only the Kadhi's courts have a sure basis for their application of Muslim law in Kenya. If Muslims go, or are taken, in a mixed case to other courts, the general law of the land is to be applied, though this includes the rules as to the conflict of laws, which may result in Muslim law being applied in some cases. Again if an appeal is taken from a Kadhi's court to the High Court or the E.A.C.A., it would appear that both those courts could quite lawfully apply the general law of the land, notwithstanding the presence of a Kadhi as an assessor. This is an even clearer indication that Muslim law too is in eclipse in Kenya, and may have more and more difficulty in surviving.

The reforms of the law contained in the Judicature Act and Magistrate's Courts Act are rather antipathetic to Kenyan law with a non-English common law origin. The approach to law with an English origin on the other hand has been very much more sympathetic. With only one exception, all the legislative developments in the field of law reform in the sixties have been in the direction of introducing portions of English law into Kenya, and in this, the African government has merely followed previous practice. In contract, the Indian Contract Act was repealed and replaced by the English common law of contract in 1960.[42] The reason given was the difficulty in discovering what the Indian law of contract was, now that India was independent. No

[41] See footnote 23.
[42] Law of Contract Act 1960, Cap. 23.

consideration was given to whether the slowly emerging class of African businessmen might not find it equally difficult to discover what the English law of contract was, and whether a Kenyan Contract Code might not help them, or whether the consumer might not be better protected by a code from which he can the more easily discover his rights. In tort the English Occupiers Liability Act was enacted into the law of Kenya in 1962.[43] In land law, the Registered Land Act 1963,[44] repeating much of the Land Registration (Special Areas) Act, introduced several concepts of English land law into former Trust land areas, including parts of the Prescription Act of 1832, and is designed to replace the Indian Transfer of Property Act 1882 in time. The Act contains a provision specifically referring the courts to so much of the common law as is in force in Kenya in the event of the Act not covering a particular situation.[45] Since the Act draws on the 1925 English land legislation, and the common law in force in Kenya is the pre-1925 English land law, the potential for uncertainty and confusion is almost unlimited. The object of the Act was to provide a simple code of land law relating to registration and transactions. One would have thought that it could have been better advanced if references to English land law were specifically forbidden, rather than specifically encouraged. The Limitation Act 1968[46] has clear affinities with the English Limitation Act 1939 despite recommendations that provisions dealing with prescription should be based on former legislation specifically devised for Kenyan conditions.[47]

The one field where a decision to move away from English law has been implemented is copyright law. The English Copyright Act 1956, extended to Kenya in 1960, was repealed and replaced by the Copyright Act 1966.[48] The reason given was that the English law was not suitable to the needs of Kenya. Even this reform was based to some extent on English initiative, for much of the impetus for the reform of the copyright laws of Commonwealth African countries had come from the British Institute of International and Comparative Law. There is, however, a moral here. The law was reformed because investigation had shown that the English law did not take sufficient account of the educational and cultural needs of developing countries. If on a subject which is somewhat marginal, investigation showed that Kenya

[43] Occupiers Liability Act No. 21 of 1962, Cap. 34.
[44] Cap. 300.
[45] Section 163. This section refers to 'the common law of England as modified by the doctrines of equity shall extend and apply to Kenya . . .' Common law is defined in the Interpretation and General Provisions Act as follows: 'Common law means so much of the common law, including the doctrines of equity, of England as has effect for the time being in Kenya'.
[46] No. 21 of 1968.
[47] *Report of the Mission on Land Consolidation and Registration*, op. cit., p. 75, para. 272.
[48] No. 3 of 1966.

should not blindly rely on English law, how much more probable it is that Kenya would have a system of law more relevant to its needs in many other fields, if it did not equate reform and modernization of the law with the introduction of English law.

The investigatory approach was again used, when in early 1967 two Commissions of Inquiry were appointed, charged with the task of inquiring into the family and succession laws of the peoples of Kenya and preparing draft unified codes on both these topics which would replace the customary laws and the special religious laws which at present exist in Kenya. There is little doubt that the present position is unsatisfactory. It is difficult to administer, the various laws are based on different conceptions of the family and inheritance, and derive from different periods of time and parts of the world, and the whole emphasizes the distinctions amongst the peoples of Kenya, and so represents a potential obstacle to building a Kenyan nation. The arguments for a reformed and unified law on these subjects are therefore strong. The Commissions produced reports in September 1968 which showed that an effort had been made to reconcile the need for modernization with the stubborn fact that it will be some time before the majority of Kenyans will cease ordering their personal lives on the basis of customary and Muslim law, a fact which was brought home to them early in their work when they encountered Muslim hostility. The Commissions attempted to solve their dilemma by recommending that persons be given wide freedom to contract marriages and make wills using their own customary or religious formalities, but that certain basic substantive rules be applied to all marriages so formed and wills so made, and that the courts (or, in the case of divorce proceedings, other tribunals) administer the new law, being given wide discretionary powers to do so. Some of the detailed recommendations certainly reflect modern English thinking on these matters—for instance, that special provisions be enacted regarding the matrimonial home, and that divorce should be granted on the single ground that the marriage has broken down beyond all hope of repair. Equally, the recommended mode of further progress—through decisions of the courts, which have been given a crucial role here—is in line with the thinking of a common lawyer, but overall, the Commissions have gone some way towards producing a blend of African and English legal notions, the first time this has been so explictly done in Kenya.

CONCLUSION

Why has law reform proceeded hitherto on such English lines; equally, why has reform of the courts taken the form that it has? There have been few clear or meaningful official statements on either matter but the following may be advanced as likely explanations. In so far as reform has proceeded in an English direction it reflects a reaction to the colonial view that the

British system of justice could not be introduced in its entirety into Kenya. What was introduced was regarded by Africans as inferior to that system, and reform is equated with making the superior British system available to all Kenyans. The maintenance of colonial characteristics may be put down to the belief that whatever judicial purists might say, the colonial legal system performed its main task of maintaining law and order, and extending the writ of government efficiently, and these are still important aims of government. A dislike of the continued existence of Indian legislation in Kenya has been a spur to reforming legislation in those branches of law in which it still plays an important part. The English training of the lawyers who have been concerned with reform, be they African, Asian or English, has been a positive spur to the introduction of English law; this is the law such people know, often better than the laws and social conditions of the country into which they introduce it. Finally the two desires of national unity and economic development have been incentives to action. The former stresses the benefits of one legal system which does not distinguish litigants according to their race, the latter, the benefits which a framework of modern statute law will provide for economic activities such as land transactions, buying and selling goods, and the creation and operation of corporate bodies, benefits which will not be obtained from a reformed customary or Muslim law.

Some of these reasons cannot be accepted uncritically. Indian legislation was devised specifically for Indian conditions. Some of these may have greater similarity to Kenyan conditions than would English legislation, and Kenya could usefully use Indian legislation as a model for its own. Using English legislation as one possible model for Kenyan reforms would be unimpeachable; equating the introduction of English legislation with reform and modernization is not. A question mark must remain against the last two reasons given, for though specifically referred to in official statements and speeches, they rest more on optimistic assumptions than empirical research.

This indeed is a criticism which may be levelled against some of the law and court reforms of the last few years in Kenya. The use of investigatory commissions, which have usually been associated with the reform of agrarian law, and more recently have been used to propose reforms in the field of family and succession law, should always be regarded as a *sine qua non* of any large scale law reform proposals. Indeed, we would go further and suggest that law reform in a developing country cannot be regarded as a once-and-for-all business, or a matter which private pressure groups such as the Law Society may be left to deal with on an *ad hoc* basis. If Government believes that there is a connection between national unity, economic development, and law reform, then law reform should be regarded as a high and continuing priority. Research into law and proposals for reform should form part of the programme of the Institute for Development Studies at the University College, Nairobi, and there should be close liaison between that, the Law Faculties of the University of East Africa and the Attorney-General's chambers, which should have a section of lawyers employed full-time on law reform. This is one area where the traditional English approach, now going out of fashion in England, should most certainly not be followed in Kenya.[49]

[49] A corollary of investigatory commissions and research into legal problems is that reforming legislation should be based on the conclusions and recommendations produced by their work. This has not always happened in Kenya.

We would stress that we are not necessarily recommending the introduction in Kenya of an equivalent institution to the English Law Commissioners. What is needed is not another statutory agency, but much more empirical research into the operation of the law in Kenya. Such research has traditionally been confined to anthropological or other investigations of customary law, but what is needed now is research into the extent to which actual practice in the field has been affected, and people's attitudes changed, by modern statutory reforms in, for example, industrial relations, land law. and commercial dealings.

CHAPTER X

The Administration of Justice: 2. The Legal Profession

INTRODUCTION

The focus of attention in this book has hitherto been on institutions and their operation rather than on personnel. But several writers on new countries have drawn attention to the important role that the small professional and educated classes play in their political development.[1] The civil service, the military, and the students are being singled out for special investigation, as they wield their power in practice. The legal profession has not been a subject of very much investigation, presumably because the likelihood of its overthrowing a government by unconstitutional means is remote. It is, however, an important profession for precisely the opposite reason to those which make the military and the students important; it is, or can be, a powerful force for constitutionalism. Lawyers tend to be conservative, and although this is not always a desirable quality in a new and fast-changing state, some of the values associated with this attitude—respect for law, and taking action only in accordance with the law—are desirable, and are well worth propagating in new states. Lawyers have also traditionally been concerned with individual human rights, and this aspect of their work in developing countries has received great prominence in the last decade through organizations such as the International Commission of Jurists and specialized agencies of the UNO. The safeguarding of human rights is a matter on which many governments in developing countries adopt a different approach to that of lawyers and their organizations, but here again, the values of the lawyer, if sufficiently pervasive in society, might temper the approach of governments. In short, in a country recently emerged from colonial rule, lawyers may be regarded as a potential pressure group for liberal democracy in a society in which its values have not in the past had a firm hold, and are under constant pressure in practice and in discussion.

A survey of the growth, and present organization and work of the legal profession in Kenya is therefore an important aspect of the theme of this book. How far has the profession contributed, or been allowed to contribute,

[1] Shils, 'Opposition in the New States of Africa and Asia', *Government and Opposition*, volume I, No. 2; Gower, *Independent Africa: The Challenge to the Legal Profession* (Cambridge, Harvard University Press, 1967), especially chapter 3.

to the growth of constitutionalism and liberal democratic values in Kenya? How has the profession regarded its role in the legal system of Kenya, and how has it responded to the advent of an African government and independence? What part does it play in the political and constitutional development of Kenya? These are the questions with which this chapter will attempt to deal.

Attention will be concentrated on the private legal profession, so at the outset it is important to distinguish it from the public legal profession, and say something of the division between the two. In Kenya, as in all British dependencies, the legal profession in the colonial period was, in effect, divided into public and private halves. The public legal profession consisted of the members of the Colonial Legal Service, and the judiciary, usually qualified at the Bar in England, in the employ of the Crown, and, as such, subject to two characteristics of the colonial service, a liability to be posted anywhere in the colonies, and so not often spending very much time in any one dependency, and a prospect of promotion up a reasonably well-defined hierarchy. A person might start his service as a probationary Crown Counsel in Fiji, rise to be Attorney-General in the Gold Coast, having had a period of service in Uganda on the way, be promoted to a puisne judgeship in Kenya, and finish his service as Chief Justice of Fiji.[2]

The private legal profession, the members of whom are known individually as advocates, and will be collectively referred to here as the Bar, served the general public, and remained in practice in Kenya. The profession was fused, an advocate performing the functions of both barrister and solicitor, but the rules governing the profession were drawn increasingly from the rules governing solicitors in England, though the vast majority of advocates qualified at the Bar in England. It was rare for a local advocate to join government service, though retirement of colonial officials from government service into private practice was not unknown. To all intents and purposes, however, the division between the two halves of the profession, despite their common educational background, was very marked; it influenced the development of the private profession, and still remains a feature of the legal profession in Kenya.

Various factors have influenced the existence of the division. First, the outlook and conception of his role of the career colonial service lawyer, in the country for a short period and serving government all the time, was inevitably different from that of the advocate. The former was a colonial

[2] Sir John Ainley, who retired from the Chief Justiceship of Kenya in 1968, saw service as a judge in the Gold Coast, Uganda, Eastern Nigeria, Sarawak, North Borneo, and Brunei before his appointment as Chief Justice in 1963. On the other hand, Mr. Justice Rudd, the senior puisne judge until his retirement in 1968 was a Resident Magistrate in Kenya (1936–44), a puisne judge in Aden (1944–51), and a puisne judge in Kenya from 1951.

officer with a specialist qualification, whose work lay mainly in the field of public law. The latter did not work for government, his work tended to lie in the field of private law, and when he did branch into public law, it was usually in the role of defence counsel 'against' the government. Secondly, advocates on the whole supported the judicial approach to the administration of justice, and were accordingly regarded with some suspicion by the colonial administration, whose lawyers, at least until they became judges, tended to support the administrative approach. Thirdly, an important, though little stressed factor was that the majority of advocates were Asian, and the colonial legal service consisted of British personnel, so to the antipathy of the colonial administrator for the lawyer was added the antipathy of the British administrator for the Asian lawyer.

A very good example of the colonial administration's attitude to advocates is provided by the policy of exclusion of advocates from native tribunals, and its legal implementation in the Native Tribunals Act of 1930. The policy was justified on the grounds that advocates had been touting for custom in the native reserves, that if they appeared in a tribunal they would try and confuse the tribunal members with technical legal points, and that their presence would impede the administration of justice.[3] There was never any recognition that the advocate was there to assist the course of justice, and that his professional ethics imposed an obligation on him to do so, quite apart from any disciplinary measures that might be taken against him for unprofessional conduct. This ban was maintained for the rest of the colonial period, and only disappeared with native and African courts in 1967, though antipathy towards lawyers softened in the late forties and thereafter.

Since independence, there have been movements of personnel from the private to the public profession and to the judiciary, but the division remains and two new factors are to some extent exacerbating it. There is the beginning of an educational difference between the two branches of the profession, between those educated locally who are tending to go into central or local government service, and those trained at the English Bar who go into private practice, though it is unlikely that this difference will persist. Secondly, the public profession is being Africanized, but the private profession remains overwhelmingly non-African.[4] It is to the development of this non-African part of the profession, seen mainly through its formal organization and control, that we now turn, for it is only by examining that, that we can understand its present position and attitudes.

[3] See Phillips, *Report on Native Tribunals in Kenya*, pp. 227–33, and the Legislative Council, *Debates*, 18 July 1930, on the Native Tribunal Bill.
[4] Out of 303 advocates who took out practising certificates in 1968, 12 were Africans. See further on this point p. 403, below.

DEVELOPMENT OF THE LEGAL PROFESSION TO 1949

The history of the Bar divides into two periods—before 1949, when the profession was subject to a measure of public control exercised primarily through the Chief Justice, and after 1949, when the profession was first given self-governing powers by law, and began its rapid progress to its present position of almost complete self-government. Legal regulation of the Bar was first provided for in 1901.[5] Barristers and solicitors from England and pleaders from the Indian High Courts were allowed to practise, and disciplinary control was to be exercised by the High Court, with an appeal to the High Court at Zanzibar, and as a last resort to the Foreign Secretary. Remuneration agreements were to be in writing, registered with the court, and if sued upon, could be reduced by the court if it thought they were unreasonable. At this early date the profession did not have a monopoly of practice, for the same regulations provided that if there were not enough legal practitioners for public requirements, the protectorate Judge (the senior judge of the High Court) could license other persons of good character and adequate capability to practise.

The first hint of monopoly appeared in 1906 when the Legal Practitioners Act[6] forbade those pleaders who had not been enrolled before an Indian High Court, and notaries public, to practise in the East Africa Protectorate. A revised and expanded version of the 1901 rules promulgated in 1911[7] omitted the licensing of non-lawyers, though it continued the licensing of *vakeels*, and from that time onwards the monopoly of the legal profession was more secure, though it was not until 1929 that penalties for wrongfully acting as an advocate, and a statutory prohibition on the claiming of fees for so doing, were introduced.[8]

The 1911 rules extended the right to practise to advocates from self-governing dominions, and to all types of lawyers from the British Isles. They also clarified the disciplinary provisions by empowering the Crown Advocate (later Attorney-General), or a person aggrieved by the action of a legal practitioner, to apply to a judge in chambers for a rule directed to that practitioner to show cause why he should not be suspended. The hearing was in open court. Other rules of court of this period laid down the rates of remuneration which could be charged, but these were in the nature of maximum rates, for there was no prohibition against undercutting them.[9]

[5] East Africa Legal Practitioners' Rules (1901), 1 E.A.L.R. 121. See, too, Native Courts Practitioners' Rules (1899), 1 E.A.L.R. 126 which regulated native *vakeels* and pleaders before the Muslim native courts at the coast. *Vakeels* had to be related to, or be the general agent of, the litigant. The 1901 Rules permitted native *vakeels* to practise on production of evidence of qualifications and good character.
[6] No. 19 of 1906.
[7] Rules of Court (Legal Practitioners) No. 2 (1911), appendix 1, 4 E.A.L.R. 3.
[8] Legal Practitioners (Amendment) Ordinance No. 7 of 1929.
[9] Rules of Court (Advocates' Remuneration and Taxation of Costs) No. 2 (1916), 5 E.A.L.R. 14.

At the same time legal practitioners were permitted to make remuneration agreements with clients to such amount and in such a manner as they might think fit, provided that the agreement did not give the legal practitioner an interest in the litigation, and did not exempt him from liability for negligence. A Taxing Master and the court could examine and vary any agreement. With two significant additions—the requirement of a six months' residence period in Kenya before commencing practice, introduced in 1926,[10] and the penalties and prohibitions for wrongful acting as a practitioner, introduced in 1929—this framework of control remained broadly the same until 1949.

During much of this period, there were two Law Societies in Kenya, the Mombasa Law Society, and the Law Society based at Nairobi. Both bodies were voluntary, and the amalgamated body, the Law Society of Kenya, which came into being in the 1920s, was also voluntary. (The Mombasa Society still continues as a separate body, although without statutory authority, and even though one lawyer from Mombasa is normally on the Council of the Law Society of Kenya.) From 1935 it was making representations to the administration that the legal profession should be organized on the lines of the solicitor's profession in England with the Law Society given a central statutory role. As a result of the first representations, a committee was established to look into the whole question, but the Attorney-General took a long time to consider the report that was produced in 1938, and the Administration seized on the war as an excuse to shelve the question indefinitely.[11] It was only after the end of the war that the Law Society began to re-apply the pressure which finally resulted in the Advocates, and Law Society of Kenya, Acts of 1949, both of which marked a fundamental change in the position of the legal profession.

Throughout the whole of this first period, and indeed well beyond it, the legal profession had remained almost wholly apart from the African population of Kenya. Indeed until the end of the war, the Nairobi Law Society was exclusively a European organization, and it was against stern opposition from some of its members that, when it was revived after temporary demise during the war, membership was opened to non-Europeans. What little professional contact it had with Africans diminished to near zero following the Native Tribunals Act 1930, and it is significant that neither the Law Society, nor any advocate, gave evidence to the Bushe Commission in 1933. Phillips did not consider it necessary to consult with, or invite evidence from the Law Society in his investigation of Native Tribunals in 1944, nor did it contribute a memorandum of its own accord.

[10] Rules of Court (Legal Practitioners), No. 3 (1926), 10 K.L.R. 184.
[11] Legislative Council, *Debates*, volume 34 (26 October 1949), col. 72 (O'Connor, A-G, introducing the Advocates Bill 1949 for its second reading).

The profession consisted wholly of non-Africans and belonged to the small comparatively wealthy non-African élite of Kenya. Its main work was to service the legal needs of this community, and thus it congregated in the main centres of non-African population, principally Mombasa and Nairobi. Its English education, and the type of law that it applied, emphasized its remoteness from the African population and their legal problems. There was consequently every incentive to emphasize the Englishness of the profession, and none to associate it with the Africans, with whom there was neither general, social, nor professional contact. This fact is of crucial importance in the development of the profession in the second period.

DEVELOPMENT OF THE LEGAL PROFESSION AFTER 1949

The Acts which were passed in 1949, which placed the organization and control of the legal profession on a new footing, closely followed drafts prepared by a committee of the Law Society set up in 1945 to press for such legislation, and had been thoroughly discussed by members of the society prior to their submission to the Attorney-General.[12] The Law Society of Kenya Act[13] established the existing Law Society as an incorporated body having among its main objects the maintenance and improvement of the standards of conduct of the legal profession in Kenya, the representation and protection of, and assistance to members of the profession as regards their conditions of practice and otherwise, and the protection of and assistance to members of the public in all matters touching law. The Society was to be governed by a Council consisting of a president, and six other persons elected at an annual general meeting, the president himself being elected by the Council and not the members directly, and a convention had grown in the 'fifties and 'sixties that a European and an Asian would be the annual president alternatively. The Council was empowered to make rules on a variety of topics, among them the grounds for expulsion from the Society. These rules did not have to be approved by any other person or body, any more than did any of the other actions of the Council. This did not perhaps matter too much, for membership of the Society remained voluntary, and expulsion therefrom did not prevent an advocate from continuing to practise. This was an important limitation on the powers of the Society.

The Advocates Act[14] was represented by the Attorney-General, in introducing it into the Legislative Council, as being mainly a repetition of the old law on the subject. It is difficult to accept this, for it established bodies and conferred powers where none had previously existed as a matter of law, whatever might have been the position in practice. The two important

[12] Legislative Council, *Debates*, ibid.
[13] No. 10 of 1949.
[14] No. 55 of 1949.

new bodies that were established were the Advocates' Committee and the Remuneration Committee. The first consisted of the Attorney-General, the Solicitor-General, and three advocates from the Law Society, and was given certain responsibilities in the field of discipline. Anyone could make a complaint concerning the conduct of an advocate. The complainant and the advocate complained of were heard by the Committee, which submitted a report to the court, together with all the evidence, if it considered that there was a prima facie case to answer. A court of two judges was to consider the report, giving the advocate a hearing if he so desired, and if it found the complaint proved might admonish, suspend, or order the advocate to be struck off the Roll of Advocates, the latter two punishments having the effect of preventing the advocate from practising. The Committee performed the function of a filter, the actual disciplinary decision being still left to the judges who acted, however, largely on the evidence collected by the Committee. Since advocates were in a majority on the Committee, they had made a significant gain in acquiring control over discipline.

The role of the Law Society in vetting entrants into the legal profession was also enhanced. A person applying to be admitted to the Roll of Advocates had first to be interviewed by the Law Society (in practice a Committee of the Council), which forwarded a report on the applicant to the Chief Justice, who was to admit him unless he thought he was not of a fit and proper character. In practice the effective power of admittance was wielded by the Law Society, for successive Chief Justices rarely departed from its recommendations. After being admitted, an advocate wishing to practise was required to obtain an annual practising certificate from the Registrar, which he might only refuse in certain specified circumstances.

The Remuneration Committee and the general law of remuneration marked, in some ways, the most important advance for the profession. The Committee consisted of five advocates nominated by the Law Society. The Chief Justice might make orders prescribing the rates of remuneration for both contentious and non-contentious business on the recommendation of this Committee. The Committee was also given an exclusive jurisdiction to enforce, or set aside, a remuneration agreement, for no action could be brought upon such an agreement in the courts by either party to it. Advocates were permitted to take security from their clients for their costs, and the court was empowered to declare an advocate entitled to a charge on property recovered through his services for his fees—two provisions which went some way towards offsetting the prohibition against maintenance. The most important new rule, however, was that an advocate might not agree to undertake work for a fee below the prescribed rates of remuneration; for an advocate to hold himself out directly or indirectly as being prepared to work for less than the prescribed rates or to make an agreement so to work, was in future to be classified as professional misconduct. By this provision maximum rates were transformed into minimum rates which the Law Society would in future have the major say in prescribing and policing.

The final point which must be mentioned relates to the tightening of the monopoly of legal practice. In future it was to be an offence to prepare documents relating to movable and immovable property in the expectation of being paid for so doing if one was unqualified. Thus the profession made sure of retaining their near-monopoly of work in connection with transactions in registered land (and all land in the modern sector of the economy is registered) and preventing the possibility of the growth of a class of land brokers or firms of non-lawyers or both lawyers and non-lawyers (for it was professional misconduct for a lawyer to act for an unqualified person) specializing in providing a cheap service in handling land transactions to the owners of registered land.[15] It is not without significance in view of this provision that since that date the Law Society has never opposed the extension of registration in Kenya whereas before that date it had on occasions apparently done so.[16] The only infringement of the monopoly of the Bar was the continued existence of *vakeels*, who, on giving a bond for good behaviour, could be licensed by the Chief Justice to appear in the Muslim subordinate courts.

Though in some respects the two Acts only placed on a legal footing what had been the practice for some time past, their total effect was to give a measure of self-government and power to the Bar, greatly in advance of anything it had had before. It had achieved this position by the continuing pressure it had brought to bear on successive Attorneys-General, the last one of whom stated, on introducing the Advocates Bill into the Legislative Council, that it was not perfect, that there were some respects in which he would have liked to see it different, but that the Law Society would not have it.[17] The major tactics of the Bar had been to argue for self-government on the

[15] Such as exist in the state of South Australia, where lawyers originally opposed the introduction of a system of land registration and refused to co-operate with it. See Paton (editor), *Australia: The Development of its Laws and Constitutions* (London, Stevens and Sons, 1952), pp. 123–7. Advocates did not have a complete monopoly of transactions in registered land, for many agricultural transactions took the form of an equitable mortgage by deposit of title deeds, in which the relevant bank drew up the necessary documents and the mortgagor did not have to use an advocate at all. It is interesting to note that the Registered Land Act contains no reference to an equitable mortgage or charge by deposit of title deeds, and that owners of land or interests in land registered under that Act may dispose of their interests (which term means any act by a proprietor whereby his rights in or over his land are affected) only in accordance with the Act and not otherwise.

[16] Maini, *Land Law in East Africa* (Nairobi, Oxford University Press, 1967), p. 34. The author does not, however, indicate his authority for this comment.

[17] It is worth noting, in the light of later events, that one particular matter which the Attorney-General wanted introduced but the Law Society was opposed to, was pupillage in chambers for barristers trained in England while they were completing their residential qualifications in Kenya. The Law Society did not obtain all that it

English solicitors' pattern, and at this point in time, colonial officials did not challenge the basic relevance of that model. It was assumed without argument that if the Bar was so organized, it would be making the most effective contribution possible to legal and other developments in Kenya.

The two Acts may have given the Bar great powers, but it was not wholly satisfied with them, for there were still some loop-holes in the system of self-government that they had established. During the fifties, the most momentous decade in Kenya's political and constitutional history to date, the Law Society, using the same pressure and tactics as before, set itself to fill these loop-holes, and was wholly successful. A series of important amendments to the Acts in 1952 further increased its power. By the first,[18] the Advocates Committee acquired disciplinary powers over advocates' clerks, and was empowered to order that no advocate should employ a clerk convicted of certain offences without the permission of the Law Society. An appeal from such an order lay to the Supreme Court. The same amending legislation provided that the Advocates' Committee need not call upon an advocate to answer a complaint made to it about his conduct if it thought that no prima facie case had been made out in the complaint.

The second amendment to the Acts[19] contained a most important concession to the Law Society; membership became compulsory. An advocate was required to pay his subscription to the Law Society to the Registrar of the High Court at the same time as he paid his fee for his annual practising certificate, and the Registrar was not to issue that until the subscription had been paid. All fees received by the Registrar in respect of the admission of, or issuing of practising certificates to, or subscriptions paid by, advocates were to be paid by him to the Law Society, and could thereafter be applied by it to the furtherance of its objects. Members of the Society were no longer permitted to resign while they were entitled to practise, but conversely they could not be expelled while entitled to practise. On the other hand, an advocate struck off the Roll ceased to be a member of the Society, and one who was suspended was no longer entitled to the rights and privileges of membership. Somewhat surprisingly, in view of the greatly increased power which these amendments to the law gave the Law Society, no restrictions or limitations, in the nature of a requirement to consult the Chief Justice or obtain his approval, were attached to the rule-making power of the Law Society. The reasons given in the Legislature for the change were that the

wanted. Mr. H. Slade, a leading figure in the Society at that time, and one who was concerned with the negotiations over the Bill from the beginning, commented in debate that there were some respects in which he would have liked to see it different.

[18] Advocates (Amendment) Act No. 20 of 1952.

[19] Advocates (Amendment No. 2) Act No. 55 of 1952; Law Society of Kenya (Amendment) Act No. 56 of 1952.

Law Society was short of funds to perform its important statutory functions, and that it would become more truly representative of the profession.[20]

The Law Society had thus achieved a position which its counterpart in England had tried in vain to achieve. The monopoly by the Bar of legal practice had been strengthened by the closed shop now given to its trade union. The Law Society's power over its members had been increased without any corresponding assertion of public supervision over how that power was to be exercised—again, a privilege not accorded to the English Law Society. Its power as a pressure-group *vis-à-vis* the government of the day was also greatly increased, for it could now claim to speak for every single advocate in the country—a power it was not unwilling to exploit when the need arose. As with other accretions of power, this had been obtained without any real consideration of the role of the whole legal profession in Kenya. In 1952, Kenya was still seen, in the circles in which the profession moved, as a 'white man's country' and if this posed any problems for it, the solution was seen in becoming even more English.

To this end further privileges and concessions of self-government were obtained. The 1952 amendments went some way towards introducing the two-counsel rule into the unified profession of Kenya by providing that Queen's Counsel were not to perform the functions of solicitors. In 1954,[21] the Advocates' Committee was empowered to exercise the disciplinary power of admonishing an advocate if it considered a prima facie case of misconduct had been made out on the complaint of any person. An advocate could, however, require a report of such proceedings to be laid before the court of two judges, which could then confirm or quash the admonition. This same amending Act introduced the principle of reciprocal enforcement of suspensions and strikings off in the East African countries.

Further amendments to the two Acts were proposed from time to time by the Law Society in the later fifties, but by the beginning of the next decade, the Society was working on two new Bills which would completely replace the existing Acts, incorporate some of the provisions of the English Solicitors Act 1957 into the law of Kenya, and obtain further powers of self-government in those few areas in which they were lacking. At this point, the Report of the Denning Committee on Legal Education for Students from Africa[22] was published, and its implementation in respect of Kenya precipitated a major row between the Government and the Bar, the first such that had occurred, and significant both for that reason and for the subject-matter of the row. The implementation of the Report was contained in the Advocates Act 1961,[23] which, except for this and one other matter,

[20] Legislative Councils, *Debates*, volume 52 (25 November 1952), cols. 321–323.
[21] Advocates (Amendment) Act No. 49 of 1954.
[22] Cmnd. 1255/1961.
[23] No. 34 of 1961, Cap. 16.

was entirely the product of the Law Society. The controversy and provisions relating to legal education and entry into the profession will be dealt with after the other main provisions of the Act have been examined.[24]

Important changes from the previous legislation were made in the key fields of discipline, remuneration, and unqualified persons' attempts to practise. In place of the Advocates' Committee with its primarily advisory and 'filter' powers, a Disciplinary Committee with full executive powers over discipline was established, with its own filter system attached. The Committee is composed of the Attorney-General, the Solicitor-General, and three advocates of at least ten years standing, of whom one is to be in practice outside Nairobi. It may act as a tribunal of three or five members, provided that either the Attorney-General or Solicitor-General is present at the sitting, and may require the President or Vice-President of the Law Society, or both, to sit, in order to make up the numbers. The secretary of the Law Society is the secretary of the Committee, which is empowered to administer oaths and make rules governing its procedure.

Complaints against the conduct of an advocate may be made to the Disciplinary Committee by any person. On receipt of the complaint it is referred to a board of inquiry consisting of three advocates of not less than five years' standing appointed by the Council of the Law Society. The board is to consider the complaint and make such inquiries as it thinks fit in so doing. If it considers that the complaint does not warrant a reference to the Disciplinary Committee it rejects it, otherwise it refers it to the Committee and in any event it reports what action it has taken to the Committee. A complainant whose complaint has been rejected by the board may refer it himself to the Committee but only on payment of a stiff fee deliberately designed to be a deterrent to prevent 'frivolous' complaints.[25] The fee is to be paid to the Society to be used for the furtherance of any of its objects.

Even when the Committee is finally seized of the complaint, it is not required to give it a full consideration and hearing. If, in its opinion, it does not disclose a prima facie case of professional misconduct, it may dismiss it without requiring the advocate complained of to answer it, and without hearing the complainant. If it does decide to hear the complaint,

[24] Legislation on the Law Society was also revised by the Law Society of Kenya Act No. 30 of 1962, Cap. 18. The only significant amendments to the law concerned the composition of the Council of the Society and the summoning of meetings. The Council, which was elected, was henceforth to include at least one non-Nairobi-based advocate amongst its membership of ten. The Council was required henceforth to hold a special meeting of the Society if any fifteen members of the Society so requested it.

[25] Legislative Councils *Debates*, volume 88 (6 December 1961), col. 1041 (Webb, Temporary Minister for Legal Affairs introducing the Advocates Bill on its second reading). It would appear that fees paid in respect of a complaint justifiably referred to the Committee are not returned to the complainant, for the Act makes no distinction between those and fees in respect of complaints held to be frivolous.

however, it must give the advocate complained of an opportunity to appear before it (there is no equivalent statutory duty imposed upon it in respect of the complainant), and may then dismiss the complaint or admonish, fine, or suspend the advocate or order him to be struck off the Roll. A report of the Committee's findings is to be sent to the court and the Registrar, and may be inspected by the advocate and the complainant but not the public. The disciplined advocate may appeal to a two judge bench of the High Court, which may refer the report back to the Committee or make orders confirming or varying or reversing its decision, and from which order, appeal lies to the E.A.C.A. The Chief Justice is vested with the power to restore an advocate to the Roll, either on his own initiative or on the recommendation of the Disciplinary Committee.

The Remuneration Committee is replaced by the Council of the Law Society, which may make recommendations on all matters relating to the remuneration of advocates. The Chief Justice is to consider these recommendations before he prescribes rates for both contentious and non-contentious business. Remuneration agreements, other than those to accept less than the prescribed rates, may be made before, after, or during the business in respect of which they are made. The client may within six months apply to the High Court to have the agreement set aside as harsh, unconscionable, exorbitant or unreasonable. The court must sit with two advocates as assessors, appointed by the Registrar after consultation with the secretary of the Law Society. Its decision is final. The problem of a client wishing to change his advocate after concluding an agreement with him receives attention for the first time. A client is at liberty to make such a change, and apply to the court to vary the agreement accordingly, but on such an application the court is to have regard to the circumstances in which the change has taken place, and unless it is of the opinion that there has been neglect, default, negligence, improper delay, or other conduct on the part of the advocate affording a reasonable ground for changing him, it is to allow the advocate the full amount stipulated for in the agreement.

These provisions would seem to impose a very heavy burden on the client, and permit a correspondingly privileged position to the advocate, for what a lay client may consider reasonable grounds for changing his advocate may well not satisfy a judge sitting with two advocate assessors. The fallacy in the provisions seems to be in regarding the agreement as an ordinary contract which the client must adhere to, or pay the penalty for breach thereof. But to view the provision of legal services by a profession having a monopoly of their supply, and the power to lay down the terms upon which they are supplied, in such simple terms, is to weigh the balance heavily against the consumer of those services, and in this situation it converts a *de jure* profession-wide monopoly into a *de facto* single advocate monopoly—

the client has little option but to continue making use of an advocate with whom he is dissatisfied, because he is going to have to pay him the full amount of the agreement in any case.

The provisions against all forms of undercutting are tightened up. The Minister introducing the Bill admitted that these provisions against undercutting were different in England, but stated that 'we do not think it [undercutting] proper in the present context of Kenya'.[26] No reasons were given for this. At the committee stage of the Bill, where an amendment was introduced to stiffen the provisions against undercutting still further, it was made clear that the prohibition extended to undercutting as a form of unofficial legal aid.[27] An advocate who offered his services at a discount for that reason would have to rely on the discretion of the Disciplinary Committee. Since the tightening-up provisions were introduced at the behest of the Law Society which wanted to stop undercutting becoming more rife than it was at that time, and the Law Society provided a majority of the Disciplinary Committee, one may be forgiven a certain scepticism as to the likelihood of that discretion being exercised favourably in such situations.

The penalties against unqualified persons acting as advocates are extended to embrace those who act without any expectation of reward, and those who merely pretend to be advocates without acting as such. Both classes of persons are deemed to be in contempt of court, and can be imprisoned or fined. The prohibition does not extend to public officers, or persons employed by advocates, for example, their clerks, but its general effect is to increase the occasions when it may be necessary to use the services of an advocate.

All these changes represented further privileges and powers of self-government for the Bar which, as a result of this Act, achieved a position of greater privilege and monopoly than the solicitor's profession in England, a hitherto little noticed side-effect of a fused profession. Far from showing any appreciation of the privileged and responsible position which they had achieved, the Bar, speaking through those of its members who were in the Legislative Council, was critical on occasions to the point of bitterness and hostility over the matters in respect of which it had failed to get its way, and considered that it had thereby suffered a loss of power. The two matters in which it did not get its way were the composition of the Council of Legal Education, and the virtual elimination for the future of lawyers qualified in Commonwealth countries other than the United Kingdom being able to come to Kenya and practise law there. On the second point, much concern was expressed that Irish and Asian lawyers would no longer be able to come to Kenya and practise, and it was suggested that anybody who wanted

[26] *Debates*, op. cit., col. 1040.
[27] Legislative Council, *Debates*, volume 88 (12 December 1961), cols. 1209–1229, at cols. 1225–1226 (Webb).

to, should be allowed to come and practise law in Kenya. There was no equivalent concern at the lack of African advocates, and the need to produce some as soon as possible. There was the barest mention of the problem of legal aid and advice for the poor—the vast majority of Kenyans—and then only as a subsidiary argument for allowing Commonwealth lawyers to practise in Kenya.[28] No mention was made of the adverse effect on legal aid of the tightening-up of provisions against undercutting.

A relatively minor matter on which the Government was not prepared to make a concession was the privileges which should accrue to a QC. The Bill repeated the prohibition against such persons undertaking solicitors' work, but in the Legislative Council, Mr Salter, QC, speaking, as he said, on behalf of the other Kenya QCs, demanded that they be given all the privileges of an English QC, and in particular that they should cease to be liable for negligence.[29] The Minister for Legal Affairs observed that this was not a demand supported by the Law Society, but that he would refer it to the Lord Chancellor's Office. That Office presumably rejected it, for the Act conferred no such immunity on the Kenya QCs.

In some respects, the most remarkable feature of the debates on the Bill was the attitude adopted by the advocate members of the Legislative Council to those parts of it on which the Law Society had failed to get its way. They pointed out to the Minister of Legal Affairs, himself a lawyer and a member of the Law Society, and chief government spokesman on the Bill, that he stood alone against the unanimous, or overwhelming, opinion of almost four hundred of his legal brethren expressed through the Law Society, that he should not go against the wishes of the profession of which he was a member, and that although the Law Society was only in an advisory position, its advice should prevail against that of members who did not practise, unless there were the strongest possible reasons to the contrary. In the circumstances, the Minister's comments in the debate were extremely mild. He stated that while he paid great attention to the views of the Law Society, it was bound to be prejudiced by considerations of its own interests, and emotions engendered by past practice, and government must therefore have the last word.

Another line of approach used in the debate was the copious reference to the law and practice of England and India, and the opinions of such bodies as the International Commission of Jurists and *Justice*.[30] References to the

[28] Second reading, *Debates*, op. cit., cols. 1048–1054 (De Souza). The connection between increasing the number of Commonwealth lawyers allowed to practise in Kenya, and providing legal advice for the poor was not spelt out, and indeed is not at all clear in view of the other provisions of the Act against undercutting and the complete absence of any system of free or heavily subsidized legal aid and advice.

[29] Second reading, *Debates*, op. cit., cols. 1042–1048, at col. 1047.

[30] See, particularly cols. 1054–1062, second reading, and 1211–1213, committee; and De Souza (cols. 1212–1215, committee).

English law governing solicitors were somewhat selective, however, for only those portions were referred to which showed the solicitors as having a greater power of self-government than the profession in Kenya was achieving, and not those portions which showed the reverse. The references, however, were used as if it were self-evident that the position in England, and to a lesser extent India, should be reproduced with no variations in Kenya. As we have seen, this has been the constant theme of the legal profession in Kenya, and it was the Minister's deliberate refusal to follow English practice in relation to legal education and entry into the profession, and his rejection of it as irrelevant to Kenya's needs, that shocked the Bar, and aroused the ire of its representatives in the Legislature, for this had never happened before. This matter, and the Bar's reaction to the Government's proposals, must be considered in some detail.

LEGAL EDUCATION AND ENTRY INTO THE PROFESSION

The Denning Committee recommended that there should be a uniform qualification to practise in East Africa, obtainable in East Africa, which should consist of a law degree from a Faculty of Law to be established at Dar es Salaam as part of the University College, one of the constituent colleges of the projected University of East Africa, followed by one year's practical training to be provided at a School of Law established for that purpose at one of the commercial centres of East Africa, to cater for the whole of East Africa.[31] It looked with favour on the establishment of Councils of Legal Education or similar bodies in the East African countries to co-ordinate qualifications for entry into the profession, and instanced, as an example, the projected Nigerian Council of Legal Education which was 'to consist of representatives from the judges, the law officers, the Bar, the faculty of law, and the school of law'.[32] It outlined, being careful not to commit itself either way, a plan for a system of articled clerkship similar to that adopted by the Law Society in England for training solicitors, which, it stated, at least one of the territories was preparing to institute.[33]

The Kenya Government established a Council of Legal Education on an administrative basis in the middle of 1961. It was composed of representatives of the Attorney-General's Chambers, the judiciary and the Law Society. The Law Society did not approve of the recommendations of the Denning Committee, and recommended that Kenya establish a School of Law and a system of articled clerkship, as an alternative to a university legal education, followed by a one year practical course. The Government accepted this recommendation, but as an additional means of entering the legal profession,

[31] *Report*, op. cit., paras. 51, 57, 60–62.
[32] ibid., para. 70.
[33] ibid., paras. 64–67.

and not, as the Law Society would have preferred, as the sole means. The Advocates Act accordingly provides for two main streams of entry into the legal profession in Kenya. A person must either have received a professional legal qualification in the United Kingdom, or hold a prescribed degree in law from a prescribed University or University College,[34] have attended for one year as a pupil and received instruction from an advocate of not less than five years' standing, and have passed such examinations as may be prescribed by the Council of Legal Education, which may, however, exempt a person from these last two requirements.[35]

The alternative is that a person may enter into articles of clerkship with an advocate who must be of not less than seven years' standing, unless the Council has given special permission to dispense with that requirement. The period of articles is to vary depending on the educational background of the individual concerned.[36] All clerks must be employed in the business of the advocate who is their principal, and must complete a course of legal education at the School of Law, through attendance thereat, and passing the prescribed examinations. The Council may waive attendance at the School where special circumstances exist—for example, when a clerk is articled to an advocate at Mombasa—and may of its own motion determine articles, all of which have to be registered with it, if satisfied that an articled clerk is morally unfit to be an officer of the court.

The bare outlines of the two streams of legal education suggest a rational system for, as has been pointed out,[37] the long-standing argument between the protagonists of professional legal training and university legal education has nowhere been finally or satisfactorily resolved, and Kenya is not alone in declining to base its system of entry into the profession on only one of the

[34] Advocates (Degree Qualification) Regulations Legal Notice 476/1963; Advocates (Qualifications) (Admissions) Regulations Legal Notice 199/1965. These regulations prescribe the LL.B. of the University of East Africa and any undergraduate law degree of any University in the British Isles that offered a law degree in 1963, when the prescribed list was compiled. For a brief period a mysterious Oxford LL.B. was on the prescribed list, but not the more common Oxford B.C.L. No other degrees have been prescribed. The Council has debated but rejected proposals to prescribe law degrees from Canada, U.S.A. and Russia.

[35] Advocates (Admission) Regulations Legal Notice 568/1963; Advocates (Admission) (Amd.) Regulations Legal Notice 262/1965. Exemptions from examinations may be granted if, in the opinion of the Council, the applicant has sufficiently covered their subject matter in his previous course. Exemptions may be granted from examinations and pupillage, however, at the unfettered discretion of the Council. In practice the Council is very ready to grant exemptions to persons who have obtained professional legal qualifications in the British Isles despite the fact that most of these persons are barristers and therefore totally unfamiliar with the solicitor-type organization and work of the profession in Kenya.

[36] Periods are as follows: three years for a person who has been an advocate's clerk for at least seven years, and for a person holding a degree other than a prescribed one; five years for a person with two passes at the principal level of the Cambridge Overseas School Certificate ('A' level); five years for a person with five passes at the ordinary level.

[37] A. W. Bradley, 1966 *Cambridge Law Journal* 291.

two possible methods. It is, however, the way the system has been run that is more open to comment.

From the first, the Law Society was opposed to university legal education and to allowing professional legal educators any say in the policy-making or administration of legal education and entry into the profession in Kenya, and was prepared to carry its opposition to great lengths. Its opposition commenced when it took strong objection to the proposed composition of the Council of Legal Education: two judges, the Attorney-General or a representative from his chambers, three advocates nominated by the Law Society and one teacher of law appointed by the Attorney-General. The Bar considered that the proposed Council had a government majority, whereas it should have an absolute majority of advocates; this was so because the Council was to be the body which in effect admitted persons into the legal profession; this was a job which the legal profession had hitherto discharged on its sole responsibility and this was the position in England and India. In particular, there should be no law teacher on the Council; his status should be that of a servant of the Council, ready to tender advice when required, but not taking an equal part in Council deliberations.[38]

The Government's position was that the English practice was irrelevant; that it was obviously right that a Council charged with exercising general supervision and control over legal education in Kenya, and advising the Government thereon, should have a law teacher among its members, the law teacher would be a university law teacher and not in the employ of the Council or the Government, that a block of three out of seven members would give the profession ample power on the Council, but that in view of their feelings, government was prepared to give them half the membership of the Council by increasing their, and thus the Council's, number by one.

The Law Society was not satisfied with that concession. It continued the fight in the legislature, appealed to *Justice*[39] and other bodies in England on the basis that the independence of the profession and the Rule of Law were under attack by government, and when it still failed to obtain an absolute majority, its representatives on the Council of Legal Education, now established under the Act, declined to attend its meetings.[40] The Council was naturally unwilling to proceed in their absence, though its quorum permitted it to, and it did in fact do so. Eventually a face-saving amendment was devised, and smuggled through in a Statute Law (Miscellaneous

[38] This summary is based on the speeches of advocate members of the Legislative Council in the debates already referred to.

[39] The details are in *Justice's 5th Annual Report* (1962). The matter is referred to again in its *8th Annual Report* (1965).

[40] In resorting to a boycott, the Law Society was following an old Kenyan tradition, for this practice had often been used by the settlers in their disputes with the Administration, and had also been used by African politicians in the later fifties. See chapter II for details of these earlier boycotts.

Amendments) Act that the law teacher should be elected by the Council, rather than appointed by the Attorney-General, thus ensuring that he would not be a 'government' man.[41] The boycott was then called off.

From this inauspicious beginning, the Council, now dominated by the Law Society nominees, pushed ahead with plans to establish the Law School and the articled clerk stream as a fully-fledged alternative to the university education stream. A certain conflict of ideas and plans surrounded the growth of this stream and the Law School. The Minister in his speech introducing the Bill appeared to see the articled clerk stream as secondary to the university stream, and the Law School as providing a wide range of differing types of legal training to all and sundry. 'We are taking steps to see that no student who comes forward in the near future, and requires its services will find us wanting'.[42] The Law Society, on the other hand, saw the speedy development of the Law School for articled clerks under the Council as the best educational means of countering the influence of university legal education, and acquiring fuller control over legal education and entry into the profession in Kenya. The educational problems of establishing a Law School and a system of articled clerkship became of secondary importance to this political objective.

Inevitably, with these different ideas and plans in being, the development of the Law School has been somewhat haphazard.[43] At its most lyrical the Denning Committee envisaged the School of Law to be established to provide post-degree professional training for law students from the Faculty of Law, as developing 'into an Inn of Court where students would not only receive practical instruction but also build up a corporate life as members of the profession . . .'[44] The Law Society shared this vision, but reality has turned out to be rather different. The first intimation of reality was the appointment of the first principal of the School; this was done by the Government without prior consultation with the Council as to the individual appointed; the Council merely ratified the appointment. There was some ill-feeling amongst the Law Society nominees on the Council over this incident, but it was the Law Society that was mainly responsible for the complete take-over of the School by the Government.

This came about because the Law Society finally convinced the Government of the desirability of supporting and building up the School. The Law Society did not, however, have the funds to develop it; the Government was able to obtain funds from the British Government, and devoted some of its own resources to it, and he who pays the piper calls the tune.

[41] Statute Law (Miscellaneous Amendments No 2) Act No. 36 of 1962.
[42] Second reading, *Debates*, op. cit., col. 1035.
[43] For a discussion of the development, see Twining 'Legal Education within East Africa' in *East African Law Today*, op. cit., pp. 115–51, at pp. 127–39.
Report, op. cit., para. 61.

The result of this was seen in developments in 1966 and 1967. In 1966, the method of appointment to the Council was changed; the appointment of the law teacher was placed in the hands of the Attorney-General once again without, however, any discussion of it in the Council or prior consultation with its chairman, the Chief Justice;[45] the immediate effect and object of this was to remove the member of the Faculty of Law of the University of East Africa from the Council.[45a] In 1967 the Attorney-General began to allocate members of his chambers to the staff of the School in the same way as he allocated them to handle certain cases, or go on assize. The School of Law became just another section of the Attorney-General's chambers. The Law Society which was so hostile to allowing a university legal educator to have anything to do with planning or supervising the education of the profession, had both acquiesced in, and encouraged, the complete governmental control of legal education in Kenya.

By the middle of 1967, however, the Law Society no longer spoke with a united voice on the future of the Law School. There were those who regretted the complete lack of contact between the Law School and the Bar on the one hand, and other institutions of higher education, particularly the University, on the other. They saw the dangers of the existing trend of developments, and believed that the best solution would be to hand the Law School over to the University which would provide the basic three-year degree course, leaving the job of organizing the post-degree practical training to the Bar. But these views were in a minority in the policy-making circles of the Law Society, which continued to view university legal education with greater suspicion than government legal education. Even the Government, however, was not entirely happy at having to look after such a sickly child, and began to look with more favour on university legal education provided it was located in Nairobi. In mid 1968, the University College there, with the full approval of the Government, decided to establish a Faculty of Law, offering a full three-year law degree. The question of the relationship between that Faculty and the School of Law, and the future role of the Council of Legal Education remained for solution however. One possible solution, similar to that proposed for Uganda, and in existence in Nigeria and Ghana, would be for the School of Law to become primarily a post-graduate practical training

[45] Statute Law (Miscellaneous Amendments) Act No. 21 of 1966.

[45a] He was replaced by a member of the Law Department of the University College, Nairobi, so to that extent University representation was retained. However, at the time of the change of personnel, there was only one law faculty in the University of East Africa, and that was providing a law degree to Kenyans which was a basic qualification to practise in Kenya. This was one important reason for the presence on the Council of a member of that law faculty, and while it was laudable to wish to involve law teachers from the University College Nairobi in the work of the Council, that could have been done by the addition of such a person and not by his substitution for a law faculty member.

school, providing required courses and exercises in Kenyan law and practice to all law graduates, wherever they came from, be it Nairobi, London or Bombay, and whatever their previous legal education, though there should be close liaison between the Faculty of Law and the Council.[46]

CONCLUSION: PROBLEMS AND PROSPECTS FOR THE PROFESSION

We have considered the development of legal education in some detail because it goes to the root of the development of the Bar in Kenya, highlighting its attitude towards its role, and society in general, and because, in retrospect, it now seems to be the first step in a slow, but unmistakable, assertion of government power over the Bar which, largely through its role in this matter, it finds itself unable to resist. While making every allowance for the fact that the leaders of the Law Society were having to deal with a matter with which they were unfamiliar, it is difficult not to conclude that they have failed, through their own deliberate decisions, to rise to the challenge provided by the Advocates Act to plan and create, in co-operation with other interested parties, a system of legal education designed to equip a student with an understanding of the law of Kenya, its social and economic problems, and the uses and limitations of the law in their solutions, so that as an advocate he would be able and willing to serve all sections of the population and play a proper public role in the development of his society. Too often they have given the impression that they are more concerned with an increase in their powers of self-government, and that they regard this as being more important than establishing a viable system of legal education. This indeed is a criticism of the Bar which can be made in more general terms, for the increase in its powers of self-government has not brought an increase in awareness of its public responsibilities in more traditional fields than that of legal education. For instance little effort has been made to provide a system of legal aid and advice for the urban poor, and such legal aid as exists is not widely publicized so that few people can take advantage of it.[47]

[46] A Faculty of Law is to be established at the University College, Nairobi in 1970. Even after it has been established there will be a need for some organized system of practical training for graduates from the University of East Africa, plus localization for graduates from abroad. Both types of training are virtually non-existent at the moment as the Council has been wholly concerned with building up the Law School as the Kenyan alternative to University legal education. It is arguable that it could make a much more significant contribution to legal education in Kenya if it developed a system of post-final practical training suited to Kenya's needs. For some suggestions on this, see Twining, 'Social Justice and the Law' in *East African Law and Social Change*, op. cit., pp. 258–78 at pp. 266–72.

[47] It was stated in a conference on Law and Social Change in East Africa, held at Dar es Salaam in April 1966, by a Kenyan that such legal aid as exists in Nairobi is deliberately not widely publicized lest the response is greater than the few advocates who take part in the service could cope with. Our information is that, despite the prohibition on it, undercutting is prevalent in Nairobi, and this no doubt operates as a form of legal aid. A suggestion that the students of the Law School might assist in a scheme of legal aid was opposed by the representatives of the Society at the Council.

Even in the field of human rights and the Rule of Law, which the legal profession generally has always claimed to be its special responsibility, and which provides the justification, in so far as any has been provided, for its privileged position in society, the Bar has never given a lead since it first acquired self-government in 1949. The harsh, and at times lawless, regime of the Emergency Regulations occasioned the Law Society no public alarm—indeed it was a leading member of the Society who, in the Legislative Council, called for still harsher measures.[48] Its appeals to *Justice* in the colonial period concerned its own supposed loss of power and independence. Since Kenya's independence it has kept quiet over the amendments to the Preservation of Public Security Act[49] which introduced preventive detention without trial, the large amount of retrospective legislation that has been produced, and the failure of government to prosecute its supporters who admit to breaking the law. The continuation of administrative magistrates, and the Attorney-General's wide power to direct the place of proceedings provided for in the Magistrate's Courts Act, passed without public comment from the Law Society. Indeed its only recorded intervention while the Bill was going through Parliament was to request an amendment to reduce the monetary limits of the civil jurisdiction of the Senior Resident and Resident Magistrate's Court on the grounds that it was too high. This was acceded to by the Government.[50] In this field then the picture is of a profession that is unwilling to stand up in public for matters of principle except where its own powers are concerned, and even there, it appears willing to compromise on the principle of independence, if, by allying itself with government, it can obtain increased powers.

It comes as no surprise therefore that a profession which has been so intimate with government for so long, and which has so little tradition of public protest or service, now finds itself unable to resist an even closer embrace. When a leading member of the profession, and a close associate and adviser of the leader of the KPU, was deprived of his citizenship and deported, the Bar took the hint. Advocates are now more chary of acting for members of the opposition in criminal or civil matters.[51] An eminent

[48] Legislative Councils, *Debates*, volume 57 (18 October 1953), cols. 67–111 at cols. 94–95 (H. Slade). Other advocate members of the Legislative Council were more dubious of the abolition of safeguards in a criminal trial contained in the Emergency Regulations in this debate, see cols. 75–78 (Madan).

[49] Cap. 57, as amended by the Constitution of Kenya (Amendment No. 3) Act No. 18 of 1966. See chapter XI.

[50] National Assembly, *Debates*, volume XII, part I (13 June 1967), cols. 880–881, section 5, Magistrate's Courts Act. The power given the Chief Justice to raise the limits of the jurisdiction of both courts, however, somewhat offsets the value of the concession.

[51] National Assembly, *Debates*, volume XIII, part II (28 November 1967), col. 2595. The whole debate on the incident is instructive (cols. 2592–2599). See, too, the question at volume XII, part II (28 July 1967), cols. 2899–2901.

QC from England was refused admission into Kenya in 1967 to take a case before the High Court. No public comment was forthcoming from a Law Society whose members a few years back had argued eloquently for an 'open house' policy on practice in Kenya, though a protest was made to the Government which rejected it, and argued that there were enough good lawyers in Kenya without having to import any. A short while after this incident, it was announced that the Government was considering vesting in the Attorney-General the power to permit foreign lawyers to take cases before the Kenyan courts. This would mean removing the power from the Chief Justice. The necessary legislation was passed soon afterwards.[52] It is by these piecemeal but significant means that the profession, and its mouthpiece, the Law Society, are slowly being manoeuvred into a position of subservience to government.

It would be easy to conclude that the Bar has not in the past represented, and does not now represent, any sort of effective pressure-group for constitutionalism and the Rule of Law, and leave it at that. It would be more useful, however, to try to state why this is so, why the Bar, in such a seemingly powerful position in 1949, did not begin to concern itself with those and allied issues, but instead concentrated on consolidating its own position, and why the maintenance of even that now appears to be beyond its powers. The basic explanation lies in the dual society of Kenya within which the Bar developed. It developed as part of the élite colonial society, its leaders were the leaders of the Asian and European communities in political and public affairs, and the bulk of its work was for these communities. It had been deliberately excluded from professional contact with the African part of society in 1930, and, inevitably thereafter, its interest in that part of society and its problems waned. Increasingly it saw itself as an integral part of the élite, and, as such, entitled to share its privileges, particularly that of self-government based on the English pattern. The colonial authorities in effect accepted this case in 1949, and the conclusion which the Bar could reasonably draw from its campaign for self-government was that so long as it confined itself to proposals for technical law reform, and its own organization and self-government, and did not, as a corporate body, become involved in contentious political issues, it would keep on the right side of government, and usually get its way. In the fifties, when Africans were beginning to push into the political arena through both political and revolutionary means, the Bar had become part of the established colonial order of things, set in its ways, and remarkably successful in the limited fields in which it had exerted pressure on government, pressure which was consistently in the direction of introducing English law and practices into

52 Statute Law (Miscellaneous Amendments) Act No. 8 of 1968.

Kenya. There was no apparent incentive to change its general outlook or policies, and so it did not.

Thus, when the era of African government arrived in Kenya, the Bar was unprepared for it or the consequent changes that it would bring in society. Most important of these from the point of view of the Bar was that its position changed from being an accepted part of the colonial society to being a rather conspicuous non-African part of an African society. This may be graphically illustrated by the fact that in 1968, just over four years after independence, of 292 advocates based in Kenya who took out practising certificates in Kenya, 11 were Africans, 224 Asians and 57 Europeans.[53] This poses problems for it. In the past it held aloof from political and constitutional developments out of choice, now it must hold aloof out of necessity, for any public comment critical of governmental action would be quickly seized upon as evidence that the Bar was not loyal to the new state of Kenya, since similar comment had not been forthcoming in the colonial era. The increasing pressure to Africanize the trading and commercial sector of the economy which provides the Bar with much of its work, and the tightening-up of conditions for non-citizens to retain, and obtain, work in Kenya are forcing the Bar more and more on to the defensive.[54] In these circumstances a continuation of the old policy of no political role, co-operation with government, and concentration on the safeguarding of its own position, may well seem to offer the best hope for survival.

The pressures which now exist on the Bar may explain its present role, but do not excuse its past deficiencies. One of the most serious of these has been its general failure to try and identify itself a little more with the African population of Kenya. While it was not the fault of the Bar that there were so few African advocates by the beginning of the sixties—it was the policy of the colonial authorities not to provide scholarships for Africans to study law, and few had the private means to do so—it was a grave mistake, stemming from its social position in Kenya, to be so uninterested in that problem, or even to recognize that it was a problem. Its conversion to the cause of legal education in Kenya owed more to its fear of losing control of entry into the profession, than to a commitment to speed the entry of Africans into the profession. The grounds of its opposition to the implementation of the Denning Report were that it was sceptical of the value of a university legal education, but the result of its opposition was that the first two or three graduating classes of Africans from the University of East Africa's law faculty did not find themselves made welcome by the Bar in

[53] There were nine advocates who took out practising certificates in Kenya who were based in either Uganda or Tanzania.

[54] The important statutes here are the Immigration Act No. 25 of 1967, and the Trade Licensing Act No. 34 of 1967, both avowedly designed to increase African participation in the commercial and professional life of the country.

Nairobi. The position was changing by 1967, and good salaries were being offered to African graduates to join some of the larger firms as articled clerks, but the damage had been done and there is now a residue of hostility between the African graduates, educated in East Africa, and the non-African Bar, educated for the most part in the United Kingdom.[55]

The failure to develop effective legal aid schemes in urban centres is another example of this non-involvement with the African population, made the more serious by the fact that there is a massive concentration of advocates in the major urban centres. In 1968, 199 had offices in Nairobi and 49 in Mombasa.[56] It is to be doubted whether all these make an adequate living from practice, certainly the turn-over of advocates is very fast, comparatively few staying in practice for any length of time, yet, properly organized, some of them could provide the nucleus of a legal aid and advice scheme, paid for by the Bar as a whole through the Law Society, on such matters as rent control, and employment problems. This failure to identify with the African population and to change its colonial image means that it will be unable to rely on much indigenous support as it comes under increasing government pressure. Since few Africans have obtained any benefit, direct or indirect from, or have a stake in, a strong and independent legal profession, few will defend it against government pressure, particularly when that is put in terms of Africanization. It will be seen for what it has always held itself out to be, part of the non-African commercial sector of the community, and as such entitled to no special privileges or attention.

Until very recently there has in fact been a marked lack of sympathetic or indeed any public interest, as evidenced by debates in the legislature, in the development of the legal profession. This has been of undoubted benefit to the Bar, and there have been times in the legislature when non-lawyers have been encouraged to take no interest in a Bill conferring powers on it, or at least not to have the temerity to suggest any alterations to it.[57] Non-lawyers have been given to understand that they are very lucky that Kenya has a legal profession willing to shoulder the burdens of self-government. There are some signs, however, that this immunity from lay opinion, in the legislature at any rate, may soon come to an end. Africanization is no respecter of persons or professions, and in the fifth and sixth sessions of the first

[55] Most of the first graduates of the University of East Africa went into central or local government service, and only in 1968 were these first graduates coming out of such service, and, together with later graduates, moving into the private sector. One of the larger firms in Nairobi was prepared to pay £600 per annum to a graduate articled clerk during his one year's pupillage, a generous offer, but not thought so by all graduates, as it was below the starting salary for a probationary state attorney.

[56] The location of others was as follows: Kisumu, 12; Nakuru, 9; Eldoret, 6; Kitale, 5; Thika, 3; Nyeri 3; Kericho, 2; Kisii, 2; Machakos, 1; Meru, 1; Kakamega, 1; Malindi, 1. Some advocates have offices in two places and these have been counted as two separate advocates.

[57] Legislative Council, *Debates*, volume 47 (1 April 1952), cols. 13–16.

Parliament of Kenya, there were several questions and short debates on the slow progress of the Africanization of the judicial service, including High Court judges, and of other public service lawyers, and other aspects of the legal profession.[58] The pressure is on the public legal profession because there are so many expatriates still in it, and it is that branch of the legal profession that African lawyers are at the moment joining. There is no reason to suppose that the private branch of the profession will not equally come under fire when Africans begin to join it in significant numbers, as may soon occur, and consider that their prospects of obtaining work are hindered by non-African advocates. Moreover in this case the Immigration Act is to hand to assist in reducing the numbers of non-African advocates.

A final weakness of the profession may be mentioned. Quite apart from its failure to associate itself with the new African society, the general work and performance of the Bar, both in the past and now, does not provide very much justification for its present position of self-government. It cannot rely on the 'Rule of Law' argument, for that has waxed and waned in Kenya irrespective of the professional or other activities of the Bar. It cannot wholly rely on the relevance of English precedents because it has been prepared to depart from them in the past, when to do so has suited its purposes. In any event a reference to English precedents is a two-edged weapon, for nowadays African governments look to them to justify an increase, but never a decrease in their own powers, and Kenya is no exception to this. It cannot rely on economic arguments—that free competition is better than a state monopoly—because all its efforts over the years have been to eliminate any form of competition both from outside, and within its own ranks.[59] Finally it cannot rely on the argument that a self-governing Bar is able to give a better service to the public than one run as a state agency, for the majority of the public are not able to obtain the services of an advocate at a price they can afford, and therefore have to go without.

The only justification that can be put forward is that other professions in Kenya enjoy somewhat similar powers of self-government. But a profession's self-government must be distinguished from the degree of freedom from government control that that profession has in its daily work. If, for instance, the Government were to introduce a National Health Service, practically all doctors would thereafter be employed by the Government or some other public authority, but this would not prevent their professional

[58] House of Representatives, *Debates*, volume IX, part II, cols. 1434-1435; National Assembly, *Debates*, volume XI (16 February 1967), cols. 36–40; 28 February, 452–454; 1 March, 605–608; volume XIII, part I (5 October 1967), cols. 176–177; volume XIV (25 March 1968), col. 996; (26 March 1968), cols. 38–46.

[59] Economists have of late turned their attention to the professions and their monopolies of practice, statutory or otherwise, in England, and have reached some rather unwelcome (to the professions) conclusions. See in particular, Lees, *The Economic Consequences of the Professions* (London, Institute of Economic Affairs, 1966).

organization from disciplining them, representing them in negotiations with the Government, and proposing changes in medical practice. Similarly if a National Legal Service were to be proposed, the questions which would then have to be asked would be: what functions do, and should, lawyers perform in Kenya; which method of organization will ensure that they perform those functions most effectively; who is to pay for the work lawyers do? In answering these questions attention will have to be paid to the role of the lawyer in assisting the individual in his contact with government as well as to his other roles, and a system would have to be devised which was both efficient and obtained the confidence of the public. It is by no means certain that answers to these questions would result in a profession organized as it is at present in Kenya—no control over the numbers entering, or where they establish their offices, a multitude of one-man offices, or very small partnerships in which the corporate pressure to maintain high professional standards which accrues from membership of a large firm is absent, no representation of consumers on the governing body of the profession, and no organized provision of legal services for the poor. A reorganized profession might be a profession with a greater degree of overt public control, but if this resulted in its performing its functions more effectively, there could be little valid criticism.

The Bar then is in a vulnerable position. It is in that position because of its racial composition, its seeming irrelevance to the needs of most Kenyans, and its apparent inability or unwillingness to do anything about improving its organization and work. Unless it can convince a significant number of people that it can perform important services for the community, it will fail to obtain the support it needs to resist present encroachments of the Government, which are not always directed to desirable ends. It may be that the Government would not tolerate a Bar which was more actively involved in society, but at least an effort could be made, and it is that which is so conspicuously lacking at present. Thus, far from being a pressure group for constitutionalism and the Rule of Law, the Bar is unable to ensure the existence of two essential prerequisites for such a role—independence from government pressure, and public understanding and support for itself.

CHAPTER XI

Human Rights and Public Order

INTRODUCTION: THE COLONIAL HERITAGE

Kenya is no stranger to the problem common to all countries, of reconciling the needs of maintaining public order and protecting human rights. This problem was not, as some wishful thinking would have had it, solved by the creation of a Bill of Rights in the self-government Constitution of 1963, and its maintenance in the independence Constitution at the end of the same year, any more than it was solved by the original Bill of Rights, introduced into Kenya in 1960 as a result of decisions taken at the first Lancaster House Conference.[1] In this chapter we shall examine the problem, considering the Bill of Rights, various sensitive areas of political and quasi-political activity which it is designed to protect, and some general laws whose tenor might appear difficult to reconcile with the letter and spirit of the Bill of Rights. As with other areas of public law, however, it is necessary first to indicate something of the colonial traditions of this part of the law which the present Government has inherited, and which the Bill of Rights was in part designed to overcome.

Human Rights, as defined and protected in the Universal Declaration of Human Rights, the European Convention on Human Rights and the Bills of Rights in the constitutions of many countries, had little place in the colonial régime established in Kenya. Part One of this book showed how the colonial administration established and maintained by means of law a governmental and social system characterized by authoritarianism, and racial discrimination in such vital fields as the administration of justice, the development of representative institutions, and agrarian administration. The necessarily repressive and discriminatory nature of the colonial system and its hostility to human rights may be illustrated here by one or two examples drawn from early legislation, some of which, however, still remains in existence, and will be looked at in more detail later in the chapter.

In one of the first exercises of his legislative power—the Native Courts Regulations of 1897[2]—the Commissioner for the East Africa Protectorate armed himself with powers of preventive detention, and restriction of movement, in respect of any persons subject to the Regulations if it was shown to the satisfaction of the Commissioner, that the person was disaffected

[1] Kenya Constitution (Amendment) (No. 2) Order in Council 2201/1960.
[2] E.A.P.G., Orders and Regulations, volume I, p. 65, sections 77–79.

to the Government, was about to commit an offence against the regulations or was otherwise conducting himself so as to be dangerous to peace and good order in the protectorate. There was no appeal against the Commissioner's exercise of this power, though he had to report on the same forthwith to the Foreign Secretary.

There are several interesting points about these provisions, paralleled in other colonial laws. First, they provide for special powers which have effect to deprive a person of the basic rights of freedom of the person, of movement, and of recourse to the courts. Similar deprivations appeared in the Vagrancy Regulations[3] which provided for the arrest and detention of any person found asking for alms or wandering about without any employment or visible means of subsistence; the Native Passes Regulations which enabled the Commissioner to make 'such general or local rules for controlling the movements of natives travelling into, out of, or within the limits of the protectorate as may from time to time appear to him to be necessary or desirable',[4] and laws empowering administrators to impose curfew or other restriction orders.[5] Under the Outlying Districts Ordinance,[6] the Commissioner or other officials to whom he delegated the power could declare districts 'closed', the effect of which was to confer power on the administration to restrict, by means of the issue of licences, persons other than natives of the area from entering the district.

Secondly, there was a complete absence of any or adequate provisions for appeal. This was going further than some laws which at least provided for an appeal from one administrator to another, but it was by no means unique. In the regulations prohibiting *ngomas* or social activities there was no appeal from the order of the District Commissioner; and there was a similar absence of appeals in the Native Passes Regulations and the Outlying Districts Ordinance. The lack of adequate provisions for appeals was to some extent offset by the residual supervisory powers of the Colonial Office, its powers of disallowance of, or prior approval for, legislation, and the requirement that the action taken by local officials had to be reported to it in certain circumstances. It is very doubtful if in practice these provisions had a significant ameliorative effect, and in most cases non-compliance with them did not bring about invalidation.[7]

Thirdly, the powers of the Commissioner were discriminatory, for they were to be used only against those subject to the Native Courts Regulations—

[3] Regulations No. 2 of 1898, replaced by No. 3 of 1900.
[4] Regulations No. 12 of 1900, repealed in 1961.
[5] Preservation of Order by Night Regulation No. 15 of 1901.
[6] Regulations No. 31 of 1899, replaced by Regulations No. 25 of 1902, now Cap. 104. A licensee who failed to comply with the terms of his licence was liable to have his building or crops seized or disposed of as considered fit by the District Commissioner; the offender, however, had a right to the residue of the proceeds—section 7 (2).
[7] *Attorney-General* v. *Kathenge*, [1961] E.A. 348; see p. 409, below.

that is, Africans. Where laws were not expressly discriminatory, of which many examples have already been given,[8] administrators were given wide discretion, and in practice could and did exercise it in a discriminatory manner. In this they were generally supported by the courts, which seemed unwilling to extend their conceptions of justice from the administration of justice into other fields. The attitude of the courts may be illustrated by two decisions, upholding the principle of racial discrimination, where in both cases the court could have opted for different interpretations on the grounds that such discrimination was repugnant to public policy or the common law.[9] The first concerned the power of the Commissioner of Lands to impose restrictions on who could bid at auctions for sales of Crown land, and their use thereafter.[10] The Commissioner had advertised the auction of town plots at which only Europeans were to be allowed to bid and purchase and had stipulated that during the terms of the grant the grantee should not permit the dwelling house or outbuilding thereon to be used for the residence of any Asiatic or African who was not a domestic servant employed by him. The Commissioner's powers to dispose of land were derived from the Crown Lands Ordinance of 1915. The Ordinance had made a distinction between the disposal of agricultural and urban land, and the power to impose racial restrictions or covenants was expressly granted only in the case of agricultural land. It was argued by the appellants that therefore there was no power to impose these restrictions on the disposal of land in towns. The Judicial Committee, saying they were concerned with law and not policy, found for the Commissioner, holding that prima facie the rights of the Crown and its servants to dispose of Crown property were analogous to those of the private owners. They had to observe the express terms of the statute, but apart from that they were free to impose what restrictions they chose. Their Lordships went on to argue that it would be valid to restrict the bidding to industrialists, or the trading community, in appropriate cases; so why not to racial groups?

The second decision concerned the validity of a curfew order whose application was restricted to Africans only.[11] It was made under the Public Order Ordinance 1950 (as amended), section 10 of which provided that the curfew orders may be applied to 'every member of any class of persons' specified therein. Without considering what might have been intended to

[8] See also Chanan Singh, 'The Republican Constitution of Kenya' (1965) 14 *I.C.L.Q.* 878, and McAuslan, 'Prolegomenon to the Rule of Law in East Africa', *Proceedings of the E.A.I.S.E.R.*, Kampala (mimeo.), 1963.

[9] See e.g. *Constantine* v. *Imperial Hotels*, [1944] 2 All E.R. 171. But see *Koinange Mbiu* v. *R.* (1951), 24 (2) K.L.R. 130 where the High Court struck down discriminatory regulations as being *ultra vires* a statute.

[10] *The Commissioner for Local Government, Land and Settlement* v. *Kaderbhai* (1930), 12 K.L.R. 12 (J.C.P.C.)

[11] *Attorney-General* v. *Kathenge*, [1961] E.A. 348.

be the proper purposes of this phraseology, the court held that it permitted racial discrimination. The court also stated its opinion that non-conformity with legislative procedures requiring the consent of the Secretary of State for specified kinds of legislation, contained in the Royal Instructions, was not an invalidating factor since it was not justiciable.

A final example of denial of human rights is contained in the laws allowing collective punishment to the disregard of individual guilt or responsibility, and the imposition of responsibility for the misconduct of others on one deemed to be in authority over them. Good examples of the first are found in the Special Districts (Administration) Ordinance, discussed below, and in the Stock and Produce Theft Ordinance, section 15 of which authorized a magistrate, though not necessarily acting in a judicial capacity, on a complaint of stock theft to order all or some members of a tribe or sub-tribe to pay compensation to the aggrieved party in specified proportions (to determine which, one of the factors to be considered was the ability to pay) if it was established that any member of that tribe or sub-tribe had been implicated in the theft.[12] An example of the second provision occurred in the Village Headmen Ordinance of 1902, under which a headman, appointed by the Commissioner, was required to keep order in areas adjacent to his village or villages, and an order against him in his official capacity was enforceable against all the inhabitants of his village or villages. If an outrage (not defined) occurred in any area in which a headman was responsible for the preservation of order, and the perpetrator of such outrage could not be discovered, the Sub-Commissioner (later Provincial Commissioner) could in his discretion impose a fine upon such a headman unless he could prove to the satisfaction of the Sub-Commissioner that the outrage could not have been prevented by reasonable vigilance on his or his people's part.[13]

These laws were made necessary by a colonial régime established to provide conditions for European settlement, and were made possible by the absence of constitutional barriers; no fundamental and justiciable limitations of power were placed on either the legislature or executive, and there was little check in the legislature to the enactment of such legislation. But in addition to these normal powers, usually granted willingly

[12] Ordinance No. 18 of 1933, now Cap. 355. (The first such law was passed in 1913, Ordinance No. 8.) The Judicial Committee has accepted collective punishment as an emergency measure. *Ross-Clunis* v. *Papadopoulos*, [1958] 1 W.L.R. 546 (Cyprus). However in *Muhuri* v. *Attorney-General* (Crown Case 1021/1964, unreported), the court had to determine the validity of an order for compensation made under section 15 of the Stock and Produce Theft Act. It was held that it amounted to deprivation of property, and since it was not an 'order of the court in proceedings for the determination of civil rights or obligations' (Constitution section 75 (6) (IV)—p. 421, below), it was unconstitutional. After this decision such provisions for collective punishment as still exist in the law must now be regarded as void.

[13] Ordinance No. 22.

enough by the legislature, the administration could and did, particularly in the fifties, exercise extensive powers which overrode the normal ones, and bypassed the legislature, powers given to it by the Emergency (Powers) Orders in Council.[14] The Orders were brought into operation either for the whole territory or part of it by a proclamation of the Governor if he was satisfied that a public emergency existed. After that he had wide law-making powers—he could make such regulations as appeared to him necessary or expedient for securing the public safety, the defence of the territory, the maintenance of public order and the suppression of mutiny, rebellion and riot, and for maintaining supplies and services essential to the life of the community. The regulations were valid even if in conflict with other laws, indeed they could modify or suspend ordinary laws and could delegate law-making powers to other persons or authorities. It was possible under such powers to provide for detention, deportation, and exclusion from the country, the requisition of property and to authorize the entering and search of any premises. The legislature had no control over any of this nor was it really possible to challenge the validity of the regulations in the courts.

A distinct system of administration—powerful and centralized—was thus firmly established in Kenya. With the imminence of independence under an African government, major reversals of policy were decided upon and carried through. Kenya was to be a country where the Rule of Law was to be supreme, individual rights in a context of a non-discriminating society were to be fundamentally safeguarded, legislative and executive powers were to be accordingly circumscribed and the judges were to be established as watchdogs over the new scheme. The new system was to be brought into being through two kinds of changes. First, the decentralization of government with its powers divided between a central administration and regional authorities.[15] Secondly, the establishment within the constitution of a Bill of Rights[16] which was to be supreme over the ordinary laws and executive action, and whose amendment was through a complex and difficult process. A Bill of Rights was also considered a particularly appropriate device for the protection of minorities, which is at the same time acceptable to the majority, for it singles out not communities but individuals as possessors of rights.

[14] These were a series of orders contained in Group 3 volume XI, Kenya R.L. See, too, Holland, 'Law and Order in Kenya' (1954) 7 C.L.P. 173, 'Emergency Legislation in the Commonwealth' (1960) 13 C.L.P. 148. Regulations made under the Order in Council could be given retrospective effect. *Corbett* v. *Floyd*, [1958] E.A. 389.

[15] Chapter V.

[16] Chapter II of the Independence Constitution, now chapter V. The words 'Bill of Rights' are not used in the Constitution, the title of the chapter being 'Protection of Fundamental Rights and Freedom of the Individual'. It is interesting to note that the Rights now appear towards the end, rather than the beginning, of the Constitution. See generally on Bills of Rights within the Commonwealth chapter V in S. A. de Smith, *The New Commonwealth and Its Constitutions* (London, Stevens and Sons Ltd., 1966) and relevant chapters in the *Annual Surveys of Commonwealth Law*, 1966–8, edited by H. W. R. Wade (London, Stevens and Sons Ltd.).

How realistic was it to expect that the system of administration would change overnight in the direction of greater liberalism? It is true that the adoption of a Bill or Rights at independence was not a totally novel departure, but the previous attempts were of little importance. Britain was a party to the European Convention of Human Rights and Fundamental Freedoms, which was signed in 1950 and came into force in 1953;[17] it guaranteed the right to life, freedom from torture or inhuman or degrading treatment or punishment, freedom from slavery or servitude, right to liberty and security of person, the right to a fair trial, freedom from retroactive legislation, right to respect for private and family life, the right to freedom of thought, conscience and religion, the right to freedom of expression, of peaceful assembly and association, to marry, found a family, and freedom from discrimination in the enjoyment of these rights. A Protocol, an essential part of the Convention, was signed in 1952 and provided for three additional rights—of the peaceful enjoyment of possessions, education, and 'free elections at reasonable intervals by secret ballot, under conditions which will ensure the free expression of the opinion of the people in the choice of the legislature'. Under the terms of the Convention and the Protocol[18] it was possible for signatory states to extend them to all or any of the territories for whose international relations they were responsible. Britain made a declaration to apply the Convention but not the Protocol (perhaps primarily because it guaranteed the right of free elections) to her various overseas possessions, including Kenya.[19] Thus from 1953 Britain was under an international obligation, enforceable regionally, to respect important human rights in its administration of Kenya. The impact of the Convention in Kenya was, however, minimal—because of several reasons.

The Convention did not automatically become a part of the municipal law of Kenya—due to the common law doctrine that a treaty does not affect the domestic law unless it has been expressly incorporated by the local legislature. The consequence was that no recourse could be had to Kenyan courts for violations of the Convention. Nor was the machinery under the Convention adequate as far as Kenya was concerned. It provides for both political and judicial methods of settlement. A case under the Convention can be brought up in one of two ways: either by another signatory or by the aggrieved individual. The second does not apply automatically; it operates only if a signatory lodges a declaration conceding such a right. Britain had not done so, and the only recourse for a person in Kenya was to persuade another member state to take up his case—an important departure from the

[17] Generally, A. H. Robertson, *Human Rights in Europe* (Manchester University Press and Oceana, Dobbs Ferry).
[18] Articles 63 and 4 respectively.
[19] Cmd. 9045 (1953).

traditional rules of international law since a state usually can only espouse the case of its own nationals, but of little use in practice to Kenya. Furthermore, Britain had not accepted the compulsory jurisdiction of the Court of Human Rights, and therefore complaints against Britain would have had to be solved through political rather than judicial means. Finally, it was possible under the Convention for a member to derogate from most of its obligations,[20] in times of emergency. Britain invoked the power of derogation in relation to Kenya in 1954 and again in 1960,[21] and so for the majority of the period the Convention did not fully apply to Kenya.

A domestic Bill of Rights for Kenya made its first appearance in 1960. Closely modelled on the European Convention, it made little difference in practice and it is difficult to trace a single case in which the Bill was successfully invoked. When Kenya's independence became imminent, and the decision was taken to incorporate a declaration of rights, models for such a declaration were sought in the constitutions of other countries, but Kenya's own Bill was largely overlooked or ignored.[22] When she obtained her Constitution for internal self-government, there was a Bill of Rights, which, with minor modifications, was subsequently entrenched in the independence Constitution.

THE BILL OF RIGHTS

Kenya's Bill of Rights is wide-ranging and written in elaborate detail. The purpose of the Bill is stated boldly as the entitlement of 'every person in Kenya . . . to the fundamental rights and freedoms of the individual, that is to say, the right, whatever his race, tribe, place of origin or residence or other local connections, political opinion, colour, creed or sex, but subject to respect for the rights and freedoms of others and for the public interest, to each and all of the following, namely: (a) life, liberty, security of the person and the protection of the law; (b) freedom of conscience, of expression and of assembly and association, and (c) protection of the privacy of his home and other property and from deprivation of property without compensation'.[23] Subsequently there is a closer definition of these rights, and exceptions to them, but the preamble-like statement is presumably to set out the tenor of the nature of government and 'the general purport of the guarantees,

[20] Article 15.
[21] Yearbook of the European Convention of Human Rights I, p. 48 (Hague, M. Nijhoff); Yearbook I, 48.
[22] Cmd. 1700. The models were Uganda and Nigeria, which in turn were based on the European Convention. Rights which appear in the Convention but are missing in Kenya's Bill are the rights to respect for private and family life, the right to marry and found a family, and the right to periodic elections, though the latter is substantively provided in other parts of the Constitution. On the other hand, the Bill's provision for non-discrimination is perhaps wider than the convention, not being confined in relation to the guaranteed rights.
[23] Constitution section 70.

lifting them above the austerity of tabulated legalism'.[24] For our purposes, it may be convenient to disregard the classification of rights indicated above, and to discuss them under five heads: personal freedoms, property rights, civil rights, the right to non-discrimination, and the protection of the legal and judicial process.

(a) *Personal freedoms*

The first of the personal freedoms and rights is the protection of life itself—no one is to be deprived of it intentionally, save in execution of a sentence of a court in respect of a criminal offence.[25] However, if death results from force reasonably needed to defend any person from violence or the defence of property in order to effect a lawful arrest or to prevent the escape of a person lawfully detained, for the purpose of suppressing a riot, insurrection, or mutiny, or in order to prevent the commission by the person of a criminal offence, or due to a lawful act of war, it is not to be regarded as coming within the prohibition of the section. It is not immediately obvious what purpose is served by the enumeration of these exceptions. It may have been thought that these exceptions were necessary to preserve the common law and statutory powers of the police and the armed forces to use reasonable force in the execution of their duties, though no powers expressly authorize them to take life. It might be that the exceptions were considered necessary to protect them from liability in those instances where death does take place as a result of the reasonable use of force[26]—which is equivalent to the entrenchment of the common law.

The second right in this group is the prohibition of slavery or servitude or forced labour, to the last one of which there are some exceptions, notably in relation to members of the disciplined forces and 'any labour reasonably required as part of reasonable and normal communal or other civic obligations'.[27] It is also provided that no person shall be subjected to torture or to inhuman or degrading punishment or other treatment.[28] There is no definition of 'inhuman' or 'degrading', and the article states expressly that any description of punishment which could have been inflicted on 11 December 1963 is not to be regarded as prohibited by this provision.[29]

[24] S. A. de Smith, op. cit., p. 194. However, the case for the plaintiff in *Madhwa* v. *City Council of Nairobi*, [1968] E.A. 406 was based in part on it.
[25] Constitution section 71.
[26] It might also be argued that the word 'intentionally' renders the exceptions redundant.
[27] Constitution section 73.
[28] Constitution section 74.
[29] Capital and corporal punishments are thus sanctioned. See *Runyowa* v. *The Queen*, [1966] 1 All E.R. 633 (J.C.P.C. from Rhodesia) where the court held that punishment was not inhuman because it appeared excessive to the crime committed. See, too, Palley, 'The Judicial Committee of the Privy Council as Appellate Court—the Southern Rhodesian Experience', 1967 *Public Law* 8. *Quaere* whether the

More important in this group, however, are the provisions protecting 'personal liberty'. There is first of all protection against arbitrary search of persons or property or entry into premises except with consent.[30] However, nothing done under a law will contravene this article if it is 'reasonably required in the interest of defence, public safety, public order, public morality, public health, town and country planning, the development and utilization of any other property in such a manner as to promote the public benefit; or that is reasonably required for the purpose of promoting the rights or freedoms of other persons', or if the law provides for a public official, including that of a public corporation, 'to enter on the premises of any person in order to inspect those premises or anything thereon for the purpose of any tax, rate or due or in order to carry out work connected with any property that is lawfully on those premises and that belongs to the Government or other public body'; or finally, entry which is necessary to carry out a judicial decision. However, there is a general proviso that the law, and the action under it, must be reasonably justifiable in a democratic society—a phrase which qualifies exceptions to several other rights as well,[31] and will be discussed later.

Secondly, personal liberty is safeguarded. Article 72 does not define personal liberty but states that no person shall be deprived of his personal liberty save as may be authorized by law in a number of specified cases, and a person unlawfully arrested or detained shall be entitled to compensation from the wrongdoer. Whenever a person is arrested or detained under the exceptions, he has to be informed as soon as is reasonably practicable, in a language that he understands, of the reasons for it. Some of these cases concern the deprivation of liberty in connection with the execution of lawful court orders. Another instance is the arrest of a person reasonably suspected of having committed or being about to commit a crime. In this case, and when a person is detained or arrested in order to bring him before a court in execution of an order of a court, he must be brought before the court as soon as reasonably practicable and unless this is done within twenty-four hours, the onus of proving that the provisions of the article have been complied with will be on the detaining authority. Once a person has been brought before a court, his further detention can be valid only after an order of the court. A person detained on reasonable suspicion of having committed or being about to commit a crime, unless tried within a reasonable

Penal (Amendment) Bill 1969 would be valid; it seeks to remove the existing restrictions on the imposition of corporal punishment (particularly on age and sex, and the amount of punishment imposed) so that everyone could become liable to it.

[30] Constitution section 76.

[31] Right to property (Constitution section 75), freedom of conscience (section 78), freedom of expression (section 79), freedom of assembly and associations (section 80), freedom of movement (section 81).

time, has to be released, without prejudice to further proceedings, either unconditionally or upon reasonable conditions, in particular to ensure his appearance at the trial or preliminary proceedings.

Other deprivations of personal liberty are permitted, in the case of a person under eighteen, for the purpose of his education or welfare; and in the case of persons reasonably suspected to be of unsound mind, addicted to drugs or alcohol, or a vagrant,[32] for the purpose of their care or treatment or the protection of the community; or of persons to prevent the spread of an infectious or contagious disease. Restrictions can also be imposed to prevent the unlawful entry of a person into Kenya or to effect his expulsion, extradition or other lawful removal. The final exception to the general principle is vague, and suggests that liberty is more than just an antithesis of detention, but seems to be more closely connected with freedom of movement. Its effect is to permit the deprivation of liberty which may be necessary in the execution of a lawful order requiring a person to remain within a specified area within Kenya or prohibiting him from being within such an area, or to such extent as may be reasonably justifiable for the taking of proceedings against that person relating to the making of any such order, or to such extent as may be reasonably justifiable for restraining that person during any visit that he is permitted to make to any part of Kenya in which, in consequence of any such order, his presence would otherwise be unlawful. No indication is given as to what would be a 'lawful order' for the purposes of this exception; orders other than under the preceding exceptions must be contemplated, otherwise there would be no need for this subsection. The execution of the order which is referred to is more likely to be one in the nature of a restriction order to a specified area, and therefore belongs more logically to the exceptions to freedom of movement.

Thirdly, freedom of movement is safeguarded. Article 81 protects freedom of movement, which is widely defined as 'the right to move freely throughout Kenya, the right to reside in any part of Kenya, the right to enter Kenya, the right to leave Kenya and immunity from expulsion from Kenya'. It is made clear that any restriction that is involved in a person's lawful detention is not to be regarded as a contravention of this section, but, for what is 'lawful detention', one has presumably to refer to Article 72—it is curious that these two sections which are so closely related in their content should be set so far apart.[33] The article does not protect non-citizens,

[32] The Constitution does not define 'vagrant'. In *Kioko* v. *Attorney-General*, Crown Appeal 633/1964 (unreported) the court upheld the Vagrancy Act, because section 72 exempts vagrants, but did not consider whether the extraordinarily wide definition of 'vagrant' in the Act is justified. See new Vagrancy Act No. 61 of 1969.

[33] In Kioko's case the High Court remarked; 'The dichotomy here achieved by the framers of the Constitution is perhaps more practical than scientific'. cf. *Ibingira* v. *The Republic*, (Uganda) [1966] E.A. 306 where the Court of Appeal discussed the relation between the exceptions to the right of liberty and the freedom of movement.

though at independence, its protection was extended to non-citizens ordinarily and lawfully resident in Kenya at that time, but a subsequent amendment restricted its operation to citizens only.[34]

There are several exceptions to the protection guaranteed by this section, excluding immunity from expulsion which is inalienable.[35] Three are serious. It is provided that nothing contained in or done under the authority of a law, which imposes restrictions on the movement or residence within Kenya of a person, or on his right to leave Kenya, that are reasonably required in the interests of defence, public safety or public order, shall be regarded as contravening this freedom. Under the second exception similar restrictions are possible but they can be imposed on 'persons generally or any class of persons' and in the 'interests of defence, public safety, public order, public morality, public health or the protection or control of the nomadic peoples'; except in so far as the law or the Act under it is reasonably justifiable in a democratic society. In relation to a restriction order under the first, but not the second exception, there is a right to review of the order at the end of three months (and thereafter at similar intervals) by an independent and impartial tribunal presided over by an appointee of the Chief Justice, qualified to be appointed a judge of the High Court. The tribunal's recommendations are binding, unless it is otherwise provided by law.[36] Again, in relation to the first exception, it is necessary to prove that the law or the action in question is 'justifiable in a democratic society', though the court has hinted that few additional limitations are imported by this phrase that are not implied by the other requirements of the exception.[37] However, it is not

[34] Act No. 14 of 1965.

[35] When the Government has wished to deport a citizen it has had to revoke his citizenship first. However, such revocation is possible only in the case of those who become citizens by registration or naturalization. Even in their case, it is doubtful if they could be deported if other countries refused to receive them. They are stateless, but their last effective nationality link was with Kenya, which continues to have some obligations towards them.

It is worth mentioning here that the Government can prevent the movement of a citizen out of the country by the simple expedient of withdrawing or withholding his passport. The leader of the opposition was prevented in this way from travelling to the United States to talk to a university. When questioned on this in the National Assembly, the Government claimed that any passport is the property of the State and not of the temporary holder and and can be withdrawn from any person at any time . . . The Attorney-General said that 'As far as the law is concerned, and as far as the Constitution is concerned, a passport is the property of the Government . . . [and] the question of its deprivation cannot be raised in a court of law'. National Assembly, *Debates*, XIX (10 April 1968), col. 1894 et seq. The Constitution, however, makes no mention of a passport and it is arguable that given the guarantee of the freedom of movement a passport is a right and cannot be arbitrarily withdrawn by the Government. Nor is it a foregone conclusion that its issue or withdrawal is not justiciable. All matters which affect the guaranteed human rights can be taken to court, see below.

[36] No such law appears to have been enacted nor has this exception been used to restrict freedom of movement. Restriction and detentions have been made under other provisions. See below.

[37] *Kioko* v. *Attorney-General*, op. cit. See footnote 64, below.

easy to understand the exact distinction between the two exceptions; in *Kioko* v. *Attorney-General,* a case in which the constitutionality of the Vagrancy Act was at issue, the High Court indicated that the first exception must refer to 'laws under which a particular individual is regarded against the background of a particular and special set of circumstances. Special circumstances inimical to public order and safety arise, or are envisaged. Against that background it is expedient and necessary that one Mr. A because of matters personal to him should suffer some restriction touching his residence . . . A distinction can be made . . . between such a law and a law which is applicable to the public generally or to a section of the public'. The court went on to hold the Vagrancy Act as falling within the second exception. While it is true that 'vagrants' are a class of people, the order operates against individuals, as does an order which is authorized by a law against 'persons engaged in subversion', under the first exception.

Another important exception is in relation to the application of the Outlying Districts Act and the Special District (Administration) Act.[38] Both Acts, part of the paraphernalia of colonial administration, are still in use in Kenya today.[38a] The former has been looked at earlier, the latter may be dealt with here. The Government can apply the Act to any area or areas but at the same time exempt any person or class of persons from its operation. Restrictions on movement similar to those under the Outlying Districts Act may be imposed, but there are, in addition, penalties for harbouring offenders. Again, if the Provincial or District Commissioner is satisfied that a person is conducting himself so as to be dangerous to peace or good order, or has a blood feud or has created a cause of quarrel likely to lead to bloodshed, he may order his removal to another place. The more significant provisions, however, are those which enable control to be exercised over whole groups of people through collective orders. If, for example, in the opinion of the Provincial or the District Commissioner any tribe or a section of it is acting in a 'hostile manner towards the Government or towards any foreign power in friendly relations with the Government or towards any persons being or residing in Kenya', he can order the arrest of all or any members of such tribe or prohibit them from leaving the areas reserved for their use and order the seizure and detention of all their property. Subsequently he has to hold or 'cause to be held' an inquiry into the circumstances relating to the alleged hostile acts and if it is 'proved' that persons who have

[38] Cap. 105. First enacted in 1934.

[38a] Several districts have remained closed. In a parliamentary answer a Minister said that there were 19 wholly or partly closed districts (though in a subsequent statement he said that the number was considerably less). He explained that these had been closed during the Emergency and the Government was now studying actively the possibility of lifting this closure. National Assembly, *Debates*, volume XII (26 May 1967), col. 252.

been arrested or whose property has been seized had acted in a hostile manner, they are to be deemed to have committed an offence and, in addition to any other punishment provided in the Act, lose their property, whose proceeds go to the consolidated fund. The rules of criminal procedure are to be followed in the inquiry, as far as possible, but those rules may be displaced by rules of 'African customary law' applicable to the person concerned. Moreover, it does not seem to be contemplated that the inquiry need comply with the rules of natural justice, since the District Commissioner might hold it himself. No further safeguards are provided, even though it appears that as a result of the inquiry not only can property be lost, but the punishment provided in the Act can be meted out. In addition to these powers the Act gives wide powers of search and arrest without warrant, impounding and destruction of cattle and in many instances creates presumptions of guilt which it is up to the accused to rebut.

Subsection 6 of Section 81 preserves both these enactments despite conflict with the freedom guaranteed by it. Their continuance, however, is subject to two limitations—first, even though they can be amended or replaced, the new legislation cannot impose greater restrictions than was possible under them at the date of self-government.[39] Secondly, their operation cannot be extended to areas which were not under restriction at the time. Beyond this, however, it is not clear what the effect of subsection 6 is. These two enactments permit the deprivation not only of the freedom of movement, but also of other important rights, such as property and the protection of the judicial process. It is probable that subsection 6 preserves only the restrictions on movement, and does not affect the other provisions of the statutes, whose validity may be in question due to the guarantee of other freedoms. Thus collective punishment is probably unconstitutional, as are provisions for the detention, confiscation or destruction of property, and conviction and sentence through inquiries under the second of the statutes, for they are contrary to the protection of the process of the law and courts given under the Constitution.

(b) *Civil rights*

We now move to the next category of rights—the 'civil rights'—which comprise the freedom of conscience,[40] expression[41] and assembly and association.[42] All these rights have some exceptions in common; they can all be qualified with the consent of the person concerned, and they can also be qualified in the interests of defence, public safety, public order, public

[39] 31 May 1963.
[40] Section 78.
[41] Section 79.
[42] Section 80.

morality or public health. Again, all these rights may be limited in so far as the limitations are reasonably required for protecting similar rights and freedoms of others. Finally the limitations are not valid if shown not to be reasonably justifiable in a democratic society.

The freedom of conscience is defined widely to include the freedom of thought and religion, freedom to change religion or belief, and freedom either alone or in community with others, and both in public and private, to manifest and propagate one's religion or belief in worship, teaching, practice and observance. No one can be compelled to take an oath contrary to his religion or belief; and no person attending any place of education shall be required to receive religious instruction in, or to take part in any religious ceremony of, a religion other than his own, though it is not specified whether a student can be compelled to receive instruction in his own religion. On the other hand, every religious community has the right to establish and maintain places of education and to manage those which it wholly maintains, and in such institutions or in any other educational course it provides, it is free to provide religious instruction for persons of the community.

The freedom of expression protects the right to hold opinions and to receive and impart ideas and information generally or to an individual or a class of persons without interference, and the inviolability of correspondence.[43] Restrictions on this right, however, can be imposed on public officers; and also for the purposes of preventing the disclosure of information received in confidence, maintaining the authority and independence of the courts, or regulating telephony, telegraphy, posts, wireless, broadcasting or television; or to protect the rights and freedoms of other persons or the private lives of persons concerned in legal proceedings.

The freedom of assembly and association is similarly widely defined; it is the right to assemble freely and associate with other persons and in particular to form or belong to trade unions or other associations for the protection of one's interests. As usual, restrictions can be imposed in the interests of public safety, etc., or to protect the rights or freedom of other persons, or on public officers or members of any disciplined force. An additional exception was introduced in 1966, the primary effect of which was to legalize developments in the trade union movement;[44] it permits the refusal to register trade unions or associations of trade unions when others sufficiently representative exist in the same area, and permits the imposition of conditions, including a minimum number of persons, before registration is granted.

[43] cf. The Zambian case, *In the Matter of the People* v. *J. U. Patel* (Constitutional Ref. 1 of 1968, unreported) where the court discussed whether it was constitutional, on provisions similar to those in Kenya, for customs officers to open mail suspected of conveying currency out of the country.

[44] Act No. 16 of 1966. See below pp. 444–5.

(c) *Protection of property*

The third category of rights is the protection of property. We have already noted the right to privacy and protection against illegal entry. Property rights are the most comprehensively protected of all the rights, and the exceptions are narrow and do not significantly affect the substance of the right. Private property or any kind of interest in it can only be compulsorily acquired or taken possession of under very stringent conditions.[45] First, the taking over must be necessary in the interests of defence, public safety, public order, public morality, public health, town and country planning, or the development or utilization of it in such manner as to promote the public benefit. Secondly, the necessity of the taking over should be such as to afford reasonable justification for the causing of any hardship to the person with an interest in the property. Thirdly, provision must be made for the prompt payment of full compensation. Property which is acquired in satisfaction of a person's tax, duty, etc., a court judgment,[46] or because it is in a dangerous state or injurious to the health of human beings, animals or plants, or temporarily for the purposes of agricultural conservation work (after the owner or occupier has been asked, but has failed, to carry it out himself) is not to be regarded as unconstitutional, so long as it is not shown to be reasonably unjustified in a democratic society. Similarly the acquisition of enemy property, or the property of a deceased, or insane person, an infant or bankrupt, or a trust for the purposes of administration on behalf of the beneficial owners, does not contravene the section. Elaborate provisions are made for access to the High Court to determine the legality of the taking over and the amount of compensation. The owner, presumably even though a citizen, has been given the right to remit the whole of the amount of the compensation to any foreign country of his choice. There are very few restrictions in this; the remission has to be 'within reasonable' time after its receipt, reasonable restrictions can be imposed on the manner of the remission, and the amount may be subject to attachment by an order of the court to satisfy a judgment or pending the determination of civil proceedings to which the owner may be a party.

(d) *Freedom from discrimination*

The next category of rights is the fundamental right to equality or non-discrimination.[47] We have already seen how racial distinctions were woven into the whole political, economic and legal fabric of Kenya. This right is therefore extremely important for it seeks to establish the law and society on a basis of equality and non-racialism. Given, however, the disparities

[45] Section 75.
[46] *Muhuri* v. *Attorney-General* 1964 (unreported) for a discussion of this exception.
[47] Section 82.

between the races at the time of independence, a formal equality under the law would have the effect of preserving the *status quo*, and thus to some extent perpetuating the unfairness and injustice of the colonial system. Africans had suffered various legal and other handicaps, and, partly as a result, their economic and social position was greatly inferior to that of the other two races. Derogations from the rights are therefore permitted in certain circumstances to redress the previous imbalances

The substance of the right is that no law shall make any provision that is discriminatory either of itself or in its effect; and no persons shall be treated in a discriminatory manner by any person acting by virtue of any written law, or in the performance of the functions of any public office, or any public authority. 'Discriminatory' is defined as affording different treatment to different persons attributable wholly or mainly to their respective descriptions by race, tribe, place of origin, political opinions, colour or creed whereby persons of any such description are subjected to disabilities or restrictions to which persons of another such description are not made subject or are accorded privileges or advantages which are not accorded to persons of another such description. The Constitution therefore protects from discrimination in two ways—first, against the enactment of any law which is discriminatory either expressly or in its effect; secondly, against discriminatory action by persons acting under written law, or in the performance of the functions of any public office or any public authority.

The second, on the face of it, would extend beyond the acts of public officials, so long as they were in pursuance of a written law, though difficult points may arise where the basic authority comes from the common law and that has been supplemented or modified by legislation. The section does indicate, however, that the constitutional protection may be available in the private domain, and it is expressly provided in another part of the section that, with one exception, no person shall be treated in a discriminatory manner in respect of access to shops, hotels, lodging-houses, public restaurants, eating houses or places of public entertainment.[48]

The protection that is given against executive action is wider than that against laws but if discrimination is necessarily involved in the implementation of a valid law, this does not contravene the section. Thus the action of the City Council of Nairobi in serving notices of eviction on its tenants of Asian origin who were holders of stalls in the municipal market in order to re-let them to Africans was held to be unconstitutional,[49] for the Council was not acting under any law authorizing discrimination, but only in the

[48] The same part similarly protects access to places of public resort maintained wholly or partly out of public funds or dedicated to the use of the general public—subsection (7).

[49] *Madhwa* v. *City Council of Nairobi*, [1968] E.A. 406.

performance of its functions as a public authority, in which capacity it could not discriminate. It is likely that if the Council had passed a by-law to implement its policy to Africanize the stall holders, its notices would have been valid, because—and this brings us to the second important distinction between the scope of the two kinds of protection—the protection against discriminatory legislation does not extend to non-citizens, while the protection against discriminatory executive action does so extend.[50]

Laws may also be valid, even though discriminatory, in the areas of personal or family law, including devolution of property or in the application of customary law in any matter to the members of a particular race or tribe exclusively. This exception validates the diversity of personal laws that existed at independence and recognizes the plural nature of Kenya's society, though it could be argued that it was not necessary for validation, on the ground that differential laws may exist without resulting in discrimination.[51] A law may also be valid even though it discriminates in favour of or against a group mentioned in the definition of discrimination, if such discrimination is reasonably justifiable in a democratic society, 'having regard to its nature and to special circumstances . . ..' The purpose of this exception must be to incorporate the principle of reasonable classification that is permissible under the equal protection clauses of the American and Indian Constitution, and when the classification involves one of the 'prohibitive' factors.[52] It is a very open ended exception and the vagueness of the justifying criteria—having regard to the nature of the discrimination and 'special circumstances'—means that it could be used extensively to render the substance of the right illusory. The necessity for the kind of exception has previously been discussed, but it may be asked whether it was not possible to frame it in more restrictive terms, with clearer criteria for the guidance both of the Legislature and the courts.

Another exception is in favour of laws which prescribe standards or qualifications for entry into any branch of the public service; but it also says that such standards or qualifications shall not specifically relate to any of the 'prohibitive' factors of discrimination. Unless the intention was to sanction some kind of discrimination, it is difficult to see the point of this exception unless it is put there *ex abundanti cautela*. The key word here is *specifically* and the effect of the exception may be to permit discrimination so long as

[50] *Madhwa*, op. cit. The judgment proceeded on the assumption that the plaintiffs were non-citizens, even though some of them had applied for, but had not yet been granted citizenship.
[51] However, the Government set up two commissions in 1967, one on succession (Gazette Notice 1095) and the other on marriage and divorce (Gazette Notice 1261), both with instructions to recommend, 'so far as may be practicable', uniform rules in those areas for all persons in Kenya. See above p. 378.
[52] See Ghai (1963), 12 *I.C.L.Q.* 1089, at 1127–8.

it is not primarily based on one of the 'prohibitive' factors but is related to the nature of the service, etc.

The final exception provides that no law will be considered inconsistent with this right if it imposes restrictions on persons on the basis of the 'prohibitive' factors, in their exercise of the following rights, the freedom against entry on private premises and search of the person, the freedom of conscience, expression, assembly and association, and movement. However, the restrictions must be such as are otherwise within the exceptions to these individual rights. In other words, these restrictions will be valid if the only objection to them is that they are discriminatory, but they will still have to satisfy all the requirements of compatibility with a democratic order of society that are necessary before legislation under an exception is valid. This provision will enable Parliament to impose restrictions on persons within an area or locality if that is all that is necessary; and would also appear to sanction the kind of racial restriction in *Attorney-General* v. *Kathenge*.[52a] There is no limitation on the power to impose racial, and other, restrictions of this kind, though it can be argued that the requirements of compatibility with a democratic society, that qualify the exceptions in the individual rights, apply to the exception to impose racial and other restrictions. If so, the authority will have to justify restrictions of this kind.

Racial and tribal restrictions on these rights are also possible under executive action, even though there may be no express authorization in the law itself. Executive discrimination is also possible in the giving or withholding of consent to a transaction in agricultural land, by the Divisional, Provincial or Central Land Boards established under the Land Control Act 1967. This is an important exception and underlines the sensitivity of the land issue and the fears of Africans of the loss of their land. Formerly the Public Service Commission could make appointments in disregard of this section for limited purposes, first, in order to ensure that a reasonable number of persons from each region and Nairobi were represented in the establishment of the Central Government, and secondly, to ensure that the establishments of regions were staffed by a substantial proportion of persons from the respective regions. With the abolition of *majimbo*, these exceptions were abolished; their express provision at independence underlines that the Commission cannot take racial and tribal factors into account, unless specifically authorized by law. Indeed, it would appear that without authority under law, it cannot even discriminate between a citizen or non-citizen. Finally, the discretion under law to institute, conduct or discontinue civil or criminal proceedings is not affected by the restriction on discriminatory executive action.

52a See above, pp. 407–9.

(e) *Protection of the law and the legal process*

These rights can be divided into the protection of the criminal law; the safeguards in a criminal trial and civil proceedings; and the special jurisdiction of the High Court. It is provided that no person can be convicted of a criminal offence unless that offence is defined and the penalty prescribed in a written law.[53] Customary criminal offences are thus abolished—the administration can no longer use this 'contingencies vote'[54]—and the relative precision of written law should make it more difficult to use the criminal process for capricious purposes. No person who has been convicted or acquitted on a criminal charge can be tried again for the same offence or any other offence for which he could have been convicted under the first charge, except for a retrial ordered by a court on appeal or review. It is further provided that laws which retrospectively establish criminal offences or increase the penalty for a criminal offence will be invalid if they expose a person to new or increased liabilities.

As to the safeguards of the criminal trial, every accused has to be given a fair hearing within a reasonable time by an independent and impartial court established by law. The section elaborates the essentials of such a trial, but there is no definition of a 'court' either here or in reference to civil proceedings. In case the question arises, it is likely that the common law notions of what constitutes a court will be referred to.[55] The safeguards of the trial are similar to the rights available to an accused under the common law but are now entrenched and comprise the presumption of innocence, though there is no reference to the burden of proof the prosecution has to discharge,[56] the right of the accused to be informed in a language he understands of the nature of the offence, the provision of adequate time and facilities to prepare his defence, the right to plead his case either himself or through a legal representative of his own choice,[57] the right to call witnesses

[53] This came into effect on 1 June 1966. It does not affect the powers of a court to punish for contempt. The Attorney-General announced in Parliament that he had instructed the African Courts that where formerly there would have been criminal liability, they should now treat it as a case for civil liability. See the circular of 18 June 1966 to African Court Presidents by the African Courts Officer. For criticism of it by back-benchers, see National Assembly, *Debates*, volume XI (10 March 1967) col. 984.

[54] Phillips, in his *Report on Native Tribunals in Kenya*, op. cit., thus described the prevalent attitude to customary criminal law. See chapter IV for details. The Cotran Report on the recording of *Customary Criminal Offences* (Government Printer, 1964), recommended that some such offences be incorporated into the Penal Code. No action has yet been taken on this report.

[55] The point arose in *Godfrey Muhuri* v. *Attorney-General*, op. cit., where the Chief Justice stated that 'throughout this puzzling Constitution the familiar court processes of law based on English law have been envisaged'. For a useful discussion of what constitutes a court and judicial proceedings, see the South African case of *Minister of Interior* v. *Harris*, [1952] (4) S.A. 769 (A.D.).

[56] It is, however, also provided that a law is not invalid if it places the burden of proving particular facts on the accused—section 77 (12) (a).

[57] There is no obligation on the state to provide the fees for a lawyer. The 'legal representative' must be a member of the Kenya bar, though the Government has refused

on his behalf and to cross-examine those of the prosecution, and the provision of an interpreter. He cannot be compelled to give evidence, and the trial cannot proceed in his absence, unless the court orders otherwise due to his own conduct which makes it impracticable to continue the trial in his presence.

As regards civil proceedings, the provisions are brief: it is provided that any court or other adjudicating authority prescribed by law for the determination of the existence or extent of any civil right or obligation shall be established by law and shall be independent and impartial; and any case before it shall be given a fair hearing within a reasonable time. The hearing is to be in public unless all the parties agree otherwise, except when the court or the authority, under powers given by law, may decide otherwise in certain specified instances in the interests of justice, privacy, defence, public safety or public order.

The main interest of these provisions lie in their applicability to those proceedings where an individual may be asserting a claim against a public authority. It is not clear how far the provisions apply to administrative adjudications, but 'the determination of the existence or extent of any civil right or obligation' would cover many decisions made by administrative tribunals and other authorities, including Ministers and officials.[58] The administrative law and practices in Kenya have been built on the principle of the supremacy of the Legislature, which can establish what system it pleases. If the present section were held applicable to the administrative system, in so far as it makes decisions about the rights and claims of individuals, it would call for important changes in many laws. For instance, in *Muhuri* v. *Attorney-General* the court held that, what was in effect administrative machinery for the settlement of claims for compensation for loss of property under the Stock and Produce Theft Act, was unconstitutional, for it lacked the essentials of the court procedure.[59] This case did not arise under section 77, but the basic principles would hold for cases under it. The section does not compel the disclosure of all information, but the

permission to a British lawyer qualified to practise in Kenya to enter the country so that he could appear in court—cf. the Nigerian case, *Awolowo* v. *Minister of Internal Affairs* (1963, unreported), where the court held that the choice is limited to legal practitioners who have the right to audience in Nigerian courts and who are in Nigeria or have right to enter Nigeria. See also chapter X, pp. 401–2.

[58] cf. Nigerian decision of *Merchants Bank Ltd.* v. *Federal Finance Minister*, [1961]. All N.L.R. 598, where the Federal Supreme Court held that rights under a licence were not 'civil rights or obligations' within a similar section. Since a considerable part of regulatory powers are exercised through licensing, this is an important decision.

[59] It was not the duty of the magistrate to fix any individual with responsibility but, as the Court put it, 'it appears . . . that once it established that some unidentified members of a class have done harm or are suspected reasonably of doing harm, the magistrate may fix all or any of them with payment of compensation'. See, on this point, Ghai, 'Judicial Protection of the Individual against the Executive in Kenya' in *Proceedings of the Colloquium on Judicial Protection of the Individual against the Executive* (Max-Planck Institute for Comparative Public Law and International Law, Heidelberg, forthcoming).

requisites of a 'fair hearing' imply that the Executive's case shall be made known to the other party who will also be given the right of rebuttal. This is not the case in many administrative proceedings at present.

It remains to consider the special jurisdiction of the High Court in matters of the fundamental rights. If any person alleges that any right is being, or is likely to be, contravened in relation to him; or, in the case of a person who is detained, if any other person alleges such contravention in relation to the detained person, then without prejudice to any other action in respect of the same matter which is lawfully available, that person may apply directly to the High Court for redress.[60] In the section dealing with property, direct access to the High Court has been expressly and separately provided for, either directly or from a tribunal or other authority, to determine the legality of the taking over and the amount of compensation, and to secure the prompt payment of the compensation. The High Court has original jurisdiction in either a direct application to it or on a reference from a subordinate court, in whose proceedings any question of a contravention of the guaranteed rights has arisen—the subordinate court may refer such matter to the High Court, and has to if a party requests it, unless it feels that the request is merely frivolous or vexatious. At independence an appeal went direct from a final decision of the High Court to the Privy Council, but was abolished in 1965; since then, appeals on constitutional matters lie to the E.A.C.A.[60a]

Who may invoke the special jurisdiction of the High Court? It is clear from the words 'contravened in relation to him' that the applicant must have some interest, but does it have to be as substantial and immediate as under the restrictive rules of standing in administrative law? Secondly, at what stage can a person, if he has an interest, come to the court? The section allows him to approach the court before he has suffered an injury, but can he seek a declaration even though there is no immediate danger of injury to him? The High Court would be justified in taking a liberal view of *locus standi* or 'ripeness', especially as there is no other way to challenge the constitutionality of legislation, though the Nigerian courts have taken a narrow view on identical provisions.[61] Given that the court accepts jurisdiction, what redress can be given? The court has wide powers in this respect—

[60] Section 84.

[60a] See chapter V, footnote 120.

[61] *Olawoyin* v. *Attorney-General of Northern Nigeria*, [1961] 1 All N.L.R. 269. The Federal Supreme Court said, 'It will be noted that a declaration can only be made in favour of an interested party and a person asking for a declaration must therefore first show that he has an interest in the subject matter', p. 273. Disregarding the precise wording which gave it jurisdiction, the court looked to Commonwealth and American cases, *Dwarkadas* v. *Sholapar Spinning Co*, [1954] A.I.R. (S.C.) 119; *Crouch* v. *The Commonwealth*, [1948] 77 C.L.R. 339; *Massachusetts* v. *Mellon*, [1923] 262 U.S. 447; *and United Public Workers* v. *Mitchell*, [1947] 330 U.S. 75, and held that there must be immediacy of injury.

it 'may make such orders, issue such writs and give such directions as it may consider appropriate for the purpose of enforcing or securing the enforcement' of the rights. This would enable the court to grant any of the remedies it can ordinarily award, for example, damages, mandamus, certiorari, injunctions and declarations, but it is not clear whether it can go beyond these conventional remedies or disregard the limitations on their award. There has so far been no occasion when the court has discussed the ambit of this power,[62] but there is no reason for the court to confine itself to the recognized remedies or their limitations. In the constitutional scheme, the provisions for human rights are considered extremely important and a wide interpretation of the court's power would not be out of place.

(f) General comments on the Bill

No attempt at a close analysis of the provisions of the Bill has been made. An indication, however, has been given of the open-endedness of many of them, and it is obvious that a court will have various options open to it in a given case. The substance of the rights has been closely and carefully qualified, and it may well be argued that in consequence little of the substance is left. It is inevitable in any system of guarantees that there would be exceptions, but the crucial question is the manner and the method of providing for them. If the Constitution itself did not contain them, the courts would have to establish them. This may place an excessive burden on the courts. If the Constitution establishes the criteria, it may tend to detract from the magnificence of the rights, but it does set out the upper limits, as it were, prohibiting, by implication, further exceptions. In most instances, moreover, the exercise or enjoyment of the rights can only be qualified by express authorization under the law. This means that the substantive provisions, unless qualified by law, significantly restrict the exercise of administrative discretion. It follows that a general power to an administrator does not enable him to exercise it in infringement of the guaranteed rights; there must be express powers for this purpose. The commitment of the Legislature to these ideals is important, for it means that the matter is not left entirely to the whim of the Executive.

All infringements or alleged infringements of the guaranteed rights can be challenged in the courts. It is therefore possible in all cases where an appeal from administrative decisions to the courts is expressly excluded, to go to the court if the complaint is appropriately presented. The courts have a key role; and they must be satisfied not only that the law is valid but

[62] In *Madhwa*, op. cit., the court gave a declaration and an injunction, but refused to grant an injunction in respect of any future notices of eviction on the ground that there was no evidence to suggest that the defendant would deliberately disregard the Constitution. In *Olawoyin* v. *Attorney-General Northern Nigeria* the court held that a declaration could be made under a similar section.

also that any action under it is justified in the circumstances of the case. It is probable that the courts will apply the presumption of constitutionality of legislation, so that it will be for the complainant to prove that it is invalid.[63] The wording of the proviso in relation to the exceptions to the rights—'except [it] is shown not to be unreasonably justifiable in a democratic society'—also appears to throw some onus on the complainant. In practice this could be a serious burden, especially in a challenge to executive action, since much of the factual information in the possession of the Executive, in cases where a threat to public safety and security is alleged, is unlikely to be disclosed in the court or given to the complainant. Moreover the courts have to perform a function which is novel to them, and the chances are that they will lean in favour of the Executive, as they have in the past on crucial issues, or interpret the provisions in the Bill in a mechanistic manner. Already the court has hinted that it does not think that any additional limitations on the Legislature or the Executive are imposed by the need to establish that the laws or actions are reasonably justifiable in a democratic society, over and above those imposed by the main exceptions.[64] The courts will also have to determine how immediate the threat to security must be before restrictions can be imposed. Is it enough to assert that the acts in question are potentially dangerous?[65]

Could the Bill be too generous to individuals at the expense of the State? Its paternity is traceable to the European Convention, which is replete with liberal and *laissez faire* philosophy[66] and may be appropriate for the advanced economies and more stable political conditions of Western Europe, but is hardly suitable for a developing fragile polity, avowedly committed to socialism.[67] Most of the rights are available to non-citizens, the exceptions being the freedom of movement and freedom from discriminatory laws. There is a heavy emphasis on protection of property, which inevitably benefits those, mainly non-citizens, who had large amounts of property at independence, and which, if strictly interpreted, would throw doubt on the operation of exchange control laws. In particular, there is an absence of the State's positive obligations to its citizenry, such as the provision of work and

[63] The U.S., Indian and the Nigerian courts have all adopted this attitude: *Ogden* v. *Saunders* (1827), 12 Wheat 213; *Chiranjit Lal* v. *Union of India* (1950), S.C.R. 869.

[64] *Kioko* v. *A-G*, op. cit., 'Very special facts indeed would be required to lead this Court to say that though a law was reasonably required in the interests of our society, it was not reasonably justifiable in a democratic society' per Chief Justice Ainley.

[65] In *D.P.P.* v. *Obi*, [1961] All N.L.R. 186, the court held that the Government did not have to prove that the threat was immediate; it was enough if it was 'potential'.

[66] Robertson, op. cit., p. 4 says that the Convention was adopted to assert liberal Western values in the face of the communist threat.

[67] Kenya's conception of socialism is outlined in *African Socialism, Its Application to Planning in Kenya*, Sessional Paper No. 10, 1965, Nairobi. The paper claims that Kenya's Constitution is 'socialist'. Tanzania has rejected proposals for a Bill of Rights on the ground that it would retard her economic development and bring clashes between the executive and judiciary. *Government Paper 1*, Dar es Salaam, 1962.

education, and an absence of the citizen's own responsibilities to the community. As to the latter point, it has been said that the criticism is misconceived in so far as it attributes a wrong significance to the omission of these provisions, for it does not connote any hostility to them. Such provisions are difficult to enforce legally and so should be left out of a constitution.[68] As to the point of fragility, the answer may be made that issues of security are well taken care of. Most of the rights and freedoms can be qualified in the interests of defence, public safety and public order; in fact the major thrust of the exceptions is in this direction. The disciplinary laws of the armed and security forces are excluded from the operation of the guarantees except for those protecting life, and against slavery or inhuman treatment. The State has adequate authority to take all necessary action to deal with any threats to public security or with the danger of subversion. If anything, it might be argued that the theme of security is more pervasive than that of liberty, and could provide a convenient cloak for oppression. To give a complete picture of the relationship between the protected rights and the needs of security, however, it is necessary to discuss the special or emergency powers of the Government.

SPECIAL POWERS TO PRESERVE PUBLIC ORDER

At independence the Emergency (Powers) Orders in Council were repealed as part of the law of Kenya,[69] but the Constitution provided for two special kinds of emergency powers for the Government. The first was in relation to the North Eastern Region[70] (now Province), whose operation was subsequently extended to the contiguous districts of Marsabit, Isiolo, Tana River and Lamu.[71] Under it, the widest possible powers are granted to the Government. The President may, by regulations, make such provision as appears to him to be necessary or expedient for the purpose of ensuring effective government in or in relation to these areas; such regulations are valid notwithstanding conflict with the Constitution or any other law. These powers have been given for an indefinite period of time; it is for the President to decide when they come to an end, though the regulations made thereunder may continue up to six months thereafter. Not only are these powers extensive, but there is little control over their exercise, the only

[68] de Smith, op. cit., p. 185. It is sometimes possible in a preamble to outline the 'social security' obligations of the state and other aspects of its philosophy. Kenya's Constitution, however, does not have a preamble. See, for an alternative method, the Constitution of Malta S.1., 1398/1964, chapter II, Declaration of Principles, which includes the right to work, and the right to social assistance and insurance. The principles are not enforceable in any court but 'it shall be the aim of the state to apply [them] in making laws'.

[69] Section 10 of the Order in Council, S.I. 1968/1963.

[70] Section 19, ibid., now Constitution section 127.

[71] Act No. 16 of 1966. These were the areas where the Somali secessionist movement was active.

stipulation being that the regulations should be published in the Gazette. Ample use has been made of them and these areas have been administered in considerable part through such regulations, which were consolidated in 1966.[72]

The Regulations state that they shall have effect notwithstanding anything in the Constitution or in any other law which is inconsistent therewith. They establish a 'prescribed area', which is the whole of the province, and a 'prohibited zone' within it which is the area along the Kenya-Somalia boundary. They make certain conduct offences, give special powers to the police, armed forces and administrative officers, provide for restriction of movement and preventive detention, and special machinery for the trial of specified offences.

If the Minister is satisfied that it is necessary for the preservation of public security in the prescribed area either to exercise control over the movement or residence of any person or to detain him, he may issue a restriction order so that the person has to live in an area prescribed in the order or he may order his detention, as the case may be. Persons so restricted or detained have to be informed of the grounds for the order, and have a right to a review of the order by a tribunal appointed by the Minister and consisting of not less than three persons, of whom the chairman and one other should have had judicial experience. The tribunal's recommendations are not binding, but the Minister has to communicate his decision to it.

As to the offences within the prescribed area, some of them are extremely vague and reverse the normal burdens of proof in criminal prosecutions. It is provided that any person who, without lawful authority or lawful excuse, carries or has in his possession or under his control any firearm ammunition or explosive, shall be guilty of an offence for which the mandatory penalty is death, the burden of proving 'lawful authority or lawful excuse' being on him. It is also an offence for a person to consort with or be found in the company of another person with firearms, in circumstances 'which raise a reasonable presumption' that he intends to act, or is about to act, or has recently acted with that other person in a manner prejudicial to the preservation of public security; the penalty for this also is death and the presumption will be raised automatically if the other person is found with firearms. A person who consorts with or is found in the company of another person whom he knows, is, or has reasonable cause to believe to be, about to act, or to have acted in a manner prejudicial to the preservation of

[72] Legal Notice 264/1966, as amended by Legal Notice 77/1967; Legal Notice 163/1967; Legal Notice 185/1968. These Regulations are purported to be made under both section 19 of the Order (now Constitution section 127) and the Public Security Act. Since the regulations apply to the areas within section 19, and since powers under section 19 are wider than under the Act, the invocation of the Act is unnecessary.

public security is guilty of an offence for which he is liable to life imprisonment. For the prohibited zone, there are additional offences—it is an offence, punishable with life imprisonment, for any person, other than authorized public officers, to be in, enter or attempt to enter the zone.

Special machinery is provided for the trial of these and other offences.[73] A court of Special Assize has been established, held by a judge of the High Court designated for this purpose by the Chief Justice. Some of the safeguards associated with a criminal trial are missing; for instance the joinder of counts is possible, even though one of the offences charged may not be a specified offence. However, if the court of Special Assize feels that, taking all relevant factors into consideration, the accused ought to be tried according to the normal procedure, it may transfer his case to an ordinary court.

The members of the armed forces and the administration have special powers of entry and search without warrant and to seize anything 'upon, in, with or in respect of which an offence has been committed or is reasonably suspected of having been committed, or which is necessary to the conduct of any investigation into an offence'. Persons reasonably suspected of having committed an offence can be arrested without a warrant and detained for a period of up to twenty-eight days under the written authority of a commissioned officer of the armed forces, or a police officer of the rank of Assistant Superintendent or above; at the expiration of twenty-eight days, he can be detained for a further similar period if authorized by a police officer in charge of a province. Any stock found in the prohibited zone may be seized and forfeited, or may be destroyed. Additional powers which an officer has are to impose a limited amount of forced labour 'on specified inhabitants or a specified class of inhabitants' in circumstances which endanger the existence or the well being of the inhabitants. An officer may also use any arms and ammunition against any person, to defend a person from violence or to defend property, to effect a lawful arrest or prevent escape from custody, to prevent the commission of a crime or to suppress a riot or an uprising or an invasion, up to the point of killing that person, if reasonably justifiable in the circumstances.

The other Regulations are designed to control movement, but apply only to the tribes scheduled in the Regulations.[74] If the Minister or any person authorized by him considers it expedient for the preservation of public

[73] Part VIII, section 17, refers to 'scheduled' offences, for which the machinery is used. There are, however, no such offences. It is probable that the word 'scheduled' is a mistake for specified, which includes all the offences described above, plus any other offence which is committed within the prescribed area and which is punishable by death or at least 7 years' imprisonment.

[74] Legal Notice 43/1967. Most of the scheduled tribes are from the North Eastern Province. An order covers all the members of the family of and residing with a person affected by it (section 5).

safety, he may order all members of any of the scheduled tribes living in any particular area to move to another area within a specified time, or to remain within the limits of a prescribed area, or to live within part of a prescribed area and to remain there during or at given hours. No appeal procedures of any kind are provided for.

The other kind of emergency powers provided for at independence were not so extensive, though they were not restricted to any geographical area. They were not ordinarily available as part of the normal law, but only came into operation when either Kenya was at war or there was in force a proclamation of a state of emergency by the President (originally, the Governor-General). Unless both houses of the National Assembly were adjourned or prorogued, the declaration of emergency could not be made without their prior authority, which was expressed by an affirmative vote of 65 per cent of all the members of the respective house.[75] The declaration would only last for two months but the two houses could, by similar resolutions, authorize further extensions of two months at a time. During these periods, the only special powers which became available were to enact or take executive action under legislation which derogated from the freedom of personal liberty and the protection from discrimination, but only to the extent reasonably justifiable for dealing with the actual situation.[76] It was not possible to derogate from other rights and freedoms, though it was otherwise possible to qualify the exercise of those rights in the interests of public safety and order, the difference being that the courts would have greater control over the latter restrictions. It is doubtful, however, whether the validity of a declaration of emergency could be effectively challenged in the courts; the provisions were that the President might proclaim an emergency but no criteria were set out. It would therefore be difficult to challenge such a proclamation, even if there were no justification for it, especially after authorization by the National Assembly. But actions taken during an emergency could be challenged if they were excessive or unrelated to the purpose of restoring and preserving order and security.[77]

After a series of amendments in favour of the Executive in relation to the procedure for the declaration of emergency and its duration, the Government introduced constitutional proposals in 1966 which are now the basis for the special and the extraordinary powers to deal with situations of crisis.[78]

[75] If the houses were adjourned, the declaration could remain in effect for seven days after which it lapsed. See chapter V.

[76] The relevant legislation could be enacted at any time, though it would remain in suspension till an emergency occurred. See the decision in the Nigerian case *Williams* v. *Majekodunmi*, [1962] W.N.L.R. 174.

[77] In the *Williams* case, ibid., and *Adegbenro* v. *Majekodunmi*, [1962] W.N.L.R. 196, the court did not discuss when an emergency could be validly declared but was prepared to test the validity of the orders to examine if they were reasonably justifiable in the circumstances of each case.

[78] Act No. 18 of 1966.

The proposals amended sections 83 and 85 in some respects, and the Preservation of Public Security Act,[79] which is now closely tied to the procedure for the use of special powers. The expression 'emergency' has been deleted and the Act refers only to 'security measures'.[80] Section 85 now provides that the President may at any time by an order in the Gazette bring the whole or part of Part III of the Preservation of Public Security Act into operation over the entire country or part of it. The order remains in force for twenty-eight days before it is necessary to have the approval of the National Assembly and the period when the Assembly is dissolved does not count towards the twenty-eight days. No special majority is specified for the approval; so a simple majority of those present and voting suffices. Unless the President revokes the order earlier, it stays in force indefinitely,[81] although the National Assembly may bring it to an end at any time, but to do so, it must muster up the support of the majority of *all* the members of the Assembly. The order also comes to an end a week after a change through elections in the holder of the office of the Presidency.

Another important change which was made in 1966 was to permit greater and wider derogations from the guaranteed rights. The rights which can now be derogated from are not only those of liberty and non-discrimination, but also the freedoms of expression, assembly and association, movement, and the protection against arbitrary search or entry, and finally, the requirement that derogation must be reasonably justifiable in the circumstances of the situation has been removed.

To understand the scope and the operation of special powers it is necessary to look at the Preservation of Public Security Act, which is a difficult and

[79] Cap. 57. It is a little misleading to say that the Act was amended; the original Act was entirely superceded by new provisions.

[80] The Government explained the change of terminology by saying that the word 'emergency' was 'unnecessary and misleading'. 'Furthermore, it has for us the most distasteful associations of memory. We prefer to talk about our public security', House of Representatives, *Debates*, volume IX, part I (2 June 1966), col. 279. Another Minister who disliked the use of 'emergency' said, 'it gives a misleading picture of a country, it gives a bad picture of a country, and it gives too many sweeping powers that might not really be necessary in dealing with a localized situation' (col. 286).

[81] Act No. 45 of 1968 deleted the provisions whereby the maximum duration of an order without further parliamentary approval was eight months.

In practice the requirement of approval by the National Assembly for an extension beyond eight months provided little protection. When the Government sought approval for extension on 21 March 1967 for an order made originally on 21 July 1966, it gave little evidence in support of its request. A member of the opposition questioned the basis on which members were going to renew the order—'Members of this House do not know why these people have been detained. These people have been in detention for 7 months and up to now the hon. Members have not been told exactly what has been going on. There was supposed to be a tribunal for these people, but no one knows what really went on. I do not see how the Members of this Assembly can make a decision on this, a matter they do not know about. They do not know whether these people have done anything or not, so how can they vote that these people should remain in detention for another 8 months'. National Assembly, *Debates*, volume XI (21 March 1967), col. 1363 et seq.

confusing enactment. The Act distinguishes between public security measures and special public security measures; the former are available under Part II of the Act and are brought into operation by a declaration of the President which does not require the approval of the National Assembly; the latter, under Part III, by an order under section 85 of the Constitution. Under either declaration it is possible to invoke all or some of the powers provided for in the Act and for the whole or part of the country. A declaration can be made when, in the opinion of the President, such powers are necessary for the preservation of public security.[82] The 'preservation of public security' is widely defined and covers situations of political instability or subversion, the breakdown of the economic order, and natural disasters. The primary effect of bringing Part II or III of the Act into operation is to confer on the President the power to make laws by regulations. The regulations can be made for all or any of the purposes specified in section 4(2). These purposes are extensive and include the detention or the compulsory movement of persons, censorship or the prohibition of communications, control or prohibition of processions and meetings, compulsory acquisition of property, forced labour, control of trade and prices, and the modification of any law. The specified purposes are wide enough to comprehend any regulations, but the Act has a residual provision which permits regulations on any matter not expressly specified which is necessary or expedient for the preservation of public security.

Even though the power to make regulations is so extensive, for the regulations to be valid they have to conform to the terms of the Constitution. Regulations under Part II are considerably more restricted than under Part III and are invalid if they are inconsistent with any provision in the Constitution or any other law. It is therefore very confusing that the Act should provide a common list under section 4(2) of the specified purposes for which regulations can be made under either Part; it is clear, for example, that the purpose specified under section 4(2)(l)—to modify or suspend the existing law—can have no relevance to Part II. Similarly, the regulation to detain cannot be made under Part II, though detention is a specified purpose. It is unfortunate that the Act is so unclear on what precise kind of regulations can be made under Part II; any doubt in the important area of human rights is undesirable, and it is not enough to state that the regulations cannot be made in contravention of the Constitution or any other law.

Confusion is confounded, however, because there are certain regulations under Part II which may be valid notwithstanding conflict with the Constitution or any other law. These are the regulations made when Kenya is at war

[82] It is not expressly so provided in relation to the declaration for the special security measures, either in the Act or the Constitution but must *a fortiori* be implied. In any case it is unlikely that it is justiciable on this point.

or made and applied to those areas of Kenya covered previously by section 19 of the independence Order in Council and now section 127 of the Constitution—when only the restrictions outlined in the Constitution will apply.[83] It would have helped clarity if the powers when Kenya is at war or under section 127 were not dealt with under Part II; it is true that the exercise of these powers does not require the approval of the National Assembly, but nor does it require a declaration by the President, and the powers are in any event of a different magnitude from those ordinarily envisaged under Part II.

Part IV makes general provision for the regulations and the rules and orders made thereunder.[84] Like all other subsidiary legislation, this has to be laid before the National Assembly after it is made, unless already approved in draft form, and can be annulled by it if it passes a resolution of annulment within twenty days. It is made clear that subsidiary legislation may be made applicable to the whole or part of the country and may discriminate between classes of persons. Subsidiary legislation, like the parent regulations, is to have effect notwithstanding conflict with other laws. The regulations may make provision for the apprehension and punishment of persons offending against them, and for the imposition of penalties, including death, and the forfeiture of any property connected in any way with the offence. The regulations may also provide for the trial of such offenders by such courts (excluding courts martial) and in accordance with such procedure as prescribed therein. The powers to provide for trials are drastic and could result in serious derogations from the right to the protection of the law and its process guaranteed by section 77 of the Constitution. This is one of the few rights that cannot be derogated from even under the 'emergency' powers, and unless the regulations incorporate all the essential safeguards provided there, both before and during the trial, they would be invalid. The regulations may also authorize the search of persons and entry of premises, etc., provide for the payment of compensation and remuneration to persons affected by the regulations, charge fees for the issue of licences, permits, etc., required under the regulations, delegate rule-making power, and contain other provisions 'as appear to the President to be necessary or expedient for the purposes of the regulations'.[85]

The Act was brought into operation soon after its re-enactment and has continued in force ever since. As far as Part III is concerned it has been

[83] Section 3 (4). In these instances the regulations may make provision for any of the matters specified in section 4 (2).

[84] What is covered by 'orders'? Would a detention order be covered? Restriction or detention orders are not laid before the Assembly. 'Order' of a legislative rather than an executive kind must be intended here.

[85] Section 7 (3). Though it is not expressly provided, subsidiary legislation under part II must be qualified by the provisions discussed above.

brought into operation only for the purposes specified in section 4(2)(a) and (b) and regulations have been made.[86] They provide that if the Minister is satisfied that it is necessary for the preservation of public security to exercise control over the residence and movement of any person, he may order him to be restricted within a specified area, which need not be his normal place of residence, and may require him to reside in a particular house or building within the area to which he is restricted, and to remain indoors during the hours of darkness. The restriction order may also contain conditions to prohibit or control the possession of, or transactions in, any movable property and restrict his association or communication with other persons, and control messages to and from him. A person may be ordered to be detained in a prison or some other designated place if the Minister is satisfied that there is need for control beyond what is possible under a restriction order.[87]

Any person who is detained or restricted has within five days to be given detailed reasons in writing in a language he understands for the order, and has to be informed of his other rights under the Constitution.[88] A Review Tribunal is established for both kinds of orders. As originally provided, the tribunal consisted of one member appointed by the Chief Justice from those qualified to be appointed as High Court judges (who also presided), one member appointed by the President who is or has been a magistrate empowered to hold a subordinate court of the first class, and not less than two or more than four others appointed by the President. In 1968 an amendment was passed allowing even the presiding officer to be appointed by the President.[89] This was *ultra vires*, for the Constitution clearly provided that the presiding officer shall be a nominee of the Chief Justice, though the 1969 Constitution Act now provides for the President to make such an appointment. Not more than one month after the commencement of his detention, and thereafter at intervals of not more than six months, a detainee's case shall be reviewed by the tribunal. The detainee has the right, but at his own expense, to consult a legal representative of his own choice and to present his case through him, or personally. The tribunal may make recommendations by a majority if necessary, about the necessity or expediency of the detention but, unless the law provides otherwise, its recommendations are not binding. It was established in *Ooko* v. *The*

[86] Section 4 (2) (a): 'the detention of persons; (b): the registration, restriction of movement (into, out of or within Kenya) and compulsory movement of persons, including the imposition of curfews'. Legal Notice 212 of 1966 as amended by Legal Notice 240 of 1966.

[87] In *Ooko* v. *The Republic* (discussed below) the court rejected the argument that a detention order can only be made after a restriction order.

[88] As far as the restriction order is concerned, this provision goes beyond what is strictly required under section 81 (4) and (5) of the Constitution.

[89] Legal Notice 278 of 1968.

Republic[90] that the detainee may have the assistance of the courts to secure these safeguards, but the court has also shown that the assistance it is ready to give is very limited.

Ooko was detained on 4 August 1966 under a detention order, with his surname but different first names, signed by the Minister. On 27 September 1966 he filed a complaint in the High Court alleging that his detention was unlawful for the following reasons: he was not given the reasons for his detention within the prescribed period; the reasons were not sufficiently detailed as required by the Constitution; he was detained under the wrong name; and outsiders were present when his detention order was being reviewed by the tribunal. The case was not finally disposed of until December 1967 due to adjournments requested by the Government, the difficulties the plaintiff experienced in finding an advocate who would take his case, and the lack of facilities at his own disposal to prepare his case. The court held that the detention was not unlawful. As to the wrong name in the order, it accepted that a warrant of arrest applied for in a name which was not the name of the person arrested and intended to be arrested does not justify the arrest of the person. The court found no authority as to whether the same principles applied to detention orders, but surprisingly found that they did not. The doubt in the law was resolved against the liberty of the subject as follows:

> I think that in view of the seriousness of the conditions precedent to the issue of a detention order in as much as the Minister must be satisfied that the detention is necessary for the preservation of public security a partial mistake in naming the person to be detained should not necessarily have the effect that that person should be released from detention when he is the person intended to be detained and there is in fact no confusion as to the real identity of that person.

The court also dismissed the next ground of the complaint that a state counsel and a senior police officer were present at the Review Tribunal; there was no reason why they should not be present, and in fact the court considered the presence of some such persons desirable and necessary. There was no evidence that these persons took part in the recommendations of the tribunal, and in any case its recommendations were not binding on the Minister.

On the two final grounds, the court found that the reasons were given within the prescribed time, but agreed with the plaintiff that they were not sufficiently detailed. It did not, however, think that this was sufficient cause for his release;[91] it might well have been otherwise if no written statement

[90] High Court, Civil Case No 1159 of 1966, unreported.
[91] The plaintiff had referred the court to the Indian case of *Ram Krishan* v. *Delhi*, [1953] A.I.R. 318, when the Supreme Court ordered the release of the detainee because of the insufficiency of the details.

at all of the grounds for the detention had ever been given. In the circumstances the plaintiff's remedy was to apply to the court for an order to obtain further and better particulars of the reasons for detention.

The court's primary concern appeared to be to ensure compliance with the procedural rights under section 83. It may be argued that it should have also concerned itself with the consequences of non-compliance. The court did in fact touch on this when it hinted that it was prepared to consider the release of a detainee if no reasons at all for detention were given. But are reasons which are so vague as to give no real indication of the real grounds any better than no reasons at all? The absence of detail suggests that the decision to detain may have been arbitrary and unjustified. The court appeared to recognize this, when it said that no argument was addressed to it on the basis that the general statement of grounds apart from the lack of details were incapable of establishing a reasonable belief and satisfaction in the mind of the Minister that the security of the Republic was adversely affected, but went on to say that such an argument would have failed. It is thus possible under this decision for the Government to detain a person on vague and general grounds, and then later to look for evidence against him. What if the particulars given later under court order try to establish a basis for detention different from the grounds originally given? When the Government did supply the plaintiff in the instant case with details, he alleged that they added new grounds; the court did not pronounce on this.

The second point which arises from the decision is how far the courts will concern themselves with the adequacy or truth of the grounds. In the present case the plaintiff had attacked the new particulars as being still vague and general and based in part on his activities as a trade unionist before independence. The court held that the new particulars satisfied the requirements of section 83. If further particulars were required, a request could be made to the tribunal, but as far as the court's limited jurisdiction was concerned, the particulars given were adequate.

> The grounds if true could justify his detention. The truth of those grounds and the question of the necessity or otherwise of his continued detention are matters for the Tribunal and ultimately for the Minister rather than for this court.[92]

Does the court mean that if the grounds do not on the face of it disclose good

[92] In *Williams* v. *Majedodunmi*, op. cit., under a similar phrase, the Nigerian Federal Supreme Court examined the evidence in favour of a particular restriction order and set it aside as being not reasonably justifiable. In *Adegbenro* v. *Attorney-General*, op. cit., under the same emergency regulations, the court held that there was sufficient reason for the restriction order. cf. The Indian Supreme Court which has said: 'Preventive detention is a serious invasion of personal liberty and such meagre safeguards as the Constitution has provided against the improper exercise of the power must be jealously watched and enforced by the courts'. *Ram Krishan* v. *State of Delhi*, op. cit., at p. 329.

cause, it will order release? Further, will it try to discover whether the restriction order bears any relation to the real needs of the situation? Before the 1966 amendment to section 83, the court would have been justified in addressing itself to this issue in some form, but now the court is excluded from it.

COMPATIBILITY OF LAWS WITH THE CONSTITUTION

In specified circumstances, the law allows serious derogations from the constitutional guarantees of human rights. It is also possible to qualify significantly the enjoyment of these rights through ordinary legislation. It may be argued that in the end little of the rights is left and that the Bill is no more than a façade concealing abuses of power. The Bill does in theory increase the individual's rights compared to the colonial period, but how much in practice depends on the attitude of the courts, no less than on that of the Government. One peculiar problem arises from the fact that the constitutional arrangements at independence provided that the existing laws should continue in force as if made under the new Constitution but should be construed with such modifications, adaptations, qualifications and exceptions as might be necessary to bring them into conformity with it.[93] Therefore, while the existing laws continue in force, they do so only as long as they are valid under the Constitution, and some of the colonial laws are clearly inconsistent with the Bill of Rights. It is possible that a law may be inconsistent with the Constitution only in part; section 4 of the Order in Council enables that part to be severed leaving the rest in force. One of the difficult tasks for the courts is to decide how many excisions are necessary before the whole statute is abrogated.[94] So much of the colonial legislation is tainted in one way or another that the burden on the courts could be enormous.

Though the Constitution affects all laws, whether enacted before or after independence, there is no method whereby their validity may be determined, save for a challenge in court on a specific case. At best this provides only for random and partial review, and in Kenya, for a variety of reasons, judicial review has not been invoked to determine questions of constitutionality—the legal profession has not shown any appreciation of the possibilities of challenging the validity of laws and their administration, individuals and political parties are seldom aware of the extent of their rights, no provi-

[93] Section 4 of Kenya Independence Order in Council S.I. 1968/1963.

[94] In *Kioko's* case, op. cit., the court hinted that at least one of the sections of the Vagrancy Act might be invalid, but nevertheless upheld the statute. cf. *Ibingira* v. *Uganda*, [1966] E.A. 306, when the East Africa Court of Appeal said that 'the inconsistencies that are alleged are of so fundamental a nature that a finding in favour of the appellants would, for all practical purposes, amount to a finding that the Ordinance was abrogated by the enactment of the Constitution'. The Uganda Constitution expressly provided that the law shall be void only to the extent of inconsistency, section 1. Kenya Constitution Act, 1969 now has a similar provision, section 3.

sions exist for legal aid, the courts lack experience in deciding litigation of this kind, and in any event are too ready to accept the arguments of the Executive. Meanwhile a great deal of suspect legislation of both pre- and post-independence periods continues to be employed and administered. In only one area has the Government responded to the imperatives of the Constitution—discriminatory laws—and has made an effort to bring the law into line with the Constitution. We shall examine this before discussing some examples of legislation which may be invalid but which is still in force and used.

(a) *Discrimination*

In 1963 the Government set up a working party to consider what laws in force in Kenya were discriminatory in themselves or in their effect and to recommend on their amendment or repeal in view of the constitutional protection from discrimination.[95] A thorough review of the legislation was undertaken. Some of the more glaring discriminatory laws or practices, however, had already been abolished or amended even before the report—for example, provisions for jury trial for Europeans, the civil service regulations, the Registered Land Act, 1963 which removed all trace of discrimination from all transactions in land covered by it;[96] and the integration of the educational system had begun. The working party still found several areas of discrimination, both in the rules of procedure and the substantive law. To give a few examples, section 16 of the Criminal Procedure Code[97] empowered the Governor-General by special appointment to confer High Court jurisdiction on first class magistrates in special districts over Africans only. Section 126 of the same Act provided that any person may be allowed to deposit money in lieu of recognisance, but only an African or Baluchi was allowed to deposit property instead. The Detention Camps Act[98] applied only to Africans. There were separate Muslim subordinate courts, and the African courts had jurisdiction only over Africans. Under the Bankruptcy Act, the priority given to the debts for labourers' wages related back further in the case of Africans.[99] The Registration of Persons Act[100] differentiated

[95] *Report of the Working Party on Discriminatory Laws*, (mimeo.), n.d., Attorney-General's Chambers, Nairobi.

[96] Section 95 makes void 'any agreement, condition or restriction contained in any instrument (whether executed before or after the commencement of the Act), whereby persons who are members of a particular race or who are not members of a particular race are prohibited from or prevented from owning or from occupying any land or from acquiring an interest therein'.

[97] Cap. 75.

[98] Cap. 91. Its purpose was to permit Africans convicted of any offence in certain circumstances to be sentenced to detention in a camp rather than be fined or sentenced to a regular jail, section 5.

[99] Cap. 53, section 38 (1) (d).

[100] Cap. 107.

Africans from other people and required any African who had reached the age or apparent age of sixteen to register; the Immigration Act[101] treated the Africans more favourably; only the Europeans were liable to compulsory military service; and the Stock and Produce Theft Act[102] applied to Africans only. In most cases the working party recommended either the deletion of the discriminatory provisions or their extension to people of all races.

The Government took prompt action on the recommendations.[103] We have already discussed the reforms to the legal system, leading to the integration of the courts; and alterations have also been made to the procedural laws.[104] The Bankruptcy Act has been amended by deleting the part which gave the African labourer priority,[105] the discriminatory sections of the Registration of Persons Act have been deleted,[106] references in the Immigration Act to Africans were replaced by references to 'citizens of countries of Africa',[107] the compulsory Military Training Act has been repealed,[108] and section 7(3) of the Auctioneers Act which limited the issue of a special kind of auctioneers' licence to Arabs and Africans only has been deleted.[109] Despite this effort at the removal of discrimination, some discriminatory laws remain. It is intended that these will eventually be removed; the delay is due to the need to make firm policy decisions on the changes, the lack of personnel to implement these, and the problems of unscrambling past discriminatory schemes and regulations.

The prompt action of the Government to remove legal discrimination is understandable: it was not to be expected that an African government would for long countenance racial laws which usually, though not always, operated to the disadvantage of Africans.

In this area, the courts have also followed the lead of the Government, and have set themselves against racial differentiation. There are two decisions of particular interest. In 1964 a European called Wilken was charged with the murder of an African, allegedly a thief, by confining him in a box with insufficient air until he could be handed over to the police.[110] By this time the right to trial by jury for Europeans had been abolished, and consequently Europeans came under the same provisions for trial by assessors as Africans and Asians. At the trial, counsel for the accused argued that all three assessors

[101] Cap. 172, section 1 (2).
[102] Cap. 355.
[103] See *Notes on steps taken or contemplated to implement the recommendations of the Working Party on discriminatory legislation in Kenya*, (mimeo.), n.d., Attorney-General's Chambers, Nairobi.
[104] e.g. Section 16 of the Criminal Procedure Code was modified to enable the President to confer special powers on a magistrate to cover *all* races, Legal Notice 374/1964.
[105] Act No. 21 of 1966.
[106] Legal Notice 236/1964.
[107] In the new Immigration Act No. 25 of 1967.
[108] Act No. 36 of 1963.
[109] Cap. 526 as amended by Legal Notice 374/1963.
[110] *R.* v. *Wilken*, [1965] E.A. 286.

should be Europeans, on the ground that the practice had grown up that when the accused was African or Asian, all the assessors were of the same race as the accused. It was only fair that a European accused should have the benefit of trial by all European assessors.

> The law, in the form of the practice of choosing assessors of the same race as the accused, had been observed before and since independence in the case of Africans. To depart from this would be to give a discriminatory effect to the law contrary to section 26 of the Constitution.[111]

The Chief Justice had little difficulty in disposing of this argument. Referring to the practice on which the accused's point was based, he said:

> All this has not conferred upon an accused of any race the right to be tried with the aid of assessors exclusively of his own race, nor has it, to my mind, established a principle that it is necessarily just and essential that a man should be so tried.

The important principle was to have such assessors as were most likely to benefit the judge. A mixed panel of assessors was often likely to be more helpful.[112]

The second case concerns an application under section 62 of the Civil Procedure Act to vary the terms of a trust which had been established by a wealthy Arab in 1940 for the benefit of European children residing in the country, and more particularly for the provision of a resort at Mombasa for the holidays, convalescence and recreation of such children.[113] The application was to remove the racial restriction. The court granted the application on the basis of the *cy près* doctrine. It was difficult to find in the trust a general charitable intention, but such intention was not necessary in this kind of trust. Less easy to understand as an application of the *cy près* doctrine was the court's finding that the trust had become impossible or impracticable, even given the wide definition of these expressions. The court referred to *In re Dominion Students' Hall Trust* v. *Attorney-General*,[114] but that case is distinguishable on at least two grounds—it concerned a company limited by guarantee and most of the shareholders agreed to the change of terms, and its primary object was not necessarily to benefit white students from the Commonwealth but to strengthen the ties of the Commonwealth. The changing racial composition of the Commonwealth meant that the racial restriction jeopardized the object of the charity, and in that sense it had

[111] p. 28. Section 26 referred to is now section 82.

[112] p. 28. The Chief Justice is reported to have stated, though this does not appear in the published report, that in some cases all assessors of the same race might be preferable, e.g., in cases where the defence is provocation. See Morris and Read, *Uganda: The Development of its Laws and Constitutions* (London, Stevens and Sons Ltd., 1966), p. 267.

[113] *In the Matter of the trusts of a deed . . . between Sir Ali Bin Salim and the Public Trustee*, Miscellaneous case No. 36/1967 (unreported). See also *Madhwa's* case, discussed above.

[114] [1947] 1 Ch. 183.

become impracticable or impossible. In the instance, the object was to benefit the European children, and the changed political and social conditions could not be held to frustrate that object. The court, however, held that

> the restriction on the charity to benefit European children only, in the context of independent Kenya, renders the trust thereunder impracticable as being in contravention of the spirit of the Constitution of Kenya.

Earlier the court had rejected the argument that the trust was unconstitutional due to section 82(6). The spirit, if not the letter, of the Constitution prevailed, therefore, and the application was granted.

(b) *Freedom of association*

Turning to possibly invalid legislation, it is proposed to examine some laws which give the Executive important powers of control over persons and their exercise of fundamental rights. To consider first the law of associations, it is provided that every society in Kenya has to be first approved by a state official before it can exist legally.[115] In addition, each society has to conform to certain standard conditions. It is possible for the Minister to exempt a society from some or all of the provisions of the law relating to registration. Every society which is not registered, unless its application for registration is pending, is an unlawful society. Applications for registration are made to the Registrar of Societies, who can reject an application if he is satisfied, *inter alia*, that the society is a branch of, or is affiliated to, or connected with, any organization or association of a political nature established outside Kenya, or that the society has amongst its objects, or is likely to pursue or to be used for, any unlawful purpose prejudicial to or incompatible with peace, welfare or good government in Kenya or that the interests of peace, welfare or good order in Kenya would otherwise be likely to suffer prejudice by reason of the registration of the society. The Registrar has extensive controls over societies which have been registered or exempt; he has to be kept informed of changes in the officers of the society or amendments to its constitution for which his approval is necessary; he can ask for the removal of persons or officers who have been associated with an unlawful society or with a society which has been refused registration, and he can call for its accounts and other documents. He can revoke the registration of a society or deprive a society of its exemptions. The grounds for revocation are similar to those which, if they existed at the time of the application for registration, would have justified refusal to register. In addition, revocation can also be based on the ground of the refusal of a society to comply with the Registrar's order for information or accounts or failure to furnish him with

[115] See, generally, Societies Act No. 4 of 1968. 'Society' includes clubs or other associations of ten or more persons, and would cover political parties but exclude registered or probationary trade unions, section 2.

information about its change of name, constitution or officers. Moreover the Minister has overriding power to ban a society by a declaration if he thinks that it is dangerous to the good government of the Republic.

Severe penalties are provided for contravention of any of the provisions of the Act either in the management or membership of an unlawful society. The police have extensive powers of entry, arrest and search without warrant if they have reason to believe that the meeting of an unlawful society is taking place. Many of the rules of evidence established for the purposes of the Act throw the onus of proof on the accused; thus, for example, when it is alleged that a society is an unlawful society, it is for the defence to prove that it is not so and where any books or other papers of a society are found in the possession of any person, it shall be presumed, until the contrary is proved, that he is a member of the society, whose existence is also similarly presumed from the existence of the books and papers.

It is open to question whether these wide measures of control are really necessary for the purposes for which control is permitted by the Constitution. Many of the provisions may be regarded as purely administrative in nature, but their effect is to impose serious constraints on the freedom to form groups and associations. Two aspects of the Act in particular are objectionable—first, the wide discretion given to the Minister and the Registrar, often without any guiding criteria. It is a well established doctrine in many countries where there are constitutional restrictions on legislative and executive competence that the discretion given to the Executive is only valid if it can be exercised solely in a manner and for the purposes permitted by the Constitution, and grants of wide discretion, capable of being exercised in a constitutional as well as unconstitutional manner, are struck out.[116] Quite apart from the wide administrative control over societies vested in the Registrar, some of the grounds on which a society can be refused registration, or have it cancelled, may be themselves unconstitutional. Thus if a registered society amends its name or its constitution without the prior consent of the Registrar (and it is nowhere provided for what reasons he can withhold his consent), he can cancel its registration. Another ground for refusal is that a person who is an officer of the society was previously an officer of some other society which was refused registration or had it cancelled; similarly the registration of a society can be cancelled if such a person becomes its officer, and the society ignores the Registrar's direction to remove him.

Secondly, the Act makes no provision for appeals to the courts with regard to the exercise of powers under it. An appeal from the refusal, cancellation or

[116] e.g. *Panama Refining Co.* v. *Ryan*, 293 U.S. 388; *Schecheter Poultry Corp.* v. *U.S.*, 295 U.S. 495 (both held the delegation of legislative power to the President by Congress unconstitutional since the enabling legislation did not contain adequate standards for the exercise of the powers). See also the discussion in *Tika Ramji* v. *State of U.P.*, [1956] A.I.R. (S.C.) 676. (An Indian case where, however, the court upheld the statute.)

suspension of registration by the Registrar can be taken to the Minister, but there is no appeal beyond him. In other instances of the decision or directions of the Registrar, there is no appeal even to the Minister. In these matters the Minister is not necessarily an independent or impartial person, particularly where the complainant may well be from an opposition political party, and the absence of appeals to an impartial and independent tribunal seems to be based on the assumption that the formation of associations is a privilege and not a right—an assumption which is contrary to the Constitution where the formation of, and participation in, associations is guaranteed.

Another aspect of freedom of association is the right to form trade unions, specifically referred to in the Bill of Rights. Trade unions enjoy wide immunities from civil and criminal proceedings,[117] which free them to pursue the rights and claims of their members without fear of legal harassment. A serious restriction on the immunities, however, is that they are not available to a trade union unless it is registered. Every trade union has to apply for registration to the Registrar of Trade Unions, appointed by the Minister. The Registrar may reject the application for various reasons, including that any other trade union already registered is sufficiently representative of the whole, or of a substantial proportion, of the interests in respect of which the application is made. A registration can be cancelled or suspended for similar reasons. An appeal against the Registrar's decision to the High Court is provided. The Registrar's powers are important and can to some extent be used to control and regulate union activity. Similar powers apply also in relation to an association or combination of trade unions.

A striking instance of control through these powers in relation to associations of unions was the dissolution in 1965 of two rival associations, the Kenya Federation of Labour (KFL) and the Kenya African Workers' Congress (KAWC) and the establishment of one central association, the Central Organization of Trade Unions (Kenya), COTU.

Until 1965 there was only one association, the KFL, but in that year differences developed within it, particularly in relation to affiliations with rival international federations of trade unions. A group broke off, applied for, and obtained, registration as the KAWC, initially with six member unions. An intense rivalry developed between the two, and there is reason to believe that there was considerable involvement on their part in the country's political activity; the KAWC, whose application for registration may have been originally accepted to weaken the KFL, contained several radical officials. The Government showed its concern in these developments

[117] Trade Unions Act, Cap. 233. For a useful account of the history and present rules of industrial law, see Livingstone, 'The Government, the Worker, and the Law in Kenya' (1967) 3 *E.A.L.J.* 282. See this article also for the Government's power to prohibit strikes. The laws appear to provide for the right to strike, but in practice the Government has been able to prohibit strikes in most key sectors, including governmental.

by the appointment of a high powered Presidential Ministerial Committee to enquire into the trade union situation. The Committee reported quickly with far reaching recommendations, including the de-registration of the two associations, and their replacement by COTU. The constitution for COTU should be drawn up by the Government, and should provide for considerable governmental participation. The President accepted the recommendations,[118] gave orders for the immediate de-registration of KFL and KAWC and instructed the Attorney-General to draw up a constitution for COTU, which was to provide, *inter alia,* for government representation on its governing council and the appointment of the Secretary-General by the President from a panel of three names submitted by the governing council. All trade union affiliations with outside bodies were also cancelled. All this was done without any fresh legislation,[119] and it was not done in strict conformity with the terms of the Trade Union Act. Theoretically the status of COTU is that of an independently registered trade union federation, but the actions of the Government have appeared at times to assume that it is an adjunct to the administration.

Further controls, especially over organizations of a political nature, are imposed by the Public Order Act.[120] Organizations equipped to usurp the functions of the police or the armed forces or for the display of force to promote political ends are prohibited and severe penalties are set out for the breach of this prohibition and others against the wearing of uniforms associated with political organizations or political objectives. It is unlawful to carry offensive weapons at public gatherings or in public places. Under this Act and the Police Act,[121] the police have wide powers of search, entry and inspection on reasonable suspicion of a contravention of the law.

The police and the administration are also given wide powers of control over public gatherings.[122] The police may control and direct the conduct of

[118] *The policy on Trade Union Organization in Kenya,* Nairobi, 1965. The Government ruled out any debate or discussion on the recommendations.

[119] Except subsequently an amendment to section 24 of the Constitution to remove doubts as to the constitutionality of the proceedings. Act No. 16 of 1966. See new Constititution section 80 (2) (d).

[120] Cap. 56.

[121] Cap. 84.

[122] 'Public gathering' means 'a public meeting, a public procession, and any other meeting, gathering or concourse of ten or more persons in any public place.' Meeting is defined as any gathering or assembly of persons convened or held for any purpose including any political purpose but excluding religious, social, cultural, trade union, etc. purposes, and 'public meeting' is also defined; it means 'any meeting held or to be held in a public place, and any meeting which the public or any section of the public or more than fifty persons are or are to be permitted to attend whether on payment or otherwise'. 'Public place' is any place to which for the time being the public or any section of the public are entitled or permitted to have access whether on payment or otherwise (section 2). In *Kaggia* v. *The Republic,* Criminal Appeals Nos. 582 and 583 of 1968 (unreported), the court had to construct whether it was necessary for a meeting in a public place to be a 'public meeting', that there should be at least fifty persons present. It held that when the meeting was in a public place, it was

all public meetings, including the specification of the route to be followed in the case of a public procession, if it appears necessary or expedient in the interest of public order to do so. No public meeting or procession can be held without the prior permission of the District Commissioner, who may refuse permission if he is satisfied that the meeting or procession is likely to prejudice the maintenance of public order, to be used for any unlawful or immoral purposes, or may give permissions with conditions attached. Permission may also be refused if the applicant or any person or organization associated directly or indirectly with the application or likely in the opinion of the District Commissioner to be concerned in the holding or organizing of the meeting or procession has, in relation to any public gathering, recently contravened the provisions of the Act or any other written law or any condition attached to a permission.

It is also illegal to advertise a public meeting or procession before the permission to hold it has been obtained; and the District Commissioner may refuse permission if a meeting has been so advertised. He may also revoke a licence or amend its conditions if he thinks this is necessary or expedient in the interest of public order or to prevent the execution of an unlawful or immoral purpose. The person to whom a licence has been given must be present at the meeting or procession from its beginning to the end and has to follow any directions the police may give him to ensure compliance with the conditions in the licence and the maintenance of public order. A police officer may stop or prevent the holding of any

> public gathering or *other meeting*, procession or gathering of persons *whatsoever and wheresoever* whether or not required to be licensed, and whether licensed or not . . . if the public gathering, meeting, procession or gathering is causing or is, in the opinion of such officer, likely to cause a breach of the peace.[123]

If the police suspect that an unlicensed gathering is likely to take place they may prevent access to the place of the gathering by any means, including physical barriers, that they think fit. Appeals to the Minister are

automatically a public meeting, regardless of the numbers involved, substituting thus, in effect, 'or' for 'and' in the definition. The court went on to say, 'We concede . . .that there appears to be a considerable amount of duplication and overlapping in this group of definitions. For example, in the definition of "public gathering", it is sufficient to give any meaning to the expression "any other meeting . . . in any public place" seeing that (if we are right), any meeting held in a public place is a public meeting. Similarly, it would appear that in the definition of "public meeting" the words "any meeting which the public or any section of the public . . . are or are to be permitted to attend whether on payment or otherwise" are surplusage, since the place of such a meeting would under the ensuing definition be a public place and that meeting would accordingly be a public meeting. We do not think that any construction of the definition is capable of removing all these superfluities. But whether this is so or not, we still do not consider that there is any other possible construction of the definition of "public meeting" than the one we have propounded.' *Quaere* whether this was the only option open to the court, and whether it ought not to have leaned in favour of the accused given the spirit of the Bill of Rights.

[123] Italics supplied.

provided in case of the refusal or cancellation of a licence or the imposition of conditions thereon, and he may 'in his discretion', confirm, reverse or vary the decision appealed against. Again, there is no appeal to the courts.

It is an offence not only to hold or convene such a gathering, but an offence also to take part in it. Given the wide discretions vested in administrative and police officers as to the holding and conduct of meetings, very severe limitations indeed can be imposed on the right to meet and discuss. It is common knowledge that permission is consistently denied to the members of the opposition to hold meetings,[124] even just before elections. The case of *Kaggia* v. *The Republic* illustrates the breadth of the operations of the Act in practice. Kaggia, the Vice-President of the opposition KPU, was invited to attend a ceremony for the opening of an office for the sub-branch of the party in South Nyanza, where he was holidaying nearby. When he arrived there, he went to a shop which also served as the office of the sub-branch and met the members of the local committee. Though there was great conflict in the evidence, it was accepted by the court that a large number of people crowded inside and outside the shop, where Kaggia made a speech of a 'strongly political flavour'. All this time, including the journey to the place of the sub-branch, he was followed by the police with whom he had been chatting previously. After he had spoken for about fifteen minutes, the senior police officer who was present asked him to stop, whereupon Kaggia 'promptly complied' and the people were asked to leave. It was 'not disputed that the meeting dispersed in an orderly manner'. On these facts, Kaggia was charged with holding an unlawful meeting or, alternatively, taking part in a such a meeting. The lower court convicted him on the first charge and sentenced him to one year's imprisonment.

On appeal, which was against both conviction and sentence, it was argued that the meeting was not of a political nature, but merely a meeting of the party officials, that there were not fifty persons present to constitute it a 'public meeting', and that the accused had not held or convened it. The High Court found that it was a political meeting for the purposes of the Act since the content of the speech was so heavily political, and that there were also present persons other than officials, whose actual number was immaterial. The Court was also of the opinion that Kaggia had 'held' the meeting; it is true that the occasion of the meeting was an invitation to him, but the meeting would not have been held without his acceptance and when he did arrive, it was he and his party who took charge of the proceedings. " 'Hold' is in its

[124] For allegations of this in Parliament, see reference in footnote 137, chapter VIII. The Government has stated that the DCs are responsible for licensing but there have been allegations that the DCs receive their orders from the Government to refuse licences to the opposition. National Assembly, *Debates*, volume XIV (28 February 1968), col. 162. The Government has prevented the leader of the opposition from talking to the University or schools.

nature one of the most general words in the English language, and it would require strong argument to show that in this context it is not wide enough to cover the activities of the appellant". The court, however, reduced the sentence, which it found excessive, to six months and was impressed by the fact that there was no premeditation, and the meeting was orderly and dispersed promptly after the request of the police.

The arguments for the appellant were confined to the interpretation and application of the Act. No arguments were offered as to its constitutionality, perhaps because no application had in fact been made for a licence to hold the meeting and hence there was no refusal. It would, however, have still been possible to base the defence on the unconstitutionality of the section of the Act under which the charged was preferred. Any form of prior censorship or approval has an inherent tendency towards denial of freedoms and rights, and it may be questioned whether the requirements in the Act do not infringe these rights under the Constitution.

(c) *Freedom of expression*

The Public Order Act restricts not only the freedom of association but also the freedom of expression and communication. We may examine here some other legislation which restricts this freedom. The Books and Newspapers Act[125] regulates the printing of books and newspapers and while few of its provisions can be said to impose a serious restraint on publication, there is one provision which has been criticized as tending to restrict the right to publish—no person can print or publish a newspaper unless he has executed a bond in the sum of sh. 10,000/- with one or more sureties as required and approved by the Registrar. The bond is required as security for any fine imposed on the printer or publisher for contravention of any law or for damages for libel. The sum of money required is quite substantial in Kenya's conditions and its requirement acts as a discouragement to individuals or small groups wishing to start newspapers.[126]

[125] Cap. 111. See also the Films and Stage Plays Act, No. 34 1962, now Cap. 222 which imposes censorship on the exhibition of films and plays, and does not provide for appeal to the courts against censorship.

[126] 'Newspapers' is widely defined but excludes publications appearing at intervals of more than 3 months, section 2. The Working Party on discriminatory laws recommended its abolition on the following grounds:—

(a) The security aspect expected to be covered by the bonds is adequately covered by the Law of Sedition under the Penal Code, sections 57–60.

(b) If a bond is intended to serve any useful purpose for protecting the members of the public, a bond of £500 is inadequate protection—

  (i) because the amount is too small,

  (ii) because there is no guarantee that when the person who entered the bond is called upon to honour it he will do so unless the bond was executed by an insurance company.

(c) The provisions are not discriminatory in wording thereof, but are discriminatory in effect, particularly against the low income groups, namely Africans and Asians.

(d) The freedom of expression provided for in the Constitution should be encouraged

The real instrument for control, however, is not this Act, but certain provisions in the Penal Code. Any person who prints, publishes, sells, offers for sale, distributes or reproduces any seditious publications, or imports such publication, unless he has no reason to believe that it is seditious, is guilty of an offence and liable to imprisonment for up to ten years.[127] It is also an offence to have a seditious publication in one's possession, punishable by imprisonment for up to seven years,[128] unless a person proves that he did not know that it was seditious when it came into his possession, and that he handed it to a police or administrative officer as soon as he realized its nature. The printing machine suspected to have been used to produce the seditious material may be seized by the police and if there is a conviction, confiscated for a year or forfeited outright by order of the court.[129] It is also possible for the court, on conviction of a person for printing or publishing a seditious publication in a newspaper, to prohibit the publication of the newspaper for a period of up to one year. These are serious penalties, even though administered by the courts, and possibly in excess even of the restrictions of the freedom allowed by the Constitution.

Much more serious, however, is section 52 of the Code, the first part of which enables the Minister, if he considers it necessary in the interests of public order or security, health or morals, the administration of justice or the maintenance of the authority and impartiality of the judiciary, to prohibit the importation of any publication, or if it is a periodical, any or all of its past or future issues, or the past or future publications of the person named in the order of the prohibition, so long as the principal occupation of that person is not publication.[130] Up to 1966 there were no comparable provisions to ban publications locally produced, but an amendment to section 52 was introduced that year which enables the Minister, for reasons similar to those mentioned above, to declare any publication a prohibited publication, and in the case of a periodical, also all its past or future issues, or in the case of the publisher, all his past or future publications, so long as publication is not his principal activity.[131] Though the grounds for prohibition in both instances

and not hindered as the passage of time will ensure that only responsible publications will survive.

[127] Cap. 63, section 57; the term of imprisonment was raised from 3 years to 10 by Act No. 24 of 1967. For definition of seditious, see below, pp. 451–2.

[128] Act No. 24 of 1967 raised the term from 3 to 7 years.

[129] *Quaere* whether it is constitutional to provide for confiscation of the machine. In *Muhuri*, op. cit., the constitutionality of the provision for a court to levy contributions in view of the protection of property was not discussed since the court found that the penalties were not imposed in respect of 'rights or duties'.

[130] *Quaere* whether Legal Notice 208/1967 which prohibits the importation of 'all past or future publications purporting to be published by Foreign Languages Press, Peking' is valid. It would seem to be too wide for any reasonable restriction.

[131] Act 41 of 1966. Among the reasons for banning, there is no mention of the administration of justice or the authority of the judiciary (because the courts can punish for contempt?) and it is provided that the ban must be reasonably justifiable in a democratic society.

are spelled out and related to the exceptions permitted by the Constitution, the Minister's power to ban all past or future issues is arguably excessive and unconstitutional.[132] The Government has not hesitated to make use of these powers, and in many of these instances it would be difficult to prove that the publications in question posed any threat which would justify the ban.[133] Moreover the very existence of such powers has an inhibiting effect on free expression, and it has indeed been suggested that threats of ban have been used to seek modifications of editorial policy or removal of staff.[134]

Mention must be made, too, of the law in respect of broadcasting. The monopoly of broadcasting, whether of sound or television, is vested in the Government and exercised through its agency, the Voice of Kenya. The Voice of Kenya is obliged under the law to provide daily news broadcasts in the English, Swahili and Hindustani languages and such other languages as the Minister may determine; and to keep a fair balance in all respects in the allocation of broadcasting hours as between different political views. Before its nationalization,[135] the broadcasting company was a public corporation legally separate from the Government; it is now part of the Government, under the Ministry of Information and Broadcasting. It is, therefore, not surprising that it has not always complied with its obligation to give fair coverage to all political views. The opposition views are rarely heard on the radio or the television.[136]

[132] The Code provides penalties for the breach of the prohibitions and authorizes a public official to detain, open and examine any article or package which he suspects to contain any prohibited publication (section 54).

[133] Among the publications banned are: *Africa Communist, Africa and the World*, W. Attwood, *The Reds and the Blacks, U.S. News and World Report, Sauti Ya Urafiki, Who Rules Kenya? News* (GDR), Mao Tse Tung, *Cheche Moja Yaweza Kuanzisha Moto Mbugani, Quotations from Chairman Mao Tse Tung, Cavalier, Men Only, Adam* and 'any publication depicting or containing any symbol, emblem, device, colours, slogan, motto, words, or letters signifying any association with or support for a political object or political organization' (void for vagueness?). *Playboy* was banned in 1968 but surprisingly, without a reason, the ban was revoked a few days later.

Recently a schoolboy and a university teacher were charged under this section for possessing certain prohibited books by Mao Tse Tung. The charge against the teacher was dropped though not until a considerable harassment had been caused to him; no reason was given, but presumably the reason was that the book was not prohibited, since the book in question was published in the U.S.A. and not China. The schoolboy was convicted and sentenced to 18 months' imprisonment.

[135] The Kenya Broadcasting (Nationalization) Act No. 12 of 1964. The Corporation was financed in part by the Government and in part by private firms.

[136] The Minister has admitted that it was the custom of political governments in developing and certain developed countries, where a mass medium is controlled by the Government, that the voice of the opposition party is not heard through such a medium. He stressed that KPU could not expect facilities on the Voice of Kenya to express its views which, in most cases, were contradictory to the Government desire to accelerate unity for effective economic development. However, if a KPU leader was 'constructive', i.e. if he preached loyalty to the Government, and the spirit of self-help to uplift the standard of living in the country, without criticizing the Government, his voice was given prominence on the radio or television. *Daily Nation*, 14 September 1968 (Nairobi).

Finally the law of sedition and treason may be discussed. It is treason for a citizen,[137] whether he is in Kenya or outside, to 'compass, imagine, invent, devise or intend' the death, wounding or imprisonment of the President, or the deposing of him or the overthrow of the Government by unlawful means, so long as the intention is expressed in some overt manner. It is also treason for a citizen to levy, or incite war against Kenya or to help her enemies. The penalty for treason is death. Similar offences by those owing allegiance are felonies punishable with life imprisonment.[138]

The crime of sedition is even more widely defined, though the penalty is not so heavy.[139] It is sedition for any person to do or attempt to do, or make any preparation to do, or conspire with any person to do, any act with a seditious intention; or to utter any words with a seditious intention; or to print or publish or sell or offer to sell any seditious publication, or import or possess any seditious publication, unless he had no reason to believe it was seditious. Seditious intention is defined as an intention to overthrow the Government by unlawful means, to bring into hatred or contempt or to excite disaffection against the person of the President or the Government, to excite the inhabitants of Kenya to attempt to procure the alteration by unlawful means, of any matter or thing established by law, to bring into hatred or contempt or to excite disaffection against the administration of justice, to raise discontent or disaffection among the inhabitants, or to promote feelings of ill-will or hostility between different sections or classes of the population. This would cover most acts of criticism of the Government;[140] and so it is important to establish what kind of intention is necessary for conviction. It is provided that an intention is not seditious by reason only that it is intended to point out that the Government is mistaken, or its errors or those of the administration of justice, so that they may be remedied, or to persuade people in favour of change through lawful means or to point out the causes of ill-will or hostility between the people with the purpose of removing them. Nevertheless, even if this is the only intention, it will still be seditious, if its effect or likely effect is any of the factors mentioned in the definition of seditious intention. It is, moreover, provided that to determine whether the intention was seditious, it will be presumed that a person intended the natural consequences of his acts.[141] It is therefore possible

[137] Even non-citizens owing allegiance to the Republic are covered by this provision. cf. *R.* v. *Casement*, [1917] 1 K.B. 98.

[138] Sections 40 and 43 of the Penal Code as amended by Act 24 of 1967.

[139] It used to be imprisonment up to 3 years, but was changed to 7 years by Act 24 of 1967.

[140] cf. *Burns* v. *Ransley*, [1958] C.L.R. 101 (Australia), where Dixon C. J. defined 'disaffection' (and presumably related expressions) as 'not merely the absence of affection and regard, but disloyalty, enmity, hostility' (p. 109).

[141] In *D.P.P.* v. *Obi*, [1961] All N.L.R. 187, the court held, on a similar provision, that its purpose is to enable the prosecution to rely on it without extrinsic evidence, but that it does not prevent the accused from showing that his only intention was as

to convict a person even though there was no *mens rea*. It would also appear from the words of the section that the truth of what is alleged is no defence, for the paramount factor is its effect—a very serious restriction on what could be legitimate, even necessary, criticism or exposure of the Government.[142] Nor is it necessary to prove that there was any incitement to violence.[143] It is not necessary to prove that the act in question had any effect at all; it is enough if it is likely to have the effect.[144]

Even though these provisions for sedition were enacted after independence, their constitutionality may be questioned. The freedom of expression and communication is seriously undermined by them; the restraints are imposed for many of the purposes not permitted under the exceptions in the Constitution to the freedom; in particular, they do not all have a relation to public order. 'Sedition' is an offence notoriously susceptible of abuse by those in authority. As the counsel in the Nigerian case of *Obi* v. *D.P.P.* said:

> Any law which punishes a person for making a statement which brings a Government into discredit or ridicule or creates disaffection against the Government irrespective of whether the statement is true or false and irrespective of any repercussions on public order or security is not a law which is reasonably justifiable in a democratic society.[145]

The result of all these provisions is that it is difficult for the opposition or even sympathetic critics to express themselves freely, and communicate their views to the public. They are hardly necessary for public security, and seem to stem from a fear that too much free speech might lead to subversion or instability. No one disputes that there must be some restrictions on freedom of expression in every state, or that more restrictions may be permissible in a state such as Kenya which can so easily be thrown into turmoil by over-zealous political activity on the part of an opposition, than in states whose political systems are older, and therefore more secure, and indeed the Bill of Rights attempts to allow that, but the laws discussed above go beyond that, and turn a right guaranteed and defined in the Constitution into a privilege, the extent and very existence of which is wholly dependent upon the Government. Both the letter and the spirit of the Constitution are ignored.

permitted under the section. It is, however, doubtful if this interpretation will be of much assistance in Kenya, as the section makes clear that even if the intention was innocent, it is deemed seditious in view of its effect or likely effect—cf., also, *R.* v. *Burns*, [1886] 16 Cox C.C. 355.

[142] It was held in *D.P.P.* v. *Obi*, op. cit., on a similar section, that truth is no defence. *Quaere*, would it be seditious to suggest that the Government was corrupt, if this could be substantiated? It is likely that allegations against individual Ministers (other than the President) cannot constitute sedition. For definition of 'Government', see *D.P.P.* v. *Obi*.

[143] *Wallace-Johnson* v. *R.*, [1940] A.C. 231, a Privy Council decision from the Gold Coast on a similar section.

[144] ibid. What if the act is not reasonably capable of such an effect?

[145] p. 191.

CONCLUSION: PROSPECTS FOR THE BILL OF RIGHTS

It is hard to escape the conclusion that the Bill of Rights has had little impact on government and administration in Kenya. Public order rather than human rights remain the dominant theme of the Government. It has been argued[146] that even if there is no overt indication of the effectiveness of the Bill of Rights, it can exert a powerful influence behind the scenes for it strengthens the hands of the Government's legal advisers and draftsmen in resisting or toning down the more authoritarian proposals of their political colleagues and masters. There does not appear to be much evidence either way that that has happened in Kenya, but in any event, such influence is dependent in the final analysis on there being, first, a legal profession alert to the protection afforded by the Bill, and willing to challenge governmental action accordingly, and second, a court imbued with the philosophy behind the Bill, and willing to implement it. Neither precondition exists in Kenya. The question was posed at the beginning of this chapter whether it was realistic to expect the colonial administration to change overnight in the direction of greater liberalism consequent upon the introduction of a Bill of Rights. The same question may be posed in respect of the independent Government of Kenya, and the answer once again has to be in the negative. Kenya became independent with a war of secession under way in the North Eastern Province, with tribal suspicions exacerbated by the constant constitutional negotiations over the preceding two or three years, and with a potentially grave economic situation stemming from the problem of the landless. Inevitably public order had to be stressed at the expense of human rights, and once the new Government had made the same choice as the old and departing administration, the legal and administrative systems were ready to hand to implement it. Thereafter, there was no turning back, and indeed, the trend has been in the direction of whittling down the effectiveness of the Bill of Rights, and recreating an unfettered administration.

It may be asked why, in these circumstances, the Bill of Rights remains a part of the Constitution, for an ineffective Bill is worse than no Bill at all, as it raises false hopes. The answer we would advance is that, from the point of view of the Government, nothing would be gained, and much lost, by formal repeal; national and international opinion would be offended, and suspicions of the Government's intentions would be aroused; yet all the powers that the Government considers necessary for its survival and the implementation of its programmes can be, and presumably have been, obtained through bypassing the Bill, or where necessary amending it. Challenges to the Government on the basis of the Bill are few, and successful challenges fewer still. The moral-cum-political benefits which accrue from

[146] Gower, *Independent Africa: The Challenge to the Legal Profession*, op. cit., p. 84.

acceptance of a setback sustained through a successful challenge in a relatively minor matter—for example, the Africanization of market stalls in Nairobi[147]—far outweighs the fact of the setback which can in any event be overcome a little later by legislation—in this case by the Trades Licensing Act.[148] Thus the total effect of the Bill of Rights in practice is occasionally to require the Government to do indirectly what it cannot do directly—a strange mutation of its normal role.

[147] *Madhwa's* case, op. cit.
[148] Act No. 34 of 1967.

CHAPTER XII

Kenya and the East African Community

INTRODUCTION

No picture of Kenya's public law is complete unless an account is given of the East African Community of which she is a member with Uganda and Tanzania. Many of Kenya's public functions are performed by the Community—the management of the railways, harbours, and posts and telecommunications, and the collection of revenue from taxes, excises, and customs. Large sums of money are raised and spent through the Community, the total budget of the Community and its related institutions being of about the same order as the national budgets.[1] Similarly, a large number of persons are employed by the Community from the member countries.[2] The development and prosperity of Kenya are intimately tied up with her economic relations with her neighbours in the Community, which in turn exercise an important influence on her political and constitutional stability. Furthermore, a significant amount of legislation is enacted for Kenya through the Community, which, with the wide executive powers of the Community, render it necessary to examine the relationship of the national legislature to the Community and its institutions.

Despite her long and intimate involvement with her neighbours, Kenya's constitutional system has not been greatly affected by it. There were possibilities at various stages in the past when Kenya's political and constitutional system could have been profoundly altered by a more organic union with Uganda and Tanzania. Even as recently as June 1963, the leaders of the three countries publicly declared their commitment to a federation of their countries.[3] In the event, however, that crucial step was not taken, largely perhaps because it was felt that it would have more fundamental consequences for the national politics and constitutions than some of the leaders were prepared to accept.[4] Since then, the inauguration of the East African

[1] In 1965/66, the total revenue and expenditure figures for Kenya, Tanzania and Uganda were as follows: K£61,961,000 and £66,005,000; T£47,378,000 and £47,083,000; U£44,729,000 and £45,832,000. Comparable figures for the Community (EACSO then) but excluding East African Airways £48,915,000 and £47,185,900.

[2] Railways and Harbours alone employed 45,060 in 1968; Posts and Telecommunications, 8,387 in 1967.

[3] 'A Declaration of Federation by the Governments of East Africa' reproduced in D. Rothchild (ed.), *Politics of Integration* (E.A.P.H., Nairobi, 1968), p. 76.

[4] See 'Conclusion' in Leys and Robson, *Federation in East Africa: Opportunities and Problems* (Oxford University Press, Nairobi, 1965).

Community on 1 December 1967 through the Treaty for East African Co-operation has established a direction for it of minimum interference with the national systems. There is a clear shift towards the economic matters, co-ordinated through governmental and bureaucratic channels, at the expense of the political factors. The fortunes of the Community will no doubt continue to have deep repercussions on the national systems, but an attempt seems to have been made through the arrangements under the Treaty to separate the politics of the member states from the regional institutions.

The Treaty, in itself, provides for an impressive degree of regional co-ordination and co-operation, though in many ways it has confirmed and re-inforced the previous machinery for co-operation. It brings together under one agreement disparate areas of co-operation and co-ordination; highlights the close connection between the common market and the common services; imposes legal obligations to consult and negotiate in spheres where previously there was only a loose understanding to do so; establishes many new features of the machinery for co-ordination and co-operation; and records the aspiration for future development. Thus though it represents an advance from the previous position, it has fallen short of expectations in some other respects, especially in the field of closer political union. The Treaty can, therefore, be seen either as a culmination of a long period of economic co-operation or as just another stage to full political union. For a proper understanding of its provisions and aspirations, however, it is necessary to look at its historical antecedents.

Various and differing forms of co-operation have existed in East Africa for a long time. They grew on an *ad hoc* basis, generally as a response to specific needs; periodically, a review would be undertaken of the degree and mechanism of co-operation, with a view to a systematic ordering of co-ordination. The *ad hoc* growth of integration without a constitutional frame-work was possible due to the common administration of these countries by the British. The complete British hegemony meant that important decisions could be pushed through by administrative action. But the pace of constitutional progress in the individual territories forced attention on a constitutional structure for matters administered on a regional basis. When action was taken in this direction, the ready models were the territorial constitutions. But the constitutional arrangements made for the common affairs did not always keep pace with the territorial developments, and were often behind them in terms of constitutional progress. As a result, in their earlier phase, they were dominated by the colonial bureaucracy. However, politics were never unimportant, and the progress (or lack of it) towards a full union is better explained in terms of political than economic or bureau-cratic factors.

There have been two strands to the growth of East African integration:

structural and functional. They proceeded at different speeds. In the beginning, when bureaucracy was more important than politics, the dissonance was unimportant, for what could not be accomplished through law, could be achieved through administrative action. Later, the dissonance produced great tension, which in turn led to increased progress. A further, but related, distinction is between provisions which facilitated a common market for the area, and those which established the administration of common services. While the latter were ultimately based on the law, the former, despite some bilateral agreements in the 1920s, were always precariously secured, depending on the goodwill of the parties. However, there was an intimate connection between the two, and the former could not be disregarded without damaging the latter. One of the main objectives of the Treaty was to produce some consonance between structures and functions, and to lay a firm foundation in law for the provisions and machinery for co-operation. Inevitably, the Treaty built on existing structures, which in turn had been influenced by their antecedents. There has thus been a remarkable degree of continuity in aims and methods since the 1930s when the ideas of a political union were modified in favour of a more functional approach to regional integration. The history of the integration can most usefully be divided into three periods—1900 to 1947 (the era of the Governors' Conferences); 1948 to 1961 (the era of the East Africa High Commission); and 1961 to 1967 (the era of East African Common Services Organization).

ERA OF THE GOVERNORS' CONFERENCES 1900–1947

This period was remarkable for the intensive studies on the schemes for closer union. A seemingly endless debate took place on the constitutional and institutional forms of the union.[5] While no particular consensus was achieved on the constitutional issues, much progress was made in the actual co-operation among the territories. Such co-operation could be secured either by agreement among the three Governors, through instructions from the Colonial Office, or by imperial legislation applicable on a regional basis. Thus the lack of a constitutional structure within East Africa for a closer union did not seriously inhibit the growth of rules and institutions for co-operation, though, as we shall see later, there were some difficulties in relation to Tanganyika due to its international status of a mandated, later trust, territory.

[5] For the history of the movement for closer union, see T. M. Franck, *East African Unity Through Law* (Yale University Press, New Haven and London, 1964); B.T.G. Chidzero, *Tanganyika and International Trusteeship* (London, Oxford University Press, 1961); D. Rothchild, *Towards Unity in Africa* (Washington, Public Affairs Press, 1960); C. Rosberg and A. Segal, 'An East African Federation', *International Conciliation*, 1963; Leys and Robson, op. cit.; *East Africa: Report of the Economic and Fiscal Commission* (The Raisman Commission) Cmnd. 1279 (1961). Much of the following historical account is based on these sources.

As Tanganyika was under the German administration until 1920, the earlier forms of co-operation existed only between Kenya (then the East Africa Protectorate) and Uganda, both of which were under British control. There was from the first (1902) a common administration for the railway line which served Kenya and Uganda. In the same year, a Court of Appeal for Eastern Africa was established by an Order in Council, to which appeals lay from both the territories.[6] A common currency was also instituted, and in 1905 the East African Currency Board was set up to issue notes.[7] In 1911 a postal union was created between Kenya and Uganda and in 1917, a customs union with the amalgamation of their customs authorities.

With the transfer of responsibility over Tanganyika to the British in 1920, it also began to be integrated into the regional schemes of co-operation. In 1922 agreement was reached on a common external tariff with the Kenya-Uganda union and the following year on the free interchange of domestic products; and in 1927 the free movement of imported goods was established. None of this, however, was provided for under any law; a common external tariff was maintained only as a result of interterritorial negotiations; and Kenya-Uganda and Tanganyika retained their separate customs administrations until 1949. In 1921 Tanganyika was admitted to the East African Currency Board, and her currency was harmonized with that of the other two countries.[8] She was also brought under the appellate jurisdiction of the Eastern Africa Court of Appeal.[9] In 1933 the Kenya-Uganda and Tanganyika postal and telegraph authorities were amalgamated. The railways, however, continued under separate administrations.

In addition to the integration of Tanganyika into the existing schemes, various new schemes were inaugurated during this period. Provisions were made in 1921 for the reciprocal enforcement of judgments;[10] and consultations took place so as to achieve uniformity in commercial and other matters of common interest. In 1925 a joint East African office for trade and information was opened in London, and a trade commissioner appointed. The British East African Meteorological Service was set up four years later. In 1937 an East African air service was established, followed later by the Airways Corporation, to run the services, and an Air Transport Authority, to control the provisions of commercial services. Income tax services were co-ordinated in 1940, when Uganda and Tanganyika levied such tax for the first time. There was also co-operation in higher education (the Makerere College being a common institution) and research, including statistics.

[6] Eastern African Protectorates (Court of Appeal) Order in Council, 1902.
[7] E.A. Currency Board Order in Council, 1905.
[8] Currency Notes Proclamation No. 22 of 1920 (T).
[9] Eastern Africa Court of Appeal Order in Council, 1921; Court of Appeal Ordinance, No. 11 of 1922 (T).
[10] Judgment Extension Ordinance No. 13 of 1921 (T); Proclamation No. 65 of 1921 (K); Judgment Extension (Amendment) Ordinance No. 15 of 1921 (U).

East African co-operation was greatly accelerated during the Second World War. A plethora of inter-territorial councils and boards came into being to co-ordinate the war effort and to secure the economic use of resources. These included the Production and Supply Council, Industrial Council, Manpower Conference, Refugee Administration, Anti-Locust Directorate, and Import and Price Control Inter-Territorial Advisory Committee. Many of them were relevant only for the war effort, but others had a wider potential, and it was partly with a view to their future administration that serious thought was once again given to constitutional questions, just as the exigencies of the post-war period in 1918 had previously focused attention on them.

While all these developments were taking place in East African integration, there was only a rudimentary constitutional and administrative machinery to support it. Though proposals for some form of closer union were propounded and discussed as long ago as the end of the nineteenth century, it was only after the First World War that the question was taken up seriously.[11] Initially, the pressure came from the white settlers, especially in Kenya, who hoped by closer union to extend their influence throughout the region, and dilute that of Whitehall, and to ensure that the newly acquired territory of Tanganyika, which until then had cut off the British possessions in eastern Africa from those in southern, was firmly secured to the British Empire so that it would not be bartered away to Germany or anyone else. It was also hoped by closer union to establish the imperial preference system for the whole region, though economic factors were never as important as the political behind the European demands for a federal union. The European settlers had anticipated official action by convening their own conferences, in which representatives from Nyasaland, Northern Rhodesia and Southern Rhodesia, in addition to the three East African territories, took part. Their demands found a responsive chord in the new Colonial Secretary, L. S. Amery, who set up a Commission in 1924, under the chairmanship of Ormsby-Gore, whose terms of reference included, *inter alia*, the consideration of measures to be taken to accelerate the general economic development of the British East Africa Dependencies and the means of securing closer co-ordination of policy on such important matters as transportation, cotton-growing, and the control of human, animal and plant diseases.[12]

The Commission encountered much hostility to the idea of federation, especially from the Indians and the Africans; it also found the proposal inexpedient due to geographical conditions and the lack of good communications, and the expense of running a federal government. Nevertheless, it

[11] See D. Rothchild, *Politics of Integration*, op. cit.
[12] *Report of the East African Commission*, Cmd. 2387 (1925).

recognized the benefits of co-ordination, and its recommendations in this respect, though re-examined more than once in the next few years, established the lines for future development. In addition to proposing the improvement of transport facilities, its main recommendation was that periodic conferences of the Governors of the various territories should be held to secure co-ordination on matters of common interest. The recommendation was accepted and a conference was convened in Nairobi in 1926; but the idea of federation was not abandoned, and the following year another commission, this time under Hilton Young, was despatched to re-examine the question of 'federation or some other form of closer union for effective co-operation between the different Governments in Central and East Africa'.[13] Any discussion of federation inevitably involved an examination of domestic, territorial matters; in particular, the policies towards Africans. The Commission was prepared to support a federation, but on terms which were repugnant to the aims of its original advocates—the settlers; the terms were the co-ordination of policies towards Africans, so that Kenya would have had to liberalize hers, and the retention of strong imperial control, especially to ensure that there was no oppression of the indigenous population. An elaborate and gradual development in three phases was proposed, but its conditions were such as to ensure its rejection by the Colonial Office and the settlers. In particular, the Kenya settlers feared a diminution of their influence, and made the grant of an unofficial majority in Kenya's Legislative Council a precondition of participation in a federal scheme.

One reason why the Hilton Young Commission had aroused such strong reactions was that it faced up to the full implications of a federation, which meant looking at it in a political rather than an economic context, in which it was impossible to discuss union without an examination of colonial policies towards Africans, the different constitutional status and progress of the territories, and imperial control. The Colonial Office attempted to depoliticize the issue by appointing one of its officials, Sir Samuel Wilson, to re-examine the recommendations.[14] He proposed the establishment of the office of the High Commissioner for the East African dependencies to exercise complete legislative and administrative control, with the advice and consent of a Central Council, over certain defined subjects such as customs, railways, posts and telegraphs, and inter-territorial research. He was to have his own headquarters and staff. Policy for Africans was to remain a territorial matter, and the Kenya Europeans were to get their majority.

A change of government in Britain prevented action on the Wilson Report, and produced a reversal of policy, with emphasis again on the imperial

[13] See *Report of the Commission on the Closer Union of the Dependencies in Eastern and Central Africa*, Cmd. 3234 (1929).
[14] *Report of Sir Samuel Wilson on His Visit to East Africa*, Cmd. 3378 (1929).

responsibility for the protection of the interests of the indigenous population. The new Labour Government drafted fresh proposals, which also included a High Commissioner assisted by a Council.[15] The Council was to consist of three officials from the High Commissioner's staff, and seven representatives from each territory appointed by the High Commissioner. He would have the power to administer and legislate in respect of some specified services in all three territories, including railways, harbours, customs, defence, posts, telegraphs and telephones, extradition, central research, and the East Africa Office in London. In addition, he was to be given general supervisory functions over the territories in the remaining matters, which were to be exercised by the scrutiny of drafts of Bills to be introduced in the territorial legislatures, and the budgets, suspending any racial discriminatory measures and being the permanent chairman of the Governor's Conference. He could also require any of the Governors to initiate any measure or legislation which he might deem necessary. In all his functions, he was to act on the instructions of the Colonial Secretary, to whom he was also to be the Chief Adviser on African policy.

As was to be expected, there was much opposition to the proposals, which would have meant increased Whitehall control and the clear subordination of the territorial legislative and administrative powers to the central authority. The Europeans had always hoped for an increased control for themselves if a federation was set up, and the Kenya settlers had expected greater influence in that country—expectations which had been encouraged by the Wilson recommendations. The other communities also continued their opposition, though for different reasons.[16] As a result, the whole question of the union was referred to a Joint Select Committee of both Houses of the British Parliament, which reported against a constitutional union on the grounds of lack of consensus, and the expense.[17] The committee appreciated the advantages of economic co-ordination, to secure which it recommended greater use of the Governors' Conference. The matter rested there for the time being, and this thorough-going Committee closed a decade of commissions on the question.

Before discussing the machinery that operated while all this debate was going on—the Governors' Conference—it is pertinent to examine whether any constraints were placed on the movement towards closer structural union by Tanganyika's special international position as a mandated or trust territory.[18] There were two possible difficulties. First, how far was Britain

[15] Cmd. 3574 (1930).

[16] The Africans and the Asians feared that in any system of closer union, the settlers would dominate; this was resented particularly in Uganda and Tanganyika.

[17] *Report of the Joint Select Committee on Closer Union in East Africa* (London, HMSO, 1931).

[18] See Chidzero, op. cit., pp. 61–112.

free to amalgamate Tanganyika into an East African union? Secondly, even if a union were permissible, how far had its structures and policies to conform to the terms and spirit of the mandate? Article 10 of the Mandate Agreement had provided that the Mandatory was authorized to constitute the territory into a customs, fiscal and administrative union or federation, with the adjacent territories under his own sovereignty or control. But a proviso was attached to this authorization—'That the measures adopted to that end do not infringe the provisions of this mandate'. Among the important provisions were those designed to protect the indigenous population from the worst forms of exploitation of colonialism, by restricting land alienation to non-indigenous people, and imposing a positive obligation to promote to the utmost the material and moral well-being and social progress of its inhabitants. Though, therefore, there were no insuperable constitutional barriers to a federation, the kind of federation permissible under the mandate was unlikely to appeal to some of its protagonists. While the Colonial Office was not always mindful of the limitations in the mandate, and indeed the failure to federate could in no sense be ascribed to the terms of the mandate, it played an important part in focusing international attention on the various proposals, and in the Labour Government's scheme, at least, there was a clear acknowledgement of Britain's international obligations, which led it to emphasize her trusteeship and the strengthening of imperial control through the High Commission.

When the mandate was replaced by a Trusteeship Agreement, provisions for inter-territorial co-operation were retained, but in slightly diluted form. Britain was entitled

> to constitute Tanganyika into a customs, fiscal or administrative union or federation with adjacent territories under this sovereignty or control, and to establish common services between such territories and Tanganyika when such measures were not inconsistent with the basic objectives of the International Trusteeship System and with the terms of this Agreement.[19]

The proviso related to the even stronger obligations of trusteeship than under the mandate, equal rights in social, economic, industrial and commercial matters for members of the United Nations and their nationals, and a more extensive machinery for supervision over the administration. By this time there was also an increased consciousness on the part of the international community of its obligations in relation to dependent territories, and it was made clear by the General Assembly of the United Nations that it did not consider the power to create administrative unions

> as giving powers to the Administering Authority to establish any form of political

[19] The Agreement is reprinted in Chidzero, op. cit., pp. 263–8. For Mandate, see p. 257.

association . . . which would involve annexation of the Trust Territories in any sense or would have the effect of extinguishing their status as Trust Territories.[20]

It was as a result of these limitations that when the Colonial Office issued its proposals on Inter-territorial Organization in East Africa after the Second World War, it was careful to point out that the final responsibility for the administration of the three countries would continue to lie with Britain, and that the proposals involved 'neither political union nor the fusion of the East African Governments'.[21] The proposals were intended to rectify the shortcomings of the then existing machinery for securing co-operation within East Africa. As has been mentioned above, this was the Governors' Conferences whose establishment had been recommended by the Ormsby-Gore Commission in 1924, and whose intensified use was urged by the Joint Select Committee of 1931. Though the Governors of Northern Rhodesia and Nyasaland also attended the Conferences for certain matters, it was primarily an East African body, with the Governor of Kenya emerging as the standing Chairman, and had certain emergency powers over all the territories. The Conference maintained a permanent Secretariat under the direction of a Chief Secretary, through which correspondence was directed and directions given; it also acted as a general inter-territorial executive staff in such matters as might be entrusted to it. The system was, however, inadequate in several respects, which were succinctly outlined by the Colonial Office in the following manner:

The Governors' Conference is a body which was established by administrative direction of the Secretary of State and which has no juridical or constitutional basis. It functions without public debate or discussion and its decisions are normally based on material available only to the Governments concerned and not to the general public. In practice, it is frequently necessary for the Governors, having agreed in the Governors' Conference to a certain course of action, to present their Executive and Legislative Councils with what amounts to a *fait accompli*. By its very nature the Conference is not well designed to enlist the support of public opinion and to take full advantage of the considerable body of expert knowledge and experience which is available in East Africa . . . When common legislation is necessary, the procedure is to present identical ordinances separately to the three legislatures. This is not only unwieldly, but it places the territorial governments in the position of being unable to accept amendments of any kind as a result of debate without destroying the very uniformity which the legislation aims to achieve. At best, the ordinance which is passed first forms the model for the other legislatures and their debates become unreal.[22]

The Colonial Office formulated proposals to meet these shortcomings. A federation, however, was ruled out, since

there exists at the present time neither the community of interests nor the public support which a scheme of political closer union would require.

[20] General Assembly Resolution 224 (III), 1948.
[21] *Inter-territorial Organization in Africa*, 1945, Colonial No. 191.
[22] ibid.

It was proposed to establish a constitution by Order in Council for the common services, which would provide for an East Africa High Commission consisting of the Governors of Kenya, Uganda and Tanganyika, a central legislature, and an executive organization supported in appropriate cases by advisory boards. The Commission was to administer the common services listed on a schedule, to which new services could subsequently be added by the Colonial Secretary. The Assembly was to be given a wide legislative competence, including appropriation, customs and excise, including tariff rates; income tax, but not the rates; licensing of industries; control of commercial motor transport; creation of boards for the control of agricultural industries, including provisions for collective marketing; inter-territorial communication, and commercial legislation. As far as finance was concerned, the existing arrangements whereby the contribution of each country on account of the common services was settled in respect of each service by negotiation and agreement, were to continue. Customs and excise collections were to be made by the joint Customs Department (which would thus amalgamate Tanganyika into the Kenya-Uganda Department), which would retain sums necessary to cover the departmental expenditure of the High Commission according to previously agreed proportions.

The proposals were wide ranging, and though the intention to create a federation was disavowed, the proposals would have produced many of the characteristics of one. As long as the whole of the East African region was under British hegemony, the definitive characteristics of a federation would be absent anyway. As it was, by an Order in Council vesting certain legislative and executive competence in the High Commission to the exclusion of the territories, the effective supremacy of the new institutions could be assured. The Colonial Office's argument to prove that a federation was not contemplated was that the territorial governments would continue to exist: but a federation does not imply that they could not. The existence of viable separate territorial governments had, however, a different kind of significance; it meant that future constitutional developments in East Africa would be more territorially orientated, which would weaken the forces for a federation. But in the 1940s with the total constitutional dominance of Britain, it was a little difficult to distinguish a federation from other forms of union.

Had the 1945 proposals been accepted in their entirety, they would have produced a high degree of economic integration—the existing common facilities would have been rationalized and consolidated, and a genuine common market would have been established in law, as the levy of tariff rates would have become a High Commission matter. When in 1947 the East Africa High Commission was established, it fell short of the proposals in several important ways. The opposition to the proposals had arisen mainly among the Europeans and was directed at the composition of the central legislature. The proposed membership was thirty-six, excluding the Speaker, of whom twelve were to be official, and twenty-four unofficial. Of the unofficial, eighteen were to represent the three major communities in equal number, due to

> the impossibility of devising any generally acceptable formula by which to decide the relative importance or the respective claims of the communities concerned.

The European and the Indian unofficial members were to be elected by the European and Indian members of the territorial legislatives respectively; while the representation for Africans was to be secured through nomination by the High Commission, though the nominees need not be Africans. The Arab interests were also to be secured through the nomination of two members. The idea of parity on which the proposals for representation were based was totally unacceptable to the Europeans; in no territorial legislature had this principle been conceded; its implementation in the High Commission would have been regarded as a major setback for them. Their vociferous and sustained opposition led to the revision of the proposals, in which the casualty was not only the principle of parity, but also certain functions and powers of the Commission.[23] In addition to the alteration in the composition of the legislature, it was emphasized that its life would initially be for four years, and that if it were continued thereafter, the form which it would take, as well as the functions with which it would then be entrusted, would be reviewed *de novo*. On the substantive side, the subjects removed from the competence of the legislature included the determining of the tariff rates, road transport, industrial licensing and commercial legislation, the common regulation of which was important for the existence and proper functioning of the common market.

THE EAST AFRICA HIGH COMMISSION 1947–1960

The East Africa High Commission was established by the East Africa (High Commission) Order in Council of 1947.[24] Though attempts, not fully successful, had been made to secure the agreement of the inhabitants of the territories, the form of legislation emphasized the imperial legislative supremacy. So did its contents, which provided that the High Commission and the Assembly were to transact their business in conformity, as far as possible, with the Royal Instructions issued to them from time to time; the power of disallowance of laws as well as the legislative power of the British monarch for the future were retained. Like other colonial constitutions, the Order was heavily dominated by the executive. The executive, known as the High Commission, consisted of the three Governors; its Chairman was the Kenya

[23] *Inter-territorial Organization in East Africa, Revised Proposals*, Colonial No. 210 (1947).
[24] East Africa (High Commission) Order in Council, S. I. No. 2863 of 1947.

Governor, who also exercised all the powers of the Commission when it was not in conference, except those which the Commission might decide should only be exercised after prior consultation with the other members. Otherwise, the decisions had to be unanimous; any brake this might have on smooth operation was overcome by the intervention of the Colonial Secretary. The chief executive officer of the Commission was the Administrator, to whom the Chairman could and did in fact delegate most of his functions, which meant that the position of the Administrator became an important and powerful one. There were six other executive officers as well, who were the heads of departments.

The functions of the Commission were to take over the administration of services set out in the first schedule, and of those of the second schedule when they were established. The list in the second schedule could be increased by the Colonial Secretary, after a favourable resolution to that effect in the territorial legislatures. The first schedule included most of the existing services, while many in the second had to await the merger of Tanganyika with Kenya-Uganda services, like the railways, and the customs and excise. The High Commission was also to take over the functions of the East African Air Transport Authority, which it replaced, and of the East African Transport Policy Board. Finally, its executive powers included the appointment of such advisory and consultative bodies as it might think fit in respect of any matter subject to its control or of common interest to the territories.

The High Commission also had certain legislative powers; before these are discussed, we should look at the normal legislative machinery. The Central Legislative Assembly was established, under a Speaker appointed by the High Commission. The seven senior executive officers of the Commission were *ex officio* members, and the remainder of the official representation was made up of one nominee from each territory, appointed by the respective Governors. The unofficial representation was made up as follows: three members, one from each of the major races from each territory, to be nominated by the respective Governors, except in Kenya where the European and the Asian members were to be elected by their elected communal members in the Legislative Council (thus introducing into the new institution Kenya's peculiar system of racial franchise, other territories till then having no elective representation); an Arab appointed by the High Commission; and one member from each of the three territorial legislatures, who had to be an elected or unofficial member, and was elected by such members—this was an ingenious way of meeting the objections of the Europeans to the 1945 proposals for the composition of the Assembly; without explicitly introducing a further racial qualification, it ensured that in each of the territories, a European would be elected under this category.

There were three different methods of making laws under the Order, though in practice only one was ever employed. This was through the High Commission with the advice and consent of the Assembly in respect of matters specified in the third schedule, which followed closely the revised proposals of 1946. Again additions to the list could be made by the Colonial Secretary, if there was sufficient support for it in the territorial legislatures. The powers under the second method of legislation were not so circumscribed; the High Commission could, with the advice and consent of the Legislative Councils of the territories, make laws for the peace, order and good government of the territories. Any law validly made under these methods would have effect notwithstanding any territorial laws inconsistent with it. Thirdly, the Commission could bring into effect any Bill or motion introduced into but not passed by the Assembly within such time and in such form as the Commission thought reasonable, if the Commission considered it expedient in the interests of public order, public faith or good government to do so. The safeguard on this form of law-making was that such action had to be reported to the Colonial Secretary, along with any statements of objections made by an official member. The dominance of the executive in the process of law-making was further emphasized by the rule that all Bills had to be approved by the Commission before their introduction in the Assembly, that is, there were no private members' Bills properly so-called.

The Assembly was also responsible for voting the appropriations—this it could do either by a resolution or by passing an Act. A separate fund was created for each of the self-contained services, like the railways and harbours, posts and telecommunications, into which all the revenues from that service were to be paid and out of which the appropriations were to be voted. A single fund was established for the non-self-contained services, which was to be financed by appropriations from the territorial legislatures and grants from other sources. Provisions were also made for the establishment of a contingencies fund. The earlier proposal that the Commission retain certain sums from the tax and revenue collected by its tax and custom departments was not incorporated. The Commission had no powers to levy taxation to meet its expenditure, and its dependence on the territorial legislatures for this purpose was a source of serious weakness.

The effect of the Order was to introduce a much needed rationalization into the system of East African co-operation. The constitution contained in the Order did not itself provide for the organization and functioning of the common services; it was the task of the Assembly to fill the gaps, and its early years saw a vast legislative output—laws were enacted defining the scope of the power of the Commission in operating a joint system of harbours and railways for East Africa, transferring the regulatory functions of the Air Transport Authority to the High Commission, setting up an East African Naval Force, making provision for postal services and telecommunication services by means of the East Africa Posts and Telecommunication Administration, and the regulation and control of radio communications, setting up a régime for developing and regulating Lake Victoria Fisheries, and establishing complex and comprehensive codes for the procedural and substantive aspects of taxation and customs revenue.[25] However, not all the regional services were brought within the new structure—thus the East African Airways Corporation was under the control of the High Commission, but the Assembly had little say in its affairs, and the East Africa Currency Board remained separate and distinct.[26]

It was, however, in relation to the common market that the most serious omissions occurred. As we have seen, the determination of tariff rates, licensing of industry, commercial legislation and currency control were kept outside the competence of the new structure. As has been well observed:

> Emphasis, however, was more definitely upon specified common services, and the reduction in the subject matter eligible for central legislation and decision, together with the withholding of any element of revenue autonomy, significantly affected the role which the High Commission might play in the general conduct of East African affairs. Most of the deleted items related to economic matters and their omission thus narrowed the range of potential initiative by the High Commission in the furthering of economic co-ordination. Some parts of a co-ordinating committee structure remained to be serviced by the High Commission Administrator, but the High Commission itself was to be concerned primarily with the provision of specific inter-territorial services, only to a minor degree with economic co-ordination and not at all with tariff rates.[27]

Despite the absence of constitutional provisions for a common market, it was in fact effectively maintained, as previously, due to the overall authority of the Colonial Secretary. As each of the member territories moved towards greater autonomy, however, tensions were aggravated. There were many causes for the tensions, but the important ones were economic, and it is therefore necessary to examine the effects of the common services and the common market. This complex of inter-territorial and economic co-operation made an important contribution to the economic development of East Africa. The provision of technical services on an East African basis undoubtedly resulted in economies of scale; while the common market provided a powerful stimulus to the industrialization of the region. This can be seen from the fact that in the post-war period, inter-territorial trade expanded at an extremely fast rate; furthermore, a large and increasing proportion of this trade was in semi-processed and manufactured articles.

However, the benefits of the development stimulated by the common

[25] See Franck, op. cit., pp. 59–62.
[26] See Raisman Commission, *Report*, op. cit.
[27] ibid., para. 19.

market were unevenly distributed among the three countries.[28] In particular, a large proportion of the manufacturing industries that came into existence to serve the common market tended to be located in Kenya. Consequently, Kenya developed a large surplus in her inter-territorial trade, while Tanganyika had a substantial and growing deficit in her trade with Kenya; Uganda's inter-territorial trade was fairly balanced. Thus in 1960, the total inter-territorial trade amounted to £22,800,000; of this the proportion supplied by Kenya was 61.2 per cent, Tanganyika 12.4 per cent and Uganda 25.9 per cent; if we take the figures of trade in manufactured goods only, the respective proportions were 80 per cent, 4 per cent and 15 per cent. Furthermore, Tanganyika has increasingly purchased more manufactured imports from its two partner territories; in 1960, for example, of the total regional trade manufactures, Kenya purchased 14.2 per cent; Tanganyika 36.4 per cent and Uganda 49.4 per cent. Thus Tanganyika gained little from the common market arrangements, and may even have lost. Due to a common external tariff without internal barriers, Tanganyika and Uganda were in fact subsidizing Kenya industry, by paying higher prices for Kenya's manufactures than if similar goods from the rest of the world were allowed in on a competitive basis. The effect of this was not only to discourage industry in these two countries, but also in so far as the Kenya goods enjoyed protection, and were imported duty free, these governments lost the custom revenue on importation.

As far as the common services were concerned, the benefits were more evenly distributed. The argument was often made that the services in Tanganyika were subsidizied by the other two countries, in particular Kenya, due to the lesser development and longer distances in the former. As against this, the headquarters of the Commission and most of its departments were located in Kenya, and about 50 per cent of its general fund expenditure was located in Kenya, as opposed to about 17 per cent in each of the other two countries. It has been estimated that Kenya and Tanganyika gained almost the same from their membership in the common services. In any case, the common services were demonstrably to the mutual benefit of all three countries, whatever the share of their respective gains.

However, despite the advantages of the common services, complaints were heard from Tanganyika and to a lesser extent from Uganda throughout the fifties about the inequitable distribution of benefits from the operation

[28] Dharam Ghai, 'Territorial Distribution of Benefits and Costs of the East African Common Market', *E.A.E.R.* (Nairobi, OUP, June 1964); P. Ndegwa, *Common Market and Development in East Africa* (Nairobi, East African Publishing House, 1965); W. T. Newlyn, 'Gains and Losses in East African Common Market', *Yorkshire Bulletin of Economic and Social Research*, November 1965; A. Hazlewood, 'The Shiftability of Industry and the Measurement of Gains and Losses in the East African Common Market', *Bulletin of the Oxford University Institute of Economics and Statistics*, May 1966; The Raisman Commission, op. cit.

of the common market. The tensions were becoming serious enough to lead to a review by an independent commission of the system of the common services and the common market in July 1960.[29] Its major recommendation led to the creation of a distributable pool, which was intended to achieve several separate objectives. It was directed at easing tension in the common market by establishing fiscal advantages for Tanganyika and Uganda. Secondly, it would produce an independent source of revenue for the High Commission and reduce its dependence on the territorial legislatures. Thirdly, it would enable the High Commission to 'charge' the three governments for its services in the collection of the tax and revenue, the first charge on the collection being these costs. The source of revenue for the distributable pool consisted of 6 per cent of the proceeds from the customs and excise duties in East Africa, and 40 per cent of the revenue derived from the taxation of manufacturing and finance companies—both sources having relevance to the common market. Half of the proceeds of the distributable pool were distributed to the three countries in equal amounts, while the other half were retained to finance the services of the Commission. In the first years of its operation, this mechanism resulted in a fiscal redistribution from Kenya to the other two countries to the tune of £500,000 or so, in addition to her increased contribution to the costs of the services financed by the pool.

While the economic inequities were being tackled by the distributable pool, the constitutional arrangements for co-operation were also facing new problems. All three countries had made significant progress towards self-government, in which the indigenous leaders were beginning to play the leading part. While this progress was registered by changes in their constitutional form, the constitution of the Commission had failed to keep pace, and became incongruous due to being executive and colonially dominated. The constitutional problem became acute in the beginning of the new decade (the sixties) with the imminence of Tanganyika's independence. The immediate problem was to devise a form which would enable an independent country to collaborate with the others in varying degrees of colonial dependence. Agreement on it was reached at a conference in London of the representatives of the three countries and Britain,[30] and led to the establishment of the East African Common Services Organization in 1961.[31] The organization was regarded as a relatively temporary expedient, even though the Agreement was specified to be of indefinite duration, for by now the old aim of a federation was revived, though of course in a totally different environment.

[29] The Raisman Commission, Cmnd. 1279.
[30] *The Future of the East African High Commission Services* (London, HMSO, 1961).
[31] The agreement between the Governments is published in EACSO Gazette (1 January 1962). It is also reproduced in the territorial implementing legislation—Tanganyika Ordinance 52 of 1961; Uganda, 22 of 1961; Kenya, 26 of 1961.

EAST AFRICAN COMMON SERVICES ORGANIZATION 1961–1967

The new Common Services Organization, though modelled on its predecessor, differed from it in some important ways. First, it was not the result of an imperial decree. Though Kenya and Uganda were not yet independent, they had been authorized by Britain to negotiate and conclude an agreement on the forms and structures for future co-operation. The agreement was, therefore, the result of the free decision of the leaders and governments of East Africa. Secondly, it was necessary for the implementation of the Agreement to enact legislation in the three countries, unlike the previous arrangements where the Order in Council was automatically made operative throughout the region. While previously therefore the powers of the territorial legislatures were to be deemed qualified by the terms of the Order, under the Common Services they were free from any but self-imposed limitations, the regional legislation having effect in each territory due to a blanket incorporation; formerly, the regional legislation was directly and automatically operative. Thirdly, the new structure was much more highly politicized than the old, both in its executive and the legislative organs. The colonial administrators and bureaucrats gave way to political leaders, and just as had happened in the territories, the bureaucracy ceased to govern the region but began to carry out the policies of the politicians. Like its predecessor, the Organization had executive and legislative institutions, but no judicial. However, the Court of Appeal for Eastern Africa did come under its purview and ceased to be a British court; it was not established to enforce the laws of the Organization, but to provide the member countries with an appellate court.[32] The new executive was the Authority, which originally consisted of the principal elected Ministers from the three countries, and which later meant the three Presidents. The Authority had responsibility for, and the general direction and control of, the performance of the executive functions of the Organization. It operated under the rule of unanimity, and any one member could block the discussion of a proposal.

The Authority was assisted initially by four Ministerial Committees, each consisting of a Minister from each country, being known as triumvirates. The chairmanship of the Committee was held by the Ministers in rotation. A serious weakness of this system, whereby there were no ministerial appointees with full time and individual responsibility for the common affairs, was alleged to be the failure to produce an East African outlook. The names of the Committees indicate the scope of their activities: the Communications Committee, the Finance Committee, the Commercial and Industrial Co-ordination Committee, and Social and Research Services

[32] The Court came under the Organization in 1962. EACSO (Amendment) (No. 2) Agreement, Legal Notice 95 of 1962, EACSO Gazette. Eastern Africa Court of Appeal Act No. 13 of 1962.

Committee. Between them, the Committees were responsible for every service of the Organization. The rule of unanimity applied also to the decisions of the Committees, and if there was a disagreement among the Ministers, it had to be referred to the Authority.

The senior executive officers of the Organization were the Secretary-General, who was the principal officer, the General Manager of the Railways and Harbours Administration, the Postmaster-General, the Legal Secretary, the Financial Secretary and the Auditor-General. The first of these was appointed by the Authority as were the others, except that in their case the appropriate Public Service Commission and the Secretary-General were consulted. There was a Public Service Commission for each of the self-contained services, and one for the non-self-contained ones, which were responsible for appointments, promotions, dismissals, etc., within their spheres.

The executive authority of the Organization extended to the administration of the common services, most of which were taken over from the High Commission. By this time the list of the scheduled services had grown most impressive, and covered activities of great importance to the economy and well-being of East Africa.[33]

The legislative institution was the Central Legislative Assembly: its composition became more politically responsive. The total membership was forty-one, excluding the Speaker, who was appointed by the Authority. Of this, fourteen may be regarded as official members, the twelve Ministers (the members of the Ministerial Committees), and the Secretary-General and the Legal Secretary. The representative members, of whom there were 27, were elected in equal numbers by territorial legislatures (in which only the elected members of these legislatures could vote) from among those qualified to be candidates in domestic parliamentary elections. These members vacated their seats on the dissolution of the legislature which had elected them, so that their tenure was fixed by the territorial constitutions. The executive lost its powers to make laws; henceforth all regional legislation had to be introduced in the Assembly, and passed therein. The procedures for law-making were very similar to those in the territorial legislatures, including the special provisions for financial measures. However, the Authority had a veto, a power which did not exist in the heads of government in all the territories; if a Bill presented to the Authority for its assent was not approved within nine months, it lapsed automatically. A limited power of disallowance was vested in the British Government, to protect the rights of the holders of stocks issued and registered in London in accordance wth the provisions of the Colonial Stock Acts, 1877 to 1948.

[33] e.g. Railways and harbours, posts and telecommunications, directorate of civil aviation, meteorology, collection of customs, excise and taxes, statistics, and research facilities.

Though the legislative powers of the Assembly were thus qualified, it was the only channel of law-making. It occupied a curious position in a structure heavily dominated by governments; not all its members were representatives of the governments, and there was no proper party organization. However, the back-benchers from the different countries found many points of contact and collaboration. The Assembly had a distinct federal flavour, and its representative members were among the strongest supporters of the idea of federation.[34] On several occasions, the Authority was embarrassed by the attitude of the members. But there were no clear lines of responsibility, and in any event the ministerial members and the unofficial members were responsible to different bodies. As long as the Organization was looked upon as a stop gap, this anomalous position could be tolerated, but in the long run, it had either to become more amenable to official directions in a government orientated, agency-type organization, or blossom into a full-blown federal representative institution. In the event, the former of the options was taken up later.

The legislative authority of the Assembly extended to subjects listed in the second schedule. Here again, the list was very similar to that for the High Commission. The provisions for finance also remained the same as before, with the separate funds, and the need for appropriation by the Assembly. The distributable pool was retained. Thus the changeover to the EACSO was not accompanied by any increase in regional power; the changes were more of form. But they were important changes of form, and represented a considerable advance upon the High Commission. Only one of its members was independent when the EACSO began; it continued through when Uganda and Kenya attained independence, by Britain transferring its residual powers and functions in relation to Uganda and Kenya to them as they became independent. There were, therefore, few serious political and constitutional problems, as far as the functioning of the Organization was concerned. But there were problems of a different kind.

There were two problems, both pointing in different directions, and yet related. There was first, a new call for closer union in the form of federation. Secondly, there were tensions within the EACSO, tending towards the demolition of the existing machinery for co-operation. The former reasons for African opposition to federation disappeared due to the constitutional and political developments since the 1930s and 1940s; a new federation would be an African federation. Public opinion throughout East Africa was strongly in favour of a federation. There was also the force of the ideology of Pan-Africanism, and in this context an East African federation was a moral virtue. There were several other factors predisposing in favour of a federa-

[34] For a different view, see Banfield, op. cit., p. 37.

tion: a common background, a shared experience of common colonialism, the artificiality of the national barriers that cut across tribes, geographical affinities, the widespread use of the language of Swahili, an impressive record of collaboration among the nationalist leaders and the history of past co-operation. The economic considerations were equally compelling—the logic of many of these had already been acknowledged in the establishment of the High Commission and the EACSO, but further economic gains were to be made from closer co-operation, especially in industrialization, agricultural development and planning. The spirit of unity was pervasive: and received a fresh impetus from the declaration of the leaders of the three countries in June 1963 that a federation would be established by the end of the year.[35]

Subsequent developments, however, led to further recession from the goal of federation. The reasons were mainly political. All of the countries were in the process of developing their national political systems.[36] There were many unknowns and uncertainties, and the leaders were not anxious to complicate matters for themselves by entry into a bigger union. The outcome might have been different if the three countries had achieved independence more or less simultaneously; as Nyerere had argued, otherwise preoccupations with national sovereignties would militate against a union. In addition, there were constitutional difficulties—both Uganda and Kenya had achieved independence at the price of complex and rigid federal constitutions. For them to enter into a federation, it would have been necessary for the central governments to have the consent of the federal units, which could have been difficult, especially in Uganda, where Buganda had been a traditional foe of an East African federation. In any event, the competence of the federation would have been severely circumscribed for the federal units in Kenya and Uganda would not have contemplated the surrender of their own powers, thus leaving only some of the central subjects which could be turned over to the proposed federation.

Another reason why the movement for a federation was arrested, was that the economic advantages of a union were already available—there was a common market and a highly integrated system of services. If these advantages could be obtained without political or constitutional sacrifices, there were no real incentives to take a plunge into the political unknown. However, as we have seen, the economic structures were not without their own tensions. It was therefore unlikely that the existing state of affairs could last for long. The Raisman Commission had pointed to the difficulties inherent in an economic union without a corresponding integration at the political level,

[35] See, J. S. Nye, *Pan-Africanism and East African Federation* (Cambridge, Harvard University Press, 1965), and Rothchild in Carter, op. cit.
[36] Leys and Robson, op. cit., pp. 183–203; Rothchild in Carter, op. cit.; A. A. Mazrui, 'Tanzania versus East Africa: A Case of Unwitting Federal Sabotage', *Journal of Commonwealth Political Studies*, III, November 1965.

in which mechanisms for equalization could redress the national and inevitable imbalance from the economic union. The Commission had tried to provide for some form of equalization within the existing framework through the distributable pool.

Tanganyika did not consider the Raisman formula an adequate compensation for her continuing and increasing trade deficit with Kenya. As long as there was a possibility that a federation might be formed, she was prepared to continue with the existing common market arrangements, in the hope that under a federation, provisions for equalization or redistribution of benefits would be made. But once it became obvious that a federation was not likely in the foreseeable future, the East African economic co-operation came under greater strain, particularly the common market provisions. Directly or indirectly, most or all of the disintegration can be attributed to the failure to federate, even though some of it had already taken place before Tanganyika's independence. In 1961 Tanganyika withdrew from the East African Navy, on the ground that it was based in Mombasa and was of no defence value to herself. Nor was Tanganyika the only complainant: in 1963 Uganda left the semi-official East African Tourist Agency, on the ground that the benefits to her from it were disproportionate to her contribution. But it was Tanganyika, as the worst off of the partners in this unequal arrangement, who caused the greatest disruption. Even since her independence, she was known to be anxious to establish a one-party state; she had held back her plans for fear that they might be disconsonant with a federation. In December 1963, however, she announced the decision to go ahead, since the federation would not materialize soon, and on 28 January 1964 the Commission on the One-Party State was announced. She also imposed restrictions on certain categories of imports from Kenya. On 17 March 1964 one of her Ministers announced that Tanganyika might leave the common market and set up its own separate currency. In June of the same year, the three Finance Ministers stated that a common currency would cease with the establishment of three national, central banks.

The dissatisfaction with the working of the common market along with its threatened disintegration led to a series of meetings among the three countries to find a basis for the equitable distribution of benefits flowing from economic integration. This eventually resulted in the 'Kampala' Agreement of 1965, which had three major provisions. The deficit countries were permitted to impose, on an agreed basis, quota restrictions against specified imports from surplus countries. It provided for a decentralization of certain manufacturing industries such as beer, shoes, soap and cigarettes, leading to their reallocation in favour of Uganda and Tanzania. At the same time a fresh start was made towards the allocation of industry on an East African basis, so that the new industries which required the whole of the common market and, it was hoped were soon to be established, were divided equitably among the three partners, with Tanganyika allocated five of them, Uganda three and Kenya two.

The 'Kampala' Agreement, however, did not work satisfactorily and only the first provision was implemented. Tanzania and to a lesser extent Uganda, unilaterally imposed quantitative restrictions against a large variety of imports from Kenya. This had the effect of considerably slowing down the expansion of inter-territorial trade, as is shown by the 1966 trade figures.[37] Faced once again with the danger of disintegration of the entire complex of economic co-operation, the East African countries moved to appoint a ministerial commission under the chairmanship of a Danish economist, Professor Philip, to review the entire range of economic relations among the three countries. After protracted negotiations, extending over fifteen months, the Commission reported to the three Heads of State. The report formed the basis of the East African Treaty of Co-operation, which completed for the time being the long process of rationalization and reorganization of economic co-operation and co-ordination begun under the Governors' Conferences and continued through the High Commission and the EACSO.

THE TREATY OF EAST AFRICAN CO-OPERATION

(a) *General*

The Treaty is a long and complex document, consisting of 126 pages, with 98 articles and 15 annexes. It is clearly the most ambitious legal ordering of East African economic relations undertaken so far; an attempt has been made to provide for large areas of these relationships, and to deal with the numerous issues that had accumulated by 1966. The length and complexity of the Treaty was therefore perhaps inevitable, though there is less excuse for the rather pedestrian and casual drafting. As economic union treaties go, it is less complex than most, for it seeks more to formalize than to establish a common market. It is important, however, to remark that the Treaty is not concerned with any form of political union. The idea of a federation has been abandoned for the time being, though expectations have been expressed that the functional co-operation under the Treaty will lead in time to a more organic union. The major significance of the Treaty lies in its attempts to provide a firm base in law for the common market among East African countries. It is not surprising, however, that this task has been approached with much caution, and the legal and judicial decisions will continue to take a secondary place to the political. Though the common services and the common market are now regulated in the same instrument, there is a clear dichotomy in the

[37] In 1965 the total inter-country exports amounted to £45,068,000; in 1966 they fell to £43,986,000.

Treaty, and the two have not been integrated, though they share some institutions and the financing of one depends on the operation of the other. Such are the differences in the consensus towards, and the machinery provided for, these two areas, that they could easily be dealt with in separate treaties. A common treaty does, however, emphasize their close interdependence, and it may be that one could not survive without the other. Thus, though the common market provisions of the Treaty are initially to stay in force for fifteen years, while the provisions for the common services are of indefinite duration,[38] it is likely that if one went, it would be difficult to maintain the other.

The Treaty initially has effect among the signatory states, which are Kenya, Tanzania and Uganda. But the possibility of associating other countries with the East African Community is left open.[39] For this purpose, the partner states negotiate with the foreign country. No steps or procedure are laid down for the conduct of negotiations, and it may be significant that partner states collectively, as opposed to the Authority, are the negotiating bodies. The Treaty is a little imprecise on the form of the association; it is clearly implied that a foreign country may participate in only some of the activities of the Community or its institutions. While there are no insuperable legal barriers to a full and complete membership by outside countries, provided the agreement of all the parties is available, such membership would probably involve major revisions of the Treaty in other respects. The new member would need to be given representation on the institutions of the Community, and the institutions may themselves have to be revised. Even if only partial association is sought by an outsider, amendments to the agreement would be necessary to accommodate its special interests. The Treaty provides no framework within which a new member may fit automatically. Though this preserves flexibility in negotiations, it may in fact make agreement on all the issues more difficult, and lead to frequent amendments of the Treaty.

(b) *The Common Market*

The second part of the Treaty establishes the common market. The common market is not a term of art, but it is usually used to define that relationship between participating countries when all tariff and other trade restrictions among them are abolished, when the countries have a common external tariff for imports from non-member countries, and when there is free mobility of the factors of production, labour and capital. With this definition in mind,

[38] Article 92. It may be modified at any time by the agreement of the parties, article 94. It is, however, provided in relation to the Development Bank that modifications to its Charter can only be made by a specified resolution of its Board of Directors.
[39] Article 93.

how far can we say that a common market has been established in East Africa? The Partner States are obliged to maintain a common external tariff in respect of all goods. A state is free to depart from the common standard in relation to particular goods if it can obtain the consent of its partners.[40] A state is, however, free to prohibit or restrict the import from a foreign country into it of goods of any particular description or derived from any particular source.[41] The ability of the states to remit custom duties is loosely regulated; remission is not allowed if the importation is by a government itself, unless it is for its own use or consumption. Duty may also be remitted on goods provided by way of aid (free or at reduced prices) by any government or organization so long as these goods are not transferred to a state other than the recipient.[42] Thus a partner state can remit duties in favour of private importation, which would help its competitiveness *vis-à-vis* manufacturers in other countries, though the revenue of the recipient state is protected by another provision whereby, when such goods enter inter-state trade, the recipient state receives from the remitting state what it would have collected as duty if the goods had been directly imported into it.[43]

As regards external trade, there are two other provisions, one of which appears unduly to restrict the freedom of policy of the partner states. This is the provision which prohibits a state from entering into arrangements with any foreign country whereby tariff concessions are available to it and not to its partners.[44] The second restriction is in relation to barter agreements—if a state enters into a barter agreement with an external body in relation to manufactured goods, in respect of which goods a significant deviation of trade away from a partner to the foreign state occurs, it has to take effective measures to counteract such deviation.[45] What constitutes significant deviation is, however, not defined, though the statistical method of determining deviation is laid down. Nor is it specified what the 'effective steps' should be. The only effective step would be to cancel the barter agreement or re-negotiate the volume of trade under it—either of which courses would probably involve the state in a breach of its contractual obligations with the outside country. In future, an East African country would be wise to include a special clause in all barter agreements to safeguard its obligations under the Treaty. In fact, barter agreements are unusual in East Africa; much more frequent are commodity credits, which are not affected by the provision.

As far as internal trade is concerned, there is a general prohibition on

[40] Article 5.
[41] Article 9 (4).
[42] Article 6.
[43] Article 10.
[44] Article 7.
[45] Article 8.

quantitative and qualitative restrictions. As to the former, the partner states were to remove all quotas, quantitative or like restrictions and prohibitions on the transfer of goods originating in a partner state to another partner state, which were in force before the Treaty came into operation, and no such restrictions are allowed now.[46] There are several exceptions to this, however. The most important is the exclusion of certain agricultural goods from the operation of this rule.[47] The agricultural products excluded from the common market are listed in an annex and are described as basic staple foods or major export crops subject to special marketing arrangements. While some of these come within the common market in one or three years from the operation of the Treaty, for most of them there is no time stipulation. The products in the latter category include maize, wheat, rice, coffee, pyrethrum, cotton, sisal, meat, milk, eggs and groundnuts. The reason for the exclusion of agricultural products is the existence which we have noticed in previous chapters of 'artificial' price structures for some products which have resulted from the operation of 'organized' marketing by statutory authorities. Systems of marketing similar to the one that we have examined in relation to Kenya operate in Tanzania and to a lesser extent in Uganda. The pursuit of different price policies by the marketing agencies, or the existence of a guaranteed price in one country and a free market price in another, makes it necessary to maintain the power to restrict inter-territorial trade if controlled marketing arrangements are not to be disrupted. While this is the most important reason for crops like maize and coffee, in other cases the reason for exclusion is the encouragement through protection for the producers of the products in the individual states; thus the exclusion of meat and milk is to help Tanzania and Uganda to develop these industries, which Kenya has traditionally provided for them.[48]

Thus for the time being the most important sector in each state's economy is unaffected by the Treaty, though it states, as its long-term objective, the aim of bringing agriculture and agricultural products within the common market including the co-ordination of marketing boards within a single system of prices.[49] However, it has been argued that the long-term establishment of a common market in agricultural produce may not lead to free trade in any real sense.

> Article 14 commits the countries to a common market in agricultural produce but not to "co-operation and consultation in the field of agricultural policy", and it refers to "trade arrangements between the national agencies and marketing boards". It is not impossible that co-operation on agricultural policy and arrangements between the national marketing boards could lead to a situation in which

[46] Article 12.
[47] Article 13, annex, III.
[48] See A. Hazlewood, in *E.A.E.R.* 3.2 (N.S.) December 1967, p. 63 et seq.
[49] Article 14.

prices are set so that there is no incentive for trade to take place between the countries.[50]

If this forecast is correct, then the agricultural policies and development in the partner states are unlikely to be significantly affected by the Treaty.

Quantitative restrictions can also be imposed on all goods for special reasons—like the application of security laws and regulations, the control of nuclear materials, transfer of precious metals, and the protection of human, animal or plant health or life, or the protection of public morality. Further, a partner state is free to impose quantitative restrictions on specified goods produced in another state in order to give effect to its contractual or other obligations incurred prior to the Treaty. Restrictions can also be imposed if a state encounters balance of payment difficulties, provided that restrictions against imports from foreign countries have been first imposed and have not helped. Such restrictions can only be imposed after consultation with the Common Market Council, and in any case should not contravene a member's obligations under the General Agreement on Trade and Tariffs or the rules of the International Monetary Fund. Normally, these obligations are not strictly observed. The Treaty, however, reinforces the obligations, making them operative *vis-à-vis* the other partner states.[51] Under article XII of the GATT, restrictions are permitted to meet the balance of payments crisis, though the importation of minimum commercial quantities must be allowed to maintain regular trade channels, and the restrictions must be such as to avoid unnecessary damage to the economic interests of other contracting parties. It is unlikely that these provisions will impose greater limitations than under the Treaty.

The final exception to the free movement of goods within the Community is in relation to external goods which have been imported into a partner state. The other partner states can restrict the transfer of such goods to themselves by any means, including licensing or control of importers.[52] The word 'restrict' is not defined and it may be asked whether it can cover a total prohibition or the ban of such goods. The answer should be in the affirmative, for as we have seen, a state has the right to forbid totally the direct import of any goods from abroad, which right would be nullified or at least modified by a narrow interpretation of the word 'restrict'. On the other hand, the means mentioned for the restriction—licensing and control of importers—would suggest that a total ban is not permissible. Perhaps a reconcilation of the two provisions is possible if we regard the second provision as qualified by the first—for example, foreign goods on which a ban has been placed cannot be transferred from within the Com-

[50] Hazlewood, op. cit., p. 69.
[51] Article 12.
[52] Article 9 (5).

munity to the prohibiting state, but if no such ban is placed, then the goods can be transferred, subject to the restrictions which may be imposed.

To turn now to qualitative restrictions, no internal tariffs can be levied on goods originating in one partner state on their transfer to another. Goods are defined as originating in a partner state if they are produced wholly in it or, if they use material imported from outside, the value of such materials does not exceed 70 per cent of the ex-factory value of the goods in question.[53] There is one important exception to the prohibition of internal tariffs—the transfer tax. This tax will operate as a levy on goods entering from a partner state, but its primary purpose is not revenue-raising, but providing protection for industry within the country which imposes this tax so as to promote industrial balance between the partner states.[54] The provisions for the imposition of the tax are therefore limited for this purpose. Moreover, the Treaty attempts to retain special advantages for a partner whose goods may be so taxed *vis-à-vis* a foreign country. Thus the tax can not exceed 50 per cent of the external tariff, which in turn is likely to have been the subject of inter-state agreement. East African goods which are liable to excise duties may, however, end up paying more duty than external goods, for the tax and the excise may together exceed the external tariff. Partner states are further protected by a provision which requires the taxing state to take appropriate measures if trade in the goods so taxed is deviated to an external country.

The transfer tax can be applied only to manufactured goods imported from the other two countries when the importing state is in deficit in its total trade in manufactured goods with the other two countries. The taxes can be imposed against another country only on goods making up a total value not exceeding the trade deficit on manufactured goods of the imposing country with respect to the other country. This qualification means that on current inter-state trade, Kenya is not entitled to impose any transfer tax, whereas Uganda can impose taxes on Kenyan but not on Tanzanian goods,

[53] Annex I sets out the rules for determining the origin of goods. Two, slightly curious, provisions in it favour the inclusion of a wide range of goods within the category of locally produced goods. Section 3 (b) states that the value of any materials that can be identified as having been imported from any foreign country shall be their c.i.f. value on clearance for home consumption *less the amount of any transport costs incurred in transit through the territory of other partner States*. (Under this provision a factory in Uganda on the Kenya-Uganda border will be better off than a similar factory on the Kenya side of the border, though the distance between them will be only a few miles.) Section 3 (e) states that the ex-factory value of the goods shall be the *price paid or payable for them to the exporter in the territory of the partner State where the goods were produced*, that price being adjusted where necessary to an f.o.b. or free at frontier basis in that territory. (Italics supplied.) It is possible that manufactured goods may pass through two or more hands before they are exported, thus artificially putting up their ex-factory value.

[54] Article II. On transfer tax, see article 20. See, also, G. K. Helleiner, 'Transfer Taxes, Tariffs and the East African Common Market', *E.A.E.R.* (N.S.) December 1967.

while Tanzania can impose taxes on both the other partners. However, a transfer tax can only be imposed if the importing country has, or will within three months of its imposition have, productive capacity of at least 15 per cent of the domestic consumption or of a total value of at least sh. 2,000,000/- of goods of similar description to those taxed. The maximum transfer tax applicable to a specified commodity is 50 per cent of the external duty on the commodity; and its maximum duration cannot exceed eight years. It is further provided that all transfer taxes must come to an end fifteen years from the imposition of the first such tax, unless they have expired or been revoked earlier. Provisions also exist for the expiration of the taxes if a certain degree of export success is attained in the tax-protected industry and for the prohibition of further taxes when a certain degree of overall export success in manufactured goods is achieved. Within five years of the operation of the system, the partners have agreed to undertake a joint review and appraisal of its effectiveness as a measure to promote a more balanced industrial development.

The transfer tax is, therefore, a serious derogation from the principle of a common market. Its inclusion in the Treaty has given rise to resentment within the Community, and businessmen and certain Ministers in Kenya, which has the most to lose from it, have officially and publicly criticized it.[55] The application of the provisions for the transfer tax is likely to cause the greatest difficulty of any article of the Treaty, both because of the drafting, and its effect on East African trade. Some of the problems which are likely to arise in the interpretation of these provisions may be briefly discussed here.

As we have seen, a state can impose a transfer tax on a particular item not only if it actually manufactures similar goods or plans to do so within three months of the imposition, but also if it has a certain productive capacity.[56] It need not presumably, however, utilize that capacity fully, but 'capacity' is not defined. Is 'capacity' to be reckoned on the basis of production per shift of labour or more? Is any regard to be had for the standards of efficiency actually obtaining in the factory, which may effect the quantum of production? Secondly, the tax can only be imposed on manufactures if goods of a 'similar description' are produced locally. Goods of 'similar description' as those which 'in addition to similar functions, constituent parts or content' are defined as of 'such a nature as will enable them actively to compete in the same market as those other goods'.[57] As to the stipulation of competition, it is not clear how relevant the price differential is to be. If the price differential between two items of similar function is vast, they may not be mutually competitive, despite the potential competition; this is especially so

[55] See, however, National Assembly, *Debates*, volume XVI (14 February 1969), col. 5060 et seq., when the Government defended the transfer tax against strong criticism from back-benchers.

[56] Article 20 (7). [57] Article 20 (6).

in East Africa where income differentials are so great. The kind of soap used for a bath by the ordinary worker or peasant is likely to be quite different from the kind used by, say, the expatriate community. What makes them mutually non-competitive is very often only the price factor. A similar distinction can be made between fur coats and ordinary ones. What meaning is to be given to the expression 'same market'? Does this refer to the general purchasing public or is it to be restricted to specialized sectors within it? Are the requirements of 'similar function, constituent parts or content' to be construed disjunctively or conjunctively? If the former, it would be necessary to prove that locally produced goods were parallel in all respects to the goods on which a tax was imposed—which would greatly restrict the right to tax and would seem in any case not to be indicated by the form of drafting. Thus it might not be possible to tax detergents if only soap is produced locally, or gin if only *waragi* is produced locally, though it could be proved that the functions were similar and they could indeed be used as substitutes for one another. Since there is a tendency for manufacturers to produce numerous varieties of the same goods, the precise meaning to be given to the above expression becomes extremely important.

A related difficulty is encountered in the paragraphs which deal with the revocation of a tax if the imposing country achieves a certain percentage of export of its own goods of the same kind. Here the expression used is 'goods of that kind':[58] is it to be construed to have the same meaning as 'goods of a similar description', or is it intended to indicate an even closer resemblance than under the former formula? Thirdly, it is provided that if as a result of a transfer tax, a significant deviation of trade occurs away from a partner state subject to such a tax, to a foreign country, the taxing state must take appropriate steps to counteract such measures, but here again 'significant' is not defined.[59] Fourthly, it is provided that if a tax is placed on goods whose production has been licensed under the East African licensing system, the Common Market Council may, at the request of the country of production, direct its revocation 'if it considers that there are such exceptional circumstances that the tax ought not to continue in force, having regard to all relevant matters and to this Treaty'.[60] The Treaty gives no guidance as to what the exceptional circumstances are, nor what are the 'relevant matters' to be taken into account. Finally, though it is provided that a tax shall come to an end if local production does not commence within three months, there is no provision as to what is to happen to the tax collected before its repeal.[61] Is the tax to be regarded as void *ab initio* and so liable to be refunded to the manufacturers who paid it or can it be kept by the

[58] Article 20 (19).
[59] Article 20 (17).
[60] Article 20 (22).
[61] Article 20 (6).

taxing country? If it is void *ab initio*, is the period of eight years which is the maximum period for which a tax can be levied, to run from its first imposition, even though void, or is this date to be disregarded?[62] Nor is it clear whether a state whose tax has lapsed due to non-commencement of production, can reimpose it later when it does commence production. A paragraph in the Treaty provides that if such a state applied to the Common Market Council within three months of the imposition, the latter may direct that, conditional upon the commencement of production within a further period of three months, such tax may be reimposed.[63] Does it by implication rule out the ability of a state unilaterally to reimpose a tax?

Most of the provisions of the Treaty that we have examined so far are aimed at preventing a state from imposing restrictions on the goods of its partners. Nowhere is a state prohibited from imposing restrictions on its own goods, as by way of an export tax or quota or even prohibition on their export to a partner state, although one of the aims of the Community is stated to be the abolition generally of restrictions on trade. It may be argued that a state is unlikely in this way to discourage export of its own goods, but it is not impossible to conceive of situations when a state may wish to do so. Export taxes may also provide a state with an opportunity, within the protection from foreign competition of an East African market, of raising revenue from its exports to the other members of the Community. In any case, these are likely to be governmental decisions in which those actually engaged in inter-state commerce may not have much say.

As regards the mobility of the factors of production, labour and capital, the Treaty also falls short of a full common market. As far as capital is concerned,[64] the states are obliged to permit payments on current accounts in the currency of the partner state in which the creditor or beneficiary resides; Annex VII sets out the current account payments that can claim the benefit of this provision, and include most of the payments that would arise due to the operation of the common market. The obligations in respect of capital accounts are not so specific. Payments or transfers on capital account are permitted, but a state is free to impose controls on certain categories of such payments and transfers, if it considers such controls necessary for furthering its economic development or an increase in trade. There are two qualifications on this, first the rather nebulous and unenforceable one that the controls should be consistent with the aims of the Community; and secondly, that the controls should not prejudice the ability of the Community, the Bank or the Corporations to perform their functions. The states therefore in effect retain their competence to regulate the flow

[62] Article 20 (14).
[63] Article 20 (6) (a) and (b).
[64] Articles 24–28.

of money out of capital accounts, and there is no obligation of prior consultation with the Common Market Council, though the Council is free to review the controls.

There is even less mobility in relation to labour. The only concession that the states have made is to waive their immigration rules for the benefit of the employees of the Community and its institutions, as agreed on by the Authority.[65] Apart from this, there is no right of movement, though the immigration laws of the states do in fact permit a fair degree of mobility. Until recently, the controls in the Immigration Acts of these countries did not apply *ipso facto* to Africans, who were defined to include people of all the indigenous tribes of East Africa.[66] However, under all these Acts, the Government could by regulation extend the controls to the Africans from the neighbouring countries, who were also liable to deportation orders. There was as a result no secure right of movement within East Africa. East African citizens of non-African descent were in any case bound by the Acts. Now, the position has been further affected by the recent Immigration Act, 1967, of Kenya which applies to all non-citizens, regardless of race. Under the immigration laws of all these countries, exemptions can be made by the Government in favour of groups or an individual and work permits can also be granted which give the right of residence. The mobility of labour therefore depends on the policies of the Governments, and is not a condition stipulated by the Treaty. It should be further mentioned that no right of establishment is provided.

It is obvious from the foregoing discussion that the common market which has been established is incomplete. As we shall see later, this was inevitable given that the partner states were at different stages of industrial development, but first we must look at some provisions designed to prevent the distortion of competition within the Community in order that the full benefits of the common market may be realized. The partner states are to establish and maintain a common excise tariff in respect of excisable goods manufactured, processed or produced in the partner states, departures from the common tariff being permissible only for revenue purposes and after consultation with the other governments.[67] The states have undertaken to co-ordinate their fiscal and monetary policies and to pursue a common scheme of fiscal incentives towards industrial development.[68] They have also agreed to promote a harmonization of their commercial laws, though the Treaty does not specify what is comprehended within this term.[69]

[65] Article 3 (4).
[66] Cap. 60 (Uganda); Cap. 534 (Tanzania); Cap. 172 (Kenya), now replaced by Act 25 of 1967.
[67] Article 17.
[68] Article 19.
[69] Article 2 (2).

Practices which are specifically outlawed, in so far as they frustrate the benefits of the common market, are one channel marketing, discriminatory rates of taxes, duties or other charges levied in a partner state on any goods originating in another, dumping, and discriminatory purchasing.[70] 'One channel marketing' is defined as any arrangements for the marketing of goods, whether regulated by law or otherwise, which, by limiting the channels by which such goods may be marketed, has effect to exclude competition in the marketing of such goods. As all three states have established State Trading Corporations, with monopolies of wholesale distribution of various items, the interpretation of this prohibition is important. It is obvious that one channel marketing is not void *ipso facto*, but only in so far as it prevents competition. The manner in which the Corporations manage their monopolies and the effects it has on the actual distribution of goods will determine the lawfulness of one channel marketing. In particular, it would be incompatible with the Treaty if the Corporations imposed any conditions or levies on the goods of the other partner states additional to those on local goods. 'Dumping' is defined as the sale of goods to another state at prices lower than those charged in the producing country, in circumstances likely to prejudice the production of similar goods in the importing state. 'Discriminatory purchasing' is any arrangement or practice whereby a partner state or any body in it gives preference to the purchase of goods originating from a foreign country when suitable goods originating within the partner states are available on comparable terms, including price. It may also be argued that import licensing is no longer possible, except where quantitative restrictions are allowed. There is no express prohibition of licensing, but its indirect effect might well be to hamper inter-state trade and commerce and to place the goods of other partner states at a disadvantage *vis-à-vis* local goods, through delays and uncertainties.

(c) *Equalization measures*

As we have hinted above, one of the principal difficulties of establishing a free and complete common market is the need to reconcile with it the other major aim of the Treaty—industrial equalization. The transfer tax has been designed to promote industry in the more industrially backward states, though doubts have been expressed as to whether it will achieve this purpose.[71] The second provision for ensuring equity is the East African Development Bank, which is established by the Treaty.[72] Of its initially subscribed capital of £10,000,000, £6,000,000 is subscribed by the partner states in equal shares; provision is made for subscription by approved institutions, but the

[70] Article 16.
[71] Helleiner, op. cit.
[72] Article 21 and annex (Charter).

total holding of the partner states is not to fall below 51 per cent. Among the objects of the Bank designed to even out industrial imbalances, is the provision that in its operations the Bank is to give priority to industrial development in the relatively less industrially developed partner states. Moreover, of its total loans, guarantees and investments, Tanzania and Uganda are to get 38¾ per cent each and Kenya 22½ per cent. The provisions of the Bank thus seek to remove the imbalance by providing capital for investment and also technical assistance. This factor could be an important boost for the underdeveloped areas, though it remains to be seen how seriously this aim is adversely effected by an operating principle of the Bank that it shall be guided by sound banking principles and shall finance only economically sound and technically feasible projects.

The East African industrial licensing system is to continue until October 1973 without any extension of its present scope.[73] Licensing was instituted by means of parallel legislation in the three countries—a course of action which was necessary since the CLA had no competence in this area—but the items listed for industrial licensing were severely restricted, and attempts to extend the schedule were unsuccessful. It is generally accepted that the system has had little impact on the location of industry within East Africa and is unlikely in future to be a significant factor for an equitable distribution of new industry.[74] Nevertheless, the real advantages of a common market among developing countries are to be found not in free competition, but in industrial planning, and if the common market in East Africa is to contribute significantly to industrialization and its equitable incidence, some central planning seems essential. Other measures for equalization are connected with the reorganization of the common services, discussed below.

(d) *Machinery of the Common Market*

We now turn to the machinery for the supervision and enforcement of the provisions of the common market. Apart from the East African Authority,[75] consisting of the Presidents of the partner states, which is responsible for, and has the general direction and control of, the performance of the executive functions of the entire Community, there are two bodies specifically established for the enforcement of the common market provisions. First, there is the Common Market Council, composed of three East African Ministers, to be described later, and three ministerial representatives from each of the partner states.[76] Its function is to ensure the observance of the common

[73] Article 23.
[74] Raisman Report, para. 100. See Ghai, 'East African Licensing Council', mimeo. (Uppsala, Dag Hammarskjöld Foundation, 1969).
[75] Articles 46–48.
[76] Articles 30–31; 54.

market provisions by the various parties, settle problems arising from their implementation and to consider references made to it about the infringement of the provisions. It is not clear who can make such references, presumably the partner states can, but are private individuals or business organizations similarly eligible? It could be argued that the latter are eligible, since there is no express exclusion of them, though the general scheme of the Treaty is based on initiative and participation by the states exclusively. Once a complaint has been made to the Council, it can dispose of it in a variety of ways—it can issue a binding directive to a partner state or states, or make recommendations to them, or promote a settlement, or record its inability to agree on a solution.

It is only in the last instance, that is, when the Council is unable to agree on a solution, that the dispute can be referred to the second common market institution, the Tribunal;[77] this must be done within two months of the Council's decision, and only a partner state can invoke the jurisdiction of the Tribunal. It is also possible for a state to bring a complaint to the Tribunal if within one month after its reference to the Council, the Council has not determined it. The Tribunal also has jurisdiction at the instance of a state in cases where it alleges that another state has not complied, within the specified time, with the binding directive of the Council disposing of a complaint referred to the Council under the provisions discussed above. Thus only states can invoke the compulsory jurisdiction of the Tribunal, and even then, in all but the last case, the Council controls the access to the Tribunal, which means that a political decision, if it is possible, takes precedence over a legal one. It is important to notice that the rule of procedure that when a member of a Council of the Community objects to a proposal for the decision of the Council, he can thereby cause it to be referred to the Authority, where the rule of unanimity prevails, does not apply to those decisions of the Common Market Council which might affect the reference of a dispute to the Tribunal under the foregoing provisions.[78] Moreover, it is possible for the Council to request the Tribunal for an advisory opinion.

The Common Market Tribunal consists of five members, of whom only the chairman need be a lawyer; others should be persons of impartiality and independence with knowledge or experience in industry, commerce or public affairs. The chairman is appointed by the Authority; of the remaining, one each are selected by the member states, and they along with the chairman select the fifth. Its functions are limited to the observance of the laws and terms of the Treaty that relate to the common market and the states have pledged themselves not to take disputes in this area elsewhere. But as we have seen, the access to the Tribunal is not automatic. The task

[77] Articles 32–42.
[78] Section 8 of annex XI—*Procedural Provisions.*

of the Tribunal is likely to be difficult. Matters of an extremely complex and controversial nature are likely to be referred to it. Nor is it absolutely clear what the Tribunal can do in a given case. It can make interim orders, and give binding decisions.[79] It is not specified what kind of final orders it can make, though presumably it can make any of the orders that an ordinary court can. The Tribunal is not allowed to deliver dissenting judgments—which may seem a curious provision to common lawyers but is perhaps considered desirable in order to promote the acceptability of the decision of the majority in controversial cases.[80] The Tribunal could play an important role in evolving the law of the common market, in an area where rules and procedures are few and far between, but the precise role the Tribunal will be called upon to play depends in large part on the Council.

(e) *The Common Services*

In many ways, the common services continue as before, the Community having succeeded to the services run by the EACSO. The legislative functions of the Community are likewise similar.[81] There have, however, been important institutional and administrative changes, which we must examine.

The East African Authority has the same composition and powers as under the former organization—in it are vested the principal executive powers. In addition to its executive responsibility, the Authority has important functions of a legislative kind, especially in relation to the common market, though these are not explicitly described as such.[82] It is assisted primarily by the East African Ministers and the Councils, to whom it can issue directions as to the performance of their functions. The rule of unanimity applies to the decisions of the Authority, so that any member can prevent discussion or action on a proposal. The rule applies in a modified way to the Councils, for any member can, by objecting to a proposal, prevent further action, unless the Authority decides otherwise.[83] The rule of unanimity detracts from the provisions for co-operation that have been established and emphasizes the 'agency' nature of the Community. The need to secure universal agreement still remains, and large sections of the new arrangements depend for their proper functioning on it.

The East African Minister is an innovation of the Treaty.[84] One of the proposals which had been made to strengthen the East African Common Services Organization was to appoint its own Ministers responsible to the Organization and its Assembly. Such Ministers were to hold the Organiza-

[79] Articles 37 and 39.

[80] The rule prohibiting the giving of dissenting judgments in the Judicial Committee of the Privy Council was abolished only in 1966, Judicial Committee (Dissenting Opinion) Order, 1966, in S.I. p. 1100.

[81] See annexes IX and X.

[82] See below, p. 495.

[83] Section 8 of annex XI.

[84] Articles 49–51.

tion's portfolios, and to replace the Ministerial Committees.[85] The East African Ministers under the Treaty are different from these proposals. Each state nominates one such Minister from among those qualified to vote under its national electoral laws. He cannot hold any other political office in the government of his own country, though he enjoys the status equivalent to that of a Minister, and can attend and speak at its Cabinet meetings, but presumably without a vote. An East African Minister is to assist the Authority whose meetings he would normally attend and to whom he is responsible; yet he can be dismissed from office by the Authority at the request of his own government. His constitutional position therefore is difficult, and a little obscure. His basic function would be to provide a link between his own government and the Community, and to strengthen the latter's executive. They are also expected to lighten the load of the Authority, by taking decision within the spheres delegated to them. For the first time the central organization has its own full time political appointees, whose primary responsibility is towards the Community; they are also its chief spokesmen in the new legislature. They are chairmen of the Community's Councils, and the Authority can assign to each one of them particular responsibilities or 'portfolios'. Given able persons, the East African Ministers can be an important factor in the strengthening of the Community, though much would depend on the degree of delegation to them by the Authority. Deputy East African Ministers, with similar qualifications, can also be appointed if the Authority deems it desirable, and have in fact been appointed.[86]

The Authority and the Ministers are assisted by five Councils, consisting of the East African Ministers and the ministerial representatives from the partner states.[87] We have already discussed the most important of these Councils, the Common Market Council. Of the others, the Communications Council and the Finance Council are the more important ones, the former having the overall responsibility for the proper and efficient running of communication services, which are now operated by four corporations. The four corporations are the East African Railways Corporation, the East African Harbours Corporation, the East African Posts and Telecommunications Corporation and the East African Airways Corporation; all but the last are new. Formerly the railways and harbours, and posts and telecommunications were run as self-contained departments, each under a Manager, with responsibility to the Ministerial Committee and the Legislative Assembly, especially for appropriations. Now the harbours have been separated from the railways, and the operation of all these services is

[85] Banfield, in Leys and Robson, op. cit., pp. 38–40.
[86] Article 52.
[87] Articles 54–55.

entrusted to corporations.[88] The one immediate effect of this change is that the Legislative Assembly no longer appropriates for the finances of the services as the corporations run their own budgets.

The Treaty sets out the principles for the operation of the corporations, and places, in particular, an obligation to run them on efficient commercial principles so that not only does their income cover the expenditure, but that a fixed profit on the investment, as determined by the Authority, is secured, though East African Airways may be exempt from the last rule.[89] The responsibility for the corporations is divided among their Director-General, the Board of Directors, the Communications Council, and the Authority, in that ascending order.[90] Though initiative in much of the day to day running is left to the former two, the Council and the Authority have to approve major changes in tariffs, etc., and development plans, and can give directions of a general nature. The advantages of corporations over government departments are thought to be that they provide flexibility and avoid bureaucratic delays, are able to harness business and commercial expertise, are not directly accountable to the legislature, and in particular obtain their financial independence. It would appear that one of the important effects of the establishment of these corporations would be to remove legislative controls, both in the states and the Community, over their activities. Since the Council and the Authority are responsible for all but small decisions, it may be doubted if the other advantages would be available. While the state governments may not have got more control over these activities than they had under the East African Common Services Organization, the removal of the competence of the Assembly over them cannot but increase the influence of the governments.

The Finance Council is responsible for consultation in common on the major financial affairs of the Community, and considers and approves major financial decisions relating to the common services, including their estimates of expenditure and related loan and investment programmes. The fourth council is the Economic Consultative and Planning Council which is to assist in the national planning of the partner states by consultative means and to advise the Authority upon the long term planning of the common services; it remains to be seen how far it performs the former of these functions, but unless this becomes its meaningful activity, many of the advantages of planned expansion and industrialization due to economies of scale will be frittered away. Finally, there is the Research and Social Council to help co-ordinate the policies of the partner states in research and social matters.

[88] Article 71.
[89] Article 72.
[90] Article 73, and annex XIII.

The Authority, the Ministers and the Councils are served by a secretariat, while each corporation has its own staff, recruited and appointed by its Board of Directors.[91] Of the Community's Secretariat, only three officers are specifically dealt with in the Treaty—the Secretary-General, who is the principal executive officer of the Community and appointed by the Authority; the Counsel, the principal legal adviser, appointed by the Authority after consultation with the Secretary-General and the Community's Service Commission, and the Auditor-General. There is a Service Commission, appointed by the Authority, which is responsible for making appointments to offices in the service of the Community and has powers of disciplinary control and dismissal over persons in such offices. Much of the success or failure of the Community depends on the calibre and dedication of the Secretariat. While some of its duties are clearly defined, others, like the co-ordination of national fiscal or economic planning, depend to a large extent on its own initiative. On the whole, the powers of the Secretariat are those of traditional international bureaucracy, with severe limitations on its ability to initiate and propose. Nevertheless, together with the East African Ministers, the Secretariat could constitute an important force for the viability and even enlargement of the Community and its purposes. Unlike the Ministers who are subject to removal by their own national governments, the civil servants enjoy security of tenure and could significantly develop an East African ethos. Moreover, they alone of the civil servants in East Africa can claim to be free of national biases, a fact which could lead to their performing important evaluation work especially in disputes arising out of the implementation and operation of the common market. However, whether the Secretariat plays a significant part will depend on its ability to recruit competent and experienced persons, which in turn depends on whether the partner states are willing to release their most efficient civil servants for employment in the Community. It is quite likely that the partner states will regard with some misgivings Community officials who show an over-zealous concern for the interests of the Community as opposed to those of the states.

The employees of the Community and the Corporations are subject to the law of the settlement of trade disputes of the state within which they are employed.[92] This replaces the previous arrangements whereby the employees of the EACSO were subject to its own law of dispute settlement which applied uniformly throughout the EACSO. It will now happen that the different groups of employees of the Community, depending on the country in which they work, will come under different industrial regimes, which may affect not only the right to strike and bargain, but the actual terms of service. While there are disadvantages to this diversity, a system

[91] Articles 61–64; 77. [92] Articles 84-85.

whereby two sets of industrial workers in a state come within different regimes has its drawbacks as well, and could affect the success of a state's policy in relation to its domestic labour. To some extent, under the present system, the danger of excessive diversity will be counteracted by another provision in the Treaty that replaces, in the case of Community employees, a national court, tribunal or other authority which has power to make final orders in respect of terms of service by the East African Industrial Court, which consists of the presidents or chairmen (or their nominees) of the national industrial tribunals. It is, furthermore, provided that the Industrial Court shall exercise its powers in accordance with the principles laid down by the Authority from time to time. The jurisdiction of the Industrial Court is not quite clear; it exercises jurisdiction only when the national tribunal of the state in question would have powers to make binding awards. However, some of the jurisdiction of the national tribunals is not binding in this sense, but may be a necessary part of the process for the settlement of disputes. Also, an award can become binding not so much by legislation as by a prior agreement of the disputants. Will the East African Court have jurisdiction in such cases?

(f) Legislative powers

The primary institution for law-making is the E.A. Central Legislative Assembly, but the Authority has some of what amount to legislative powers in relation to the common market, where the Assembly has no competence, except some ill-defined powers over the Tribunal.[93] The Authority's power derives from its competence to alter the terms of the Annexes concerning the common market. The Authority can, for example, amend or add to Annex I, which sets out the rules to determine which goods qualify as originating within East Africa, so as to be exempt from internal tariffs. Similarly the Annex providing for exemption from quantitative restrictions in relation to agricultural product can be altered by the Authority. The Authority also has powers of veto over Bills passed by the Legislative Assembly, which are discussed below.

The Assembly consists of a Chairman appointed by the Authority, the East African Ministers, their deputies, if appointed, the Secretary-General and the Counsel, and twenty-seven appointed members, nine from each state.[94] The Treaty does not specify the method of appointment of these members, but leaves the procedures to be determined by each of the states.

[93] The Common Market Tribunal is listed as one of the matters with respect to which the Assembly can legislate (annex X, item 21), but section 23 of the Statute of the Tribunal (annex VIII) provides that the Authority may, after consultation with the Tribunal, amend or add to the Statute. It may be that the Assembly can provide for the detailed functioning of the Tribunal, but its basic constitutional rules can only be altered by the Authority.

[94] Articles 56–60.

Under the East African Common Services Organization, such members were elected by the state legislatures, and resulted in the election of back-benchers who were often critical of the Authority. Now, depending on the method chosen by a state to appoint its members, their nomination could be used as a means of patronage and to play down the expression of public opinion, and the members, mindful of their 'benefactors', may turn out to be more docile. However, whatever the method of the appointment,[95] the members continue in office till the legislature of their state is next dissolved and first meets after the dissolution. This provision is a little curious. If in fact these members are not to be elected by the state legislatures, why should their term of office be tied to them? If the intention was to give the new government that might be formed after the general election an opportunity to appoint its own nominees, then the principle is only imperfectly implemented, since there can be occasions other than a general election when a new government could be formed. If the intention was to give some security of tenure, this could have been better achieved by specifying a fixed period for the appointment.

There are other provisions, too, which can be seen as reducing the significance of the Assembly. The presiding officer, formerly the 'Speaker', is now called the 'Chairman', the corporations are largely independent of it and it has little jurisdiction over the common market. True, it continues to legislate (including appropriations), but legislative power is not the only sign of a legislature's importance and even there the veto of the Heads of State to Bills passed by the Assembly is retained—if their assent is not given within nine months, a Bill automatically lapses. Furthermore, the Assembly does not make its own rules of procedures—these, including the Standing Orders, are made by the Authority. The rules which have been made are very restrictive of the functions and powers of the Assembly.[96] It can discuss only those matters which relate to the services administered by the Community or to matters over which it has legislative competence. Its predecessor had shown great enthusiasm for motions urging the establishment of an East African Federation; but it is possible that under the new Standing Orders, such motions or questions would not be admissible. Also, as we have seen, the effect of putting the major common services under the control of corporations is to dilute the Assembly's power of accountability over them, and the Standing Orders expressly provide that the operations of the corporations shall not be the subject of questions or motions except where their reports and accounts are tabled.[97] It is quite likely,

[95] Tanzania provided for its members to be chosen through elections by the National Assembly; in Kenya and Uganda, the Governments nominated their members.
[96] Rules 26 (1) and 35 of the Standing Orders.
[97] Rule 54 (5).

however, that despite these limitations, the Assembly will see its role as larger than is strictly constitutional. The Central Legislature was always seen as the one common institution which was directly responsible to an East African public opinion and had developed a strong 'federal' ethos. It may be that the new Assembly will continue the tradition despite its limitations.

(g) Decentralization, Financial Provisions and Equalization of Benefits

As we have seen, the centralization of EACSO activities in Nairobi meant that Kenya benefited disproportionately from the expenditure of the Organization's budgets and incomes. Now provisions are made for the decentralization of the operations of the Community and the reallocation of its various institutions. The headquarters of the Community itself are now located in Arusha in northern Tanzania (as a special concession to Tanzania for her rather unequal benefits from the common market); that of the Bank in Kampala in Uganda; of the East African Airways Corporation in Nairobi in Kenya; the East African Harbours Corporation in Dar es Salaam in Tanzania; the Posts and Telecommunications in Kampala, and the Airways Corporation in Nairobi. In addition, there has been some degree of decentralization; the Railways, and Posts and Telecommunications Corporations are to establish regional headquarters; while for the Departments of Income Tax and Customs and Excise and the Directorate of Aviation, there is now a Commissioner or Director for each in each of the partner states.[98]

It has been calculated that the effect of these changes will be the net loss to Kenya annually of £1,347,800 to £1,750,100; the gain to Uganda of between £394,400 and £722,900; and the gain to Tanzania of between £953,800 and £1,027,200, without taking into account the capital expenditure in Uganda and Tanzania due to the building of the new headquarters now allocated to them.[99] Moreover, most of the corporations of the Community are instructed in the Treaty to give priority to development in Uganda and Tanzania.[100]

These measures of equalization, plus those we examined in relation to the common market—the transfer tax and the policy of the Development Bank—involve a considerable sacrifice on the part of Kenya. As a result, the system of the Distributable Pool of the EACSO, whereby part of Kenya's revenue was distributed to Tanzania and Uganda, is abolished, though the Distributable Pool, in a modified form, continues till mid-1969.

The major financial provisions of the Community are as follows.[101] The

[98] Articles 86–87.
[99] A. R. Roe, 'The Impact of the East African Treaty on the Distribution of the EACSO Benefits', *E.A.E.R.* (N.S.) December 1967, p. 39.
[100] Annex XIV, part B.
[101] Articles 65–70.

Corporations are expected to be self-sufficient, just as the services they administer were 'self-contained' previously. For the other services of the Community, a General Fund has been established. The primary source of revenue for the General Fund are certain charges on the revenue collected by the Community—income tax and customs and excise. First, an amount equal to the cost of the collection of the taxes and duties (excluding the transfer tax, the expense of which collection the imposing country has to reimburse) is paid into the General Fund. Whatever the remaining deficit between the Fund and the expected expenditure from it, is met by a first charge on the tax on profits of companies engaged in manufacturing or finance business, and the customs and excise dues—the amount to be divided between the two sources in a fixed proportion laid down in the Treaty. Apart from this, each state receives taxes and other revenue that can be ascribed to income or dues accruing in that state. Thus while the Community's financial needs are secured on the income of the states, there is no redistribution of one country's revenue to another. It is estimated that under the new system, compared with that under the EACSO, Kenya stands to gain about £550,000, and Tanzania and Uganda to lose about £300,000 and £250,000 respectively.[102]

CONCLUSION

Looking at the Treaty over-all, one can say that Kenya has made the greatest sacrifice—she is the only country which cannot impose a transfer tax, while her own goods are liable to be taxed by both her partners. She has surrendered the location of the headquarters and certain other institutions to Tanzania and Uganda, and she stands to lose from the provisions regarding the investment policies of the Development Bank and the corporations, though she does gain slightly from the eventual abolition of the Distributable Pool. All this can be regarded not only as a measure of equity, given Kenya's past dominance of the regional institutions, but it can also be argued that Kenya stands to gain the most from the Treaty in the long run. Her goods seem to be in the greatest need for protection from foreign competition and her lead in industrialization will continue to give her dominance in the East African markets. In fact the chances are that her partners will realize or at least feel that their own industrialization is hampered by Kenya's dominance and the dissatisfaction with the operation of the Treaty arrangements may lead to new tensions and a threat to its continuance. What seems to have been realized by the Philip Commission was that the viability of regional co-operation and institutions depends on their producing mutual advantages. Whatever the legal provisions, a partner state can frustrate the

[102] P. Robson, 'The Reshaping of East African Economic Co-operation', *E.A.J.* August 1967.

operation of the Community if it feels that it has little to gain and much to lose from its membership. Whether the arrangements of the Treaty will be a sufficient safeguard against such a state of affairs remains to be seen, but it can reasonably be stated that the Community's prospects are dim if such a state of affairs arises.

Under the Treaty, the states have undertaken as far as they can to secure the enactment and continuation of legislation to give effect to it.[103] In East Africa treaties do not automatically become part of the law of the state, but require incorporation by Parliament for this purpose. All three Parliaments have now passed legislation to implement the Treaty.[104] Due to the simplification of the constitutions of Kenya and Uganda, there were no constitutional difficulties in the way of the implementation. Only Tanzania had to amend her constitution for full effect to be given to the Treaty in order to provide for full participation by Zanzibar.[105]

Under the national implementation legislation, legal capacity has been conferred on the Community, as opposed to the Authority, under the East African Common Services Organization. The position as to the immunities and privileges of the Community is unclear, in particular whether it partakes of the privileges and immunities of the states which make up the Community.[106] The assets and liabilities of the EACSO have been transferred to the Community, the laws of EACSO have been kept in force, subject to the necessary modifications, and enactments of the Community will apply automatically in the states. Whenever the laws of the Community conflict with the national laws, the former are to prevail, unless in any given case, the state legislature had declared a contrary intention. Nevertheless, it would seem that the Community law will not be valid in a member state if it is inconsistent with that state's constitution, since neither the government nor the legislature of that state has powers to authorize the enactments of such laws. It may therefore be doubted whether the Community's regulations which discriminate against non-African citizens of East Africa in its employment is valid, since it is inconsistent with Kenya's Constitution. Most of the laws of the Community will be enacted by its Assembly, and

[103] Article 95.

[104] Act No. 42 of 1967 (T); Act No. 28 of 1967 (U); Act No. 31 of 1967 (K).

[105] Zanzibar is now for the first time brought integrally into a system of East African co-operation, and in order to make this possible, the list of Union matters in Tanzania's Interim Constitution had to be expanded. Act No. 35 of 1967.

[106] A similar problem in relation to the EACSO arose in *Re General Manager EAR and H*, [1966] E.A. 110 but the decision is unhelpful.

On the international plane, the Community has been authorized to negotiate with outside bodies or states, but it is doubtful how far it has power to conclude international agreements, e.g. Articles 51 (5), which authorizes the Community to negotiate bilateral air service agreements on behalf of partner states, but the agreements are actually signed by the territorial government. See, also, the agreement with the E.E.C. and the East African Governments, 1968.

have application throughout the region, but the implementation legislation allowed for the incorporation of decrees of the Authority concerning the corporations promulgated before 31 December 1967. All this involves a significant surrender of their power by the state legislatures. But even more important is the provision they have passed, that any amendments of the Treaty will automatically come into operation in the state, provided that a notice of the amendment is published in the local Gazette and laid before the National Assembly without delay. This provision gives the Authority very wide powers.

There are other ways too in which national laws and obligations are affected by the Treaty. The states have undertaken to co-ordinate their fiscal and monetary policies; and though the state legislatures continue to legislate on these matters, their hands will in fact be tied by the agreements their governments may have made with the other states. The commercial laws of the states may also be revised to achieve harmony, though the Treaty does not specify what laws are comprehended within this term, and in any event, there is already a large measure of uniformity.[107] In the long term, the whole of the arrangements for commodity and marketing boards may come under review; no immediate changes seem necessary, but if the Community's long term aim to co-ordinate agriculture gets under way, the existing arrangements will need radical modifications. We have already discussed the limitations on the partner states in formulating and implementing their economic and industrial policy because of the restrictions of the common market provisions. Further, there is the potentiality of the clash between the judicial tribunals of the Community and the states. Difficult questions of competing jurisdictions can arise; and there is need in particular to clarify the competence of the Industrial Court, since its decisions, unlike those of the Tribunal, will automatically apply to individuals and organizations within the states.

In conclusion, two general comments may be offered. First, though the economic and industrial plans and policies of the partner states are so greatly determined by the provisions of the Treaty, its direct effect on the political systems of the partner states is likely to be small. The strong position given to the governments of the partner states insulates the Community and its institutions against proper political pressures. As we have seen, the national legislatures have lost important powers, and the central legislature is unlikely to exact much accountability from the Authority. The national legislatures can still question their governments on the affairs of the Community, but the responsibility for these affairs is too diffuse to be effectively controlled by them. It would have been desirable to have

[107] W. C. Whitford, 'Harmonization of Commercial Laws under the Treaty for East African Co-operation', *E.A.L.R.* 1 (N.S.) 2, August 1968.

required the East African Ministers to be members of the legislatures of their own countries, *ex officio* if need be, and answerable there for Community affairs.

Secondly, while the Treaty is a remarkable achievement in terms of economic co-operation and its provisions for the common market and the common services constitute East Africa as one of the most advanced areas of regional co-operation, it falls short of the hopes of many East Africans which have transcended forms of merely economic union and extended to the establishment of a federation. It is obvious from the examination of the provisions of the treaty, that there has been only a small surrender of sovereignty, the most significant being the jurisdiction of the Tribunal to give binding decisions—which, however, has not yet begun to function. The principle of unanimity, the weakness of Community institutions, and the basing of the common market on consent rather than strictly on legal obligations, the many exceptions to the general restrictions of national competence, all point towards the supremacy of national governments over the Community, and of a reluctance to take steps that might lead to further economic or political integration. It is true that the Treaty does not preclude a federation, but it might be argued that the Treaty itself is an admission of the failure to federate. The success of the Treaty, paradoxically, may drive further away the hopes of a federation.

Most of the national leaders have made the claim that the Treaty has brought full East African unity nearer. It is true that the Community has wider powers than the East African Common Services Organization, but these powers are wielded through a highly bureaucratic and government-dominated machine. The Assembly of the EACSO had always held out hope as one institution which could readily blossom into a full federal legislature; its downgrading is significant in the attempt to exclude back-bench politics from the new Community. The lack of a proper institution responsive to an East African opinion is a backward step. Nor are the other Community institutions likely to build strong regional loyalties, since the respective governments so dominate them.

PART III

Conclusions

CHAPTER XIII

Conclusions: Constitutionalism, Retrospect and Prospect

The preceding chapters of this book have been concerned with describing and analysing the development of public law in several significant fields in Kenya since that country was first carved out of the African continent some eighty years ago. This has been done in the conviction that law and attitudes towards law have hitherto been rather neglected in studies of developing nations, yet are relevant in any attempt to understand how these nations are governed today. In the common law world in particular, there has been a great willingness to accept at their face value, assertions as to the benefits conferred by the reception of the common law, assertions usually made by those trained in that subject,[1] and little attempt to examine or investigate the effect of such reception on attitudes towards law, government and power, or to consider the relationship between methods of government in African states, including breakdowns and revolutions, and the imported system and concepts of law used in governing.[2] It cannot be claimed that the preceding chapters themselves cover that whole field of investigation, but they do lay the groundwork for some conclusions about the role of law in the development of Kenya, which are put forward in this chapter.

These conclusions may be considered in the context of the question of legitimacy. To what extent are the institutions and procedures of government regarded with trust and confidence by the people of Kenya and what role has the public law of Kenya played, and is playing, in developing the legitimacy of these institutions and procedures? Most new nations are faced with a problem of legitimacy; the institutions of government are new, the people who run them are inexperienced, and the population as a whole has only recently been able to take part in the political process, and then at a period when colonial institutions and authorities were under constant attack. The combination of these factors means that the institutions of government are fragile, and not generally accepted or understood by the populace.

[1] e.g. Roberts-Wray, 'The Adaptation of Imported Law in Africa', 4 *J.A.L.* 66. But see Gower, *Independent Africa: the Challenge to the Legal Profession*, op. cit., pp. 26–30.

[2] One exception is Pye, *Aspects of Political Development* (Boston, Little, Brown & Co., 1966), chapter 6.

Their existence may be known but their relevance, the connection between them and the daily life of the peasant or worker and his attempts to better himself, are not perceived, or are misunderstood. An important task for a new government is to create confidence in, and respect for the institutions of government as such so that they become legitimate in the eyes of the populace who begin to distinguish between the permanent institutions and the transient members of those institutions. The role of law here is crucial for it is usually the means whereby these institutions are used and altered, so that both rulers and ruled will come to associate law and its processes with the development or otherwise of legitimacy. It is for this reason too that the colonial past of the law cannot be neglected. The institutions of an independent government may be new, but the legal system available to that government—the laws and the ways they are used—are not, and it is a fair assumption that people's attitudes towards the new institutions and the new rulers will be affected by their experience of the legal system and whether it continues as before.

The question posed above may be answered first; the reasons for that answer will be discussed in the rest of the chapter. The legitimacy of the institutions of government, and the legal processes whereby they are created, altered, and operated, in short the Constitution and public law of Kenya, hang in the balance. Whereas confidence in the institutions and mode of government was generated in the first two and a half years of independence, a turning point seems to have occurred in mid 1966. From that time, the Government has become increasingly careless of the need for legitimacy, and the dictates of constitutionalism, in their alterations of the Constitution and their administration of the laws relating to government and administration, and there is a corresponding loss of confidence in, and increase in cynicism about, these matters amongst some important sections of the ruled. Although an analysis of the underlying trends of Kenya's constitutional and legal inheritance cannot provide a full explanation for this present state of affairs, it will provide a background which in turn may help towards an understanding of the Government's and the governed's attitude, the institutions of government, and their operation at present. We may consider first some general conclusions about public law in Kenya and the reception of the common law as described in the earlier chapters.

The role of public law in the colonial era, when looked at through the eyes of the colonized, provides one of the best examples there is of the operation of law as expounded by adherents of the Austinian theory of law. 'Orders backed by threats', 'the gunman situation writ large', these phrases most adequately describe what is more usually but less accurately called the reception of the English common law. Law was second only to weapons of war in the establishment of colonial rule, and for the early settlers and officials there was little difference between the two; they were both useful implements to coerce the African. Acceptance of this role of the law was not universal amongst colonial officials, but it was the dominant view. The conflict between administrative and judicial viewpoints on the administration of criminal justice discussed in chapter III occurred in other fields as well, notably in the discussions preceding the drafting of the Foreign Jurisdiction Act, and the Orders in Council made thereunder in the 1890s, and was basically a conflict between those who saw law as a system of orders backed by threats, and those who knew that law had traditional associations, at least in the metropolitan country, with notions of justice which in turn were concerned with equality before the law, regularity and impartiality in the administration of the law, and the use of the law to protect the citizen against oppression, public or private, economic or political. Looking at the development of colonial power in the areas discussed in the first part of this book there is little doubt as to which conception of law prevailed for which category of people in the colonial era.

It is important to appreciate that more was involved here than just the fact that different sets of rules were applied to Africans and non-Africans. A different philosophy and style of law and its administration applied to the two groups. The Austinian philosophy inspired the former set of rules, but something akin to a philosophy of natural rights, derived from a belief that English settlers took the common law and representative government with them and were entitled to all their rights and privileges, inspired the latter set of rules. In relation to agrarian administration, these sets of rules have been characterized as coercive and co-operative, and these terms well sum up the two approaches of the colonial law giver. Africans were to be coerced into performing their required role in society, whether it was to work, to pay taxes, to live in a particular place or to move about the country, and thus the criminal law, and courts to enforce it, were in many respects the key institutions in native administration for they underpinned the whole approach of the colonial administrator. Hence these administrators spent much time in tinkering with the native courts, to make them more efficient, and resisted attempts to remove them from their control, or radically alter the function which they themselves performed as magistrates and supervisors of the native courts.

Europeans on the other hand were invited to, perhaps a more accurate description would be, were conceded as a result of their demands, a great degree of co-operation in the administration of the law, whether in the field of government, in the Legislative and Executive Councils, in agrarian policies, on boards and committees, or in the judicial system via the jury, a legally qualified judge, and the application to them of all the safeguards of an English criminal trial. The dual system of administration in Kenya therefore was derived in part at least from these two different philosophies of law, and their practical implementation.

A matter of major significance for the development of public law in Kenya is that the inequalities in the administration of the law to which the coercive and co-operative approaches gave rise were also inherent in the introduction of the common law system into Kenya. One of the characteristics of any legal system from the point of view of the ordinary citizen, which is often also one of its defects, is that it can be activated only if one knows one's rights, knows the mechanics of doing something about protecting those rights, and has the money to pay somebody to take the necessary action. This characteristic or defect is accentuated in the common law system with its great emphasis on the protection of private rights, and its system of case-law which increases the difficulty of knowing what one's rights are. In the field of public law matters are made worse by the tradition of administrative disinclination to have discretion bound by legal rules, and the complexity of the remedies available to control the administration.

To introduce such a system into Kenya together with a whole battery of repressive and regulatory laws on Africans was to introduce an unequal system of law from the start. It was a system which the ruling minority knew and could operate, and the ruled majority did not know and could not operate. Thus a rule which the former class of persons would regard as basic to the system, and evidence of its essential fairness—for example, the right to challenge the actions of government officials in open court—was virtually denied to the latter class, either by the iniquitous doctrine of Act of State, itself a rule of the common law, or by the ignorance of this class coupled with the fact that the courts and access to them were often controlled by the very administrators whose conduct one wished to challenge. Such concessions as were made to Africans—for example, the use of assessors in criminal trials, or the application of customary law to land disputes—were more apparent than real, for the extent of their actual, as opposed to their formal, use depended on the willingness of colonial officials to use them, and in any event customary law did not apply to disputes with the administration. Executive discretion unfettered by law was, to some extent, controlled by political means as far as Europeans were concerned through their system of co-operative administration, but such a system did not apply to Africans for most of the colonial period. Thus Africans in Kenya came to political awareness within a legal system whose rhetoric praised equality and justice but whose practice sharply distinguished between those with, and those without, power, wealth and influence. The reception of the common law into Kenya in short created a two class society as regards law whose resultant development can be summed up in a paraphrase of Belloc's famous couplet:

> Whatever happens, we have got
> The common law, and they have not.[3]

Such an inheritance cannot but breed cynicism and a lack of respect for the processes of the law. The law is seen solely as being a tool of the wielders of power who use it as they think fit, legalizing their own illegal exercises of power, and attempting to prevent the acquisition of power by, and the development of, the powerless. Only superior power, in the shape of Her Majesty's Government, could alter this state of affairs, and that was called into play by 'illegal' protests against the law, and not by adherence to lawful or constitutional forms.

Such an inheritance has also been inimical to the development of constitutionalism. To understand how this has come about, the development of constitutional law in Kenya must be analysed. In so far as a constitution is generally accepted as being a body of rules which define and limit the exercise of governmental power, and regulate major political activity in the state, it may be said that until very late in the colonial era, Kenya had no constitution, and political activity took place without regard to a constitutional framework. The ultimate arbiter of power was the Colonial Secretary in London, and he was not bound by legal rules, though political considerations at home and in Kenya might have a limiting effect on his exercise of power. The Orders in Council and Royal Instructions which provided the legal backing for administration in Kenya were not concerned with limitations on power or even very often with the way power was to be exercised; rather they were concerned firstly with broad divisions of functions between Executive, Legislature, and Judiciary, always reserving final power for the Executive in the person of the Governor, and secondly, with providing outlets for the ventilation of a small section of public opinion. The autocratic basis of colonial rule coupled with frequent changes of Governor and Colonial Secretary—there were eighteen of the former and thirty of the latter between the declaration of the protectorate in 1895 and independence in 1963—with the consequent shifts in policy which that entailed, hindered the development of the idea of a government of laws, and not of men. Whatever the rules might say, politicians in Kenya knew that if they applied sufficient

[3] The original couplet is:

> Whatever happens, we have got
> The Maxim gun, and they have not.

Written in 1898, the incident in verse from which the couplet is taken is thought to be based on Lugard's use of the Maxim gun in storming Mengo in 1892. Hilaire Belloc, *The Modern Traveller* in *Verse* (London, Nonesuch Press, 1954), p. 184. See the interesting correspondence on the matter in *The Times Literary Supplement*, 26 September, 3 and 10 October 1968.

pressure for a sufficient length of time on key individuals, the rules would be quietly ignored or changed to suit their convenience. Thus, although important issues were often debated in the Legislative Council so that the idea of a representative legislature was early in existence in Kenya, both sides there—colonial officials and politicians, first settlers, and later Asians and Africans—knew that power lay elsewhere, and pressure had to be applied through other channels. At the same time, therefore, as the idea of a representative legislature was being ventilated, its irrelevance to the exercise of power was also being demonstrated. Again, although the constitutional system established by Order in Council was used from time to time to present claims to the colonial authorities, these claims were often directed to the demolition of the system; where such claims were successful, and they usually were, they demonstrated both the efficacy and the impermanence of constitutional rules at one and the same time. Generally, however, constitutional law appeared to be like any other part of imported law; it provided benefits for those with power, but it could be altered by a sufficient display of force.

Not until the late fifties did a colonial constitution in Kenya address itself to the problems of the limitation of executive power, and go into considerable detail on how power was to be exercised. But if this made the 1958 Kenya (Constitution) Order in Council more recognizable as a constitution, it still suffered for another of its predecessors' defects, in that no one in Kenya regarded it as permanent, and few regarded agitation by all possible means against its continuance as being wrong. Indeed at the very time when constitutional law was becoming more and more detailed, and covering a wider and wider area of public and political conduct in Kenya so that it was more and more necessary that it be seen as a set of rules different from, and more fundamental than, the ordinary law, constitutional Orders in Council came and went with bewildering frequency. Far from being the most fundamental law of the land, the constitutional law of Kenya from 1958 to independence was the least fundamental, undergoing major changes two or three times a year.

At independence, however, a complete change of attitude towards the constitution was assumed to have taken place and statements were made by the independent government which led the unwary to believe that such a change had indeed taken place. It was only later that the old pattern of a contrast between rhetoric and practice was seen to be still in existence, but precisely because hopes had been raised at independence of a new approach, the continuance of the old has come as that much of a greater let-down.

The new approach to the constitution, put forward by both the departing colonial authorities and incoming new authorities, was that the constitution was henceforth to be regarded as permanent, as being the basic and fundamental law of the land hammered out by agreement between all relevant political groups in the various pre-independence constitutional conferences. It was deemed to have fixed once and for all the divisions of power between the various governing authorities in Kenya, provided an elaborate set of checks and balances, and topped the whole thing off with a wide ranging Bill of Rights, and a Supreme Court, composed of a judiciary whose appointment was utterly insulated from any taint of political factors.

It may readily be admitted that the independent Government of Kenya was as aware as the governments of other new nations of the importance of starting off independent nationhood with a new constitution. As has been remarked by several political commentators,[4] the process of constitution making is a symbol of a new state; a constitution transforms a population living within a colonial territory into an independent state, and it is the first and most important step on the road towards the legitimacy of the institutions of government. It is, in short, a symbol of nationhood. But to regard a constitution as a symbol of nationhood, and to regard it as a fundamental and immutable law are two different things, not always clearly distinguished in the rhetoric put out about the importance of a constitution. The Government of Kenya may have regarded the Constitution as the first; it did not regard it as the second, as previous chapters have shown. It has brought to its operation of the Constitution something of the traditional approach. The Constitution is not in practice seen as an umpire above the political struggle, but as a weapon in that struggle which can be used and altered in order to gain temporary and passing advantages over one's political opponents. Looking at the alterations to the Constitution, and the changing administration of several allied laws, for example those concerned with elections and the holding of meetings, it seems undeniable that while the inspiration of changes in the first two years of independence was to escape from the straitjacket of the independence Constitution that was deliberately designed to prevent the government from exercising powers available to all previous governments, changes since then have had as their main aim an increase in the powers of the Executive, a decrease in the powers or status of those institutions whose function it is to try and control the Executive, and a whittling away of legal safeguards on the exercise of power by the Executive. It must be doubted if effective controls exist now on even the most obvious abuse of power. Increasingly, executive authority is exercised through powers and procedures which the Constitution contemplates as exceptional. In many important respects, whole sections of the Constitution

[4] Shils, 'The Fortunes of Constitutional Government in the Political Development of New States' in Hallowell (ed.), *Development For What?* (Durham, Duke University, 1964); Friedrich, 'Some Reflections on Constitutionalism for Emergent Political Orders' in Spiro (ed.), *Patterns of African Development: Five Comparisons* (Englewood Cliffs, N. J., Prentice Hall, 1967).

have been suspended; and the suspension has been in effect for so long that they have ceased to have any influence on the practice of law and administration, and remain only as sad reminders of earlier hopes.

Though the traditional approach to the constitution may be in evidence, there is one vital difference from the colonial period. Then, the contestants in the political struggle ignored the constitutional law and appealed to the supreme political power, the Governor or the Colonial Secretary. Now, one of the contestants is the supreme political power, so that an alteration to the law in favour of that side is much more obviously partial, and likely to lead to greater disillusionment with the idea of a constitution, and hence to the whole system's forfeiture of legitimacy. This process may well be hastened by the method and rhetoric used by the government when it alters or operates the Constitution. Great stress is laid on the continuity of legal forms. The basic constitutional document was still, after ten amending Acts, the second schedule to the Kenya (Independence) Order in Council 1963. When a revised version of the Constitution was finally published as a Bill in November 1968, it was made clear that this was merely a tidying up operation of no particular political significance and in the presentation of the new Constitution Act of 1969, its consolidating nature is what was emphasized by the Government, to the extent that it overlooked to bring to the attention of Parliament all the changes it introduced. The previous form was retained moreover; the Constitution was enacted as the second schedule to an Act of Parliament. This is part of a deliberate policy of emphasizing that Kenya is not a revolutionary state, but is dedicated to orderly constitutional progress in the British tradition. Stress is also often laid in speeches on the government's willingness to abide by the Constitution in its daily work, and the high regard in which it holds Parliament and the courts. But the contrast between form and speech which assumes a constitution limiting government's power and respected by the Government, and substance and practice which shows a reverse position is very obvious: less hypocrisy on the part of the Government, which is indeed in the British colonial tradition, might mean less disillusionment with the direction of its changes.

One change which the Government has not introduced by law, though sometimes pressed to by its more ardent supporters, is a one party state, and this may be taken as a very good illustration of the gap between rhetoric and practice. To introduce a one party state by law, to ban all opposition parties and proclaim KANU the one lawful party would be to alter drastically Kenya's image as an evolutionary mature state, and it is therefore opposed by the Government. But the Government is not opposed to the gradual introduction of a one party state, and increasingly the administration of many of the rules of public law has discouraged the expression of dissent, or the formation of political groups opposing KANU. A legal ban on opposition parties is a rather crude use of law to maintain oneself in power, though it would be perfectly possible under the law in Kenya now; a more sophisticated approach is so to exercise powers under the law that an opposition party finds itself virtually unable to carry on because it cannot reach its supporters, who for their part find that they are suffering through lack of government development funds and projects. The form of opposition is left with a minuscule opposition party in the National Assembly, but the substance has disappeared, or at least, disappeared from view. That this is possible within a constitutional framework which appears to safeguard rights of opposition and dissent further serves to undermine its legitimacy.

The decision not to create a one-party state, or to elevate the ruling party into a formal constitutional role, reflects another important facet of constitutional development. Party politics of any sort are increasingly being played down so that even KANU does not have an active political role in government, e.g. in mobilizing the people for development. Kenya is becoming once again a bureaucratic state in which administrators, a term which here includes Ministers, take precedence over politicians, particularly MPs and local party officials. This development too is not without its dangers, for the party which achieved independence has often served the function of bringing a nation into being by making people aware of their national as opposed to their tribal, racial or local identity. To allow the party to atrophy is to run the risk of allowing this national outlook to atrophy and parochialism to reassert itself. In Kenya, a national identity is to some extent still preserved in the office, and more particularly in the present holder of the office, of President, but how will it be preserved when he is gone, and KANU is moribund?

We have so far looked at the colonial and post-colonial approaches towards constitutions, and have seen that whatever bright hopes there were at independence of a new dawn, they have not been fulfilled. Politicians, whose early experiences were under the former approach, are not going to change when they reach a position where they can benefit from it. There are, however, two further factors to be considered which affect the long-term prospects for constitutionalism in Kenya. The first is the basic conflict that exists between the philosophies of the constitution—certainly as it was at independence, and as the rhetoric has it that it still is—and the administrative process.

In older countries, a constitution and its values emerge from the values of the society at large so that its values reflect those of society or a large part of it. In Kenya, however, the Constitution was designed to introduce liberal democratic values, of which constitutionalism (the limitation of the powers of government, the assurance of the rights of the citizens) and representation (the government must be regularly elected by, and responsive to, the people) are among the most important, and these were values which, while they may have existed in traditional societies in Kenya, did not exist in the society established by colonial rule. For the vast majority of the population, the values of colonial society were autocratic, and took the form of an authoritarian administrative structure. Thus this structure and its values were at variance with the Constitution and its values, and it is the Constitution which has been adjusted to the administrative structure, and not, as was clearly envisaged, the other way round. Indeed, as the chapter on the administrative system has shown, while the segregated administrative system has been brought to an end, the co-operative approach to administration which was a characteristic of the European side of it has tended to be played down. Ministers have sought and obtained more powers over administrative institutions such as public corporations and licensing authorities, and have used these powers to reward their supporters and penalize their opponents. Far from the Constitution being instrumental in introducing greater standards of objectivity into administration, its existence has coincided with an increase in political partiality in administration. The seeming irrelevance of the Constitution in these circumstances will again adversely affect its legitimacy.

Secondly, it would appear that not enough thought has been given to the effects that the implementation of the economic policies contained in the Development Plan may have on the confidence accorded the Constitution. The implementation of the Development Plan necessitates both an increase in central governmental control over the administration, and the passage of many new laws. There is less autonomy for local authorities or public corporations, more central direction and an increase in legal regulation of many daily activities. The administration is being overloaded with work and legislation is being passed which then remains either a virtual dead letter or is bypassed and ignored through the lack of administrators to enforce it. The later passage of retrospective amendments may correct administrative shortcomings but hardly increases respect for the law. Every increase in the legal regulation of economic activities brings a corresponding increase in attempts to circumvent the law, and engage in extra-legal activities. Failure to deal with this brings the law into contempt, and lessens respect for its enforcers.

It may be argued, however, that the disciplines of the Development Plan require increased administrative power and discretion and increased enforcement procedures, and that the law cannot be allowed to impede the taking of such decisions and the execution of such policies as the exigencies of the Plan demand. It may readily be conceded that no system of public law, least of all that in a developing country, should be designed so as to impede necessary governmental action, but this would be an argument for restructuring, not whittling down, the safeguards the law provides in respect of administrative action. The objects of legal regulation of governmental decision-making and administration are to ensure that decisions are rationally made, after all points of view have been considered, and if necessary reconsidered on appeal; that their implementation is efficient, and imposes no avoidable inconvenience on the administered; that where benefits are to be conferred the criteria for their conferment are publicly known and defensible; and that where administrators are negligent or actuated by malice they can be brought to book. Such objects are perfectly compatible with effective government by plan, and indeed should be regarded as an essential precondition to the success of the Plan.

Unfortunately this point does not appear to be understood by the Government, for in an attempt to increase the effectiveness of the administration, wider discretions are conferred upon officials by law, and these officials are prepared to take, and can get away with taking, short-cuts. It is here that a glaring discrepancy exists between the rhetoric and the practice of the exercise of power. Few actions could have better demonstrated the sincerity of government's intention to keep within the spirit of the Constitution than a broadening, simplifying and cheapening of the remedies available to challenge administrative action, and in particular, a replacing, with something more straightforward, of the archaic formalism of the prerogative orders, surely the most ludicrously inadequate remedies to exist in a nation of peasant farmers and ill-paid workers, which has no system of legal aid. Rather than wait for the development of a system of administrative law through the decisions of courts—the traditional common law approach which is being questioned even in its original home where there is a greater willingness to challenge, and understanding of, the mechanics of challenging administrative action in the courts—the government could give consideration to introducing a simple code of administrative procedure, covering such points as right to a hearing, time-limit for the giving of administrative decisions, opportunities and methods of challenging administrative decisions, powers of officials to enter one's land, search one's papers, etc., or demand facilities for doing so, liability of officials for negligence, and establishing a general administrative appeal tribunal or Ombudsman, with power to act on complaints, formal or informal, or even on no complaints at all, to exercise general supervision over the administration. Far from taking such action, however, the Government has cut down, in several statutes, the possibility of challenge to administrative action in the courts and has peremptorily dismissed suggestions that an Ombudsman or equivalent institution might be established.[5] Yet development can only take place if peasants and workers co-operate in government plans, and this is more likely to happen if they have

[5] National Assembly, *Debates*, volume XV (31 May 1968), cols. 987–989.

some opportunity of satisfying themselves that the increasing powers of the Government are being used wisely and honestly, and of seeking redress if they are not so satisfied. This use of the law to increase the power of Government and decrease the opportunities of challenge to it in the name of development will result in development itself becoming suspect, and losing its legitimacy as a unifying force in, and rallying call to, the nation.

Much of this analysis of the trends of public law in Kenya seeks to relate the present to the past. To that extent therefore it is arguable that the Government should not be criticized for its present performance. But there are factors present which prevent such a convenient position being adopted. Though the legal framework and traditions of colonial authoritarianism and partiality might remain, the independent Government of Kenya is an elected government, brought into being as the end product of a long period of political agitation whose driving force was the inherent unfairness of the colonial system and the need to replace it with representative institutions and government. It might be expected therefore that such a government would make strenuous efforts to avoid following colonial traditions as far as possible, and it is a valid cause for criticism that that has not occurred.

Over and above that fact, however, is the threat to the legitimacy and stability of the whole political system that the continuation of the colonial approach entails. Precisely because expectations of a new approach to governing were raised by the Government in 1963, and because of its continued reference in speeches to its commitments to the law and the Constitution, the Government's falling back on colonial rules and practices, its harassing of political opponents, its blatant conferring of benefits on its own supporters and its manipulation of the Constitution for its own ends comes as a greater disillusionment to people. The Government has been well aware of the need energetically to tackle long-standing economic problems, particularly those of land ownership and use, and the relationship between them and political stability, but does not seem to have the same awareness of the need to foster constitutionalism, its role therein, and the relationship between that and political stability. This is the more surprising because the Government of Kenya, more than any other government of an independent country within the Commonwealth, should be only too well aware of the dangers of a widespread loss of confidence in the efficacy of the Constitution and the impartiality of legal processes.

Notwithstanding these points, it may be thought that this final chapter has been unduly critical of the conduct of the Government. It could be argued that the preceding chapters have shown that the Government has made great strides in removing the grosser inequalities of the colonial system, particularly the dual system of administration and justice, and if it has failed so far to remove some of the basic inequalities inherent in the reception of the common law into Kenya, it has at least made a start in that direction, and has received little assistance from the legal profession, whom one might suppose ought to be more concerned with the matter, in so doing. It has done this during a period for part of which it was saddled with an unwieldy Constitution. Moreover at independence, the country was deeply divided and there was armed rebellion along parts of its borders. It is to the credit of the Government that it was able to maintain the integrity of its territory, and then to create unity and consensus out of the bitter strife of the immediate pre-independence period.

But a consideration of the underlying trends of constitutional and legal developments, also indicated in preceding chapters, makes it difficult to take an optimistic view of Kenya's constitutional future. The dual system may have been dismantled, but so have many safeguards against abuse of power. The running sore of the *shifta* may have been ended, but the emergency powers first applied, with the approval of Parliament, to the North Eastern Province to deal with it, now extend in an amplified fashion throughout the whole country, with no requirement of a parliamentary check on them. The Constitution is altered in a lawful manner after a full debate in the National Assembly, but the substance of the alterations reduces its significance as a set of checks and balances on executive power. Parliament and the courts continue to be praised for the performance of their functions, but their power significantly to affect executive action continues to be whittled away. The Government claims that it has the support of the people, but deferred general elections, the disqualification on technical grounds of all opposition candidates in local elections in the middle of 1968, and the constant alteration of the laws on elections make this claim seem increasingly questionable.

Indeed, the electoral laws and their administration pose the crucial issues for the legitimacy of the constitutional system and therefore of the future political stability of Kenya. As the law stood at the coming into effect of the Constitution Act 1969, Parliament was to stand dissolved by 7 June 1970, and presidential and parliamentary elections would have taken place after that date.[6] Elections have been postponed once—from 1968 to 1970—and while there is no particular virtue in a five year cycle of elections as opposed to a six or seven year cycle,[7] further postponement would extend the period since the last general elections to beyond seven years, and the longer the period since the last elections, the more difficult it is to justify further

[6] Constitution section 128. See 'Postscript' for General Elections, December 1969.
[7] Senators in the U.S.A. are elected for six year periods, the President of France, under the Fifth Republic, for seven years. From time to time amendments have been proposed in Congress in the U.S.A. which would lengthen the President's term to six years. Parliaments in the United Kingdom could last for up to seven years between 1716 and 1911.

postponements. It might be argued, however, that there was a sufficiently representative parliamentary election in 1966, that elections are in any event time and administration consuming, and that the business of economic development necessitates unpopular decisions from time to time which it would be impossible to take if elections were to intervene before their benefits could be seen. But such arguments would overlook that the National Assembly of 1969 has been transformed out of all recognition from the National Assembly elected in 1963. It is unicameral rather than bicameral, many electors are not represented by the MPs for whom they originally voted, and others are no longer represented by the party—KADU—for whom they originally voted. These facts alone might seem to justify elections. But over and above them, arguments questioning the use of elections have to face the unpalatable fact that experiences in other parts of Africa suggest that the alternative to elections is not the continuation of strong government, but repression or revolution or both, and no one in government today can be sure that he may not be the victim of either tomorrow. Elections on the basis of universal adult suffrage were one of the main goals of African politicians when in opposition and the institution now appears to be too much a part of the political culture of African nations to be done away with.

A decision to have elections by 1970, however, will raise some of the following questions: what sort of elections shall there be; shall they be contested and, if so, by whom; who is to stand for the Presidency if President Kenyatta does not; should President Kenyatta stand for re-election? These are not idle questions, for many of the more recent constitutional amendments and practices have had as one aim the elimination of chance in the succession to the Presidency, and the assurance, so far as rules can assure such things, that party and government leaders will be able to effect a smooth succession, and then continue with the business of running the government. Elections could pose a threat to this arrangement, as they do to the whittling down of effective methods of control over, and accountability of, the Executive, and a reduction in the political influence of the Legislature, other aims of constitutional amendments and practices; so it is reasonable to suppose that the decision to have elections, and if so, what kind, will be considered in this context.

At the back of most politicians' considerations about elections lies the threat they pose to their retention of power. This is in fact the crux of the problem not merely for elections, but for the whole trend of constitutional development in Kenya. Whether power is seen and used as an avenue for the acquisition of wealth or as providing an opportunity to assist in the development of one's country, or both, there seems to come a point when the politician, especially if he is a Minister, decides that he is indispensable, and that this justifies postponing or 'managing' an election. No provision of any constitution limiting the number of occasions a person may stand for office would be very effective here (and Kenya's Constitution contains no such provisions) for they would be the first provisions to be changed in any programme of managed elections. Yet without an acceptance of the possibility of loss of office and/or seat in the National Assembly by Ministers and MPs it is doubtful whether meaningful elections can take place.

We have argued earlier in the chapter that the legitimacy of the constitutional system is threatened by the way the political leaders of Kenya are exercising their powers. Legitimacy can refer to two distinct situations, charismatic legitimacy and institutional legitimacy.[8] The former refers to an acceptance, as valid and proper, of a constitutional system only because certain political leaders, in this context, usually those who obtained independence, occupy key positions within it, the latter to the acceptance, as valid and proper, of a constitutional system as such. We did not distinguish between the two because the way in which political leaders exercise power within a constitutional system affects both, but of the two, the latter is the more important, much the more difficult to create, yet much the more necessary to create if the constitutional system is to have any chance of survival. What has to be done is to transform charismatic into institutional legitimacy and elections can play an extremely important role here for they can be used as the mechanism whereby one generation of political leaders can gradually hand over power to another within the framework of a constitution. In order to be used for this purpose, however, some acceptance of loss of office is clearly necessary.

This cannot be brought about by the enactment of a constitutional rule providing for compulsory retirement from office, but it may be assisted into being by an example of a voluntary retirement; indeed it may be that only a dramatic example of voluntary retirement at the top would make the point in a forceful enough way. If the constitutional system is significantly to outlive its creators, its legitimacy must be divorced from that of theirs. While one way of achieving this is by meaningful elections, another is via voluntary relinquishment of office, which might, besides demonstrating confidence in and enhancing the status of the constitutional system, materially assist towards the acceptance of the former method.

Parliamentary elections should, however, be held by 1970; MPs like Ministers are reluctant to risk losing their position through the polls. In

[8]These terms are adopted from Weber's 'three pure types of legitimate authority', legal authority, traditional authority, and charismatic authority. See his *The Theory of Social and Economic Organization* (New York, Free Press of Glencoe, 1964), p. 328 et seq. See, too, Singham, *The Hero and the Crowd in a Colonial Polity* (New Haven, Yale University Press, 1968), for a useful discussion on the problem of legitimizing a constitutional system in a colonial and post-colonial situation.

the past, this might have occurred through the perennial Kenyan problem—brought about through weak party discipline—of party 'independents' standing against and winning a seat from the official party candidate, but the 1968 constitutional amendment eliminating all independents and unofficial party candidates should prevent that happening again. But this in turn could give great power to the central organs of the political parties, and in practice, therefore, virtual control over the composition of the next Parliament to the central organ of KANU. Were this to happen, another important aspect of the creation of institutional legitimacy—that of participation by the people in the formation of the Legislature and the Executive—would have been put aside. The introduction of party primaries, also provided for in 1968, could however, offset this by ensuring a meaningful participation by local party members in the electoral process, as well as making slightly more palatable to MPs their failure to be re-nominated, if such be the case. It is essential therefore that these primaries be conducted openly and fairly, and their results generally accepted by the president of the party—the official nominating authority.[9]

Elections contribute to the legitimacy of the constitutional system by allowing for popular participation, and succession to power within it. But another important function of elections is to provide a channel for the expression of demands and grievances by the people to the government, and the medium through which this is generally done is the Legislature. An active and politically influential legislature can itself be a major legitimizing factor in the constitutional system, and for all its shortcomings, the Kenyan National Assembly has so far performed this role. As we have seen, its lack of docility has not been entirely welcome to the Government, and the electoral system now provided for by law gives the Government another opportunity to try and ensure that the National Assembly consists only of obedient MPs. But whatever short-term benefits this seems to bring, the long-term effects of deactivating the National Assembly on the legitimacy of the constitutional system may be severe. This is yet another reason for holding meaningful elections.

In the final analysis, however, the future of Kenyan constitutionalism depends not upon the rules of the Constitution, nor the opinions of the commentators, but largely on the actions of the politicians. Given the colonial heritage of a society divided along economic, racial and tribal lines, and an administration that paid scant regards to the wishes of the majority, saddled with an overweight and unrealistic Constitution at independence, and facing

[9] This was the position in the Tanzanian General Elections of 1965. See McAuslan and Ghai, 'Constitutional Innovation and Political Stability in Tanzania: A Preliminary Assessment' (1966) 4 *J.M.A.S.* 479 at pp. 488–93; L. Cliffe (ed.), *One Party Democracy: The 1965 Tanzanian General Elections* (Nairobi, East African Publishing House, 1967).

almost insurmountable problems of development, the political leaders of Kenya have made striking progress, and have much to be praised for. But they run the risk of throwing much of their good work away by slipping into an unnecessary authoritarianism. Elections by 1970 will provide an opportunity for a reconsideration of this trend, and will show whether that opportunity has been accepted or rejected. It is for this reason that their conduct is of crucial importance to the future of constitutionalism in Kenya.

POSTSCRIPT:

General Elections, December 1969

When the constitutional amendment abolishing the independent candidates for Parliament was proposed, the MPs were rather apprehensive of the way in which the new rules requiring party nomination might be operated. They wanted to know the detailed provisions affecting nomination, and so the Government published a bill which set out the procedure.[1] It gave a considerable say to the officials and the committee members of the party, and followed largely the system that was used in the local government elections of 1969. Alarmed, however, by the practices at that election, and, as they saw it, the possibilities of manipulation of nomination, the back-benchers agitated for a more democratic method of nomination. There was also the feeling that the KANU failure in the Gem by-election in May 1969 was as a result of an undemocratic method of nominating KANU's candidate.

As a result a new Bill was introduced in July 1969 which provided that all the supporters of a party in the constituency should participate in the preliminaries for that constituency. There were still a few provisions of the Bill which the MPs found unacceptable, including the proposal that the votes might be cast by queuing behind a candidate of one's choice. MPs also objected to the wide powers given to the Minister to make regulations and determine certain points unresolved in the Bill, which they regarded as usurpation of the constitutional functions of the Electoral Commission, despite an assurance from the Speaker that he thought otherwise.

Both these criticisms were met to some extent by the Government; the provision about queuing was abolished and voting was to be by secret ballot, and though the Minister's powers were not removed, it was provided in the Act that the regulations had to be laid before the National Assembly for approval before they came into effect. One provision, however, on which the Government refused to compromise concerned the role of the party in the nomination process. No rules were provided in this respect in the Bill, it being specified that a candidate had to be validly nominated in accordance with the rules of the party, so that presumably the party was free to determine any rules it wished. The Attorney-General had indicated that once a candidate was electorally qualified and a member of the party, he could put himself up for nomination, but several members expressed their anxiety and felt that whatever concession the Government had made in the new Bill

[1] See p. 317, above.

might be nullified if the party leaders were free to manipulate the party rules for nomination.[2] As the Act now stands, it is merely provided that a candidate has to be qualified under, and has to comply with, any provisions of the constitution or rules of the political party concerned relating to members of that party who wished to stand as candidates at preliminary elections. Furthermore, the Act is silent on the nomination process for the Presidency.

The Act[3] came into force on 21 August 1969, and at a meeting of the Governing Council of KANU on 28 August at Mombasa, the Party nominated Mzee Kenyatta as its sole presidential candidate, and set out its own rules for party nomination. All prospective candidates had to make an oath of loyalty to the Party and the President, and declare their support for the constitution and the policies of KANU. They had to notify party officials in advance of their intention to stand, and deposit a non-returnable shs. 1,000/- with the party headquarters. On compliance with these provisions, the party headquarters would issue the candidate with a certificate of compliance.[4]

The situation changed dramatically in October. Following certain disturbances on the visit of the President to Kisumu, the stronghold of the KPU, the Government proceeded to arrest all the KPU MPs, plus some other officials. This was on 28 October and two days later the KPU was banned, and its leaders put under preventive detention. Kenya thus once again became a one-party system, and the Government soon announced its intention to go to the polls before the end of the year, though it had generally been assumed previously that elections would not be held until 1970. Registration of voters had been carried out in September, and on 7 November the President dissolved Parliament.

Despite the fact of only one lawful party, keen interest was shown in the elections, and a large number of people indicated their intention to contest the KANU preliminaries, success in which would be tantamount to election to the National Assembly. However, several of the prospective candidates were disappointed when the Party issued further rules for nomination:[5] civil servants, unless they resigned, were barred; if a candidate already occupied a public position to which he had been elected with party support, he was not eligible for nomination—this particularly affected the local government councillors; and finally, it was stipulated that a candidate had to show that he had been a member of KANU six months before the nomination, which rule, however, could be waived by the President of the Party, and was in fact so waived in a small number of cases, the outstanding being those of

[2] See National Assembly, *Debates*, 22 July 1969.
[3] The National Assembly and Presidential Elections Act, No. 13 of 1969.
[4] *E.A. Standard*, 30 August 1969.
[5] *E.A. Standard*, 17 and 18 November 1969.

the former deputy leader of the KPU, Mr. Kaggia, and a former KPU member and mayor of Kisumu, Mrs. Onyango. Elections were held under the auspices of the party; candidates had to share the platform, and individual candidates were not allowed to issue their own manifesto. The party had avowed not to support any particular candidates, though in practice important leaders campaigned in favour of particular candidates. In the end altogether 616 candidates satisfied party rules and contested the preliminaries; and only in eight constituencies, including that of the President and the Vice-President, was there one candidate.

Even though the KANU rules had the result of disqualifying some prospective candidates, most members were able to contest the preliminaries, and the rule of the abolition of the independents was to some extent mitigated, since in the past the independents tended to be party members anyway. The right to vote was available widely, since a voter did not have to produce evidence of membership to the KANU party; a verbal declaration of support for it was enough to qualify as a voter. Thus, despite the ban on the KPU, the elections provided for a large element of choice to the voters. In the result, 5 Ministers, 13 Assistant Ministers, and more than 60 other MPs lost their seats.

It may thus be said that the authoritarianism implied in the ban of the KPU has been offset by relatively free elections, in which people have had a chance to throw out leaders in whom they had lost confidence. There has been choice, but the whole series of circumstances surrounding the elections must cast some doubt on how much of a change of heart the Government has undergone. A significant point of view was excluded from competing; the only opposition party was banned just before the election and not allowed to contest the elections. The elections were therefore not to provide for a new government; President Kenyatta was to continue as head of government, though individual Ministers might lose. The elections have, consequently, not solved the succession problem. Another outcome of the elections might be the continued fluidity of KANU politics, as several former KPU members have now joined it, and can participate in politics only through it. KANU may thus continue to provide an umbrella for all; and allow for some democracy within its framework. It must be borne in mind, however, that a large influx of new MPs will, initially at least, place the back-benchers at a disadvantage—in terms of parliamentary procedure and tactics—to the Government, the key members of which have been returned to power, and this may detract from the effectiveness of the National Assembly.

Appendix

Footnote 57 (Chapter 5)

Region	*Major Tribes*	*Population*
Central	Kikuyu	1,233,343
	Embu	91,684
	Meru	435,434
	Kamba	39,325
	Total	1,909,603*
Coastal	Mijikenda	413,489
	Teita	81,119
	Pokomo	22,311
	Arabs	30,261
	Kamba	30,120
	Luo	17,743
	Swahili	11,171
	Kikuyu	10,719
	Total	727,844*
Nyanza	Luo	1,061,621
	Luhya	925,370
	Kisii	530,728
	Kipsigis	286,113
	Iteso	64,080
	Kuria	40,482
	Kikuyu	21,032
	Total	3,012,468*
Rift Valley	Kikuyu	278,728
	Nandi	137,924
	Tugen	109,041
	Luhya	106,440
	Elegeyo	100,294
	Pokot	76,317
	Marakwet	66,747
	Kipsigis	35,671
	Total	1,049,136*

Region	*Major Tribes*	*Population*
Southern	Kamba	821,466
	Masai	139,913
	Kipsigis	16,676
	Kikuyu	10,768
	Total	1,013,977*
Northern Province	Turkana	169,279
	Ogaden	121,235
	Hawiyah	84,208
	Boran	56,881
	Samburu	47,174
	Gurreh	34,565
	Ajuran	19,885
	Rendille	13,645
	Total	590,084*
North East Province	Kikuyu	65,560
	Luhya	26,332
	Luo	24,870
	Kamba	23,864
	Total	314,760*

**Source: Kenya Population Census, 1962, Advance Report* of vols. I and II (Nairobi, Ministry of Finance and Economic Planning, 1969). Total tribal figures do not include minor tribes, and are thus higher than the sum of the tribes shown.

In the May 1963 elections, in which the North-Eastern Region did not take part, KANU obtained majorities in the following regional assemblies: Central, Eastern and Nyanza, while KADU won the Coast, Rift Valley, and Western. In the House of Representatives, KANU had 83 seats to the 33 for KADU and 8 for APP; while in the Senate KANU held 23 as opposed to KADU's 15.

For a discussion of the elections, see Sanger and Nottingham, *J.M.A.S.* (1964), 2, 1, at p.1.

Index

Printed by The English Press Limited, P.O. Box 30127, Nairobi, and published by Oxford University Press, Eastern Africa Branch, P.O. Box 12532, Nairobi